The Psychology
of Separation and Loss

Jonathan Bloom-Feshbach
Sally Bloom-Feshbach
and Associates

Foreword by Joseph D. Lichtenberg

The Psychology of Separation and Loss

Perspectives on Development, Life Transitions, and Clinical Practice

Jossey-Bass Publishers

San Francisco • London • 1987

THE PSYCHOLOGY OF SEPARATION AND LOSS
Perspectives on Development, Life Transitions, and Clinical Practice
by Jonathan Bloom-Feshbach, Sally Bloom-Feshbach, and Associates

Copyright © 1987 by: Jossey-Bass Inc., Publishers
433 California Street
San Francisco, California 94104
&
Jossey-Bass Limited
28 Banner Street
London EC1Y 8QE

Library of Congress Cataloging-in-Publication Data

The Psychology of separation and loss.

(The Jossey-Bass social and behavioral science series)
Includes bibliographies and index.
1. Separation (Psychology) 2. Loss (Psychology)
3. Developmental psychology. 4. Psychology, Pathological.
I. Bloom-Feshbach, Jonathan. II. Bloom-Feshbach, Sally.
III. Series. [DNLM: 1. Child Development. 2. Family.
3. Object Attachment. 4. Parent-Child Relations.
5. Psychoanalytic Theory. WS 105.5.F2 P974]
BF575.G7P78 1987 155 87-3786
ISBN 1-55542-040-0 (alk. paper)

Manufactured in the United States of America

The paper in this book meets the guidelines for
permanence and durability of the Committee on
Production Guidelines for Book Longevity of the
Council on Library Resources.

JACKET DESIGN BY WILLI BAUM

FIRST EDITION

Code 8715

The Jossey-Bass
Social and Behavioral Science Series

Contents

Foreword

Much has changed since Freud solved the Sphinxlike riddle of the nineteenth century: Why are so many bright capable people afflicted with neurotic symptoms? When psychoanalytic theory and treatment were conceived, people assumed the essential stability of their political and social world. Dynastic succession in the Austro-Hungarian Empire and in Czarist Russia had survived the threat of the Industrial Revolution, the sun never set over Britannia's rule, and the revolutionary fervor of colonial America and Robespierre's France had spent itself. In this zeitgeist an illusion of continuity and predictability was reasonable, if false. Throughout most of the world, people lived in the same area for generations. In neighborhoods in New York as well as in their native land, Roumanians lived with Roumanians. Grandparents, parents, aunts, uncles, and children lived in the same house, sharing the same bedroom, bathroom, and, often, bed.

Editors' Note: Joseph D. Lichtenberg, M.D., is a practicing psychoanalyst in Washington, D.C., a faculty member of the Washington Psychoanalytic Institute, and editor in chief of the journal *Psychoanalytic Inquiry.* He is author of *Psychoanalysis and Infant Research* and *The Talking Cure* and is editor of several books and articles on empathy and self-psychology.

Lust, incest, and overexcitement, a netherworld of unconscious fantasy triggered by the close proximity of the child to procreation, birth, and frequent death kept the pot boiling with Faustian questions, walpurgisnachts, and other phantasmogoric conceptions of the universe. The oedipal heroes—George Washington, Eli Whitney, Sigmund Freud—challenged the establishment in the fields of government, technology, and science. They pushed against the confinement of stability and tradition. The penalty was guilt—hurting or destroying someone or something valued and loved.

Then came the twentieth century, with two world wars, the attempted genocide of the Jews, the scattering of people all over the Western world. Now the bomb's mushroom cloud hangs over us all, threatening the final "loss"—annihilation. In the home, mother and father may be struggling to make a go of the first, second, or third marriage for each. The grandparents live alone or are in nursing homes and require an obligatory visit from time to time. Ideally, if not in fact, the children have separate beds, rooms, even bathrooms. The Roumanian district has been cut in half by a highway—and the young people moved out anyway, seeking work in the Sunbelt. In Europe as in America, people are on the move. Turks are paid to go to Germany to work and then, no longer wanted, are paid to go back to Turkey, where no jobs are available and little welcome awaits them. Workers' attachment to their trades—the family farm, the steel mill, the automobile plant—has proven a shaky reed for individuals, families, and communities to rely on. In the cultural climate of the twentieth century *The Psychology of Separation and Loss*—a serious, sober study of the underpinnings of people's struggle to live with and apart from each other—should find a receptive audience.

The number of emotions humans feel is finite and unchanging. Philosophers and psychologists select from the range of emotions particular experiences to best characterize the problems of their era which they wish to investigate. Kohut tried to flag the distinctions between the conflicts of closeness and the despair of isolation in his dramatic conceptions of Guilty Man and Tragic Man. Although Guilty Man derives from the nineteenth-century conception developed by Freud and others, Guilty Man and Tragic Man do not designate two men (or women), one of the nineteenth, one of the twentieth century, but two ways to regard the strivings of all people. In Kohut's view, if human beings are regarded as motivated largely by drives to seek sensual satisfaction and to exert domination over others, then parents, authorities, and therapists are seen as necessary civilizers and therefore breeders of guilt and other discontents. But, if a human being is depicted as motivated to seek his or her personal destiny, derived from a blueprint laid down in the "nuclear self," then parents, authorities, and therapists, by their empathic responsiveness, are seen as facilitators of strivings, unsuccessful (tragic) though they may ultimately be. The Bloom-Feshbachs opt for a choice close to the second depiction, that of Kohut's Tragic Man, yet distinctly different. The question they ask is Does the infant begin life motivated to struggle through stages of increasingly complex relatedness to caregivers and others, seeking closeness and its refuge at one moment and separateness and the risk of loss at another moment?

If loss is the central tragedy of our times, how is it manifest? Freud described a hierarchy of dangers—the loss of the object, the loss of the love of the object, the loss of physical integrity (castration), and the loss of the approval of the superego. Dangers trigger fear, and fear, or more particularly anxiety, its internally generated counterpart, became the affect most investigated. The ability to anticipate danger and signal its potential through anxiety became recognized as a potent function of the ego—the demarcation point for a consolidated structural hypothesis. In the literary domain, W. H. Auden spoke of the Age of Anxiety; Sartre described existential anxiety, a consequence of the terrifying freedom of choice of the individual set adrift in a universe devoid of the meanings once offered in a believable form by religious or governmental institutions. The popularity of the works of Franz Kafka, Eugene O'Neill, and the authors of the Theatre of the Absurd attest to the responsiveness of twentieth-century man to explorations of admixtures of guilt and angst. These works and the studies of self-psychology indicate that loss need not be experienced as guilt and anxiety alone. When associated with narcissism in the form of normal self-esteem or exaggerated egocentricity, loss of affirming, empathic responsiveness may be experienced as deflating, fragmenting, humiliating, or shame inducing. When associated with narcissism in the form of runaway ambition for money, power, or self-display, divorced from concern for others or ethical principle (the evils of me-ism), either gaining or losing the tokens of success may be experienced as loneliness, isolation, the icy despair of internal bankruptcy.

Central to Freud's investigations was the distinction between normal sadness consequent to mourning and pathological depression associated with melancholia. Freud's suggestions in "Mourning and Melancholia" are seminal to major developments in contemporary psychoanalytic theory. Brenner has borrowed from Freud's concept of mourning and designated signal depression, a sense of a loss that has already occurred, to be on a par with signal anxiety, a sense of a potential future loss. From the mechanism of identification in mourning described by Freud, Kohut derived his concept of transmuting internalizations, by which small losses of empathy and support lead to the internalization of the capacity to perform a missing function. This has led to a debate about whether psychic structure or internalized functions develop as a result of optimal frustration (separation, loss, absence) or optimal cooperation and caretaking, or a combination of the two, optimal flexible responsiveness. The shadow of this debate can be found in this book, which addresses both the positive and negative effects of separation.

Still another question follows from "Mourning and Melancholia": Can a baby or small child mourn? This question sparked the great debates over Bowlby's assertion that a baby *can* mourn because, contrary to the Freudian canon, a baby forms an attachment the loss of which leads to mourning. This issue casts more than a shadow over *The Psychology of Separation and Loss;* it constitutes a major and recurrent theme. Mahler's separation-individuation theory is the editors' main conceptual base, but Bowlby's theory and Ainsworth's experimental studies receive searching review. Observations of the manner in which infants react to moments of separation and reunion by secure reattachment, avoidant-anxious reactions, or ambivalent clinging to and pushing off, are juxtaposed to observations of the effects of infants' increasing locomotion and exploratory inclinations, which lead to separations of the infants' own making. Sadness, distress, and anger tinge the momentary response. Mahler's low-keyedness describes the more prolonged reaction. The rich combination of Mahler, Bowlby, and others gives the book a broad foundation of observations on which to build its exploration of later-life responses to separation and loss.

The thematic source for separation-individuation theory, on which the Bloom-Feshbachs rely heavily, follows a distinguished but tortuous course. It begins with Freud's forthright, courageous, self-confrontal question in *Beyond the Pleasure Principle:* If repressed libido is responsible for neuroses, why, when insight as to its source in infantile life is provided, does it not relieve the symptoms and personality distortions in some cases while in others the results confirm libidinal theory so well? Is another factor present in those who seem impervious to change? Is the twig so bent at the beginning that the tree will not form normally or resume its normal shape after correction? The search for the factor causing an alternate bending of the twig led in many directions. One pursued by Melanie Klein followed Freud's suggestion that a death instinct vied with Eros and pulled the libido off its normal path. In no clinical disturbance does the loving attachment to need-satisfying others seem more pulled off its course than in autistic or schizophrenic children who resist all efforts at primitive relatedness, much less intimacy. It was logical for Klein to begin her observations with these unrelating children and for Mahler to follow with similar initial research subjects. Throughout the psychoanalytic field the universally accepted assumption was that each pathological situation resembled a stage or phase of development the limitations of which the adversely affected individual had failed to overcome. Taking this focus, the effort to investigate problems in forming relationships forces attention on issues of establishing boundaries between self and others, on the role of aggression, and on primitive mechanisms for warding off or regulating stimuli (projection, introjection, splitting, denial).

In addition to the wide-ranging theories Freud presented in *Beyond the Pleasure Principle,** he made telling direct observations of infants and children. In offering these few observations, Freud planted a significant seed whose flowering is a direct link to this book through Klein and Mahler, A. Freud and Winnicott, Bowlby and Ainsworth, and a vast array of other infant researchers as well. One of Freud's observations is immediately relevant: A little boy of one and a half, "greatly attached to his mother" invented a game of throwing small objects out of sight and then hunting for them while giving "vent to a loud, long-drawn-out 'o-o-o-o' accompanied by an expression of interest and satisfaction" (p. 14). O-o-o-o stood for *fort* —"gone" in German. "I eventually realized that it was a game and that the only use he made of any of his toys was to play 'gone' with them. One day I made an observation which confirmed my view. The child had a wooden reel with a piece of string tied round it. It never occurred to him to pull it along the floor behind him, for instance, and play at its being a carriage. What he did was to hold the reel by the string and very skilfully throw it over the edge of his curtained cot, so that it disappeared into it, at the same time uttering his expressive 'o-o-o-o.' He then pulled the reel out of the cot again by the string and hailed its reappearance with a joyful 'da' ['there']. This, then, was the complete game—disappearance and return" (p. 15). Freud's formulations about the meaning of the toddler's behavior interest us to this day. Is the little boy making it possible to not make a fuss at his mother's departure by mastering his distress through turning passive into active? Is he expressing his anger at his loss by resentfully throwing the offending mother away?

In determining the path to a contemporary understanding

*Sigmund Freud. "Beyond the Pleasure Principle." In J. Strachey (ed.), *The Complete Psychological Works of Sigmund Freud.* Vol. 18. London: Hogarth Press, 1955. (Originally published 1920.)

of separation and loss, Freud's methodological excursion into infant observation is more significant than was recognized at the time. Stimulated by the desire to understand and relieve psychopathology, informed by problems he encountered in the existing theories of development, Freud turned to naturalistic observations of normal infants and children. This small turn generalizes in time to an important addendum to the scope of psychoanalytic inquiry. Freud's first great discovery was that symptoms and dreams are not random occurrences but have significant psychological meaning and are governed by precise rules. To this dictum we can add a counterpart: Infant behaviors are not random activities but have significant psychological meanings and thus may be governed by precise rules also. During the 1920s and 1930s, psychoanalytic treatment through play therapy techniques was already under way to explore the meanings of behaviors in older children. But it is the infant who more slowly has become the increasingly interesting subject of research. It was not until the fourth and fifth decades of this century that the arena for these studies guided by psychoanalytic formulations began to spread to wherever babies and infants might be found separated from their families, such as foundling homes, pediatric facilities, and war-time fostercare hospitals, and also to places where babies and infants might be brought, such as experimentally arranged observational free-play nurseries or observational settings arranged for fixed-design-situation testing.

Simultaneously observers guided by theories peripheral or oppositional to psychoanalysis began to report independent findings. More important, these observers devised increasingly sophisticated technology for studying physiological, perceptual, cognitive, affective, and motoric behaviors in the youngest babies (and even *in utero*). Affect theorists examined facial patterns and autonomic nervous system responses in social and asocial situations. Because researchers inspired by Pavlov and Skinner proved that babies can be conditioned, it became possible to ask babies whether a certain stimulus was familiar or new, whether a particular stimulus served as an interest-arousing re-

ward or an aversive turn-off. Learning theorists, many guided
by Piaget, others not, had many other questions, which babies
answered by turning their heads, altering their sucking rates,
fixing their gaze, remembering activity patterns for certain
lengths of time but not longer, and so on.

Answers to little questions help to answer big questions,
and big questions help to formulate little questions. Freud
asked how the child's throwing-seeking game tied in to his
mother's comings and goings. Piaget asked when the child
knows to search behind a screen for an object. These "little"
questions built to bigger questions—What is the influence of environment and what is the influence of innate givens on intrapsychic development? Out of the multitude of concepts inherent in the nature-nurture dilemma, the editors and authors of
this book choose one: the psychology of separation and loss.
This choice implies a number of decisions. First, separation and
loss is an important nodal point where caregiving conjoins with
internalized response potentials. Second, the authors believe
sufficient conceptual and experimental-observational work has
been accomplished to make this compilation a fruitful study.
Third, the authors wish to explore patterns that stand at the
edge of normal vicissitudes and pathological responses. And
fourth, the authors want to take a life cycle approach, offering
perspectives on development, life transitions, and clinical practice.

In keeping with their life cycle approach, the editors sub-
scribe to a *modified* separation-individuation model in which
self- and object constancy is not to be regarded as completed
after the third year or at any time, but rather in which the individual remains motivated by wishes for intimacy-in-depth. This
conception, that modes of relatedness common to early childhood persist in the patterning of intimacy-seeking throughout
life and are needed for successful passage through life transitions, places the authors in close consonance with Erikson, Kohut, Gedo, and Stern. The editors thereby lay open the question
of psychic structure: How much is completed, organized, and reorganized by oedipal resolution and superego formation; how

much remains in the realm of intersubjective needs and wishes? They place their emphasis on representations rather than on macrostructures (id, ego, superego), thus slipping by one thicket of psychoanalytic conundrums while opening another Pandora's box of questions about the timing, type (presymbolic, symbolic), and permanence or flexibility of representational encoding.

The Psychology of Separation and Loss is written at a time of pronounced diversity among the theories that are believed by their adherents to represent psychoanalysis. Possibly another way to express this is that the willingness to contain and entertain controversy prevents the major splits and purifying excommunications of the early days. Given this historical fact the editors made a clear-cut choice. They built the diversity directly into their study both in writing their own contributions and in choosing contributors who range widely across the spectrum of American psychoanalysis and cognitive theory.

The Bloom-Feshbachs place their hopes for enlightenment on an ecumenical approach. Since each author takes as his or her point of departure the Rorschach-like cue "separation and loss" and proceeds to tell a story based on his or her area of expertise, the overlap tends to validate proposals in some respects while the contradictions provoke informed further discourse. But the reader is not simply a passive guest at this rich and varied feast. He or she must serve as individual judge and jury for the visions of separation and loss that are presented. This is as it should be. When we formulate psychoanalytic theories, we are not enunciating truths but offering strategies that we hope will best explicate meanings. Readers must "sense their way" into the ideas and observations and clinical examples presented to them. They must match their personal and clinical experiences with the ways in which the experiences of separation and loss are portrayed. Following this approach readers will find that theories presented in *The Psychology of Separation and Loss* are timely and, wherever possible, well grounded in empirical data. This is a virtue, but it is not the greatest virtue of this fine book. Its strong appeal derives from the great care exercised by the editors and the authors in choosing their material with a constant feel for clinical relevance. They never lose sight of the significance of the human encounter with separation and loss as a condition of life for secure and troubled individuals alike.

Washington, D.C.   Joseph D. Lichtenberg
June 1987

Preface

The role of separation in human development and behavior is complex and extensive. Separation is an experience, a developmental process, a dimension of life transitions, a symbolic mental event. Separations can be expectable or unpredictable, growth-promoting or destructive. Separation defines interpersonal relationships by demarcating their boundaries, or end points; and this definition of human relationships is far-reaching, because attachments are the catalysts and media of human development.

How one thinks about separation raises difficult issues for the researcher, the clinician, the social policy analyst, and the layperson. To what extent is human personality influenced by experiences of separation and loss, and to what extent is the early childhood shaping of personality enduring? What kinds of early parent/child relationships are crucial for healthy development, and how much parent/child separation is reasonable? Is distress at separation healthy, and if so, how much and for how long? How does the symbolic meaning of separation shape reactions to events as disparate as leaving a job, terminating a psychotherapy, or coping with death?

The goal of this book is to provide a conceptual framework for the various domains and directions relevant to the study of separation. This framework includes a life-span developmental view of separation, a focus on critical life transitions, and a clinical emphasis on the psychological sense of separateness. Contributors to the volume were invited to go beyond accustomed research and clinical areas of expertise to present integrated views of their subareas within the field of separation, incorporating relevant theory and research and, where appropriate, providing clinical illustration. In order to address an interdisciplinary audience of scholars and mental health professionals concerned with separation, the emphasis has been on distilling important currents of theory, research, and practice, not on presenting comprehensive literature reviews or detailed case summaries. Each chapter is preceded by an "Editors' Note" designed to provide the reader with an overview of that contribution that places it within the broader framework of the field of separation and loss.

The volume should be of interest to a wide variety of professionals concerned with separation and loss in clinical, research, and educational settings. Psychologists, psychiatrists, psychoanalysts, social workers—indeed, all mental health professionals—may find this book informative and useful in their therapeutic work. The clinician interested in personality change, whose focus goes beyond specific problems of loss, should also find this book valuable in its broad conceptualization of the developmental and therapeutic significance of psychological separateness. The volume's diverse contributions should be of interest to research investigators of separation, including those studying child, personality, and social development. In addition, this book may be useful for mental health trainees and for graduate and professional students in psychology, medicine, social work, and counseling, in providing an overview of the field of separation and loss. As a text, the book may be useful in bringing together an integrated sampling of an otherwise fragmented domain of inquiry. Finally, assorted other professionals may find this book valuable, ranging from educators interested in nursery school entry to professionals working with issues of bereavement, cultural dislocation, and divorce.

The book is organized into three main parts, along with introductory and concluding sections. In the introduction, we provide a theoretical overview that outlines the developmental and clinical significance of psychological separateness and experiences of loss. Mental representation of self and other is suggested as an integrative psychological level that cross-cuts otherwise divergent disciplinary perspectives on separation. Part One, on development, takes a life-span perspective. It opens with a provocative article devoted to animal studies of separation that offers useful analogues relevant to our understanding of human reactions to separation. The next two chapters are devoted to early childhood, which has received the lion's share of attention in both psychoanalytic and attachment/ethological approaches to the study of separation. A chapter on later childhood and adolescence follows. The final chapter in this section addresses the role of separation issues through the adult years, a period when development and separation are not typically considered in tandem.

Part Two departs from the more familiar developmental focus on separation and examines the role of separation in normal and crisis life transitions. These include the expectable experiences of nursery school entry, leaving home, and parental absence due to work demands. Other chapters consider the role of separation in unexpected crises for the family and the individual such as cultural migration and divorce. The last contribution in Part Two examines the traumatic experience of childhood bereavement. In contrast to the existing literature on life transitions, these chapters focus primarily on the *separation* component.

Part Three examines the role of separation in the etiology and treatment of psychopathology. This part brings the clinical implications of separation and psychological separateness into focus, drawing extensively on psychoanalytic contributions about the role of separation in psychopathology, in personality disorders, and in the psychotherapeutic process. Such topics as mourning, severe psychopathology, mental representation, and gender differences in response to attachment and loss are considered. Although these issues may be of greater interest to the clinician, we hope that these chapters will also be relevant to the researcher, who may find new hypotheses or new sources of converging evidence in the clinically oriented discussions of separation phenomena. Finally, the afterword briefly highlights converging themes in the study of separation, including intrapsychic, developmental, and ecological issues.

The genesis of this book was our graduate and internship training years at Yale University, where our theoretical biases and substantive interests were developed. Sidney Blatt ignited an interest in mental representation and object relations theory and demonstrated how psychoanalytic theory, empirical research, and clinical practice could productively interact. Daniel Levinson encouraged a developmental view of the life span and a preference for conceptual and qualitative analysis, as opposed to immersion in quantitative inquiry. Our interest in separation grew, in large part, out of (Sally's) research on separation and nursery school entry. Also adding to our interest in separation was theoretical work (primarily Jonathan's) elaborating a representation-based, development-oriented theory of personality functioning. This work on the multiple dimensions of intrapsychic organization (with Alan Sugarman's collaboration) clarified the central importance of psychological schemata and the developmental role of separation in the internalization of caregiving transactions. Our respective research and policy work on parenthood and work/family interaction fostered an interest in life transitions and a deepening awareness of the ubiquitous role of separation. Along the way, teachers, supervisors, colleagues, and supervisees have helped to clarify our understanding, and we acknowledge the gratitude we owe to all of them.

We also want to express our thanks to our patients, who have provided a window into a usually shaded psychological universe. The psychoanalytically oriented psychotherapy process has expanded our conceptions of separation and psychological separateness. Although one learns something from every therapeutic encounter, the psychology of separation has been especially evident in working with young children, adolescents, college students, foreign service families, and seriously disturbed patients.

In addition, we thank Allen Jossey-Bass for his openness

and encouragement and William Henry for his editorial assistance at a conceptual level. To the entire staff at Jossey-Bass who have facilitated this project, we would like to express our gratitude for their patience, encouragement, and help on many matters—small as well as important. Lynn Klinger and Sandra Nolte also deserve thanks for their timely assistance with typing.

Completing this book is an ending and, in a symbolic sense, a kind of separation. We are reminded again that every ending shapes a new beginning, that separation is part of every transition, part of death and of birth, and that beginnings and endings are the dialectic of life.

Washington, D. C.   Jonathan Bloom-Feshbach
June 1987   Sally Bloom-Feshbach

*To the developing child,
who poignantly feels
the pain of separation and
the joy of emerging separateness*

The Authors

Jonathan Bloom-Feshbach is an assistant clinical professor in the Departments of Psychiatry and Behavioral Sciences and of Child Health and Development at the George Washington University School of Medicine, clinical consultant to the Georgetown University Counseling Center, and a practicing psychotherapist, specializing in psychoanalytically oriented treatment of adults and couples. Formerly, he served as a Congressional Science Fellow of the Society for Research in Child Development. A recipient of a Ph.D. degree in clinical psychology from Yale University, he has conducted research and published articles and chapters on separation, the father's role in development, and psychological differentiation. Most recently, he has written about the implications of developmental research for psychoanalytic treatment of adults. Bloom-Feshbach has a particular interest in disentangling the role of separation and loss in the development of representation and psychological structure.

Sally Bloom-Feshbach is an assistant clinical professor in the Department of Psychiatry and Behavioral Sciences at the George Washington University School of Medicine. She conducts a private practice that includes treatment of adults and children and consultation to parents and preschools. Formerly, she was co-director of Post-graduate Training at the Center for Psychological and Learning Services of American University and research associate for the Committee on Child Development Research and Public Policy of the National Academy of Sciences. Bloom-Feshbach received a Ph.D. degree in clinical psychology from Yale University. She has been engaged in research on separation and nursery school adjustment, psychological change over the course of long-term therapy, and ego and object relations functioning of substance abusers. Her background in developmental psychology and work with seriously disturbed patients contributed to interests in separation. She has published articles and chapters on various topics, including separation in early childhood, work/family interactions, and severe psychopathology.

Beatrice A. Beebe, Ph.D., is associate professor at the Ferkauf Graduate School of Psychology, Yeshiva University, New York.

Michael V. Bloom, Ph.D., is director of behavioral sciences at the Sioux Falls Family Practice Residency and associate professor in the Departments of Family Medicine and Psychiatry, University of South Dakota School of Medicine.

Bertram J. Cohler, Ph.D., is William Rainey Harper Professor of Social Sciences in the College, and professor in the Departments of Behavioral Science (Committee on Human Development), Education, and Psychiatry, University of Chicago.

Jesse D. Geller, Ph.D., is director of Yale Psychological Services Clinic, Department of Psychology, Yale University.

Lisa K. Gornick, M.A., is a candidate for the Ph.D. in the Department of Psychology, Yale University, and is serving her internship at New York Hospital, Cornell Medical Center.

Doris S. Jacobson, Ph.D., is professor in the School of Social Welfare and principal investigator with PROJECT STEP, University of California, Los Angeles.

Gerald F. Jacobson, M.D., Ph.D., is executive director of the Bidi-Hirsch Community Mental Health Center and associate clinical professor in the School of Medicine, Department of Psychiatry, University of Southern California.

Lee S. Jaffe, Ph.D., is staff psychologist at Mesa Vista Hospital, San Diego, California.

Eugene H. Kaplan, M.D., F.A.P.A., is professor in the Division of Psychoanalysis, Department of Neuropsychiatry and Behavioral Science, School of Medicine, University of South Carolina.

Janice L. Krupnick, M.S.W., is assistant clinical professor in the Department of Psychiatry, Georgetown University School of Medicine.

Frank M. Lachmann, Ph.D., is senior supervisor and training analyst in the Postgraduate Center for Mental Health, New York City.

Howard D. Lerner, Ph.D., is assistant professor in the Department of Psychiatry, University of Michigan.

Paul M. Lerner, Ed.D., is a faculty member of the Toronto Psychoanalytic Institute and assistant professor in the Department of Psychiatry, School of Medicine, University of Toronto.

Marsha H. Levy-Warren, Ph.D., is a faculty member of the Child and Adolescent Analytic Training Program, Postgraduate Center for Mental Health, and adjunct assistant professor in the Department of Psychology, Barnard College.

Helen Block Lewis, Ph.D., was professor emeritus (adjunct) of the Department of Psychology, Yale University, and editor of *Psychoanalytic Psychology,* Cambridge Hospital, Cambridge, Massachusetts, prior to her death in 1987.

Alicia F. Lieberman, Ph.D., is associate professor in the Department of Psychiatry, School of Medicine, University of California, San Francisco, and senior psychologist in the Infant-Parent Program at San Francisco General Hospital.

Chaya S. Piotrkowski, Ph.D., is associate professor in the Department of Psychology, St. John's University, New York City.

Edward H. Plimpton, Ph.D., is a fellow in pediatric psychology in the Department of Pediatrics, Bay State Medical Center, Springfield, Massachusetts.

Sally Provence, M.D., is professor of pediatrics, Yale University Child Study Center, and faculty member of the Western New England Institute for Psychoanalysis, New Haven, Connecticut.

Leonard A. Rosenblum, Ph.D., is professor in the Department of Psychiatry and director of the Primate Behavior Laboratory, State University of New York, Downstate Medical Center, Brooklyn, New York.

Fredric Solomon, M.D., is director of the Division of Mental Health and Behavioral Medicine at the Institute of Medicine, National Academy of Sciences, Washington, D.C.

Robert D. Stolorow, Ph.D., is psychoanalyst in private practice and a member of the Southern California Psychoanalytic Society, Los Angeles.

Frances M. Stott, Ph.D., is a faculty member of the Erikson Institute, Chicago, Illinois.

Alan Sugarman, Ph.D., is clinical associate in adult and child psychoanalysis at the San Diego Psychoanalytic Institute and associate clinical professor of psychiatry, University of California, San Diego.

The Psychology
of Separation and Loss

Introduction:
Psychological Separateness
and Experiences of Loss

Jonathan Bloom-Feshbach
Sally Bloom-Feshbach

Separation: An Introductory Sketch

The significance of separation for each individual originates in the nature of the caregiving relationships of early life. These relationships create a psychological foundation that functions as a cognitive and affective template, shaping later interpersonal experience and emotional well-being, including response to separation. Depending on one's theoretical view, a sound psychological foundation is labeled differently: object constancy, a cohesive sense of self, a secure attachment. This healthy emotional core does not insure against later traumatic loss, nor does it describe the more subtle aspects of individual variation in response to separation. But successful traversal of early developmental milestones shifts the meaning of loss from a psychological focus on the availability of interpersonal resources to a focus on the nature and characteristics of others in relation to the self.

Theoretically, we support a modified separation-individuation model, in which symbiosis and lack of self/object differentiation are not complete or basically cognitive and perceptual

1

but, rather, are founded in part on emotional, motivational wishes for merger and the comfort of psychological union. Even for adults with a solid emotional foundation, the continued course of development requires further self-definition, with increasing degrees of separateness, autonomy, and relatedness. The role of separation in facilitating the construction of an inner world of mental representations of self and object, through identification with love or attachment figures, is central to early childhood but continues throughout life.

The dynamics of separation responses include anxiety at being apart from the love object; anger, rage, and sadness at the loss; conflict over negative feelings toward the yearned-for figure; defensive detachment; and depression. The cues instigating separation reactions, and the intensity of the responses, are rooted in the individual's psychological history, including the quality of the early foundation, parenting transactions at later ages, and the history of separation and loss experiences. This psychological heritage shapes the way that objective, or realistic, elements of separation or loss in life events are subjectively filtered or amplified.

Response to separation exists at such a fundamental level of the entire personality organization that its influences can be discerned in many symbolic or disguised forms. The individual's sensitivity to separation may be reflected in the ease of letting go of noninterpersonal attachments, of relinquishing ties to old furniture, familiar buildings and neighborhoods, sports teams, or accustomed routes of travel; the pressured need to move on and continually experience new settings and relationships, a compulsion to separate and be separate, is but another way of responding to similar internal issues. When development calls for reevaluation and change, how readily can one relinquish a self-image, a political value, a theoretical tenet, or a vision of life? When life calls for commitment and responsibility, how readily can one feel satisfied with continuity and be content with letting go of potentially exciting opportunities? We suggest that noninterpersonal objects, even psychological phenomena such as attitudes, images, and dreams, become familiar attachments and prompt separation reactions—direct *or* defensive—at the threat of their loss. Because development and growth necessitate the giving up of old friends, old self-concepts, and old habits, difficulty with the emotional struggles that separations evoke may impede development in indirect or camouflaged ways. For example, adolescent delinquent behavior may be less a struggle with authority than a struggle with separation; the child who does not protest school entry may in fact be suffering considerably; a patient's resistance to a therapeutic interpretation may not be related to the content of the interpretation or to the dynamics of accepting assistance but may reflect the individual's struggle with relinquishing an enduring conception of the self that, however outworn and painful, is like an old, familiar friend.

Thus, the capacity to master separation facilitates growth by permitting an openness to losing the familiar, be it people or their support. Separation mastery allows the individual to face the specter of ambiguity and aloneness that accompanies surrendering ideals, hopes, or self-images. Thus, coping with loss is inextricably tied to creative transformation, as Robert Jay Lifton (1975, p. vii) suggests: "There is no love without loss. And there is no moving beyond loss without some experiencing of mourning. To be unable to mourn is to be unable to enter the great human cycle of death and rebirth."

The purpose of this chapter is to provide a conceptual overview of theories and issues relevant to the study of separation. In particular, we will discuss the backdrop in psychoanalytic and attachment theory to the evolution of separation as a field of inquiry. Some complicated and conceptually murky issues will be reviewed in this process of examining basic theoretical assumptions. Because psychoanalytic theory and clinical practice have been such rich sources of understanding about separation, we also grapple with general issues beyond separation itself, such as the validity of psychoanalytic and clinical knowledge, the benefits and limits of empiricism, and conflicts in psychoanalytic theory itself. Psychological representation (what others term the internal working model, schema, script, or self and object world) emerges as a cross-cutting concept, holding promise for unifying the disparate clinical, research, and theoretical approaches to the study of separation phenomena.

Historical Overview. The psychology of separation has roots in psychoanalytic theory and observation. Freud initiated the notion that early experience has formative effects on personality development and the adult emergence of psychopathology. However, Freud did not pay sufficient attention to the importance of the early parent/child bond, instead emphasizing later oedipal phenomena. In addition, his treatment of the relationship between infant and parent was based on notions of instinctual gratification. This fundamental issue of what motivates, maintains, and disrupts the intense parent/infant (and later parent/child) relationship has been a controversial question producing evolving answers both in psychoanalytic thinking and in academic psychology.

Freud's instinct theory paralleled the experimental psychologist's view of hunger and thirst as fundamental motivations for the infant. Social motivation in both traditions was thought of as a secondary drive; that is, if mother feeds you, you develop an attachment to her based on her repeated satisfaction of hunger and thirst (see Maccoby and Masters, 1970, for a review of psychoanalytic and social learning theory views of this issue). As Eagle (1984) notes, in traditional psychoanalytic theory it is not only the reinforcement principle that underlies the mother's importance but also her role in preventing the infant from being overwhelmed by excessive stimulation and her role as exciter of erotogenic zones (Freud, 1940/1964). Although Freud did at times emphasize the fundamental affectional nature of the early relationship of infant and mother, the basic thrust of his theory, as Bowlby (1969) points out, was that love originates in attachment to the satisfier of nourishment needs (Freud, 1940/1964).

In the 1940s and 1950s a variety of mental health clinicians, both American and English, observed the negative effects evident in infants and children who had experienced impoverished maternal contact through institutionalization, war-related separations, or other traumatic losses. These studies, conducted almost entirely by psychoanalysts, showed how extensive institutional infant care or repeated changes in mother figures during the child's earliest years impaired personality development (Bender and Yarnell, 1941; Bowlby, 1940, 1944; Burlingham and Freud, 1942; Levy, 1937; Skodak and Skeels, 1949; Spitz, 1945). For the first time, a body of evidence began to accumulate pointing to separation as a key factor in child development.

These studies of prolonged institutional care and frequent maternal separations contributed to several lines of disciplinary development. For mainstream psychoanalysis, René Spitz's work helped to initiate a major reorientation toward exploring and elucidating the importance of the pre-oedipal period of the child's life. This pre-oedipal emphasis has led to new developmental observation and theory, to a greater psychoanalytic interest in understanding and treating severe psychopathology, and to a theoretical shift toward greater emphasis on object relations and theories of the self. Another major pioneer, John Bowlby, conducted extensive studies of separation, loss, and early parent/child relations that led to his departure from traditional psychoanalytic theory. Bowlby put forward a new theory of attachment (for example, Bowlby, 1958, 1969), presented as an alternative to a psychoanalytic model of development and of the formation of psychopathology. This ethologically oriented attachment theory helped to spawn a new field of research on attachment phenomena in behavioral science, especially in developmental psychology. Another disciplinary line originating in the early studies of prolonged maternal separation has been a subfield focused on maternal deprivation. This body of research has better delineated the various factors accounting for deficits observed in children who have experienced significant early trauma and loss. Finally, there has been a distinct, nontraditional body of psychoanalytic theory also relevant to our topic, the British object relations school. During this same historical period, object relations thinkers have contributed to the mainstream psychoanalytic reemphasis on pre-oedipal phenomena. Although these theorists (including M. Klein, Fairbairn, Winnicott, and Guntrip) have worked outside the central psychoanalytic circles, Otto Kernberg (1975, 1976) in particular has sought to integrate many of their ideas into the mainstream of contemporary psychoanalytic ego psychology.

Given these and other subfields that bear on the study of

separation, it is impossible to do full justice to the currents, persons, and ideas that influence separation research and theory today. However, in this chapter we will briefly discuss these different disciplinary lines, some of which will be elaborated in greater detail in other chapters of this volume.

The Evidence on Early Deprivation. Both the immediate and the long-term consequences of institutional child rearing include profound deficits in intellectual and social development. For example, Goldfarb (1943, 1944, 1945) conducted an early series of follow-up studies of older children who had spent their first three years in an institution. The children had trouble developing social relationships, showed limited and superficial emotional responses, and had poor capacity for social discrimination (for example, as infants they failed to discriminate caregivers from strangers). Many were socially withdrawn and were unable to form deep relationships with caregivers and later with peers. In a contrasting but still problematic pattern, other children did develop relationships with caregivers but in an indiscriminate manner. These children presented an insatiable need for social stimulation and affection (what Spitz called "affect hunger"). Follow-up data on these children during adolescence revealed serious cognitive, affective, and social deficits, including disturbances in ability to form relationships, lack of anxiety or guilt over antisocial behavior, poor impulse control, and delinquency. Goldfarb's (1955) findings were consistent with evidence compiled in other studies of children reared in institutions (for example, Freud and Burlingham, 1944; Spitz and Wolf, 1946).

In response to these studies by Spitz (1945), Bowlby (1944), Freud and Burlingham (1944), and others, researchers began to study a range of traumatic early experiences (such as adoption and brief hospitalization) in more rigorous attempts to differentiate whether these untoward consequences for the developing child followed from the parent/child *separation* or from other factors, such as inadequate emotional or cognitive stimulation. These studies found that maternal separation was not the only factor accountable for the effects of early institutionalization; many variables interacted with the loss of maternal contact. For example, the age of the child makes an important difference. Yarrow (1964) reviewed several studies and concluded that the most vulnerable period for hospitalization is seven months to three years of age and that hospitalization of children as old as seven years may cause susceptibility to serious psychological disturbance. Wachs and Gruen (1982) summarize other important factors that have been identified, such as the quality of care before (Rutter, 1971, 1979; Yarrow, 1964), during, and after a major separation (Tizard and Hodges, 1978), the duration of parental loss (Spitz and Wolf, 1946), the quality of the marital relationship (Rutter, 1971, 1979), and the child's own contribution, including sex and temperamental differences (Rutter, 1971, 1979; Tizard and Hodges, 1978). These mitigating factors, in combination with various methodological critiques of such studies and some disconfirming evidence (for example, that some effects of institutionalization are reversible—Hunt, 1979), have led researchers to be much more cautious about identifying maternal deprivation or parent/child separation alone as responsible for the effects of long-term hospitalization (Hunt, 1979; Rutter, 1979; Wachs and Gruen, 1982). Lacks in perceptual, cognitive, and social stimulation have been alternatively cited as important contributing or central elements. Nonetheless, the striking negative effects of separation are evident even in a well-conducted more recent study (Tizard and Hodges, 1978) of a rather good institution (generous staff/child ratio, toys and books plentiful, and so forth). Such findings suggest that "institutions like this still fail to provide the warm, intimate, and continuous one-to-one relationship with a mother substitute that Bowlby (1944) and others have stated is necessary for healthy development" (Wachs and Gruen, 1982, p. 123). Thus, although long-term institutional care represents a nonnormative data base for studying separation, one that is not applicable to the average parent/child relationship, these studies dramatically highlight the importance of separation.

Separation and Psychoanalytic Theory

The Separation-Individuation Process. Contemporary psychoanalysis places considerable emphasis on the impact of the mother/infant relationship and on the pre-oedipal basis of personality formation and vulnerability to psychopathology. In the context of Freud's elaboration of the oedipal conflict and his emphasis on the father's role in childhood intrapsychic conflicts, Spitz has been credited with introducing the mother into psychoanalysis (Pine, 1985). Among other contributions, Spitz first identified the infant's phase of heightened separation anxiety at eight to ten months of age and identified a type of depression related to object loss—anaclitic depression (Spitz and Wolf, 1946). More important, Spitz helped to create a climate of psychoanalytic emphasis on early, and hence typically mother/infant, object relations. Among the many psychoanalysts who have contributed to this shift are those who have studied and/or treated children (for example, Burlingham, Erikson, Fraiberg, A. Freud, Greenspan, M. Klein, Provence, Solnit), those who have treated adult patients with severe psychopathology (Fromm-Reichmann, Knight, Lidz, Searles, Sullivan), and those who have elaborated developmental theories focused on early object relations (in America, Jacobson, Kernberg, and Kohut are examples, and abroad, Fairbairn, Guntrip, and Winnicott).

Preeminent among the many contributors to a psychoanalytic illumination of pre-oedipal development has been Margaret Mahler. Mahler's initial studies of child autism and child psychosis (Mahler, 1952; Mahler and Elkish, 1953; Mahler and Gosliner, 1955) led her to pursue an extensive longitudinal investigation of the normative mother/infant relationship over the child's first years of life. This research by Mahler and her colleagues on the separation-individuation process (Mahler, Pine, and Bergman, 1975) has contributed an entirely new framework to the study of separation. Separation is viewed more broadly than as discrete events of loss: it is cast into a larger developmental process of psychological differentiation.

Mahler's Theory. Although other contributors to this volume explain and discuss Mahler's theory of the separation-individuation process (especially Provence, Chapter Two), her theory is so fundamental that it warrants consideration in some detail here. The studies by Mahler and her colleagues of the parent/child relationship examined how the developing child not only gradually becomes more *behaviorally* independent but undergoes a *psychological* progression from a relatively undifferentiated sense of self and other to a more differentiated, articulated representation of both the self and important others. According to Mahler's theory, the newborn's subjective world is initially self-absorbed; this is the stage of "normal autism." As an infant develops an attachment to the mother, Mahler posits a subjective experience of "symbiosis," a sense of merger with the parent that invokes fluid, poorly defined self/other boundaries. Through several other phases of increasing interpersonal separation, the child gradually achieves a sense of psychological separateness. The final stage that Mahler and her collaborators delineate in this psychological "gestation" results in the establishing of a critical emotional foundation around the age of two and a half to three years. This foundation, termed "libidinal object constancy" (Fraiberg, 1969), is the psychological basis for the child's growing independence, for consolidation of a separate identity, and for the capacity to relate to others in an interpersonally meaningful and mutual way. Separation and individuation are seen as two intertwined and interacting, but distinct, developmental lines: "Separation consists of the child's emergence from a symbiotic fusion with the mother . . . and individuation consists of those achievements marking the child's assumption of his own individual characteristics" (Mahler, Pine, and Bergman, 1975, p. 4).

In common-sense terms, the infant's initial great need for and total dependence on the parent for comfort and affection, in combination with limited cognitive capacities, leaves the infant feeling linked to the parent and vulnerable to parental separation. As the child comes to internalize the parent's external provision of emotional security, the child becomes more separate as a psychological entity and is able to tolerate more interpersonal separation. The separation-individuation process thus entails interacting interpersonal and psychological events (Fraiberg, 1971). The achievement of object constancy is thought to bring about an entire reorganization of the organism that affects all of development and is so fundamental that Mahler labels this stage "the psychological birth of the infant."

The hypothesized stages of separation-individuation and the factors that lead to attainment of object constancy are based on both observation and inference and have been debated by skeptics even within psychoanalysis (Klein, 1981; Peterfreund, 1978). Nonetheless, Mahler's developmental model is widely accepted in psychoanalytic circles and has been illustrated with enormous frequency in observations of parent/child interaction and in the developmental reconstructions of adult patients. These ideas have taken hold in the clinical community by proving useful in psychoanalytic treatment. Hence, various chapters in this book do rely on Mahler's theory of the separation-individuation process in describing the etiology and treatment of psychopathology.

According to Mahler, the child needs a substantial dose of parental nurturance balanced by a reasonable degree of frustration and limit setting. The child who receives sufficient love is able to develop positively toned mental images of the parent that can become internal psychological sources of comfort. The construction of integrated inner representational images of caregivers who are both loving and frustrating is facilitated by, and facilitates, separation. The capacity to soothe and comfort oneself, by relying on positively toned parental imagos, helps the child cope with concrete separation events. In a broader sense, the child's long-term increasing separateness and independence from the parent promotes the very internalization process by which affectively integrated representations of the parent can be realized.

It is important to note that Mahler's "psychological birth process" occurs developmentally in the context of other critical shifts. The increase in representational capacity her theory requires is corroborated by the progression at this time in cognitive level from Piaget's sensory-motor to preoperational thought. Similarly, the cerebral hemispheres are thought to become lateralized, with more specific and heightened linguistic functions, around this two- to three-year time frame. Increased linguistic capacity provides a better medium for representation and serves an important emotional function in helping the child to delay gratification and control impulses (Katan, 1961; Mischel, 1974).

Further, the child's motoric development, curiosity, and exploratory urges prompt more physical distance from the parent, more autonomous play activity, and hence more mini-experiences of separation and reunion.

Separation and Internalization. Central to the separation-individuation process is the link between separation and internalization. In "Mourning and Melancholia," Freud (1917/1957) discussed the notion that one way of coping with the grief of a loved one's death is to identify with that longed-for individual. The pain of this total, permanent separation is diminished by internalizing a part of the lost person. This phenomenon of identification with a mourned individual is central to normal development as well. The child copes with the many mini-separations of parental unavailability by creating an abstract internal representation of the caregiver's presence. However, it should be noted that the dynamics of identification with generally available attachment figures differ from the dynamics of identification instigated by bereavement; see Chapter Twelve.

Many psychological theories of social influence on development emphasize the interaction between parent and child through which modeling, imitation, and identification occur. The psychoanalytic concept of internalization requires a mix of interaction *and* separation experience to promote representations of the attachment figure (for example, Behrends and Blatt, 1985; Sandler and Rosenblatt, 1962). Among child developmentalists, Michael Lewis and his colleagues have elaborated Sigel's (1970) "distancing hypothesis," advancing the view that the child's representational world is spurred by the combination of what are termed (1) direct effects, or direct contact, and (2) indirect effects, or parental separation and absence (Lewis and Feiring, 1978; Lewis, Feiring, and Weinraub, 1981; Weinraub and Frankel, 1977). For example, it has been shown that infants tend to say the word for "daddy" before the word for "mommy" (Jakobson, 1962) and will label pictures of fathers before those of mothers (Brooks-Gunn and Lewis, 1979). Lewis considers an array of explanations for these findings and concludes that the father's greater interpersonal distance, generally due to work absence, fosters children's capacities to represent him. Lewis, Feiring, and Weinraub (1981, p. 282) state that "representation may be best constructed with the child experiencing both presence (interaction) and absence in some as yet unknown ratio." In a study of infant labeling of parental pictures, Brooks-Gunn and Lewis (1979) found that fifteen months was the age at which labeling first occurred. At this age, 25 percent of the infants correctly labeled pictures of their fathers, while no pictures of mothers were correctly labeled. By eighteen months of age, all paternal pictures were labeled accurately, and only a few maternal pictures were correctly identified. In fact, it was the children of the mothers who left home most frequently (for example, for employment) who used the "mother" label earliest!

This notion that separation or loss fosters representation is well accepted in diverse psychoanalytic circles and is reflected in the conceptualization of such phenomena as mourning, introjection, identification, identification with the aggressor, the psychology of the self, depression, and the therapeutic process (Axelrad and Maury, 1951; Freud, 1923/1961; Kernberg, 1976; Kohut, 1971; Loewald, 1960; Meissner, 1979). Further, many observers report that bereaved spouses often adopt behaviors, attitudes, or mannerisms of the lost loved one and that children imitate behaviors of siblings who have died (Bowlby, 1980; Furman, 1974; Weinraub and Frankel, 1977). Introjection (a form of internalization more basic than identification) spurred by separation is a central component of Jesse Geller's elaboration of the role of mental representation, internalization, and separation in the psychotherapy process (see Chapter Fifteen, this volume; and Geller, Smith-Behrends, and Hartley, 1982). Empirical research on the role of separation in facilitating representation has been relatively scant, however, perhaps because it is counterintuitive for the behavioral scientist to study how a *moderate lack* of interpersonal interaction fosters parental influence.

In the face of limited data, Lewis and his colleagues (1981) cite a number of incidental experimental observations that support what they term the "distancing hypothesis" (Sigel, 1970). First, they note Rosenblum's observation that "macaque monkeys reared only with their mothers—never seeing another monkey—have difficulty in finding her (recognizing) when placed in a situation where their mother and other female monkeys are present" (Lewis, Feiring, and Weinraub, 1981, p. 282). This finding is consistent with the hypothesis that lack of distance impedes development of differentiated mental representations. Lewis and his colleagues (1981) report another provocative observation, this time of human infants, that demonstrates a different aspect of the relation between separation and internalization. They report that when mothers of one- and two-year-olds leave their children in the laboratory playroom, over 23 percent of children seen in the laboratory move to sit in the chair recently vacated by their mothers, even though the chair is not close to the exit door! This finding illustrates how children may cope with even a brief separation by attempting to identify with an element of the absent caregiver. Although the child's move to occupy the mother's chair is an active behavior, not an inner thought, one can consider it a psychological phenomenon, reflecting the child's sensory-motor level of mental representation.

These ideas about mourning and internalization, about coping with loss by bringing back or reconstructing an element of an absent person, have a direct bearing on the theory of separation-individuation. According to Mahler's theory, a cyclical process ensues wherein coping and development interact and foster each other. In normal development, the child's increasing psychological separateness and autonomy necessitate, and are facilitated by, internalization of the parent's loving and comforting attributes. In order to cope with the myriad mini-experiences of object loss that growing up entails, the child constructs affectively integrated (and hence soothing) inner images of the parent. More internalization fosters increasing representational capacity, which, in turn, fosters the development of new levels of separateness. Thus, separation-individuation theory recasts separation and loss into a fundamental, psychological, "self-generating" developmental process—self-generating even in the sense that the child's self or self-image is developed through this process.

Criticisms of Separation-Individuation Theory. As already noted, Mahler's developmental sequence of psychological stages

culminating in object constancy has been widely criticized
(Bowlby, 1982; Eagle, 1984; Klein, 1981; Lichtenberg, 1983;
Peterfreund, 1978; Stern, 1983, 1985). The criticisms focus
mainly on (1) the inaccuracy of the theory in light of experimental research on infant perception, cognition, and social behavior, (2) the arbitrary nature of stage definition, and (3) the
problems inherent in inferring early childhood mental events
and structures from reports by adult clinical patients or childhood nonverbal behavioral data. Although some aspects of these
criticisms are legitimate, the theory's contribution remains compelling.

One convincing criticism of separation-individuation theory concerns Mahler's assumption of an early phase of normal
autism. This phase, conceptually linked to Freud's views on primary narcissism, is directly contradicted by mounting evidence
of the neonate's highly organized perceptual, cognitive, and
communicative capacities (see Chapter Sixteen). For example,
infants less than two days old can repeat a sound pattern associated with their mothers' voices and distinguish their mothers'
voices from the voices of other people (DeCasper, 1979). Further, Stern (1983, 1985) presents a variety of evidence suggesting that even at birth the infant does not exist in an undifferentiated state. He examines a range of findings about neonatal
capabilities that he believes point to early differentiation. For
example, Stern notes that neonates can recognize an object in
one modality that was previously experienced in a different
modality, can maintain the identity of a three-dimensional object despite spatial rotation, and can remember, with minimal
cues, an event experienced several days before. Stern shows that
these kinds of mental capacities are the very abilities that form
the basis of a rudimentary but separate sense of self and other.
This kind of evidence is contrasted to Mahler's notion of the
young infant's lack of self/other differentiation. In addition,
Stern (1983) and Klein (1981) further indicate how the lack of
self/object differentiation evident in adult psychopathology is
morphologically dissimilar to infant developmental stages. Klein
describes the "pathomorphic myth" in psychoanalysis as a tendency to attribute adult pathological states to normative infant

psychological functioning; consider, for example, such constructs as symbiotic merger, selfobjects, and part objects. Peterfreund (1978) has also noted such tendencies in psychoanalytic views of infant and child development.

In this light, many of the criticisms directed at Mahler's theory are applicable more broadly to psychoanalytic developmental theory in general. Stern (1983, 1985) and others (Eagle, 1984; Klein, 1981; Peterfreund, 1978) believe that even when psychoanalysts such as Mahler study behavior directly, rather than relying on retrospective developmental accounts from patients, they nonetheless tend to fit data into preconceived theoretical constructs. Stern (1985) voices this criticism in spite of his sympathy with the psychoanalytic effort to capture overarching, phenomenologically relevant dimensions of human experience that transcend observable behavior. Such concepts are clearly vital for clinical intervention. Thus, although Stern is cautious about the appearance of subjective bias in drawing theoretical inferences, he does not discourage constructing models of infant subjective experience. Rather, he distinguishes a developmental from a clinical view of the infant, the developmentalist's understanding of development being research-oriented and behavior-linked (hence, more affiliated with the views of academic developmental psychology) and the clinician's being more phenomenological and better able to characterize the subjective world of the developing child (hence, more reflective of the psychoanalytic approach to development).

In fact, promoting understanding between students of the clinical and developmental approaches to the study of separation is a major purpose of this book. However, in contrast to Stern (1985), and more in concert with Lichtenberg (1983), our bias is toward the clinical side and toward the application of developmental principles to the understanding and treatment of adult psychopathology—still a speculative enterprise. Encouraging fertilization between the different perspectives on the study of separation requires a sympathetically critical examination of alternative approaches. With this view, we find much of value in Mahler's theory and much that needs refinement—just as, in a later section of this introduction, we suggest that, despite some limitations, Stern's developmental model and Bowlby's theory contribute much to the understanding of separation.

A balanced critique of Mahler's theory suggests that *autism* is certainly the wrong word and likely the wrong concept to apply to the normal infant. The research evidence clearly points to a modification in Mahler's description of the first phase of life. But, rather than quibble about the extent of neonate autism or self-absorption, and rather than debate how complete infant undifferentiation is, we suggest that it is more productive to emphasize the general principle Mahler's theory enunciates: that the neonate has a relatively diminished sense of the other and a relatively undefined sense of self and that, through development, awareness of self and other increases tremendously, as does differentiation between the two. Thinking about Mahler's work from this less rigid perspective brings her theory more into line with the research evidence and with general theories of human evolution and development, aligning her model with the psychological differentiation theory of Werner (Werner, 1957; Werner and Kaplan, 1963). In Werner's theory, all living systems, both biological and mental, originate in states of undifferentiation and gradually evolve toward states of greater differentiation, articulation, and hierarchical integration.

Mahler and her colleagues' (1975) framing of the separation-individuation process narrowly emphasizes the child's total lack of self/object differentiation and the achievement of object constancy. More recently, Pine (1985) continues to restrict the definition of separation-individuation problems to those patients who have not achieved object constancy. In contrast, we think it more productive, and more congruent with related theory and evidence on psychological differentiation, to consider separation and individuation developmentally extended processes, certainly continuing through adolescence (Blos, 1967) and likely into adulthood. Within this extended model, object constancy is a critical nodal point but not the end point of psychological differentiation. Similarly, in regard to self psychology, the establishment of a cohesive self does not preclude further developmental progressions in the degree of individuation, autonomy, and capacity for object relatedness in the structure of the self.

Our reframing of separation-individuation theory does not alter fundamental notions about object constancy—the dynamics and processes governing achievement of a sense of separateness and the far-reaching import of object constancy for understanding personality organization and psychopathology (for example, Burgner and Edgcumbe, 1972; McDevitt, 1980; McDevitt and Settlage, 1971; Masterson, 1976; Stolorow and Lachmann, 1980). Rather, extension of the separation process beyond early childhood suggests a recapitulation of differentiation at increasingly more abstract cognitive levels and at emotionally more autonomous levels of functioning (Blatt, Wein, Chevron, and Quinlan, 1979; Loevinger, 1976; Selman, 1980). This process is analogous to Kernberg's (1975, 1976) account of how formation of the superego recapitulates the affective and representational processes that bring about ego formation. More specifically, Blatt (1974) details a model of psychological differentiation in the development of self- and object representations that integrates the developmental theories of Werner, Piaget, and psychoanalysis (also see Greenspan, 1982). Blatt and his colleagues have demonstrated the empirical applicability of this developmental model to parental representation and depression in adults (Blatt, Wein, Chevron, and Quinlan, 1979) and to severely disturbed patients as well (Blatt, Brenneis, Schimek, and Glick, 1976; Blatt and Lerner, 1983; Blatt and Wild, 1976; Spear and Sugarman, 1984). Proceeding from these research findings and from theoretical considerations, Behrends and Blatt (1985) also take the position that separation-individuation and the mechanisms of internalization spurred by separation continue throughout life. They account for differences in the process of internalization at different life stages by (1) reframing and extending the motivation for secure attachments, or the wish for symbiosis, into a need for coherence, order, and integration of sense of self and identity, and (2) reconceptualizing separation, or breaches in the experience of unity and coherence, in terms of "experienced incompatibilities." Such "separations" include experiences of object loss but also entail other forms of internal and external conflict that require relinquishing old representations and building new structures. In addition to this psychoanalytic perspective, Weiss (1982) provides theoretical and empirical evidence for the proposition that adult attachment bonds have the same dynamic properties as parent/child relationships, further supporting the view that separation/internalization mechanisms may continue to operate in adulthood (see Chapter Five for a discussion of the role of separation in adult development).

The theory of separation-individuation and its extension through later developmental stages receive additional support from the huge literature on field dependence (for example, Witkin and others, 1972, 1974), which conceptually rests on Werner's developmental theory of psychological differentiation. The degree of individuation of a person's sense of self, as well as the degree of differentiation of self from object, is reflected not only in performance of basic perceptual tasks of spatial discrimination but also in cognitive, affective, and interpersonal behavior (Witkin and Goodenough, 1977; Witkin and others, 1974) and even in the form psychopathology takes (Witkin, 1965). Although individual differences are emphasized in the study of degree of differentiation (or what is called field independence), the average level of differentiation across the population as a whole increases through development, certainly through adolescence. Helen Block Lewis (see Chapter Sixteen) has been especially interested in the link between differentiation theory and individual differences in social and affective functioning, including responses to separation.

As Mahler's theory is relatively recent and is based on one of the few longitudinal psychoanalytic explorations of development, its need for revision and refinement is not surprising. For example, Fred Pine (1985), one of Mahler's original collaborators, has already reframed the concept of stage. Rather than viewing a psychological stage as the sole or constant affective theme for a chronological epoch, Pine proposes the notion of critical psychological "moments." Such moments are the heightened affective experiences associated with crucial interpersonal and/or intrapsychic events relevant to a given psychological thrust. Thus, what characterizes a given stage of separation-individuation might be particular incidents during which the child struggles with the issue of how much distance from the caretaker to tolerate or initiate. Not all of parent/child interaction during a given age period will be suffused with the dynamics or meaning typical of that stage.

Pine's view of psychological stages (psychosexual, separation-individuation, and so forth) suggests that stages are overlapping and not mutually exclusive. Stern (1985) notes that such ambiguity in stage definition makes it even more difficult to develop empirical parameters for deriving stage categories. But in contrast to Stern, we feel that such ambiguity and multidimensionality do not invalidate the stage concept but, rather, underline the complexity of psychological development and suggest the limits of empirical methodology. Although the relevant epistemological issues cannot be addressed here, our view is that validation of at least some portions of psychoanalytic theory will rest on clinical and inferential, rather than empirical, modes of evaluation. Although behavioral research can inform theoretical inference, ultimately it does only inform.

Thus, even though we recommend openness to future revision of Mahler's model, the fundamental theoretical view of the evolution of the self seems compelling: that the infant begins with a limited, relatively undifferentiated sense of self and other, that the connection with the parent deepens profoundly, and that the basis of identity is achieved through a psychological separation from the parent based on internalization of affectively integrated images of the parent/child bond.

Stern's Model of Infancy: An Alternative to Mahler. A variety of developmentalists have proposed stage sequences that modify certain aspects of Mahler's theory (such as Greenspan, 1981), but these models do not alter the fundamental propositions that bear on separation phenomena. The one major alternative to separation-individuation theory warranting discussion here is Daniel Stern's (1985) developmental framework of infant stages of self-experience. Stern proposes a model of infant subjective experience that he believes is both clinically informed and more compatible than Mahler's with the research findings documented by behavioral scientists. Stern rejects Mahler's stages of normal autism, symbiosis, hatching, practicing, rapprochement, and object constancy. Instead, he emphasizes a

neonatal self that has "emergent relatedness" and proposes that
this newborn interpersonal capacity for relatedness develops
through several crucial stages dependent on qualitative shifts in
the subjective experience of self (the core, subjective, and intersubjective self).

Stern takes issue both with the concept of normal infantile autism and with the psychoanalytic concept of symbiosis.
He believes that the infant has a degree of other-relatedness and
differentiation at birth (and soon thereafter) that contradicts
these stage concepts. Further, he argues with stage sequencing
and presumes that the qualitative shifts in self-experience that
he describes exist as evolving, retained developmental lines.

In general, Stern's theory has a more scientific flavor than
much of psychoanalytic theorizing, in its thoroughness, level of
specification and articulation of concepts, attention to research
evidence, and careful comparison with alternative models. In
addition to the clarity of his model, the emphasis on the self as
a focal point for developmental theorizing seems to hold considerable promise for integration with other conceptual thrusts
in psychoanalytic and academic psychology (such as self psychology, object relations theory with its emphasis on self-representation, and research on self-esteem and self-concept).

The view of the aware infant presented in Stern's model
is strikingly different from the image of the passive infant, seeking tension reduction, presented in traditional psychoanalytic
theory. Consistent with Lichtenberg's (1983) integration of psychoanalytic theory and contemporary infant research, and with
Bowlby's and Ainsworth's emphasis on the reciprocity of par-
ent/child exchange, Stern looks carefully at the mutual cuing
and interactional sensitivity between parent and child. Stern
helps to resolve theoretical contradictions by emphasizing the
primacy of the child's interpersonal motivation. In practice, the
clinical underpinnings of Mahler's work clearly highlight parent/
child interchange and illustrate her sensitivity to the subtle messages communicated between parent and child. From a theoretical perspective, however, Mahler embeds her views in an ego-
psychoanalytic framework, obscuring what her contributions
imply for object relations.

Stern's (1985) review of research on infant cognition suggests, for example, that the psychoanalytic timetable of dynamic conflict be pushed forward and that primary process thinking be considered a developmental emergence, not a first stage. Lichtenberg (1983) proposes a modification in psychoanalytic theory based on such evidence, indicating how infants' representational capacities point to a tandem appearance of primary and secondary process thinking. Such data-based revisions of clinical theory are certainly useful, but it is also important to examine how Stern's research bias may circumscribe his perspective. In particular, Stern's outright rejection of the notion of psychological symbiosis neglects considerable contradictory clinical evidence and empirical research. For example, many parents have the experience, in comforting their young children, that the child is soothed by a psychological state that does approach something of merger. Perhaps Stern's theory is useful in pointing out that the infant is *capable* of more differentiation but incomplete in not recognizing the psychological *need* or predilection to find comfort in a state of being emotionally or physically held in a womblike way. Although Mahler's presumptions that such a symbiotic stage occurs only during months four through six and that infants are incapable of more differentiation may well be erroneous, we may lose ourselves in research data by ignoring a nearly universal observation of the infantile gratification that a boundaryless psychological state engenders. As a clinical example, consider a psychotherapy patient who reported the childhood habit of comforting herself by lying against her mother and aligning her breathing in unison with mother's, letting go of all thought apart from this special closeness. This experience, which was both regressive and nurturing for the patient, goes beyond the "core self" or "intersubjective union," as Stern might label it, to a level of psychological unboundedness that defies verbal description. In fact, words such as *symbiosis* or *merger* may be inherently deficient in describing such nonlinear experiences, and may contribute to scientific difficulty in defining such internal states.

The issue of symbiosis is important because it is critical in understanding the quality of infantile attachment, the nature of primitive self-experience, and the implications such experiences have for separation and separation-individuation. In further defense of the idea of symbiosis, we note that, in addition to the many qualitative observations about merger experiences, a large body of empirical research by Lloyd Silverman and his colleagues (summarized in Silverman, Lachmann, and Milich, 1982) addresses this issue. Their work constitutes a major empirical test of various psychoanalytic propositions and shows that wishes to merge are powerful unconscious forces. Experimental presentations, at a subliminal or unconscious level, of messages that gratify or frustrate a wish for symbiosis consistently shape the psychological responses and even the psychiatric symptoms of normal and disturbed research subjects in directions predicted by psychoanalytic theory. This research lends considerable support to the import and ubiquity of the "symbiotic" experience Mahler emphasizes. Although it may well be that union experiences originate at a developmental point different from that postulated by Mahler or that such experiences occur in a more differentiated manner or that they persist through later ages, as Stern (1985, p. 10) suggests, we believe that such modifications in Mahler's model do not crucially alter the role of separation-individuation in the development of the self. As we have suggested, psychological separateness may be less a cognitive-perceptual phenomenon than an emotional-motivational developmental achievement (taking place on a subjective *psychological* level).

One overarching issue that divides scientists and clinicians is the credence given to evidence of early development derived from adult patients. Detailed exploration of fantasy and emotional functioning in long-term psychotherapy patients provides clinicians with compelling illustrations of key dynamics of the separation-individuation process that Mahler describes. (Several such cases are provided in this volume; see especially Chapters Twelve and Thirteen.) The progression through some kind of separation-individuation sequence, even if such a sequence is only similar to, and not morphologically the same as, actual infant development, is so clearly evident to psychoanalysts and dynamic psychotherapists that the "pathomorphic" assumption may contain some truth as well as some illusion. Although practitioners and theoreticians may be infused with subjective bias, and although adults' psychological functioning may not be structurally equivalent to children's developmental experience, there are enough converging empirical data and theoretical logic to suggest that clinical findings have something important to offer. It is not in accord with the strictest conventions of scientific caution, but there is still something useful to learn from psychoanalytic speculations that order the nature and severity of psychopathology on the basis of a theoretical view of infant developmental stages (see Chapter Fourteen).

In sum, separation-individuation theory needs revision and rethinking as the field of infant developmental research progresses. The special contribution of Stern is his effort to propose a clinically meaningful alternative to Mahler's model that is more compatible with the research evidence. However, in our view he omits a crucial dimension of psychological development central to the psychology of separation. The ongoing validity of separation-individuation theory is highlighted in Eagle's (1984, p. 22) rebuttal to his own critique of Mahler: "In developing the concept of separation-individuation, Mahler has identified a truly universal dimension applicable to all members of the species and, in appropriate form, to members of other species. Further, in describing the unfolding of this dimension, Mahler has suggested certain relationships (for example, between 'safe anchorage' and exploratory behavior) which . . . have received wide and systematic support. Finally, . . . concepts such as symbiotic gratification and particularly separation-individuation are most meaningfully understood, not in terms of (sexual or aggressive) drive gratification, but in terms of attachment behavior. As I will try to show, although Mahler often employs the language of libido and drive, one can essentially ignore this language in understanding her more basic formulations."

Controversy and Convergence in Psychoanalytic Thought. Viewed under a microscope, the debates and controversies within psychoanalysis are manifold and the schisms broad. Through a wider lens, basic propositions relevant to the study of separation appear more coherent than an initial glance would suggest.

For example, although Kohut's branch of analytic thought and treatment has diverged from mainstream psychoanalysis, for our purposes many similarities exist. The concept of the "selfobject" and the need for interpersonal relationships that function as cohesion-inducing agents to provide more integrated self-experience are quite similar to the ego-analytic view of how others are experienced in the face of inadequate object constancy. Although critics have attacked the focus on empathy in Kohut's treatment approach and compared it simplistically with Rogerian therapy, Kohut's writings stress that the interpretation of the patient's experience of therapeutic empathic failure is crucial. Perceived or actual unavailability of the therapist provides mini-experiences of loss that become opportunities for working through the history of inadequate parenting. This idea, elaborated by Geller in Chapter Fifteen, is quite consistent with the ego-analytic emphasis on interpretation of negative transference, which may be evoked by physical or psychological separation, even in patients who have significant conflicts on an oedipal level. Further, although Kernberg retains the structural theory in his object relational model (Kernberg, 1975, 1976), his embrace of Mahler and his incorporation of Fairbairn's work and other object relational ideas bring object love to the fore. Thus, although Mahler and Kernberg still place themselves within traditional psychoanalytic instinct theory, their emphasis on early parent/child relations (and hence on separation events) is in line with the central emphasis on attachment and separation experiences in Bowlby's theory. These issues hark back, in spirit if not in actual word, to the early psychoanalytic debate between primary object love and primary narcissism (Balint, 1937/1965; Fairbairn, 1952; Ferenczi, 1950).

In general, then, psychoanalysts recognize the importance of the child's earliest caretaking relationships and the role of separation in promoting development or in creating psychological difficulty. Separation-individuation theory is consistent with modern biological views of development in which all living organisms develop from states of relative undifferentiation to states of greater differentiation and hierarchical integration (Blatt, 1974; Werner, 1957). The notion that the self emerges through internalization of, or through psychological reconstruction of, key elements of the primary parenting relationship points to a formative role for attachment and separation processes in the older self theories (Cooley, 1902; Mead, 1934; Sullivan, 1953), in the contemporary psychoanalytic self psychology of Kohut, in the developmental theory of Mahler, in the self- and object representational system of Kernberg, and in the analytic theories of Klein (1976) and Gedo (1979, 1980).

Common to all these approaches, and to psychoanalysis from its beginnings, is the focus on mental representation (Fraiberg, 1969). The traditional psychoanalytic view is that the infant's first mental schemata evolve out of experiences of frustrated need fulfillment (A. Freud, 1952; Spitz, 1966). As already noted, representational processes are central to the evolution and differentiation of the self in Mahler's theory. But mental representation is essential to any model of how the individual constructs a sense of self and of others. Accordingly, there has been an increasing focus on mental representation in cognitive, developmental, and social psychology (Bretherton and Waters, 1985; Main, Kaplan, and Cassidy, 1985; Mandler, 1983; Schank and Abelson, 1977; Singer, 1985), as well as within psychoanalytic and clinical theory (Blatt, 1974; Horowitz, 1983; Kernberg, 1976; Sandler and Rosenblatt, 1962). In an earlier epoch, when behavioral science was embedded in exclusively behavioristic theories of human functioning, the emphasis on mental representation alienated psychoanalysis from academic psychology. The more recent explosion in cognitive psychology and the computer-oriented information sciences has brought the return of "psyche" to psychology. Considerable interest in mental representation has resulted, especially in the developmental research stemming from attachment theory. In a later section, we will return to the issue of representation because of its centrality and its key discipline-bridging role, but first we will address the main alternative to a psychoanalytic conception of separation—Bowlby's attachment theory. (We do not review the social learning view of separation because it is less clinically relevant and less conceptually heuristic; this approach to separation is reviewed in Ainsworth, 1969.)

Attachment Theory

Basic Assumptions. From his seminal paper "The Nature of the Child's Tie to His Mother" (1958) through his three-volume series *Attachment* (1969), *Separation* (1973), and *Loss* (1980), John Bowlby has sought to provide an alternative conceptual approach to the study of object relations (what he calls affectional relations). The resulting "attachment theory" has been buttressed with strong empirical support, ranging from Harlow and Harlow's (1965, 1969) classic studies of rhesus monkeys to research on the mother/infant relationship (for example, Ainsworth, Blehar, Waters, and Wall, 1978; Bretherton and Waters, 1985; Sroufe, 1983) and studies of the father/infant tie (for example, Lamb, 1977, 1978; Parke and Tinsley, 1981).

The concept of an attachment behavioral system implies a set of psychological structures that motivate a person to attain or maintain "proximity to some other clearly identified individual who is concerned and better able to cope with the world" (Bowlby, 1982, p. 668). Bowlby posits that this motivational system exists at the level of a psychoanalytic instinct and believes that attachment is at least as powerful as feeding, sexual, and aggressive urges, if not more so. Attachment behavior in humans becomes organized during the second half of the first year of life, although the component behaviors exist from birth—vocalizing, eye contact, responsiveness to tactile and kinesthetic stimulation, crying, clinging, and so forth. These behaviors all serve the function of bringing the infant into closer contact and increased interaction with a caregiver. The preferential activation of these behaviors in regard to certain caregiving figures (for example, crying when mother, but not a stranger, leaves the room) and the resistance of this focused response to change define the attachment bond.

In theory, the attachment response is an evolutionary heritage, balancing the infant's increased locomotive capacity with the need not to stray too far from a protective figure (Freedman, 1974). Such increasing orientation to a central caregiver around six to seven months of age has been empirically demonstrated in both experimental and field studies. For example, Yarrow (1964) found that a move from foster to adoptive home care before age six months creates only temporary distress, while shifts in caregivers at age seven to twelve months lead to more serious disturbance.

The attachment response has been classically illustrated in Harlow's (1958) studies of "contact comfort" in infant monkeys. This well-known body of work showed that infant monkeys developed attachments to terrycloth surrogate mothers that provided tactile contact in preference to wire surrogate mothers that offered food. Monkeys would go to the milk-dispensing surrogates when hungry but would cling to the cloth mothers for comfort and security. (See Chapter One, this volume, for a contemporary research approach to separation in nonhuman primates.)

The importance of tactile stimulation has been demonstrated at a physiological level as well. For example, inadequate parental attention despite adequate nutrition and medical care can produce psychosocial dwarfism, a psychologically based decrease in body size (Thoman and Arnold, 1968). Similarly, tactile stimulation of premature babies has been associated with increased weight gain (White and La Barba, 1976), and even biochemical evidence reveals the effects of maternal deprivation in rats (Schanberg and Kuhn, 1980). This evidence on the tactile/physiological dimension of attachment behavior underlines the biological/evolutionary origins of the attachment system. In this respect, attachment theory is conceptually akin to the psychoanalytic attempt to place development in a biological context but theoretically divergent in Bowlby's claim that the attachment drive is a separate motivational system. Although attachment theory radically departs from the traditional psychoanalytic emphasis on libidinal and aggressive instincts, Bowlby's focus on the early parent/child tie is consistent with current psychoanalytic attention to pre-oedipal object relations. For example, Bowlby's reframing of Freud's case of Little Hans in terms of separation anxiety would not be very different from some object relations rerenderings of the case.

Attachment and Separation. Clinical and experimental

observations of responses to separation by Bowlby (1973) and others (for example, Robertson, 1970) have revealed a universal sequence of reactions to separation: protest (anger), depression (sadness and mourning), and eventual detachment (defensive avoidance of the feelings associated with the loss of the attachment figure). Bowlby's (1973) extensive work on separation reviews the research and clinical literatures on this topic from an attachment theory perspective. For example, Bowlby outlines several theories of separation anxiety, including Freud's signal theory (1926/1959), Rank's (1929) birth-trauma theory, Melanie Klein's (1932/1949) depressive and persecutory anxiety, and the theories of frustrated attachment suggested by James (1890) and Suttie (1935). Bowlby's (1973, p. 377) own view, which he terms a combination of Freud's signal theory of anxiety and the frustrated attachment model, "regards separation of a young child from an attachment figure as in itself distressing and also as providing a condition in which intense fear is readily aroused. As a result, when a child senses any further prospect of separation, some measure of anxiety is aroused in him." Thus, in this view a key determinant of distress over object loss is simply the loss itself. In contrast, the psychoanalytic perspective emphasizes anger at loss and the complex dynamic conflicts instigated by such anger, which we will elaborate later in the chapter.

The separation response depends on the development of a preferential attachment figure. Before sixteen weeks of age, differential separation responses are limited. By six or seven months, the infant displays a full range of responses to separation. The child's response to strange surroundings or strange people does not alter "in form or in intensity, much before the third birthday" (Bowlby, 1973, p. 56)—the same age as establishment of libidinal object constancy. Thus, the child's third and fourth years of life constitute a critical transitional stage for Bowlby as well as for Mahler. According to Bowlby, reactions to separation from loved ones continue throughout life, but with advancing age only longer separations will evoke a significant response, except in someone particularly vulnerable to loss.

Alicia Lieberman (this volume, Chapter Three) reviews

the attachment field's theoretical and methodological approach to the study of separation, comparing this literature with psychoanalytic theory's view of separation. In research on attachment, the child's response to separation emerges as a characterizing feature of the parent/child bond. The quality of parenting shapes the intensity and nature of separation reactions, and hence the separation response is an index of key qualitative features of the parent/child relationship. Further, the child's laboratory response to separation correlates with maternal and infant behavior in the home: laboratory-derived categories of the quality of the parent/child bond, based on separation response, are associated with many significant dimensions of the child's later adjustment (for example, Ainsworth, Blehar, Waters, and Wall, 1978; Sroufe, 1983).

Experimental measures of the quality of the attachment relationship are based on assessment of the reunion response following separation (Ainsworth, Blehar, Waters, and Wall, 1978). Secure early attachment, as measured by the separation/ reunion response, predicts longer attention spans in children, more display of positive affect during free play, and both more autonomous play activity and better use of parental help in problem solving (Bretherton, 1985; Matas, Arend, and Sroufe, 1978). In general, the research evidence shows that the quality of the early caregiving relationship influences the child's overall adjustment and the quality of relationships developed with peers and secondary caregivers (Bretherton, 1985; George and Main, 1979).

The strength and formative influence of the child's earliest attachment and separation experiences are evident in research documenting effects on the child-rearing behavior that children show when they grow up to become parents themselves (Ricks, 1985). Such intergenerational transmission of interpersonal patterns supports the psychoanalytic principle of the consistency of personality and the repetition of core interpersonal patterns (that is, transference). The social transmission of adverse relationship patterns is especially troubling in light of the evidence on psychological unavailability. Egeland and Sroufe (1981a, 1981b) studied attachment relationships in three groups of children who suffered different types of parental maltreatment and in a normal control group. The three types of maltreatment were (1) physical abuse and hostility, (2) psychological unavailability and depression, and (3) neglect, or failure to provide proper care. All three troubled groups were insecurely attached compared with the control group at eighteen months of age, but psychological unavailability appeared to be the most damaging—even more damaging than psychological unavailability paired with physical abuse. The authors suggest that *any* kind of relationship or contact is preferable to no contact or attention. Lack of contact might be viewed as too much separation. Because separation defines the boundaries of the attachment bond, too much unavailability or too much separation shrinks that bond to an insufficient level. Viewing separation as a defining feature as well as a reflection of the attachment relationship illustrates why the separation response has been a pivotal factor, both conceptually and empirically, in the study of attachment.

Representation: Linking Attachment Theory and Clinical Views of Separation

Representations are mental models or schematic constructions of individual experience. Research psychologists emphasize the cognitive and external event components of representation, while psychoanalysts emphasize the interpersonal, emotional, and fantasy properties of representation. Although the lion's share of research on attachment and separation has focused on behavioral indexes of these phenomena, a current trend in the attachment field is the study of the "internal working model," the child's psychological representation of his or her repeated transactions with the world and especially with significant others. Bowlby's (1969, 1973, 1980) "internal working model," derives from Craik's (1943) idea of the construction of a mental model that guides and regulates human functioning. However, Bowlby primarily emphasizes the mental schemata of attachment relationships. His selection of the term *working model* suggests the dynamic evolving nature of the individual's conception of significant others and of the self. Bowlby's "internal working model" is compatible with Piaget's (1954) theory of representation and the representational framework in Peterfreund's (1971) systems/cybernetic revision of psychoanalytic theory. Although the working-model concept differs from psychoanalytic models of representation, it is important because it provides a link between clinical and research perspectives of development and, in particular, of separation.

The internal working model can be considered a "macroscopic" representational structure through which behavior is mediated and motivated—macroscopic in the sense of embodying representations of other persons, of self, and of dynamic interactions between the two. Other theorized mental models vary in the "level" of phenomena represented or in the degree of emphasis on affective or social variables. The idea of level can be noted in linguistics, where one can analyze language processing at a sensory/phonemic level, a cognitive/morphemic level of word meaning, or a more complex pragmatic level of intended communicative meaning. Similarly, different conceptions of mental models range from basic perceptual-memory units of representation to more complicated and emotionally significant psychological structures. Work on representation includes such ideas as event schemata (Mandler, 1979), active structural networks (Norman and Rumelhart, 1982), representations of interactions that have been generalized (Stern, 1985), scripts (Schank and Abelson, 1977), and generalized event schemata (Nelson and Gruendel, 1981). The multilevel nature of representation is evident in script theory. Scripts themselves are seen as composite constructs of event patterns but also can be elaborated into emotionally influential scripts or vignettes (scenes); in turn, the emotionally dominant themes of our lives are termed metascripts or nuclear scenes (Abelson, 1983; Carlson, 1981; Tomkins, 1979).

This recent explosion of interest in mental schemata, within developmental, social, and cognitive psychology and within the field of artificial intelligence, supports the long-held psychoanalytic emphasis on the fundamental role of the psyche in motivating and mediating behavior. Research exploration of

the representational world is a new area of the attachment field
and eventually may become more useful clinically. For example, Main, Kaplan, and Cassidy (1985) examined six-year-olds'
representations of their relationships with parents, using a family picture measure and a projective test of separation reaction.
This parent/child representation was strongly predicted by direct behavioral assessment of the child's attachment classification at one year of age. Such a study adds support for the psychoanalytic proposition that psychological representation of
the parent/child relationship is an enduring, shaping behavioral
influence. But the study adds another, more curious element: it
differentiates maternal and paternal representation. The attachment classification with mother, but not with father, at age
one predicted the child's attachment representation at age six.
This finding raises the substantive issue of multiplicity and nonconcordance of object representations—a topic to which we will
return—and also provides a methodological illustration of how
the attachment field might begin to develop and test hypotheses
of interest to the psychoanalytic developmentalist and clinician.
However, the attachment approach is not likely to conceptually
recognize, or use methods capable of assessing, the more unconscious structural elements of psychological organization that
psychoanalytic theory posits. The psychoanalytic literature on
representation is far more thorough and integrative in its specification of the developmental ordering of the representational
world and in its articulation of theoretical links between representation and psychological functioning, both normal and
pathological (Blatt, 1974; Blatt and Lerner, 1983; Kernberg,
1975, 1976; Sugarman and Jaffe, this volume, Chapter Fourteen). Moreover, psychoanalytic research studies have explored
the representational world using empirical methods (Blatt,
Wein, Chevron, and Quinlan, 1979; Burke, Summers, Selinger,
and Polonus, 1986; Krohn and Mayman, 1974; Mayman, 1967,
1968; Sugarman, Quinlan, and Devennis, 1981; Urist, 1977).
Linking traditional developmental research with the clinical approach should foster more shared knowledge between scholars
operating from different vantage points.

In this light, it is useful to return to the issue of multiple representations raised by the research finding that maternal but not paternal attachment was linked to later representational structure. This finding and other supporting evidence (Ricks, 1985) point to the inconsistency or multiplicity of psychological structure. This multidimensionality of psychological organization, a perspective we have outlined elsewhere (Bloom-Feshbach, 1979; Bloom-Feshbach and Bloom-Feshbach, 1985; Sugarman, Bloom-Feshbach, and Bloom-Feshbach, 1980), refines the issue of enduring cross-situational consistency in personality and behavior. Working from clinical observation, from review of the research literature, and from theoretical inference, we proposed that because psychological organization is based on the internalization and elaboration of early parenting experience, variations within and across the attachment relationships that form the basis of fundamental self- and object representational structures will result in variations in the structures themselves. Within this psychoanalytic developmental model, no one developmental vulnerability or fixation point is pivotal in the shaping of inner representational structures; rather, the entire set of early developmental relationships has the potential to affect the psychological structures that evolve. Hence, adult character structure and vulnerability to development of psychopathology will be influenced by all important early object (attachment) relationships. Further, the inner variability that each significant object or caregiver manifests (both the variability within the caregiver's representational structure and the variation in external stressors impinging on the caregiver), along with the existence of multiple parenting objects, creates a vehicle for considerable variation in the patterning of the child's self- and object representations—the building blocks, or modules, of psychological structure. This multidimensional model may help explain the complex variations of borderline personality organization, at times a source of diagnostic dispute; some "borderline" individuals display transient psychotic symptoms and others do not, some "borderline" personalities are organized predominantly at the mid-level of character pathology, and some characteristics of "borderline" psychopathology appear to coexist with higher-level neurotic functioning (Bloom-

Feshbach, 1979). The degree of variability in the formative caregiving transactions internalized through the early years shapes the degree of consistency in the psychological structure. Such a multidimensional model speaks to the debate between personality theory and social learning theory by positing the existence of multiple enduring "internal working models."

This multiple view of the representational world is based in part on attachment research demonstrating the importance of multiple attachment figures. The bias toward the mother's developmental importance was once evident in both psychoanalytic theory and developmental psychology, but child development researchers came to recognize and explore the father's pre-oedipal role. Research has shown that the father/infant relationship not only is important as a differentiating complement to the potentially engulfing mother/child union (Abelin, 1971; Mahler and Gosliner, 1955) but can even be primary (Schaffer and Emerson, 1964). Thus, even though it is true that in most families the father/child tie will differ from the mother/child bond in fostering more exploratory and play activity (Lamb, 1981), for some children the father may serve the child's basic security needs. Such variation and overlap in parent/child relationship patterns will complicate and multiply the self- and object representational patterns that the child internalizes and elaborates. In psychotherapy, the resulting complexity accounts for the rigidity of certain relationship patterns, for the startling resilience of some patients, and for the coexistence of very disparate levels of functioning within the same individual (for example, an individual with substantial self-observational capacities as well as primitive self- and object representational patterns). Researchers are increasingly interested in the wide range of important interpersonal ties during development, including the child's relationship with father (for example, Bloom-Feshbach, 1981; Lamb, 1977, 1978; Parke and Tinsley, 1981), with siblings (Lamb and Sutton-Smith, 1982), with peers (Berndt, 1981; Bloom-Feshbach and Bloom-Feshbach, 1985), and with alternative caregivers such as grandparents and babysitters (Kellam, Ensminger, and Turner, 1977). The question of how differential relationships with many significant others may shape the representational bases of psychological organization is compelling; as Bretherton (1985) emphasizes, studying the development of "nonconcordant" working models is an exciting direction for future research exploration.

The multidimensionality of attachment relationships and the resulting disparities in the representational world imply greater complexity for our picture of separation; consideration of how the internal templates of relationships filter and mediate reactions to separation is complicated indeed. Depending on the individual or on the issue at hand, the inner representational structures that govern response to separation may be coherent and unified or may be disparate and divergent. The many influential factors include early experience, contextual cues, gender of the abandoning and abandoned objects, and impinging psychological and external factors. One must consider the coexistence of oedipal and pre-oedipal issues, or, in Stern's language, the various levels of self-experience. Thus, a neurotic patient may have a slight symbiotic tendency (alternatively understood as a moderate need for selfobjects or a partial core vulnerability) that contributes to a subtle lack of identity definition, especially when self-definition and assertion foster conflict with a significant object and raise the threat of loss of love, either practical or symbolic. Another level of complexity that the multidimensional model raises is reflected in considering how such a mild pre-oedipal vulnerability might exist as a result of one parent's, perhaps the father's, struggles with lack of differentiation. What might result is a process whereby an individual's tendency toward a symbiotic loss of self-definition occurs primarily in relationships with persons who resemble the father. This abstract example illustrates how a person's level of individuation and separateness might vary, depending on the interpersonal and dynamic context and the complicated history of attachment relationships. Another element of complexity is the balance between degree of vulnerability and degree of other, healthier elements of psychological structure. Consider an individual with a mild symbiotic (selfobject, core) vulnerability who also has the capacity for ready self-observation, compared with an individual with a more profound vulnerability that remains beyond conscious awareness because other representational structures are limited and not sufficiently differentiated to allow for self-reflection.

The complexity of the representational world as briefly sketched here suggests that the psychological bases of the sense of separateness, and the psychological residue of specific separations, may be consistent or nonconcordant, depending on a wide constellation of factors. In the clinical context, where individual variation, not group data, is paramount, complexity in the etiology of separation reactions must be carefully considered along with general principles governing response to separation.

Summary: The Psychology of Separation and Separateness

To separate means literally "to set apart," to detach, disengage, divide, or sever. In this book, we look at separation in different ways. The specific experiences through the life cycle of being set apart from loved ones, of being disconnected from significant others or objects, captures the "separation event" dimension of psychological separation. In contrast, the "separation process" dimension reflects the countless normal mini-separations—some interpersonal, some intrapsychic—that accumulate through life. Developmental psychologists focus on separation within the context of the attachment system, while psychoanalytic thinkers emphasize subjective transformation in the degree of *separateness of the self.* This psychoanalytic view of separateness, a non-event-oriented view of separation, captures the etymological origin of *separate: se,* "without," "apart"; *parara,* "make ready," "prepare." The process of psychological separation in Mahler's sense readies, prepares the child to be apart, to be an individual—that is, to be a separate entity, a single person. Similarly, Kohut's notion of the need for a "selfobject" reflects a person's lack of readiness for separateness, the inability to experience an individual, cohesive self. The psychological processes of individuation (of becoming distinct or individual) and of differentiation (of being different and distinguishable) are based on the process of separation-individuation.

Bowlby and Mahler agree on the fundamental observation that mastery of separation events improves considerably around the time of the child's third birthday. The evolution of "object constancy" in Mahler's model provides a way to conceptualize the evolution of the internal schemata, the inner world of cognitive and affective representations, that underpin the child's behavioral capacity to adapt to separation events. Bowlby's model and the research on neonatal cognitive and perceptual competence and interpersonal capacity (Emde and Harmon, 1982; Lichtenberg, 1983; Stern, 1985) point to a new conception of the infant that suggests modification in various aspects of Mahler's theory; nonetheless, we believe the theory retains validity and utility. Because the conceptual and theoretical basis of separation-individuation is relatively new and because empirical research is only now exploring the complexities of mental representation, we hope that future research and theory will better specify the timing, stage categorization, and defining characteristics of the child's behavioral mastery of separation. Basic studies assessing the links between separation problems, social adjustment, and the degree of differentiation and integration in the child's self and object imagos have only begun to be conducted. Similarly, future researchers and theoreticians must eventually resolve the central question of the conditions under which separation fosters intrapsychic internalization and clarify the role of such internalization in the formation of the self (see Harter, 1983, for an extensive discussion of the development of the self).

Biases inherent in the disciplines approaching separation discourage open inquiry and mutual exchange. The classical psychoanalytic tendency to remain fixed on instinct theory is a case in point. Although we happen to agree that aggression and sexuality must be important components of a theory of personality, we believe that much benefit would derive from an atmosphere promoting theoretical divergence, rather than one that discourages questioning of basic assumptions. The literature on attachment relationships, especially the biological/physiological evidence, suggests that psychoanalysts ought to consider whether the motivation for object love or attachment should be thought of as a basic drive, separable from sexuality. This volume is not a context in which to reconsider psychoanalytic theories of motivation and personality formation but, rather, a place to raise the hope that a more open-minded, reciprocal exchange of ideas will be fostered.

An example of the anti-Bowlby view held by some psychoanalysts is an article by Sylvia Brody (1981), which criticizes Bowlby's attachment theory for not considering, among other key omissions, psychic energy, intrapsychic processes, unconscious motivation, infantile sexuality, conflict, and rage. A rebuttal would note that many psychoanalysts now dispense with the notion of psychic energy (for example, Holt, 1975; Schafer, 1976), that Bowlby does address intrapsychic processes (he has a representational model), that he proposes his own theory of the unconscious (unconscious motivation and conflict), and that he devotes significant attention to the affect of anger. To this extent, Brody reads or reports Bowlby's ideas inaccurately. Brody is correct, however, in emphasizing that Bowlby does omit sexuality from his understanding of human relationships and inadequately addresses the problem of aggression. Although Bowlby acknowledges that his work does not provide a general theory of anxiety or an overall theory of personality and psychopathology, he does present his work in a way that fosters the view of attachment theory as an alternative to psychoanalytic theory. For psychoanalytic critiques of attachment theory as mechanistic and nondynamic, see, among others, Engel (1971), A. Freud (1960), Hanly (1978), Rochlin (1971), Roiphe (1976), and Spitz (1960). In particular, we find Bowlby's theory lacking in its omission of a structural dimension of mental representation.

Nonetheless, the research literature on attachment offers a variety of contributions to psychoanalytic developmental and clinical views of separation. For example, reunion responses following separation are important behaviors reflecting the deeper attachment/adjustment dimension of reactions to separation (for example, Lamb, 1979). Reunion behavior may be a useful but often overlooked assessment criterion for evaluating separation problems during clinical inquiry about object relationships and when such behavior is observed during the treatment process. The research literature also provides useful information about differential attachment patterns that supports, expands, and contradicts the traditional psychoanalytic view of object ties. Such findings emphasize the importance of thinking in terms of parental functions, not roles, and analyzing patients' transferential and current interpersonal patterns with an eye toward complex and nonstereotypical object relations histories (Bloom-Feshbach and Bloom-Feshbach, 1985; Bloom-Feshbach, Bloom-Feshbach, and Gaughran, 1980). The attachment field's idea of "nonconcordant working models," or multiple self- and object representations, complicates and clarifies the nature and influence of representational psychological structures. In addition, the research literature offers a potpourri of interesting experimental information about the underpinnings of children's separation reactions and about how responses to separation and loss evolve with development and predict social adjustment (DeLozier, 1982; Henderson, 1982; Pound, 1982). More generally, empirical researchers provide the study of separation with a model of intellectual clarity and scientific rigor, wherein hypotheses are specified and tested (for example, the disentanglement of the influence of the separation factor from other variables in maternal deprivation).

Unfortunately, research clarity is often achieved at the expense of a narrow focus and a comparative lack of depth. Behavioral science has finally acknowledged mental representation, but psychoanalysis has long been exploring the intricacies of the psyche. One of the main contributions of the attachment field may be in serving as a bridge between the empirical research world and the hypothesis-generating, theory-rich clinical/ developmental psychoanalytic literature. The psychoanalytic world gave birth to the study of separation, first identified the role of separation in fostering internalization, drew the first maps of the mental landscape, and first explored how unconscious self- and object images define the emotional software of human information processing. As Loevinger (1976) notes, psychoanalysis is the only developmental theory to demonstrate that regression is essential for development, that one step back may be necessary before two steps forward are taken. The separation behavior of two-year-olds and adolescents amply illustrates this pattern of developmental movement. The psychoanalytic psyche is a symbolic mind, in which separation or loss may be symbolically or metaphorically felt in any experience that marks an ending. Transitional events such as geographical relocation, divorce, retirement, psychotherapy termination, and school entry entail physical separation and would more obviously lead to loss reactions, but many other events involve separation in subtle or symbolic ways. Body changes, new self-realizations during adolescence or during psychotherapy, creative ideas or new problem-solving approaches, and finishing a novel all entail surrendering an attachment of some kind, leaving behind the familiar. Letting go of an accustomed self-image, attitude, or habit may instigate the dynamics of separation reactions. The psychoanalytic model also provides us with the concept of the transitional object (Winnicott, 1953; see also Chapter Fourteen, this volume)—a blanket, stuffed animal, toy, or other such object invested by the child with properties that serve to soften the pain of separateness and bridge the distance between closeness and aloneness. This and many other naturally occurring separation-related phenomena are considered and studied within psychoanalytic theory. For the researcher, though, and especially for the skeptical reader, the contributions of psychoanalysis are inaccessible. Harvesting the richness that psychoanalysis offers about separation requires filtering the excesses and identifying the digestible components. To accomplish this requires a capacity to translate unfamiliar but important jargon (such as *object, cathexis,* and *introjection*); this connotative recasting requires, perhaps not a Rosetta stone, but the patience to learn an obscure dialect. The clinical information base, lack of scientific rigor, and academic isolation of psychoanalytic theory have facilitated creative but at times inexact and rigid thinking, exemplified by strict definitions of concepts like "normal autism" and "symbiosis." However, the convergence of developmental psychology with many basic psychoanalytic propositions about separation adds to their weight. Attachment research not only provides a testing ground for these ideas but also offers an independent, more scientifically rigorous source of findings and perspectives for psychoanalysis to incorporate. The attachment field offers a bridge between psychoanalysis and mainstream academic developmental psychology, which is only beginning to tackle the complexity that clinicians have long faced.

Representation and the Phenomenology of Separation. As we have suggested, an integrated view of the psychology of separation rests on the notion of cognitive/affective schemata, a concept with wide acceptance in psychoanalytic theory (self- and object representations, in attachment theory (internal working models), in social psychology (scripts), and in related fields. One can imagine a complex hierarchical network of generalized and specific dynamic representations that shape perception, motivate behavior, and form the basis of interpersonal relating, self-esteem, and inner well-being. The deepest and most far-reaching, in its influence on separation reactions, interpersonal patterns, and emotional adjustment, would be the pre-oedipal (or security of attachment) set of representational structures. According to the nuances of separation-individuation theory, these self- and object representational structures shape more than secure, ambivalent, or anxious attachment. Rather, each individual's unique set of inner representations carries a subtle mix of predispositions, vulnerabilities, and resiliences regarding loss, closeness, affect regulation, and the boundaries of the self. The nonconcordance of representational structures based on variability in caregiving interactions suggests that there may be multiple basic-level structures. Within a representational model, one can incorporate psychosexual stages by considering the modes of bodily experiences that give meaning and shape to internalized interpersonal transactions, which are then psychologically elaborated into representational structures (see Lichtenberg, 1983). Mental constructions begin at a bodily, or sensory-motor, level and shift representational level in a Piagetian cognitive-developmental manner though perhaps not in accord with Piaget's original timetables. As others note, representations exist in different modalities and need not be symbolic (Blatt, 1974;

Geller, Smith-Behrends, and Hartley, 1982; Horowitz, 1983). Thus, criticisms of symbiosis that note the infant's incapacity to represent merger wishes until the second year of life (for example, Lichtenberg, 1983; Stern, 1985) may underemphasize the affective/motoric nature of early representation. If attachment relationships form by six or seven months of age, it is likely that the psychological structures underlying these bonds, including sensory-motor encodings of merger wishes, are also in evidence.

The foundation structures, or basic representational configurations, involving attachment and separation have multiple effects. First, as the literature shows, responses to separation provide an index of overall adjustment. Second, we suggest that development of a vulnerability to separation in the early years not only negatively affects later adjustment but creates a specifically heightened difficulty in coping with life events that entail separation. Thus, school entry, summer camp, and leaving home may be more problematic for the separation-vulnerable individual than functioning in school with a familiar teacher or attending college while living at home. Although the representational schemata regarding separation that develop after age three may not carry so great a shaping influence, continued life experience and the representations it spawns will reinforce, modify, or counter the early structures. Changes in the caregiving environment in childhood are central to the expansion or alteration of these schemata. Such changes include enduring traumatic shifts in the family system, such as divorce or remarriage (Chapter Ten, this volume) and parental death (Chapter Eleven). Other caregiving alterations may originate in fluctuations within the parents themselves, including emotional crises that temporarily disrupt parental availability (such as depression) or variability in the capacity to respond to children's different developmental needs (see Chapter Seven, this volume, and Stierlin, 1981, for discussions of parental difficulties in coping with the separation of adolescents leaving home).

Negative self- and object images and vulnerability to loss can be modified by later experience. For example, a child with early separation problems related to extended maternal illness might become less sensitive to loss with nurturant, consistent corrective parenting experiences at a later age. However, given the central shaping influence of the earliest caregiving transactions, problematic early experience may still leave a mark on adult personality. A different but likewise mutative scenario is evident when a relatively solid emotional foundation is rocked by later familial instability, such as repeated geographical moves or marital disruption and divorce. In most families, however, it is likely that the emotional resources available to children are relatively stable across time, resulting in positive or negative cycles. The parent who is both nurturant and firm provides a healthy influence throughout the child's development, while the parent with emotional difficulties may provide problematic transactions throughout.

The cyclic increase in separation mastery or separation problems is further intensified by the subjectivity of perceptions filtered through the internal working model. The child with early vulnerability to separation will experience separation events as more difficult and painful and will have fewer emotional resources available for mastering these separations. The child with a solid emotional foundation will perceive separation events as less threatening and less difficult to master; a pattern of healthy adaptation will be set in place, and later adjustments will be easier.

The inner affective dynamics pertaining to separation reflect this same polarization. Secure attachment, cohesive self-experience, and object constancy all imply the capacity to tolerate rage toward the lost or depriving object. When there are sufficient positive feelings toward the separated figure to balance the negative feelings engendered by the loss, loss is less threatening and separation is facilitated. But the less one is loved, the more rage and anger are produced; heightened rage originating from inadequate nurturance is inherently disturbing because internalized loving and soothing self- and object structures are fewer. Hence, it is harder to become separate and harder to separate from relationships when loving internalizations have been scarce. In contrast, when love has been plentiful and non-conflictual, it is easier to become separate and easier to separate .

from attachments. An early foundation of separation difficulty —of lack of separateness, in Mahler's sense, or insecure attachment, in Bowlby's model—explains why adolescents have a harder time leaving pathological homes, why marital abuse may not motivate divorce, and why it is hard for patients to weather therapists' silences, pregnancies, and vacations. Rage evoked by the experience of loss is overwhelming when one lacks the capacity to maintain an integrated imago of the lost love object— that is, an image that includes loving attributes that help to balance or neutralize the rage. Or, from another perspective, scarce resources must be protected, and when the internalized sense of having been loved is limited, the risk of jeopardizing any available opportunities for nurturance is rendered more threatening.

Anger and separation are intertwined, and they create an inherent dynamic conflict regarding response to loss. Anger or conflict entails a subjective state of distance from others; the lack of closeness experienced during anger is itself a separation experience. Thus, not only does loss evoke anger and also raise the specter of further loss by threatening the bond with the absent loved one, but *the angry state itself intrinsically involves additional feelings of loss* (which produce more anger, implying more distance and hence more anger, and so on). In this way an intense cycle of feelings of separation and anger builds to a climax of heightened rage that may be too threatening to be consciously experienced or expressed, especially when the scales tip in the direction of separation and loss rather than closeness and nurturance. When rage cannot be expressed, it becomes hidden and transformed, most often into depression and frequently from depression into anxiety or psychosomatic complaints, obsessional thought cycles, or other symptoms. Such transformations make up the mosaiclike puzzle of the interpersonal maze of psychotherapy or psychoanalysis, which recapitulates the dyadic transactional history underlying the representational patterns that govern the meaning of separation.

The psychological dynamics of reaction to separation are complicated by many other factors, including familial, societal, and cultural influences on, and meanings ascribed to, interpersonal closeness, affect expression, and loss. Some of these dimensions are discussed in detail in this volume; consider the issue of family systems' responses to the child's adolescent struggle with separation and individuation (Chapter Seven), the work on family functioning and separation (Chapter Eight), and the role of mental representations of culture in the psychological adaptation of immigrants experiencing culture loss (Chapter Nine). The larger net of social forces impinging on the individual, from the family to social class to culture to societal events, cannot be ignored in considering the psychological meaning of separation and the factors that influence separation behavior (Bergmann and Jucovy, 1982; McCubbin and others, 1974; Mitscherlich and Mitscherlich, 1975).

Unconscious dispositions regarding separation resonate both to interpersonal events of loss and to any experience that entails surrendering something familiar or loved. It is necessary to distinguish a resilient, well-integrated stance toward separation from the many individual variants of defensive avoidance of the threat of loss. Individuals who suffer from inadequate nurturance and conflictual early relationships but deny the attendant separation anxiety and dependent longings may flee into new transitions, take excessive risks, or compulsively seek creative outlets while maintaining a rigid self-reliance. Both counterdependent and dependent means of coping with actual or potential loss preclude the healthy mastery of separation experience. Because development and growth intrinsically require adaptation to change, successful mastery of the conflictful affects stirred by separation and loss may promote new capacities for autonomous thought and new avenues for creative expression, laying the groundwork for continued positive transformations of the self (Becker, 1973).

In *Three Essays on the Theory of Sexuality,* Freud (1905/1953) suggests that anxiety in children is, in essence, a reaction to the loss of the person they love. Bowlby (1973) reminds us of William James's (1890) observation that "the great source of terror in infancy is solitude." The study of separation pursues this core problem of human existence through the normative and pathological pathways of the development of the self, from the functions and features of reactions to separation and loss to theories of the psyche in which transformation of root experience describes a labyrinthine, but predictable, emotional course. We hope that conceptual integration of disparate disciplinary methods and epistemologies, with less attachment to any single approach, will facilitate understanding of separation phenomena.

References

Abelin, E. L. "The Role of the Father in the Separation-Individuation Process." In J. B. McDevitt and C. F. Settlage (eds.), *Separation-Individuation: Essays in Honor of Margaret S. Mahler.* New York: International Universities Press, 1971.

Abelson, R. P. "Whatever Became of Consistency Theory?" *Personality and Social Psychology Bulletin,* 1983, *9,* 37-54.

Ainsworth, M. D. S. "Object Relations, Dependency, and Attachment: A Theoretical Review of the Infant-Mother Relationship." *Child Development,* 1969, *40,* 969-1025.

Ainsworth, M. D. S., Blehar, M. C., Waters, E., and Wall, S. *Patterns of Attachment: A Psychological Study of the Strange Situation.* Hillsdale, N.J.: Erlbaum, 1978.

Axelrad, S., and Maury, L. M. "Identification as a Mechanism of Adaptation." In G. B. Wilbur and W. Muensterberger (eds.), *Psychoanalysis and Culture.* New York: International Universities Press, 1951.

Balint, M. "Early Developmental States of the Ego: Primary Object Love." In A. Balint and M. Balint (eds.), *Primary Love and Psychoanalytic Technique.* New York: Liveright, 1965. (Originally published 1937.)

Becker, E. *The Denial of Death.* New York: Free Press, 1973.

Behrends, R. S., and Blatt, S. J. "Internalization and Psychological Development Throughout the Life Cycle." *Psychoanalytic Study of the Child,* 1985, *40,* 11-39.

Bender, L., and Yarnell, H. "An Observation Nursery." *American Journal of Psychiatry,* 1941, *97,* 1158-1174.

Bergmann, M. S., and Jucovy, M. E. (eds.). *Generations of the Holocaust.* New York: Basic Books, 1982.

Berndt, T. J. "Relations Between Social Cognition, Nonsocial

Cognition, and Social Behavior: The Case of Friendship." In J. H. Flavell and L. D. Ross (eds.), *Social Cognitive Development: Frontiers and Possible Futures*. Cambridge, England: Cambridge University Press, 1981.

Blatt, S. J. "Levels of Object Representation in Anaclitic and Introjective Depression." *Psychoanalytic Study of the Child*, 1974, *29*, 107–157.

Blatt, S. J., Brenneis, C. B., Schimek, J., and Glick, M. "Normal Development and Psychopathological Impairment of the Concept of the Object on the Rorschach." *Journal of Abnormal Psychology*, 1976, *85*, 364–373.

Blatt, S. J., and Lerner, H. "The Psychological Assessment of Object Representation." *Journal of Personality Assessment*, 1983, *47*, 7–28.

Blatt, S. J., Wein, S. J., Chevron, E., and Quinlan, D. M. "Parental Representations and Depression in Normal Young Adults." *Journal of Abnormal Psychology*, 1979, *88*, 388–397.

Blatt, S. J., and Wild, C. M. *Schizophrenia: A Developmental Analysis*. Orlando, Fla.: Academic Press, 1976.

Bloom-Feshbach, J. "Object Relations Theory and the Multiple Dimensions of Intrapsychic Organization." Unpublished manuscript, Department of Psychology, Yale University, 1979.

Bloom-Feshbach, J. "Historical Perspectives on the Father's Role." In M. E. Lamb (ed.), *The Role of the Father in Child Development*. (2nd ed.) New York: Wiley, 1981.

Bloom-Feshbach, J., and Bloom-Feshbach, S. "Psychodynamic Psychotherapy and Research on Early Childhood Development." In G. Stricker and R. H. Keisner (eds.), *From Research to Clinical Practice: The Implications of Social and Developmental Research for Psychotherapy*. New York: Plenum, 1985.

Bloom-Feshbach, S., Bloom-Feshbach, J., and Gaughran, J. "The Child's Tie to Both Parents: Separation Patterns and Nursery School Adjustment." *American Journal of Orthopsychiatry*, 1980, *50*, 505–521.

Blos, P. "The Second Individuation Process of Adolescence." *Psychoanalytic Study of the Child*, 1967, *22*, 162–186.

Bowlby, J. "The Influence of Early Environment in the Development of Neurosis and Neurotic Character." *International Journal of Psycho-Analysis,* 1940, *21,* 154-178.

Bowlby, J. "Forty-Four Juvenile Thieves: Their Characters and Home Life." *International Journal of Psycho-Analysis,* 1944, *25,* 107-128.

Bowlby, J. "The Nature of the Child's Tie to His Mother." *International Journal of Psycho-Analysis,* 1958, *39,* 350-373.

Bowlby, J. *Attachment and Loss.* Vol. 1: *Attachment.* New York: Basic Books, 1969.

Bowlby, J. *Attachment and Loss.* Vol. 2: *Separation: Anxiety and Anger.* New York: Basic Books, 1973.

Bowlby, J. *Attachment and Loss.* Vol. 3: *Loss: Sadness and Depression.* New York: Basic Books, 1980.

Bowlby, J. "Attachment and Loss: Retrospect and Prospect." *American Journal of Orthopsychiatry,* 1982, *52*(4), 664-678.

Bretherton, I. "Attachment Theory: Retrospect and Prospect." In I. Bretherton and E. Waters (eds.), "Growing Points of Attachment Theory and Research." *Monographs of the Society for Research in Child Development,* 1985, *50*(1-2, Serial No. 209).

Bretherton, I., and Waters, E. (eds.). "Growing Points of Attachment Theory and Research." *Monographs of the Society for Research in Child Development,* 1985, *50*(1-2, Serial No. 209).

Brody, S. "The Concepts of Attachment and Bonding." *Journal of the American Psychoanalytic Association,* 1981, *29*(4), 815-829.

Brooks-Gunn, J., and Lewis, M. "Why Mama and Papa? The Development of Social Labels." *Child Development,* 1979, *50,* 1203-1206.

Burgner, M., and Edgcumbe, R. "Some Problems in the Conceptualization of Early Object Relationships." *Psychoanalytic Study of the Child,* 1972, *27,* 315-333.

Burke, W. F., Summers, F., Selinger, D., and Polonus, B. S. "The Comprehensive Object Relations Profile: A Preliminary Report." *Psychoanalytic Psychology,* 1986, *3*(2), 173-185.

Burlingham, D. T., and Freud, A. *Young Children in War-Time.* London: Allen & Unwin, 1942.

Carlson, R. "Studies in Script Theory: I. Adult Analogs of a Childhood Nuclear Scene." *Journal of Personality and Social Psychology,* 1981, *40,* 501–510.

Cooley, C. H. *Human Nature and the Social Order.* New York: Scribner's, 1902.

Craik, K. *The Nature of Explanation.* Cambridge, England: Cambridge University Press, 1943.

DeCasper, A. J. "The Mommy Tapes." *Science News,* 1979, *115*(4), 56.

DeLozier, P. P. "Attachment Theory and Child Abuse." In C. M. Parkes and J. Stevenson-Hinde (eds.), *The Place of Attachment in Human Behavior.* New York: Basic Books, 1982.

Eagle, M. N. *Recent Developments in Psychoanalysis: A Critical Evaluation.* New York: McGraw-Hill, 1984.

Egeland, B., and Sroufe, L. A. "Attachment and Early Maltreatment." *Child Development,* 1981a, *52,* 44–52.

Egeland, B., and Sroufe, L. A. "Developmental Sequelae of Maltreatment in Infancy." In R. Rizley and D. Cicchetti (eds.), *Developmental Perspectives on Child Maltreatment.* New Directions for Child Development, no. 11. San Francisco: Jossey-Bass, 1981b.

Emde, R. N., and Harmon, R. J. (eds.). *The Development of Attachment and Affiliative Systems.* New York: Plenum, 1982.

Engel, G. L. "Attachment Behavior, Object Relations, and the Dynamic Point of View: A Critical Review of Bowlby's *Attachment and Loss.*" *International Journal of Psycho-Analysis,* 1971, *52,* 183–196.

Fairbairn, W. R. D. *Psychoanalytic Studies of the Personality.* London: Tavistock, 1952.

Ferenczi, S. *The Selected Papers of Sandor Ferenczi.* New York: Basic Books, 1950.

Fraiberg, S. "Libidinal Object Constancy and Mental Representation." *Psychoanalytic Study of the Child,* 1969, *24,* 9–47.

Fraiberg, S. "Separation Crisis in Two Blind Children." *Psychoanalytic Study of the Child,* 1971, *26,* 355–371.

Freedman, D. G. *Human Infancy: An Evolutionary Perspective.* Hillsdale, N.J.: Erlbaum, 1974.

Freud, A. "The Mutual Influences in the Development of Ego and Id." *Psychoanalytic Study of the Child,* 1952, 7, 42–50.

Freud, A. "Discussion of Dr. John Bowlby's Paper." *Psychoanalytic Study of the Child,* 1960, *15,* 53–62.

Freud, A., and Burlingham, D. T. *Infants Without Families: The Case For and Against Residential Nurseries.* New York: International Universities Press, 1944.

Freud, S. "Three Essays on the Theory of Sexuality." In J. Strachey (ed. and trans.), *The Standard Edition of the Complete Psychological Works of Sigmund Freud.* Vol. 7. London: Hogarth Press, 1953. (Originally published 1905.)

Freud, S. "Mourning and Melancholia." In J. Strachey (ed. and trans.), *The Standard Edition of the Complete Psychological Works of Sigmund Freud.* Vol. 14. London: Hogarth Press, 1957. (Originally published 1917.)

Freud, S. "Inhibitions, Symptoms and Anxiety." In J. Strachey (ed. and trans.), *The Standard Edition of the Complete Psychological Works of Sigmund Freud.* Vol. 20. London: Hogarth Press, 1959. (Originally published 1926.)

Freud, S. "The Ego and the Id." In J. Strachey (ed. and trans.), *The Standard Edition of the Complete Psychological Works of Sigmund Freud.* Vol. 19. London: Hogarth Press, 1961. (Originally published 1923.)

Freud, S. "An Outline of Psychoanalysis." In J. Strachey (ed. and trans.), *The Standard Edition of the Complete Psychological Works of Sigmund Freud.* Vol. 23. London: Hogarth Press, 1964. (Originally published 1940.)

Furman, E. *A Child's Parent Dies: Studies in Childhood Bereavement.* New Haven, Conn.: Yale University Press, 1974.

Gedo, J. E. *Beyond Interpretation.* New York: International Universities Press, 1979.

Gedo, J. E. "Reflections on Some Current Controversies in Psychoanalysis." *Journal of the American Psychoanalytic Association,* 1980, *28,* 363–383.

Geller, J. D., Smith-Behrends, R., and Hartley, D. "Images of the Psychotherapist: A Theoretical and Methodological Perspective." *Imagination, Cognition, and Personality,* 1982, *1,* 123-146.

George, C., and Main, M. "Social Interactions of Young Abused Children: Approach, Avoidance, and Aggression." *Child Development,* 1979, *50,* 306-318.

Goldfarb, W. "The Effects of Early Institutional Care on Adolescent Personality." *Journal of Experimental Education,* 1943, *12,* 106-129.

Goldfarb, W. "Effects of Early Institutional Care on Adolescent Personality: Rorschach Data." *American Journal of Orthopsychiatry,* 1944, *14,* 441-447.

Goldfarb, W. "Psychological Privation in Infancy and Subsequent Adjustment." *American Journal of Orthopsychiatry,* 1945, *15,* 247-255.

Goldfarb, W. "Emotional and Intellectual Consequences of Psychologic Deprivation in Infancy: A Reevaluation." In P. Hoch and J. Zubin (eds.), *Psychopathology of Childhood.* Orlando, Fla.: Grune & Stratton, 1955.

Greenspan, S. I. *Psychopathology and Adaptation in Infancy and Early Childhood.* Clinical Infants Reports, no. 1. New York: International Universities Press, 1981.

Greenspan, S. I. "Three Levels of Learning: A Developmental Approach to 'Awareness' and Mind-Body Relations." *Psychoanalytic Inquiry,* 1982, *1,* 659-694.

Hanly, C. "A Critical Consideration of Bowlby's Ethological Theory of Anxiety." *Psychoanalytic Quarterly,* 1978, *67,* 364-380.

Harlow, H. F. "The Nature of Love." *American Psychologist,* 1958, *13,* 673-685.

Harlow, H. F., and Harlow, M. K. "The Affectional Systems." In A. D. Schrier, H. F. Harlow, and F. Stallnitz (eds.), *Behavior of Non-Human Primates.* Vol. 2. Orlando, Fla.: Academic Press, 1965.

Harlow, H. F., and Harlow, M. K. "Effects of Various Mother-Infant Relationships on Rhesus Monkey Behaviors." In B. M. Foss (ed.), *Determinants of Infant Behavior.* Vol. 4. London: Methuen, 1969.

Harter, S. "Developmental Perspectives on the Self-System."

In E. M. Hetherington (ed.), P. H. Mussen (series ed.), *Handbook of Child Psychology*. Vol. 4: *Socialization, Personality, and Social Development.* (4th ed.) New York: Wiley, 1983.

Henderson, S. "The Significance of Social Relationships in the Etiology of Neurosis." In C. M. Parkes and J. Stevenson-Hinde (eds.), *The Place of Attachment in Human Behavior.* New York: Basic Books, 1982.

Holt, R. "The Past and Future of Ego Psychology." *Psychoanalytic Quarterly,* 1975, *44,* 550-576.

Horowitz, M. J. *Image Formation and Psychotherapy.* New York: Jason Aronson, 1983.

Hunt, J. M. "Psychological Development: Early Experience." *Annual Review of Psychology,* 1979, *30,* 103-143.

Jakobson, R. "Why 'Mama' and 'Papa'?" In *Selected Writings of Roman Jakobson.* The Hague: Mouton, 1962.

James, W. *The Principles of Psychology.* (2 vols.) New York: Holt, 1890.

Katan, A. "Some Thoughts About the Role of Verbalization in Early Childhood." *Psychoanalytic Study of the Child,* 1961, *16,* 184-188.

Kellam, S. G., Ensminger, M. E., and Turner, R. J. "Family Structure and the Mental Health of Children." *Archives of General Psychiatry,* 1977, *34,* 1012-1022.

Kernberg, O. *Borderline Conditions and Pathological Narcissism.* New York: Jason Aronson, 1975.

Kernberg, O. *Object Relations Theory and Clinical Psychoanalysis.* New York: Jason Aronson, 1976.

Klein, G. *Psychoanalytic Theory: An Exploration of Essentials.* New York: International Universities Press, 1976.

Klein, M. *The Psycho-Analysis of Children.* London: Hogarth Press, 1949. (Originally published 1932.)

Klein, M. "On Mahler's Autistic and Symbiotic Phases: An Exposition and Evaluation." *Psychoanalysis and Contemporary Thought,* 1981, *4,* 69-105.

Kohut, H. *The Analysis of the Self.* New York: International Universities Press, 1971.

Krohn, A., and Mayman, M. "Object Representations in Dreams and Projective Tests: A Construct Validational Study." *Bulletin of the Menninger Clinic,* 1974, *38,* 445-466.

Lamb, M. E. "Father-Infant and Mother-Infant Interaction in the First Year of Life." *Child Development,* 1977, *48,* 167–181.

Lamb, M. E. "Influence of the Child on Marital Quality and Family Interaction During the Prenatal, Perinatal, and Infancy Periods." In R. M. Lerner and G. B. Spanier (eds.), *Child Influences on Marital and Family Interaction: A Life-Span Perspective.* Orlando, Fla.: Academic Press, 1978.

Lamb, M. E. "Separation and Reunion Behaviors as Criteria of Attachment to Mothers and Fathers." *Early Human Development,* 1979, *3/4,* 329–339.

Lamb, M. E. (ed.). *The Role of the Father in Child Development.* (2nd ed.) New York: Wiley, 1981.

Lamb, M. E., and Sutton-Smith, B. (eds.). *Sibling Relationships: Their Nature and Significance Across the Lifespan.* Hillsdale, N.J.: Erlbaum, 1982.

Levy, D. "Primary Affect Hunger." *American Journal of Psychiatry,* 1937, *94,* 643–652.

Lewis, M., and Feiring, C. "The Child's Social World." In R. M. Lerner and G. B. Spanier (eds.), *Child Influences on Marital and Family Interaction: A Life-Span Perspective.* Orlando, Fla.: Academic Press, 1978.

Lewis, M., Feiring, C., and Weinraub, M. "The Father as a Member of the Child's Social Network." In M. E. Lamb (ed.), *The Role of the Father in Child Development.* (2nd ed.) New York: Wiley, 1981.

Lichtenberg, J. D. *Psychoanalysis and Infant Research.* Hillsdale, N.J.: Analytic Press, 1983.

Lifton, R. J. "Preface." In A. Mitscherlich and M. Mitscherlich, *The Inability to Mourn.* New York: Grove Press, 1975.

Loevinger, J. *Ego Development: Conceptions and Theories.* San Francisco: Jossey-Bass, 1976.

Loewald, H. W. "On the Therapeutic Action of Psycho-Analysis." *International Journal of Psycho-Analysis,* 1960, *41,* 16–33.

Maccoby, E. E., and Masters, J. "Attachment and Dependency." In P. H. Mussen (ed.), *Carmichael's Manual of Child Psychology.* Vol. 2. New York: Wiley, 1970.

McCubbin, H. I., and others (eds.). *Family Separation and Re-*

union: *Families of Prisoners of War and Servicemen Missing in Action.* Washington, D.C.: Naval Health Research Center, 1974.

McDevitt, J. B. "The Role of Internalization in the Development of Object Relations During the Separation-Individuation Phase." In R. F. Lax, S. Bach, and J. A. Burland (eds.), *Rapprochement: The Critical Subphase of Separation-Individuation.* New York: Jason Aronson, 1980.

McDevitt, J. B., and Settlage, C. F. (eds.). *Separation-Individuation: Essays in Honor of Margaret S. Mahler.* New York: International Universities Press, 1971.

Mahler, M. S. "On Child Psychosis and Schizophrenia: Autistic and Symbiotic Infantile Psychoses." *Psychoanalytic Study of the Child,* 1952, *7,* 286–305.

Mahler, M. S., and Elkish, P. "Some Observations on Disturbances of the Ego in a Case of Infantile Psychosis." *Psychoanalytic Study of the Child,* 1953, *8,* 252–361.

Mahler, M. S., and Gosliner, B. J. "On Symbiotic Child Psychosis: Genetic, Dynamic, and Restitutive Aspects." *Psychoanalytic Study of the Child,* 1955, *10,* 195–212.

Mahler, M. S., Pine, F., and Bergman, A. *The Psychological Birth of the Human Infant: Symbiosis and Individuation.* New York: Basic Books, 1975.

Main, M., Kaplan, N., and Cassidy, J. "Security in Infancy, Childhood, and Adulthood: A Move to the Level of Representation." In I. Bretherton and E. Waters (eds.), "Growing Points of Attachment Theory and Research." *Monographs of the Society for Research in Child Development,* 1985, *50*(1–2, Serial No. 209).

Mandler, J. H. "Categorical and Schematic Organization in Memory." In C. R. Puff (ed.), *Memory Organization and Structure.* Orlando, Fla.: Academic Press, 1979.

Mandler, J. H. "Representation." In J. H. Flavell and E. M. Markman (eds.), P. H. Mussen (series ed.), *Handbook of Child Psychology.* Vol. 3: *Cognitive Development.* (4th ed.) New York: Wiley, 1983.

Masterson, J. *Psychotherapy of the Borderline Adult: A Developmental Approach.* New York: Brunner/Mazel, 1976.

Matas, L., Arend, R. A., and Sroufe, L. A. "Continuity of Adaptation in the Second Year: The Relationship Between Quality of Attachment and Later Competence." *Child Development,* 1978, *49,* 547–556.

Mayman, M. "Object Representations and Object Relationships in Rorschach Responses." *Journal of Projective Techniques and Personality Assessment,* 1967, *31,* 17–24.

Mayman, M. "Early Memories and Character Structure." *Journal of Projective Techniques and Personality Assessment,* 1968, *32,* 303–316.

Mead, G. H. *Mind, Self, and Society.* Chicago: University of Chicago Press, 1934.

Meissner, W. W. "Internalization and Object Relations." *Journal of the American Psychoanalytic Association,* 1979, *27,* 345–360.

Mischel, W. "Processes in Delay of Gratification." In L. Berkowitz (ed.), *Advances in Experimental Social Psychology.* Vol. 7. Orlando, Fla.: Academic Press, 1974.

Mitscherlich, A., and Mitscherlich, M. *The Inability to Mourn.* New York: Grove Press, 1975.

Nelson, K., and Gruendel, J. "Generalized Event Representations: Basic Building Blocks of Cognitive Development." In M. E. Lamb and A. Brown (eds.), *Advances in Developmental Psychology.* Vol. 1. Hillsdale, N.J.: Erlbaum, 1981.

Norman, D. A., and Rumelhart, D. E. "Memory and Knowledge." In D. A. Norman and D. E. Rumelhart (eds.), *Explorations in Cognition.* New York: W. H. Freeman, 1982.

Parke, R. D., and Tinsley, B. R. "The Father's Role in Infancy: Determinants of Involvement in Caregiving and Play." In M. E. Lamb (ed.), *The Role of the Father in Child Development.* (2nd ed.) New York: Wiley, 1981.

Peterfreund, E. "Information, Systems, and Psychoanalysis." *Psychological Issues,* 1971, Monographs 25 and 26.

Peterfreund, E. "Some Critical Comments on Psychoanalytic Conceptions of Infancy." *International Journal of Psycho-Analysis,* 1978, *59,* 427–441.

Piaget, J. *The Construction of Reality in the Child.* New York: Basic Books, 1954.

Pine, F. *Developmental Theory and Clinical Process.* New Haven, Conn.: Yale University Press, 1985.

Pound, A. "Attachment and Maternal Depression." In C. M. Parkes and J. Stevenson-Hinde (eds.), *The Place of Attachment in Human Behavior.* New York: Basic Books, 1982.

Rank, O. *The Trauma of Birth.* London: Kegan Paul, 1929.

Ricks, M. H. "The Social Transmission of Parental Behavior: Attachment Across Generations." In I. Bretherton and E. Waters (eds.), "Growing Points of Attachment Theory and Research." *Monographs of the Society for Research in Child Development,* 1985, *50*(1-2, Serial No. 209).

Robertson, J. *Young Children in Hospital.* (2nd ed.) London: Tavistock, 1970.

Rochlin, G. "Review of Bowlby, J., *Attachment and Loss. I: Attachment." Psychoanalytic Quarterly,* 1971, *50,* 504-506.

Roiphe, J. "Review of J. Bowlby, *Attachment and Loss. II: Separation: Anxiety and Anger." Psychoanalytic Quarterly,* 1976, *65,* 307-309.

Rutter, M. "Parent-Child Separation: Psychological Effects on the Children." *Journal of Child Psychology and Psychiatry,* 1971, *12,* 233-260.

Rutter, M. "Maternal Deprivation, 1972-1978: New Findings, New Concepts, New Approaches." *Child Development,* 1979, *50,* 283-305.

Sandler, J., and Rosenblatt, B. "The Concept of the Representational World." *Psychoanalytic Study of the Child,* 1962, *17,* 128-145.

Schafer, R. *A New Language for Psychoanalysis.* New Haven, Conn.: Yale University Press, 1976.

Schaffer, H. R., and Emerson, P. E. "The Development of Social Attachments in Infancy." *Monographs of the Society for Research in Child Development,* 1964, *29*(3) (Serial No. 94).

Schanberg, S. M., and Kuhn, C. M. "Maternal Deprivation: An Animal Model of Psychosocial Dwarfism." In E. Usdin, T. L. Sourkes, and M. B. Youdin (eds.), *Enzymes and Neurotransmitters.* New York: Wiley, 1980.

Schank, R. C., and Abelson, R. P. *Scripts, Plans, Goals, and Understanding.* Hillsdale, N.J.: Erlbaum, 1977.

Selman, R. L. *The Growth of Interpersonal Understanding: Developmental and Clinical Analyses.* Orlando, Fla.: Academic Press, 1980.

Sigel, I. "The Distancing Hypothesis: A Causal Hypothesis for the Acquisition of Representational Thought." In M. R. Jones (ed.), *Miami Symposium on the Prediction of Behavior, 1968: Effect of Early Experience.* Coral Gables, Fla.: University of Miami Press, 1970.

Silverman, L. H., Lachmann, F. M., and Milich, R. H. *The Search for Oneness.* New York: International Universities Press, 1982.

Singer, J. L. "Transference and the Human Condition: A Cognitive-Affective Perspective." *Psychoanalytic Psychology,* 1985, *2*(3), 189–219.

Skodak, M., and Skeels, H. M. "A Final Follow-Up Study of One Hundred Adopted Children." *Journal of Genetic Psychology,* 1949, *75,* 85–125.

Spear, W., and Sugarman, A. "Dimensions of Internalized Object Relations in Borderline and Schizophrenic Patients." *Psychoanalytic Psychology,* 1984, *1,* 77–92.

Spitz, R. A. "Hospitalism: An Inquiry into the Genesis of Psychiatric Conditions in Early Childhood." *Psychoanalytic Study of the Child,* 1945, *1,* 53–74.

Spitz, R. A. "Discussion of Dr. John Bowlby's Paper." *Psychoanalytic Study of the Child,* 1960, *15,* 85–94.

Spitz, R. A. "Metapsychology and Direct Infant Observation." In R. M. Loewenstein, L. M. Newman, M. Shure, and A. J. Solnit (eds.), *Psychoanalysis: A General Psychology.* New York: International Universities Press, 1966.

Spitz, R. A., and Wolf, K. "Anaclitic Depression: An Inquiry into the Genesis of Psychiatric Conditions in Early Childhood, II." *Psychoanalytic Study of the Child,* 1946, *2,* 313–342.

Sroufe, L. A. "Infant-Caregiver Attachment and Patterns of Adaptation in Preschool: The Roots of Maladaptation and Competence." In M. Perlmutter (ed.), *Minnesota Symposium in Child Psychology.* Vol. 16. Hillsdale, N.J.: Erlbaum, 1983.

Stern, D. N. "The Early Development of Schemas of Self, Others, and 'Self with Others.' " In J. D. Lichtenberg and S. Kaplan (eds.), *Reflections on Self Psychology.* Hillsdale, N.J.: Analytic Press, 1983.

Stern, D. N. *The Interpersonal World of the Infant: A View from Psychoanalysis and Developmental Psychology.* New York: Basic Books, 1985.

Stierlin, H. *Separating Parents and Adolescents.* New York: Jason Aronson, 1981.

Stolorow, R. D., and Lachmann, F. *Psychoanalysis of Developmental Arrests: Theory and Treatment.* New York: International Universities Press, 1980.

Sugarman, A., Bloom-Feshbach, S., and Bloom-Feshbach, J. "The Psychological Dimensions of Borderline Adolescents." In J. Kwawer, H. Lerner, P. Lerner, and A. Sugarman (eds.), *Borderline Phenomena and the Rorschach Test.* New York: International Universities Press, 1980.

Sugarman, A., Quinlan, D. M., and Devennis, L. "Anorexia Nervosa as a Defense Against Anaclitic Depression." *International Journal of Eating Disorders,* 1981, *1,* 44–61.

Sullivan, H. S. *The Interpersonal Theory of Psychiatry.* New York: Norton, 1953.

Suttie, I. D. *The Origins of Love and Hate.* London: Kegan Paul, 1935.

Thoman, E. B., and Arnold, W. J. "Maternal Behavior in Rats." *Journal of Comparative Physiological Psychology,* 1968, *65,* 441–446.

Tizard, B., and Hodges, J. "The Effect of Early Institutional Rearing on the Development of Eight Year Old Children." *Journal of Child Psychology and Psychiatry,* 1978, *19,* 99–118.

Tomkins, S. S. "Script Theory: Differential Magnification of Affects." In H. E. Howe, Jr., and R. A. Dienstbier (eds.), *Nebraska Symposium on Motivation.* Vol. 26. Lincoln: University of Nebraska Press, 1979.

Urist, J. "The Rorschach Test and the Assessment of Object Relations." *Journal of Personality Assessment,* 1977, *41,* 3–9.

Wachs, T. D., and Gruen, G. E. *Early Experience and Human Development.* New York: Plenum, 1982.

Weinraub, M., and Frankel, J. "Sex Differences in Parent-Infant Interaction During Free Play, Departure, and Separation." *Child Development,* 1977, *48,* 1240–1249.

Weiss, R. S. "Attachment in Adult Life." In C. M. Parkes and J. Stevenson-Hinde (eds.), *The Place of Attachment in Human Behavior.* New York: Basic Books, 1982.

Werner, H. *Comparative Psychology of Mental Development.* New York: International Universities Press, 1957.

Werner, H., and Kaplan, B. *Symbol Formation: An Organismic-Developmental Approach to Language and the Expression of Thought.* New York: Wiley, 1963.

White, G. L., and La Barba, R. C. "The Effects of Tactile and Kinesthetic Stimulation on Neonatal Development in the Premature Infant." *Journal of Developmental Psychobiology,* 1976, *9,* 569–577.

Winnicott, D. W. "Transitional Objects and Transitional Phenomena: A Study of the First Not-Me Possession." *International Journal of Psycho-Analysis,* 1953, *34,* 89–97.

Witkin, H. A. "Psychological Differentiation and Forms of Pathology." *Journal of Abnormal Psychology,* 1965, *70,* 317–336.

Witkin, H. A., and Goodenough, D. R. "Field Dependence and Interpersonal Behavior." *Psychological Bulletin,* 1977, *84,* 661–689.

Witkin, H. A., and others. *Personality Through Perception.* New York: Harper & Row, 1972.

Witkin, H. A., and others. *Psychological Differentiation: Studies of Development.* New York: Wiley, 1974.

Yarrow, L. J. "Separation from Parents During Early Childhood." In L. Hoffman and M. Hoffman (eds.), *Review of Research in Child Development.* Vol. 1. New York: Russell Sage Foundation, 1964.

Part One

The Role of Separation in Development

A toddler in her second year is upset and furious at her father after he shaves off his beard. She refuses to look at him and cries when he tries to initiate contact. Another individual, a college student, excels at structured classroom activity but becomes paralyzed in the face of term papers. What links these two response patterns is the effects of separation experiences for those with only partially developed psychological separateness. The first example illustrates the connection between representation and attachment, the power of the visual dimension of representation, and the separation response evoked by loss—in this case, the loss of the concretely represented father. The second example highlights the fact that a lack of psychological autonomy may prevent someone from functioning in solitary contexts. Working on conceptual tasks that require initiative, self-reflection, and independent activity may prove impossible when negative affect overwhelms a vulnerable, underdeveloped sense of self.

The attachment and psychoanalytic literatures delineate how psychological separateness, or autonomy, and the capacity to form and maintain healthy attachments are predicated on successful mastery of separations in the course of the early parent/child relationship. Less attention has been devoted to the question of the continued role that separation plays in later childhood, adolescence, and adulthood. At the least, the psychological foundation developed through the attachment and separation experiences of early childhood functions as a historical influence, shaping later interpersonal and affective experience. Although it is likely that separation experiences exert continued developmental influences throughout middle childhood and adolescence, it is more difficult to determine the nature and source of developmental change in adulthood. The inclusion in Part One of a chapter on the role of loss in nonhuman primates is meant to add an evolutionary developmental perspective to the consideration of separation and loss in the human life cycle.

1

Maternal Loss in Nonhuman Primates: Implications for Human Development

Edward H. Plimpton
Leonard A. Rosenblum

Editors' Note: *A major premise of this volume is that experiences of separation and loss universally exert an influence on human behavior, and, moreover, that this influence operates at the most fundamental level of social adaptation. Research on nonhuman primates has been a touchstone for this perspective. The classic Harlow studies of thirty years ago demonstrated that maternally deprived infant monkeys prefer tactile nurturance to nutritive nurturance offered by mother substitutes—a bold illustration of the basic and compelling nature of attachment motivation. Subsequent research has examined how nonhuman primates respond to maternal loss with protest and depression, calling attention to the biological, evolutionary heritage of the human attachment system. In this chapter, the authors explore various factors that shape reactions to loss, emphasizing that adaptation to separation involves a number of potentially competing adjustment pressures. For example, high work demands associated with obtaining food mitigate the depression of infant macaques separated from their mothers. The chapter also explores the dynamics of the affective detachment that often follows loss. The striking parallels between infant macaques' and infant humans' reactions to loss suggest behavioral similarity and, likely, a common psychological conflict between anger and love toward the absent attachment figure. The reader might compare the ecological and temporal influences on macaque infants with similar findings on nursery school children's reactions to separation (see Chapter Six).*

For a human or nonhuman primate infant, separation from the mother, who is usually the primary caregiver, can be a traumatic and even life-threatening event. Furthermore, it is unusual for maternal loss to occur in the absence of other major changes in the infant's life, such as the introduction of new caretakers or a new living environment. In the relatively controlled laboratory studies of maternal separation, the effects of disruption of the social bond can be examined in isolation, but in naturally occurring cases of maternal loss, a number of environmental changes ensue. Although maternal and other types of loss have been widely implicated in the development of emotional disorders, little attention has been given to how concomitant changes affect the outcome.

Substantial research has been conducted over the past twenty-five years on response to maternal loss in nonhuman primates (see Mineka and Suomi, 1978; Rosenblum and Plimpton, 1981). Investigators have been impressed by the similarities in the pattern of protest followed by despair found in both nonhuman primates and human infants (Bowlby, 1969). Immediately after maternal loss, both human and nonhuman primate infants engage in protest behavior during which they attempt to regain contact with mother. When reunion is not achieved, these infants sometimes become depressed. In addition to the behavioral research on the effects of separation in primates, several investigators have examined the physiological response to maternal loss (Coe and Levine, 1981; Reite and others, 1978; Coe, Mendoza, Smotherman, and Levine, 1978; Suomi, Kraemer, Baysinger, and De Lizio, 1981). A striking feature of these studies has been the frequent disparity between behavioral and physiological responses. For example, a separated infant that has been adopted by an adult female of its social group and is

showing no overt behavioral distress may nevertheless have highly elevated cortisol levels (Coe and Levine, 1981) and disturbances in temperature regulation (Reite, Seiler, and Short,
1978). As with human infants who have formed an attachment
(Yarrow and Goodwin, 1973), the separation response of nonhuman primates is tied to the absence of a particular individual
rather than to a lack of caregiving.

The impressive variability in separation behavior (Rosenblum and Plimpton, 1981) suggests the importance of enlarging
both the physical and temporal contexts in which events of loss
are examined. In this chapter, we would like to present a conceptual and empirical basis for understanding the relationship
between maternal loss and other variables that may change with
that event. We will show that most existing theories of the effects of separation have focused exclusively on the response to
the loss of mother as a psychological object. In contrast, we will
discuss experiments with nonhuman primates that illustrate
ways in which environmental variables of different kinds can influence the response to loss.

Before we begin our review, some general comments
about the objectives of comparative research may provide a useful orientation. The basic premise in comparative research with
nonhuman primates is that behavior as well as morphology has
been influenced by natural selection and other evolutionary
principles. A variety of environmental pressures, such as the distribution and availability of food and the presence of predators,
influence the expression of behavior over the course of evolutionary time. As with morphology, behavior that enhances the
organism's reproductive success—that is, the probability that its
genes will appear in subsequent generations—will be favored
through the principles of natural selection. As Gould (1983) has
consistently pointed out, an organism is not a collection of
separate parts on which natural selection can act but, rather, a
hierarchically organized and interrelated totality. An environmental change, such as an alteration in the presence of predators or maternal loss, will affect not only the behavioral systems
most directly involved but also the entire functioning of the
organism. In theory, at least, by virtue of their common evolu-

tionary background, all primates have faced a number of similar selective pressures and consequently share a host of similar behavioral adaptations. Perhaps the most striking example of behavioral continuity found among primates is the relatively intense bond that develops between mother and infant and, as we shall presently discuss, the similarity in the form of the separation response.

Once behavioral continuity among primates is accepted, the value of comparative research rests less on its use as a tool to establish further parallels between species than on its potential as a heuristic device in suggesting hypotheses we might consider at the human level. We must recognize, of course, that in any particular domain of inquiry the behavioral diversity among primates may be just as extensive as any similarities that have been found. Nonetheless, if a given behavioral phenomenon or relationship is found at the nonhuman primate level, the probability of a similar relationship at the human level is increased.

Conceptual Issues in the Study of Maternal Loss

The historical context in which such major theorists as Bowlby developed an interest in the effects of loss was the aftermath of the First World War (Newcombe and Lerner, 1982); this was a point when a number of British investigators found inadequate the prevalent psychoanalytic explanations of shell shock in terms of infantile sexual trauma. Subsequently, the importance of specific emotional ties in the experience of loss was demonstrated in several studies (Spitz and Wolf, 1946; Robertson, 1953; Rosenblum and Kaufman, 1968). Thus, the initial studies of maternal loss in both human and nonhuman primates were significant in demonstrating the emergence of a specific bond to mother as well as the importance of this bond during the first year of life. In addition, the pattern of response to prolonged separation was viewed as an exemplar of adaptation to stress at a variety of levels (Bowlby, 1973). In Bowlby's view (1969, 1973), the pattern of response to early loss consisting of three successive phases, characterized as protest, despair, and detachment, is a prototype of responses to separation in adult life. In our initial review of the separation literature (Rosenblum and Plimpton, 1981), we characterized the conservation/withdrawal model (Kaufman, 1977), the opponent-process model (Solomon and Corbitt, 1974), and Bowlby's control system models as "ballistic," in that all these theories viewed the infant, upon losing its mother, as launched on a predetermined adaptive trajectory. Since our work builds mainly on Bowlby's contributions, we will restrict our discussion here to his theoretical perspective.

Bowlby (1969, 1973, 1980) has developed his theory of attachment and separation within the context of evolutionary theory. As stated earlier, from this perspective, behavior patterns, as well as morphological structures, are seen as subject to the laws of natural selection. Animals evolve behavior patterns that serve to maximize their reproductive success in the environment in which they live. As a by-product of a common reproductive strategy of single, slowly developing offspring, intensively cared for early in life, young primate infants cannot survive on their own (Martin, 1975). As a consequence of this dependent state and in order to protect themselves from predation and from other types of danger, primate infants have evolved a signaling system (the protest pattern) designed to reestablish proximity with their caregivers. According to Bowlby, this reaction of protest and its sequelae of despair and detachment, which occur when an infant fails to achieve rapid contact when separated from its mother or other primary caregiver, are "phases of a single process and . . . only when they are treated as such is their true significance grasped" (1973, p. 27). In addition, the three phases of response to separation have been viewed as prototypes of adult anxiety, mourning, and defense (Bowlby, 1973, p. 26). Although in his most recent work Bowlby (1980) has emphasized the mediating role of environmental variables, his basic conceptual model remains a "unidirectional type of process" (Bischof, 1975, p. 804).

To the degree that separation responses do reflect a unitary process, one would expect positive correlations in the intensity of expression among the various phases of the response pattern. In other words, infants who protest the most vigorously upon separation would be expected to become the most depressed and despairing, the most detached, and the slowest to recover, and all infants would be expected to show all three phases of the response. However, this is clearly not the case. We found that virtually all studies of separation in nonhuman primates did document a protest reaction, whereas only one fourth of these studies showed any subsequent indication of despair (Rosenblum and Plimpton, 1981). Variability in behavior following protest is also typical of human infants. For example, in Spitz and Wolf's original study (1946), only one fourth of the subjects developed "anaclitic depression" after the separation. It seems critical that our conceptual orientation be able to account for this variability in a major portion of the separation response, as well as to pose new questions that will help to illuminate it. In the following discussion, we will consider two factors that may add to understanding of these fundamental variations in the separation response.

The first factor concerns the temporal context of behavior. At any given moment an organism is *simultaneously* confronted with multiple demands and must decide what behavior or combination of behaviors to engage in next. For example, juvenile monkeys in the wild typically spend a substantial part of each day engaged in various forms of play. However, when free-ranging monkeys are confronted by a drought or food shortage, all juvenile play stops and these youngsters spend their time searching for food (Baldwin and Baldwin, 1974). Typically, at a given moment, the most pressing biological consideration, such as finding food, takes precedence over less urgent needs, such as play. However, the fact that an animal cannot simultaneously engage in two complex activities does not mean that *sequentially* they are incompatible. Some Japanese macaques live in an area that is covered with snow in winter and hence have very little food available then. Females typically breed annually and give birth in the spring. Toward the end of summer, mothers prematurely wean their infants, thus freeing themselves to rebreed and put on necessary fat reserves for the coming winter. As winter sets in, mothers take back their infants and nurse them during the hard winter months, when food is extremely scarce. The potentially incompatible activities of nursing an infant and rebreeding and putting on appropriate fat reserves are sequentially integrated over time. Thus, one element to be considered in our effort to understand variability in separation patterns is the ability of subjects to accomplish several otherwise incompatible but vital needs over time.

The second factor we will consider is how social and nonsocial aspects of the separation environment influence the infant's capacity to confront diverse demands simultaneously and sequentially.

Effects of Multiple Demands:
Avoidance of Mother in Separated Infant Macaques

The "detachment" response sometimes seen in human infants provides an interesting focus for our consideration of the ways infants reconcile their responses to conflicts arising simultaneously from internal drives and impulses. We will begin with a brief explanation of this pattern as addressed in the human literature and will follow with a review of a nonhuman primate study that provides evidence for a similar response in macaque infants. This study illustrates one way in which differences in the separation environment can affect an infant's adjustment.

A basic attribute of an attachment object is that it serves both as a secure base for an infant's explorations into the environment and also as a safe haven in moments of stress. However, in a variety of circumstances, some human infants have been observed, after a separation from their parents, either to avoid them or to behave in an emotionally detached manner in their presence (Robertson, 1953; Heinicke and Westheimer, 1966). This appears to be an unusual and paradoxical event. But Main (1977) has suggested that avoidance of mother may be a part of a particular pattern of sustained mother/infant interaction. She suggests that an infant who is frequently rejected in his or her attempts to achieve physical contact with the mother may develop a pattern of avoidance when in proximity to her. And, in fact, the Ainsworth Strange Situation has shown that infants who avoid their mothers during reunion episodes tend to be those who have more rejecting mothers. More recently, Main has suggested that avoidance "permits the infant to maintain organization, control, and even flexibility in behavior" (Main and Weston, 1982, p. 51). The infant therefore may have two incompatible tendencies activated simultaneously—in this case, the impulse to achieve physical closeness with the mother and the wish to avoid her engendered by her past rejections.

In laboratory studies of nonhuman primates, after an enforced separation of infant and mother, at reunion the mother almost always immediately retrieves her infant. Thus, the infant has very little opportunity to avoid the mother. However, during the last few years we have conducted several studies that allowed us to observe an avoidance response in macaque infants at least suggestive of the "detachment" behavior seen in human infants. In these studies, two infants at a time were separated from their mothers and housed together in their home pen. During the period of separation (which lasted a number of weeks), one mother at a time was returned briefly to the home pen in an open-wire cage that prevented her from retrieving her infant. These "reunion" episodes lasted twenty to thirty minutes. Comparisons were made of each infant's response to its own mother and its response to the return of the other infant's mother. Only one mother was introduced into the pen at a time, and the order of introduction alternated from day to day. We used two observers during the introduction of each mother so that we could attend closely both to the infant whose mother was being introduced and to the other infant in the pen.

The results showed several forms of avoidance response to the mother in pigtail and bonnet macaque infants and suggest that the way the avoidance expresses itself depends on the nature of the separation environment. Specifically, when foster caretakers were present, the infants tended to avoid the mother by moving to these substitute figures. In contrast, when the infants had not been "adopted," they often avoided mother by failing to move toward her, by averting their gaze from her, and by assuming a "depressed posture." Thus, it is our initial contention that the social and, as we shall subsequently suggest, also the inanimate features of the separation environment influence the avenues by which an infant expresses avoidance. It should be pointed out that, as with all complex behavior of this type, intersubject variability is high; the reader should be aware that the following cases focus on the clearest instances of this form of expression, which are not seen in all infants. However, grappling theoretically with such extreme variations has often proved useful as a first step in understanding basic psychological processes.

Rosenblum (1971, 1978) has provided evidence that separated pigtail infants respond to brief reunions with their mothers by becoming depressed. For example, five seven- to eight-month-old pigtail infants were separated from their mothers for eight weeks. During the basic separation condition, the range of depressive affect (as evidenced by eye closure and posture collapse) varied: three infants showed a severe response, two showed more limited reactions. When pigtail infants are separated from mother and returned to their social groups, they are not usually adopted by other females; indeed, none of these five infants was adopted. (It should be noted that there is one limitation to our "mother return" data. Because the mother was prevented from carrying out the normal response of immediately retrieving her infant, we cannot be certain what elicited the infant's avoidance response. The infant's avoidance behavior might be due to the mother's "strange behavior," that is, her failure to retrieve or other unusual behaviors elicited by her restraint, rather than to her identity as the infant's "lost" mother. However, since we observed the same responses in more recent studies when we presented a color videotape of a mother to her separated infant, edited to contain only normal, relaxed behaviors, we believe that the results recounted here do represent the infants' responses to their own mothers, not merely to a constellation of strange, stressful behaviors elicited by her confinement to a cage.)

In keeping with prior separation research in this species (Rosenblum and Kaufman, 1968), during the baseline separation observations, in which the separated infants' mothers were not present, most infants had recovered from any depressive affect by the twentieth day of separation. In several cases, however, introduction of the mother after this period repeatedly re-invoked the depression in these apparently recovered infants. Infants often moved to the restraining cage when it contained the mother of another infant but not when their own mother was presented. Moreover, the depressive pattern of collapsed posture, immobility, and withdrawal from involvement with the environment persisted only while the infant's own mother was in the pen and terminated when she was removed. Similar to human infants described by Main and Weston (1982), infants averted their gaze from their mothers by slowly closing their eyes.

One infant, #10, exhibited the phenomenon of reinvoked depression much more dramatically than the four others. Figure 1 illustrates the responses of pigtail #10 (based on a composite behavioral index) to the reunion episodes and during normative observations. It is impressive that, particularly on days three through fifty, the presence of this infant's mother resulted in more negative affect than the presence of the other mother or the absence of any mother. One important implication of these findings is that depressive behaviors such as postural collapse are indeed a psychological response to the loss of mother, rather than a physiological phenomenon related to such factors as nutrition or sleep disorders.

In any event, we now know that depression can be re-invoked in separated pigtail infants during caged reunion episodes. It is important to note that the responses of these infants to their mothers were essentially self-directed. When the mother was in the pen, the infant closed its eyes, assumed a collapsed posture, and ceased any dynamic interaction. This response was almost identical to the one observed following the initial protest phase in the basic separation condition.

In contrast to the relative indifference of their social group suffered by pigtails, separated bonnet infants are frequently adopted by females remaining in the group. How does an infant respond to its mother during a reunion episode when it has been adopted by another female during the separation? In one study, identical to that described above with pigtail infants, bonnet infant #8 quickly established an intense adoptive rela-

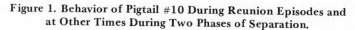

Figure 1. Behavior of Pigtail #10 During Reunion Episodes and
at Other Times During Two Phases of Separation.

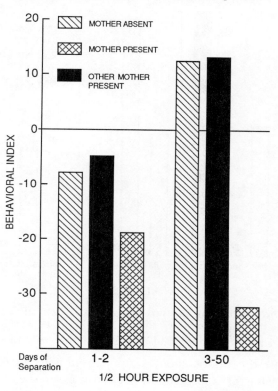

The index scores are based on behaviors observed during a half-hour exposure trial. A positive score on the behavioral index indicates the predominance of play and object exploration; a negative score, the behaviors of depressed posture, distress vocalizations, and physical immobility. Note that
the behavioral index is the most negative during the mother-present condition.

tionship with an adult female after the loss of its mother. As is
generally true of adopted bonnet infants following loss of the
biological mother, this infant established levels of ventral/ventral
contact that were not appreciably different from those it had
maintained with its mother before separation. It can be seen in
Figure 2 that during the separation, when the biological mother

Figure 2. Behavior of Adopted Bonnet #8 During Reunion Episodes
and at Other Times During Separation.

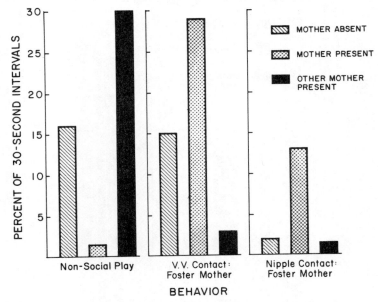

Note that the infant spent the most time in ventral/ventral and nipple contact with its foster mother when the biological mother was present. Nonsocial play was also lowest during the mother-present condition.

was absent, the infant spent a substantial amount of time off the foster mother, engaged in activity play, social play, and inanimate-object exploration. However, the return of the biological mother produced a marked intensification of ventral/ventral and nipple contact with the foster mother. Like the repeated depression of pigtail #10, this intensification of the relationship with the foster mother appeared consistently over the eight-week experimental period whenever the biological mother was introduced but not when the mother of another separated infant was.

It is also striking that, after the permanent return of its biological mother, bonnet #8 remained with its foster mother! Although such complete transfers of filial response have been described in other situations (Dolhinow, 1980; Rosenblum, 1971; Mason and Kenney, 1974), very little is known about the process by which they take place. One interpretation of our data is that the return of the biological mother, after a traumatic separation, induces marked stress in the infant and that, at least for some period, her sudden reappearance is quite disturbing. When primate infants are upset or afraid, they seek and maintain physical and usually oral contact with their attachment objects; indeed, such proximity-seeking behavior is a central element in most definitions of attachment. Only when the infant feels calm and secure does it move off its caregiver. The heightened contact of bonnet #8 with its foster mother when its biological mother was returned strongly suggests that the latter had taken on aversive properties to her infant. That this same infant often remained free of the foster mother when other females were returned in the same manner indicates the selective arousal induced by its own mother.

Our approach in explaining the behavior of these infants is to assume that depression and heightened contact with the foster mother are expressions of the same internal state and that the nature of the environment influences how this common affective state is expressed. A typical infant, when aroused or afraid, returns to its secure base, the primary caregiver, in order to regulate its level of internal stimulation. However, in the absence of an attachment object, often the only available means by which an infant can modulate arousal is by reducing the assault of environmental stimulation. In its efforts to reduce this potentially overwhelming stress, the infant comes to avert its gaze from particular stimuli or the environment as a whole by hunching over and rolling itself into a ball. Both forms of response, one socially directed and one self-directed, may serve to decrease the level of stressful stimulation for the infant and keep it to manageable proportions.

Both Main (1977) and Bowlby (1973) have suggested that the detachment response in human infants is the result of a conflict between behavioral systems of anger and attachment. This conflict constitutes a form of aversive stimulation in that the infant may fluctuate in an unmodulated manner between these competing systems unless it finds some way to reconcile them. Although the same conflict between behavioral systems appears to be operating in our separated nonhuman primate infants in that they are avoiding their mothers, we lack direct confirming evidence. Main (1977), for instance, found that during a brief laboratory separation some infants acted aggressively immediately after the mother's departure, hitting the chair she had been sitting on. We have not observed any noticeable increase in aggression in our separated infants. However, consistent with a prediction made by Main and Weston (1982), we have indeed found "an active avoidance of all reminders of mother during her absence" (p. 57). Although our data base is at present too narrow to confirm unambiguously the parallel between the internal states of human and nonhuman primate infants, we do feel that our findings strongly suggest this relationship, and that hypothesis should stimulate further research, focusing on both behavioral and physiological dimensions.

Our macaque infants' avoidance responses exemplify a consistent psychological response to a lost attachment figure despite varying environmental circumstances. However, it is clear that environmental conditions affected both the way the avoidance response was expressed and the infant's eventual adjustment to maternal loss (Kaufman and Stynes, 1978). The presence of females willing to adopt bonnet infants certainly facilitated their recovery, whereas the recovery of the pigtail infants was impeded in an environment in which they could not turn to other caretakers for support.

Sequential Integration of Incompatible Activities

In keeping with the material just described, it is our view, therefore, that a separated infant can be understood as being confronted with two simultaneous tasks: first, to adjust to the psychological loss of mother and, second, to reestablish itself in an environment altered by her absence. How the infant deals with the tasks of separation depends on the social and nonsocial demands of the environment and on the infant's own characteristics, which may help or hinder the adjustment. The infant must make decisions about how to act at a particular moment ("What's important now?") and also about how to organize diverse behavioral systems sequentially across time. Although it is true that behaviors that are incompatible simultaneously may not be incompatible over a longer period, it also seems likely that the solutions found at one moment are relevant to long-term integration and may influence the expression of other behavioral systems. In the experiment to be presented in this section, we consider how imposing demands on the infant during separation influences the way it responds to maternal loss. To provide a context for this experiment, we need to consider some of the ways in which the infant can sequentially integrate incompatible behavioral systems.

When the problem arises of how a choice is made between multiple demands, investigators such as Bowlby have generally considered the problem with reference to the immediate moment (Bowlby, 1969, pp. 97–101). Bowlby (1969) outlines several ways an organism can deal with the simultaneous activation of incompatible behavioral systems. When an infant engages in protest immediately following separation from its mother, other activities are momentarily preempted but not necessarily superseded over the long run. Although it would be premature to try to construct a comprehensive theory of how such broad temporal organization occurs, the concern with biological rhythms found in current infancy research provides a useful starting point for such thinking.

One perspective in which to view the ideas just outlined derives from the ideas of Sander (1977, 1983) in his work on infant state regulation. Sander's research provides an interesting perspective on the importance of viewing behavior within a temporal frame. From this point of view, initially the infant's basic problem is to bring its semi-independent physiological subsystems into coordination with one another. The infant needs to coordinate its various activities such as swallowing and breathing so that they do not interfere with one another. In addition, the infant and caretaking environment must achieve some organization and coordination in order to function effectively. Coordination between systems, whether they are different physiological systems of a single organism or the systems of the mother and the infant, involves interdependent timing and temporal organization. With regard to the mother and infant, the temporal patterns of their interaction provide the mechanism through which basic rhythmicity is established. Since, as a system, the mother/infant dyad has to coordinate many different elements, stability is not achieved at a single point in time around a particular set goal but, rather, "as relative stability about a trajectory over time" (Sander, 1983, p. 336). However, as Cairns (1972, p. 45) has also pointed out, "stimuli distinctive to the mother may also serve a more general role in the support of response patterns of the young in which she was not directly involved." Hence, one of the essential tasks that confront a separated infant is the reestablishment of a number of basic rhythms to which the mother was an essential contributor. Reite and others (1978) have shown with the pigtail macaque infant that many basic rhythms, such as REM patterns in sleep, diurnal cycles of body temperature, and heart rate, are markedly disrupted by maternal loss.

Whereas support is potentially available to separated human infants or primates studied under laboratory conditions, when a nonhuman primate infant loses its mother in its natural habitat, it will probably die unless it is adopted by another female in the group (Rhine, Norton, Roertgen, and Klein, 1980). Even if it is adopted, it will most likely have to search for all or most of its food, since the availability of a female who is lactating sufficiently and not supporting her own infant is unlikely. Indeed, when very young infants are adopted by nonlactating females, they may starve to death while remaining in the foster mother's "care." Thus, in the course of events triggered by a loss, the infant must reorganize itself on several fronts in order to coordinate its behavior with its changed environment. Although multiple changes following a loss may be the typical state of affairs, it is frequently quite difficult to predict what effect the concomitant changes will have. In the case of the infant separated from its mother in its natural habitat, one might predict with equal plausibility that the additional demand of having to search for food would either be "the straw that breaks the camel's back" or provide a "helpful distraction." In either case, in order to understand the response to separation and loss, we must clearly delineate how the changes that accompany the loss influence adaptation.

The following study illustrates how the separation response may be affected by the nonsocial environmental variable of foraging demand—that is, the degree of difficulty in finding food. We have been investigating this variable in recent studies because it is one of the major influences on the pattern of social interaction between animals (Clutton-Brock, 1977; Altmann, 1980). Whether food is located abundantly and ·uniformly throughout the animal's habitat or is found sparsely in small patches influences, in varying degrees, group size and composition, social organization, and patterns of interaction in primates as well as nonprimates.

In one of our foraging studies, we separated five infant pigtail macaques from their mothers into either a high- or a low-foraging-demand environment (Plimpton, 1981). In the high-foraging-demand separations, infants had to spend a substantial part of their day searching for food, whereas food was easily available with minimal search requirements in the low-foraging-demand separations. All prior studies of separation in primates, as well as normative developmental studies, have maintained subjects under constant, *ad lib* feeding conditions. The object of the current study was to learn what effect imposition of a high foraging demand would have on an infant after losing its mother. Two effects were possible: either the additional demand would overload the infant and result in greater debilitation, or the necessity of searching for food would counteract the behavioral effects of the loss.

The five infants lived with their mothers in a single group before the experiment began. As part of the mechanics of imposing a foraging demand, the subjects were housed on alternate days in one of two identical adjoining pens, connected by a small door. The door was opened only to move the subjects into the adjoining pen at the beginning of each test day. The pen floors were covered with a six-inch layer of sawdust bedding, which was changed once a week when the pens were cleaned. Food was either placed on the surface of the sawdust bedding, for the low-foraging-demand condition, or hidden three to four inches under the surface, for the high-foraging-demand condition. In order to find the food in the high-demand situation, infants had to dig. In the low-demand situation, food was readily visible. The amount of food available in both conditions was sufficient to maintain the body weight of all animals.

The infants were separated from their mothers six times in six successive weeks. Each separation lasted four days, followed by a three-day reunion period. The infants received high- (HF) and low- (LF) foraging-demand separations in the following sequence: (1) LF, (2) HF, (3) HF, (4) LF, (5) LF, (6) HF. All reunions with mother took place in a low-foraging-demand situation. In keeping with our interest in examining behavioral organization across time, the focus of this study was not simply an assessment of whether these separated infants could, in a manner of speaking, "pat their heads and rub their bellies" at the same time. That is, we were not concerned merely with whether the infants would show fewer signs of depression or behavioral disruptions while actually engaged in the incompatible behaviors required for foraging. Rather, we wished to learn how foraging at a given time would affect behavior during later periods when the foraging activity was laid aside.

Immediately following separation from mother, all infants engaged in high levels of protest (coo vocalizations and vigorous locomotion) regardless of the level of the foraging demand. Indeed, no foraging took place while the infants were engaged in protest behavior during any of the separations. As the separation proceeded, infants spent an average of 20 percent of their time searching for food in the HF situation and only 4 percent in the LF. During LF separations, infants engaged in substantially higher levels of self-directed behavior (which is a reflection of negative affect in these infants) and passive peer contact than during HF separations. In general, the evidence supported the hypothesis that engagement in higher levels of foraging during separation prevented or ameliorated the expression of negative affect at other times during the separation. The lower incidence of negative affect in these infants during HF separations could not be attributed merely to the fact that a greater percentage of their time was filled with searching for food, since this abatement was also evident during times when they were not foraging. Rather, these results suggest that the experimentally varied need to find food influenced the infant's overall adjustment to the loss; in other words, it was the integrative effects of disparate behavioral systems, including the disrupted bond with mother and the consequent urgency of obtaining all nutrition from the inanimate environment, that served to structure the infants' behavior during the period of separation.

At the human level, investigators have found with widows that having to care for children after a loss is a "mixed blessing" (Parkes, 1972; Glick, Weiss, and Parkes, 1974). Providing care for children does give a certain meaning and direction to the life of a widow. However, it also takes up time and thus may prevent the widow from forming new adult relationships. The "demand" characteristics of the separation environment in some cases have positive carryover effects and in others minimize time availability and hence may exacerbate the difficulties in adjustment, but the net result represents the integrated influence of numerous variables operating simultaneously.

Conclusion

Maternal loss in both human and nonhuman primates is not an event that occurs in isolation from other major changes in the infant's life. The mother/infant dyad is a system, rather than two independent entities; however, this system is itself part of a larger structure involving the social group and physical habitat. The separated infant must reorganize itself not only with regard to the absence of its mother but also with regard to this larger context. Given the numerous internal and external demands made on the infant following maternal loss, and given the variable nature of the separation environment, it is not surprising that recent investigators have been impressed with variability in behavioral expression in the separation response.

In an attempt to broaden our understanding of this variability, we have developed two themes. The first is the nature of the separation environment and how it influences the infant's behavior. In the first study reviewed, we observed the effect of the presence or absence of females willing to adopt a separated infant; specifically, infants who are adopted become less depressed than infants who are not. In the second study, we noted that differences in the nonsocial environment—namely, high or low foraging demand—also result in differences in affective expression: infants faced with the necessity of finding food for themselves become less depressed.

The second theme is the existence for the infant of multiple and often competing demands arising both from its internal drives and impulses and from external survival demands, together with the ways infants integrate these demands either at a given moment or over a longer period of time. In our consideration of the detachment response, we maintained that the avoidance of mother during the controlled reunion episodes represents a conflict similar to that which Main and others have described in human infants: an effort to balance the incompatible feelings of need for closeness to the mother and the aversive qualities produced by her absence. Avoidance of the mother, we feel, represents an effort by the infant to maintain behavioral organization in the face of the incompatible response tendencies activated by the reintroduction of the mother.

The foraging-demand study showed that some types of incompatible responses can be integrated over time and that the expression of one can influence the expression of the other. That is, active engagement in foraging at one time seemed to inhibit expression of negative affect in our infants even at a later time when they were not looking for food.

The way in which either an infant monkey or a human responds to a traumatic event such as maternal loss depends both on how its behavior is organized in response to immediate challenges and on how its behaviors are coordinated over time to deal with diverse problems. A focus on behavioral expression at a given point in time permits hypotheses about how the infant is reconciling a momentary conflict. Unless behavior adjustment is viewed over longer periods, however, the total significance of any short-term adaptation cannot be determined. The presence or absence of a particular set of behaviors, such as those involved in protest immediately following loss, is not informative unless viewed across the broader temporal context of the individual's existence. Only when behavior is viewed across time can the enduring and persistent effects of a trauma on development be sorted out from momentary disruptions.

References

Altmann, J. *Baboon Mothers and Infants*. Cambridge, Mass.: Harvard University Press, 1980.

Baldwin, J., and Baldwin, J. "Exploration and Social Play in Squirrel Monkeys (*Saimini*)." *American Zoologist,* 1974, *14,* 303–315.

Bischof, N. "A Systems Approach Toward the Functional Connections of Attachment and Fear." *Child Development,* 1975, *46,* 801–817.

Bowlby, J. *Attachment and Loss.* Vol. 1: *Attachment.* New York: Basic Books, 1969.

Bowlby, J. *Attachment and Loss.* Vol. 2: *Separation: Anxiety and Anger.* New York: Basic Books, 1973.

Bowlby, J. *Attachment and Loss.* Vol. 3: *Loss: Sadness and Depression.* New York: Basic Books, 1980.

Cairns, R. "Attachment and Dependency: A Psychobiological and Social-Learning Synthesis." In J. L. Gewirtz (ed.), *Attachment and Dependency.* Washington, D.C.: Winston, 1972.

Clutton-Brock, T. (ed.). *Primate Ecology Studies of Feeding and Ranging Behavior in Lemurs, Monkeys, and Apes.* London: Academic Press, 1977.

Coe, C., and Levine, S. "Normal Responses to Mother-Infant Separation in Nonhuman Primates." In D. Klein and J. Rakkin (eds.), *Anxiety: New Research and Changing Concepts.* New York: Raven Press, 1981.

Coe, C., Mendoza, S., Smotherman, W., and Levine, S. "Mother-Infant Attachment in the Squirrel Monkey: Adrenal Response to Separation." *Behavioral Biology,* 1978, *22,* 256–263.

Dolhinow, P. "An Experimental Study of Mother Loss in the Indian Langur Monkey (*Presbytis entellus*)." *Folia Primatologica,* 1980, *33,* 77–128.

Glick, I. O., Weiss, R. S., and Parkes, C. M. *The First Year of Bereavement.* New York: Wiley-Interscience, 1974.

Gould, S. J. *Hens' Teeth and Horses' Toes.* New York: Norton, 1983.

Heinicke, C. M., and Westheimer, I. J. *Brief Separations.* New York: International Universities Press, 1966.

Kaufman, I. C. "Developmental Considerations of Anxiety and Depression: Psychological Studies in Monkeys." In T. Shapiro (ed.), *Psychoanalysis and Contemporary Science.* New York: International Universities Press, 1977.

Kaufman, I., and Stynes, A. "Depression Can Be Reduced in a Bonnet Macaque Infant." *Psychosomatic Medicine,* 1978, *40,* 71–75.

Main, M. "Analysis of a Peculiar Form of Reunion Behavior Seen in Some Daycare Children: Its History and Sequelae in Children Who Are Home-Reared." In R. A. Webb (ed.), *Social Development in Childhood: Daycare Programs and Research.* Baltimore: Johns Hopkins University Press, 1977.

Main, M., and Weston, O. "Avoidance of the Attachment Figure in Infancy: Descriptions and Interpretations." In C. M. Parkes and J. Stevenson-Hinde (eds.), *The Place of Attachment in Human Behavior.* New York: Basic Books, 1982.

Martin, R. "Strategies of Reproduction." *Natural History.* Nov. 1975, pp. 48–57.

Mason, W., and Kenney, M. "Redirection of Filial Attachments in Rhesus Monkeys: Dogs as Mother Surrogates." *Science,* 1974, *183,* 1209–1211.

Mineka, S., and Suomi, S. "Social Separation in Monkeys." *Psychological Bulletin,* 1978, *85,* 1376–1400.

Newcombe, N., and Lerner, J. "Britain Between the Wars: The Historical Context of Bowlby's Theory of Attachment." *Psychiatry,* 1982, *45,* 1–12.

Parkes, C. M. *Bereavement: Studies of Grief in Adult Life.* New York: International Universities Press, 1972.

Plimpton, E. H. "Environmental Variables and the Response to Maternal Loss." Unpublished doctoral dissertation, Department of Psychiatry, Downstate Medical Center, Brooklyn, N.Y., 1981.

Reite, M., Seiler, C., and Short, R. "Loss of Your Mother Is

More than Loss of a Mother." *American Journal of Psychiatry,* 1978, *135,* 370–371.

Reite, M., and others. "Heart Rate and Body Temperature in Separated Monkey Infants." *Biological Psychiatry,* 1978, *13,* 91–105.

Rhine, R., Norton, G., Roertgen, W., and Klein, H. "The Brief Survival of Free-Ranging Baboon Infants (*Papio cynocephalus*) After Separation from Their Mothers." *International Journal of Primatology,* 1980, *1,* 401–409.

Robertson J. "Some Responses of Young Children to the Loss of Maternal Care." *Nursing Times,* 1953, *49,* 382–386.

Rosenblum, L. A. "Infant Attachment in Monkeys." In R. Schaffer (ed.), *The Origins of Human Social Relations.* Orlando, Fla.: Academic Press, 1971.

Rosenblum, L. A. "Affective Maturation and the Mother-Infant Relationship." In M. Lewis and L. A. Rosenblum (eds.), *The Development of Affect.* New York: Plenum, 1978.

Rosenblum, L. A., and Kaufman, I. "Variations in Infant Development and Response to Maternal Loss in Monkeys." *American Journal of Orthopsychiatry,* 1968, *38,* 418–426.

Rosenblum, L. A., and Plimpton, E. H. "The Infant's Effort to Cope with Separation." In M. Lewis and L. A. Rosenblum (eds.), *The Uncommon Child.* New York: Plenum, 1981.

Sander, L. "The Regulation of Exchange in the Infant-Caretaker System and Some Aspects of the Context-Content Relationship." In M. Lewis and L. A. Rosenblum (eds.), *Interaction, Conversation, and the Development of Language.* New York: Wiley, 1977.

Sander, L. "Polarity, Paradox, and the Organizing Process in Development." In J. Call, E. Galenson, and R. Tyson (eds.), *Frontiers of Infant Psychiatry.* New York: Basic Books, 1983.

Solomon, R., and Corbitt, J. "An Opponent-Process Theory of Motivation: I. Temporal Dynamics of Affect." *Psychological Review,* 1974, *81,* 119–145.

Spitz, R. A., and Wolf, K. "Anaclitic Depression: An Inquiry into the Genesis of Psychiatric Conditions in Early Childhood, II." *Psychoanalytic Study of the Child,* 1946, *2,* 313–342.

Suomi, S. J., Kraemer, C., Baysinger, C., and De Lizio, R. "Inherited and Experiential Factors Associated with Individual Differences in Anxious Behavior Displayed by Rhesus Monkeys." In D. Klein and J. Rakkin (eds.), *Anxiety: New Research and Changing Concepts.* New York: Raven Press, 1981.

Yarrow, L. J., and Goodwin, M. "The Immediate Impact of Separation: Reactions of Infants to a Change in Mother Figures." In L. J. Stone, H. T. Smith, and L. B. Murphy (eds.), *The Competent Infant.* New York: Basic Books, 1973.

2

Psychoanalytic Views of Separation in Infancy and Early Childhood

Sally Provence

Editors' Note: *In this chapter on the psychoanalytic view of separation in early childhood, the author, herself a pioneering investigator of separation and child development, outlines fundamental issues about the role of separation in psychological growth. These central propositions about separation and psychological separateness form the assumptions on which many chapters in this volume are based. Provence discusses how the parent/child relationship influences personality development, emphasizing the reciprocity of parent/child communication, the extended period of childhood dependence, and the biological endowment that influences psychosocial phenomena. She examines object constancy within the separation-individuation process, highlighting its role in identity formation.*

This chapter clarifies the distinction between general anxiety and stranger anxiety and presents a developmental view of anxiety based on progressive differentiation in level of object-relatedness. This developmental model, which incorporates object loss, separation-individuation, and internalization, is elaborated further in Part Three of this volume (the "clinical" section). Provence also compares the developmental significance of mourning, bereavement, and grief, which are especially relevant to the section of the book that addresses specific transitions in-

87

volving loss (Part Two). Finally, she presents several clinical vignettes that illustrate a variety of separation problems, including maternal overinvolvement, a lack of separateness that stifles individuation, and insecure attachment that may foster aggressive or risk-taking behavior.

Separation as a concept in psychoanalytic child psychology refers to a process through which the individual child develops a sense of his or her physical and mental self—an awareness of being a person apart from others. The term is often used in association with the term *individuation* to describe the maturational and developmental process during which intrapsychic representations of the self and the love object are gradually formed and differentiated. Separation also refers to events in the life of the child in which he experiences being parted from those on whom he is dependent and to whom he is most strongly attached by bonds of love.

Coping with experiences of separation from those we love is a lifelong task for each of us, not only inevitable but necessary for normal development. In childhood, some separation experiences facilitate psychological growth by mobilizing new opportunities for learning and adaptation. Other separation experiences, especially those involving loss of important persons, precipitate states of bereavement, grief, and mourning and can be painful and traumatic. Between growth-promoting experiences and bereavement there are many separation experiences involving varying degrees of psychological and psychobiological stress, depending on such factors as the nature of the relationship between the child and the adults who are most important to him or her, on the developmental period during which they occur (including age-specific competencies and vulnerabilities), on previous experiences with separation, on the immediate condition of the child—health, fatigue, and so forth—and on the intensity and duration of the separation event.

The development of the child, according to psychoanalysis, proceeds as a result of the interaction between innate and experiential factors. After birth, the psychic and somatic systems become increasingly organized and differentiated from each other as development progresses, and the functions of each become more clearly discernible, although their interdependence persists throughout life. The development of the mind, anchored in the biological equipment, is strongly influenced by environmental factors. Endowment, maturational processes, and experience in continuous and complex interaction codetermine the developmental process and outcome. The psychic agencies—id, ego, and superego—are structured gradually out of the relatively undifferentiated state of the newborn.

Although one can, for purposes of study or emphasis, focus on ego development or instinctual development or object relationships as though they were distinct and separate, psychoanalysis holds that they are interwoven and that their influence on one another must be taken into account at every stage. For example, the interdependence of object relations, drive, and ego development is illustrated in the fact that the baby's ability to recognize the mother, respond emotionally, and "read" nonverbal cues reflects the object relation but also involves cognitive abilities and instinctual energies. Perception and intelligence are involved in the infant's social relationships from the beginning. Similarly, the infant's drive endowment and its development partly determine his or her needs and behavior, including aspects of interaction with others; the nature of the infant's object relationships either facilitates or interferes with drive development and organization. Thus it must be emphasized that psychoanalytic developmental psychology embraces a complex theory in addressing the intricacy of human development. The four dimensions selected for discussion in this chapter are therefore admittedly arbitrary. They were chosen because they are useful in organizing clinical and observational data on separation in young children. They are (1) the central role of object relationships, (2) the separation-individuation process and identity formation, (3) developmental aspects of separation anxiety, and (4) separation, loss, and bereavement.

The Central Role of Object Relationships

In psychoanalytic developmental theory and practice, the child's human relationships occupy a centrally important position because of their influences on physical, mental, and emotional development. These relationships during infancy and early childhood, especially those with parent figures, exert a powerful effect at any given moment as well as on future development. The prolonged dependency of the human child intensifies the importance of the child's nurturers for his or her development and adaptation. Children are predisposed by inborn characteristics to be responsive to and become attached to their caregivers. They have a readiness for social contact that is coordinated with the responsiveness of the parents to the infant's needs and with phases in their development as parents. Both Erikson's psychosocial theory (1950, 1953, 1959) and Hartmann's adaptation theory (1939/1958) assume the biological preadaptedness of the human infant to an average expectable environment. Erikson's concept of the mutuality of adaptation between child and parent is generally accepted and has been examined in a number of landmark research studies of infant/parent interaction (Korner, 1974a, 1974b; Sander, 1970, 1980; Stern, 1974; Brazelton, 1974; Brazelton, Koslowski, and Main, 1974; Lewis and Lee-Painter, 1974; Emde, Gaensbauer, and Harmon, 1976; Emde, 1980).

Through his or her human relationships the child receives not only life-sustaining physical nurturance but also the stimulation, guidance, training, and protection that enhance cognitive, emotional, and social development. No matter how promising a child's endowment, if he or she is to flourish, the quality of object relations must be at least reasonably good. And, in the early years, the most important figures are the parents who love and nurture the child, to whom the child makes his or her first strong attachments, and whom he or she comes to love and to trust.

The first love relationship formed by the infant is to the person who provides nurturance in accordance with his or her bodily and social/emotional needs. Gradually and through many interactions that person, usually the mother, becomes a recognized, differentiated object whose absence may engender anxiety in the child. Freud (1926/1959) identified two stages in the development of object relations: the first stage, in which the infant recognizes and relates to the need-satisfying object, and the later stage of the psychologically permanent object—the stage of object constancy.

Memory and Object Constancy

The stability and permanence of the child's psychic representations of the love objects are only gradually achieved during the early years. The construct of object constancy is important for issues of separation because it is believed that children's ability to cope with the stress of separation depends significantly on the capacity to evoke the mental images of those to whom they attribute their sense of security and well-being. As Fraiberg (1969) pointed out, the term *object constancy,* introduced by Hartmann (1952/1965), has been used variously by different psychoanalytic writers, ranging from those who use the term to mean simply a firm attachment to the love object to those who define it as a libidinal and cognitive acquisition in which mental representations of the mother have attained a high level of stability. Mahler (1966) proposed that a certain degree of object constancy is attained during the fourth subphase of separation-individuation (around twenty-four months to thirty or thirty-six months). Memories of the mother are present that "enable the child to remain away from the mother for some length of time and still function with emotional poise, provided he is in a fairly familiar environment" (p. 156). Fraiberg emphasized the usefulness of distinguishing between recognitory and evocative memory in this process—the latter being a point in the development of intelligence when an image can be evoked with relative autonomy from stimulus or sign. Recognitory memory is illustrated when the baby clearly affirms his awareness of the mother as a specific person when she reappears after a brief absence. This behavior occurs first at a time when there is no evidence that he can remember her in her absence—that is, when evocative memory is not yet operating. Evocative memory is probably a necessary though not sufficient condition for the child's awareness that the loved figure from whom he is separated has not been lost. It appears that children at around eighteen months of age have achieved the capacity for symbolic

operations required for evocative memory. Piaget's (1952) formulations on (inanimate) object permanence are relevant. The
cognitive capacity for object permanence, in concert with the
strengthening of the libidinal tie, leads gradually to the achievement of object constancy in its psychoanalytic sense, when
mental representations are stable enough to sustain the child
during brief separations. Solnit's (1982) definition is useful in
this context: "Object constancy is that state of object relations in which the child has the capability to retain the memory of and emotional tie to parents, his primary love objects,
and to feel their nurturing, guiding presence even when they are
a source of frustration or disappointment or when they are absent" (p. 202).

But the child's separation experience is a more complex
issue than one of memory alone, because while he moves toward
object constancy, he has also a growing awareness of his own
feelings of anger and his sense of shame at disapproved behavior. These feelings make separation more difficult, and he needs
reassurance that those to whom he is closely attached will not
abandon him.

Minde and Musisi (1982) have emphasized the role of
cognition as well as affect in the young child's mediation of attachment and responses to separation and loss. They point out
that the development of general cognitive skills, including object permanence in Piaget's (1952) sense, provides some of the
necessary conditions for phases of attachment in early childhood. A second role of cognition, in their view, is that relationships are increasingly controlled or shaped by expectations built
up through earlier experiences with others. These expectations
may either alleviate or exacerbate the effects of loss or threat of
loss.

The Separation-Individuation Process
and Identity Formation

In recent years, the separation-individuation process as an
essential aspect of the child's development has been the focus of
much attention from psychoanalytic clinicians and theoreti-

cians, well illustrated by the observational research of Margaret Mahler and her colleagues (Mahler, 1963, 1968; Mahler, Pine, and Bergman, 1975; Pine and Furer, 1963). Mahler, Pine, and Bergman (1975), in describing their view that the "psychological birth of the human infant" is the separation-individuation process, spoke of "the establishment of a sense of separateness from, and relation to, a world of reality, particularly with regard to the experience of *one's own body* and to the principal representative of the world as the infant experiences it, the *primary love object*" (p. 3). Though emphasizing that the separation-individuation process is never finished in that it reverberates through the life cycle, they placed the principal psychological achievements of this process within the period from the fourth or fifth month of life to the thirtieth or thirty-sixth month, a period they called the "separation-individuation phase." "The normal *separation-individuation* process . . . involves the child's achievement of separate functioning in the presence of, and with the emotional availability of, the mother. . . . In contrast to situations of traumatic separation, however, this normal separation-individuation process takes place in the setting of developmental readiness for, and pleasure in, independent functioning" (Mahler, 1963, pp. 3, 4). To cite one example: The child who walks away from his mother or waves good-bye and then interests himself in something else when she leaves experiences something quite different than does the child left in an alien setting or with a person of whom he is afraid or uncertain. In the first instance, whatever signal anxiety the child feels at mother's departure mobilizes the adaptive and defensive resources he has developed in her presence, and he busies himself with actions or thoughts that he enjoys or that reassure him. In the second instance, the stresses of the situation are too great for the child's psychological resources, and he feels upset, anxious, and perhaps overwhelmed. Whether this second experience becomes a traumatic event will depend on its context, its duration, antecedent events in the mother/child relationship, and the extent to which others can substitute effectively for the mother in her absence.

A sense of separateness of self and other, an awareness of

a body and a mental self, and the development of an identity are concepts referring to aspects of the individual's view of his or her totality as a person. The self as a cohesive psychological organization is, as Loewald (1980) has emphasized, contingent on the differentiation between self and other. The infant's capacity to make this distinction develops slowly, in the process of hundreds of transactions between the infant and those who nurture him. Awareness of the bodily self precedes, but is continuous with, awareness of the mental self as distinct from all others. The awareness or *sense* of identity is very much influenced by factors affecting perception of the external world—psychological factors as well as stability and change in the environment. In myriad day-to-day experiences with persons, with action, with material objects, the child builds mental images of his body and its sensations, of competencies, thoughts, and feelings. The child comes to identify with his parents and wishes to be like them while defining his own uniqueness. Comparisons and contrasts with others are made more vivid by the child's intellectual development and are stimulated by heightened awareness of the child's own body and mental states. Similarly, as the child is able, he weighs and compares real and wishful images of himself and adjusts them. Greenacre (1971) pointed out that although the individual's self-image forms the core of identity, identity is maintained and vitalized by the continual redefinement accompanying comparison and contrast with others. The child's recognition of likeness with others and differences from them is fundamental to the development of identity. Experiences of likeness arise from the child's intimacy with those who nurture (Jacobson, 1964) and are strengthened by the mutual affective identifications between them (Greenacre, 1971). Love and admiration for parents, siblings, and other important objects and wanting to acquire what they possess and do what they do reinforce the child's looking for likenesses between himself and others. But there is also the significant role of aggression in the development of identity. The frustration, envy, rivalry, and hostility felt by the child in relation to loved ones impel him toward recognition of differences, including differences between wishful images of the self and the other. Concomitant with the growth of cognitive functions, these experiences stimulate his learning about these differences that may account for his frustrations and feelings of inferiority and, in time, for feelings of superiority and competence. There is wide agreement among psychoanalytic theorists and clinicians that it is those to whom the child is strongly attached with whom the most important patterns of separation and individuation are played out as part of the process through which awareness of the separate self, identity, and self-esteem come into being.

Developmental Aspects of Separation Anxiety

In psychoanalytic theory anxiety is of great significance in the psychological life and development of the child. The studies of Benjamin (1961, 1963) and Spitz (1957, 1965) in particular contributed much of the background of current efforts to understand developmental aspects of anxiety. Their research as well as others' followed Freud's (1926/1959) exposition of his general theory of anxiety. Freud introduced the idea of anxiety, psychological pain, and mourning as differential responses to object loss with the words "So little is known about the psychology of emotional processes that the tentative remarks I am about to make on the subject may claim a lenient judgment" (p. 169). In Freud's view, pain is the reaction to actual loss; anxiety is the reaction to the danger that that loss entails and, by further displacement, a reaction to the danger of the loss of the object itself (p. 170). Both Spitz and Benjamin, from observational and experimental data, distinguished two overlapping but different anxiety responses during the first year of life, defined operationally as *infantile stranger anxiety* and *infantile separation anxiety.* The phenomenon of stranger anxiety has been described by many workers with considerable agreement on its characteristics and timing but with expectable disagreement about its theoretical implications. Benjamin (1963), in his cogent discussion, pointed out that to psychoanalysts, but not exclusively to them, stranger anxiety assumes a very special significance because of its intimate connection with the field of object relationships. Benjamin's highly condensed summary of his view is instructive: "On the psychological level anxiety, realistic or unrealistic, is the response to a perceived danger. It is the ego that perceives (or anticipates) the danger and the ego that 'feels' the affect of anxiety, whatever its physiological concomitant may be. Therefore, one can reasonably speak of anxiety as soon as the ego is sufficiently developed to permit the perception of danger and the felt differentiated affect. This clearly seems to be the case for many three- and four-month-old infants, to judge by behavioral criteria. Later, the anticipatory function of the ego as well as the signaling function plays an increasingly important role . . . , both of these in close relationship to memory."

The progression of normal ego development and differentiation, as well as object and drive differentiation, dictates that the anxieties of the infant will occur in new forms as he grows older. Among the early disturbances are those of psychophysiological equilibrium, of which anxiety is a part. Such disturbances of homeostasis may be caused by separation of the infant from the mother before he can discriminate her from others, particularly if her substitute has a different caregiving style. The developmental progress in the psychological life in regard to anxiety is from reaction to loss of a "preobject" (a person or persons who reduce tensions and provide comfort and pleasure through appropriate care) to fear of loss of a differentiated object—a particular person whom one knows and loves. Sequential aspects of this normal process over the first five or so years of life are (1) anxiety in an interaction with one who *does* things differently—that is, who does not fit with what the infant is accustomed to, (2) fear of the strange and of the stranger, (3) fear of the loss of the loved person in reality, (4) fear of loss of that person's love and approval, (5) fear of loss of the loved self—that is, both castration anxiety and anxiety about death—and (6) fear of one's own disapproval—that is, superego anxiety. Benjamin's hypothesis that fear of object loss, loss of the person whom one loves and depends on, is the immediate dynamic determinant of separation anxiety appears valid. With its later derivative, the fear of loss of love, it is universal or nearly universal in our culture.

Anxiety at separation characterizes the infant and pre-school child from approximately the last quarter of the first year, with phase-specific peaks; slowly but progressively, more effective means of coping with the feelings involved develop. Inherent in the fear of object loss is the mixture of feelings that characterize love relationships: loving, tender feelings are mingled with hostile feelings. Libidinal and aggressive cathexes of the mental representation of the loved person coexist. Longing for that person and sadness at the thought of loss, as well as shame or guilt over one's hostile wishes and feelings, stimulate eagerness for reunion.

Anxiety, however, is not a disaster, nor is it necessarily traumatic, although emphasis on its troublesome aspects tends to make us less appreciative of its importance as a signal affect through which adaptive and defensive mechanisms are prepared and mobilized. If not overwhelming at a given point, anxiety can sharpen the perception of the self, of the other, and of the world of reality. Separation for a four-year-old in nursery school, for example, though engendering some degree of anxiety, also provides the child with appropriate opportunities for mastery and for acquiring skills that enhance development. Such opportunities are best realized when the child has achieved a level of self-awareness and self-esteem that, when combined with object constancy and trust in parent figures and with an awareness of a past and future (memory and anticipation), enable him or her to make good use of new experiences. In contrast, the plight of the young child who has experienced physical abuse is especially poignant. Many children are strongly attached to parents who abuse them, and even though they may show relief and begin to thrive when placed with adults who provide protection and better care, they may nonetheless feel the loss deeply and show separation anxiety. Their psychological resources for coping with that anxiety are impaired, and they require substantial experience with adults who love and nurture them in order that the healing process may occur.

Robert White's (1959) paper emphasized the high adaptive value of effectance motivation (competence) as one of the processes through which the individual learns to interact effectively with his or her environment. This topic has more recently been studied primarily by developmental psychologists (Harter, 1978; Harter and Zigler, 1974; White, 1975; Yarrow, 1981; Yarrow and Pederson, 1976; Yarrow, Rubenstein, and Pederson, 1975), who have contributed to views on the origins of competence, motivation for mastery, and relations between cognition and motivation. These studies, together with studies of coping, well represented in Lois Murphy's work (1974), can be usefully coordinated with Hartmann's (1939/1958) adaptation theory and the role played by learning in the adaptation process. Learning and motivation for mastery are processes that not only provide satisfaction and enhance self-esteem but also enable the child to cope with stress and adversity, including the stress of separation. In this process the elaboration of play and fantasy is significant. Play and fantasy are examples of the beneficial function of "detour" activities that both prepare and facilitate better mastery of reality situations, including experiences of separation or the fear thereof. Thus, the child's awareness of the separateness and the feelings of vulnerability and helplessness that may threaten to overwhelm him are counterbalanced by feelings of competence and mastery that he acquires when he is in a situation that not only is protective but also facilitates effective interaction with his environment.

Separation, Loss, and Bereavement

There is a large literature on separation, loss, and bereavement in young children. Studies of infants without families, of children who have lost one parent through death, divorce, or illness, and children with physically present but psychologically absent parents with depressive illness or other severe psychiatric disorders are examples (Freud and Burlingham, 1944; Spitz, 1945, 1950; Spitz and Wolf, 1946; Bowlby, 1951, 1973; Provence and Lipton, 1962; Benjamin, 1963; Yarrow, 1964; Mahler, 1966; Pavenstedt, 1967; Anthony, 1970; Goldstein, Freud, and Solnit, 1973; Furman, 1974; Wallerstein and Kelly, 1975, 1980). Children separated from parents because of hospitalization of the child form another frequently encountered group.

The question of the emotional experience involved in loss of a parent and how early in life the child can be said to mourn has occupied psychoanalysts, among others. Bowlby (1960), in a paper on grief and mourning in infancy, took the position that "the responses to be observed in young children on the loss of the mother figure differ in no material respect (apart probably from certain consequences) from those observed in adults on the loss of a loved object" (p. 10). Bowlby used the term *mourning* to denote the psychological processes set in motion by the loss of a loved object, while *grief* denotes the sequence of subjective states that follow loss and accompany mourning. Bowlby described a reaction to loss in children from approximately six months of age onward in which feelings of grief are intimately related to separation anxiety, and he described three phases of behavior after separation: protest (a first phase of angry, loud, tearful behavior), despair (a second phase of acute pain, misery, and diminishing hope), and detachment (a third phase in which the child behaves as if he or she had ceased to care). Anna Freud (1960), in responding to Bowlby's ideas, proposed that the term *bereavement* be used to designate the reactions of infants and that the term *mourning* be reserved for later stages of development. She said that the nearer the child is to object constancy and the higher the level of object relationship and ego maturity the child has developed, the longer the duration of grief reactions will be, "with corresponding approximation to the adult internal processes of mourning" (p. 59).

The feelings engendered by separation and loss of the loved person include anxiety, anger, and depression. There is general agreement among psychoanalysts that bereavement reactions of infants and young children may follow the three-phase process of protest, despair, detachment (withdrawal) and that there is no doubt that the emotional experience of loss of the loved person is a difficult one from the early months onward.

Leon Yarrow's (1964) discussion of separation from parents in early childhood presents a valuable point of view congenial with psychoanalytic propositions: "Separation in the purest sense involves a break in the continuity of relationship with a mother figure after a meaningful, focused relationship has been established . . . [and] involves the loss of a significant loved person. . . . In analyzing the effects . . . not only is it important to distinguish separation from other kinds of deviations in maternal care . . . but to distinguish among different kinds of separation experiences" (p. 90). Yarrow emphasized that a traumatic separation event may be followed by other experiences that are equally or at times even more devastating—for example, placement in an impersonal institution, hospitalization with the associated stress of illness or surgery, and changes in foster homes. Individual factors such as the child's vulnerability, sensitivities, and resiliences stemming from earlier experiences partly determine the effect of separation, as does his or her stage of development at the time. The degree of concomitant trauma and the duration of the separation are other significant determinants of impact.

Case Examples

The following case vignettes illustrate some of the forms of behavior commonly seen in young children caused by unresolved separation issues. The variation in behavioral manifestations requires that early childhood specialists keep in mind the frequency with which separation issues may become pathogenic and remember that there is no single set of behaviors that manifests them.

Anna—Separateness and Failure to Thrive. Anna, age eleven months, was hospitalized for failure to grow normally after a good start. The study revealed that the mother/infant relationship was a very disturbed one in which maladaptive patterns of interaction, most apparent in but not limited to the feeding situation, were conspicuous. The mother allowed the infant scarcely any social interaction with anyone except herself; the infant was by turns apathetic and irritable. It became clear as the study proceeded that the mother's clinging to the babyhood of her daughter had been expressed in behavior that interfered with the child's steps toward more independent functioning and the normal progression of separation and individuation. A treatment plan was carried out in which the mother was relieved of all responsibilities for feeding and bodily care for a period of about a week, and the baby slowly began to take more food from a skilled nurse, who also encouraged her to be active with toys and around such experiences as bathing and dressing. She was encouraged to creep and to explore her surroundings. Mother and child were enabled to interact around activities other than feeding and at first to tolerate and later to enjoy social contact across a space. For each, it was believed, the interruption of the exclusiveness of the interaction and the recognition of separateness were important elements in the steady improvement that occurred during the continuing treatment. Bodily manifestations of psychological stress and conflict are common, especially in infancy and early childhood.

Jamie—a Tyrant at Age Two. Jamie, at age two and a half years, had become a tyrant in his family, primarily because his imperious and frequent demands for his mother's attention placed considerable stress on the entire family. His protest and clinging to his mother whenever she tried to leave him with his father or a babysitter was the immediate reason for their seeking help. His conscientious parents felt desperate, were very angry at him, and feared that they must be doing something terribly wrong. Evaluation of Jamie revealed that, in contrast with his overt behavior, he had many fears, relieved primarily by his mother's comforting presence. This physically sturdy and intelligent two-year-old had developed very few strategies for coping with psychological distress and quickly dissolved into tears at the least frustration or anxiety. Both parents, tense and overanxious, were appalled at the intensity of their dissatisfaction with him and with themselves and feared they had damaged him forever. Individual treatment for Jamie and counseling for the parents extended over a twelve-month period and were successful. He was enabled to enjoy and to benefit from a morning nursery school program during that time. It became clear that Jamie felt insecure about his parents' love and compared himself unfavorably with his sister, two years older. His discomfort at separation and his clinging were closely linked with his fear that, he was able to say, he would "go away like ice" or would be thrown on the garbage heap if he did not hold on tight. Behind his imperious, demanding, and aggressive behavior were overwhelming feelings of fear, shame, and inadequacy. As his parents were helped to understand his behavior more clearly, they were able to respond in ways that enabled Jamie to feel their love for him, and conflicts were diminished.

George and Emily—Bravado Masking Separation Anxiety. George, age three and a half, and Emily, age four and a half, were children whose unresolved separation problems were expressed in counterphobic behavior. George was seen by his parents and others as a fearless, risk-taking child who responded only to severe reprimands when his behavior was difficult. Treatment revealed that much of his behavior was an expression of his anxious efforts to stay in emotional contact with his depressed mother and that his greatest fear was of separation from her. Emily responded in many social situations by running away from her mother, scaling dangerous heights on the playground, or making undiscriminating contacts with other adults. At the root of her problems was a relationship in which the mother's ambivalence toward her less than perfect daughter from infancy onward had interfered with the normal separation-individuation process, heightened anxiety at every level, and interfered with the development of normal adaptation and coping and the creation of stable defenses.

Mary—an Ill-Cared-For and Abused Child. Mary, age three and a half, had lived all her life with her psychiatrically disturbed parents and four older siblings except for a six-month period in foster care at age two years. History revealed that during foster care placement her development, which had been delayed in several ways, had improved dramatically. She was brought to the attention of the clinic by the child protective services of the state when she was again placed in foster care because of physical abuse (a severe burn). Her parents thought of her as their favorite child—the baby—and resented the foster placement and any thought that she might be better off away from them. Many months of work with the parents, using a variety of supportive services, resulted in little benefit. The clinical evaluation of the parents, the lack of improvement in their ability to care for her, and Mary's dramatic improvement in foster care led to a strong recommendation that parental rights be terminated and that she be adopted. One year after placement

Mary was adopted by her foster parents. Follow-up at age six years revealed that her few memories of her biological parents were primarily anxiety-producing and she needed much reassurance that she did not have to return to them. Her ties to her adoptive parents became strong and positive.

Although one cannot fully appreciate what Mary had experienced in her psychological life, it seems clear that she has been given a second chance at life and that the results thus far are good. Forced separation from parents and permanent placement elsewhere, though a grave and sobering step for clinicians to recommend, is necessary in some instances for a child's psychological as well as physical survival.

Summary

The psychoanalytic view of separation in the life of the infant and young child presented in this chapter focuses on emotional and psychological experiences. Of central importance are the child's relationships with loved ones in determining how he or she will experience, cope with, and defend against separation from them. Levels of psychosexual and psychosocial development as expectable sources of conflict, anxiety, and adaptation in the early years have an important role in the child's emotional experience, as does the line of maturation and development that includes concepts of the growth of intrapsychic representations of the self and the love objects. In spite of their vulnerability and need for emotional as well as physical nurturance, young children possess adaptive capacities that enable them to develop effective ways of coping with and defending against the psychological consequences and discomforts of separation.

References

Anthony, E. J. "The Influence of Maternal Psychosis on Children: Folie-à-Deux." In E. J. Anthony and T. Benedek (eds.), *Parenthood: Its Psychology and Psychopathology.* Boston: Little, Brown, 1970.

Benjamin, J. D. "Some Developmental Observations Relating to the Theory of Anxiety." *Journal of the American Psychoanalytic Association,* 1961, *9*(4), 652–668.

Benjamin, J. D. "Further Comments on Some Developmental Aspects of Anxiety." In H. S. Gaskill (ed.), *Counterpoint: Libidinal Object and Subject.* New York: International Universities Press, 1963.

Bowlby, J. *Maternal Care and Mental Health.* Monograph 2. Geneva: World Health Organization, 1951.

Bowlby, J. "Grief and Mourning in Infancy and Early Childhood." *Psychoanalytic Study of the Child,* 1960, *15,* 9–52.

Bowlby, J. *Attachment and Loss.* Vol. 2: *Separation: Anxiety and Anger.* New York: Basic Books, 1973.

Brazelton, T. B. "Does the Neonate Shape His Environment?" In S. Bergsma (ed.), *The Infant at Risk.* Birth Defects: Original Article Series, *10*(2), 131–140. New York and London: Intercontinental Medical Book Corporation, 1974.

Brazelton, T. B., Koslowski, B., and Main, M. "The Origins of Reciprocity." In M. Lewis and L. A. Rosenblum (eds.), *The Effect of the Infant on Its Caregiver.* New York: Wiley, 1974.

Emde, R. "Toward a Psychoanalytic Theory of Affect: II. Emerging Models of Emotional Development in Infancy." In S. I. Greenspan and G. H. Pollock (eds.), *The Course of Life: Psychoanalytic Contributions Toward Understanding Personality Development.* Vol. 1: *Infancy and Early Childhood.* Washington, D.C.: National Institute of Mental Health, 1980.

Emde, R., Gaensbauer, T. J., and Harmon, R. J. "Emotional Expression in Infancy: A Biobehavioral Study." *Psychological Issues,* 1976, Monograph 37.

Erikson, E. H. *Childhood and Society.* New York: Norton, 1950.

Erikson, E. H. "Growth and Crisis of the Healthy Personality." In C. Kluckhohn, H. A. Murray, D. Schneider (eds.), *Personality in Nature, Society, and Culture.* New York: Knopf, 1953.

Erikson, E. H. "Identity and the Life Cycle." *Psychological Issues,* 1959, Monograph 1.

Fraiberg, S. "Libidinal Object Constancy and Mental Representation." *Psychoanalytic Study of the Child,* 1969, *24,* 9–47.

Freud, A. "Discussion of Dr. John Bowlby's Paper." *Psychoanalytic Study of the Child,* 1960, *15,* 53-62.

Freud, A., and Burlingham, D. T. *Infants Without Families: The Case For and Against Residential Nurseries.* New York: International Universities Press, 1944.

Freud, S. "Inhibitions, Symptoms and Anxiety." In J. Strachey (ed. and trans.), *The Standard Edition of the Complete Psychological Works of Sigmund Freud.* Vol. 20. London: Hogarth Press, 1959. (Originally published 1926.)

Furman, E. *A Child's Parent Dies: Studies in Childhood Bereavement.* New Haven, Conn.: Yale University Press, 1974.

Goldstein, J., Freud, A., and Solnit, A. J. *Beyond the Best Interests of the Child.* New York: Free Press, 1973.

Greenacre, P. "Early Physical Determinants in the Development of Identity." In *Emotional Growth: Psychoanalytic Studies of the Gifted and a Variety of Other Individuals.* Vol. 1. New York: International Universities Press, 1971.

Harter, S. "Effectance Motivation Reconsidered: Toward a Developmental Model." *Human Development,* 1978, *21,* 34-64.

Harter, S., and Zigler, E. "The Assessment of Effectance Motivation in Normal and Retarded Children." *Developmental Psychology,* 1974, *10,* 169-180.

Hartmann, H. *Ego Psychology and the Problem of Adaptation.* New York: International Universities Press, 1958. (Originally published 1939.)

Hartmann, H. "The Mutual Influences in the Development of Ego and Id." In H. Hartmann, *Essays on Ego Psychology: Selected Problems in Psychoanalytic Theory.* New York: International Universities Press, 1965. (Originally published 1952.)

Jacobson, E. *The Self and the Object World.* New York: International Universities Press, 1964.

Korner, A. F. "The Effect of the Infant's State, Level of Arousal, Sex, and Ontogenetic Stage on the Caregiver." In M. Lewis and L. A. Rosenblum (eds.), *The Effect of the Infant on Its Caregiver.* New York: Wiley, 1974a.

Korner, A. F. "Individual Differences at Birth: Implications for Child Care Practices." In D. Bergsma (ed.), *The Infant at Risk.* Birth Defects: Original Article Series, *10*(2), 51-61.

New York and London: Intercontinental Medical Book Corporation, 1974b.

Lewis, M., and Lee-Painter, S. "An Interactional Approach to the Mother-Infant Dyad." In M. Lewis and L. A. Rosenblum (eds.), *The Effect of the Infant on Its Caregiver.* New York: Wiley, 1974.

Loewald, H. W. "Book Review: Heinz Kohut, *The Analysis of the Self.*" In *Papers on Psychoanalysis.* New Haven, Conn.: Yale University Press, 1980.

Mahler, M. S. "Certain Aspects of the Separation-Individuation Phase." *Psychoanalytic Quarterly,* 1963, *32,* 1–14.

Mahler, M. S. "Notes on the Development of Basic Moods: The Depressive Affect." In R. M. Loewenstein, L. M. Newman, M. Schur, and A. J. Solnit (eds.), *Psychoanalysis—a General Psychology: Essays in Honor of Heinz Hartmann.* New York: International Universities Press, 1966.

Mahler, M. S. *On Human Symbiosis and the Vicissitudes of Individuation.* Vol. 1: *Infantile Psychosis.* New York: International Universities Press, 1968.

Mahler, M. S., Pine, F., and Bergman, A. *The Psychological Birth of the Human Infant: Symbiosis and Individuation.* New York: Basic Books, 1975.

Minde, K., and Musisi, S. "Some Aspects of Disruption of the Attachment System in Young Children: A Transcultural Perspective." In J. Anthony and C. Chiland (eds.), *The Child in His Family.* New York: Wiley, 1982.

Murphy, L. "Coping, Vulnerability, and Resilience in Childhood." In G. V. Coelho, D. A. Hamburg, and J. E. Adams (eds.), *Coping and Adaptation.* New York: Basic Books, 1974.

Pavenstedt, E. (ed.). *The Drifters.* Boston: Little, Brown, 1967.

Piaget, J. *The Origins of Intelligence in Children.* New York: International Universities Press, 1952.

Pine, F., and Furer, M. "Studies of the Separation-Individuation Phase: A Methodological Overview." *Psychoanalytic Study of the Child,* 1963, *18,* 325–342.

Provence, S., and Lipton, R. *Infants in Institutions.* New York: International Universities Press, 1962.

Sander, L. "Early Mother-Infant Interaction and 24 Hour Patterns of Activity and Sleep." *Journal of the American Academy of Child Psychiatry,* 1970, *9,* 103–123.

Sander, L. "Investigation of the Infant and Its Caregiving Environment as a Biological System." In S. I. Greenspan and G. H. Pollock (eds.), *The Course of Life: Psychoanalytic Contributions Toward Understanding Personality Development.* Vol. 1: *Infancy and Early Childhood.* Washington, D.C.: National Institute of Mental Health, 1980.

Solnit, A. J. "Developmental Perspectives on Self and Object Constancy." *Psychoanalytic Study of the Child,* 1982, *37,* 201–218.

Spitz, R. A. "Hospitalism: An Inquiry into the Genesis of Psychiatric Conditions in Early Childhood." *Psychoanalytic Study of the Child,* 1945, *1,* 53–74.

Spitz, R. A. "Relevancy of Direct Infant Observation." *Psychoanalytic Study of the Child,* 1950, *5,* 66–73.

Spitz, R. A. *No and Yes: On the Beginnings of Human Communication.* New York: International Universities Press, 1957.

Spitz, R. A. *The First Year of Life: A Psychoanalytic Study of Normal and Deviant Development of Object Relations.* New York: International Universities Press, 1965.

Spitz, R. A., and Wolf, K. "Anaclitic Depression: An Inquiry into the Genesis of Psychiatric Conditions in Early Childhood, II." *Psychoanalytic Study of the Child,* 1946, *2,* 313–342.

Stern, D. N. "Mother and Infant at Play: The Dyadic Interaction Involving Facial, Vocal, and Gaze Behavior." In M. Lewis and L. A. Rosenblum (eds.), *The Effect of the Infant on Its Caregiver.* New York: Wiley, 1974.

Wallerstein, J., and Kelly, J. "The Effects of Parental Divorce: The Experience of the Preschool Child." *American Academy of Child Psychiatry,* 1975, *14*(4), 600–616.

Wallerstein, J., and Kelly, J. *Surviving the Breakup.* New York: Basic Books, 1980.

White, R. W. "Motivation Reconsidered: The Concept of Competence." *Psychological Review,* 1959, *66,* 297–333.

White, R. W. "Critical Influences in the Origins of Competence." *Merrill-Palmer Quarterly,* 1975, *21,* 243–266.

Yarrow, L. J. "Separation from Parents During Early Childhood." In M. L. Hoffman and L. W. Hoffman (eds.), *Review of Child Development Research.* New York: Russell Sage Foundation, 1964.

Yarrow, L. J. "Beyond Cognition: The Development of Mastery Motivation." In S. Provence (ed.), *Zero to Three: Bulletin of the National Center for Clinical Infant Programs.* Washington, D.C., 1981, *1*(3), 1-5.

Yarrow, L. J., and Pederson, F. A. "The Interplay Between Cognition and Motivation in Infancy." In M. Lewis (ed.), *Origins of Intelligence.* New York: Plenum, 1976.

Yarrow, L. J., Rubenstein, J. L., and Pederson, F. A. *Infant and Environment: Early Cognitive and Motivational Development.* New York: Halsted Press, 1975.

3

Separation in Infancy and Early Childhood: Contributions of Attachment Theory and Psychoanalysis

Alicia F. Lieberman

Editors' Note: *With a primary focus on explicating attachment theory, Lieberman considers the complementary contributions of the two primary approaches to the study of separation in early childhood. Basic assumptions, methods of inquiry, and substantive findings of the attachment literature are discussed. The chapter reviews the factors that shape response to separation, including the child's developmental stage, length of the separation, familiarity of the surroundings, and quality of the preexisting parent/child relationship. The widely used experimental method of the "strange situation" is described, as is a theoretical framework for why children's brief separations and reunions with attachment figures, along with their confrontations with strangers, capture such a deep psychological dimension of relatedness and personality functioning. Lieberman characterizes attachment relationships as providing both a secure base from which the child explores and a secure haven to which the child returns.*

The chapter outlines the three patterns of parent/child relationship emerging from attachment research: the securely attached, the anxious/ambivalently attached, and the anxious/ avoidant attached. Studies of these three patterns reveal striking links between quality of attachment in infancy and later childhood play behavior, interaction with peers, and social competence in nursery school and kindergarten (see Chapter Six for an examination of separation problems and preschool adjustment). Lieberman also notes parallels between the characteristics of separation reactions observed in children with different attachment patterns and the three stages of mourning that Bowlby postulates during any experience of object loss (protest, despair, detachment).

In spite of theoretical disagreements in conceptualizing issues like separation anxiety and mourning, Lieberman finds considerable convergence in the clinical observations and conclusions put forth by the psychoanalytic and attachment theory approaches to separation. It is clear that long-term or repeated separations under certain conditions will be traumatic and may have detrimental effects on personality functioning. However, Lieberman complicates the picture of separation as negative by (1) emphasizing the growth-promoting aspects of separation, especially the process of separation-individuation, and the positive impact that developmentally appropriate transitions involving separation may have for the child and (2) presenting clinical situations in which even permanent separation may be the preferred course for children.

The term *separation* has two major uses in the psychoanalytic literature, each of them related to the child's relationship with a primary object, or attachment figure, most commonly the mother (Allen, 1955). One meaning is the normal developmental process of gradual psychological differentiation from the mother following the physical separation of birth. The second use refers to separation not as process but as event: the premature and prolonged removal of a child from the mother, this physical absence having far-reaching psychological consequences.

As Provence points out in Chapter Two, the two meanings of separation—as process and as event—represent polar experiences in a spectrum of separation situations that include many gradations in their potential for promoting growth versus producing stress. In the present chapter, the focus will be on the psychological impact of separation as an untimely external event that disrupts, sometimes permanently, the emotional relationship between a child and his or her principal caregiver. The contributions of attachment theory (Bowlby, 1969, 1973, 1980; Ainsworth, 1972a) will be discussed as pivotal in expanding our understanding of the intense grief experienced by a child on separation from this central attachment figure, with possible long-term consequences for the ability to form and sustain other love relationships. At the same time, it will also be argued that this perspective on the pathogenic potential of separations is most useful when read in the context of other contributions that emphasize the growth-promoting aspects of separation when this event occurs under conditions that do not violate the age-appropriate and individual competencies and vulnerabilities of the child (for example, Mahler, Pine, and Bergman, 1975; Spitz, 1965; Benjamin, 1963; A. Freud, 1960). In this regard, the viewpoints of attachment and psychoanalytic theorists may be seen as mutually enriching and complementary in spite of fundamental theoretical disagreements (for example, Bowlby, 1960, 1980; A. Freud, 1960; Schur, 1960; Spitz, 1960). Attachment theory highlights the emotional impact that a reality event —that is, a major separation—has on the child's psychological functioning and emphasizes the possibility of pathological repercussions for the child's personality formation. In complementary fashion, psychoanalytic contributions have stressed that the child's unique individuality must be seen as a filter through which reality events acquire highly personalized meanings as organizers of psychological experience (Chapter Two, this volume). It is easy to unwittingly play down the importance of one perspective in the process of fully exploring the contributions of the other. Nevertheless, an awareness of how reality and the mind continuously and simultaneously mold each other is crucial for understanding both how separation can function as an external pathogen for personality development and how such an event is shaped into a unique psychological configuration by the subjective experience of each individual child.

Attachment Theory

Major Characteristics. The cornerstone of attachment theory is the effort to explain the intense emotional reactions experienced by children between about six months (the age when a focused relationship to a discriminated mother figure begins to be reliably reported in studies of socioemotional development) and three years of age when they are separated from their mother figure (Bowlby, 1969). The method of inquiry is characterized by four main features: a prospective approach, the focus on a pathogenic event and its repercussions for personality formation, the use of direct observations of young children as a basis for theoretical hypotheses as well as clinical data, and an evolutionary perspective that draws on ethological principles and the observation of animal behavior for understanding the formation of social bonds. Using separation from the mother as a point of departure for his thinking, Bowlby has relied on observations of young children's responses in order to trace the psychological sequelae of this event and its long-term consequences for personality formation. He has also compared young children's behavior in separation and reunion situations with the behavior of other primates, finding similarities and differences that can be understood in the context of evolutionary adaptations that maximize survival.

According to attachment theory, the intense bond (or attachment) between a child and its mother is mediated by behaviors that promote the child's proximity and contact with her—the so-called attachment behaviors, which include, for example, seeking, approaching, grasping, clinging, and following. This attachment behavioral system is activated most readily in situations that arouse wariness and fear and is postulated to serve a specific biological function: protection from predators. The protection from physical dangers has psychological correlates as well: in Bowlby's words, "The knowledge that an attachment figure is available and responsive provides a strong and pervasive feeling of security" (1982, p. 668). The tendency to seek proximity and contact with an attachment figure is most apparent in early childhood but remains present throughout life, particularly in situations of stress or emergency.

The attachment system is postulated to be a distinct motivational system comparable to feeding and mating in its biological importance (Bowlby, 1982). In this sense, the term *attachment* has a specialized, technical meaning that is different from its generalized use as a synonym for *social bond* (Bretherton, 1985). Attachment relationships involve specifically the regulation of protection and security and are therefore qualitatively different from social relationships where this is not a primary component (such as a relationship with a playmate). The attached person seeks the attachment figure for the purpose of security and protection, using behaviors that promote proximity and contact in order to do so. The attachment figure, in turn, is a source of protection and of its psychological correlate, felt security. This process takes place in the context of a dynamic balance between the attachment system and other behavioral systems, particularly exploration and fear. Attachment behaviors tend to be mobilized in situations that arouse wariness and fear, and attainment of the set goal of proximity and contact brings about both a decline in fear (by establishing distance from the situation perceived as dangerous) and a psychological experience of security (by establishing closeness to the perceived source of protection). Attachment behaviors are thus attenuated, and distance from the attachment figure may then be restored in order to explore.

The view that the attachment system is a distinct motivational system with the biological function of promoting survival has profound implications for our understanding of separation anxiety and of distress following separation from the attachment figure. In the "environment of evolutionary adaptedness" in which humans evolved, separation from the attachment figure represented an increase in physical risk, since her absence signaled her unavailability as a protector. Separation thus served as a natural clue to potential danger. In this context, separation anxiety and distress upon separation evolved as adaptive responses to forestall such an increase in risk. In Bowlby's words: "Because being alone carries an increased risk of danger, especially for young individuals and others who are weak, the fear response to inaccessibility of mother can usefully be regarded as a basic adaptive response, namely a response that during the course of evolution has become an intrinsic part of man's behavioral repertoire because of its contribution to species survival" (1973, p. 178).

What is the evidence that led to giving separation such an important place in attachment theory? The earliest systematic documentations of children's responses to separation were made by psychoanalytically informed observers in very dramatic situations: children evacuated from London during World War II (Burlingham and Freud, 1942, 1944) and children of imprisoned women at a penal institution in South America, who at six months of age were arbitrarily separated from their mothers, having been reared by them in prison since birth (Spitz, 1946). The methods involved detailed behavioral observations in naturalistic conditions and in longitudinal sequence. The data made clear that babies separated from their mothers from the second half of the first year onward experienced severe grief. When this grief was not assuaged either by the mother's return or by adequate surrogate care from a reliable caregiver, the grief became depression: the babies withdrew from human contact, failed to progress in their development, and within a few months to a year seemed irreversibly damaged by the morbid conditions compounding the original maternal loss.

The pervasive changes brought on by maternal loss and subsequent maternal deprivation were irrefutably captured on films of individual children by Spitz (1947). Although the clinical observations were impossible to deny, however, the reasons for them were the focus of much controversy. The naturalistic conditions that had given rise to the observations also conspired against methodological soundness because the multiple variables affecting the babies' responses could not be systematically controlled. As a result, there was heated debate over just which variables were causally linked to the babies' developmental decline: Separation or a strange environment? Separation or deprivation of maternal care? Separation from the mother or separation from a familiar person? Separation from mother or absence of an adequate caregiver? (Rutter, 1972). These questions generated a voluminous body of naturalistic studies conducted in institutions such as hospitals and residential nurseries, where some of the variables could be more systematically controlled. Useful distinctions have been made in the light of those studies. Whereas the term *maternal deprivation* had long been used to denote a variety of conditions, including separation, neglect, and institutional care, it is currently accepted that different environmental circumstances have different short- and long-term consequences for personality development and need to be carefully and explicitly described rather than subsumed under a single, seemingly homogeneous category (Rutter, 1972).

The methodologically sounder studies have both confirmed and refined the earlier finding that disruption of a bond with the mother figure (whether she is the biological mother or not) causes severe distress in young children. This information became the basis for Bowlby's efforts to understand why "mere separation" from the mother should have such strong emotional repercussions. It is now time to examine the evidence.

Responses to Prolonged Separation from Mother. Bowlby (1969) has reviewed several decades of studies describing the response of young children to separation from their mothers. The studies differ on many variables, such as the children's age (although the range is between approximately twelve and thirty-six months), family characteristics, type of institution in which they lived while away from home, quality of substitute care, length of the separation, and health status of the children. Despite these differences, there is a remarkable uniformity among the observations reported. Children's responses to separation may be divided into three major phases, called, respectively, protest, despair, and detachment (Robertson and Bowlby, 1952). These phases merge, overlap, and alternate with one another but are relatively distinct in terms of the child's predominant attitude toward the absent mother. The phases were derived from observations by James Robertson of children in their second and third years who were hospitalized for minor procedures or placed in residential homes, but their basic features apply to other separation situations as well.

In the initial phase, *protest,* the child shows severe distress (crying loudly, flailing, shaking the crib) as well as search behavior (standing next to the door or trying to open it, looking for mother in different rooms, calling out to her or asking about her, listening intently for noises that may signal her return). Some children reject efforts by surrogate figures to console them, although others cling to an available adult or allow themselves to be held. This phase may occur immediately on separation or may be delayed, but its hallmark is the child's distress coupled with a simultaneous expectation that the mother will return. The child's behavior can thus be interpreted as an all-out effort to bring the mother back by displaying the full range of behaviors that in ordinary circumstances restore proximity to and contact with the mother.

The second phase, *despair,* shows increasing hopelessness about the mother's return. Activity and the intensity of crying decrease, and the child appears subdued and withdrawn. He or she shows little interest in the surroundings and makes few demands on attentive caregivers, suggesting a continued preoccupation with thinking about the mother. This behavior is construed as the child's grieving for the mother's absence with little expectation that his or her actions will help to bring her back.

In the third phase, labeled *detachment,* the child shows renewed interest in the physical and social environment. He or she explores toys, accepts care from others, and may be sociable, friendly, and outgoing. The main sign that the separation is still a source of anger and pain is the child's response to a visit from the mother. In earlier phases, such an event would have triggered intense efforts by the child to regain proximity and contact through hugging the mother, clinging to her, and protesting her efforts to leave again. In the detachment phase, in contrast, the child fails to greet the mother, turns away or walks away from her, and may seem not to recognize her. Often there is intense absorption in the gifts brought by the mother with a concomitant absence of social interaction with her. These responses accomplish the opposite of attachment behaviors: they fail to restore and may actively preclude proximity and contact. This is clearly not due to a simple process of forgetting who the mother is: the same children tend to show instant recognition of other relatives (siblings, father, grandmother) from whom they have also been separated for comparable periods of time. Thus, detachment is interpreted as serving a defensive function against the intense negative emotions experienced during the separation and against the anxiety triggered by the expectation of losing the mother again.

When reunion finally occurs, the children's responses often show persistent effects of the separation experience. The initial response is often detachment—the previously mentioned lack of recognition or turning or walking away from the mother. This period may last hours or days and is commonly followed by a phase of ambivalence in which the child alternates between, on the one hand, clinging to the mother, following her from room to room, and crying bitterly on brief separations and, on the other hand, being hostile, defiant, and rejecting of the mother. After the child's behavior returns to normal, there may be periodic exacerbations of anxiety when the child is faced with unexpected situations that evoke fear of a new separation. Very frequently, children become frightened when they encounter the caregiver who was assigned to them during the separation, and they ignore or actively avoid proximity to and contact with her (Heinicke and Westheimer, 1966; Robertson and Robertson, 1971).

Bowlby (1961, 1980, 1982) argues that the responses of children to separation are simply variations of basic mourning processes that occur in similar form and in the same sequence regardless of age. He points to a basic difference between mourning in childhood and in adulthood: "In childhood the processes leading to detachment are very apt to develop prematurely, inasmuch as they coincide with and mask strong residual yearning for and anger with the lost object, both of which persist, ready for expression, at an unconscious level. Because of this premature onset of detachment, the mourning process of childhood habitually takes a course that in older children and adults is regarded as pathological" (1961, p. 269). In this premature onset of detachment in childhood lies, in Bowlby's view, the key to the significance of separation for the onset of psychiatric conditions. The intense yearnings coupled with anger are not given free expression, are suppressed, and continue to exert a hidden negative effect on the child's unfolding personality.

Mitigating Conditions. The disturbance that tends to follow a major separation is influenced by a number of factors (Ainsworth, 1972a). These include age or maturity of the child, whether the separation is permanent or temporary, number and length of temporary separations, whether the child remains in familiar surroundings during the separation period, whether a mother substitute is available, whether the mother visits periodically, and the quality of the mother/child relationship both before and after the separation.

In most separation studies, three concomitant factors interacted to increase the child's distress: mother's absence, the child's removal from familiar surroundings, and lack of alternative caregiving from a consistently available (and preferably familiar) figure. A study by Robertson and Robertson (1971) shows that separation responses persist but are ameliorated under more favorable conditions—namely, when care is provided by a familiar and consistent caregiver and when the child's own cherished possessions accompany him or her to the new setting.

The Robertsons undertook to act as foster parents to four children, aged seventeen to twenty-nine months, whose mothers were having a new baby. All the children were first-born, were living with both parents, and had not had previous separations. The length of separation ranged from ten to twenty-seven days. In each case, the Robertsons met the child a month or so before the separation and acquainted themselves with the child's developmental stages and with the details of everyday life, such as likes and dislikes, daily routines, and the mother's caregiving practices. The child visited the foster home before the move. During the separation, the father visited frequently. Every effort was made to keep alive a positive affective connection with the mother by talking about her, looking at her photograph, and giving reassurance that the child would return home as soon as possible. The child's own bed, blankets, and toys were brought to the foster home, and the daily routine was patterned after the home routine as much as possible.

Under these conditions, the children showed far less distress during the separation and less separation anxiety and developmental disturbances after reunion. Nevertheless, the experience of separation was clearly a painful one for them. The high quality of surrogate care and the frequent reference to the mother and to impending reunion with her seemed to serve a preventive function that fended off despair and detachment, but the coping mechanisms of these children were clearly strained by the mother's absence, as indicated, for example, by explicit expressions of sadness and longing, intermittent rejection of the foster mother's care, and the emergence of new fears (such as the fear of being lost). These observations have reinforced both the Robertsons and Bowlby in their belief that prolonged separations in the first three years are "dangerous and whenever possible should be avoided" (Bowlby, 1973, p. 22).

Brief Separations: Experimental Studies. The problems of methodological soundness that mar even careful naturalistic studies can be more easily solved in experimental studies of brief separations. These separations, lasting only a few minutes and consonant with a baby's everyday experiences, are ethically permissible in the laboratory and allow for rigorous control of relevant variables and for systematic and detailed observation.

The most influential instrument for studying infants' responses to brief separations is the "strange situation" (Ainsworth and Wittig, 1969; Ainsworth and Bell, 1970; Ainsworth, Blehar, Waters, and Wall, 1978). This is a laboratory situation that consists of eight episodes, lasting three minutes each. The episodes are designed so that various sources of stress for the baby are introduced gradually and have a cumulative effect that tips the behavioral balance from a predominance of exploratory behaviors to a predominance of attachment behaviors. In Episode 1 an observer introduces the mother and baby to the test room and then leaves. The sources of stress are: mother and baby occupying an unfamiliar playroom in Episode 2; the entrance of a stranger in Episode 3; mother's departure, leaving the baby alone with the stranger, in Episode 4; mother's second departure after a brief reunion in Episode 5; the baby staying alone in the playroom in Episode 6; and the stranger's return when the baby is actually expecting the mother in Episode 7.

The strange situation ends with a final reunion with mother in Episode 8.

The strange situation was designed to assess one-year-olds, and it has proved to be a reliable and valid instrument for detecting both normative trends and individual patterns in the organization of attachment behaviors. These characteristics have made the strange situation the instrument of choice in the experimental study of attachment in infancy, and it has been used with toddlers and preschoolers as well as with one-year-olds.

When behavior in the strange situation is analyzed to determine the infant's responses to separation and reunion, several findings emerge (Ainsworth, Blehar, Waters, and Wall, 1978). Among one-year-olds, separation from the mother is associated with an increase in crying and searching behavior and a decline in exploratory behaviors. These effects are intensified when the baby is left alone (Episode 6) rather than with the stranger (Episode 4). However, there are significant differences between the incidence of these behaviors in the mother's presence and in her absence, indicating that separation from the mother leads to a shift in the organization of fear, attachment, and exploratory behaviors that is consonant with the predictions of attachment theory. Similarly, reunion with the mother (in Episodes 5 and 8) is associated with significant increases in the baby's effort to seek proximity to her and maintain contact with her. A comparison of the relevant episodes also shows that these behaviors are much more frequently addressed to the mother than to the stranger. Thus, the baby's behavior is specifically organized around the mother's presence or absence, although the stranger serves a palliative function for distress in the mother's absence.

When normative trends are compared for strange-situation behaviors among one-, two-, three-, and four-year-olds, some predictable developmental changes appear. In a study by Marvin (1977), two-year-olds resembled one-year-olds in the incidence of crying upon separation. Upon reunion, they sought proximity to and contact with the mother even more strongly than one-year-olds, but they were less insistent in their efforts to maintain physical contact after it was achieved. The three-year-olds, in contrast, were not distressed by the first separation, and they tended to maintain high levels of exploration during the first part of the situation. They did cry when left alone (with a consequent decline in exploration), but they were consoled more readily than younger children by the stranger's return in Episode 7. In spite of this readiness to rely on the stranger for comfort, three-year-olds resembled the younger groups in seeking proximity to the mother in the final reunion episode. Four-year-olds, in general, were little distressed by the separations and tended to maintain high levels of exploration across the different episodes.

Behavior in the strange situation is interpreted as an indication of how the mother/child relationship is organized around the issues of maternal physical and emotional availability and the child's felt security. Two closely related concepts are relevant in this context: the mother as a secure base from which to explore and the mother as a secure haven in which to seek shelter (Ainsworth, Blehar, Waters, and Wall, 1978). "Secure base" behavior refers to the contextually determined balance between attachment and exploratory behaviors that allows the baby to use the mother as a reliable anchor from which to explore, returning to her periodically for social exchanges and reassurance. This pattern is observed even in the absence of wariness or fear. In the "secure haven" pattern, in contrast, the implication is that the baby experiences at least some alarm, and this impels him to seek proximity to and contact with the mother. The patterns of secure haven and secure base may be mobilized in succession. The baby may use the mother as a secure haven from a frightening experience and be so reassured by her presence and behavior that he can then leave the mother's side in order to explore, using her as a secure base from that point on.

As the infant's social competence and cognitive capacities increase with age, the external circumstances experienced as dangerous (fear-arousing) will differ in degree and kind, in keeping with the child's capacity to appraise danger and seek protection. In the course of development, the child develops an increasingly sophisticated internal working model of the mother's availability as a protector (Bowlby, 1980). When the mother is reliably available as a protector, the features that make her so become an integral part of the working model, providing the child with an internalized sense of security. Conversely, when a mother is unable to provide reliable protection from danger through contingent responsiveness to the child's signals of fear or distress, the child fails to attain a consistent state of felt security and cannot internalize such a state into the features of the working model of the attachment relationship.

The developmental trends in responses to separation and reunion observed in the strange situation suggest that older children become less distressed by the brief separations involved because they have learned, through repeated experiences of brief separations in different contexts, that the mother is consistently available and will return. They are also presumed to have more recourse, in the mother's absence, to the internalized sense of protection that is part of their working model of the attachment relationship. Because these older children are less distressed, they experience less need to seek proximity and contact with the mother on her return; their social skills also enable them to use distal behaviors (such as talking to the mother) as a means of restoring psychological contact. The younger children, still in the early stages of developing an internal working model, are more easily undone by even brief separations in an unfamiliar setting and need reassurance through physical proximity and contact upon reunion (Marvin, 1977; Ainsworth, Blehar, Waters, and Wall, 1978).

In addition to shedding light on developmental changes in the responses to separation and reunion, the strange situation illuminates the meaning of individual differences in these behaviors. This is particularly so among one-year-olds, the age for which the instrument was explicitly designed. Specifically, the strange situation permits a classification of one-year-olds according to the quality of their attachment to the mother. Three such groups were originally described (Ainsworth, Blehar, Waters, and Wall, 1978). These groups (labeled A, B, and C) differ not so much in the amount of intensity of distress upon separation as in the quality of the response to the mother upon reunion. The groups are not homogeneous, and indeed each comprises subgroups for greater accuracy of classification, but the main features are uniform within each group.

The normative group, called Group B, is considered to be securely attached. These babies use the mother as a secure base from which to explore the unfamiliar environment of the strange situation. They may or may not cry when the mother leaves the room, but when she returns, they immediately seek physical proximity and close body contact. Such closeness is an effective soothing mechanism for these babies, who may resist being put down if the mother attempts to do so prematurely.

During home observations conducted throughout their first year and prior to the strange situation, these babies were found to be unlikely to cry when the mother left the room. Their mothers were observed to be sensitively responsive to the baby's signals, whether in the context of feeding, response to distress, face-to-face social exchanges, or close bodily contact. Ainsworth and her colleagues hypothesize that these experiences led the baby to develop a confident expectation of the mother's availability. When these expectations were negated in the strange situation by her departure from an unfamiliar setting, the babies responded with protest and/or search behavior but were quickly reassured again by the mother's return, which reconfirmed for them the accuracy of their expectations.

Babies considered anxiously attached were classified in two groups. One group showed avoidance of the mother upon reunion (Group A, labeled "anxious avoidant"). The babies looked away, turned away, moved past the mother, or ignored her when she reentered the room. They showed little tendency to seek proximity to or contact with the mother or to interact with her. They made little effort to maintain contact with the mother when picked up and then released. Avoidant babies, distressed by separation in the strange situation, also tended to cry at home when the mother left the room. They tended to show more anger at home than the other babies. Their mothers, in turn, were described as rejecting, showing indications of submerged anger, uncomfortable with physical contact, and showing rigid, compulsive patterns of overall adjustment. These and other findings led Ainsworth and her colleagues to postulate that the avoidance of mother shown by A babies upon reunion in the strange situation serves a defensive function, protecting them from the negative emotions triggered by their mothers' emotional unavailability and consistent rebuff of the baby's signals (Ainsworth, Blehar, Waters, and Wall, 1978; Main, 1977). Ainsworth and Bell (1970) also noted the similarity between avoidance of the mother in the strange situation and the defensive "detachment" observed when reunion follows a long separation.

A different behavioral configuration of anxious attachment is observed in babies who resist and reject their mothers upon reunion (Group C—"anxious resistant"). These babies cry more than those in the other groups, both in the strange situation and at home. In the reunion episodes of the strange situation, they resist contact and interaction through behaviors such as hitting, pushing away, squirming to be put down, temper tantrums, or rejection of toys offered by the mother. At the same time, these behaviors are intermingled with efforts to seek and maintain proximity and contact. The resulting effect conveys a strong impression of ambivalence. The mothers of C babies tended to be less contingent to the baby's signals and communications, less responsive to crying, and more inept in holding the baby. The C babies are thus likely to experience a constant sense of uncertainty about the mother's availability, generating both an urgent wish to secure contact with the mother and anger about the mother's poor timing in responding to their needs.

These individual differences in patterns of attachment are strong predictors of individual differences in later years. Strange-situation classifications have been found to be stable across a six-month period when family circumstances remain relatively unchanged (Waters, 1978); to change in ways that are consonant with changing family circumstances that alter maternal availability to the child (Thompson, Lamb, and Estes, 1982; Vaughn, Egeland, Sroufe, and Waters, 1979); to be related to the child's competence in other areas of functioning, such as play (Belsky, Gardugue, and Hrncir, 1983), interaction with peers (Lieberman, 1977; Easterbrooks and Lamb, 1979), internalized controls (Londerville and Main, 1981), and compliance (Stayton, Hogan, and Ainsworth, 1971); and to predict competence in negotiation of the changing developmental tasks facing the toddler, preschooler, and kindergarten-age child (Matas, Arend, and Sroufe, 1978; Marvin, 1977; Sroufe, 1979, 1983; Waters, Wippman, and Sroufe, 1979).

What do these findings say about separation? How can a research instrument featuring two three-minute separations and two three-minute reunions with the mother illuminate the role of separation in the unfolding personality of the child? To answer these questions, we must remember that the strange situation functions as a stressor that mobilizes the child's coping resources in a situation perceived as dangerous: the mother's departure, leaving the child alone in an unfamiliar setting. The behaviors that the child uses in response to this event allow inferences about the child's state of felt security and his or her perception of the mother's availability. Thus, the strange situation offers a window through which to study the child's susceptibility to separation anxiety and the degree to which the mechanisms used to cope with it incorporate anger, ambivalence, and mistrust.

Separation Anxiety: Perspectives from Attachment Theory and Psychoanalysis

In his influential volume on separation, Bowlby (1973) presents an extensive discussion of Freud's (1926/1959) general theory of anxiety. He is in basic agreement with Freud's views that anxiety is a response to the danger of losing the love object, pain or mourning (grief) is the response to the actual loss, and defenses are the psychological processes mobilized as ways of coping with anxiety and pain. From here on, however, the different motivational models underlying psychoanalytic and attachment theories lead to a divergence in their accounts of the mechanisms that trigger separation anxiety.

In Freud's view, the ultimate danger situation is a "recognized, remembered, expected situation of helplessness" (Freud, 1926/1959, p. 166) that is associated with the mother's absence because the mother is perceived, through experience, to be the person who satisfies all the child's needs. In this view, fear of loss of the mother is rooted in the child's expectation that the mother's absence will result in a deprivation of satisfaction for his needs. In Freud's model of motivation, the achievement of a quiescent psychophysiological state is a basic aim of the organism; Freud argues that, if feasible, the nervous system would "maintain itself in an altogether unstimulated condition" (1915/ 1957, p. 120). A corollary of this position is that anxiety stems from the child's dread of a painful increase in psychic stimulation when the mother is not available to satisfy his needs through timely ministrations.

Freud's position on separation anxiety is embedded in his broader discussion of realistic and unrealistic, or neurotic, anxiety (Freud, 1926/1959). Realistic anxiety is that which is triggered by a known danger; neurotic anxiety is that triggered by unknown dangers. Freud classifies fear of being alone and fear of strangers as fear of unknown dangers. These fears are equated with fear of losing the love object and hence with fear of psychic helplessness to cope with increasing psychic stimulation. Since all children experience fear of these unknown dangers, Freud considers neurosis a universal childhood condition. Neurosis is "grown out of" in the course of healthy development as unrealistic fears are assuaged through an accurate appraisal of their lack of foundation in a known danger. Within this theoretical context, separation anxiety is the key to the problem of understanding neurotic anxiety.

Provence (Chapter Two, this volume) reviews subsequent psychoanalytic contributions to an understanding of the developmental progression of anxiety in the course of ego development and object and drive differentiation in the infant, toddler, and preschool child. Major contributors to the question of separation anxiety and distress in children are Anna Freud (1960), Benjamin (1963), and Spitz (1945, 1946, 1960). A basic theme in this thinking is that responses to separation must be understood in the context of the child's developmental stage, including ego development and libido development. A corollary of this position is that young children are not capable of engaging in mourning over the loss of the object because mourning is a complex psychological process that requires the function of a fairly developed ego. Thus, these authors consider the sequence of responses to separation in childhood and adulthood to be similar at a descriptive, but not a psychodynamic, level (A. Freud, 1960; Spitz, 1960).

Bowlby's (1973) formulation of the underpinnings of separation anxiety differs almost step by step from the account above. As mentioned earlier in this chapter, Bowlby espouses a Darwinian motivational model in which the attachment system has a distinct biological function in promoting survival. Within this framework, separation anxiety, far from being a neurotic response to an unknown danger, is an adaptive response to the increased dangers that attend the child in the mother's absence: "The heart of the theory here advanced, which derives directly from ethology, is that each of the stimulus situations that man is genetically biased to respond to with fear has the same status as a red traffic light or an air-raid siren. Each is a signal of potential danger; none is intrinsically dangerous . . . far from being irrational or foolhardy, to rely initially on the naturally occurring clues to danger and safety is to rely on a system that has been both sensible and efficient over millions of years" (pp. 138–139). Mother's presence is a natural clue to safety; her absence, a natural clue to danger. Responding differentially to these clues is adaptive indeed.

Because separation anxiety and distress are postulated to have evolved as survival mechanisms and because they are observed in nonhuman primates, Bowlby believes that "explanations of human responses that presume cognitive processes at a specifically human level are . . . called into question" (1973, p. 74). In other words, grief and mourning can occur before the ego is fully developed. Bowlby also argues that, once established, the pattern of responses to separation does not undergo marked change either in form or in intensity until after the third year, and then these responses decline gradually.

Bowlby (1973) uses these conclusions as the basis for understanding some psychiatric conditions, such as phobias and anxiety states, as originating in an anxious attachment to the mother figure—namely, in a relationship where the child has been unable to develop a stable sense of the mother's availability. Such children experience heightened separation anxiety and, in an effort to cope with it, mobilize maladaptive psychological processes such as rationalization and projection. Some conditions that, in Bowlby's view, promote anxious attachment are the absence of a permanent mother figure, experiences of separation or unstable daily substitute care, and parental threats of abandonment or suicide. The work of Ainsworth and her colleagues shows that anxious attachment may also be attributable to patterns of mother/infant interaction in which the infant's signals and communications are consistently ignored, rejected, or responded to in ways that are not contingent on the child's needs (Ainsworth, Blehar, Waters, and Wall, 1978).

The connections linking actual separation experiences, anxious attachment, and later psychopathology are by no means linear. Nevertheless, Bowlby finds that, despite individual variability, the causal effects are clearly established and strong preventive efforts are called for. He warns: "The effects of separation from mother can be likened to the effects of smoking or of radiation. Although the effects of small doses appear negligible, they are cumulative. The safest dose is a zero dose" (1980, p. 73).

Clinical Implications: Some Suggestions for a Synthesis

In spite of disagreements over theoretical issues, the clinical observations and clinical conclusions derived from psychoanalytic theory and from attachment theory show substantial areas of agreement. There is a consensus that separation from the mother after a differentiated relationship has been formed causes strong negative emotional reactions in the infant. There is also agreement that separations may be traumatic events with long-term repercussions and detrimental effects on personality development. Obvious as they may now appear, these conclusions have been of monumental importance for the theory and practice of infant mental health. The interest in prevention of psychopathology has led to a serious quest for the conditions that have a negative effect on development, and untimely separations have emerged as just such a factor. Social policy has been slowly shaped by this discovery: more efforts are made now to avoid arbitrary separations of a child from the mother figure.

This being said, there is still much well-warranted confusion over when a separation may be in the best interests of the child. At the Infant-Parent Program, my colleagues and I have repeatedly witnessed the blossoming of a child after being removed from a worrisome family situation and placed with more adequate caregivers (for example, Lieberman and Pawl, 1984). Such observations have been made by many other clinicians. Given these findings, can one really agree with Bowlby (1980, p. 72) that when it comes to separation from mother, "the safest dose is a zero dose"? This is certainly true of prolonged separations from a "good enough mother" (Winnicott, 1941) to whom the child is attached and who is capable of supporting and promoting the child's development. The less these optimal conditions apply, the more ambiguous the relative costs and benefits for the child of a separation from the mother. Thus, there are difficult ethical and psychological issues to untangle when the child is clearly attached to neglecting or abusing parents who have failed to improve in spite of intensive intervention or when the attachment is loving and intense but the child's personality is being distorted by interactions with a parent who has a psychosis or a pervasive thought disorder. The question of what is more detrimental for the child—to be removed or to remain in that surrounding—has unfortunately met with only elusive attempts at answers. All we can do is grapple with the individual circumstances to make a painful and uncertain but somewhat informed guess.

Even in less extreme situations, Bowlby's prescription of a "zero dose" of separation is easily misinterpreted. Again, the truth of this position is inescapable when one is speaking of a prolonged separation from an adequate mother figure. But what does a "zero dose" mean in everyday terms? Does it preclude a parent's "night out"? Does it preclude nursery school before age three? Maternal employment? Full-time day care? These questions are made urgent by the anxiety experienced by many mothers attempting to find the right balance between sensitivity to the emotional needs of their child and respect for their own individual and family needs.

In this context, it is wise to remember Provence's statement (Chapter Two) that anxiety need not be a crippling experience for the child but may, on the contrary, serve as a stimulus for mastery of age-appropriate developmental challenges. Gradual negotiation of increasingly longer separations from the mother is such a developmental task. It is optimally growth-promoting when external and psychological conditions coincide in such a way that a child need not be faced with separations that are longer than he or she can accommodate without undue distress. However, children can be helped to a successful adjustment even when circumstances necessitate exposing them to longer separations than seem desirable (as in full-time day care for toddlers and preschoolers). Crucial ingredients in the achievement of such mastery are empathetic acknowledgment of the child's feelings as understandable and legitimate, reassurance that the mother loves him and will return, and availability of a stable substitute caregiver who serves as a secondary attachment figure and as an external support and reliable extension of the child.

The question of the child's chronological and developmental age at the time of separation is also a complex one, but one in which a synthesis between the psychoanalytic and the attachment theory approaches seems to best resolve the clinical issues involved. Bowlby's position that young children's responses to separation remain largely unchanged until after the third year is well supported. It is also plausible to postulate, as he does, that these responses are phylogenetically evolved mechanisms representing adaptive responses to a danger situation. Such a viewpoint is not inconsistent with the equally cogent psychoanalytic argument that the child's developmental stage and individual characteristics play a crucial role in the child's perception of the reasons for the separation, his or her role in causing it, his or her ability to come to grips with it, and the way the separation experience will be incorporated into the evolving sense of the self. Phylogeny and ontogeny interact, just as nature and nurture do.

In summary, a balanced reading of the evidence suggests that, in conjunction with the basic phenomenon of distress upon separation, there are many gradations of individual experience and circumstance that may either increase the chances of a pathological outcome or increase the likelihood of an adaptive adjustment to an admittedly painful event. Bowlby and Ainsworth have trained a zoom lens on a phenomenon that, until their contributions, was not fully appreciated as a major risk factor in the affective landscape of infancy. Their work has enriched our understanding of the roles of evolution and external reality in shaping the psychological experience of the child. As a result, we currently think about influences on development in increasingly multidimensional ways. Perhaps the best summary of such a multidimensional approach is that the effects of separation are not necessarily problematic, but rather depend on the nature of the parent/child relationship (Rutter, 1972). Such an emphasis on the individual experience and the multiple factors that affect it should foster the balanced perspective needed to surmount two polar tendencies: on one hand, the wishful impulse to dismiss the burden of pain imposed on the child by even brief separations and, on the other hand, the compensatory tendency to highlight the dangers of separation at the expense of an equally important respect for the nuances of separation experiences and for the self-righting developmental tendencies of the child.

References

Ainsworth, M. D. S. "Attachment and Dependency: A Comparison." In J. L. Gewirtz (ed.), *Attachment and Dependency.* Washngton, D.C.: Winston, 1972a.

Ainsworth, M. D. S. "The Effects of Maternal Deprivation: A Review of Findings and Controversy in the Context of Research Strategy." In *Deprivation of Maternal Care: A Reassessment of Its Effects.* Public Health Papers, No. 14. Geneva: World Health Organization, 1972b.

Ainsworth, M. D. S., and Bell, S. M. "Attachment, Exploration, and Separation: Illustrated by the Behavior of One-Year-Olds in a Strange Situation." *Child Development*, 1970, *41*, 49–67.

Ainsworth, M. D. S., Blehar, M. C., Waters, E., and Wall, S. *Patterns of Attachment: A Psychological Study of the Strange Situation.* Hillsdale, N.J.: Erlbaum, 1978.

Ainsworth, M. D. S., and Wittig, B. A. "Attachment and Exploratory Behavior of One-Year-Olds in a Strange Situation." In B. M. Foss (ed.), *Determinants of Infant Behaviour IV.* London: Methuen, 1969.

Allen, F. H. "Mother-Child Separation—Process or Event." In G. Caplan (ed.), *Emotional Problems of Early Childhood.* New York: Basic Books, 1955.

Belsky, J., Gardugue, L., and Hrncir, E. "Assessing Performance, Competence, and Executive Capacity in Infant Play: Relations to Home Environment and Security of Attachment." *Developmental Psychology*, 1983, *20*, 406–417.

Benjamin, J. D. "Further Comments on Some Developmental Aspects of Anxiety." In H. S. Gaskill (ed.), *Counterpoint: Libidinal Object and Subject.* New York: International Universities Press, 1963.

Bowlby, J. "Grief and Mourning in Infancy and Early Childhood." *Psychoanalytic Study of the Child*, 1960, *15*, 9–52.

Bowlby, J. "Processes of Mourning." *International Journal of Psycho-Analysis*, 1961, *42*, 317–340.

Bowlby, J. *Attachment and Loss.* Vol. 1: *Attachment.* New York: Basic Books, 1969.

Bowlby, J. *Attachment and Loss.* Vol. 2: *Separation: Anxiety and Anger.* New York: Basic Books, 1973.

Bowlby, J. *Attachment and Loss.* Vol. 3: *Loss: Sadness and Depression.* New York: Basic Books, 1980.

Bowlby, J. "Attachment and Loss: Retrospect and Prospect." *American Journal of Orthopsychiatry*, 1982, *52*, 664–678.

Bretherton, I. "Attachment Theory: Retrospect and Prospect." In I. Bretherton and E. Waters (eds.), "Growing Points of Attachment Theory and Research." *Monographs of the Society for Research in Child Development*, 1985, *50*(1–2, Serial No. 209).

Burlingham, D. T., and Freud, A. *Young Children in War-Time.*
London: Allen & Unwin, 1942.

Burlingham, D. T., and Freud, A. *Infants Without Families: The Case For and Against Residential Nurseries.* London: Allen & Unwin, 1944.

Easterbrooks, M. A., and Lamb, M. E. "The Relationship Between Quality of Infant-Mother Attachment and Infant Competence in Initial Encounters with Peers." *Child Development,* 1979, *50,* 380–387.

Freud, A. "Discussion of Dr. John Bowlby's Paper." *Psychoanalytic Study of the Child,* 1960, *15,* 53–62.

Freud, S. "Instincts and Their Vicissitudes." In J. Strachey (ed. and trans.), *The Standard Edition of the Complete Psychological Works of Sigmund Freud.* Vol. 14. London: Hogarth Press, 1957. (Originally published 1915.)

Freud, S. "Inhibitions, Symptoms and Anxiety." In J. Strachey (ed. and trans.), *The Standard Edition of the Complete Psychological Works of Sigmund Freud.* Vol. 20. London: Hogarth Press, 1959. (Originally published 1926.)

Heinicke, C. M., and Westheimer, I. J. *Brief Separations.* New York: International Universities Press, 1966.

Lieberman, A. F. "Preschoolers' Competence with a Peer: Relations with Attachment and Peer Experience." *Child Development,* 1977, *48,* 1277–1287.

Lieberman, A. F., and Pawl, J. H. "Searching for the Best Interests of the Child: Intervention with an Abusive Mother and Her Toddler." *Psychoanalytic Study of the Child,* 1984, *39,* 527–548.

Londerville, S., and Main, M. "Security of Attachment, Compliance, and Maternal Training Methods in the Second Year of Life." *Developmental Psychology,* 1981, *17,* 289–299.

Mahler, M. S., Pine, F., and Bergman, A. *The Psychological Birth of the Human Infant: Symbiosis and Individuation.* New York: Basic Books, 1975.

Main, M. "Analysis of a Peculiar Form of Reunion Behavior Seen in Some Daycare Children: Its History and Sequelae in Children Who Are Home-Reared." In R. A. Webb (ed.), *Social Development in Childhood: Daycare Programs and Research.* Baltimore: Johns Hopkins University Press, 1977.

Marvin, R. S. "An Ethological-Cognitive Model for the Attenuation of Mother-Child Attachment Behavior." In T. M. Alloway, L. Krames, and P. Pliner (eds.), *Advances in the Study of Communications and Affect*. Vol. 2: *The Development of Social Attachment*. New York: Plenum, 1977.

Matas, L., Arend, R. A., and Sroufe, L. A. "Continuity of Adaptation in the Second Year: The Relationship Between Quality of Attachment and Later Competence." *Child Development*, 1978, *49*, 547-556.

Robertson, J., and Bowlby, J. "Responses of Young Children to Separation from Their Mothers." *Courrier du Centre International de L'Enfance*, 1952, *2*, 131-142.

Robertson, J., and Robertson, J. "Young Children in Brief Separation: A Fresh Look." *Psychoanalytic Study of the Child*, 1971, *26*, 264-315.

Rutter, M. *Maternal Deprivation Reassessed*. London: Penguin Books, 1972.

Schur, M. "Discussion of Dr. John Bowlby's Paper." *Psychoanalytic Study of the Child*, 1960, *15*, 63-84.

Spitz, R. A. "Hospitalism: An Inquiry into the Genesis of Psychiatric Conditions in Early Childhood." *Psychoanalytic Study of the Child*, 1945, *1*, 53-74.

Spitz, R. A. *Grief: A Peril in Infancy* [Film]. New York: New York University Film Library, 1947.

Spitz, R. A. "Discussion of Dr. John Bowlby's Paper." *Psychoanalytic Study of the Child*, 1960, *15*, 85-94.

Spitz, R. A. *The First Year of Life: A Psychoanalytic Study of Normal and Deviant Development of Object Relations*. New York: International Universities Press, 1965.

Spitz, R. A., and Wolf, K. "Anaclitic Depression: An Inquiry into the Genesis of Psychiatric Conditions in Early Childhood, II." *Psychoanalytic Study of the Child*, 1946, *2*, 313-342.

Sroufe, L. A. "The Coherence of Individual Development: Early Care, Attachment, and Subsequent Development Issues." *American Psychologist*, 1979, *34*, 834-841.

Sroufe, L. A. "Infant-Caregiver Attachment and Patterns of Adaptation in Preschool: The Roots of Maladaptation and

Competence." In M. Perlmutter (ed.), *Minnesota Symposium in Child Psychology.* Vol. 16. Hillsdale, N.J.: Erlbaum, 1983.

Stayton, D. J., Hogan, R., and Ainsworth, M. D. S. "Infant Obedience and Maternal Behavior: The Origins of Socialization Reconsidered." *Child Development,* 1971, *42,* 1057–1069.

Thompson, R. A., Lamb, M. E., and Estes, D. "Stability of Infant-Mother Attachment and Its Relationship to Changing Life Circumstances in an Unrelated Middle-Class Sample." *Child Development,* 1982, *53,* 144–148.

Vaughn, B., Egeland, B., Sroufe, L. A., and Waters, E. "Individual Differences in Infant-Mother Attachment at Twelve and Eighteen Months: Stability and Change in Families Under Stress." *Child Development,* 1979, *50,* 971–975.

Waters, E. "The Reliability and Stability of Individual Differences in Infant-Mother Attachment." *Child Development,* 1978, *49,* 483–494.

Waters, E., Wippman, J., and Sroufe, L. A. "Attachment, Positive Affect, and Competence in the Peer Group: Two Studies in Construct Validation." *Child Development,* 1979, *50,* 821–829.

Winnicott, D. W. "The Observation of Infants in a Set Situation." *International Journal of Psycho-Analysis,* 1941, *22.* Reprinted in D. W. Winnicott, *Through Paediatrics to Psychoanalysis.* New York: Basic Books, 1975.

4

Development of the Sense of Separateness and Autonomy During Middle Childhood and Adolescence

Eugene H. Kaplan

Editors' Note: *In this chapter, the author focuses on the biological, cognitive, and psychological changes during latency and adolescence that continue to foster the sense of separateness and capacity for autonomy begun in the early years of life. Kaplan discusses how the pathways of development differ for boys and girls and how the emotional resources of the family affect the individual's ability to master necessary developmental transitions. For the latency-age child, cognitive/perceptual development (such as the shift from egocentrism toward objective realism) combines with superego development (the move away from external parental control of regulation toward internal self-regulation) to promote more independent functioning. In latency, dependence on parents lessens markedly; object relationships expand, the capacity for aloneness develops, and the ability to view others realistically begins to unfold. Kaplan examines the meaning of typical latency-age separation experiences, such as travel, camp attendance, school vacations, and day care, and classic separation-related phenomena, such as the family romance fantasy, keeping secrets, and running away. Separation reactions will depend on the ratio of "strangeness" to "familiarity" in the environment and the degree of family stability shaping the child's sense of security.*

Moving on to adolescence, Kaplan again highlights the complex interplay among physical, cognitive, and emotional factors that govern the continuing separation-individuation process. He outlines three phases of adolescence. The first entails redefining the self and the relationship to parents in light of intense bodily transformations; the second, developing the sense of being one's own self and owning one's own body (consolidating sexual identity and beginning to experience intimacy); and the third, defining independent standards and goals in relation to society. The meanings of masturbation, sexual intimacy, menstruation, and the crisis of falling in love are discussed. Kaplan emphasizes the inevitable anxiety and mourning that the necessary separations of adolescence evoke. (These are expanded further, from a family perspective, in Chapter Seven.)

This chapter is especially useful in its discussion of developmental progression and regression, illustrating how the tasks of each stage of development may either facilitate mastery of successive stages or pose challenges that interfere with the individual's ability to cope with the need for increasing separateness and independence.

To examine and understand psychological development, I shall use an organizing framework based on psychoanalytic developmental theory. After a brief review of some salient concepts of that theory, my focus will narrow to one specific issue of psychological development: How does the child develop a tolerable sense of separateness and the capacity to function autonomously as a separate individual?

Development is the outcome of the interaction between

My deep appreciation to my family, for the grandfatherly privilege of observing and participating in the joyous interactions of Saul and Susan with Rachel, and of Bob and Jean with Anna and Leah. Susan's authoritative and insightful accounts of second- through fifth-graders put me further in her debt—E. H. K.

maturation and environment. Maturation is the innate, genetically programmed component that provides the potentialities
of, and sets the limits to, development. The developmental process advances at all levels of the organism's organization, from
the molecular to the psychological.

Psychological development may be viewed as an evolving
series of changes through which an infant totally dependent on
parenting at birth gradually acquires self-parenting capacities.
An autonomously functioning adult is able to take care of both
his bodily and his emotional needs. He is capable of recognizing his emotional state—sadness, anger, worry, depression—and
figuring out the reasons and then acting to dissipate the disturbance of mental equilibrium. The mature adult, in effect, parents himself.

A useful framework for understanding this complex evolution is drawn from psychoanalytic developmental theory,
Piagetian cognitive psychology, and developmental neurology.
Despite gaps and flaws in each and difficulties in their integration, this combination provides the best approach at hand for
organizing and making sense of a very complicated and confusing area (Brody, 1982).

Freud's structural theory (1923/1961) and anxiety theory (1926/1959b) are fundamental psychoanalytic concepts. In
the structural theory, Freud posits a tripartite division of the
mind into id, ego, and superego. These three functional groups
are called "structures" because of the relative constancy of their
objectives and because of their consistency in modes of opera-
tion. This division is based on observations of how the mind
functions in conflict over an instinctual drive. The 1926 theory
defines anxiety as a biologically rooted affect that develops a
signal function: the anxiety signal serves to alert the ego to danger. Freud listed a developmental series of dangers: annihilation, abandonment, loss of love, castration or mutilation, and
guilt. When a conflict arises among the three agencies of the
mind, danger is signaled by anxiety. For example, a murderous
or incestuous wish arises from the drive repository, the id. This
triggers signal anxiety in the ego, anticipating conflict with and
danger of retaliation from the love objects (abandonment, loss

of love, castration) and/or from the superego (guilt). The ego's function is then to mediate, accommodate, and compromise these conflicting demands. Since the conflict is within the mind, it is termed intrapsychic.

Separation-individuation theory also provides insights into development prior to latency. The purview of separation-individuation theory (Mahler, Pine, and Bergman, 1975) is object relations and object representations: how representations within the mind, of the self and others, evolve and differentiate in early mental functioning. The separation process includes boundary formation, distancing, and disengagement from the mother, culminating in the realization that mother and others are outside the boundaries of the self. Individuation comprises the organization and control of perception, memory, cognition, and reality testing.

Reciprocal interaction between separation and individuation is optimal, but Mahler (1972) emphasizes the potential for disjunction of these two distinct processes. She describes how precocious motor development propels a toddler into premature awareness of separateness, without the cognitive ability to cope with this awareness. In the reverse, individuation develops unimpeded while separation is retarded by an overprotective, infantilizing mother, for example (see also Speers and Morter, 1980).

Autonomy, the capacity of the young child to function satisfactorily in mother's absence, is postulated to require the presence in the child's mind of a stable representation of mother clearly differentiated from the self. External separations are tolerable because this internalized maternal representation is a resource for the child's self-comforting.

In the third year, this representation normally acquires permanence during the fourth subphase of separation-individuation ("on the way to object constancy"). *Object constancy* refers to the persistence of the object representation in the child's mind despite mother's absence in reality and/or the child's angry feelings toward her.

Mahler theorizes that this achievement requires the merger of two separate mental images of mother into one. The representation of the good, giving, loving and lovable, approving mother coalesces with that of the bad, frustrating, hating and hateful, condemning one. These separate images are the developmental prototype of the splitting defense. As they fuse into one maternal representation incorporating both "good" and "bad," the child becomes capable of authentic ambivalence.

The term *on the way to object constancy* reflects the tentativeness and incompleteness of the achievement and the proneness to regression. If the child gets angry enough at mother, he or she may succumb to magical, omnipotent thinking and feel convinced that this angry, wishful sentence of banishment or death will do mother in. Then, and especially at bedtime, reassurance requires her physical presence.

Although this regressive tendency diminishes with age, the regressive wish for reunion with the mother of early childhood is never fully outgrown (Mahler, 1966). Reverberations of the separation-individuation process occur throughout all subsequent phases of life.

The contrast between the rapprochement-phase toddler and the oedipal-phase preschooler illustrates the difference that evolving object constancy makes. In rapprochement, the toddler is assailed by the anxiety of separation and even annihilation, threatening the extinction of the object representations and thus the collapse of the child's intrapsychic world. Even during heated contentions with parents, the oedipal child has the constant buttress of the comforting mental representations and therefore is spared separation and annihilation anxiety. Castration anxiety predominates in this phase.

Concluding this brief review of prelatency development, we turn now to latency and adolescence.

Latency

Latency corresponds roughly to the grade school years, ages six to eleven. The designation of this period as the time for grade school is society's institutionalized response to the child's developmental advances in self-control, tractability, cognition, and socialization. The latency child is capable of functioning for hours away from home and parents, of sitting, listening, and learning, and is therefore considered educable.

Freud (1905/1953) used the term to denote a sexual latency, an abatement of the sexual drives between the oedipal phase and their resurgence at puberty. He postulated a biological decrease in the instinctual drives as the maturational component of latency development. Current thinking considers biological advances in brain function, notably in perception and cognition, to provide the maturational underpinning for the advances of latency. Freud attributed the shift toward quiescence in the drive-control equilibrium to an innate decrease in the drives. Today, we attribute the shift to an innate increase in the mechanisms of control.

Biological Maturational Factors. Shapiro and Perry (1976) marshal impressive research findings in support of biological maturational factors underlying the inhibition and control of drives characteristic of latency. The frontal lobes of the brain, the seat of verbal self-regulation, undergo significant structural differentiation between six and seven. The alpha-wave pattern of the electroencephalogram becomes stabilized at this time. The connection between the thinking cerebral cortex and the thalamus, locus of affects, acquires the myelin layer that speeds impulse transmission between them, enhancing their interaction (Kaplan, 1965). At age seven spatiotemporal orientation matures and two-point face/hand discrimination improves dramatically. Thinking changes from associational, egocentric, preoperational to ideational, concrete operational (in Piaget's terms) between seven and eight. Right/left discrimination, time sense, temporal order, and discrimination (in Piaget's sense) are present by age eight. Shapiro and Perry believe these new cognitive structures provide the means for the inhibition and control that characterize latency.

Cognition and Perception. Piaget (1955) found that whereas 40 percent of the conversational speech of four- to seven-year-olds was egocentric echolalia and monologue, nearly all eight-year-olds conversed in socialized speech; they sought communication with the other. Piaget speculates that the phase-specific thrust toward peer socialization facilitates the shift from egocentric thought to logical thinking. The child from eight to twelve, in the stage of concrete operations, can deal with classes and relations as long as the objects are present. Although semantic conceptions are evident, they are essentially stimulus-bound, dependent on sensory input (Piaget and Inhelder, 1958). As Wolfenstein (1958) puts it, the child before age twelve adheres to a concrete visual image evoked by words, which precludes a shift of meaning from the literal to the figurative. Therefore, proverbs are not understood. Riddles are enjoyable because the answer involves word play while the original question is forgotten. Thinking at this stage is literal and limited.

The cognitive advance to concrete operational thinking provides a new capacity for objective realism. At first, this newly acquired aptitude for categorization and causality gives the youngster a scientific grasp of the realities of life. However, as the latency child comes to realize the personal implications of procreation, birth, and death, omnipotence suffers another necessarily painful reduction. The conflicted wishes that reality testing proves impossible are then expressed in play and fantasy, in which prelogical, primary process thinking still holds sway.

Superego and Ego. Most authors follow Bornstein (1951) in dividing latency into two subphases, early and late. The division is around age eight, after the aforementioned maturational changes. Our review of cognitive and perceptual maturation quickly brought us to the midpoint of latency, so let us go back. The oedipal preschooler has the advantage over the rapprochement toddler of structuralized—that is, enduring—mental representations of the parents. Latency may be said to begin with the resolution of the oedipus complex and the formation of the superego. The superego is an internal regulator of self-esteem. This structural addition to the mind makes the latency child less dependent on the parents than the oedipal preschooler, whose definition of good and bad depends exclusively on external parental approval and punishment.

Nevertheless, the trade-off is painful for the early-latency youngster. The superego is initially harsh, rigid, and unintegrated, like a foreign body. Caught between it and the drive impulses, the child typically alternates obedience with rebellion followed by self-reproach. Guilt feelings are novel and poorly tolerated, and so youngsters in this first subphase often tend to regress. They try to transform their internal conflict back to an external clash with their parents: they misbehave and feel relieved by the parental punishment, enabling them to avoid the unbearable guilty feelings.

Alongside the solacing maternal representation for self-comfort, latency adds to the mind the superego for self-direction. This internalization of moral standards develops by identification with the attitudes of the parents and other significant persons in the child's environment. As latency progresses, the superego becomes depersonified, gradually losing the quality of a forbidding or reproachful person; its rigidity and harshness soften as well. Kohlberg (1964) characterizes the normal attitude of the latency child (age seven to ten) as one of fixed concrete interpretation of, and submission to, "the rules" and "law and order" for its own sake. This is reflected in the collective regard for obeying the rules in school and peer group.

Ego functioning is enhanced by the maturational advances, and so we observe a relative strengthening of the ego vis-à-vis the drives and superego around the midpoint. Between seven and ten, the ego's defense mechanisms are developed and strengthened, notably obsessive-compulsive defenses, reaction formation, displacement, and fantasy. This enhancement is reflected in less conflict, greater frustration tolerance, and better impulse control in the second half of latency.

Self-Representation and Object Representation. The latency child's predominant identification is typically with the parent of the same sex, significantly advancing the resolution of bisexuality so that sexual identity is stabilized. Identification with the peer group promotes the sense of separateness from the parents: "us kids versus them grownups." Since the group is of the same sex, identification strengthens the sense of masculinity or femininity. By age nine or ten, the youngster typically has developed a more objective self-awareness. Thus the concept of self (as distinguished from self-awareness and self-experience) first appears in latency (Kramer and Rudolph, 1980). A parallel and proportional shift occurs from an egocentric to a more differentiated view of the other as separate and different, and the capacity for empathy appears. *Egocentricity* means obliviousness to the feelings of the other. Only when the distinction of separateness is realized can one try to bridge the gap by putting oneself in the other's shoes. The salient latency change in the object representations is their deidealization and loss of omnipotence.

Object Relationships. The intrapsychic developments of latency facilitate broadening of object relationships beyond the family circle to peers, teachers, and others in the community. Separation is promoted not only by this expansion of object relationships but also by another fundamental consequence of object constancy, the capacity to be alone (Brody and Axelrad, 1978).

Latency is the time when complete dependence on the parents comes to an end. Brody (1982) suggests that entry into latency is a better time than earlier to evaluate the child's quality of autonomy. In this phase object relations extend beyond the family, deepening later. The older latency child loses his or her belief in parental omnipotence. This necessary deidealization has far-reaching consequences, not only resulting in the common family romance fantasy (discussed later) but also making the child malleable to the influence of extrafamilial others, both adults and children (Kaplan, 1965). By late latency, the primary focus of interpersonal interest moves from the parents to the best friend. The child can depend more on himself or herself and on extrafamilial others.

Note well, however, that the change is from total to partial dependence. Significant, though progressively diminishing, dependence on parents and parent surrogates is essential and normative until adulthood.

The latency child needs parental support and approval, especially after frustration, failure, and rejection, to refuel and return to the fray. Oedipal resolution is also strengthened by parental availability. Ideally, this intrapsychic devolution takes place in a nexus of secure, continuing relationships fostering structuralization and minimizing regression. Unfortunately, the erosion of family and social networks leaves increasing masses of youth with a less than adequate holding environment in which to experience comfortable separation and practice separateness.

The older latency child's enlarged object relations capacities expand the potential for sustaining separations from the parents. Cultural responses to this developmental advance include segregation of eight-year-old boys in cohorts by many nonliterate tribes; apprentices sent to the master's household or aboard ship as cabin boys or powder monkeys in our own historical past; our prep schools and their English prototypes. The allocation of parenting functions between adults and other children varies widely. Their familiarity to and with the child and their parenting capabilities are crucial in determining the outcome of separation.

The expansion of object relationships in latency includes the first manifestations of institutional transference—to school, camp, team, and other organizations. How well the child makes the transfer depends not only on the stability of self- and object constancy and on superego/ego-ideal development and trust but also on the internalization of parental attitudes about the novel and strange, whether enthusiastic, matter-of-fact, or fearful and mistrustful.

Further, the external factor of strangeness, or, more precisely, the proportion of the strange to the familiar, is decisive in all stages of development. *Strange* (Latin *extraneus*, "foreign") means previously unknown, while *familiar* derives from the Latin *familia* ("family," "household"). Greenacre (1975) describes the vulnerability of the solitary traveler in settings of extreme unfamiliarity to severe identity disturbances and depersonalization and the psychological wisdom of traveling to exotic places in pairs. Even a successful negotiation of separation-individuation leaves mature, well-functioning adults with the enduring requirement for significant stability, predictability, and familiarity in their social context (or holding environment).

From this viewpoint, the preference of many foreign tourists for group travel, bringing the familiar along, or of domestic travelers for well-advertised fast-food and motel chains becomes more understandable. Other reservoirs of familiarity, stability, and predictability when people and surroundings are strange include our prized possessions (with transitional-object qualities) and ritual. The comic stereotype of the solitary Imperial Englishman dressing for dinner in some remote jungle vastness illustrates this self-cloaking in familiarity through ritual clothing and behavior.

After a bout of homesickness during his first camp summer, a boy subsequently brought a sandwich from home, which he ate at his first camp meal. He attributed his freedom from homesickness the summers following to this symbolic link between home and camp. Thus, circumstances of separation and strangeness put object constancy under pressure, and the object representations summonable through evocative memory commonly require reinforcement employing the older recognition memory (Fraiberg, 1969). Although it appears that transitional objects are given up as object constancy firms by the child between four and seven (Winnicott, 1953; Busch, 1977), there is some evidence that transitional phenomena and use of transitional objects may arise in adults under the stress of separation from significant current objects (Kahne, 1967).

Evaluation of separation experiences requires consideration of internal and external circumstances. Judgment of the latter attends to what the child is separating from as well as separating to. A child leaving a stable, intact family for a place she can easily view as a contiguous or connected extension of her world, with assurance of communication with her family during the separation, is under the least strain.

The greater the gulf of difference and the fewer the bridges of familiarity, the greater the burden. To illustrate, Bowlby's prediction of increased separation reactions (separation anxiety and depression) in kibbutz youngsters resulting from early sequestration into the children's house from their parents' homes was not borne out. Separation reactions and school phobia were indeed rare in latency (Neubauer, 1965).

An early-latency child who may enjoy a week or two away from home in the company of familiar peers and extrafamilial adults is usually not comfortably ready for the one to two months' separation of summer camp. And although a teen tour abroad poses no problem to the healthy midadolescent, individual foreign-study exchange programs lasting six months to a year are usually too much. This experience is much better assimilated four years later, in the junior year of college. There is a developmental progression in the capacities for autonomous functioning and tolerating separation.

In early grades, classes show much tension and regressive behavior in anticipation of the separation from the teacher and peers during the long Christmas vacation. Children from one-parent households or with two working parents expect to be left with babysitters and to lose their school-based peer contacts. For them the separation is also a deprivation, whereas more supportive, intact families make provision for their children. The resumption of relationships after Christmas recess involves several days of jockeying with peers and teacher, testing the limits. By spring vacation, the children are older and their relationships more rooted, so that the class separation reaction is significantly milder.

The great increase in marital separation and divorce makes the threat of parental loss realistically palpable for hosts of children today. Because of the security derived from the regularity and predictability of the daily school schedule, teachers are singled out as parent substitutes. With the approach of the summer recess signaling the loss of the teacher, early-latency children cling to the teacher—figuratively, with an uninterrupted flow of words, or literally, hanging onto her skirts. Many of these children suffer both infrequent visits with separated or divorced parents—usually fathers—and three to four hours daily in an after-school day-care center until mother returns from work.

Day-care-center staffs are often deficient both in number and in parenting qualities. So children arriving tired from school receive juice and cookies but frequently no quiet time alone with a familiar, empathic adult. Nor is there consistent staff presence to impose order and fairness. Such a deprived child will be extremely self-centered, mistrustful, unable to share possessions or adult attention with peers, unable to be alone and to concentrate on learning.

The diagnostic criteria for the separation anxiety disorders of childhood and adolescence in *DSM-III* treat separation or its threat from "major attachment figures and home."

Rather than "school phobias," day-care children develop "home phobias." Even though the familial is familiar, school and the day-care center seem more stable and predictable.

Children vary not only in the capacity to accept extra-familial objects but also in the capacity to actively seek them out. This is especially evident in those who thrive despite their disturbed or psychotic families. They are somehow able to exact some parenting from their own parents and, in addition, from those of friends. These relationships with the parents of peers may even amount to a tacit, informal adoption.

In the family romance (Freud, 1909/1959a), a common latency fantasy, the child deals with the deidealization of the parents by imagining that he is adopted and that his "real" parents are of exalted status (celebrities, millionaires, royalty). The fantasy of having a twin (Burlingham, 1945) is also typical of latency. Mark Twain combined these two themes in *The Prince and the Pauper*. The family romance is a fantasy about separation as well, a vehicle for expression of the regressive sense of abandonment and the wish to abandon. The fantasy thus serves defensively to maintain the object constancy strained by phase-appropriate disillusionment with the parents. Even when the disappointment is reinforced by the real defects of the parents, and the child approximates realization of the fantasy in securing "adoption," the relationship to parents is preserved.

The normative latency runaway episode is typically brief and impulsive. Hiding in some familiar location (even within the home), the protagonist fantasizes about the impact of the disappearance with vengeful self-pity. The adolescent version is usually overnight in the home of a friend, whose parents are then drawn into the negotiations for the return home. There is no genuine destination; salient is the action itself, a mild, limited acting out of abandonment.

Before latency, extrafamilial objects become familiar to the child through the agency of the family. Nursery schoolers' after-hours play with peers is usually initiated by their parents, and contacts with neighborhood children ordinarily are not sustained without parental sanction. A facet of the latency child's greater autonomy is the more independent choice of friends from among neighborhood and school peers.

Latency children apply their cognitive powers of classification to themselves, knowing exactly their class and group standing in physical development, athletic prowess, school performance, combativeness, and popularity, further diminishing the self-representation. The peer group and institutions are endowed with this surrendered narcissism in addition to what is displaced from the original family; the children then borrow it back, sporting their team caps and school jackets.

The obsessive form of latency rituals reflects the rawness and lack of integration of the superego, but the latent content is the harnessing of rivalry, to permit the capacity for sharing and mutuality of interest. The extent to which the group is peer-organized or structured by adults varies from the ghetto gang affording doorkey youngsters a haven from their fragmented families to overorganized middle-class children, carpooled from school to Scouts and Little League.

Preschoolers commonly embarrass their parents by greeting friendly strangers egocentrically with the news of mother's pregnancy, grandmother's visit, or father's hangover. They do not draw a line of privacy or secrecy. The latency child heightens his or her sense of separateness from parents and community through privacy and secrecy. The classic latency uncommunicativeness is celebrated in the humorous cliché: "Where did you go?" "Out." "What did you do?" "Nothing." At the same time, boys form secret clubs with passwords and handshakes, girls find secrets to divulge to the best friend. In addition, the capacity to be alone acquires some measure of enjoyment that is not solely defensive. The latency child may come to look forward to some solitary play, fantasy, reading, or other activity in a further positive accentuation of separateness.

Gender differences in the preference for playmates of the same sex are observable early. This is more pronounced in boys; by age six or seven they have as little as possible to do with girls. Given the choice, girls are less exclusionary. Some boys and girls pair off in imitation of older couples. Spontaneous play between the sexes includes the perennial "house" and "doctor" games.

The strong, stable group formation of boys, with collective submission to the rules and acknowledgment of a leader, stands in clear contrast to girls' less cohesive, transient exclusionary triangles. Girls seem to come together with little in common save the wish to win agreement to be best friends at the expense of other girls. The best-friend pair may expand to become an exclusionary clique. On the collapse of the friendship, the bereft girl tearfully informs mother at bedtime. Among boys the best-friend phenomenon occurs in late latency, typically from among the cohesive peer group. Should a boy and girl pair off, they tend to conceal it.

Scrutiny of a child's object relationships provides an important sampling of the extent to which the tasks of latency have been achieved. Inability to form extrafamilial relationships; exclusion of, or strong preference for, extrafamilial adults, other-sex peers, or dyadic peer relationships; and rejection and ridicule by the peer group—all indicate significant disturbances in the separation-individuation process.

In the successful passage through latency, continued separation-individuation sees the child ceasing total dependence on the parents, extending social relationships beyond the family, and expanding ego and superego functions in a significant augmentation of autonomy.

Adolescence

Biological Maturational Changes. Adolescence, a psychological developmental phase, is initiated by puberty, a biological maturational process originating in the neuroendocrine system. The hypothalamus secretes hormones stimulating the pituitary to increased production of a growth hormone, leading to the adolescent growth spurt. Pituitary production of gonadotrophins is actuated as well. These gonad-stimulating secretions stimulate the testes or ovaries to synthesize the appropriate sex hormones responsible for the physical changes of sexual maturation.

Reviewing the data of physical maturation (Katchadourian, 1977), the average age of puberty onset is ten to eleven for girls, eleven to twelve for boys. The average age at which the growth spurt peaks is twelve for girls, fourteen to fifteen for boys. The average girl of fourteen and boy of sixteen have attained 98 percent of their adult heights. Continuing with the average, menarche at 12.8 years will be followed by the capacity for normal pregnancy by fourteen to fifteen; 90 percent of boys have the first ejaculation between eleven and fifteen, approximately one year after rapid growth of the testicles. Mature sperm is detectable by fifteen or sixteen. Levels of testosterone increase twentyfold between ten and seventeen, rising most rapidly between twelve and sixteen.

Cognitive and Perceptual Changes. Piaget and Inhelder (1958) found a significant developmental advance from concrete to abstract thinking between twelve and sixteen, which they attribute to central nervous system maturation. In this new stage, termed "formal operational," thinking no longer depends on perceived objects or stimuli. Freed from the here and now, information becomes spaceless and timeless. The adolescent is capable of thinking of the possible and the potential and about propositions about thinking itself. Propositions exhibit four kinds of transformation in this stage: identity, negation, reciprocity, and correlation. These transformations are necessary for dealing with proportionality and analogies and imply an increasing ability to deal with complexity (Guilford, 1967). A puzzling phenomenon will touch off numerous abstract hypotheses involving the cognition and production of implications in terms of variables and multiple determination of events.

To recapitulate, this developmental advance in thinking between twelve and sixteen is from the more concrete, present-oriented, simplistic, right/good versus wrong/bad to the general, formal, logical, and abstract. Piaget's genetic epistemology focuses on cognition (problem solving, direct thinking), not on a broader definition of thinking that encompasses motivations, affects, or fantasy (Dulit, 1972). In the broader view, the capacity to think about thinking and to work with ideas not immediately tied to concrete examples leads to a greater appreciation of cause and effect. Thus, the historical view appears—a sense of the causal significance of the past in viewing the present. This cognitive development would seem to correlate with Wolfenstein's (1966) thesis that true mourning, implying the capacity to both relate to and separate from objects, does not develop until at least midadolescence. However, I find the evidence more convincing for the opposing view, that both latency children and adolescents have the intrapsychic capacity to mourn but require the external support of trusted adults encouraging and facilitating open reactions to the loss (Bowlby, 1960; Garber, 1985; Pollock, 1977, 1978; Raphael, 1983).

Tasks of Psychological Development in Adolescence. Laufer (1968, 1976) makes a tripartite statement of the overall tasks of adolescence: changing one's relationship to parents and to contemporaries and accepting sole responsibility for one's sexually mature body. Separation from the family requires one to relinquish both external and intrapsychic childhood dependent ties; assuming control of one's own life implies more autonomous self-esteem regulation, effectively divorced from the parental figures. Mastering aggression, achieving heterosexual love relationships, and planning and commitment to future goals are other phase-specific developmental tasks.

Attaining these mature, adult capacities requires intrapsychic expansion and reorganization. The process involves a combination of progression and regression, with unavoidable anxiety and mourning. Overt manifestations of this inner stress in the form of emotional and behavioral disturbances show marked individual variation.

Optimal progress through adolescence simultaneously embraces transformation and continuity. An empathetic, collaborative family in a compatible sociocultural context minimizes stress without thwarting the developmental process. The principle of appropriate dosages of stress, anxiety, and frustration holds not only for childhood but also for all developmental stages of life.

Emphasis on the developmental task of release from the infantile tie to the original objects should not obscure appreciation of the adolescent's need for stable, reliable parents. Lidz, Lidz, and Rubenstein (1976) suggest that latency peer involvement and adolescent essays in independent action are like latter-day "practicing periods" of separation-individuation, during which the parents continue as a delimiting influence and a reliable source of security in moments of fear and failure.

Subphases of Adolescence. In defining adolescent subphases—early, middle, and late—the propositions following are overschematized to help the reader get his or her bearings. In early adolescence one must redefine oneself and one's relationship to parents in the wake of the momentous physical transformation of puberty. The middle adolescent must venture from the protective scaffolding of the peer group into one-to-one heterosexual love relationships. Sexual identity is further delineated in this intimacy. The late adolescent must define his or her spiritual and worldly standards and goals of achievement, while initiating their implementation. To summarize these redefinitions: first, the body and parents; second, sexual identity and the relationship to the other sex; third, goals, standards, and the relationship to society (Kaplan, 1980).

The psychological predicament of the early adolescent, burdened with the consequences of withdrawal from the parents and rejection of the comforting parental introjects, physical maturation, and the surgence of frightening and unacceptable impulses, prepares the way for the phase-specific shift to the peer group. At this point, the adolescent's needs are primarily narcissistic, with a touchy need for total approval from peers suitable for idealization, in order to shore up fallen self-esteem. These peer involvements are quasi relationships. When disillusionment sets in, they are dropped without a backward glance or a trace of mourning (Freud, 1921/1955), giving group formation at this stage its fickle, unstable character.

In the train of the inevitable devaluations of idealized figures, allegiance is transferred to another group or back to the family temporarily. Youths with more psychopathology either are unable to make the initial peer involvement or quickly withdraw for good. Alternatively, such disturbed youngsters may attach to a "pseudo group," in which some stereotyped behavior, as drug abuse, delinquency, or gang fighting, confers a sense of belonging and identity without intimacy (Meeks, 1974).

The shift to contemporaries is a phase-specific develop-

mental progression; the normative adolescent launches himself
or herself outward from the stable, empathetic family. By contrast, when supports are removed by death, divorce, parental
pathology, or social upheaval, the youngster often turns to age
mates as a substitute family. Precocious peer-group formation is
an outgrowth of deprivation and family disorganization (Bronfenbrenner, 1974) typical of the impoverished families of the
inner city (Minuchin and others, 1967). With increased separation and divorce, this phenomenon is becoming more prevalent
among middle-class youth as well.

Psychological midadolescence begins as biological adolescence comes to an end. Lidz, Lidz, and Rubenstein (1976) list
its phase-specific tasks as accomplishing separation from the
family, assuming control of one's own life, and achieving a firm
ego identity and capacity for intimacy with a significant heterosexual extrafamilial love object, while tolerating inevitable anxieties and feelings of loneliness.

As the young person feels more secure with his body and
his impulses in midadolescence, peer relations tend to jell. The
peer group becomes the mirror of the body image, the social
monitor and behavioral arbiter. Midadolescents are preoccupied
with living up to the group ideal of masculinity or femininity
and concerned with whether the other sex finds their behavior
and appearance attractive (Hofmann, Becker, and Gabriel,
1976). Only gradually are peers perceived more realistically as
separate, distinct, and imperfect individuals whose friendship is
valued notwithstanding; only gradually does the capacity for intimacy evolve.

During midadolescence the sense of personal identity, of
being one's own self and owning one's own body rather than
being defined solely as the child of one's parents, is worked out
in peer-group relationships that ideally offer support, confidence, and distancing from the original objects (Solnit, 1976).
As the peer group takes over from the parents in serving as the
ideal standard, the self-esteem regulator, and the controller of
impulses, it becomes the mirror for defining the body image and
the sense of identity. The sense of identity, involving both a
feeling of uniqueness and a feeling of similarity, requires at least

one other similar person for its preservation (Greenacre, 1975). Identifications, which in early adolescence have a holistic, imitative quality, become more selective and partial as the mid-adolescent continually borrows and experiments in the reshaping of the self.

Adolescent Sexuality and Masturbation. Sexuality is a powerful stimulus to the psychic reorganization of adolescence, and masturbation serves to facilitate this reorganization. In early-adolescent males beset by erections from wrestling with a classmate, the vibrations of a bus, or a glimpse of mother in a state of partial undress, masturbation promotes a sense of mastery, for the pleasurable sensations of erection and ejaculation are initially experienced as a frightening loss of control. The act furthers integration of the mature genitalia into the body image, advancing the development of the self-concept and sharpening the delineation of inner and outer reality.

Masturbation helps bring the pregenital drives under the regulation of the genital function. Fantasies during masturbation connect earlier autoerotic experiences with images of objects, advancing object-relatedness. Fantasies about a particular object known to the adolescent evolve slowly, peaking in mid-adolescence (Francis and Marcus, 1975).

In adolescence, the psychological significance of masturbation changes appreciably. Early, masturbation serves as a defense against internal genital sensations and the wish for/fear of penetration. Later, the act fosters the repeated experience of focal stimulation, spreading genital excitement and gratification. Not only is readiness for coitus promoted, but also the conviction that the body belongs to the self and not the parents is strengthened, facilitating dissolution of symbiotic infantile ties (Clower, 1975).

Thus, the capacity to masturbate alone in adolescence deepens the developing sense of autonomy and is a developmental prerequisite for mature sexual relations. Early engagement in coitus with avoidance of masturbation often reflects deficiencies in the sense of autonomy. Borowitz (1973) attributes the incapacity to masturbate alone in adolescence to early disturbances in object relationships. Solitary masturbation may be viewed, therefore, as a developmental achievement in the transition from infantile to adult sexuality and from narcissism to mature object-relatedness. The capacity for intimate closeness with another requires a firm sense of oneself as autonomous and separate.

During adolescence, oedipal wishes are tested in the context of the possession of mature genitalia. Adolescent masturbation is both a trial action experienced within one's own thoughts and a way of testing which sexual thoughts, feelings, or gratifications are acceptable to the superego. The compromise solution found defines the person's sexual identity. This becomes irreversible in the consolidation of late adolescence, when masturbation is relinquished for true object attachment (Laufer, 1976).

Menstruation. Menstruation undermines the girl's denial of the introitus and initiates a regressive confusion of the inner genital with bladder and rectum in cloacal fantasies (Kestenberg, 1980). The differentiation of these organs in the body image and their acceptance in the self develop with time in the normal girl. Menstruation is a badge of arrival that typically advances the girl's sense of grown-up separateness. In adolescents with severe problems in separation-individuation, menarche may trigger significant regressive and even psychotic reactions.

Sexual Intimacy. The capacity for intimacy requires fusion of genital strivings with tenderness and resolution of the intensified oedipal wishes. Other necessary intrapsychic changes include modification of the mental representations of the parents to more realistically acknowledge their sexual activities and parallel superego revisions allowing the adolescent a sexual life of his or her own. At the beginning of midadolescence, heterosexual relationships are more narcissistic, with greater investment in oneself and peer-group approval than in the partner. As midadolescence ends, the couples should manifest considerable empathy, tenderness, and responsibility.

All mating behavior originates in mother/child behavior: the nursing dyad is the prototype of lovemaking (Sarlin, 1970). In sexual intimacy, the adolescent becomes dependent on the body of the partner in a form that has not been experienced

since infancy. Coitus shifts the balance between the reality principle and the pleasure principle, from gratification and discharge
associated with fantasy and autoplastic masturbation to gratification in the context of the external alloplastic relationship.
For the late adolescent, the new object serves functions resembling those served by the object of infancy and early childhood,
as a stabilizer of physiological and affective processes, but at a
higher level (Ritvo, 1971).

Since these implications of intimacy are anxiety-laden
with regressive potential, falling in love is a developmental crisis.
The typical manifestations of sexual conflicts in adolescence
are dissociation of tenderness from sexual excitement, dichotomy of asexual idealized objects and sexually devalued objects
(madonna versus whore), and the coexistence of excessive guilt
and impulsive expression of sexual urges. Falling in love produces an experience of transcendence in the normal adolescent.
The capacity to experience in depth the nonhuman environment, to appreciate nature and art, and to experience the self
within a historical and cultural continuum are intimately
linked to the capacity for being in love (Kernberg, 1974).

Late Adolescence. By the end of midadolescence, the individual should be more or less at ease in his or her sense of self
and identity, self-esteem, self-regulation, independence from
parents, and heterosexual love relationships. Yet the adolescent
process is far from complete. The restructuring and synthesis of
late adolescence, the period of consolidation and implementation, involve further changes in superego and ego ideal, with
coalescing of the hierarchy of defenses and the character. The
midadolescent's unfinished quality is reflected in her mood
swings and open emotional display. She remains unable to reveal her emotions to intimates while hiding them from public
display, without feeling divided; she still lacks a life plan's pur-
posive striving toward reasonable goals, an obligatory feature
of adolescent closure (Blos, 1976). Identity does not incorporate definitively the sense of where she belongs in her particular
society. The move to college or a job at around age eighteen is
the beginning of the period of implementation (Gould, 1972),
of taking action to achieve the goals chosen.

The early childhood ego ideal counters the narcissistic mortification of loss of omnipotence through recourse to an illusory self-perfection. In the oedipal phase, perfection is borrowed from the idealized parents and their narcissistic overestimation of the child. The childhood ego ideal, which depends partly on this external regulation, undergoes a radical and lasting change in the second individuation process of adolescence. The emotional disengagement from the internalized objects of early childhood leads to the heightened narcissistic state, idealizations, and rebellious self-assertion typifying adolescence (Blos, 1972).

In the final stages of adolescence, the striving after perfection of the ego ideal evolves into a direction-giving function, relatively independent of objects and of instinctual pressures (Hartmann and Loewenstein, 1962). From dependent, personalized, and concretized, the ego ideal becomes autonomous, impersonal, and abstracted. Excessive self- and object idealization are reduced to more realistic appraisals as the ego ideal loses its more primitive wish fulfillment quality. At the end of adolescence, the maturing ego ideal has taken over some value functions from the superego and ego, while the ego has expanded at the expense of the superego and the id.

Summary

The capacity of the toddler to function satisfactorily in mother's absence is presumed to derive from self-comforting based on an internal, mental representation of the mother. This capacity is enhanced by the significant stability of mental representations that develops "on the way to object constancy" around the time of the oedipal phase.

Complete dependence on the parents comes to an end in latency. As the superego forms, self-esteem regulation no longer depends exclusively on external parental approval. Maturation of cognitive perceptual functions by midlatency affords the ego increasing control over the inhibition, modulation, and discharge of instinctual (sexual and aggressive) drive derivatives. The capacity for objective self-awareness and the self-concept appear in late latency, together with the beginnings of empathy.

In early adolescence the self and the relationship to the parents require redefinition in the wake of the momentous physical transformation. The middle adolescent must venture from the protective scaffolding of the peer group into the dyadic heterosexual love relationship. The late adolescent must define personal standards and goals of achievement, while initiating their implementation. These developmental redefinitions involve, first, the body and the family; second, sexual identity and intimacy; third, standards, goals, and one's relationship to society.

In successful negotiation of the midadolescent subphase, continued separation-individuation finds the young person at ease in his or her sense of self and identity, with relatively stable and autonomous self-esteem and self-regulation, emotionally emancipated from childish dependence on family, and capable of heterosexual intimacy.

These developmental achievements of midadolescence involve extensive intrapsychic reorganization. Further restructuring, notably of superego and ego ideal, and the coalescing of character and of the hierarchy defenses take place before final closure at the end of late adolescence. The accretions to autonomy from more mature superego controls and ego-ideal directives equip the late adolescent to continue the journey of separation-individuation away from the original matrix. The move is toward further self-definition in terms of a life plan in the larger social context. As development shades into adulthood, the self has coalesced and wider horizons are contemplated with comfort in separateness and confidence in autonomous functioning.

References

Blos, P. "The Function of the Ego Ideal in Adolescence." *Psychoanalytic Study of the Child,* 1972, 27, 93–97.

Blos, P. "When and How Does Adolescence End?" *Journal of the Philadelphia Association for Psychoanalysis,* 1976, 3, 47–58.

Bornstein, B. "On Latency." *Psychoanalytic Study of the Child,* 1951, 6, 279–285.

Borowitz, G. H. "The Capacity to Masturbate Alone in Adolescence." *Adolescent Psychiatry*, 1973, *2*, 130–143.

Bowlby, J. "Grief and Mourning in Infancy and Early Childhood." *Psychoanalytic Study of the Child*, 1960, *15*, 9–52.

Brody, S. "Psychoanalytic Theories of Infant Development and Its Disturbances: A Critical Evaluation." *Psychoanalytic Quarterly*, 1982, *5*(4), 526–597.

Brody, S., and Axelrad, S. *Mothers, Fathers, and Children.* New York: International Universities Press, 1978.

Bronfenbrenner, U. "The Origins of Alienation." *Scientific American*, 1974, *231*(2), 123–126.

Burlingham, D. T. "The Fantasy of Having a Twin." *Psychoanalytic Study of the Child*, 1945, *1*, 205–210.

Busch, F. "Theme and Variation in the Development of the First Transitional Object." *International Journal of Psycho-Analysis*, 1977, *58*, 479–486.

Clower, V. L. "Significance of Masturbation in Female Sexual Development." In I. M. Marcus and S. J. Francis (eds.), *Masturbation from Infancy to Senescence.* New York: International Universities Press, 1975.

Dulit, E. "Adolescent Thinking à la Piaget." *Journal of Youth and Adolescence*, 1972, *1*, 281–301.

Fraiberg, S. "Libidinal Object Constancy and Mental Representation." *Psychoanalytic Study of the Child*, 1969, *24*, 9–47.

Francis, S. J., and Marcus, I. M. "Masturbation: A Developmental View." In I. M. Marcus and S. J. Francis (eds.), *Masturbation from Infancy to Senescence.* New York: International Universities Press, 1975.

Freud, S. "Three Essays on the Theory of Sexuality." In J. Strachey (ed. and trans.), *The Standard Edition of the Complete Psychological Works of Sigmund Freud.* Vol. 7. London: Hogarth Press, 1953. (Originally published 1905.)

Freud, S. "Group Psychology and the Analysis of the Ego." In J. Strachey (ed. and trans.), *The Standard Edition of the Complete Psychological Works of Sigmund Freud.* Vol. 18. London: Hogarth Press, 1955. (Originally published 1921.)

Freud, S. "Family Romances." In J. Strachey (ed.), *The Standard Edition of the Complete Psychological Works of Sig-*

mund Freud. Vol. 9. London: Hogarth Press, 1959a. (Originally published 1909.)

Freud, S. "Inhibitions, Symptoms and Anxiety." In J. Strachey (ed. and trans.), *The Standard Edition of the Complete Psychological Works of Sigmund Freud.* Vol. 20. London: Hogarth Press, 1959b. (Originally published 1926.)

Freud, S. "The Ego and the Id." In J. Strachey (ed. and trans.), *The Standard Edition of the Complete Psychological Works of Sigmund Freud.* Vol. 19. London: Hogarth Press, 1961. (Originally published 1923.)

Garber, B. "Mourning in Adolescence: Normal and Pathological." *Adolescent Psychiatry,* 1985, *12,* 371–387.

Gould, R. L. "The Phases of Adult Life: A Study of Developmental Psychology." *American Journal of Psychiatry,* 1972, *129,* 521–531.

Greenacre, P. "Differences Between Male and Female Adolescent Development." *Adolescent Psychiatry,* 1975, *4,* 105–120.

Guilford, J. P. *The Nature of Human Intelligence.* New York: McGraw-Hill, 1967.

Hartmann, H., and Loewenstein, R. M. "Notes on the Superego." *Psychoanalytic Study of the Child,* 1962, *17,* 42–81.

Hofmann, A. D., Becker, R. D., and Gabriel, H. F. *The Hospitalized Adolescent.* New York: Free Press, 1976.

Kahne, M. "On the Persistence of Transitional Phenomena into Adult Life." *International Journal of Psycho-Analysis,* 1967, *48,* 247–258.

Kaplan, E. B. "Reflections Regarding Psychomotor Activities During the Latency Period." *Psychoanalytic Study of the Child,* 1965, *20,* 220–238.

Kaplan, E. H. "Adolescents, Age Fifteen to Eighteen: A Psychoanalytic Developmental View." In S. I. Greenspan and G. H. Pollock (eds.), *The Course of Life: Psychoanalytic Contributions Toward Understanding Personality Development.* Vol. 2: *Latency, Adolescence and Youth.* Washington, D.C.: National Institute of Mental Health, 1980.

Katchadourian, H. *The Biology of Adolescence.* New York: W. H. Freeman, 1977.

Kernberg, O. "Mature Love: Prerequisites and Characteristics." *Journal of the American Psychoanalytic Association*, 1974, *22*, 743–768.

Kestenberg, J. "Eleven, Twelve, Thirteen: Years of Transition from the Barrenness of Childhood to the Fertility of Adolescence." In S. I. Greenspan and G. H. Pollock (eds.), *The Course of Life: Psychoanalytic Contributions Toward Understanding Personality Development.* Vol. 2: *Latency, Adolescence and Youth.* Washington, D.C.: National Institute of Mental Health, 1980.

Kohlberg, L. "Development of Moral Character and Moral Ideology." In M. L. Hoffman and L. W. Hoffman (eds.), *Review of Child Development Research.* New York: Russell Sage Foundation, 1964.

Kramer, S., and Rudolph, J. "The Latency Stage." In S. I. Greenspan and G. H. Pollock (eds.), *The Course of Life: Psychoanalytic Contributions Toward Understanding Personality Development.* Vol. 2: *Latency, Adolescence and Youth.* Washington, D.C.: National Institute of Mental Health, 1980.

Laufer, M. "The Body Image, the Function of Masturbation, and Adolescence: Problems of the Ownership of the Body." *Psychoanalytic Study of the Child*, 1968, *23*, 114–137.

Laufer, M. "The Central Masturbation Fantasy, the Final Sexual Organization, and Adolescence." *Psychoanalytic Study of the Child*, 1976, *31*, 297–316.

Lidz, T., Lidz, R. W., and Rubenstein, R. "An Anaclitic Syndrome in Adolescent Amphetamine Addicts." *Psychoanalytic Study of the Child*, 1976, *31*, 317–348.

Mahler, M. S. "Notes on the Development of Basic Moods: The Depressive Affect." In R. M. Loewenstein, L. M. Newman, M. Schur, and A. J. Solnit (eds.), *Psychoanalysis—a General Psychology: Essays in Honor of Heinz Hartmann.* New York: International Universities Press, 1966.

Mahler, M. S. "Rapprochement Subphase of the Separation-Individuation Process." *Psychoanalytic Quarterly*, 1972, *41*, 487–506.

Mahler, M. S., Pine, F., and Bergman, A. *The Psychological*

Birth of the Human Infant: Symbiosis and Individuation. New York: Basic Books, 1975.

Meeks, J. T. "Adolescent Development and Group Cohesion." *Adolescent Psychiatry,* 1974, *3,* 289–297.

Minuchin, S., and others. *Families of the Slums: An Exploration of Their Structure and Treatment.* New York: Basic Books, 1967.

Neubauer, P. B. *Children in Collectives.* Springfield, Ill.: Thomas, 1965.

Piaget, J. *The Language and Thought of the Child.* New York: World, 1955.

Piaget, J., and Inhelder, B. *The Growth of Logical Thinking from Childhood to Adolescence.* New York: Basic Books, 1958.

Pollock, G. H. "The Mourning Process and Creative Organizational Change." *Journal of the American Psychoanalytic Association,* 1977, *25,* 30–34.

Pollock, G. H. "Process and Affect: Mourning and Grief." *International Journal of Psycho-Analysis,* 1978, *52,* 255–276.

Raphael, B. *The Anatomy of Bereavement.* New York: Basic Books, 1983.

Ritvo, S. "Late Adolescence: Developmental and Clinical Considerations." *Psychoanalytic Study of the Child,* 1971, *26,* 241–263.

Sarlin, C. N. "The Current Status of the Concept of Genital Primacy." *Journal of the American Psychoanalytic Association,* 1970, *18,* 285–299.

Shapiro, T., and Perry, R. "Latency Revisited: The Age Seven Plus or Minus One." *Psychoanalytic Study of The Child,* 1976, *31,* 79–106.

Solnit, A. J. "Inner and Outer Changes in Adolescence." *Journal of the Philadelphia Association for Psychoanalysis,* 1976, *3,* 43–46.

Speers, R. W., and Morter, D. C. "Overindividuation and Underseparation in the Pseudomature Child." In R. Lay, S. Bach, and J. Burland (eds.), *Rapprochement: The Critical Subphase of Separation-Individuation.* New York: Jason Aronson, 1980.

Winnicott, D. W. "Transitional Objects and Transitional Phenomena: A Study of the First Not-Me Possession." *International Journal of Psycho-Analysis,* 1953, *34,* 89–97.

Wolfenstein, M. "Children's Understanding of Jokes." *Psychoanalytic Study of the Child,* 1958, *13,* 296–308.

Wolfenstein, M. "How Is Mourning Possible?" *Psychoanalytic Study of the Child,* 1966, *21,* 93–123.

5

Separation, Interdependence, and Social Relations Across the Second Half of Life

Bertram J. Cohler
Frances M. Stott

Editors' Note: *This chapter is unique, viewing separateness and autonomy from the vantage point of adult relatedness. The authors dispute the notion that adult personality is shaped by early experience alone. They also take issue with the separation-individuation stance that independence and autonomy are the culminations of healthy development. Instead, they suggest that interdependence and mutuality better characterize successful adult relationships and that the significance of relatedness and aloneness changes throughout the life course. Cohler and Stott assume that development need not reflect a linear progression from infancy onward, while nonetheless acknowledging the roots of mature adult mutuality in the active interchange between infant and caregiver.*

The authors review the extensive survey literature on adult relationships. Most older adults are not socially isolated, as commonly perceived; they are actively embedded in networks of family and peers. Nevertheless, as people age, they increasingly prefer aloneness and find it harder to seek assistance from others. Actual social contact may become less important than reminiscences about time spent with others; memories serve a self-soothing function in the face of "role exits" (such as retirement) and "role losses" (such as the death of loved ones). Interestingly, Cohler and Stott point out that relationships with offspring are often less satisfying to the older person than relationships with spouse and peers; access to confidantes, not ties to family, appears to foster psychological well-being in later life.

Attachments to others remain central throughout life, with the capacity for emotionally sustaining adult relationships determined by the early internalization of self-comforting mechanisms and the assurance that others can provide solace. We would add that the quality of caregiving relationships also provides the foundation for a rich world of internal representations of self and other—which appear to be central in maintaining happiness, given the inevitable losses of later life. Further, we think it may be possible to reconcile the authors' theoretical emphasis on adult interdependence and mutuality with a life-course view of separation-individuation by recasting the individuation process in terms of (1) a general theory of psychological differentiation that includes multiple levels of self-transformation beyond object constancy and (2) a theory of adult development that emphasizes the interplay between psychological structure and life experience.

Although relations with others are important across the life course, there may be significant changes from the first to the second half of life in the experience of ties to others in relation to feelings of well-being. The present chapter considers the interplay between psychological and social factors in determining the experience of being alone and with others across the second half of life. Whereas survey studies are valuable in describing the variety of social relationships in adulthood, psychodynamic perspectives can contribute to understanding of the psychological significance of these relationships.

Work on this chapter was facilitated by Grant 00039 from the National Institute on Aging. The authors wish to thank Bonnie Litowitz for her comments on an earlier draft.

Developmental Change and the Life Course

During the past two decades, study of development has shifted from an interest in childhood to consideration of the life course as a whole, from earliest childhood to oldest age. Inspired in part by findings from longitudinal studies that provided an opportunity to examine personality change over time, such as those reported by Kagan and Moss (1962), Jones, Bayley, MacFarlane, and Honzik (1971), and Eichorn and others (1981), there has been increased interest in the study of personality development across the adult years.

Chronological change, as such, is largely unrelated to the course of adult lives. Indeed, socially determined perception of place in the course of life may be more important than age in understanding the process of change in adult lives (Neugarten and Hagestad, 1976; Cohler and Ferrono, forthcoming). Central to the perception of place in the course of life is awareness of particular life tasks to be performed by persons attaining particular "life stations" (Riley, Johnson, and Foner, 1972; Neugarten and Hagestad, 1976). Even young children are aware of a progression through these tasks according to a socially shared timetable of development (Farnham-Diggory, 1966; Roth, 1963), and in adulthood this sense of social timing largely determines both the course of personality change and feelings of well-being.* As a consequence of expected time of entrance into such characteristic adult roles as work, marriage, and parenthood, together with later timing of exit from these roles in middle and later life, individuals continually evaluate for themselves the extent to which they are "on" or "off" time with regard to the timetable of life. It is possible to characterize people as being largely on time regarding major life attainments or as

*There has been marked controversy over the use of morale or well-being as a measure of adjustment in later life (George, 1979; Lawton, 1982). In this chapter, feelings of life satisfaction or well-being are viewed as representing feelings of self-integrity or cohesiveness (Kohut, 1977). As a result of this sense of cohesiveness or well-being, people are able to preserve a positive outlook on the future, characterized by cheerfulness, appropriate optimism, and confidence that inner tensions can be contained.

off time early or late. Women widowed in their fifties are off time early for this expectable role transition, while women becoming a parent for the first time in their forties are viewed by themselves and others as off time late for entrance into this characteristic adult role.

One of the areas of social timing on which greatest agreement has been realized is the expected duration of life itself, including the point in life at which persons are young, middle-aged, or elderly (Neugarten, Moore, and Lowe, 1965). Not only can people agree on the age at which one is young, middle-aged, or old, but they also agree on the expectable duration of life itself. Indeed, it is just this shared agreement on the duration of lives that makes possible the construction of social timetables.

At some point in the adult years, characteristically in the late forties or early fifties, acknowledged finitude of life (Munnichs, 1966) assumes new meaning. Neugarten and Datan (1974) have characterized this changed perception of life as the "personalization of death." Neugarten (1979) observes that people begin to look backward to time already lived, rather than forward to time left to live. Levinson and associates (1978) have noted that this period of life is characterized by the "end of the dream of hoped-for attainments."

Increased awareness of the reality of mortality (Jaques, 1965, 1980) is associated with efforts to grieve over goals not attained and with making peace with life as lived. Neugarten (1973, 1979) has portrayed the effect of this grieving as leading to increased "interiority," or turning inward, of mental life. In contrast to earlier formulations of disengagement of self and society (Cumming and Henry, 1961), this perspective suggests that there may be little change in actual social relations. However, there does appear to be a change in the way relationships are experienced, including increased concern with time available for oneself as well as increased reluctance to continue relationships demanding great sacrifice of time and effort.

Developmental Perspectives on Social Relations

Two assumptions have been made in the psychological study of social relations: (1) the formation of social ties during earliest infancy largely determines later well-being, and (2) concepts derived from the study of infant development are relevant in studying psychological development in later childhood and in adulthood. The present section considers some contemporary psychological perspectives on relationships, informed by our present knowledge of the course of adult life, calling into question the relevance of an infancy-based model for understanding relationships in adulthood and pointing to the problems involved in applying concepts used in the study of infant psychological development to complex adult lives.

Much of our present understanding of the impact of earlier experience on adult lives has been based on a social learning perspective (Hull, 1943; Miller and Dollard, 1941; Sears, 1951), sometimes additionally informed by psychoanalytic formulations stressing the importance of critical periods in human learning (Antonucci, 1976; Weiss, 1982a). This biological formulation, in turn, has been based on Freud's own first research in developmental neurobiology (Sulloway, 1979), which led to a reductionistic philosophy of science determining subsequent psychoanalytic developmental study, such as Abraham's (1924/1953) extension of Freud's (1905/1953) initial formulation of development.

Recent psychosocial formulations of personality development across the life course, such as Erikson's (1963, 1980) epigenetic formulation of development, have been based on a similar natural science perspective on development (Gill, 1976; Klein, 1976), emphasizing a linear relationship between early experiences and later outcomes (Vaillant, 1978). Alternative formulations of development, such as that derived from social psychology emphasizing performance of adult roles (Sarbin and Allen, 1968; Blumer, 1969), though describing the structure of adult social relations, may fail, as George (1980) has observed, to portray the personal meaning contained in performance of expected roles.

Attachment, Dependence, and Independence. To date, much of our understanding of the significance of adult social ties, including the psychological effect of loss and mourning, has been based on study of the mother/infant tie. Learning theory, ethology, and psychoanalysis all have pointed to the importance of events in earliest life for later experience of social ties. The social learning approach to the study of attachment (Maccoby and Masters, 1970; Yarrow, 1972; Gewirtz, 1972, 1976) focuses mainly on the development of attachment in early childhood. Particularly in Gewirtz's formulation, a distinction has been made between attachment, referring to a particular other, and dependence, referring to ties to a group of others, such as mother and teachers, viewed by the child as functionally equivalent and understood in accordance with the same laws of learning.

Ethological and social learning formulations both assume primacy of early experience, with little acknowledgment of the possibility of development after the first years of life. Bowlby's (1969) ethological perspective on attachment departs both from social learning and from psychoanalytic perspectives in emphasizing attachment as an instinctual response to maintain proximity to and seek protection from the caretaker. Central to Bowlby's view is the assumption that later relationships are based on this relationship with the caretaker, constructed on the basis of component instinctual responses designed to maintain proximity.

Bowlby (1969, 1973a, 1973b, 1980) and Ainsworth (1969, 1982; Ainsworth, Blehar, Waters, and Wall, 1978) have charted the course of attachment behavior and documented the importance of the interactions between mother and infant for the infant's well-being. *Attachment* refers to "the affectional bond or tie that an infant forms between himself and his mother figure" (Ainsworth, Blehar, Waters, and Wall, 1978, p. 302) and is most evident when the child is frightened, fatigued, or sick and his distress is assuaged by comforting and caregiving. The infant perceives threats to accessibility or separation from the attachment figure as a threat to his well-being, resulting in protest and anxiety and, in the absence of sustained care, apathy and despair. Even though attachment behavior is not always prominent, awareness that an attachment figure is available and responsive provides a strong and pervasive feeling of security, causing the child to value and continue the relationship.

Although attachment behavior is most obvious during the second and third years of life, Bowlby (1969, 1982) claims that it persists throughout the life course, especially in emergencies. Parents are likely to continue as attachment figures, although they are less likely to be central in the person's life than in childhood. Bowlby says that "intimate attachments to other human beings are the hub around which a person's life revolves, not only when he is an infant or a toddler or a school child, but throughout his adolescence and his years of maturity as well, and on into old age" (1980, p. 442).

Other attachment theorists have questioned whether relationships after infancy do meet the criteria of attachment. Ainsworth (1982) and Hinde (1979, 1982) both observe that attachments can form only to others perceived as stronger or wiser (Bowlby, 1977). This perception may be realized in adult relationships in which each partner on occasion plays the role of stronger and wiser figure, but it is not so characteristic of adult relationships as of childhood ties. Furthermore, Hinde (1979, 1982) notes the confusion between attachment as a bond between two persons and the behavioral system of the infant. Although attachment theory emphasizes the infant's contribution to the mother/infant relationship, this relationship involves both partners. Finally, as the attachment theorists point out, attachment is not the only type of relationship. It is tempting to look for continuities in interpersonal bonds, but the child's development leads to a variety of relationships in addition to those based on attachment (Hinde, 1982).

Extrapolation from infant/mother attachment to later relationships have nonetheless been made (Antonucci, 1976; Kalish and Knudtson, 1976; Lerner and Ryff, 1978; Troll, 1980; Marris, 1982; Weiss, 1982a). Weiss's (1982a) formulation of adult attachment emphasizes (1) that the person wants to be with the attachment figure, especially when under stress, (2) that the person associates the attachment figure with comfort and security, and (3) that he or she experiences anxiety when inexplicable separations occur. Weiss suggests that although attachment in adults may not meet all the criteria of attachment in infants, adults do maintain bonds showing these three important criteria. Attachment bonds may not be found in all adult relationships of emotional significance, but Weiss believes they are to be found in important relationships such as those of husband and wife, "buddies" under stress, and, often, very close friends.

Attachment perspectives have provided the impetus for study of such important issues in adulthood as loss and mourning (Glick, Weiss, and Parkes, 1974; Bowlby, 1980; Parkes and Weiss, 1983). To a large extent, however, the theoretical framework has been that of the formation of ties in earliest infancy extended to the study of adult lives. Additional study is required of how adult experiences transform one's understanding of self and others in ways that may not be consistent with previous experiences (Cohler, 1982; Marris, 1982).

Separation, Individuation, and Psychological Autonomy. An alternative perspective on the development of social ties has been proposed by Mahler and her colleagues (Mahler, 1979; Mahler, Pine, and Bergman, 1975). This formulation of the child's developing sense of self as a separate person has been the most clearly articulated discussion of the developmental line from dependence to independence (A. Freud, 1965). On the basis of longitudinal study of both psychotic and well children and their mothers over the first three and a half years or so of life, Mahler has described a number of stages whose resolution results in the more or less successful attainment of psychological autonomy.

According to Mahler's formulation of the process of separation and individuation, the infant moves from the first phase of normal autism during the early weeks of life into a close relationship with the mother in which the infant develops a symbiotic bond in order to obtain satisfaction of basic needs. The ensuing phase of separation and individuation is divided into four subphases: differentiation, practicing, rapprochement, and "on the way to libidinal object constancy." Beginning at about four or five months of age, and influenced by increased locomotion, the child begins the process of demarcation of self from other. The intrapsychic track of separation includes differentiation, distancing, boundary formation, and disengagement from mother; individuation represents "the evolution of intrapsychic

autonomy, perception, memory, cognition, reality testing"
(Mahler, Pine, and Bergman, 1975, p. 63).

Extrapolations to adulthood from Mahler's separation-individuation formulation have often been attempted (Panel, 1973b, 1973c). Settlage (Panel, 1973a) has proposed that human psychological development may be characterized as a life-long process of separation-individuation—beginning with the "hatching" from the social symbiosis with the mother and ending with the ultimate separation, one's own death. When object constancy is attained, during the preschool years, enduring mental representations of maternal care become available as sources of comfort and assistance even in the physical absence of others with whom intimate relationships are formed. As a result, there is a continuing sense of psychological autonomy separate from others. However, even in optimal development, there may still be tension between the wish to merge with the idealized mother and the fear of engulfment and loss of identity (Panel, 1973a). Later feelings of panic and anxiety may be viewed as the consequence of threatened separations, interfering in the search for a return to the comfort of the original symbiosis. Failure to resolve issues in the attainment of separation-individuation may, in adulthood, result in inability to differentiate between one's own needs and those of others, so that the person seeks comfort from relationships in ways similar to that experienced in the original undifferentiated mother/child unit (Lewis and Landis, 1979; McDevitt and Settlage, 1971; Panel, 1973a, 1973b, 1973c).

This portrayal of separateness in adulthood presents a number of problems. The adequacy of a formulation of early infancy that emphasizes such concepts as autism and symbiosis has been questioned as the competence displayed in infancy has been increasingly recognized (Peterfreund, 1978; Klein, 1981; Bowlby, 1982). Use of the separation-individuation approach in studying social relations presents two other problems. First, just as with social learning and attachment approaches, extrapolations to adjustment and social relations in later life are believed to be based on events taking place in earliest childhood. These early childhood experiences may become overvalued as the sole determinants of personality development and change across later childhood, adolescence, and adulthood (Pollock, 1964; Lewis and Landis, 1979). Second, as Cohler and Grunebaum (1981) have noted, the developmental line from dependence to independence cannot account for the reality of interdependent ties to others in adulthood.* Adult family members continue to care for each other (Fandetti and Gelfand, 1976; Troll and Smith, 1976; Brody, 1977; Brody, Johnsen, Fulcomer, and Lang, 1983) and recognize enduring bonds, or "invisible loyalties" (Boszormenyi-Nagy and Spark, 1973), in a manner that is inconsistent both with perspectives emphasizing the isolation of the nuclear family and with perspectives emphasizing autonomy and independence as the goal of development to adulthood (Goldfarb, 1969). Social relations in adulthood might better be characterized as interdependence than as independence and autonomy.

Inner Regulation and the Development of the Self. A final problem with the separation-individuation paradigm is the extent to which psychological development is viewed as a consequence of interactional processes in which a passive infant is animated from outside by the caretaker. In a series of papers, consistent with renewed emphasis on competence in infancy, Winnicott (1953, 1960, 1965a) has emphasized the importance both of the child's own contribution to developing capacity for regulation of self and of the continuing interplay of self and other as an interdependent dyad.

The capacity to make psychological use of attributes of others begins with the attainment of a shared illusion of "potential space" (Winnicott, 1953; Davis and Wallbridge, 1981) midway between maternal care and the baby's needs, fostering the baby's consolidation of sense of self. The mother's caring ac-

---

*Theories of personality and psychopathology reflect enduring values of particular societies. Certainly, emphasis on attainment of psychological autonomy or individuation and object constancy is more pronounced in Western than non-Western social science and psychoanalytic formulations, which more often emphasize the capacity to become interdependent as the distinctive attainment of psychological development (Clark, 1972; Doi, 1973; Rudolph and Rudolph, 1978; Kaker, 1978).

tions lead to the baby's experience of a matrix of care appropriate for his or her needs, or a "holding environment" (Winnicott, 1960), which both joins the baby to the mother and fosters separateness (Spitz, 1972; Metcalf and Spitz, 1978). Sense of self develops at the same time as awareness of nonself, leading to increased understanding of self in relation to others.

Illustrative of the child's contribution to the relationship is the formation of the transitional object. According to Winnicott (1953), the child creates this first "not-me" possession in the sense that he or she chooses the object and ascribes symbolic meaning to it, at the same time that it remains a real object. With the attainment of the transitional object, the child can create the illusion of maternal care as a means of providing comfort or solace (Horton, 1981).

Although Winnicott limited his discussion of the transitional object to earliest childhood, the metaphor of an illusory or potential space was maintained as a concept useful in the study of creativity, intimacy, and the capacity to be alone (Winnicott, 1965a, 1965b) in adult lives. It is in the overlap of potential spaces of separate persons that mutuality is experienced, making meaningful communication possible.

In contrast to Winnicott's contributions, limited largely to development during the first years of life, Kohut (1971, 1977) has emphasized the use of others as a means of comfort across the entire life course. Important for Kohut's formulation of the course of development is the extent to which the child experiences the caretaker's actions as a part of his or her developing self, rather than as a function provided from without. Only later in toddlerhood does the child begin to realize that self and mother are separate (Cohler, 1980). The quality and adequacy of maternal care, experienced by the child as a part of self, or selfobject (Kohut, 1977; Wolf, 1980), become an important determinant of the capacity for self-soothing in times of personal distress during later childhood and adulthood.

Problems in providing adequate regulation of tension are experienced by the child not as the consequence of deficient maternal care but as the consequence of the child's own inability to modulate or regulate this tension. Depending on the nature of the child's experience of maternal care, understood as a selfobject, variations may be expected in the later capacity for providing this comfort for oneself. However, since maternal care is never experienced as perfectly "dosed" (Tolpin and Kohut, 1980), some problems in tension regulation are intrinsic to the human condition. Initial variations in the child's experience of receiving what feels like "good enough" care provided by the child for himself (Winnicott, 1960; Tolpin and Kohut, 1980) lead to later differences in the adult's capacity for getting comfort and solace from others.

Psychology of the self, as formulated by Kohut and his colleagues, provides an opportunity for understanding mature modes of interdependence in ways that may be more consonant with adult experience than other psychodynamic formulations allow. However, it should be noted that this perspective has been derived almost entirely from transference reenactments of adults and has seldom extended to study of adult development in nonclinical contexts. Though based on the study of adult lives using the empathic method of clinical psychoanalysis and pointing toward a psychoanalytic developmental psychology of adulthood, psychology-of-the-self explanations of the origins of the capacity for social ties, as portrayed by Kohut, Goldberg, and their colleagues, maintain the metapsychological perspective characterizing earlier psychoanalytic accounts of development, stressing the supposed direct relationship between infantile life and adult personality. This assumption, initially derived by Freud from his work in developmental neurobiology, may be better understood as a statement of Freud's philosophy of science than as a theory of personality and psychopathology (Klein, 1976; Gill, 1976; Sulloway, 1979; Cohler, forthcoming). Clarification of the relative contributions of clinical theory and metapsychology to psychoanalytic explanations of development and construction of a psychoanalytic developmental psychology of adulthood based on the clinical theory remain tasks of central importance for the study of adulthood and aging.

Further, just as other psychological perspectives on social relations have attempted to extend concepts derived from the study of infancy to the study of adulthood, psychology-of-the-self perspectives have attempted to portray the course of development during earliest childhood on the basis of the study of adult lives. As with other psychological perspectives, it is assumed that earlier and later events are directly related in a linear manner. However, there is little evidence that lives are organized in this way (Neugarten, 1969; Kagan, 1980; Cohler, 1982). As Thomas and Chess (1980) have observed, it is possible for events taking place at particular points in the course of life to be important in the present without determining later outcomes. At the same time, clinical psychoanalytic approaches, informed by careful, empathic observation of lives over time, may be uniquely able to portray the particular meanings that individuals attach to relationships, providing increased understanding of the changing significance of social ties for well-being across the course of life.

Adult Social Relations and Psychological Well-Being

The first use of others as a soothing function of self, or selfobject (Kohut, 1977; Wolf, 1980), is a developmental achievement of the first years of life. The significance of others as a means of solace continues throughout life, changing together with place in the life course. Particularly during the first half of life, the use of others as a means of comfort may be best realized through seeking help from such others as parents and friends. The network of such support and assistance, or social convoy (Kahn, 1979; Kahn and Antonucci, 1980), appears to reduce both the stressful impact of adverse life events and also the strain of transition to such new roles as that of spouse or parent (Caplan, 1974; Cobb, 1976, 1979; Eckenrode and Gore, 1981; Turner, 1981; Aneshensel and Stone, 1982; Greenblatt, Becerra, and Serafetinides, 1982; Kilillea, 1982; Parkes, 1982; Weiss, 1974, 1982b; Cohler, 1982).

Being Alone and Loneliness Across Later Life. There has been little study of possible changes in the use of social supports corresponding to changing place in the course of life. Much less is known about the experience of others as a form of soothing during the second half of life than during the first half.

However, proceeding from concepts such as interiority or personalization of death, one might expect changes in the way others are used as a source of comforting. For example, accompanying the shift toward interiority, there is a tendency across the second half of life to seek solace and to master problems with the help of reminiscence, or memories of the past, as well as continuing social ties (Lieberman and Falk, 1971; Cohler, 1982). There is also increased preference for being alone, which facilitates the process of reminiscence. In late life, reminiscence may take the form of a life review, which further assists the process of making peace with life as lived and mourning unrealized attainments (Levinson and others, 1978).

One important and often overlooked function of representations of solace and comforting is the capacity to be alone as well as with others (Winnicott, 1965a; Cohen, 1982). As with other representations, it may be that first experiences, during early childhood, of receiving what is experienced as "good enough" maternal care permit the child sufficient capacity for regulation of tension states that he or she becomes able to be quiet rather than to act. With attainment of adulthood, being alone implies being with others, as when relishing a moment of quiet intimacy or at times of shared reflection, as well as being by oneself, mourning and reminiscing about the past.

From a life-course perspective, there are developmental changes not only in the significance of contact with others but also in the significance of being alone and maintaining aloneness that is satisfying. Attainment of comforting aloneness becomes more important during the second half of life, with the realization of the finitude of life (Jaques, 1965, 1980; Munnichs, 1966) to some extent replacing contact with others as a source of "emotional refueling" (Mahler, Pine, and Bergman, 1975). This increased preference for solitude must be understood as different from feelings of social isolation, which are often assumed to be inevitable in later life. It should also be noted that older persons appear somewhat less comfortable than younger persons with seeking help from others (Kastenbaum and Cameron, 1969) or with having to be physically dependent on others in order to manage everyday tasks (Munnichs and van den Heuvel, 1976).

Relations between elderly parents and their middle-aged offspring are less often characterized by reciprocity and interdependence than by continued expectations of the younger generation for assistance by the older generation. Indeed, while studies of social support have often emphasized the extent of assistance available within the family, it is less often realized that provision of such help, often the responsibility of older family members, leads to increased role strain and overload for those expected to be helpers (Cohler and Lieberman, 1980). This is a particular problem for older family members whose wish for increased time alone may conflict with demands from other family members for assistance and support. Invisible loyalties felt by older family members (Boszormenyi-Nagy and Spark, 1973) may lead them to try to continue providing such assistance (Troll, Miller, and Atchley, 1979) despite their developmentally determined increase in concern with self and need for time to be alone.

A number of studies of older persons have shown little relation between feelings of loneliness and time spent alone (Townsend, 1957; Lowenthal, 1964; Lowenthal and Robinson, 1976). Munnichs (1964) distinguishes between internal and external social isolation: external isolation may be imposed by a change in social environment, including deaths of spouse and friends or a move to a new neighborhood, whereas internal isolation, or loneliness, may reflect increased vulnerability in which older persons feel unable to establish new social ties. The social context, including age discrimination, enforced early retirement, and poverty (Rosow, 1974), may compound feelings of vulnerability, leading to increased feelings of isolation (Shanan, 1976).

It is often assumed that, beginning in late middle age, people may experience increased feelings of loneliness, in part because the very social supports that were so important in promoting increased morale during the first half of life may drop away. Certainly, among very old persons experiencing role exits such as retirement from work, which had provided meaningful activity, and role losses, particularly the deaths of spouse and close friends, there is clearly increased exposure to the conditions that breed loneliness. However, it is not true that the old feel more lonely than the young (Mancini, 1979; Mancini, Quinn, Gavigan, and Franklin, 1980). As Townsend (1957) has noted, feelings of desolation observed among some older persons, resulting from the death of significant others, may be mistaken for feelings of loneliness.

It should also be noted that death of spouse may have greater consequences for morale among men, who have always depended on their wives for social contacts and assistance with daily routine, than among women (Elwell and Maltbie-Crannell, 1981). Indeed, for some older women, having cared for their husbands through a lengthy illness, widowhood may bring increased free time as well as the opportunity to renew social ties that they could not maintain while nursing their husbands. Among those housebound women, widowhood may lead to increased social participation and may reduce, rather than increase, feelings of social isolation (Atchley, Pignatiello, and Shaw, 1979).

Perhaps the most detailed and thoughtful studies of loneliness and aging have been reported by Marjorie Fiske-Lowenthal and her colleagues (Lowenthal, 1964; Lowenthal and Boler, 1965; Lowenthal and Haven, 1968; Lowenthal and Robinson, 1976; Fiske, 1980). Consistent with the views of Townsend (1957), Fromm-Reichman (1959), Munnichs (1964), and Cohen (1982), Fiske-Lowenthal emphasizes the distinction between being alone and being lonely. Because of increased role losses in later life and a developmentally determined wish for increased time alone, older people generally spend more time alone than younger people. Fewer than 5 percent of a randomly selected group of community-living elders over age sixty showed social isolation, and most of these socially isolated older persons were men who had consistently been socially isolated during adulthood. Most social isolates were characterized by membership in the lowest socioeconomic status group and by the greatest objectively scored physical impairment. However, even among these most socially isolated older persons, there was little indication that social isolation was associated with lower morale. Indeed, many of those rated as most socially isolated reported no feelings of loneliness or of low morale.

Perhaps morale is unrelated to social isolation because, in most respects, people deal with the problems of aging in much the same way they have dealt with other challenges (Maas and Kuypers, 1974; Lowenthal and Robinson, 1976). To the extent that impairments in the ability to get around and loss of old friends create a sense of increased social isolation among persons who formerly enjoyed much social involvement, it is likely that aging might be associated with lowered morale.

Being with Others and Psychological Well-Being Across Later Life. Although it is widely assumed that the old are necessarily both lonely and socially isolated (Cohen, 1982), findings reviewed in this chapter show that the psychological significance of "being alone" may be quite different for younger and older people. Social support, particularly that involving the family, may also function in quite different ways in fostering well-being among younger and older people. Misconceptions about the availability of social support to older persons are influenced by widely held beliefs that the traditional extended family has been disrupted and that older persons in particular are isolated from family ties.

Although it has been claimed that traditional forms of family organization are threatened by social changes associated with industrial society, there is little evidence to support such claims. A number of survey studies (Sussman, 1976; Litwak, 1965; Shanas, 1961, 1973, 1979a, 1979b; Shanas and others, 1968) have documented the extent to which American families remain bonded across generations, with continuing exchange of resources across generations as well as frequent contact. Further, as Haller (1961), Blau (1981), and Bengston and Treas (1980) have all suggested, urban life-styles may enhance, rather than reduce, the opportunity for close relationships with relatives. Not only is it less likely in cities than in small towns that younger family members will have to move away in order to find jobs, but also mass transit and housing density make it possible for older and younger generations to maintain close and sustained contact, even though they may not share a household (Cohler and Grunebaum, 1981).

There is also little evidence to support the popular belief

that older persons in contemporary urban families are particularly isolated from family ties. Shanas (1961, 1973, 1979a) found that more than 90 percent of a sample of older persons in the United States with children had seen at least one of their children within the week preceding the survey. Similar findings have been reported by Adams (1968). Reviewing the literature on intergenerational relations, Cohler and Grunebaum (1981) note that frequency of contact is generally reported as somewhat greater among working-class than among middle-class families and more frequent with relatives of the wife than those of the husband, supporting Sweetser's (1963) concept of the "matrifocal tilt" in American kinship.

Rather than feeling neglected by their offspring, older people often experience the obligations to and demands of their adult offspring as problematic, at least as long as they are able to live independently (Smith and Lipman, 1972). In addition to providing material assistance and babysitting, older women in particular are expected to be responsible for kin-keeping in highly bonded urban families (Firth, Hubert, and Forge, 1970; Cohler and Grunebaum, 1981). The greater the responsibility assumed, the greater the risk for encountering additional life stress (Cohler and Lieberman, 1980). Further, roles such as that of grandparent are ascribed rather than elected (Rosow, 1967, 1974).

Thus, role strain and overload may be much more a problem than social isolation among older women in contemporary family life (Dunkel-Schetter and Wortman, 1981). Demands from young adult offspring for assistance and care may lower morale rather than raise it. Indeed, as Rosenmayr and Kockeis (1963) have suggested, the preferred mode of relationship between older parents and their offspring may be "intimacy at a distance." Both Tunstall (1966) and Johnson and Catalano (1981) report that childless older women do not differ in morale from older women who have children. Being married appears more important than having children as a factor contributing to morale and adjustment in later life (Palmore, 1976; Atchley, Pignatiello, and Shaw, 1979; Lopata, 1978, 1979; Ward, 1979; Kivett and Lerner, 1980; Beckman, 1981; Beckman and Houser, 1982).

Further, although it has been assumed that particular functions for older persons are fulfilled by particular significant others in the family, including care of older parents by their middle-aged offspring (Litwak and Szelenyi, 1969; Streib, 1972; Cantor, 1979), Shanas (1979b) has questioned this view. She has suggested a principle of serial substitution rather than functionality in the delegation of care for older persons. Indeed, as Knipscheer (1976) and Beckman (1981) have shown, when there are no children, friends may step in to provide the care ordinarily provided by offspring. Other members of the same ethnic community are also viewed as a significant source of help, carrying out responsibilities often assumed to be those delegated to family members (Weeks and Cuellar, 1981). Jonas and Wellin (1980), Johnson (1983), and Johnson and Catalano (1981) have reported that the spouse continues to be the most important caretaker for older persons, even when the spouse is also somewhat physically incapacitated.

Age peers and siblings may also serve an important role in the provision of such care (Ward, 1978; Scott, 1983). However, as Johnson (1983) notes, the spouse provides care with less sense of obligation than any other family member or friend. Matthews (1979) provides rich interview data documenting the degree of resentment that may be felt, particularly among off-spring, in providing care for the elderly, which is in striking contrast with the attitude reported by the spouse or even by close friends (Johnson, 1983). Findings reported by Johnson and Bursk (1977) suggest that the quality of the tie between elderly parents and their middle-aged offspring is mediated by the physical health of the parents, with greater conflict reported where parents have greater health problems and attendant needs for help and support. Smith and Bengtson (1979) note that one benefit of institutional placement of the parent is that a major source of conflict between generations may be removed, facilitating greater harmony and closeness.

To date, there has been little consideration of the emotional needs of older persons. In their review of family ties in later life, Hess and Waring (1978) have emphasized the importance of the change from obligatory to voluntary modes of relationship as an important determinant of satisfaction obtained from social ties across the second half of life. For example, in contrast to ties with offspring, characterized by quite specific expectations and strong sanctions for failure to provide expected forms of help and support, relations with brothers and sisters, more distant relatives of the same generation, and close friends or confidants are characterized by more informal norms and sanctions. These voluntary ties are a source of morale for older persons to an extent not possible for more obligatory ties to adult offspring.

Little association has been reported between voluntary contact with brothers, sisters, or other relatives and morale in later life. However, friends and, particularly, confidants have been found to be important to morale. Study of friendships among older people suggests that, next to the spouse, friends may be the most important source of solace and comfort. Nowhere is this better documented than in Myerhoff's (1978) Academy Award documentary film and the accompanying volume on a senior center. Central to this narrative is the death of one member of the center on his ninetieth birthday. This man had been determined to enjoy his birthday with his close friends and to die among those who had provided support and comfort over a period of many years. It is clear that these friendships were important determinants of the longevity and activity observed among participants in this remarkable setting.

There has been remarkably little study of friendship relations across the second half of life. One reason is the belief that the family is the most important source of assistance in late life and that older people tend to withdraw from social contacts (Cumming and Henry, 1961; Rosow, 1974). However, findings reported by Cantor (1979) suggest that friends and neighbors may be more important than family as a source of help with the daily round. Requests for assistance from family may be limited to major life crises.

Access to one or two confidants is particularly important in preserving psychological well-being in late life (Bell, 1981; Strain and Chappell, 1982). In contrast to ties with family, which show little positive (or negative) association with morale, friendship ties show a significant positive association (Lowenthal and Haven, 1968; Pihlblad and Adams, 1972; Moriwaki, 1973; Arling, 1976; Wood and Robertson, 1978; Strain and Chappell, 1982; Chappell, 1983).

Homans (1961) and Blau (1968) have noted the importance of establishing reciprocity in social relations. Relations with spouse and confidants in late life may be characterized by such reciprocity in that each partner is able to be of help to the other (Cantor, 1979); such balance is less likely to be realized in relations with offspring. Contrary to what might be expected, older parents continue to give more to their adult offspring than they receive. Older parents continue to provide a degree of assistance that is incompatible with their emotional needs (Quinn, 1983). This lack of reciprocity may, in part, explain the particular satisfaction reported among older people living in age-homogeneous communities, such as retirement villages (Rosow, 1967; Hochschild, 1973).

Structural factors, particularly gender and social class, also determine contact with friends. For example, women appear to have more contact with friends than men (Blau, 1981) and more confidants (Lowenthal and Robinson, 1976). This gender difference reflects both lifelong differences between men and women in the importance placed on friendship ties (Pleck, 1981) and also the fact that retirement disrupts long-standing ties to co-workers, who are so important as a source of friendship among men. Further, both men and women who are widowed early report fewer friends and a greater sense of crisis than women experiencing widowhood "on time" (Glick, Weiss, and Parkes, 1974). Having a convoy of consociates experiencing similar events at similar points across the life course facilitates maintenance of friendships (Kahn, 1979; Kahn and Antonucci, 1980; Plath, 1980), and it is fairly uncommon for men to outlive their wives or for women to be widowed early.

Social-class differences also exist in the maintenance of friendships in late life (Rosenberg, 1970; Lopata, 1979; Rubin, 1976; Blau, 1981). In general, in the working class, whose family life appears to be much more close-knit than in the middle class, kin and friends tend more often to be the same persons. Further, the greater homogeneity in working-class neigh-hoods may narrow an already restricted social world. Among working-class men and women, social ties are found close to home, among friends and neighbors. It may be for this reason that both Lopata (1973) and Blau (1981) report that widowhood is more constraining among working- than middle-class women; with a social world focused more directly on household and family, these women have fewer social resources to call on after widowhood.

Findings on the association between social status and being with others among older people are ambiguous. Some studies (Bell, 1957; Rosenberg, 1970; Atchley, Pignatiello, and Shaw, 1979; Lopata, 1973) report an association between social isolation and lower social status among older people, but other studies document the greater sense of community present in working-class life (Miller and Reissman, 1961; Komarovsky, 1962; Patterson, 1964; Fried, 1973; Cohler and Grunebaum, 1981). Certainly, it is clear that since people in lower-social-status communities tend more to rely on close ties with relatives and neighbors, all living in the immediate area (Rosenberg, 1970), if the social composition of the neighborhood changes or if the older person becomes less able to get around, working-class persons may be more vulnerable than middle-class persons to sustained social isolation; they also lack the financial resources to visit relatives and friends who have moved away. Finally, within the black community, higher rather than lower social status may be associated with lessened contact with relatives and friends (Wolf and others, 1983).

A major problem in the study of friendships across the course of life concerns the psychological significance of these ties. As Lowenthal and Robinson (1976), Conner, Powers, and Bultena (1979), George (1980), Liang, Dvorkin, Kahana, and Mazian (1980), Beckman (1981), and Strain and Chappell (1982) all have noted, much more effort has been devoted to determining the frequency of contact than to studying the psychological significance of friendships. Even when efforts have been made to evaluate the meaning of these ties, survey methods have not been very successful in providing increased understanding of this issue.

Further development of a life-course perspective requires that the findings of survey studies be augmented with understanding of the personal and psychological meanings of friendships and other relationships in later life. This understanding can best be obtained by theoretical formulations that are consonant with adult experience. Thus far, as suggested earlier, Kohut's (1959, 1971, 1982) clinical methods relying on careful, empathic observation of lives over time seem to offer the most promise.

Conclusion

Study of personality and social relations across the course of life suggests a complex interrelationship between nature and duration of contacts with others and the significance of these contacts for continued feelings of well-being. It is generally assumed that the capacity for emotionally sustaining relationships in adulthood is gradually attained over the first years or life as a result of the child's experiences with caretakers and that considering the origins of these social ties in early childhood will help us understand the psychological significance of adult social relations. Contrasting developmental perspectives suggest either that the motivation for attachments to others is innate, as represented by the work of Bowlby (1969, 1973a, 1977), Ainsworth (1969, 1982), and their colleagues, or that this need for closeness is learned during the first years of life, as represented both by social learning and by psychoanalytic formulations (Gewirtz, 1976; Mahler, Pine, and Bergman, 1975).

While attainment of a sense of cohesion, including the capacity to regulate inner tensions and to seek comfort, is a key developmental achievement of early childhood, there are important changes during the course of life that are most useful in enhancing feelings of well-being. Issues of interpersonal separateness and autonomy have become important in the study of social life as a result of the assumption that attainment of autonomy is necessary in order to rationally realize individual achievement within the constraints of the social and geographical mobility often assumed intrinsic in industrial society. As

Clark (1972) has observed, this concern with autonomy and independence, rather than with dependence on others and interdependence, is unique to society in Western Europe and the United States.

Concepts such as interpersonal separateness and autonomy, for example, may be less useful in the study of how social relations affect feelings of well-being than the concept of "invisible loyalties" (Boszormenyi-Nagy and Spark, 1973) or interdependence (Cohler and Grunebaum, 1981), which emphasize the concern that adults in our society show for those they care about. Indeed, much of older family members' feeling of being burdened, reflecting their continued concern and sense of responsibility for the welfare of adult offspring (Rosow, 1967), as well as the reciprocal concern expressed by adult offspring regarding the lives of parents (Brody, 1977; Brody, Johnsen, Fulcomer, and Lang, 1983), reflects the value placed in our society on interdependence. It is precisely because people care so much for each other that provision of care may take precedence over developmental needs for increased time for self, leading to lowered morale, particularly during middle and later life (Neugarten, 1973, 1979).

Particularly through early adulthood, continuing contact with others may be important in providing comfort and solace (Weiss, 1974, 1982a). Survey studies have documented the significance of contact with others in fostering well-being (Cobb, 1976; Greenblatt, Becerra, and Serafetinides, 1982). However, many of these studies have not considered issues of social timing and perceived place in the expected course of life as factors related to the kind of social support most important in fostering feelings of well-being at any particular point in the course of life.

Studies of older adults suggest that actual social contacts may be less important in sustaining the capacity for solace and comfort than memories of time spent together in the past (Lieberman and Falk, 1971; Neugarten, 1979; Cohler, 1982). At least to some extent, reminiscence replaces actual contacts with others as a major determinant of solace or self-soothing in later adulthood and may become particularly adaptive as the loss of loved ones and impairment in physical mobility (Munnichs and van den Heuvel, 1976) make continuing contact with others more difficult.

Changed life circumstances may partly account for changes in the tendency to turn to others. It is also likely that increased awareness of the finitude of life and personalization of death lead to increased preoccupation with one's inner world, thereby diminishing satisfaction from social ties that make demands on one's time and energy (Neugarten, 1973, 1979; Cohler and Lieberman, 1980). The spouse emerges as the single most important significant other in fostering comfort and well-being in later life. Voluntary ties, particularly those with a few confidants or close friends, may be more important in fostering a sense of well-being in later life than obligatory ties with relatives, particularly those with younger adult offspring who continue to seek precisely the degree of assistance that, as a reflection of continuing invisible loyalties within the family, parents continue to offer.

Study of adult lives highlights problems involved in the use of theories of personality development based on earliest childhood and extended to study of the life course as a whole. Detailed clinical study relying on empathically informed observation (Kohut, 1959, 1971, 1982) may provide additional important information about changes in how social support functions over time. Reliance on a life-course perspective on personality development must emphasize the continuing interplay among person, historical context, and issues of social timing (Riegel, 1979), as well as recognize the importance of studying both continuities and discontinuities in development. This inclusive perspective may yield increased understanding of the place of relations with others, and of being alone, in adjustment from earliest childhood to oldest age.

References

Abraham, K. "A Short Study of the Libido, Viewed in the Light of Mental Disorders." In K. Abraham, *Selected Papers on Psychoanalysis.* New York: Basic Books, 1953. (Originally published 1924.)

Adams, B. N. *Kinship in an Urban Setting.* Chicago: Markham, 1968.

Ainsworth, M. D. S. "Object Relations, Dependency, and Attachment: A Theoretical Review of the Infant-Mother Relationship." *Child Development,* 1969, *40,* 969–1025.

Ainsworth, M. D. S. "Attachment: Retrospect and Prospect." In C. M. Parkes and J. Stevenson-Hinde (eds.), *The Place of Attachment in Human Behavior.* New York: Basic Books, 1982.

Ainsworth, M. D. S., Blehar, M. C., Waters, E., and Wall, S. *Patterns of Attachment: A Psychological Study of the Strange Situation.* Hillsdale, N.J.: Erlbaum, 1978.

Aneshensel, C., and Stone, J. "Stress and Depression: A Test of the Buffering Model of Social Support." *Archives of General Psychiatry,* 1982, *30,* 1392–1396.

Antonucci, T. "Attachment: A Life-Span Concept." *Human Development,* 1976, *19,* 135–142.

Arling, G. "The Elderly Widow and Her Family, Neighbors, and Friends." *Journal of Marriage and the Family,* 1976, *38,* 757–768.

Atchley, R. C., Pignatiello, L., and Shaw, E. "Interactions with Family and Friends." *Research on Aging,* 1979, *1,* 84–95.

Beckman, L. "Effects of Social Interaction and Children's Relative Inputs on Older Women's Psychological Well-Being." *Journal of Personality and Social Psychology,* 1981, *41,* 1075–1086.

Beckman, L., and Houser, B. "The Consequences of Childlessness on the Social Psychological Well-Being of Older Women." *Journal of Gerontology,* 1982, *37,* 243–250.

Bell, R. *Worlds of Friendship.* Beverly Hills, Calif.: Sage, 1981.

Bell, W. "Anomie, Social Isolation, and the Class Struggle." *Sociometry,* 1957, *20,* 105–116.

Bengtson, V. L., and Treas, J. "The Changing Family Context of Mental Health and Aging." In J. E. Birren and R. B. Sloane (eds.), *Handbook of Mental Health and Aging.* Englewood Cliffs, N.J.: Prentice-Hall, 1980.

Blau, P. "Interaction: Social Exchange." In D. Shils (ed.), *International Encyclopedia of the Social Sciences.* Vol. 7. New York: Macmillan, 1968.

Blau, Z. *Aging in a Changing Society.* (Rev. ed.) New York: Franklin Watts, 1981.

Blumer, H. *Symbolic Interactionism.* Englewood Cliffs, N.J.: Prentice-Hall, 1969.

Boszormenyi-Nagy, I., and Spark, G. *Invisible Loyalties: Reciprocity in Intergenerational Family Therapy.* New York: Harper & Row, 1973.

Bowlby, J. *Attachment and Loss.* Vol. 1: *Attachment.* New York: Basic Books, 1969.

Bowlby, J. *Attachment and Loss.* Vol. 2: *Separation: Anxiety and Anger.* New York: Basic Books, 1973a.

Bowlby, J. "Self-Reliance and Some Conditions That Promote It." In R. Gosling (ed.), *Support, Innovation, and Autonomy.* London: Tavistock, 1973b.

Bowlby, J. "The Making and Breaking of Affectional Bonds." *British Journal of Psychiatry,* 1977, *30,* 201-210.

Bowlby, J. *Attachment and Loss.* Vol. 3: *Loss: Sadness and Depression.* New York: Basic Books, 1980.

Bowlby, J. "Attachment and Loss: Retrospect and Prospect." *American Journal of Orthopsychiatry,* 1982, *52,* 664-678.

Brody, E. *Long-Term Care of Older People.* New York: Human Sciences Press, 1977.

Brody, E., Johnsen, P., Fulcomer, M., and Lang, A. "Women's Changing Roles and Help to Elderly Parents: Attitudes of Three Generations of Women." *Journal of Gerontology,* 1983, *38,* 597-601.

Brody, S. "Transitional Objects: Idealization of a Phenomenon." *Psychoanalytic Quarterly,* 1980, *49,* 561-605.

Brown, A. "Satisfying Relationships for the Elderly and Their Patterns of Disengagement." *Gerontologist,* 1974, *14,* 258-262.

Brown, R. "Family Structure and Social Isolation of Older Persons." *Journal of Gerontology,* 1980, *15,* 170-174.

Cantor, M. "Neighbors and Friends." *Research on Aging,* 1979, *1,* 434-463.

Caplan, G. *Support Systems and Community Mental Health.* New York: Behavioral Publications, 1974.

Chappell, N. "Informal Support Networks Among the Elderly." *Research on Aging,* 1983, *5,* 77-99.

Clark, M. "Cultural Values and Dependency in Later Life." In
    D. O. Cowgill and L. D. Holmes (eds.), *Aging and Moderniza-
    tion.* New York: Appleton-Century-Crofts, 1972.
Cobb, S. "Social Support as a Moderator of Life Stress." *Psy-
    chosomatic Medicine,* 1976, *38,* 300–314.
Cobb, S. "Social Support and Health Through the Life Course."
    In M. W. Riley (ed.), *Aging from Birth to Death: Interdisci-
    plinary Perspectives.* Boulder, Colo.: Westview Press, 1979.
Cohen, N. "Loneliness and the Aging Process." *International
    Journal of Psychoanalysis,* 1982, *63,* 149–155.
Cohler, B. J. "Developmental Perspectives on the Psychology of
    the Self." In A. Goldberg (ed.), *Advances in the Psychology
    of the Self.* New York: International Universities Press, 1980.
Cohler, B. J. "Personal Narrative and Life-Course." In P. B.
    Baltes and O. G. Brim, Jr. (eds.), *Life-Span Development and
    Behavior.* Vol. 4. Orlando, Fla.: Academic Press, 1982.
Cohler, B. J. "Approaches to the Study of Development in Psy-
    chiatric Education." In S. Weissman and R. Thurnblad (eds.),
    *The Role of Psychoanalysis in Psychiatric Education: Past,
    Present, and Future.* New York: Guilford Press, forthcoming.
Cohler, B. J., and Ferrono, C. "Schizophrenia and the Life-
    Course." In N. Miller and G. Dohen (eds.), *Schizophrenia and
    Aging.* New York: Guilford Press, forthcoming.
Cohler, B. J., and Grunebaum, H. *Mothers, Grandmothers, and
    Daughters.* New York: Wiley, 1981.
Cohler, B. J., and Lieberman, M. "Social Relations and Mental
    Health." *Research on Aging,* 1980, *2,* 445–469.
Conner, K., Powers, E., and Bultena, G. "Social Interaction and
    Life Satisfaction: An Empirical Assessment of Late-Life Pat-
    terns." *Journal of Gerontology,* 1979, *34,* 116–121.
Cumming, E., and Henry, W. E. *Growing Old: The Process of
    Disengagement.* New York: Basic Books, 1961.
Davis, M., and Wallbridge, D. *Boundary and Space.* New York:
    Brunner/Mazel, 1981.
Doi, T. *The Anatomy of Dependence.* (J. Bester, trans.) New
    York: Kodansha International Press, 1973.
Dunkel-Schetter, C., and Wortman, C. "Dilemmas of Social Sup-
    port: Parallels Between Victimization and Aging." In S. B.

Kiesler, J. N. Morgan, and V. K. Oppenheimer (eds.), *Aging: Social Change.* Orlando, Fla.: Academic Press, 1981.

Eckenrode, J., and Gore, S. "Stressful Events and Social Supports: The Significance of Context." In B. H. Gottlieb (ed.), *Social Networks and Social Support.* New York: Russell Sage Foundation, 1981.

Eichorn, D., and others (eds.). *Present and Past in Mid-Life.* Orlando, Fla.: Academic Press, 1981.

Elwell, F., and Maltbie-Crannell, A. "The Impact of Role Losses upon Coping Resources and Life Satisfaction of the Elderly." *Journal of Gerontology,* 1981, *36,* 222–232.

Erikson, E. H. *Childhood and Society.* (2nd ed.) New York: Norton, 1963.

Erikson, E. H. "Elements of a Psychoanalytic Theory of Development." In S. I. Greenspan and G. H. Pollock (eds.), *The Course of Life: Psychoanalytic Contributions Toward Understanding Personality Development.* Vol. 1: *Infancy and Early Childhood.* Washington, D.C.: National Institute of Mental Health, 1980.

Fandetti, D., and Gelfand, D. "Care of the Aged." *Gerontologist,* 1976, *16,* 544–549.

Farnham-Diggory, S. "Self, Future, and Time: A Developmental Study of the Concepts of Psychotic, Brain-Injured, and Normal Children." *Monographs of the Society for Research in Child Development,* 1966, *33*(Whole No. 103).

Firth, R., Hubert, J., and Forge, A. *Families and Their Relatives: Kinship in a Middle-Class Sector of London.* London: Humanities Press, 1970.

Fiske, M. "Tasks and Crises of the Second Half of Life: The Interrelationship of Commitment, Coping, and Adaptation." In J. E. Birren and R. B. Sloane (eds.), *Handbook of Mental Health and Aging.* Englewood Cliffs, N.J.: Prentice-Hall, 1980.

Freud, A. *Normality and Psychopathology in Childhood: Assessment of Development.* New York: International Universities Press, 1965.

Freud, S. "Three Essays on the Theory of Sexuality." In J. Strachey (ed. and trans.), *The Standard Edition of the Com-*

plete Psychological Works of Sigmund Freud. Vol. 7. London: Hogarth Press, 1953. (Originally published 1905.)

Fried, M. *The World of the Urban Working Class.* Cambridge, Mass.: Harvard University Press, 1973.

Fromm-Reichman, F. "Loneliness." *Psychiatry,* 1959, *22,* 1–15.

George, L. "The Happiness Syndrome: Methodological and Substantive Issues in the Study of Social-Psychological Well-Being in Adulthood." *Gerontologist,* 1979, *19,* 210–216.

George, L. *Role Transitions in Later Life.* Monterey, Calif.: Brooks/Cole, 1980.

Gewirtz, J. L. "Attachment, Dependence, and a Distinction in Terms of Stimulus Control." In J. L. Gewirtz (ed.), *Attachment and Dependency.* Washington, D.C.: Winston, 1972.

Gewirtz, J. L. "The Attachment Acquisition Process as Evidence in the Maternal Conditioning of Cued Infant Responding (Particularly Crying)." *Human Development,* 1976, *19,* 143–155.

Gill, M. "Metapsychology Is Not Psychology." In M. Gill and P. Holzman (eds.), "Psychology Versus Metapsychology: Essays in Memory of George S. Klein." *Psychological Issues,* 1976, Monograph 36.

Glick, I. O., Weiss, R. S., and Parkes, C. M. *The First Year of Bereavement.* New York: Wiley-Interscience, 1974.

Goldfarb, A. "The Psychodynamics of Dependency." In R. Kalish (ed.), *The Dependencies of Old People.* Occasional Papers in Gerontology, No. 6. Ann Arbor: Institute of Gerontology, University of Michigan, 1969.

Greenblatt, M., Becerra, R., and Serafetinides, E. "Social Networks and Mental Health: An Overview." *American Journal of Psychiatry,* 1982, *139,* 977–984.

Haller, A. O. "The Urban Family." *American Journal of Sociology,* 1961, *66,* 621–622.

Hess, B., and Waring, J. "Changing Patterns of Aging and Family Bonds in Later Life." *Family Coordinator,* 1978, *27,* 303–314.

Hinde, R. *Towards Understanding Relationships.* Orlando, Fla.: Academic Press, 1979.

Hinde, R. "Attachment: Some Conceptual and Biological Issues." In C. M. Parkes and J. Stevenson-Hinde (eds.), *The Place of Attachment in Human Behavior.* New York: Basic Books, 1982.

Hochschild, A. *The Unexpected Community.* Englewood Cliffs, N.J.: Prentice-Hall, 1973.

Homans, G. P. *Social Behavior: Its Elementary Forms.* New York: Harcourt Brace Jovanovich, 1961.

Horton, P. *Solace: The Missing Dimension in Psychiatry.* Chicago: University of Chicago Press, 1981.

Hull, C. L. *Principles of Behavior: An Introduction to Behavior Theory.* New York: Appleton-Century-Crofts, 1943.

Jaques, E. "Death and the Mid-Life Crisis." *International Journal of Psycho-Analysis,* 1965, *46,* 502–514.

Jaques, E. "The Mid-Life Crisis." In S. I. Greenspan and G. H. Pollock (eds.), *The Course of Life: Psychoanalytic Contributions Toward Understanding Personality Development.* Vol. 3: *Adulthood and the Aging Process.* Washington, D.C.: National Institute of Mental Health, 1980.

Johnson, C. "Dyadic Family Relations and Social Support." *Gerontologist,* 1983, *23,* 377–383.

Johnson, C., and Catalano, D. "Childless Elderly and Their Family Supports." *Gerontologist,* 1981, *21,* 610–618.

Johnson, E., and Bursk, B. "Relationships Between the Elderly and Their Adult Children." *Gerontologist,* 1977, *17,* 90–96.

Jonas, K., and Wellin, E. "Dependency and Reciprocity: Home Health Aid in an Elderly Population." In C. Fry (ed.), *Aging in Culture and Society.* New York: Praeger, 1980.

Jones, M. D., Bayley, N., MacFarlane, J., and Honzik, M. P. (eds.). *The Course of Human Development.* New York: Wiley, 1971.

Kagan, J. "Perspectives on Continuity." In O. G. Brim, Jr., and J. Kagan (eds.), *Constancy and Change in Human Development.* Cambridge, Mass.: Harvard University Press, 1980.

Kagan, J., and Moss, H. *From Birth to Maturity.* New York: Wiley, 1962.

Kahn, R. "Aging and Social Support." In M. W. Riley (ed.), *Aging from Birth to Death: Interdisciplinary Perspectives.* Boulder, Colo.: Westview Press, 1979.

Kahn, R., and Antonucci, T. "Convoys over the Life Course: Attachment, Roles, and Social Support." In P. B. Baltes and O. G. Brim, Jr. (eds.), *Life-Span Development and Behavior.* Vol. 3. Orlando, Fla.: Academic Press, 1980.

Kaker, S. *The Inner World: A Psychoanalytic Study of Childhood and Society in India.* Delhi: Oxford University Press, 1978.

Kalish, R., and Knudtson, F. "Attachment Versus Disengagement: A Life-Span Conceptualization." *Human Development,* 1976, *19,* 171–181.

Kastenbaum, R., and Cameron, P. "Cognitive and Emotional Dependency in Later Life." In R. Kalish (ed.), *The Dependencies of Older People.* Occasional Papers in Gerontology, No. 6. Ann Arbor: Institute of Gerontology, University of Michigan, 1969.

Kilillea, M. "Interaction of Crisis Theory, Coping Strategies, and Social Support Systems." In H. C. Schulberg and M. Kilillea (eds.), *The Modern Practice of Community Mental Health: A Volume in Honor of Gerald Caplan.* San Francisco: Jossey-Bass, 1982.

Kivett, V., and Lerner, R. "Perspectives on the Childless Rural Elderly." *Gerontologist,* 1980, *20,* 708–716.

Klein, G. *Psychoanalytic Theory: An Exploration of Essentials.* New York: International Universities Press, 1976.

Klein, M. "On Mahler's Autistic and Symbiotic Phases: An Exposition and Evaluation." *Psychoanalysis and Contemporary Thought,* 1981, *4,* 69–105.

Knipscheer, K. "The Primary Relations to Old Age: Children, Brothers, Sisters, Other Relatives, Friends, and Neighbors." In G. Dooghe and J. Helander (eds.), *Family Life in Old Age.* The Hague, The Netherlands: Martinus Nijhoff, 1976.

Kohut, H. "Introspection, Empathy, and Psychoanalysis: An Examination of the Relationship Between Mode of Observation and Theory." *Journal of the American Psychoanalytic Association,* 1959, *7,* 459–483.

Kohut, H. "The Analysis of the Self." *Psychoanalytic Study of the Child,* Monograph 4. New York: International Universities Press, 1971.

Kohut, H. *The Restoration of the Self.* New York: International Universities Press, 1977.

Kohut, H. "Introspection, Empathy, and the Semi-Circle of Mental Health." *International Journal of Psycho-Analysis,* 1982, *63,* 395–407.

Komarovsky, M. *Blue-Collar Marriage.* New York: Random House, 1962.

Lawton, M. P. "The Well-Being and Mental Health of the Aged." In T. Field and others (eds.), *Review of Human Development.* New York: Wiley, 1982.

Lerner, R., and Ryff, C. "Implementation of the Life-Span View of Human Development: The Sample Case of Attachment." In P. B. Baltes (ed.), *Life-Span Development and Behavior.* Orlando, Fla.: Academic Press, 1978.

Levinson, D. J., and others. *The Seasons of a Man's Life.* New York: Knopf, 1978.

Lewis, A., and Landis, B. "Symbiotic Pairings in Adults." *Contemporary Psychoanalysis,* 1979, *15,* 230–248.

Liang, J., Dvorkin, L., Kahana, E., and Mazian, F. "Social Integration and Morale: A Re-examination." *Journal of Gerontology,* 1980, *35,* 746–757.

Lieberman, M., and Falk, J. "The Remembered Past as a Source of Data for Research on the Life-Cycle." *Human Development,* 1971, *14,* 132–141.

Litwak, E. "Extended Kin Relations in an Industrial Democratic Society." In E. Shanas and G. Streig (eds.), *Social Structure and the Family: Generational Relations.* Englewood Cliffs, N.J.: Prentice-Hall, 1965.

Litwak, E., and Szelenyi, I. "Primary Group Structures and Their Functions: Kin, Neighbors, and Friends." *American Sociological Review,* 1969, *34,* 465–481.

Lopata, H. *Widowhood in an American City.* Cambridge, Mass.: Schenkman, 1973.

Lopata, H. "Contributions of Extended Families to the Support Systems of Metropolitan Area Widows: Limitations of the

Modified Kin Network." *Journal of Marriage and the Family,* 1978, *40,* 355-361.

Lopata, H. *Women as Widows: Support Systems.* New York: Elsevier-North Holland, 1979.

Lowenthal, M. F. "Social Isolation and Mental Illness in Old Age." *American Sociological Review,* 1964, *29,* 54-70.

Lowenthal, M. F., and Boler, D. "Voluntary Versus Involuntary Social Withdrawal." *Journal of Gerontology,* 1965, *20,* 363-371.

Lowenthal, M. F., and Haven, C. "Interaction and Adaptational Intimacy as a Critical Variable." *American Sociological Review,* 1968, *33,* 20-30.

Lowenthal, M. F., and Robinson, B. "Social Networks and Isolation." In R. H. Binstock and E. Shanas (eds.), *Handbook of Aging and the Social Sciences.* New York: Van Nostrand Reinhold, 1976.

Maas, H. S., and Kuypers, J. A. *From Thirty to Seventy: A Forty-Year Longitudinal Study of Adult Life Styles and Personality.* San Francisco: Jossey-Bass, 1974.

Maccoby, E. E., and Masters, J. "Attachment and Dependency." In P. H. Mussen (ed.), *Carmichael's Manual of Child Psychology.* (3rd ed.) Vol. 2. New York: Wiley, 1970.

McDevitt, J. B., and Settlage, C. F. (eds.). *Separation-Individuation: Essays in Honor of Margaret S. Mahler.* New York: Van Nostrand Reinhold, 1971.

Mahler, M. S. *The Selected Papers of Margaret S. Mahler.* Vol. 2: *Separation-Individuation.* New York: Jason Aronson, 1979.

Mahler, M. S., Pine, F., and Bergman, A. *The Psychological Birth of the Human Infant: Symbiosis and Individuation.* New York: Basic Books, 1975.

Mancini, J. "Family Relationships and Morale Among People 65 Years of Age and Older." *American Journal of Orthopsychiatry,* 1979, *49,* 292-300.

Mancini, J., Quinn, W., Gavigan, M., and Franklin, H. "Social Network Interaction Among Older Adults: Implications for Life Satisfaction." *Human Relations,* 1980, *33,* 534-543.

Marris, P. "Attachment and Society." In C. M. Parkes and J.

Stevenson-Hinde (eds.), *The Place of Attachment in Human Behavior.* New York: Basic Books, 1982.

Matthews, S. *The Social World of Old Women.* Beverly Hills, Calif.: Sage, 1979.

Metcalf, D., and Spitz, R. A. "The Transitional Object: Critical Developmental Period and Organizer of the Psyche." In S. Grolnick, L. Barkin, and W. Muensterberger (eds.), *Between Reality and Fantasy.* New York: Jason Aronson, 1978.

Miller, N. E., and Dollard, J. *Social Learning Theory and Imitation.* New Haven, Conn.: Yale University Press, 1941.

Miller, S., and Reissman, F. "The Working Class Subculture: A New View." *Social Problems,* 1961, *9,* 86-97.

Moriwaki, S. "Self-Disclosure, Significant Others, and Psychological Well-Being in Old Age." *Journal of Health and Social Behavior,* 1973, *14,* 226-232.

Munnichs, J. "Loneliness, Isolation, and Social Relations in Old Age." *Vita Humana,* 1964, *7,* 228-238.

Munnichs, J. *Old Age and Finitude: A Contribution to Psychogerontology.* New York: Karger, 1966.

Munnichs, J., and van den Heuvel, W. J. A. (eds.). *Dependency or Interdependency in Old Age.* The Hague, The Netherlands: Martinus Nijhoff, 1976.

Myerhoff, B. "A Symbol Perfected in Death." In B. Myerhoff and A. Simic (eds.), *Life's Career—Aging: Cultural Variations in Growing Old.* Beverly Hills, Calif.: Sage, 1978.

Neugarten, B. L. "Continuities and Discontinuities of Psychological Issues into Adult Life." *Human Development,* 1969, *12,* 121-130.

Neugarten, B. L. "Personality Change in Late Life: A Developmental Perspective." In C. Eisdorfer and M. P. Lawton (eds.), *The Psychology of Adult Development and Aging.* Washington, D.C.: American Psychological Association, 1973.

Neugarten, B. L. "Time, Age, and the Life-Cycle." *American Journal of Psychiatry,* 1979, *136,* 887-894.

Neugarten, B. L., and Datan, N. "The Middle Years." In S. Arieti (ed.), *American Handbook of Psychiatry.* Vol. 1: *The Foundations of Psychiatry.* New York: Basic Books, 1974.

Neugarten, B. L., and Hagestad, G. "Age and the Life Course."

In R. H. Binstock and E. Shanas (eds.), *Handbook of Aging and the Social Sciences.* New York: Van Nostrand Reinhold, 1976.

Neugarten, B. L., Moore, J., and Lowe, J. "Age Norms, Age Constraints, and Adult Socialization." *American Journal of Sociology,* 1965, *70,* 710–717.

Palmore, E. "Total Chances of Institutionalization Among the Aged." *Gerontologist,* 1976, *16,* 504–507.

Panel (M. C. Winestine, reporter). "The Experience of Separation-Individuation in Infancy and Its Reverberations Through the Course of Life. I: Infancy and Childhood." *Journal of the American Psychoanalytic Association,* 1973a, *21,* 135–154.

Panel (M. Marcus, reporter). "The Experience of Separation-Individuation in Infancy and Its Reverberations Through the Course of Life. II: Adolescence and Maturity." *Journal of the American Psychoanalytic Association,* 1973b, *21,* 155–167.

Panel (I. Sternschein, reporter). "The Experience of Separation-Individuation in Infancy and Its Reverberations Through the Course of Life. III: Maturity, Senescence, and Sociological Implications." *Journal of the American Psychoanalytic Association,* 1973c, *21,* 633–645.

Parkes, C. M. "Role of Support Systems in Loss and Psychosocial Transitions." In H. C. Schulberg and M. Killilea (eds.), *The Modern Practice of Community Mental Health: A Volume in Honor of Gerald Caplan.* San Francisco: Jossey-Bass, 1982.

Parkes, C. M., and Weiss, R. S. *Recovery from Bereavement.* New York: Basic Books, 1983.

Patterson, J. "Marketing and the Working-Class Family." In A. Shostak and W. Gomberg (eds.), *Blue-Collar World: Studies of the American Worker.* Englewood Cliffs, N.J.: Prentice-Hall, 1964.

Peterfreund, E. "Some Critical Comments on Psychoanalytic Conceptualizations of Infancy." *International Journal of Psycho-Analysis,* 1978, *59,* 427–441.

Pihlblad, C., and Adams, D. "Widowhood, Social Participation, and Life Satisfaction." *International Journal of Aging and Human Development,* 1972, *3,* 323–330.

Plath, D. "Contours of Consociation: Lessons from a Japanese

Narrative." In P. B. Baltes and O. G. Brim, Jr. (eds.), *Life-Span Development and Behavior*. Vol. 3. Orlando, Fla.: Academic Press, 1980.

Pleck, J. *The Myth of Masculinity*. Cambridge, Mass.: M.I.T. Press, 1981.

Pollock, G. H. "On Symbiosis and the Symbiotic Neurosis." *International Journal of Psycho-Analysis*, 1964, *45*, 1–30.

Quinn, W. "Personal and Family Adjustment in Later Life." *Journal of Marriage and the Family*, 1983, *45*, 57–73.

Riegel, K. F. *Foundations of Dialectical Psychology*. (J. A. Meacham, ed.) Orlando, Fla.: Academic Press, 1979.

Riley, M. W., Johnson, M., and Foner, A. "A Sociology of Age Stratification." In M. W. Riley, M. Johnson, and A. Foner (eds.), *Aging and Society*. New York: Russell Sage Foundation, 1972.

Rosenberg, G. S. *The Worker Grows Old: Poverty and Isolation in the City*. San Francisco: Jossey-Bass, 1970.

Rosenmayr, L., and Kockeis, E. "Predispositions for a Sociological Theory of Action and the Family." *International Social Science Journal*, 1963, *15*, 410–426.

Rosow, I. *Social Integration of the Aged*. New York: Free Press, 1967.

Rosow, I. *Socialization to Old Age*. Berkeley: University of California Press, 1974.

Roth, J. *Timetables: Structuring the Passage of Time in Hospital Treatment and Other Careers*. Indianapolis: Bobbs-Merrill, 1963.

Rubin, L. *Worlds of Pain: Life in the Working-Class Family*. New York: Basic Books, 1976.

Rudolph, S., and Rudolph, L. "Rajput Adulthood: Reflections on the Amar Singh Diary." In E. H. Erikson (ed.), *Adulthood*. New York: Norton, 1978.

Sarbin, T. R., and Allen, V. "Role Theory." In G. Lindzey and E. Aronson (eds.), *Handbook of Social Psychology*. (2nd ed.) Vol. 1. Reading, Mass.: Addison-Wesley, 1968.

Scott, J. P. "Siblings and Other Kin." In T. H. Brubaker (ed.), *Family Relationships in Later Life*. Beverly Hills, Calif.: Sage, 1983.

Sears, R. R. "Social Behavior and Personality Development." In

T. Parsons and E. Shils (eds.), *Toward a General Theory of Action.* Cambridge, Mass.: Harvard University Press, 1951.

Shanan, J. "Levels and Patterns of Social Engagement and Disengagement from Adolescence to Middle Adulthood." In K. F. Riegel and J. A. Meacham (eds.), *The Developing Individual in a Changing World.* Vol. 2: *Social and Environmental Issues.* Hawthorne, N.Y.: Aldine, 1976.

Shanas, E. "Living Arrangements of Older People in the United States." *Gerontologist,* 1961, *1,* 27–29.

Shanas, E. "Family-Kin Networks and Aging in Cross-Cultural Perspective." *Journal of Marriage and the Family,* 1973, *35,* 505–511.

Shanas, E. "Social Myth as Hypothesis: The Case of the Family Relations of Old People." *Gerontologist,* 1979a, *19,* 3–9.

Shanas, E. "The Family as a Social Support System in Old Age." *Gerontologist,* 1979b, *19,* 167–174.

Shanas, E., and others. *Old People in Three Industrial Societies.* New York: Atherton Press, 1968.

Smith, K. F., and Bengtson, V. L. "Positive Consequences of Institutionalization: Solidarity Between Elderly Parents and Their Middle-Aged Children." *Gerontologist,* 1979, *19,* 438–447.

Smith, K. S., and Lipman, A. "Constraint and Life-Satisfaction." *Journal of Gerontology,* 1972, *29,* 454–458.

Spitz, R. A. "Bridges: On Anticipation, Duration, Meaning." *Journal of the American Psychoanalytic Association,* 1972, *20,* 721–735.

Stack, C. *All Our Kin: Strategies for Survival in a Black Community.* New York: Harper & Row, 1974.

Strain, L., and Chappell, N. "Confidants." *Research on Aging,* 1982, *4,* 479–502.

Streib, G. "Older Families and Their Troubles." *Family Coordinator,* 1972, *21,* 5–19.

Sulloway, F. *Freud: Biologist of the Mind.* New York: Basic Books, 1979.

Sussman, M. "The Family Life of Old People." In R. H. Binstock and E. Shanas (eds.), *Handbook of Aging and the Social Sciences.* New York: Van Nostrand Reinhold, 1976.

Sweetser, D. "Asymmetry in Intergenerational Family Relationships." *Social Forces,* 1963, *41,* 346-352.

Thomas, A., and Chess, S. *The Dynamics of Psychological Development.* New York: Brunner/Mazel, 1980.

Tolpin, F. "Social Involvement and Other Corrrelates of Psychological Health: A Prospective Study of Persons over 65." Unpublished doctoral dissertation, Department of Psychology, University of North Carolina at Chapel Hill, 1972.

Tolpin, M., and Kohut, H. "The Disorders of the Self: The Psychopathology of the First Years of Life." In S. I. Greenspan and G. H. Pollock (eds.), *The Course of Life: Psychoanalytic Contributions Toward Understanding Personality Development.* Vol. 1: *Infancy and Early Childhood.* Washington, D.C.: U.S. Government Printing Office, 1980.

Townsend, P. *The Family Life of Old People.* London: Routledge & Kegan Paul, 1957.

Troll, L. "Intergenerational Relations in Later Life: A Family Systems Approach." In N. Datan and N. Lohmann (eds.), *Transitions of Aging.* Orlando, Fla.: Academic Press, 1980.

Troll, L., Miller, S., and Atchley, R. C. *Families in Later Life.* Belmont, Calif.: Wadsworth, 1979.

Troll, L., and Smith, J. "Attachment Through the Life-Span: Some Questions About Dyadic Relations in Later Life." *Human Development,* 1976, *9,* 156-170.

Tunstall, J. *Old and Alone.* London: Routledge & Kegan Paul, 1966.

Turner, J. "Social Support as a Contingency in Psychological Well-Being." *Journal of Health and Social Behavior,* 1981, *22,* 357-367.

Vaillant, G. E. *Adaptation to Life.* Boston: Little, Brown, 1978.

Ward, R. "Limitations of the Family as a Supportive Institution in the Lives of the Aged." *Family Coordinator,* 1978, *27,* 365-373.

Ward, R. "The Never Married in Later Life." *Journal of Gerontology,* 1979, *34,* 861-869.

Weeks, J., and Cuellar, J. "The Role of Family Members in the Helping Networks of Older People." *Gerontologist,* 1981, *21,* 388-394.

Weiss, R. S. *Loneliness: The Experience of Emotional and Social Isolation.* Cambridge, Mass.: M.I.T. Press, 1974.

Weiss, R. S. "Attachment in Adult Life." In C. M. Parkes and J. Stevenson-Hinde (eds.), *The Place of Attachment in Human Behavior.* New York: Basic Books, 1982a.

Weiss, R. S. "Relationship of Social Support and Psychological Well-Being." In H. C. Schulberg and M. Kilillea (eds.), *The Modern Practice of Community Mental Health: A Volume in Honor of Gerald Caplan.* San Francisco: Jossey-Bass, 1982b.

Winnicott, D. W. "Transitional Objects and Transitional Phenomena: A Study of the First Not-Me Possession." *International Journal of Psycho-Analysis,* 1953, *34,* 89–97.

Winnicott, D. W. "The Theory of the Parent-Infant Relationship." *International Journal of Psychoanalysis,* 1960, *41,* 585–595.

Winnicott, D. W. "The Capacity to Be Alone." In D. W. Winnicott, *The Maturational Processes and the Faciliating Environment.* New York: International Universities Press, 1965a.

Winnicott, D. W. "From Dependence Towards Interdependence in the Development of the Individual." In D. W. Winnicott, *The Maturational Processes and the Facilitating Environment.* New York: International Universities Press, 1965b.

Wolf, E. "On the Developmental Line of Selfobject Relations." In A. Goldberg (ed.), *Advances in Self Psychology.* New York: International Universities Press, 1980.

Wolf, J., and others. "Distance and Contacts: Interactions of Black Urban Elderly Adults with Family and Friends." *Journal of Gerontology,* 1983, *38,* 465–471.

Wood, V., and Robertson, J. "Friendship and Kinship Interaction: Differential Effect on the Morale of the Elderly." *Journal of Marriage and the Family,* 1978, *40,* 367–375.

Yarrow, L. J. "Attachment and Dependency: A Developmental Perspective." In J. L. Gewirtz (ed.), *Attachment and Dependency.* Washington, D.C.: Winston, 1972.

Part Two

Separation and Loss
in Major Life Transitions

Every transition in life, however growth-promoting or painful, involves leaving something behind. Because change necessitates loss, the dynamics of separation can be discerned in all the major life changes an individual experiences. Part Two focuses on the separation aspect of a selection of life transitions—nursery school entry, the adolescent's departure from home, work-related parental absence, cultural migration, divorce, and childhood bereavement. Although these transitions inherently evoke a separation response, the nature of that response depends on contextual factors as well as on the individual's inner resources. Objective features of these life transitions are magnified or filtered by the individual's psychological structure, and the structure of the inner world is, in turn, influenced by new confrontations with issues of continuity, loss, and self-definition. The representational world that defines the separation response includes images of self, of others, of family, and of culture. Thus, life transitions may simultaneously require adjustment to many new people, contexts, or things and hence demand psychological accommodation at many levels.

6

From Family to Classroom: Variations in Adjustment to Nursery School

Sally Bloom-Feshbach

Editors' Note: *This chapter offers a research investigation of a major transition involving separation—the child's entry into nursery school. This particular transition is special in timing, occurring in the midst of the consolidation of libidinal object constancy and the consequent growth in capacity for independent functioning. Although the study is empirical, the methodology and analysis of results incorporate clinical observation and theory. For example, the measurement of separation reaction includes assessment of defensive behaviors not directly linked to the separation event. Further, in distinguishing healthy, adaptive reactions to separation from separation problems, the author uses a multidimensional model of what constitutes the dividing line between expectable distress and emotional difficulty. By using a short-term longitudinal design, the author is able to consider such factors as the intensity of distress, its developmental course over time, and its mode of expression. This composite index of separation behavior turns out to be conceptually important and empirically powerful as a predictor of separation problems.*

Children with separation problems exhibit general emo-

tional difficulty in the school setting, showing apathy and with-drawal as well as problematic expressions of aggression. The quality of the preexisting mother-child relationship is found to predict separation problems, as would be expected by both psy-choanalytic and attachment theory approaches to separation. Various findings of interest are reported, including how chil-dren's mastery of separation is related to use of the classroom teacher as an alternative caregiver and how the father's family involvement is related to the child's psychosocial adjustment. In addition to studying children and their interpersonal relation-ships, the research examined dimensions of the setting, finding that these factors also influenced the scope of separation reac-tions.

The transition from home to nursery school occurs at a critical stage in children's social and emotional development, as they are learning to function more independently, with growing ini-tiative and an evolving identity. Given its timing, nursery school entry provides a fertile context for studying the natural inter-play between a particular *event* requiring physical separation of child and parent and the ongoing developmental *process* through which the child becomes increasingly separate and independent. Thus, nursery school may provide a natural laboratory for study-ing how the child's experience of separation and way of master-ing the challenges posed by the need for separateness help to determine how the child eventually copes with the complex in-terpersonal world beyond the family.

Although psychodynamic and developmental perspectives suggest that later competence has its roots in successful mastery of the stresses of early separation experiences (for example, Blatt, 1974; Escalona, 1968; Mahler, Pine, and Bergman, 1975; Matas, Arend, and Sroufe, 1978), the empirical literature gener-ally offers little documentation of the natural course of separa-tion reactions and the meaning of alternative modes of express-ing distress during the transition to nursery school. In this chapter I briefly review the literature on nursery school entry and then outline a research study undertaken to explore the broader implications of responses to separation in nursery school.

This research, though empirical, was guided by psychoanalytic insights about the dynamics, behavioral patterning, and developmental modifications of responses to separation. As will be discussed later in more detail, the response to nursery school separation was examined, not as an isolated phenomenon, but as a reflection of the overall parent-child relationship, a personality/ adjustment factor central to the child's capacity to adapt. Further, response to separation was considered in both behavioral and psychological terms. Hence, indirect reactions to separation identifiable only by theoretical (psychoanalytic) inference were measured along with the more familiar behavioral reactions. The short-term longitudinal design enabled study of the evolving pattern of separation responses within the broader context of nursery school adjustment.

Literature on Nursery School Entry

The problematic nature of separation for the young child has long been recognized by educators and mental health professionals concerned with facilitating preschool adjustment (Adams and Passman, 1983; Gross, 1970; Provence, 1974; Read, 1971; Signell, 1976). Currently, with widespread maternal employment creating heightened needs for child care outside the home, the effects of daily mother-child separations increasingly interest not only researchers and clinicians but policy makers as well (Anderson, 1980; Hayes and Kamerman, 1983; Kamerman and Hayes, 1982). This impetus has helped to focus a large body of investigations on the psychological, behavioral, and cognitive consequences of separation for children under age two; Lieberman's discussion of separation in infancy (Chapter Three) details this line of inquiry.

For the infant and toddler, effects of child care remain controversial. However, most three-year-olds are deemed ready to venture beyond the home sphere and into the nursery school, the separation from mother being viewed as a stressful but growth-promoting experience. Investigators report many manifestations of separation distress at nursery school entry. Studies by developmental psychologists focus on direct expressions like crying, clinging, and verbal protest (Blurton Jones and Leach, 1972; Doris, McIntyre, Kelsey, and Lehman, 1971; Field and others, 1984). In contrast, clinically informed observers have focused on indirect or defensive expressions of separation distress, such as reluctance to join in school activities (Furman, 1972; Miller, 1968), initial smooth entry followed by extreme distress (Janis, 1964), and reliance on transitional objects in school (van Leeuwen and Pomer, 1969). Theoreticians, both developmental and psychoanalytic, agree that some sadness, fear, and anger are *expectable* responses to separation (for example, Ainsworth and Wittig, 1969; Bowlby, 1973; Furman, 1972) and must be distinguished from separation *problems,* which interfere with overall school adjustment and personality functioning.

Along this line, Weinraub and Lewis (1977) make a useful distinction between departure protest and separation distress, noting that many children react negatively to the parent's leave-taking but readily adjust once the parent is gone. The picture of a nursery schooler actively registering dismay at the prospect of mother's departure and then happily turning toward classroom activities does not portray a separation *problem.* Rather, the child's protest at leave-taking may be part of an emotionally expressive style that should not be considered a reflection of anxiety over separation. Thus, departure protest in itself may reveal little about the child's capacity to function independently and eventually to adjust well to school. Indeed, on the contrary, the ability to clearly identify and openly express distress may reflect a healthy, adaptive style. From this perspective, the meaning of distress at separation can be best understood by studying it within a natural context over time.

Unfortunately, some empirical studies of the transition to nursery school have taken a narrow focus on separation-related behavior, viewing overt distress as a sign of adjustment difficulty. From this perspective, minimal distress at separation should be correlated with better adaptation. In fact, this is the view held by many parents of nursery schoolers. The children's painful crying and clinging looks like a problem and feels distressing to the separating parent as well. Such a perspective seems to have guided the research by Schwarz and Wynn (1971), who measured children's separation response solely by crying manifested on the first day of school and one week later. They concluded that adjustment to school was rapid, and separation distress insignificant. Other studies (Barry and Barry, 1974; Peery and Aoki, 1982; van Leeuwen and Tuma, 1972) also focused on initial nursery school entry, with occasional follow-up ratings limited to discrete sessions.

Doris, McIntyre, Kelsey, and Lehman (1971), in a broader investigation of separation and nursery school entry, observed direct manifestations of separation distress over the first two weeks of nursery school and at intervals into the second semester. Entrance distress during the first two weeks of school was positively associated with parental ratings of proneness to separation anxiety (for example, reactions to strangers and to babysitters) rated before school entry. Doris and his colleagues concluded that responses to separation from parents played an important part in nursery schoolers' entrance distress and that distress at initial school entry was heightened by unfamiliarity with the school setting. By studying separation response over a longer adjustment period, Doris tried to disentangle expectable protest at separation from separation anxiety.

Focusing the lens still further, Bloom-Feshbach and Blatt (1982) conducted a short-term longitudinal study examining how separation reactions at nursery school entry related to social/emotional functioning in school. We found that direct distress (crying, clinging, verbal protest) in the early weeks of school was an expectable and seemingly adaptive response to separation, eventually giving way to healthy school adjustment. In contrast, distress at separation expressed later in the school year was associated with eventual poor school adjustment. Further, the study suggested that some problematic separation responses occurred at points other than actual leave-taking from parents and took an indirect or defensive form. We concluded that nursery school children's responses to separation should be considered in terms of the form they take and when they occur in the adjustment process, examining the separation event itself as well as points other than departure from the parent.

The value of examining behavior outside of the actual

leave-taking has been emphasized by data emerging from Ainsworth's strange-situation paradigm for assessing mother/infant attachment. Ainsworth and her colleagues (for example, Ainsworth, Blehar, Waters, and Wall, 1978; Main and Weston, 1981; Schwartz, 1983; Waters, 1978) consistently find that reunion behaviors are very reliable indicators of security of attachment. Lewis and Ban (1971) also highlight the difference between the process of leave-taking (when mother departs) and the state of being separate (when mother is absent). In addition to looking beyond the explicit behavioral event of separation for separation responses, it is also important to look beyond the strict "separation" meaning of these responses, by understanding their implications for personality and adjustment more broadly. Both psychoanalytic and attachment theories suggest that (1) the child's separation reactions reflect the overall quality of the parent/child relationship and (2) the nature of that relationship is the central influence on the child's social and emotional adjustment. Hence, I hypothesized that distinguishing the normative course of separation distress from separation problems would also differentiate normative from problematic adaptation to nursery school.

An Empirical Examination of Separation at Nursery School Entry: Approach, Methods, and Hypotheses

A research project was developed to study the entry and adjustment process at two nursery schools, taking into account the richness and complexity of separation phenomena for three-year-olds. Personnel at these schools, sensitive to the importance of this first organized school experience for the families, used similar procedures to prepare the children for the transition. Teachers made home visits before the start of the school year, and parents were encouraged to remain at school with their children as long as they deemed necessary.

Sample. The sample of thirty-six children (nineteen male) had an average age of thirty-nine months at the start of school. They came from middle-class families and attended two private nursery schools in an urban university community. At school A, classes met two or three half-days a week, with two teachers staffing a group of sixteen children. School B held classes three or five half-days a week, with three teachers each staffing five children. It was therefore possible to use frequency of school attendance and differential student/teacher ratio as variables in data analyses; see Bloom-Feshbach (1980) for reliability data as well as more detail about other elements of the methodology.

Design. The study followed a short-term longitudinal design, beginning with home interviews before the start of the school year and culminating in observations of adjustment at the end of the first semester. The broad-grained methodological approach centered on systematic observation of behaviors occurring naturally in the nursery school setting, sampling information from the salient domains of the child's world. The study considered characteristics of the child's family relationships and experience with separations before school entry, several dimensions of separation-related behavior in nursery school, and the child's seeking of the classroom teacher during the adjustment process. In addition to exploring the potential predictors of children's separation reactions, the study focused on whether, and in what ways, such separation responses would be related to eventual social/emotional functioning in school.

Separation-Related Data Predating Nursery School Entry. Information likely to shape the child's response to separation was gathered before school began. Home interviews conducted and rated according to preestablished criteria yielded data about (1) children's peer experience before nursery school entry, (2) their reactions to strangers, (3) maternal employment status, (4) quality of the mother-child relationship, (5) magnitude of maternal psychopathology, and (6) degree of paternal involvement in child rearing. Clinical judgment was required in gleaning and evaluating the interview material for these qualitative assessments. For example, the rating of the quality of the mother-child relationship took into account the degree and balance of nurturance and firmness (Baumrind, 1967), sensitivity to the child's particular needs at this developmental stage (Paul, 1970), ability to relate to the child as a separate person, rather than as an extension of self (Dally, 1976; Mahler, Pine, and Bergman,

1975), calmness or tension in manner of relating to the child (Ainsworth, 1973), and ability to balance the mother's and the child's needs (Stierlin, Levi, and Savard, 1971). In this last example, ratings were based on questions concerning the mother's feelings about nursery school entry (spending less time with the child, seeing the child's growing independence, and so on) as well as on clinical observation during the interview. Similarly, ratings of paternal involvement (based primarily on maternal report) considered the father's affective relationship with the child, his practical caregiving responsibilities, and his interest and motivation in performing tasks around the household. Paternal involvement was deemed important both in its direct effect on the child's ability to master separation (Lamb, 1981) and in its indirect effect, by moderating maternal stress (Carew, 1978; Garbarino, 1976; Pederson, Anderson, and Cain, 1980).

The Separation Problems Index: Separation-Related Behavior and Teacher Seeking. One goal of the study was to develop a quantifiable index of overall separation-related behavior. A central function of this composite index was to distinguish separation *problems* from among the body of separation-related responses. Theory and research suggested three important dimensions of the nursery school child's response to separation: the *nature* of separation distress (direct versus indirect or defensive), the *pattern* of distress (decreasing versus increasing over time), and the *magnitude* of distress (mild versus intense). The Separation Problems Index was created to capture the complex and changing elements of separation reactions by considering how, when, and to what extent these responses manifest. This measure, combining the three salient dimensions of separation distress, was hypothesized to predict the quality of nursery school adjustment.

The importance of specifying the form that a child's distress takes is evident from a clinical perspective. Not all children express their distress directly; distress that must be disguised or defended against is no less severe despite its indirectness. This idea receives empirical support from a laboratory study of two-year-olds (Weinraub and Lewis, 1977) and a field study of three-year-olds (Bloom-Feshbach and Blatt, 1982). Indeed,

Weinraub and Lewis (1977) found that children's distress while separated from mother (reflected in crying and inability to engage in play when mother was absent) was linked only to "passive distress" at leave-taking, not to "active distress" at leave-taking (departure protest). Hence, one might hypothesize that open expression of problematic affect reflects a healthier coping style during this developmental stage. In fact, Lutkenhaus, Grossman, and Grossman (1985) recently found that securely attached three-year-olds tended to display sadness more openly than insecurely attached children after failing in a game.

Children who loudly protest separation from parents, actively demonstrating their feelings, need not mask or deny the natural sadness, anger, and anxiety sparked by the parent's departure (for example, Bowlby, 1969; Furman, 1972). In contrast, other children show little or no overt discomfort. The defensive nature of their acquiescence to separation may be evident only after the parent has departed. For example, the child may remain rooted to the spot where mother left, seemingly oblivious to surrounding play opportunities. This difficulty in making the transition to independent functioning reflects a pattern of underlying insecurity and distress at separation, even though no overt departure protest is apparent. Only when feelings of distress are more directly acknowledged can the adaptive process of school adjustment proceed. Thus, this view suggests that indirect expressions of separation distress are more problematic than direct expressions of distress, a crucial distinction in light of a narrow emphasis on direct separation protest in much research on adjustment.

A second important dimension of the separation response is its *pattern* of expression. In other words, beyond the expectable distress at initial school entry, does the child's distress mount or does it diminish over time? Naturalistic empirical studies of nursery school entry show that group levels of separation distress consistently decrease over time (Bloom-Feshbach and Blatt, 1982; Doris, McIntyre, Kelsey, and Lehman, 1971; Field and others, 1984). As children grow familiar with school and its routines, they become accustomed to functioning apart from their parents. Hence, separation distress declines naturally.

Some children, however, do not follow this typical pattern. As the weeks go by, their distress at separation mounts rather than diminishes. Clinical observers of this phenomenon have noted that children who express distress openly later in the school year may have defensively denied their fear and sadness at initial school entry (Furman, 1972; Janis, 1964). On this basis, it was hypothesized that a pattern of distress increasing over time is more problematic than a pattern of decreasing distress.

The third salient dimension of separation distress is its intensity, or *magnitude*. Although some distress at separation is expectable and indeed is a healthy reflection of attachment, sustained high levels of distress signal separation problems. In fact, most developmental studies of nursery school entry focus only on this dimension of separation distress (for example, Miller, 1968; Schwarz and Wynn, 1971). Thus, higher levels of separation distress, whatever their nature, were hypothesized to be more problematic than lower levels.

The Separation Problems Index was computed as a composite of these three dimensions of separation response, using data from a twenty-item behavioral rating scale (the Direct and Indirect Separation Anxiety Rating Scale for Teachers) completed by teachers after each nursery school session for the first eight weeks of school. The scale included items assessing children's direct responses to separation from parent (for example, clinging and crying), indirect responses to separation (for example, looking for parents after they had left school; using transitional objects in school), and teacher-seeking behavior not necessarily linked to separation (for example, seeking teacher's affection through attention; turning to teacher for help in dealing with peers).

The Separation Problems Index incorporated observational data measuring direct and indirect separation distress over the first two months of nursery school attendance. Thus, children with high scores on the Separation Problems Index showed high levels of both direct and indirect distress, expressed distress more indirectly than directly, and increased their expressions of distress over time. Reliability data for the separation measures and computational procedures for the Separation Problems Index can be found in Bloom-Feshbach (1980).

Separation and Eventual School Adjustment. As already noted, the goal of the research was to understand how children with separation problems would fare in the nursery school classroom as the year progressed. To measure school adaptation, the widely used Kohn Social Competence Scale and Kohn Problem Checklist (Kohn and Rosman, 1972a, 1972b) were independently rated by observers during a two-week period at the end of the semester. On these measures, the child's social and emotional functioning is characterized by two main factors: (1) interest versus apathy and (2) cooperation versus defiance. On theoretical grounds, I presumed that separation problems would likely interfere with adjustment along both dimensions. Both psychoanalytic views of the interpersonal competence afforded by the firm establishment of libidinal object constancy (Mahler, Pine, and Bergman, 1975) and attachment research findings on separation mastery and overall adjustment (Ainsworth, Blehar, Waters, and Wall, 1978; Bowlby, 1969, 1973; Matas, Arend, and Sroufe, 1978) suggested that children with less separation difficulty would be more involved with peers and teachers and more invested in school activities. In addition, those children who had experienced a healthy caregiving relationship, which leads to fewer problems with separation, would likely adhere better to classroom work, structure, and norms. Consistent with this view, the child with more separation difficulty would likely harbor heightened anger or hostility resulting from frustrations in the parent/child relationship. Thus, I hypothesized that defiant as well as apathetic social and emotional functioning at the end of the first semester would be associated with separation difficulties, as measured by the Separation Problems Index. I predicted that symptoms of both apathy and defiance, falling outside the range of behaviors normally exhibited in school, were even more likely to be associated with separation *problems,* though not with separation responses more broadly.

It should be noted that the Kohn Social Competence Scale reflects behaviors normally exhibited by preschoolers, while the Kohn Problem Checklist measures clinically significant behaviors. For example, symptoms of apathy include "fails to play with other children," and symptoms of defiance include "bullies other children or hits or picks on them." Thus, the two

Kohn adjustment measures provide a means of assessing the normative distribution of adjustment responses as well as more troublesome symptoms of adjustment difficulty.

Results: Separation Responses Versus Separation Problems— School and Family Correlates

The pattern of results showed that the three elements of separation response—its nature, timing, and intensity—were meaningful indicators of eventual school adjustment. Direct expressions of distress at separation were highest during the first two weeks of school and decreased steadily thereafter. In contrast, indirect expressions of distress remained constant in their intensity over the first eight weeks of school. Separation distress manifested in the first two weeks of school, regardless of its nature, was not significantly associated with eventual social/emotional functioning. Thus, as hypothesized, some separation-related behavior, however distressed the child may appear, poses no problem for adjustment. However, direct distress in weeks seven and eight and indirect distress beyond week two were correlated with problematic adjustment. This finding suggests that some separation responses may indicate ongoing difficulties that do warrant concern.

The Separation Problems Index provided a concise, comprehensive, and statistically powerful way to examine the meaning of the children's separation-related behavior. Children with high scores on the index—those whose separation-related behavior was relatively intense, who showed distress more indirectly, and whose distress mounted rather than diminished over the first two months of school—were less interested and participated less in their school environment. Children with separation problems also exhibited clinical symptoms of both apathy and defiance at the end of the first semester of nursery school. In a forward stepwise multiple-regression analysis of social/emotional adjustment, the child's separation behavior emerged as the most powerful predictor of social/emotional functioning; having fewer separation problems (as indicated by the index) was associated with healthy school participation. The other variables combining to predict adjustment were degree of maternal psychopathology, maternal employment, father's involvement with the child, and quality of the mother-child relationship. When alternative separation indexes (such as total distress, total direct distress, total indirect distress, direct distress in weeks seven and eight, and indirect distress in weeks seven and eight) replaced the Separation Problems Index as independent variables in equivalent multiple-regression procedures, none of these one-dimensional variables accounted for as much variance as the index in predicting social/emotional functioning. When these alternative separation variables were entered as predictors along with the Separation Problems Index, the greater predictive power of the index prevented their entry into regression equations. Evidently, then, by integrating theoretically predictable ideas about separation, the Separation Problems Index empirically measures a more meaningful configuration of separation-related behavior.

It is also interesting to ask what factors account for separation problems during nursery school entry, considering such disparate domains as the school, the family, and the history and behavior of the individual child. The data showed that the quality of the mother-child relationship, the extent of the father's family involvement, and the student/teacher ratio in the classroom were the most important predictors of the child's score on the Separation Problems Index. The better the relationship between mother and child, the less the child manifested separation problems during the school entry process. It is noteworthy that a better mother-child relationship was related to a lower degree of maternal psychopathology and to a lesser history of stranger anxiety in the child. These latter variables were not themselves significant predictors of separation problems, suggesting that the effects of stranger anxiety and maternal psychopathology are derivatives of the more essential overriding impact of the quality of the maternal relationship.

This major predictor of separation problems—the quality of the maternal relationship—was also highly correlated with teacher-seeking behavior early in the entry process. Early teacher seeking was associated with a strong mother-child bond and, as might be expected from the pattern of findings, with fewer separation problems as well. Thus, the child's reliance on classroom teachers early in the adjustment process appears to serve an adaptive function. A stronger relationship with the mother may foster the child's seeking of attention and contact from other adults in the face of novel, stressful experience, reflecting healthy dependency. This strong tie appears to enhance children's trust, enabling them to avail themselves of the teacher's help in the new environment. Returning to the data, it is interesting that teacher-seeking variables do not enter into the multiple-regression equation for the Separation Problems Index; this suggests that variance predictive of separation problems is commonly shared by the mother-child relationship and the early teacher-seeking variables.

Beyond initial school entry, the child's seeking of the classroom teacher was not significantly related to separation problems. However, by the second month of school, teacher seeking was predictive of anger and defiance, suggesting that motivations for seeking the teacher's attention may be different as the adjustment process proceeds. Children who consistently seek out the teacher after the first few weeks of school may be overly dependent or indiscriminate in their attempts to gain adult attention. This kind of behavior may be distinguished from more differentiated attempts to engage *particular* others during stressful transitions.

One factor related to the environment—the student-teacher ratio of the classroom—emerged as an important predictor of separation problems. When there are fewer children per teacher, there are fewer separation problems. The better ratio yields easier access to the classroom teacher, which may facilitate the separation process. The high correlation between student/teacher ratio and teacher-seeking behavior shows that, over and above the impact of a crucial family antecedent of separation behavior (the mother-child relationship), the school environment exerts a substantial influence on the separation process as well. It is curious to note that the environmental variable of significance at nursery school entry is the opportunity for access to the teacher, not the sheer amount of time away from mother; attending school two, three, or five half-days a week did not affect separation reactions. This underscores the interpersonal meaning of the separation experience for the child, since mastery is facilitated by opportunities for developing alternative object relations.

A final result to consider is that children of more involved fathers also manifest fewer separation problems. Paternal family involvement was a significant predictor of the child's separation behavior, even beyond the variance attributable to the mother-child relationship. Further, in this sample, fathers whose wives were employed outside the home were more involved in family functioning, suggesting that the influence of the father-child relationship may be especially salient in the mother's absence. Thus, the paternal relationship, along with the maternal one, appears to be a central antecedent variable that shapes the child's response to separation, which, in turn, is highly predictive of nursery school adjustment.

Separation, Separateness, and Emotional Adjustment

It comes as no surprise to clinicians and educators that many children who vigorously protest separation from their mothers when beginning nursery school nonetheless adjust well and eventually thrive in the school environment. Of greater interest are the variations in children's responses to separation, the antecedents of these different patterns, and the links between separation-related behavior and school behavior that is clinically symptomatic.

There are many reasons that children protest the parent's departure when nursery school begins. The environment is novel, and classmates and teachers are unfamiliar. Parental leave-taking may anger the child, threatening the three-year-old's developing and still precarious sense of control. The nursery schooler may be fearful of being left alone, perhaps uncertain about whether mother will return. On an even more basic level, the need to function autonomously at school may be difficult for a child still dependent on mother for help with affect regulation. Psychoanalytic theories of development suggest that the former two reasons for distressful protest (novelty and control) are likely to dissipate without undue difficulty as long as the image of the absent parent has been internalized in a manner incorporating both frustrating and gratifying elements. Such integrative parental representations facilitate the child's natural experience of anger and protest at the loss of the parent. In other words, the achievement of object constancy should mitigate separation anxiety, permit the working through of troubled affect, promote a healthy reliance on the teacher as a substitute attachment figure, and thereby facilitate the transition to nursery school.

The research reported in this chapter supports the theoretically predicted distinction between distress at separation and true separation difficulty, and it elaborates some features of both healthy and pathological separation reactions during the school adjustment process. In the sample studied, no single dimension of separation distress predicted eventual adjustment as well as a composite, taking into account the intensity of the distress, the form of its expression, and the course the distress took over time. Use of this composite index to capture a complex psychological phenomenon reflects the view that research will be more efficacious in assessing real-life phenomena and will yield clinically meaningful findings to the degree that the means of measurement integrate divergent elements, much as the human observer would.

Our understanding of separation and loss suggests that such experiences can provide a spur to development, fostering further internalization and continuing healthy growth. This appeared to occur for many of the nursery schoolers under study, children who actively cried, protested, and clung to their mothers during the first two weeks of school and sought help and attention from their teachers during this initial school entry period. By the end of the first semester, these children were thriving in the school environment, actively involved in classroom life, and less dependent on the teacher.

In contrast, for other children, nursery school entry was not so smooth, and adaptation to school was marked by the emergence of clinically symptomatic behavior. Interestingly, separation problems were associated *both* with extremely defiant classroom behavior and with extreme apathy. Although a much larger sample would be needed to empirically identify different constellations of problematic separation-related behavior, this study provided observational evidence of individual differerences in maladaptive separation reactions. These different ways of responding to separation seem to reflect both temperamental differences and distinct defensive styles. We observed three variations of separation problems, two involving direct separation distress and one involving indirect manifestations of separation difficulty: (1) overt separation protest continuing unabated over the first two months of school, (2) initial leave-taking with apparent ease, followed by vigorous protest emerging after several weeks, and (3) indirect manifestations of distress occurring consistently over the first two months of school.

These problematic separation response patterns all reflect a developmental lack of readiness for the level of independent functioning needed for healthy school adjustment. Some children experience parental absence as abandonment or rejection (Ainsworth and Wittig, 1969); insufficient parental nurturance makes the separation an overwhelming anaclitic deprivation. For other children, a central underlying dynamic may be conflicts over hostile impulses toward the absent parent. A troubled early parent-child relationship evokes an abundance of aggressive feelings in the child, making the additional rage at separation unmanageable (Mahler, Pine, and Bergman, 1975; Main, 1977). These different emotional difficulties reflect a failure to achieve the level of object constancy, and the consequent psychological organization, expectable for the three-year-old.

All of the relevant theoretical approaches—attachment, self psychology, object relations, and ego psychology—embed the separation response in the nature of the early mother-child relationship. The findings of this research lend further support to this emphasis, illustrating that the quality of the tie with the mother is the strongest predictor of a healthy response to separation. Perhaps of greater interest, we find that a positive tie with the father facilitates separation at this juncture as well. The finding that children of more involved fathers have less problematic separation reactions may be understood in several ways. Research studies show that infants cared for by father *and* mother, and human and monkey infants with less exclusive attachments, are less distressed by separation (Kaufman and Rosenblum, 1969; Mead, 1962; Spelke, Zelazo, Kagan, and Kotelchuck, 1973). In addition, fathers may serve as alternative, compensatory attachment figures when the maternal relationship is troubled, providing a secure base that facilitates separation at nursery school entry (Bloom-Feshbach, Bloom-Feshbach, and Gaughran, 1980; Schaffer, 1971). Also important is the father's role in helping the young child separate from the more engulfing early tie with mother (Abelin, 1971; Mahler and Gosliner, 1955).

Good parent-child relationships enhance children's trust in the ability of adults to meet their needs when they are distressed, providing a backdrop for appropriate reliance on the nursery school teacher at the start of school. Thus, we find a negative association between early teacher seeking and separation problems. In other words, a good primary attachment relationship facilitates the child's ability to rely effectively on substitute caregivers in a stressful situation like the transition to nursery school. However, as the school year progresses, healthy adaptation depends on the child's motivation and ability to actively investigate the environment and interact confidently with peers; this process of moving away from exclusive reliance on the primary caregiver in school parallels the mother-child separation. We find that children who seek high levels of attention from their teachers later in the adjustment process are angry and defiant by the end of the first school semester. Such children may be considered overly dependent and reflect the emotional difficulties one would expect in children who do not have a secure nurturant foundation.

Attempting to disentangle the concepts of attachment, dependency, and overdependency, Sroufe and his colleagues (Sroufe, Fox, and Pancake, 1983) found that four-year-olds who had been securely attached as infants showed less emotional dependence on their teachers, although they readily sought help from their teachers when appropriate. Describing these children, they report: "Despite their substantial amount of initiated contact, teachers did not view 'secure' children as highly emotionally dependent . . . their contact was smooth, situationally appropriate, and effective. When they needed nurturance, they sought it directly and found the contact reassuring" (p. 1625). In contrast, preschoolers who had been anxiously attached in infancy were overly dependent on their teachers: "Their need for contact, approval, and attention from adults interfered with other developmental tasks, such as peer relations and environmental mastery" (p. 1626).

Easy access to the teacher—afforded by a low number of children per teacher—also appears to help with the separation process. This finding suggests that modifications in the school environment are important in mitigating separation difficulties, exerting an influence over and above the children's predispositions to avail themselves of adult help. Indeed, with elementary school children, a lesser number of new students in a classroom is associated with reduced adjustment problems (Hughes, Pinkerton, and Plewis, 1979). Further, in a small classroom, more attention can be given to the needs of each individual, making school interactions more similar to home life. These findings underscore the importance of taking a systems perspective: by looking at the whole configuration of a child's life—home *and* school conditions—we can better understand the child's ability to cope with a potentially stressful transition like nursery school entry.

In sum, nursery school entry provides an especially rich array of data about children's capacities to cope with separation, coming at a time in life when separation reactions should be diminishing, according to both ethological (Bowlby, 1973) and psychoanalytic (Mahler, Pine, and Bergman, 1975) theories. At this critical juncture of development, nursery school experience offers an opportunity to solidify the psychological sense of separateness and the capacity for developing independence. Alternatively, the stress of this transition may contribute to an ongoing negative cycle of inadequate nurturance and heightened frustration that exacerbates both internal difficulties in differentiation and behavioral struggles with dependency.

Future research on separation and preschool adjustment will need to go a step further, finding a window into the child's internal world by exploring the self- and object representational level that mediates observable behavior. In this direction, recent work by attachment researchers (Main, Kaplan, and Cassidy, 1985) and psychoanalytic theorists (Behrends and Blatt, 1985) converges, offering promise for deepening our understanding of the psychological processes that govern the meaning of separation.

References

Abelin, E. L. "The Role of the Father in the Separation-Individuation Process." In J. B. McDevitt and C. F. Settlage (eds.), *Separation-Individuation: Essays in Honor of Margaret S. Mahler.* New York: International Universities Press, 1971.

Adams, R. E., and Passman, R. H. "Explaining to Young Children About an Upcoming Separation from Their Mother: When Do I Tell Them?" *Journal of Applied Developmental Psychology,* 1983, *4*(1), 35–42.

Ainsworth, M. D. S. "The Development of Infant-Mother Attachment." In B. M. Caldwell and H. N. Ricciuti (eds.), *Review of Child Development Research.* Vol. 3. Chicago: University of Chicago Press, 1973.

Ainsworth, M. D. S., Blehar, M. C., Waters, E., and Wall, S. *Patterns of Attachment: A Psychological Study of the Strange Situation.* Hillsdale, N.J.: Erlbaum, 1978.

Ainsworth, M. D. S., and Wittig, B. A. "Attachment and Exploratory Behavior of One-Year-Olds in a Strange Situation." In B. M. Foss (ed.), *Determinants of Infant Behavior.* Vol. 4. London: Methuen, 1969.

Anderson, C. W. "Attachment in Daily Separations: Reconceptualizing Day Care and Maternal Employment Issues." *Child Development,* 1980, *51*(1), 242–245.

Barry, A., and Barry, R. J. "Easing the Child's Entry into Kindergarten." *Perceptual and Motor Skills,* 1974, *38*(3), 762.

Baumrind, D. "Child Care Practices Anteceding Three Paterns of Preschool Behavior." *Genetic Psychology Monographs,* 1967, *75,* 43–88.

Behrends, R. S., and Blatt, S. J. "Internalization and Psychological Development Throughout the Life Cycle." *Psychoanalytic Study of the Child,* 1985, *40,* 11-39.

Blatt, S. J. "Levels of Object Representation in Anaclitic and Introjective Depression." *Psychoanalytic Study of the Child,* 1974, *29,* 107-157.

Bloom-Feshbach, S. "Separation Reactions and Nursery School Adjustment." *Dissertation Abstracts International,* 1980, *41-B*(11), 4251-B.

Bloom-Feshbach, S., and Blatt, S. J. "Separation and Nursery School Adjustment." *Journal of the American Academy of Child Psychiatry,* 1982, *21,* 58-64.

Bloom-Feshbach, S., Bloom-Feshbach, J., and Gaughran, J. "The Child's Tie to Both Parents: Separation Patterns and Nursery School Adjustment." *American Journal of Orthopsychiatry,* 1980, *50,* 505-521.

Blurton Jones, N., and Leach, G. M. "Behavior of Children and Their Mothers at Separation and Greeting." In N. Blurton Jones (ed.), *Ethological Studies of Child Behavior.* London: Cambridge University Press, 1972.

Bowlby, J. *Attachment and Loss.* Vol. 1: *Attachment.* New York: Basic Books, 1969.

Bowlby, J. *Attachment and Loss.* Vol. 2: *Separation: Anxiety and Anger.* New York: Basic Books, 1973.

Carew, M. C. "Employment and Mothers' Emotional States: A Psychological Study of Women Reentering the Work Force." Unpublished doctoral dissertation, Department of Psychology, Yale University, 1978.

Dally, A. *Mothers: Their Power and Influence.* London: Weidenfeld and Nicolson, 1976.

Doris, J., McIntyre, A., Kelsey, C., and Lehman, E. "Separation Anxiety in Nursery School Children." *Proceedings of the Annual Convention of the American Psychological Association,* 1971, *6,* 145-146.

Escalona, S. *Roots of Individuality: Normal Patterns of Development in Infancy.* Hawthorne, N.Y.: Aldine, 1968.

Field, T., and others. "Leavetakings and Reunions of Infants, Toddlers, Preschoolers, and Their Parents." *Child Development,* 1984, *55*(2), 628-635.

Furman, R. A. "Experiences in Nursery School Consultations." In K. R. Baker (ed.), *Ideas That Work with Young Children.* Washington, D.C.: National Association for the Education of Young Children, 1972.

Garbarino, J. "A Preliminary Study of Some Ecological Correlates of Child Abuse: The Impact of Socioeconomic Stress on Mothers." *Child Development,* 1976, *47,* 178-185.

Gross, D. "On Separation and School Entrance." *Childhood Education,* 1970, pp. 250-253.

Hayes, C. D., and Kamerman, S. B. (eds.). *Children of Working Parents: Experiences and Outcomes.* Washington, D.C.: National Academy Press, 1983.

Hughes, M., Pinkerton, G., and Plewis, I. "Children's Difficulties on Starting Infant School." *Journal of Child Psychology and Psychiatry,* 1979, *20,* 187-196.

Janis, M. *A Two-Year-Old Goes to Nursery School.* London: Tavistock, 1964.

Kamerman, S. B., and Hayes, C. D. (eds.). *Families That Work: Children in a Changing World.* Washington, D.C.: National Academy Press, 1982.

Kaufman, I. C., and Rosenblum, L. A. "Effects of Separation from Mother on the Emotional Behavior of Infant Monkeys." *Annals of the New York Academy of Sciences,* 1969, *159,* 681-695.

Kohn, M., and Rosman, B. L. "A Social Competence Scale and Symptom Checklist for the Preschool Child: Factor Dimensions, Their Cross-Instrument Generality and Longitudinal Persistence." *Developmental Psychology,* 1972a, *6*(3), 430-444.

Kohn, M., and Rosman, B. L. "Relationship of Preschool Social-Emotional Functioning to Later Intellectual Achievement." *Developmental Psychology,* 1972b, *6*(3), 445-452.

Lamb, M. E. (ed.). *The Role of the Father in Child Development.* (2nd ed.) New York: Wiley, 1981.

Lewis, M., and Ban, P. "Stability of Attachment Behavior: A Transformational Analysis." Paper presented at the meeting of the Society for Research in Child Development at the Symposium on Attachment: Studies in Stability and Change, Minneapolis, April 1971.

Lutkenhaus, P., Grossmann, K. E., and Grossmann, K. "Infant-Mother Attachment at Twelve Months and Style of Interaction with a Stranger at the Age of Three Years." *Child Development*, 1985, *56*, 1538–1542.

Mahler, M. S., and Gosliner, B. J. "On Symbiotic Child Psychosis: Genetic, Dynamic, and Restitutive Aspects." *Psychoanalytic Study of the Child*, 1955, *10*, 195–212.

Mahler, M. S., Pine, F., and Bergman, A. *The Psychological Birth of the Human Infant: Symbiosis and Individuation.* New York: Basic Books, 1975.

Main, M. "Analysis of a Peculiar Form of Reunion Behavior Seen in Some Daycare Children: Its History and Sequelae in Children Who Are Home-Reared." In R. Webb (ed.), *Social Development in Childhood: Daycare Programs and Research.* Baltimore: Johns Hopkins University Press, 1977.

Main, M., Kaplan, N., and Cassidy, J. "Security in Infancy, Childhood, and Adulthood: A Move to the Level of Representation." In I. Bretherton and E. Waters (eds.), "Growing Points of Attachment Theory and Research." *Monographs of the Society for Research in Child Development*, 1985, *50*(1–2, Serial No. 209).

Main, M., and Weston, D. R. "The Quality of the Toddler's Relationship to Mother and to Father: Related to Conflict Behavior and the Readiness to Establish New Relationships." *Child Development*, 1981, *52*, 932–940.

Matas, L., Arend, R. A., and Sroufe, L. A. "Continuity of Adaptation in the Second Year: The Relationship Between Quality of Attachment and Later Competence." *Child Development*, 1978, *49*, 547–556.

Mead, M. "A Cultural Anthropologist's Approach to Maternal Deprivation." In *Deprivation of Maternal Care: A Reassessment of Its Effects.* Public Health Papers, No. 14. Geneva: World Health Organization, 1962.

Miller, J. "Separation Anxiety and Adjustment to Nursery School: A Study of 100 Children." *American Journal of Orthopsychiatry*, 1968, *38*, 339.

Paul, N. "Parental Empathy." In E. J. Anthony and T. Benedek (eds.), *Parenthood: Its Psychology and Psychopathology.* Boston: Little, Brown, 1970.

Pederson, F. A., Anderson, B. J., and Cain, R. L. "An Approach to Understanding Linkages Between the Parent-Infant and Spouse Relationships." In F. A. Pederson (ed.), *The Father-Infant Relationship: Observational Studies in a Family Context.* New York: Holt, Rinehart and Winston, 1980.

Peery, J. C., and Aoki, E. Y. "Leave-Taking Behavior Between Preschool Children and Their Parents." *Journal of Genetic Psychology,* 1982, *140*(1), 71–81.

Provence, S. "A Program of Group Day Care for Young Children." *Psychosocial Process,* 1974, *3,* 7–13.

Read, K. H. *The Nursery School: A Human Relations Laboratory.* (5th ed.) Philadelphia: Saunders, 1971.

Schaffer, H. R. "Cognitive Structure and Early Social Behavior." In H. R. Schaffer (ed.), *The Origins of Human Social Relations.* Orlando, Fla.: Academic Press, 1971.

Schwartz, P. "Length of Day-Care Attendance and Attachment Behavior in Eighteen-Month-Old Infants." *Child Development,* 1983, *54,* 1073–1078.

Schwarz, J. C., and Wynn, R. "The Effects of Mother's Presence and Previsits on Children's Emotional Reaction to Starting Nursery School." *Child Development,* 1971, *43,* 871–881.

Signell, K. A. "Kindergarten Entry: A Preventive Approach to Community Mental Health." In R. Moos (ed.), *Human Adaptation.* Lexington, Mass.: Heath, 1976.

Spelke, E., Zelazo, P., Kagan, J., and Kotelchuck, M. "Father Interaction and Separation Protest." *Developmental Psychology,* 1973, *7,* 83–90.

Sroufe, L. A., Fox, N. E., and Pancake, V. R. "Attachment and Dependency in Developmental Perspective." *Child Development,* 1983, *54,* 1615–1627.

Stierlin, H., Levi, L. D., and Savard, R. J. "Parental Perceptions of Separating Children." *Family Process,* 1971, *10,* 411–427.

van Leeuwen, K., and Pomer, S. L. "The Separation-Adaptation Response to Temporary Object Loss." *Journal of Child Psychiatry,* 1969, *8,* 711–733.

van Leeuwen, K., and Tuma, J. M. "Attachment and Exploration: A Systematic Approach to the Study of Separation-

Adaptation Phenomena in Response to Nursery School Entry." *Journal of Child Psychiatry,* 1972, *11,* 314–340.

Waters, E. "The Reliability and Stability of Individual Differences in Infant-Mother Attachment." *Child Development,* 1978, *49,* 483–494.

Weinraub, M., and Lewis, M. "The Determinants of Children's Responses to Separation." *Monographs of the Society for Research in Child Development,* 1977, *42*(4, Serial No. 172).

7

Leaving Home: A Family Transition

Michael V. Bloom

Editors' Note: *This chapter takes a true family perspective on separation, viewing the family as the locus of difficulties and the most effective site for intervention. The stages of the separation process, the variables affecting how necessary losses will be experienced, and the treatment interventions delineated are all considered from the vantage point of parents as well as teenagers. Bloom reviews the literature on adolescent/parent separation, highlighting the key role of this transition in development. Although the separation process in many ways resembles other experiences involving loss, the adolescent's move toward autonomy is a natural life change, initiated by healthy development and encouraged by the culture.*

The author has developed a five-stage theory of adolescent/parent separation that begins with the ambivalent struggle to remain attached. As parents and teenager gradually accept the latter's emerging independence, the new sense of separateness stirs grief and pride. Eventually the adolescent's identity changes, as qualities of the parents are internalized; parents also expand their sense of self, finding new sources of gratification. In the final stage of the separation process, the former child/parent relationship recedes and a less dependent relationship between adults *is established. Bloom identifies several factors that determine how parents and adolescents will negotiate this de-*

232

velopmental sequence, including psychodynamic, cognitive, familial, and cultural dimensions. Vignettes of family therapy interventions, presented throughout, illustrate interesting clinical dynamics of the nature of boundaries, family communication patterns, displaced conflict, and confused family roles. Working from the theoretical model elaborated in the chapter, the author offers concrete ideas for facilitating adolescent/parent separation. The issues raised by Bloom emphasize that the process of separation holds unique meanings not only for those who initiate separation but also for those who are "left behind." Hence, the implications of separation experiences inevitably depend on the interplay among all who participate in the rearranging of intense interpersonal ties.

Janice is fifteen years old. Three years ago, her parents saw her as an "ideal" child, and she saw them as "ideal" parents. Now she and her parents argue all the time. She is quick to criticize everything her parents do, and yet, away from home and their ears, she supports much of what they believe. She is always saying she wants to be "left alone," but her actions constantly call her parents' attention to her. Her mother and father profess the desire to have their teenagers become more independent; at the same time, they find themselves helping their offspring much more than necessary, thus encouraging dependency.

It is evident that adolescence is a time of rapid change and, for many, a time of great turmoil. Of the many factors that contribute to the psychology of adolescent development, the most important is the interaction between parent and teenager. During this stage, the child/parent relationship develops into a more adult-to-adult relationship. The majority of serious problems develop during this period as a result of difficulty that parents and adolescents have in negotiating the transition to the more autonomous adult-to-adult relationship.

Many explanations have been offered for the seemingly contradictory behaviors of this period, including psychoanalytic psychosexual, psychoanalytic psychosocial, peer influence, and cognitive developmental. Indeed, many of these perspectives no doubt contribute to the story. However, reviewing this process of the transition to autonomy makes clear that it shares much with other separation processes, such as bereavement. Indeed, as I will describe, most of these perplexing behaviors become quite understandable within the separation (bereavement) framework. In fact, within this context the apparent contradictions emerge as necessary steps toward adult independence. In this chapter I describe the stages of adolescent separation and how they are related to the stages of bereavement. In this context, I discuss the variables that influence the process. I then discuss intervention for cases of problematic separation.

Studies of Adolescence

In the past, most explanations of adolescent rebellion have come from a psychoanalytic perspective. Blos (1962) has been a leader in describing adolescence from a traditional psychoanalytic, psychosexual viewpoint. He sees adolescent development as fueled by heightened libidinal energy, which brings out oedipal conflicts. Resolution of these conflicts occurs as the teenager withdraws the focus of the libidinal energy from parents and redirects it toward peers. Paris (1976) and Bowlby (1961, 1969) were among the first to suggest that many of the issues that Freud saw as oedipal were in fact issues of separation-individuation. Erikson (1950, 1968) shifted his psychoanalytic framework from a psychosexual to a psychosocial paradigm, with a focus on the identity diffusion that occurs during the move from childhood to adulthood. In the process of these changes, the self-identity moves from being established mainly within the context of the relationship to the parents to being based on the relationship with peers and finally settles as an integration of both.

Offer and Offer's study (1975; Offer, Ostrov, and Baker, 1981; Offer, 1969) of over seventy boys, ages fourteen to seventeen, is one of the few comprehensive studies of "normal" adolescence. The Offers not only did psychological testing and interviewing of the teenagers but interviewed the parents as well. They found adolescent/parent separation to be a central issue to the teenager and the parents. For example, they point out the nature of rebelliousness as being directed primarily toward separation from parents.

Pepitone (1981) studied object relational changes in adolescents from age twelve to the early twenties. Using a questionnaire to test these changes in cognition, she found that during the early stages of separation the relationship with parents was looked on from a very egocentric dependency/counterdependency viewpoint. The counterdependent pattern entails projecting an image of independence that defensively masks underlying dependency needs. By the early twenties, the research revealed a cognitive ability for mature empathy and acknowledgment of family loyalty, with a marked decrease in the egocentric dependency/counterdependency descriptions of the relationships.

Sullivan and Sullivan (1980) report on a questionnaire study comparing teenagers in high school with teenagers after they have left home to go to college. They found that boys, after leaving home, exhibited increased ability to express affection, more open communication, and more satisfaction with their relationship to their parents. Mothers reported increased ability to express affection. However, some fathers showed increases in dependency when their sons moved over 200 miles away. The Sullivans' overall conclusion was that the process had proceeded in a way that allowed the family greater communication of closeness while also facilitating a greater sense of independence.

The results of Kurash's (1979) study closely parallel the Sullivans' findings. Kurash surveyed 142 college freshmen before leaving home and again after being in college nearly six months. She found that there was more aggression toward parents before leaving home than after and that feelings of closeness were expressed more when physical distance was greater.

Many studies have demonstrated the key role of the adolescent move toward autonomy in the development of psychological problems. Hoffman (1984) found that emotional independence from parents strongly influenced work performance in female college students and love relations in both sexes. A study by Murphy and others (1962) suggested that many of the emotional problems teenagers face have roots in lack of preparedness among both them and their parents for issues of independence and separation. Mallnow (1981) studied teenagers, ages fourteen through eighteen, using a questionnaire measure of Mahler's separation-individuation theory. Mallnow found, as Mahler had with younger children, that rejecting and negative control by parents during individuation correlated with a high degree of depression among the teenagers. Stierlin (1974) has studied adolescent separation within the context of family systems. He sees the inability of the family system to deal with teenage separation as a central component in development of many of the problems of teenagers, including running away and other behavioral problems.

Many family therapists—for example, Haley (1980) and Minuchin, Rosman, and Baker (1970)—point to adolescent/parent separation as the key factor in the development of problems during this period of life. Haley implicated a host of associated problems, such as drug abuse and suicidal behavior, as being related to problems of "leaving home." Minuchin found that problems in separation were among the major contributors to psychosomatic illness.

Studies of Grief and Separation

It has become increasingly clear that adolescent/parent separation plays a key role in adolescent development. Bowlby and his associates have pointed out that the processes of separation, bereavement, and grief cross-cut various losses, including the loss of a parent, a spouse, or a friend. In fact, a review of descriptions of the process of separation shows remarkable similarity, whether they refer to termination of psychotherapy, limb loss, divorce, or even a move away from a close friend. It follows that an understanding of the general processes of separation and bereavement should shed light on adolescent/parent separation. In this section I review studies of separation and grief with an eye toward the common features that will enlighten our understanding of adolescent separation.

Charles Darwin (1859/1962) was the first to suggest that there was a universal grief reaction in humans. Observing similar body language in responses to the loss of a "close associate" in various cultures throughout the world, he postulated that there was a universal reaction to grief which was, at least in part, innate.

John Bowlby's (1961, 1969) studies of grief reactions in children, along with those of his colleagues exploring parallel processes in adults, together suggest delineating various stages in the bereavement process. Bowlby outlined three stages—protest, despair, and detachment. In the child, the stage of protest is characterized by a heightened emotional response, primarily anger and fear. The overall aim of this stage is reattachment to the lost parent. The second stage is despair. Its goal is coming to terms with the reality of the separation. The child is sad, distant, and unresponsive. The final stage is detachment. During this stage, the child moves from depressed affect and lack of interest in other people to an attenuation of the attachment feelings, return of activity, and openness to new relationships. If the parent returns before the third stage, the child remains as attached as ever. However, during the second stage, much anger is expressed toward the parent on reunion, which Bowlby believes is aimed at discouraging separation in the future. During the third stage, when the orientation is toward detachment, parental return is no longer greeted with hostility and eventual restoration of closeness. Behaviors in the third stage are aimed at the child's becoming open to a new attachment to a new adult parental figure. Researchers note that the one major difference between responses to separation in childhood and separation in later life is the child's greater need to form a new attachment as part of the final stage of the separation process. Adults are much more able to learn to provide for their own needs in a fulfilling way on completion of the separation process, and so they may do for themselves many of the things that the bereaved individual used to do. However, for the adult, as well as the child, the final stage usually entails a greater openness to new relationships.

As a result of his study of widows and widowers in London, Parkes (1972) developed a five-stage concept of the bereavement experience that closely corresponds to Bowlby's three stages. Parkes's first stage of bereavement is an "alarm" phase, characterized by a generalized fear response. In this stage there is a pervasive disbelief that the loss has occurred. The first stage passes quickly. The person then enters the second stage, which Parkes entitles the "searching" phase, marked by outward acceptance of the loss. In this stage there are episodic pangs of grief that become rather severe at times. There remains an inner disbelief that the love object is gone and a feeling of wanting to search for him or her. There is, furthermore, a sense of inner incompleteness. Descriptions of affect during this period often include the feeling of being pulled in two directions—avoidance and search. The main purpose of this stage is getting control over the desire to search for the lost person. This leads to the third stage, "mitigation," characterized by the general feeling that the love object is nearby although he or she cannot be seen or heard. Bereaved individuals have frequent episodes of pining and feelings of nostalgia. During this period the person is working to accept the loss and make sense of it. Parkes describes this stage as having three main components: preoccupation with memories of the person; painful, repetitious recollections of the loss experience, which continue until the loss is accepted; and an attempt to give the loss meaning within the context of one's life. Philosophy, religion, and creative activity often come into play at this stage of mourning, as the person sees his or her world in chaos and works to give it some kind of order. This stage ends with a true acceptance of the loss at both a conscious and an unconscious level.

This acceptance frees a strong affective response to the loss, which begins the fourth stage. Parkes calls this stage "anger and guilt"; it includes depressive withdrawal. Feelings of apathy and a depressive mood are much different from the pangs of fear felt in earlier stages. This depression is described by the bereaved as a dull, withdrawn feeling of sadness and despair. During this period, feelings of guilt come to the forefront, since all relationships involve some degree of ambivalence. How this guilt is dealt with may have a significant effect on whether pathological mourning develops.

When the loss has been dealt with on an affective level and the individual has come to grips with anger and guilt, the fifth stage begins. With the reality of the loss rationally and affectively incorporated, the griever reintegrates his or her identity as separate from the lost object. In doing this, bereaved individuals must learn to provide for themselves the benefits, both psychic and physical, that the deceased had formerly been depended on to provide. In some instances the bereaved introjects strengths of the other person into the self, and in other instances such qualities are sought in other individuals. The beginning of this period is characterized by feeling empty and lost and by a desire to find oneself. The phase concludes with establishment of a new identity and new patterns of behavior.

In a series of studies of divorce, Weiss (1975) has found a similar stage process of separation. This is true even though often the divorcing individuals are electively making the decision to separate. Marris (1974) has developed a similar set of stages for individuals migrating from their traditional neighborhoods to modern high-rise apartments in an African city. Parkes (1972) has conducted a similar study with parallel findings on limb loss. Many others have developed separation stages for all types of experiences from termination of psychotherapy to changing jobs. The dynamics are similar no matter what the circumstances of the separation. Because the process of separation in human relationships follows a similar pattern independent of the circumstances, the recurring theme of separation can teach us much about adolescent/parent interaction.

To summarize the recurring themes in separation studies: The initial response to separation is emotional intensity and an attempt to reattach to the lost object. This may include protests, alarm, panic, fear, and hyperactivity. The affect is not directed at anything but is free-floating. There is a general identity diffusion and an apathetic attitude toward new relationships, which lasts until the bereavement period is at least somewhat resolved. As the panic subsides, the person feels disbelief that the object is lost and a desire to search for it. When reattachment attempts fail, the individual must grapple with the reality of the loss. This is done by alternately embracing memories of the lost object (and feeling overwhelmed by these feelings) and avoiding the memories. When the loss is cognitively accepted, energy turns to the affect associated with the loss. This entails what we commonly call depression and despair. As ambivalence is involved in all close relationships, feelings of anger and guilt are also prominent during this period. When the affect has been confronted, the person, by a process of identification and internalization, gives up the attachment. That is, individuals begin to gratify for themselves the needs that the lost relationship used to meet. Next is the final stage, which brings a sense of separation, a new identity, and an opening up to new relationships and new activities.

The Process of Adolescent/Parent Separation and the Variables Affecting It

For the most part, adolescent/parent separation follows the course just outlined for separations generally. However, this separation process differs in some ways from other separations. It is a natural part of the life course. It is initiated by personal development and capabilities for self-sufficiency. It is encouraged by the culture, especially the peer culture, which shares in the experience. The separation process is also different in that it entails not a complete disengagement of the relationship but a change from a child/parent relationship to a more symmetrical adult-to-adult relationship. The powerful child/parent relationship so necessary to child development must be relinquished in order to allow the young adult to pursue independence in his or her future. In order to permit these changes to take place, many needs that were previously fulfilled by the parents must be given up so that other ways of relating can be established. This change is experienced as a loss, and therefore a bereavement reaction is triggered. Like all bereavement processes, this experience can evoke a mild response or a powerful, overwhelming one. It can be a developmental experience or a constricting one. The variables affecting this process are similar to those that affect all bereavement processes. This considerable similarity of variables can help in understanding what can go wrong.

Most descriptions of adolescent/parent separation are from the perspective of the teenager's development. However, the separation process is a powerful experience for the parents as well. As Erikson (1950, pp. 266–267) points out, "The fashionable insistence on dramatizing the dependence of children on adults often blinds us to the dependence of the older generation on the younger one. Mature man needs to be needed, and maturity needs guidance as well as encouragement from what has been produced and what must be taken care of." The parents as well, then, must learn to separate themselves from their own dependency on the teenager. Furthermore, the meaning for the parents of their separation from the teenager profoundly influences how the teenager experiences the separation, and vice versa. We must therefore study the move toward autonomy from both the parents' and the teenager's perspective.

In my studies of adolescent/parent separation (Bloom, 1980), I found it useful to divide this process into five stages: stage one, control of the impulse to remain attached; stage two, cognitive realization of the separation; stage three, affective response to the separation; stage four, identification; and stage five, attenuation of the child/parent relationship and corresponding development of a new relationship. It is well to keep in mind, as with all stage theories, that the stages represent shifts in emphasis rather than clear-cut changes in behavior. Further, as with all developmental processes, teenagers and parents proceeding through the stages of separation vacillate between progression and regression.

Stage One: Control of the Impulse to Remain Attached. By pubescence, the child is an expert at being a child, having developed comfortable ways of getting needs met and reliable expectations of parental responses to various behaviors. The onset of the separation process is often a perplexing experience for both child and parent, disrupting well-established patterns. Ways of interacting and behaving that were useful and successful in childhood are no longer satisfying to the emerging adolescent. More is open to question. The real cause of this dissatisfaction is often unclear initially, although many explanations may be used to reduce anxiety.

The process of separation begins with an ambivalent push/pull experience by both parents and teenager. The novice adolescent tests limits and is more oriented toward the peer group. Teenagers frequently become hypercritical of their parents as idealization of the parents breaks down. During this period, teenagers also experience discomfort with themselves. They find their own behavior less predictable, since they are acting in new ways, and they face uncertainty about how others will respond to their changing behavior. The pubescent's ambivalence about childhood dependency is reflected in vacillation between playing down the need for parental help and behaving in ways that exaggerate dependence. Since the teenager has depended on parental guidelines for self-identity, new attitudes toward parental guidance may result in identity diffusion.

Parents often respond to adolescent push/pull behavior with ambivalence as well as perplexity. They may be uncertain about how to understand the adolescent, who is clearly no longer a child nor yet capable of consistent adult functioning. The adolescent push/pull is often a confusing message for parents, generating frustration and anger on both sides. Emotional uproars by parents and teenagers are not uncommon. In time, most young adolescents and parents either consciously or unconsciously recognize this behavior as movement toward independence. The stage ends with an acceptance that the process of separation is beginning. This does not mean that the ambivalence about letting go has been resolved but that the commitment to the ultimate goal has shifted from maintenance of the attachment to eventual independence.

Consider the case of Barbara, thirteen. Just last year, Barbara's mother remembers, she was telling a friend what a perfect child her daughter was—loving, well disciplined, considerate. Now she has become "a real snot." Her mother complains that nothing she [the mother] ever does is "right" anymore. Barbara regards her father as bossy. She complains continually that her parents are always seeing her as a child. The parents argue that she certainly is no adult and point out to her, in heated arguments, all the things she does that are irresponsible. Then there are other times when Barbara seems to be her "old self" again—loving, well disciplined, considerate. At these times, she feels apologetic for her other behavior. As time passes, arguments become more frequent. A realization begins to dawn on the parents. Barbara's arguments have a purpose. Barbara is trying to prove to them how grown-up she is. Their little girl is no longer a little girl. This is met with a bit of sadness but a growing recognition that their stance toward their daughter must change. They must begin to find ways to help her feel more independent while not allowing her premature independence. They are not quite sure how this is to occur, since Barbara is their eldest and therefore their first teenager. This shift in orientation represents the change to stage two. The arguments between Barbara and her parents continue but now are seen from the perspective of the youngster's attempts to become more independent. Barbara's parents are not consciously aware of how they have made this shift; it just occurred over the past year without ever having been talked about. The orientation thus has shifted from maintaining closeness, security, and dependence within the relationship to a gradual letting go.

Families who are too rigid to make this shift usually develop patterns in which there is more and more exaggerated oscillation between rebellious and clinging behavior. Therapists will frequently find families perplexed by typical adolescent behaviors and/or attaching pathological meaning to them. Recognizing this as a stage one problem and helping them to accept the change in orientation to letting go is often one key to successful therapy with families presenting such difficulties. Giving positive connotations to the common behaviors of the stage is essential.

Stage Two: Cognitive Realization of the Separation. The main objective of stage two is the cognitive proof of the separation. Adolescents are very concerned with proving to themselves, their parents, and the world that they are indeed separating and becoming more independent. Parents are also involved in gaining a cognitive acceptance of the adolescent's emerging independence. The initial tentative questioning of limits becomes a continual bickering between adolescent and parent over household rules and limits. The disagreements may be over anything—politics, morality, philosophy of life, limit setting, and how soon the teenager may take on a new activity that entails greater responsibility. Infractions vary depending on how the adolescents need to prove to themselves and to their parents that they are indeed separating. At times, the cognitive proof of separation will lead adolescents to try alternative styles of dress, philosophical viewpoints, life goals, ego ideals, ethics, morality, and life-styles. Differences between teenager and parents are often exaggerated by the adolescent when interacting with parents. For example, Offer and Offer (1975) found that the boys they studied would often bicker and disagree on issues at home, while outside the home many of their allegiances remained true to the basic views of the parents. Further, parent surrogates such as teachers and the police are often rebelled against as a projection of the struggle to prove separation and self-sufficiency. This may occur when the parent/child relationship cannot tolerate conflict or when conflict is so great that it cannot be contained within the boundaries of the family. There is a wide diversity in the degree and type of rebellion that takes place, given the family dynamics. What is uniform, however, is that adolescents have to find a way to prove to themselves and their parents that they are becoming independent *in thought* as well as in action. At this point, adolescents equate being different from parents with being separate and independent. It is only after they have proved to their own satisfaction that they are separate that, in the later stages of separation, the rebelliousness will attenuate and commitment toward other goals will become possible. Caught in feeling the need to be less dependent on parental values yet still uncertain of their own values, adolescents look more to peers to provide guidelines. However, although parents frequently blame the peer group for the changes in the adolescents, adolescents usually choose peers to reflect and support the degree of rebelliousness that they find necessary during this stage to prove their independence.

Gradually relaxing their control, parents must experiment with allowing the adolescent more responsibility in response to his or her changing abilities. As much as adolescents protest parental authority, they derive needed security from it. Parents who too quickly give up control find their adolescents becoming more insecure and forcing more limits by increased acting out. Sensitive parents then provide more limits despite protest. During this stage, some parents also initiate arguments at times to show both their caring and their different point of view. Parents who accommodate their views to those of their adolescent in order to avoid conflict only make their adolescent's divergence more extreme, since its purpose is to demonstrate differences. Successful parents then either consciously or unconsciously find a dynamic stability in their rate of allowing greater independence, increasing and decreasing controls depending on the adolescent's fluctuating ability for self-control. In offering greater parental structure, it is important to keep in mind that the adolescent, though demonstrating a need for it, will not welcome it.

When Dave was sixteen, he had saved $300 from his part-time job, and he wanted to use it to buy a car. However, when his father went with him to look at the car, he found that it had almost no brakes. Dave did not have the money at the time to fix them. He said that he could easily downshift and drive very slowly and that the brakes would be good enough to stop him. His father stated that he could buy a car when he had enough money to buy a proper car and to take care of it. Dave did not feel his father had any right to interfere with his purchase. A big fight ensued, which concluded with Dave not talking to his father for several days. Then their relationship returned to normal. Another battle that erupted frequently between Dave and his father and mother was over going to church. Dave's parents were regular churchgoers, but Dave felt bored most of the time in church and found little value in it. His parents were angry about this and initially felt that Dave was overthrowing the most important values in their life. They considered it a personal rejection. However, when the dust settled, they recognized that Dave was trying to discover his own sense of ethics and values, and although they felt bad about his not going to church, they allowed him to decide. Another frequent fight was over how late he could stay out with his friends. During the week, he was expected to be home for dinner and then homework. Only after his homework was finished was he allowed to go out with his friends, to return by 9:30 P.M. Frequent, heated arguments took place about this rule, but the parents stuck with it. At calmer times, Dave's parents were able to maintain perspective, recognizing that these disagreements were related to Dave's growing independence and not seeing his behavior as a rejection of themselves. The parents were able to be both flexible at times and firm at others. Such flexibility and a basic trust in the relationship are critical factors in negotiating this stage of separation.

By the time Dave had turned eighteen and had been at college for several months, he recognized that he and his parents were fighting less. The parents had basic confidence in Dave's ability to take care of himself. They gave him a certain amount of money to augment his own summer earnings for his college expenses, and he was expected to make it last, which he did. At times, they still got into disagreements—for example, over his church attendance—but these were no longer regular occurrences. Dave and his parents had become much more comfortable with their sense of separateness from each other. Dave, therefore, markedly reduced his rebellious behavior, since he no longer had anything to prove.

The problems of this stage most commonly develop either when the changes and the proofs of growing independence are responded to too rigidly or when independence is allowed to develop too rapidly. Another common problem is parental conflict over how rapidly independence should be allowed. This conflict frequently reflects underlying conflict between the parents in other areas. For example, a teenager may be much more rebellious during this stage if one parent feels overly controlled by the other parent or if one parent is overcompensating for the other's strictness by being too lenient. When teenager and parents have a secure sense of separation, the second stage concludes.

Stage Three: Affective Response to the Separation. The sense of separateness, though long sought after by parents and teenager, stimulates strong feelings about the change in the relationship. Feelings most often described by both parents and adolescents during this stage are those of nostalgia for the past relationship. There is no desire to return to it. In fact, the nostalgia is usually felt openly when the separation is most secure.

The nostalgia then is a feeling response to the acknowledged loss of the former child/parent relationship. There is marked variability in how powerfully this nostalgia is felt, ranging from periodic rambling remembrances of the good times spent together to despair and depressive withdrawal. Associated anger and guilt are also common during this stage. Each of the participants is acutely aware of the pain that the separation has brought about in the other. As in all bereavements, each mourns the unfinished business and lost opportunities of the past relationship. When depression is prominent during this period, more powerful feelings of anger and guilt related to the separation are also likely to occur.

In this stage, parents and adolescent are searching for the meaning of the change in their relationship. Before a successful outcome of this stage can be reached, guilt and other strong affects must be fully resolved. There must also be a basic trust in the relationship so that the change toward greater autonomy is not felt as total rejection. The adolescent's goal is to be independent but still loved. The parents also want to know that if they accept the adolescent's autonomy, they will still be loved. Counterbalancing the emotions associated with grief are feelings of pride by both the parents and the adolescent in seeing the emergence of adulthood. This aids the mitigation process.

Dave is now eighteen years old. He has been 200 miles away at college for six months. Dave has noticed a marked decrease in the amount of arguing between himself and his parents. He has been home twice during school vacations. He now comes home to find that the bedroom that had been his has been rearranged: his belongings are neatly set on shelves, and the bedroom looks like a guest room. His mother, on the telephone the month before, had asked him whether this arrangement would be okay, and he had agreed. He also notices changes in the way his parents treat him. It is much closer to the adult-to-adult relationship he had been striving for. This is a marked change from when he had lived at home six months ago. Dave feels good about the sense of independence he is developing. He finds himself showing more affection toward his parents than he has shown in years. As he is driving back to school later, all of a sudden he starts to cry. He cannot understand his tears. For years, he has been trying to get his parents to see him as more independent, and on this trip home they clearly demonstrated that change. He likes the change in their relationship and yet feels sad. Some feelings of nostalgia for the good old days when his family did things together flood him; a sense of being all alone in the world, of being completely alone in his decision making, also runs through his mind. His nostalgia continues for an hour or so and gradually passes. As he nears school, his thoughts turn to the homework he needs to complete and the date he has to get for the dormitory dance next week.

Problems during this stage are most common in individuals and families who have difficulty handling strong emotion. A useful approach to such problems is to reframe the strong emotions as positive and constructive. For example, a therapist might say, "It's not necessary to try to save Sandy from her sad feelings or to feel bad because at those times she gets so irritable. At those times, she's recognizing how much she has enjoyed her childhood but that it is behind her—she's growing up. You can all feel good about the fact that she has something to miss."

When more serious problems arise at this point, it usually is a reaction to powerful ambivalent feelings within the family. For example, the adolescent's separation may be seen as rejection by a family member. These issues must be addressed and resolved before the separation process can effectively proceed.

When the affective response to the separation has been confronted and adequately mitigated, there is a shift to the fourth stage.

Stage Four: The Identification Process. Secure and more comfortable in independence, the youth is ready to develop a new sense of identity. There is strong motivation, both conscious and unconscious, to internalize those qualities of the parents that are of value. The adolescent may, in fact, internalize some previously rebelled-against qualities, although they may be integrated in a somewhat altered form. For example, the quality of orderliness, which may have been learned in childhood in relation to keeping the house clean, may now be applied to keeping order on the job, while the personal living situation may remain messy. Traits in parents that are not felt to be valuable in getting needs met will probably not be reintegrated. Much of this identification is unconscious.

Parents, in their process of separation, must also develop a new sense of family. They must find alternative ways of achieving the gratifications previously derived from the close, dependent parent/child relationship. For example, if the parents had enjoyed vacation camping trips with the children, they must learn to go on camping trips themselves or find satisfying alternative holiday plans. The parental task at this stage is to gain self-esteem from acknowledging that they are successful parents and to internalize the valued aspects of the former relationship with the child by finding alternative outlets for it. Through this process, the former relationship is relinquished.

Dave is now twenty years old. After his summer job as a camp counselor, he reports a recent realization. He remembers thinking and saying frequently just a year or two ago that he would never raise his own kids the way his parents had raised him. Yet, as a camp counselor, he found himself on a number of occasions treating his charges similarly to the way he remembered his parents treating him. He was surprised to find that not only was he comfortable with this, but his parents' approach was effective. His mother and father, finding that they miss camping but not wanting to go by themselves, have joined a church group that goes on trips, among its other activities.

Problems usually do not occur in this stage unless rejection has occurred. Reidentification with a person one has been rejected from can only occur ambivalently. When these problems occur, psychotherapy is most successful when the therapist can bring the parties together and let them reseparate in a less rejecting way.

Stage Five: Development of a New Relationship. The final stage of separation is the development of a new relationship between parent and offspring based on adult/adult interaction. For the young adult, this allows a new openness to intimate relationships with others, the ability to make genuine commitments, and a new sense of stability and identity. The parents may also be developing new identities such as mother-in-law or grandfather. Closeness and distance can be more comfortably acknowledged, and the closeness can therefore be more comfortably acted on by both parties.

Dave and his parents, after a long suspension, now find it much more comfortable to embrace each other at homecomings or departures. Dave has recently taken on a steady girlfriend and is considering marriage after he graduates from college next year. He has decided to go to law school and plans to specialize in business law. He now finds it enjoyable to talk with his father about business practices, as his father is an experienced and successful businessman. Dave is beginning to feel that he takes part in these discussions on an equal basis, teaching his father some new things as well as learning from him. At times, the relationship may temporarily slip back to a more child/parent one, but most often Dave and his parents relate to each other as adults.

Thus, the stages of adolescent/parent separation, both in function and in process, are isomorphic with stages of bereavement. Although biological, cultural, and peer influences push the teenager toward separation, the attachment mechanisms so important to child development are strong. The first stages of this separation, as of all separation processes, are aimed primarily at confronting the mechanisms that maintain the attachment. Later stages of separation are aimed at integrating qualities that are more likely to help the person be successful when independent of the relationship. As stated earlier, although most people find adolescent/parent separation stressful, the process usually proceeds in a way that allows both parent and offspring to better adapt and to be able to meet their needs in the future. For some it can be an extremely painful experience, but later adaptation is nevertheless successful. In other families, however, the separation process leads to the development of pathological behavior patterns. The next section of the chapter will address the factors that help to distinguish the healthy separation process from its variants associated with serious psychological problems.

Variables Affecting Adolescent/Parent Separation

Because the process of adolescent/parent separation parallels other separation processes, the variables identified as most influential in other separations can be applied to this separation process as well. Six variables stand out as most important in adolescent/parent separation: (1) the readiness of the individuals for independence, (2) the cognitive development of object constancy and the assimilative and accommodative modes of adaptation, (3) the nature of the parent/child relationship, (4) the past separation experiences of the parents and the adolescent, (5) cultural influences on the separation process, and (6) the family system's impact on the separation process.

Readiness for Independence. Those teenagers who feel most confidence in their ability to care for themselves, based on gradually increasing separation experiences in childhood, are best prepared to face the issues of adolescent separation. For example, Offer and Offer (1975) found that teenagers who had had happy experiences away from home—for example, at summer camp or part-time jobs—felt most comfortable facing the adolescent/parent separation. These types of independent experiences are no doubt valuable aids to independence. However, they are also important markers of parental commitment to provide youngsters with age-appropriate separation experiences. Murphy and others' (1962) studies confirm this and also indicate that teenagers who were pushed by their parents into premature independent activities had more problems with adolescent independence.

For parents, the issue of "readiness for independence" primarily addresses the confidence they have in finding alternative modes for their own generative activity as well as other satisfactions previously derived from their children. Those who have the least experience with activities separate from their children have the most difficult time—for example, parents who went directly from living with their own parents to being married with children. The transition is facilitated when parents take up new activities as the child enters pubescence which gradually provide greater focus for their interest as their children get older. Again, this needs to be gradual, as too quickly withdrawing attention from teenagers leaves the child insecure and the parent ungratified. Parents who have confined all their generative activity to their children (the so-called supermoms) may have the most difficulty in letting go if they do not develop new outlets. However, even working parents do better when they add new activities as their child reaches pubescence.

Cognitive Influences. Directly affecting the success of the separation process is the cognitive ability to maintain object constancy. The adolescent must have a clear cognitive image of his parents from which to separate. Indeed, as stated previously, part of the process of dealing with adolescent/parent separation, for the teenager, is that identity diffusion occurs because the child defines himself in relation to the parents and must now redefine himself as separate. The teenagers who have the most difficulty are those who cannot maintain an inner cognitive image of their parents, which usually entails the ability to predict the parents' behavior, proceeding from perception of patterns of past behavior. In families where parenting is extremely chaotic, children's development of cognitive representations of the father or mother is impaired because the parents are so inconsistent. It is impossible to redefine oneself as separate, because the adolescent's own pattern of behavior cannot be adequately differentiated as separate from the parent's. Without awareness and recognition of these patterns, a sense of separateness cannot occur. In addition, in the later stages of the separation process, the necessary parental identification is impaired, since identification requires internalizing recognized and valued patterns. This makes becoming independent even more difficult. Further, as Piaget notes, the cognitive ability to assimilate and accommodate new information is essential for adaptation to new situations, such as separation.

Nature of the Relationship. As Bowlby (1973), Parkes (1972), and Marris (1974) all point out, studies of grief and separation show that the most problematic separations entail strong ambivalence toward the attachment figure. This is especially true in adolescent separation. As stated earlier, ambivalence, rebelliousness, and anger are quite normal parts of the developmental process. If there is a basic security that it is legitimate to have such negative feelings and that they can be expressed without destroying the relationship, the storms are weathered successfully. However, powerful ambivalence in the relationship can allow these feelings to undermine basic trust in the relationship, and a pathological pattern is likely to develop. It is essential that anger, ambivalence, and rebelliousness not be seen by either the child or the parents as rejection. If anger and ambivalence have been acceptable parts of the relationship before adolescence, they can be openly expressed and are less dangerous feelings to have during this time.

Past Separation Experiences. Bowlby (1973), as well as many others, has pointed out that early experiences of traumatic loss make subsequent separation extremely difficult. Early losses such as painful divorce experiences in which the children have been rejected or deserted by a parent usually increase the likelihood of pathological adolescent separation (see Chapter Ten). Death of a family member or close friend can be traumatic and disrupting to a child and can lead to anxiety about separation from parents. This is especially likely if the parents were intolerant of the child's sadness at the time of the loss. Parents then send the child the covert (sometimes overt) message "Your sadness disturbs me," and the child comes to equate feeling sad with being bad. The normal sad periods during adolescence and youth thus become especially distressing and feared.

For parents the most important and influential past experience with separation is the experience they themselves had as teenagers separating from their parents. Parents who were themselves rejected or had poor experiences in separating may consciously or unconsciously re-create a similar circumstance with their own adolescent. To protect themselves from expected rejection, these parents reject their children at the first signs of independence, thus creating a self-fulfilling prophecy. Or they frequently make the teenager feel so guilty about moves toward independence that the teenager aborts attempts at separation. In either case, problems in the separation process frequently develop.

Cultural Influences. A variety of cultural factors influence the separation process, including the current rapid rate of cultural change, wide cultural diversity, the new and often burdensome expectations placed on children by adults, and the lack of rituals for the passage to adulthood. The length of dependent childhood and the abrupt change from child to adult responsibility in contemporary Western culture are profound. In the past, the separation process usually began much earlier and proceeded more slowly, allowing a greater continuity between children's and adults' responsibilities. Studies conducted in nonindustrialized cultures show that children frequently become involved in some adult activities while quite young and gradually increase participation in adult activities, so that by adolescence the additional responsibility acquired is minimal compared with the amount acquired in postindustrial society. In today's culture, children are mostly separated from adults and adult activity until their eighteenth year.

The cultural rites of passage, once marked, are now less well defined. As a result, parents and adolescent do not often agree on when separation is taking place. For example, in a study in which eighteen-year-olds and their parents were asked whether the adolescents were independent, the majority of the youth answered that they were, while the majority of the parents answered that they were not (H. Peskin, Wright Institute, Berkeley, Calif., personal communication, 1976). As a result, in today's culture there is a much greater need for the young adult to define and prove separation, often through more rebellious behavior. In the past, mentor relationships were frequently built into the cultural system. The apprentice relationship would serve as a gradual introduction into an adult role. At present, as Levinson and his colleagues (1978) have pointed out, even those who do have a mentor usually develop this relationship during adulthood, long after it can facilitate separation from parents.

In addition, the fluid identity characteristic of adolescence combined with wide cultural diversity encourages teenagers to turn to peer groups for support. This makes good peer relationships especially important to the adolescent, and the teenager without good peer relationships is lost in today's society. In fact, if modern culture becomes less diverse and the rate of change slows, future generations may display less rebellious-ness during the separation process.

All these factors together mean that today's culture puts greater stress on parents and adolescents than in previous times. The parent/child relationship is therefore even more significant today than it has been in the past.

Effect of the Family System. The family system is the most important of all the variables, both because of its potential for generating problems and because it provides an effective place for intervention. Family systems research has shown that a family is more than the sum of its members and must there-fore be understood on a different level from the individuals in-volved. As Haley (1980) points out, any organization undergoes its greatest turmoil when a member or members enter or leave the system. The process of the adolescent's leaving home re-quires the family to reorganize, and this, in turn, puts homeo-static pressures on the teenager and parents not to separate.

Related subissues include the following: Is the family flexible or rigid? Does it try to insulate itself, thus isolating its family members from the support of the peer group, making separation more difficult? What has been the role of the teen-ager in the family (for example, bad boy, mediator, helper)? How secure are the generational boundaries? For example, in an intact family with separation problems, have the parents com-municated through the child? Separation of the child in this family could require more direct communication between the parents. If the parental relationship cannot tolerate intimacy, the adolescent may be unconsciously discouraged from separat-ing. If the children have been a reason or an excuse to maintain the marriage, again there may be pressure on the adolescent not to separate in order to avoid directly confronting the marital problems. Teenagers who have been the center of the family's communications may find their position powerful and therefore difficult to give up. Adolescents' desires to leave home may con-flict with the motivations maintaining their positions within the family. When one child leaves home, another child still at home may step into the relinquished role, sometimes postponing fam-ily conflict until the youngest child must face separation.

In the case of a single parent, the separation process may

require the parent to adapt to living alone and hence face the possibility of severe loneliness. Perhaps the child has occupied a parental position and the parent resists the separation because of his or her own dependency needs. Parental dependency may be expressed through pathological solutions such as developing somatic illnesses, in conscious or unconscious attempts to forestall adolescent separation. However, the adolescent's leave-taking may lead to healthier parental solutions, freeing the parent to become involved in organizations or relationships that meet his or her dependency or caretaker needs more acceptably.

In all cases, the child's leaving home will require a reorganization of the family: family members will communicate in new ways and get their needs met in new ways. Families sometimes avoid separation when it is extremely difficult by developing problems—behavioral, emotional, or physical—to provide an excuse to avoid the separation and thus maintain the family homeostasis. Or the child may express familial ambivalence toward separation by leaving in a way that will almost certainly lead to a return to dependency, such as failing at work or school. Or, if adolescents do separate but still feel they have hurt the family seriously, severe guilt and possibly depression may ensue, especially during the affect-oriented stage three. Another problematic possibility is that the teenager will leave and the parent will develop some form of illness or problem that requires a "parental youth" to return to the family, thus again maintaining homeostasis and avoiding separation.

The way the family communicates is also an important factor. Verbal communication that is consistent with other forms of communication, such as body language, is most easily dealt with. The most difficult communication for family members to handle is communication that is contradictory on different levels (often called "paradoxical communication"). For example, a parent tells the teenager, "If you'd rather go to the football game with your friends than go fishing with the family on Saturday, that's okay with me." If this is said with just the right tone of voice, the adolescent will overtly hear permission while experiencing (frequently unconsciously) the contradictory message. In the rare circumstance when the teenager will directly confront the parent about a mixed message, the adult will, of course, deny the covert meaning, usually because the adult is unaware of it.

Most family systems have enough flexibility, permeability, functional generational boundaries, and consistency of communication to promote adolescent separation without the development of serious problems. In fact, most adolescent separations, like other separations, though challenging and at times painful, progress to a positive resolution. When problems develop as a result of one or more of the variables described here, therapeutic intervention can reestablish a corrective route toward resolution. The most successful therapeutic interventions for the more common problems are described below (therapeutic interventions for more serious problems of separation are discussed in Bloom, 1980).

Therapeutic Change for Adolescent/Parent Separation Problems

Different types of problems in the family characteristically occur during different stages of the separation process. During the early phases of separation, when the need to prove separation is preeminent (stages one and two), rebellious behavior leads to the most common problems. Frequently the interpretation of the meaning of rebellious behavior sets off the problems. Parents sometimes have trouble perceiving their adolescent's rebelliousness as movement toward separation and instead view it as a sign of rejection. One factor in this parental misunderstanding is generational differences: parents who presently have adolescent children likely grew up at a time when teenagers in general were much less contrary toward their parents and parental figures. Therefore, using their own background as the standard, they see their adolescents' behavior as a rejection of their values.

Take the case of Jerry, seventeen. Jerry was brought to therapy by his parents after he had been arrested and placed at the local detention center for a driving while intoxicated (DWI) violation. The parents said they had suspected during the past year that Jerry had on a number of occasions smoked marijuana and on several more come home drunk. He occasionally violated his curfew, sometimes coming in an hour or two late at night. When this occurred, his parents would ground him for the next weekend. A long, drawn-out argument would usually follow, sometimes lasting all evening, at the end of which the parents would finally "give up" trying to help Jerry "understand" how they were trying to help him. They would continue with the restriction, while feeling very bad because their teenager could not understand. Jerry had a C+ average in school. He was graduating within six months and was planning to go to vocational-technical school in electronics. One last complaint the parents made was that although Jerry did have a part-time job at which he had done very well for the past year, he spent all his money on cars and, according to the father, was too "fun loving." Overall, the parents felt very bad over Jerry's having rejected their way of living, and they had great fears for his future.

In evaluating this case, it seems apparent that, despite a considerable degree of rebelliousness, the process of adolescent/parent separation is proceeding adequately. This is not to say that the DWI should not be seriously dealt with. However, what was problematic was that the parents began to brand their son a "sick child." This interpretation of attempts at separation often serves only to exacerbate the adolescent's need for more rebellion, since the teenager then feels forced to prove that he does have a mind of his own. In this particular case, the therapist tried to reframe the rebelliousness from *rejection* to seeing it as a normative process of *separation*. The parents were complimented for the structure they were providing. They were able to accept this reframing of family events. A follow-up call six weeks later revealed that things were unchanged, except for the boy's license having been suspended, but that the parents in general felt better because of the context in which they now viewed his behavior. The therapist met the mother approximately a year later by accident. At that time, she said that her son was away from home and doing well at vocational-technical school. In fact, she said, relations between her and her son were getting better since he had moved out of the house. Frequently, reframing of the "problem" within the context of a normative process allows separation to then proceed adequately.

When the separation process gets stuck and problems develop, it is likely that an evaluation of the six variables discussed in the previous section will reveal where the problem lies. Therapeutic intervention should then be directly related to making changes within the family system aimed at correcting the problem variable. This is an alternative to viewing the problem in the context of psychiatric diagnosis—for example, conduct disorder or depression. Therapy usually is much more successful in the long run if one treats the root of the problem rather than its consequences. For example, it is more effective to treat the lack of peer relations or lack of independent activity rather than treating the same adolescent for the frequent sequelae of these problems, such as depressive symptoms of withdrawal, lack of energy, and trouble sleeping.

Tom's family came for therapy because his parents reported that Tom was becoming depressed and withdrawn. He spent his days in his room by himself. Separation was progressing poorly, as he spent all his time at home, being very demanding of his parents' attention. This had caused his mother, the recipient of most of these demands, to become irritable toward him. Her recognition of Tom's overdependence on her and her guilt over her irritated response to the dependency motivated their quest for help. Tom was fifteen and looked rather immature for his age. He was of very short stature, being below the first percentile in height (for this he was referred to an endocrinologist and was found to have inherited late maturation). The year before, the family had moved from a very small town. After a review of the variables with the family, the primary problem was found to be that Tom's peer relations were undeveloped. Having grown up in a small town with the same small group of children from kindergarten on up, the boy had never learned how to develop new relationships. This problem was exacerbated by his small stature and late physical maturation. Tom did not stand out in anything. He was an average student. His slow physical development made him a poor athlete. He did have an interest in computers, as well as radio-controlled air-plane models. A therapeutic plan was developed to encourage his entry into clubs centered on these two activities. He made a couple of friends and began spending more time away from home. The depressive symptoms soon disappeared.

Another common problem of adolescent/parent separa-tion results when parents have marital problems and/or have be-come distant from each other. The children then become the one area of common interest for the parents. The child's growth toward independence threatens that connection, and therefore independence is covertly discouraged in the teenager. Usually in such families the marital problems and distance are denied, but what emerges is that the parents spend no time together with-out the children.

Sally, thirteen, was seen initially by her family physician and then by a neurologist for severe headaches as well as for a 20 percent loss of visual field in one eye, which had persisted for several months and had grown increasingly worse. A com-plete medical work-up indicated no organic etiology. The head-aches were causing Sally to drop out of her usual activities at school. She was confined at home, where she would be con-stantly "taken care of" by mother. It appeared that the head-aches were reflecting and contributing to an arrest in her devel-oping independence. During the initial family interview, it was revealed that the girl's headaches had started coincident with the problems that her fourteen-year-old brother was having in getting along with his parents as a result of his movement toward independence. The brother was very rebellious, fre-quently getting into arguments over household rules. Sally, teary-eyed, reported that, after one of these battles between her brother and the parents, her mother had yelled, "Maybe I should be the one that leaves home!" Sally said that she was in fact fearful that her mother would "run away from home." A related issue was the parents' disagreement over discipline. Fa-ther was very strict and mother rather lenient. This reflected an even larger disagreement between the parents over how impor-tant decisions were to be made. The father felt that he ought to make the decisions; the mother resented this. This conflict was played out with the children in that the father would make a number of very rigid rules; the mother, feeling that these rules were too strict, would fail to enforce them, thus effectively okaying the children's breaking the rules. Over the past several months, the father had reacted by withdrawing from the children almost completely, having nothing to do with them and no longer setting any rules. He expressed sadness over his lack of contact with the children but saw little hope that they could see him in any way other than as a rigid disciplinarian. During our first three meetings, most of our time was directed at helping the parents learn to make rules for the children that were more mutually arrived at. The father agreed that it was worth giving up some control to have better relations with his wife and children. Much more important than the actual rules they developed was the experience they had finding a new way to resolve differences between them. The children witnessed the parents' agreement.

Sally went back to more normal behavior within a few weeks. She said that her headaches no longer bothered her all day but perhaps bothered her from five to fifteen minutes in the evening, which no longer caused alterations of her behavior or life-style. Her vision impairment cleared up as well. To prevent a relapse, we then moved into the larger issue of the parents' marital problem. We did this by first suggesting that, as a reward for helping their children, the parents should spend a weekend together alone, something they had not done for at least six years. After several more meetings, they finally went out on two occasions in the evening and enjoyed each other. They also found that their ability to make some decisions together regarding the children's discipline was rubbing off in that they were making other decisions together. After seven sessions, we terminated family therapy. Follow-up two months later revealed that the family was pleased with how things were going.

Family therapy is very effective in resolving such separation problems. Generally my strategy in the initial stages is to bring the parents together to take charge of their teenager. During the later stages of therapy, the focus shifts to the parents working together to help their teenager achieve increasing independence. This keeps the parents' focus on the teenager, while the therapist's focus is on how the parents work together. Directly shifting the focus to the parents' problems may be unwise, as it may increase their guilt for their failure, further incapacitating them or adding to their resistance to therapy, since the expressed motivation for treatment was to help their child. As presented in the example, the parents can be helped to alter their relationship with each other while never needing to acknowledge their discord. Once the adolescents see their parents interacting better with each other, they move forward toward independence.

Most problems in adolescent/parent separation require the involvement of the family, or at least the parents, in therapy. There are, however, circumstances in which individual therapy may be preferred, either alone or in combination with family therapy. This is true particularly when the parents are so opposed to therapy that they only obstruct it. Sometimes they simply refuse to participate no matter what attempts are made to involve them in the therapy process. In this case, trying to change the family by using one individual as a change agent can be effective.

When only the adolescent is seen, the therapeutic relationship can be used as a practice ground for moving toward independence. That is, once the therapeutic alliance (attachment to the therapist) has been established, the focus of attention immediately switches to facilitating independence within the therapeutic relationship. Although insight may be useful, the most important focus of attention needs to be on the relationship between the therapist and the patient, within which independence is generally encouraged. Individual therapy is usually a much lengthier means of accomplishing the goal of independence but is sometimes the only alternative. It tends to be most useful when the teenager is about to move out of the home to college or job.

In summary, in providing therapy for adolescent/parent separation problems, it is more effective to zero in directly on the variables that are known to disrupt the separation process than to diagnose the symptom complex within a medical model.

Reframing the symptoms within the context of separation problems and then directing the family toward corrective experience is usually much more effective than insight-oriented therapy for these problems.

Conclusion

Parent/adolescent separation is the process through which the important child/parent attachment is disengaged, allowing the teenager to become an independent adult. I have described the similarities of this process to other separations, such as the death of a loved one. In reviewing the stages of adolescent/parent separation, we find that the process not only allows the bonds of childhood to be loosened but also encourages incorporation of valuable parental traits into adult behavior patterns just when they are most needed. It is this dynamic of integrating the necessary and valuable aspects of one's heritage into one's future that is the most important benefit of the separation process.

Peter Marris, in his book *Loss and Change* (1974), makes this point profoundly:

> Once we recognize that loss cannot be made good merely by substitution, the logic of mourning becomes apparent. If life is to seem meaningful again, it is not enough that the present should still be notionally worthwhile. The bereaved must be able to identify, in each concrete event they experience, some response worth making. The vitality of that response depends upon a commitment of purpose, which has already been given and cannot now be wished away, even though the relationships which incorporated it have been disrupted. Hence ... grief works itself out through a process of reformulation, rather than substitution. Confidence in the original commitment is restored by extracting its essential meaning and grafting it upon the present. This process involves repeated reassurances

of the strength and inviolability of the original commitment, as much as a search for the terms on which reattachment would still make life worth living. Until this ambivalent testing of past and future has retrieved the thread of continuity, it is itself the only deeply meaningful activity in which the bereaved can be engaged. . . .

Mourning for a death is a special instance of the management of loss, but its principles can be generalized. It recognizes, first, that loss generates a conflict which must be worked out, so as to restore a vital sense of continuity to experience; second, that the resolution of this conflict cannot be preordained, since the resolution only becomes meaningful through the ambivalent exploration by which it is realized; and so, finally, that until grief is worked out, the conflict itself becomes the only meaningful reference for behavior [pp. 91-92].

For the adolescent, separation from parents represents a major experience of loss and a major development in assuming adult responsibility and status. As such, it serves as a prototype for future separation experiences and is an important transition in the life course. It is obvious, then, that a successful resolution of these tasks is essential for healthy development.

References

Bateson, G. *Mind and Nature.* New York: Bantam Books, 1979.

Bloom, M. *Adolescent-Parental Separation.* New York: Gardner Press, 1980.

Blos, P. *On Adolescence: A Psychoanalytic Interpretation.* New York: Free Press, 1962.

Bowlby, J. "Childhood Mourning and Its Implications for Psychiatry." *American Journal of Psychiatry,* 1961, *118,* 481-498.

Bowlby, J. *Attachment and Loss.* Vol. 1: *Attachment.* New York: Basic Books, 1969.

Bowlby, J. *Attachment and Loss.* Vol. 2: *Separation: Anxiety and Anger.* New York: Basic Books, 1973.

Darwin, C. *The Origin of Species.* New York: Macmillan, 1962. (Originally published 1859.)

Erikson, E. H. *Childhood and Society.* New York: Norton, 1950.

Erikson, E. H. *Identity: Youth and Crisis.* New York: Norton, 1968.

Haley, J. *Leaving Home: The Therapy of Disturbed Young People.* New York: McGraw-Hill, 1980.

Hoffman, J. "Psychological Separation of Late Adolescents from Their Parents." *Journal of Counseling Psychology,* 1984, *31*(2), 170–178.

Kurash, C. "The Transition to College: A Study of Separation-Individuation in Late Adolescence." Unpublished doctoral dissertation, Department of Psychology, City University of New York, 1979.

Levinson, D. J., and others. *The Seasons of a Man's Life.* New York: Knopf, 1978.

Lorenz, K. *Behind the Mirror.* New York: Harcourt Brace Jovanovich, 1977.

Mallnow, V. "Adolescent Separation-Individuation and the Parent-Child Relationship." Unpublished doctoral dissertation, Department of Psychology, University of Cincinnati, 1981.

Marris, P. *Loss and Change.* New York: Pantheon Books, 1974.

Minuchin, S., Rosman, B. L., and Baker, L. *Psychosomatic Families.* Cambridge, Mass.: Harvard University Press, 1970.

Murphy, E. B., and others. *Development of Autonomy and Parent-Child Interaction in Late Adolescence.* Washington, D.C.: National Institute of Mental Health, 1962.

Offer, D. *The Psychological World of the Teenager.* New York: Basic Books, 1969.

Offer, D., and Offer, J. B. *From Teenage to Young Manhood.* New York: Basic Books, 1975.

Offer, D., Ostrov, E., and Baker, L. *The Adolescent.* New York: Basic Books, 1981.

Paris, J. "The Oedipus Complex—a Critical Re-examination."

Canadian Psychiatric Association Journal, 1976, *21*, 173–179.

Parkes, C. M. *Bereavement: Studies of Grief in Adult Life.* New York: International Universities Press, 1972.

Pepitone, L. A. "Adolescent Separation: A Developmental and Intergeneration Study of Relationship." Unpublished doctoral dissertation, Department of Psychology, Bryn Mawr College, 1981.

Stierlin, H. *Separating Parents and Adolescents.* New York: Quadrangle, 1974.

Sullivan, K., and Sullivan, A. "Adolescent-Parent Separation." *Developmental Psychology,* 1980, *16*, 93–99.

Weiss, R. S. *Marital Separation: Managing After a Marriage Ends.* New York: Basic Books, 1975.

8

Effects of Work-Related Separations on Children and Families

Chaya S. Piotrkowski
Lisa K. Gornick

Editors' Note: *In this chapter, the authors discuss a separation experience that is nearly universal in our society: the time family members spend apart because of work responsibilities. Two rapidly expanding new family forms—the two-earner family and the single-parent family headed by a working mother—both add to the amount of time family members are separated in daily routines. Work roles structure family separation both in the sheer amount of time they demand and in the particular pattern of time spent at home and at work.*

After reviewing the extensive literature on maternal employment, Piotrkowski and Gornick conclude that ordinary *patterns of work-related separation do not necessarily have adverse consequences for children. Thus, given good substitute care and emotionally responsive working mothers, maternal employment itself does not appear to be a crucial factor for a child's well-being. However, certain work-related factors do interfere with the child's ability to tolerate separation—for example, work patterns that are nonstandard or rotating, making it more difficult for children to anticipate with regularity mother's departure and return. Further, some coping strategies, like ritualizing sepa-*

267

ration and reunion, facilitate children's adaptation to maternal work.

In contrast to ordinary work-related separation is "extraordinary separation," which includes shift work, moonlighting, weekend work, commuter marriage, and job-related travel. Although little is known about mothers whose work requires extraordinary separation, research on work-absent fathers reveals a host of negative implications for wives and children. Unless fathers compensate for their absence by intense involvement or can control their work schedules so as to accommodate intermittently heightened family needs, considerable work-related separation can create tension and distance for blue-collar families and families of executives alike. Interestingly, research on military families has shown that experience with extended separations does not "inoculate" against negative effects.

Clearly, many factors modify the effects of work-related separation. Two cross-cutting elements stand out: the magnitude of the separation (a factor highlighted in all the chapters in this section) and the degree to which separation is under personal control (also a factor in the effects of divorce and bereavement). Work-related separation need not have ill effects, but extended, inflexible, or unpredictable work absence may be problematic. In contrast to the conclusions of this chapter, it should be noted that other experts in this field (such as Jay Belsky) find that significant work-related separation of mother and infant during the first year of life may have some negative consequences for the developing child.

Family life is structured, in part, by the regular absences of family members engaged in work for which they are paid. Increasingly, family members go their separate ways each day—parents off to their respective workplaces, children to school or to substitute caregivers. Such work-related separations are part of the invisible background of everyday family life. With the exception of mothers' employment, they have not been studied systematically.

The purpose of this chapter is to examine the ways work-related separations can facilitate or constrain adequate family functioning and the development of children. The focus is on separations from family members due to the normal requirements of paid work, as distinct from unpaid work, such as housework.

First we shall outline the historical context of modern work-related separations and present a framework for thinking about such separations and some data about the structure of work schedules. Following that, we shall discuss what is known about the consequences of work-related separations for families and children. Since empirical research in this area shows only that work-related separations might or might not be *associated* with familial or individual functioning, conclusions about causal relations must be treated as tentative and as awaiting further confirmation.

Historical Context

Two important social and economic changes during the past 150 years shaped the modern context of work/family relations. The first was the separation of work from family-based activities. Many historians believe that this separation had its roots in industrialization and the centralization of work (for example, Scott and Tilly, 1975; Thompson, 1966; Smelser, 1959). In subsistence societies, work life and life among kin were not clearly demarcated. For example, in preindustrial agrarian societies in England and the United States, subsistence activities and production for exchange (when it existed) centered on the family "homestead" (Turner, 1971). All family members, even young children, participated in the production of goods, food, and clothing. Although there are early examples of protracted work-related separations, they too were based on family prototypes. Such was the case for the young apprentice who lived for six or seven years with a master craftsman responsible for his moral development (Pleck, 1976; Ariès, 1965). But as the factory system became established, most family-based ways of organizing work gave way to relatively impersonal modes of production. The (male) worker eventually went to work with strangers and came to be treated as if he had no family (Kanter,

1977). Separation of work life from family relationships became the norm during the twentieth century.

The second important change involved women's labor-force participation. The introduction of so-called protective legislation at the turn of the century restricted the hours women could be employed in certain industries (Baron, 1981). By the early twentieth century, only about one tenth of white women in the U.S. were employed outside the home, although employment rates were higher for nonwhites (Chafe, 1976; Degler, 1980; Beckett, 1976). Most employed women were single and left the labor force upon marriage. Working-class married women often relied on home-based work such as taking in boarders and doing laundering at home (Tentler, 1979). Still, for most families, the new "traditional family," in which the wife and mother worked at home doing housework and child care while the husband and father worked outside the home, was the norm.

This situation changed during and after World War II. While the employment rates of single women remained relatively stable, the labor-force participation of married women grew steadily and, after 1960, dramatically. Most dramatic was the increased participation of *mothers* in the labor force, particularly mothers of young children. By 1981, over 60 percent of married women with school-age children were employed. Among married mothers of preschoolers, about 47 percent were employed (Moore, Spain, and Bianchi, 1984). Among single mothers, employment rates were even higher. Rather than leaving work until their children are in school or grown, many women are remaining in the labor force when their children are young. The so-called traditional male-breadwinner family is giving way to two new family forms—the dual-earner family and the single-parent family headed by an employed woman.

Understanding Work-Related Separations

Work-related separations involve the regular absence of sustained face-to-face contact between family members due to the requirements of market work. Thus, they are distinguished from emotional inaccessibility, which may be related to work experiences (Piotrkowski, 1979; Piotrkowski and Katz, 1983). Unlike losses, which mean permanent inaccessibility, such separations are temporary (see Bowlby, 1973). In addition to the actual *period* of absence are regular departure and reunion *events*, which themselves are patterned and may be meaningful for understanding the impact of absence on families and children.

Face-to-face contact is emphasized, rather than simple accessibility, for two related reasons. First, the widespread availability of telephones at the workplace makes vocal access to family members during the workday possible for many employees. Such access varies with the nature of the job and its setting—for example, the ease of getting to a telephone—as well as the degree of control employees have over when and how they perform their tasks (Piotrkowski, 1979). Thus, it is possible for family members to have lengthy separations each day while having relatively easy access to each other by telephone. Still, it is important to note that many employees have little opportunity for even minimal contact with family members during work time and that variations in such accessibility probably moderate the impact of work-related separations.

Second, face-to-face contact has some critical properties. Among adults it allows for displays of physical affection and support, as well as subtle forms of communication. For young children, face-to-face contact is a requisite for meaningful interaction with parents. Thus, it is the interruption of ongoing face-to-face contact that gives work-induced separations potential psychological importance.

The work role structures separations in several ways. First, it structures the length of absences, thereby affecting the time available for family activities. With industrialization, the working day of male laborers increased dramatically; it then declined slowly during the twentieth century (Wilensky, 1961; Hedges and Taylor, 1980). Currently, nonagricultural, nonsupervisory employees in the United States work about thirty-five hours a week (U.S. Bureau of the Census, 1983). In general, married men work longer hours than employed married women and are more likely to hold a second job, especially if they have children or if they work in managerial, professional, or technical occupations (Staines and Pleck, 1983; Sekscenski, 1980). Thus, the problems that may be created by long working hours are especially pertinent in the case of husbands and fathers.

Second, the work role structures the weekly timing of separations by affecting the pattern of days at home and at work. Staines and Pleck (1983) have divided the pattern of days worked into (1) a nonvariable pattern that excludes weekends, (2) a nonvariable pattern that includes a weekend day, and (3) a pattern of variable days. In over one third of the dual-earner couples sampled in their study, one or both spouses regularly worked on the weekend. Men, more than employed women, were likely to work on the weekend.

Finally, the work role structures the pattern of daily hours at home and at work. The Bureau of Labor Standards defines shift work as a full-time schedule with more than half the hours worked not falling between 8 A.M. and 4 P.M. (Presser and Cain, 1983). At least one in six full-time workers, particularly in the service and manufacturing sectors, regularly works a nonstandard shift—that is, during evenings, nights, or both (Finn, 1981; Presser and Cain, 1983). It has been suggested that some husbands and wives choose to work different shifts in order to manage child-care responsibilities (Working Family Project, 1978). In fact, in a national sample of dual-earner families, Presser and Cain found that at least one spouse worked a shift in approximately one-third of couples employed full-time with children under age fourteen.

These variations in work schedules have important implications for families and children. Although the majority of employed adults have "ordinary" work schedules—that is, they work eight hours or less and have weekends off—many do not. Instead, their work schedules are characterized by a second job, by weekend work, or by a nonstandard shift. These "extraordinary" work schedules also create extraordinary separations for family members. Schedules of weekend work or shift work fit poorly with the normal rhythms of social and family life. Commuter marriages, in which spouses are separated regularly for several days each week because of their jobs, constitute yet another form of extraordinary separation (Gerstel and Gross,

1984). Unfortunately, with some few exceptions, the familial implications of these variations in work scheduling have not been examined systematically. They are important because they help to establish the parameters around which family-based activities occur, as well as the possibilities for face-to-face contact between family members.

Parents and Children

Social and behavioral scientists, as well as clinical practitioners, share the biases and concerns of their culture. Not surprisingly, such biases have shaped research on the effects of work-related separations on children and on parent/child relations. It has long been assumed that a constant maternal presence is required for children to develop normally. This belief has spawned heated debate and over three decades of research on the supposed effects of maternal employment. In contrast, there has been almost no research on the effects of normal *paternal* absences due to work, for only deviations from the norm have been viewed as potentially harmful. Similarly, non-married employed mothers have also been neglected, for they were invisible until recently. These gaps in the research mean that the discussion of fathers and children is necessarily speculative. In the case of mothers and children, firm conclusions apply primarily to children in two-parent families.

Separations of Mothers and Children. Research on maternal employment has followed the patterns of women's labor-force participation. Most research has focused on children already in school because mothers with preschoolers were not employed in large numbers until recently. Now there is an emerging research literature on preschoolers. Numerous excellent reviews of these research literatures exist (see Hoffman, 1974, 1979, 1980, 1983, 1984; Heyns, 1982; Bronfenbrenner and Crouter, 1982). Consequently, only general conclusions will be described and discussed here. Historically, investigations of older children preceded those of younger children. However, our discussion of mothers and children begins with children under six in order to place maternal work-related absences in a

developmental context and because younger children are believed to be more vulnerable to separations from their mothers.

Predictions about the negative consequences of maternal
employment rest partly on clinical and developmental theories
that locate the mother/infant bond at the heart of healthy child
development. John Bowlby (1951, 1973) and Selma Fraiberg
(1972), in particular, have been concerned with separations of
infants from mothers. They have argued that the infant's attachment ("love" in Fraiberg's terms) to a stable, loving, accessible, sensitive adult forms the bedrock of healthy personality
and of the ability to love in adulthood. In Fraiberg's view, maternal employment deprives children of love because sensitive,
loving caregivers cannot be found for most babies of employed
mothers. Without such love, children become aggressive adults
incapable of genuine affection. In Bowlby's view, daily and repeated separations from mother figures create anxious, rather
than secure, attachments that are linked to emotional and cognitive difficulties later. Children who have experienced repeated
or long separations are, as Bowlby describes them, fearful, anxious, depressed, and cognitively backward. In adulthood, their
lack of internal models of dependable intimacy may create
problems in relationships.

The existing research evidence, however, does not support these dire predictions. Generally, babies appear to be as
securely attached to employed as to nonemployed mothers
(Hoffman, 1984). Two other bodies of research indicate that
daily separations from parents do not inevitably lead to harm.
First, children in good-quality day care are as securely attached
to mothers and as well adjusted as home-reared children, despite
regular separations from their mothers (Belsky and Steinberg,
1978; Clarke-Stewart, 1982). Moreover, they form their primary attachments to parents rather than to substitute caregivers.
Second, recent research shows that infants become securely attached to their employed fathers (Lamb, 1976), suggesting that
work-related separations themselves do not dramatically interfere with babies' attachments to caring parents.

The few studies of personality development in young
children show a similar pattern: children of employed and non-

employed parents do not differ in significant ways (for example, Schachter, 1981; Farel, 1980). Although Schachter did find that toddlers with nonemployed mothers performed better on a cognitive measure than toddlers with employed mothers, tests of early intelligence are not very reliable (Hoffman, 1984).

Where differences between groups do exist, they appear to be related to methodological problems in the study (for example, Cohen, 1978) or to factors related to mothers' employment status, including instability in substitute care arrangements (Moore, 1969), poor-quality substitute care (Farber and Egeland, 1982), and maternal role dissatisfaction, especially among *non*employed mothers (Hoch, 1980; Farel, 1980; Lerner and Galambos, 1985).

Recently, several studies of middle-class dual-earner families have found that sons in such families may be viewed less positively than daughters and may receive less positive attention than sons in traditional families (Bronfenbrenner, Alvarez, and Henderson, 1984; Stuckey, McGhee, and Bell, 1982; Zaslow, Pedersen, Suwalsky, and Rabinovich, 1983). Again, the issue does not appear to be maternal separation or absence as such. Instead, it may be that the higher activity level of boys and parental perceptions of their independence may interact with parental role strain caused by too much to do and too little time to do it. When energy and time are scarce, young sons may get shortchanged if they are viewed as less needy than girls. Moreover, the parent who comes home tired after a long day at work simply may find her active young son too much to handle. In such cases, role overload, rather than separation itself, is the culprit. These studies also highlight the importance of reunion events and behaviors. The absence itself is probably less important than the way reunions occur.

Studies of school-age and adolescent children generally confirm the picture presented above. There are few reliable differences between the children of employed and nonemployed mothers on measures of closeness with parents or on measures of adjustment (Hoffman, 1974, 1979). The group differences that have been found, once again, are related to factors other than absence. For example, boys and girls from lower-class homes benefit academically when their mothers are employed, probably because the additional income is critical for the quality of life in these families (Heyns, 1982). Daughters from all social classes do better when their mothers are employed, perhaps because of the greater childhood autonomy fostered in dual-earner families (Hoffman, 1980). In contrast, sons of white, middle-class employed mothers do less well academically than sons of nonemployed mothers, perhaps because they receive too much of a push toward independence (Hoffman, 1980). In a similar vein, the meaning of having an employed mother may explain why sons of lower-class and working-class employed mothers express greater disapproval of, or admire their fathers less than, sons in traditional families (McCord, McCord, and Thurber, 1963; Propper, 1972). These sons may view their mothers' employment as an indicator of their fathers' failure or as a threat to their parents' marriages (Hoffman, 1979; King, McIntyre, and Axelson, 1968). Finally, as with young children, maternal role satisfaction and job-related morale seem to be related to the quality of mothering (Hoffman, 1963; Yarrow, Scott, De Leeuw, and Heinig, 1962; Piotrkowski and Katz, 1983). Again, what is important is not maternal absence but a mother's satisfaction with what she is doing—inside the home or outside it.

Given the strong theoretical and cultural basis for believing that children—especially young ones—need a constant maternal presence, how can we account for the research evidence to the contrary? One possibility is that the proposition has not been adequately tested. For older children, the child's age with regard to maternal employment history has not been examined (Heyns, 1982). For younger children, attachment behavior has sometimes been assessed improperly (Farber and Egeland, 1982), and studies have relied heavily on middle-class white samples and on quality day-care centers. Presumably, these children receive the scarce, high-quality care that Fraiberg deemed necessary. It is also possible that the relevant variables have not yet been examined. "Capacity for intimacy and love" is difficult to assess, but according to clinical theories, it is just such a capacity that needs to be considered. Finally, the categorization and study of work-related absences remain relatively crude. Most studies focus on the *fact* of work-related separation (not even the duration of the separation) and do not directly measure amount of parent/child contact. Many employed mothers work full-time, but others work fewer hours—especially if they have young children—and some work more. For some women, shift work is the norm, while for others it is not. These variations in the length and timing of daily separations surely need to be considered.

Such methodological and substantive issues should be addressed. Still, the preponderance of currently available evidence indicates that ordinary work-related separations of mothers and children are not necessarily harmful. The clinical and developmental theories are correct in their substance—that children need stable relationships with attentive, sensitive, loving, responsive adults—but may be incorrect in the conclusion that full-time mothering is invariably the best way to ensure responsive parenting. Under some conditions, full-time mothering is oppressive and results in less than adequate caretaking. Isolated young mothers do not fare well with their children (Gavron, 1966; Minturn and Lambert, 1964), nor do mothers who prefer to be employed but are not (Yarrow, Scott, De Leeuw, and Heinig, 1962). In truth, we do not know how much time together, at minimum, parents and children need for loving relationships to develop (Parke, 1981; Ainsworth, 1979).

Clinical and developmental theories stress the importance of responsive mothers, in addition to physical presence. Empirical evidence on the antecedents of attachment also demonstrates the preeminence of responsive mothering for children's development (Ainsworth, Blehar, Waters, and Wall, 1978). Although nonemployed mothers spend more time with their young children than employed mothers, all that time together, as many reviewers have noted, does not ensure quality contact. And many employed mothers give parenting precedence over other roles and activities (Piotrkowski and Katz, 1982), ensuring quality interaction between themselves and their children. In fact, Pedersen, Cain, Zaslow, and Anderson (1982) found that the interaction between employed mothers and young in-

278 The Psychology of Separation and Loss

fants at homecoming was so intense that fathers may have been literally "crowded out." Children's preference for parents over substitute caregivers also suggests that it is the gleam in mom's and dad's eyes that helps to cement the parent/child bond, not simply the amount and constancy of contact.

Given loving, consistent substitute care and mothers who are emotionally responsive to their young children, it appears that employed mothers can provide a "good enough" environment for adequate development. Parents also evolve strategies to facilitate young children's adaptation to daily work-related departure and reunion events. Informal observations suggest that some parents help children manage separations successfully by the use of compensatory rituals—a special time with a parent in the morning, waving good-bye at the window, and so forth. Ritualization of daily departures and reunions can help the young child feel some control over the separations, thereby increasing mastery. As children mature, they come to understand that their parents will, indeed, return each day. Eventually, they come to understand that work is a necessary instrumental activity. Older children may even value their mothers' financial contributions to their families (Woods, 1972). A mother's work-related absences become increasingly congruent with the adolescent child's growing need for autonomy (Maccoby, 1958; Hoffman, 1974). It may be the mother whose children are her "job" who will have a difficult time with emerging adolescent autonomy.

If this alternative scenario is correct, then more critical than ordinary work-related separations are the factors that (1) influence the quality of parenting, (2) interfere with a child's ability to tolerate separation events, and (3) affect the quality of substitute care a child receives. In the first category are such factors as role satisfaction and job morale, as well as resources available to help at homecomings. In the second category may be such factors as nonstandard shifts or, worse yet, rotating shifts that do not allow a young child to anticipate mother's comings and goings. In the final category are social policies and inequities that do not provide employed parents with sufficient resources to ensure quality care for their children while they are at work.

Separations of Fathers and Children. The long-standing belief that men's role in child rearing was of little significance resulted in low interest in the work-related separations of fathers and children. If we begin, instead, with the assumption that fathers play a crucial role in their children's development, it becomes meaningful to ask what effects fathers' work-related absences have on children. From what is known about maternal employment, as well as infant/father attachment, it is likely that ordinary work-related separations have no ill effects on children. More important are the quality of parenting and substitute care, as well as what occurs at homecoming (see Pedersen, Cain, Zaslow, and Anderson, 1982).

More pertinent than ordinary work-related separations are fathers' extraordinary absences from home due to work. Fathers, more than mothers, are likely to work long hours and on weekends (Staines and Pleck, 1983). Long hours are especially common among men with young children (Moen and Moorehouse, 1983), and moonlighting, weekend work, and shift work each decrease the time men spend doing things with and for their children (Staines and Pleck, 1983). A father's shift work, long working hours, or extensive job-related travel all represent some degree of father absence more extreme than that posed by standard work schedules, and mothers worry about the effects of such prolonged absences on their children, especially sons (Cohen, 1977; Piotrkowski, 1979). There is some consensus that father absence due to divorce, desertion, or death can have deleterious effects on children (Shinn, 1978; Biller, 1981; Radin, 1981). Can work-related absences have similar effects? Two types of extraordinary schedules are discussed here: (1) shift work and (2) extraordinary separations due to long working hours or job-related travel.

Although most research on shift work has focused on its effects on employees, several studies have found shift work to be associated with work/family conflict (Staines and Pleck, 1983). In a study of blue-collar, service, and clerical employees, almost half of all shift-work parents with minor children at home reported that work interfered moderately or a great deal with their family life (Piotrkowski and Stark, 1984). Shift workers tend to report feeling especially inadequate as parents (Mott, Mann, McLoughlin, and Warwick, 1965).

In assessing the consequences of parents' shift work for children, a child's age is a critical consideration. Before a child enters school, the father who is home and awake during the day has the opportunity to maximize the time he spends with his young child. Hood and Golden (1979) describe a couple who worked different shifts in order to manage child-care responsibilities, an arrangement that is not uncommon. The father was home during the day, became involved in caring for his pre-schoolers, and developed a very close relationship with them. The amount of time fathers spend in caretaking activities is related to infants' greater interaction, proximity seeking, and lessened separation protest, at least in laboratory settings (Parke 1981). Thus, a father's ability to maximize his involvement in caretaking could benefit his children.

Whereas an afternoon/evening work schedule may facilitate paternal involvement with a preschooler, it can mean lessened contact for the school-age child who comes home from school after the father has left for work. In fact, Mott, Mann, McLoughlin, and Warwick (1965) found that fathers on an afternoon/evening shift, especially those with younger children, perceived more difficulty being companions to their children, teaching them skills, maintaining close relationships, and controlling and disciplining them than fathers who worked the day shift. Fathers on shift work, especially if they work on a weekend day as well, can become absentee parents. The possible detrimental consequences of such excessive absence are apparent in a study by Landy, Rosenberg, and Sutton-Smith (1969). Female college students whose fathers had worked a night shift before they were ten had quantitative achievement scores similar to those whose fathers were totally absent from home. Although their method and data analysis were problematic, the authors reasonably conclude that shift work constitutes some degree of father absence.

This discussion of the developmental context of shift work suggests that the transition to school may create a problem for some children of shift workers. Entry into school is an important role transition for children and parents. The child must learn to negotiate the roles of a new institution, to perform in accordance with impersonal criteria, and to get along with strangers. For children with parents on nonstandard shifts, this transition may be doubly difficult. If the parents have been heavily involved in caretaking, these children move from prolonged daily contact with their parents to minimal contact, except for weekends. In this situation, some children might perceive the school as responsible for their loss, perhaps being aggressive or showing signs of depression or anxiety. Parents, too, might have feelings of loss. These remarks are speculative; given the large numbers of parents on nonstandard shifts, however, such transitions certainly are worth some attention for the developmental hurdles they present. It should also be noted that these remarks apply equally to mothers and fathers on nonstandard work schedules.

Among men, excessive working hours are reported to be the major source of work/family conflict (Pleck, Staines, and Lang, 1980). Moreover, some men travel extensively for their jobs, and in certain occupations they may be absent regularly for days, weeks, or even months at a time. But little is known about the impact of such prolonged absences on children.

Some limited research suggests that these extraordinary separations of fathers and children may have costs that need to be examined. At the less extreme end of the separation continuum, Piotrkowski and Stark (1984) found that the greater the number of hours that working-class fathers reported working regularly, the more symptoms of depression were reported by their preadolescent and adolescent daughters and the poorer were daughters' school performance. These daughters might experience their fathers' absences as a form of rejection or as a loss. Blanchard and Biller (1971) found that third-grade boys who spent, on average, at least two hours a day interacting with their fathers performed significantly better on achievement tests than boys who interacted infrequently with their fathers (that is, less than six hours a week, on average). Contributing to relative father absence was the time fathers spent at work.

Work-related travel also creates extraordinary separations of fathers from children. Cohen (1977) found that young managerial and professional fathers who traveled frequently or worked long hours did not play a significant role as companions or disciplinarians for their children. Several British studies have found decreased cognitive performance in children whose fathers are frequently away from home (see Shinn, 1978).

At the extreme end of the absence continuum are fathers who work as maritime workers, as long-distance truck drivers, or for the military. These fathers may be away from home for weeks or months at a time. Lynn and Sawrey (1959) studied the eight- and nine-year-old children of Norwegian maritime officers, who regularly were away nine months each year or more. They found, as expected, that the "father absent" boys showed greater immaturity and strivings for father identification in a doll-play situation than control boys with fathers who had more ordinary work schedules. Interviews with mothers indicated that the sons of the sailors were "hypermasculine" and showed poorer peer adjustment than the control boys. In the doll-play situation, the sailors' daughters showed greater dependency on their mothers than girls in the control group. Birth order and sibling gender may further moderate the effects of fathers' absence (Hillenbrand, 1976).

Several factors can influence the impact of fathers' extraordinary work-related absences from home. Job control is one such variable. Piotrkowski (1979) describes a supervisor/technician who had enough autonomy in his job to have his children visit him at work and to take frequent telephone calls from them. In this way he was able to mitigate the potential negative consequences of working long hours at two jobs. Staines and Pleck (1983) found that schedule control increased the time spent in child care thirteen hours per week and more among shift workers. For a child experiencing the transition to school, schedule control could allow an afternoon-shift father to delay his regular starting time, at least temporarily, in order to be home when his child arrives from school and to share the child's new experiences. Such flexibility might facilitate a potentially difficult adjustment to school. Unfortunately, for most employees such changes in work schedules are difficult to make. In addition, a mother's reaction to extended separation from her husband may influence her child's response to father absence (Hunter, 1982).

A child's own adaptive efforts should not be overlooked. As every parent knows, children are not merely acted upon. Instead, they are competent, forceful actors in their home environment. For example, one father who worked an afternoon/evening shift reported that his six-year-old daughter woke him up at night to show him a picture she had drawn at school and to ask about the tooth fairy (Piotrkowski, 1979). She knew her father would be home at two in the morning, and she cleverly initiated the face-to-face contact she needed from him.

Finally, the quality of parent/child relations is also important. Shinn (1978) has suggested that compensatory attention from mothers (and alternative male figures) may help children with absent fathers. But parental involvement does not always operate in predictable ways. Reuter and Biller (1973) studied the effects of paternal unavailability and nurturance on the personality adjustment of white male young adults from "intact" families. The poorest outcomes were associated with available fathers who were not nurturant and, surprisingly, with nurturant fathers who were not available. In this latter case the authors suggest that sons felt frustrated by their fathers' absence. Although it is unwise to generalize from a single study, at minimum the findings make us aware that contextual factors may modify the effects of extensive work-related separations of fathers and children.

Husbands and Wives

Managing intimacy and tension and developing some consensus about familial roles and values are tasks that couples face in marriage. Accomplishing them in mutually satisfying ways requires some face-to-face contact and opportunities for communication and decision making. Ordinary work schedules allowing spouses to be together during evenings and weekends seem to allow sufficient contact, as most married people report satisfying marital relationships. Wives' employment need not change the amount of contact that partners have, if both spouses have standard work schedules. With some exceptions, few reliable differences currently exist in marital adjustment and individual well-being between dual-earner and male-breadwinner couples (Staines, Pleck, Shepard, and O'Conner, 1978; Simpson and England, 1981; Booth, 1977; Kessler and McRae, 1982; Locksley, 1980).* Extraordinary work schedules, however, can alter this situation dramatically. Considered here are the effects on marriage of shift work and of extraordinary work-related absences due to long hours, travel, or separate living arrangements.

Afternoon/evening-shift workers are not home during weekday evenings, and night-shift workers may need to prepare for work early in the evening. These schedules infringe on or eliminate precious evening time—when children are asleep, household chores are complete, and husbands and wives can be alone together. Rotating shifts also curtail evening time because they involve both nighttime and afternoon/evening work, as well as instability in social rhythms. Thus, shift work may limit opportunities for husband/wife contact that are necessary for developing consensus and managing tensions and intimacy. Consistent with these notions, Mott, Mann, McLoughlin, and Warwick (1965) found that husbands in blue-collar jobs who worked a nonday shift reported greater difficulty in coordination of family roles, greater difficulties with tension management, and lower marital happiness than husbands on the day shift. The night shift and rotating shifts posed special difficulties for marriage. Couples with husbands on these shifts reported greater difficulties in achieving mutual understanding and in their sexual relations than couples with husbands on the afternoon/evening shift. These wives also reported difficulty providing emo-

---

*Differences that have persisted appear to result from variables other than separation. These include social class interacting with wives' employment, role strain, values regarding women's employment, role satisfaction, age of children, and husbands' participation in child care.

tional support for their husbands, and husbands on night and rotating shifts felt they could not protect their wives adequately at night. Piotrkowski (1979) found that some wives coped with their "night fears" by sleeping with one of their young children. This effort to reduce fearfulness introduced unintended complexities into the relationships between mothers and their children.

Development of consensus and regulation of intimacy and disagreement may be further disrupted when husbands and wives work different shifts, perhaps to facilitate child care. If the wife works during the day, for example, and the husband works evenings, contact between partners is severely restricted. The situation is further exacerbated when one spouse also works on the weekend. Since the separate-shifts arrangement is most common among young couples with children and among lower socioeconomic groups (Staines and Pleck, 1983; Presser and Cain, 1983), it affects marriages that are most vulnerable: those in the formative years and those with few economic resources. Such couples, therefore, may be at increased risk for developing marital problems or at least for being unable to resolve them successfully. Of course, shift work as a refuge for the unhappily married should not be overlooked (Mott, Mann, McLoughlin, and Warwick, 1965). Individuals who are made anxious by intimacy also may find shift work agreeable.

Are long working hours similarly disruptive? Booth, Johnson, and White (1984) found reduced marital cohesion when wives were employed more than forty hours per week. Keith and Schafer (1980) found that the more hours per week husbands work, the more role strain employed wives reported. However, Clark, Nye, and Gecas (1978) found no association between wives' marital satisfaction or perception of husbands' role competence and the number of hours husbands worked. Husbands' working hours may have their strongest negative impact at the extremes, which may not have been well represented in the study. However, the authors speculate that husbands compensated their wives for their absences by giving their marriages high priority when they were present.

This theme of compensatory involvement also emerged in

a British study of long-distance truck drivers who were absent for long periods. Hollowell (1968) found that poor marital adjustment occurred when husbands did not compensate their families for their absences. In these cases, the wives became extremely self-sufficient and the families adjusted by creating lives in which husbands had no part. The men became interlopers who disrupted the family when they were home. Under these conditions, husbands' sense of duty toward their families diminished, and they were more likely to seek emotional and sexual gratification outside marriage.

More positive adjustments occurred when husbands compensated wives for their absences by intensive participation in the family when they were home. The absences of such husbands were disruptive for the family, but the men remained important family members. The wives dealt with loneliness by turning to kinfolk or children for company during their husbands' absences. Wives accepted the separation during times of financial need but viewed the situation as temporary. When economic pressures decreased, husbands frequently returned to local trucking.

Studies of managers and their wives have also emphasized the stresses on marriage of husbands' extensive job-related travel. Strains include fears of being alone, worry, fatigue, guilt among husbands, and increased responsibilities for wives (Renshaw, 1976). Under these conditions, some corporate wives are unable to cope adequately (Seidenberg, 1975). Others, however, are relatively successful in managing marital separations. Wives who appear to cope with their husbands' extensive travel are those who alter their expectations of marriage and accept this life-style—doing what husbands and corporations expect of them. They also develop their social networks and become more independent and self-sufficient (Boss, McCubbin, and Lester, 1979; Cohen, 1977). Such women seem to subordinate their own needs to those of their spouses' jobs and try to develop some sources of gratification within that context. One must ask, however, about the consequences of this coping strategy for wives' self-esteem (Macke, Bohrnstedt, and Bernstein, 1979).

Studies of military families, especially navy families, find that wives may feel depressed, angry, abandoned, sexually frustrated, and lonely—especially at night and on weekends—when husbands are away on normal tours of duty (for example, Decker, 1978; Hunter, 1982; Isay, 1968). Interestingly, experience with extended separations does not necessarily enhance wives' abilities to cope with them (Decker, 1978). Reunions after long separations also pose special tasks for couples: During the separation, wives assume full responsibility for disciplining children, making household decisions, and so forth. On reunion, spouses may have differences regarding partners' independence, discipline of children, or the structure of household tasks, all requiring renegotiation. The longer and easier the separation is, the more difficult the reunion can be (Hunter, 1982). As Gerstel and Gross (1984) noted in studying couples with husbands in the merchant marine, in traditional marriages wives expect to make complex accommodations to their husbands' sailing schedules, but the task is not a simple one.

Even when husbands travel extensively in their jobs, couples generally maintain one household—the place they call home. More extreme separations can occur, as in the case of migrant workers and public figures who maintain separate residences from spouses. Until recently, such extreme separations have been occasioned by husbands' jobs. But with the rise of dual-career families, in which wives also have important career commitments, have come "commuter marriages." In these cases, spouses maintain separate residences and are apart for several days each week (Gerstel and Gross, 1984). Generally, such separations come about because of the career needs of *both* spouses and thus reflect an egalitarian view of marriage. The separations are viewed as necessary for career development but as temporary solutions (Gross, 1980). The commuting arrangement can benefit work life by allowing long stretches of involvement without the distraction of family responsibilities. It works best when there are no children at home, when career commitments are high and are accepted by both spouses, when work schedules are flexible, when spouses see each other every week or so, and when both careers and marriage are well established (Gross, 1980; Gerstel, 1977; Kirschner and Walum, 1978). Douvan and Pleck (1978) even describe several cases in which temporary commuting arrangements were helpful in facilitating wives' personal and professional development. By strengthening wives, the separations benefited the marriages.

Young marriages appear most vulnerable to the commuting arrangement (Gerstel, 1977; Gross, 1980). Career pressures are intense, and wives miss the intimacy and emotional protection of their husbands as they face career hurdles alone, while husbands may feel abandoned (Gross, 1980). Young couples in this circumstance express fears of growing apart and of sexual infidelity (Farris, 1978), for young marriages are not yet on a firm base and important marital tasks remain. Maintaining separate residences, however, does not seem to increase sexual infidelity (Gerstel, 1979), and couples evolve strategies for maintaining intimacy and communication, including frequent telephone calls, letters, and diaries (Kirschner and Walum, 1978). Even in the face of extreme separations, these marriages remain viable, as individuals pursue career paths that are important to them.

Concluding Remarks

Ordinary separations between family members resulting from standard nine-to-five work schedules by themselves have no necessary detrimental consequences for parent/child relations or for marriages. Despite assumptions about the necessity of a constant maternal presence for healthy child development, even young children are not invariably harmed by work-related daily separations from mothers. Employed mothers probably make up in quality and intensity of interaction what children miss in sheer quantity of contact. Factors such as a mother's satisfaction with what she is doing seem to be more critical for children than how much time she spends with them, at least within reasonable limits.

Still, this picture is overly simple, for it does not take into account the effects of spouses' combined work schedules. In traditional families, a mother may welcome a father's return home from work. She gets some relief from child-care responsibilities and can attend to dinner and chores, while he reunites with his children. They greet their father with glee, and—as several investigators have noted—these reunions may involve intense, joyous bouts of play. Whereas fathers become playmates with whom contact is scarce and desirable, mothers remain sources of pressure and conflict from whom children, young ones at least, cannot escape (Abelin, 1971; Piotrkowski, 1979). How such differences in children's experiences of each parent play themselves out in psychic development is an interesting question.

In contrast is the situation of the two-career family, where both parents are separated from their children during the day. At homecoming, do parents compete for the attention of their children, or—consistent with Pedersen, Cain, Zaslow, and Anderson's (1982) study—does the traditional primacy of the mother mean that the father is crowded out, interfering with the father/child bond? As the patterns of interaction that Pedersen and his colleagues found in early infancy did not persist, it is likely that families eventually work through these homecomings so that they are more satisfying. These two portrayals of homecoming events suggest, however, that different patterns of separation during the day affect reunion patterns at night.

The picture becomes even more complex when extraordinary work schedules are considered. Though incomplete, the existing research evidence indicates that extraordinary work schedules and the separations they entail have costs for children and families. The afternoon/evening shift is especially difficult for school-age children, while the night shift is costly for marriage. The uneven impact of work schedules on families makes policy planning difficult and indicates the importance of assessing multiple research outcomes. Excessive travel and long hours also may have negative effects, especially on children and on some marriages. Although the discussion of extraordinary work-related separations centered on husbands/fathers, inquiry needs to be extended to wives/mothers, who also work nonstandard shifts and, increasingly, hold second jobs (Sekscenski, 1980). We may find that mothers' and fathers' extraordinary absences affect families differently. Moreover, the combined work schedules of husbands and wives are important. Identified as high risk are those young marriages in which husbands and wives work different shifts and rarely see each other.

Despite the obvious difficulties created by nonstandard work schedules and extraordinary separations, many families manage to maintain their integrity and to provide a good enough environment for children. Commuting couples are a prime example of the ability of families to withstand extreme periods of separation, by using a variety of strategies to maintain intimacy and communication. Of course, these couples are relatively affluent and have chosen this path to career development. Still, coping strategies are reported in other contexts as well. Strategies include placing a high priority on family interaction when members are together, developing social networks and independent activities to cope with husbands' absences, and providing children with compensatory rituals to ease the distress of daily separations. Children too may develop their own ways of coping with parents' work-related absences. Such coping strategies have important practical effects and form a fruitful arena for research. It should also be noted that the necessity of developing elaborate coping strategies depends on how disruptive taxing work schedules are for any given family. This, in turn, depends on the importance a family places on togetherness and regularity (Kantor and Lehr, 1975) and on whether the absence is viewed as a rejection or as a contribution to familial well-being.

In addition to coping strategies, three critical factors have emerged as modifying the impact of work-related separations. The first is gender. Boys and girls may respond differently to parental absence, and some parents may treat boys and girls differently at homecoming. Similarly, the impact of men's and women's absences may differ because of their different family roles. Gender must not be overlooked as an important category when trying to assess the effects of work-related absences.

A second factor is the developmental context in which separation occurs—that is, the developmental stage of children and the stage of families in the life course. Individuals and families undergo changes through the life span that alter the fit between their needs and the adults' work schedules. For example, the afternoon shift can facilitate parents' contact with pre-schoolers while dramatically curtailing contact with school-age children. Commuter marriages are more stressful for young couples still negotiating important marital tasks than for older, more established couples. Important life events can also alter family members' needs for contact with each other. In Piotrkowski's (1979) study, several wives mentioned their pregnancies as a time they needed increased daily contact with their husbands, and another woman recalled her sorrow at her father's inability to attend her high school graduation because he was at work. A developmental view necessarily complicates our understanding of work-related separations.

The third critical factor is job control—including control over work schedules. Because the needs of individuals and families change over time, jobs that allow workers to exert some control over their work situation enable them to make "micro-adjustments" that can mitigate the negative effects of taxing work schedules, thereby improving the fit between familial or individual needs and work schedules (Staines and Pleck, 1983). Job control, for example, allows employees to bring children to work and to receive phone calls from family members. Moreover, control over work schedules can decrease the negative impact of shift work on parent/child contact. Time off during important life events such as pregnancy is especially important. Such policies as paternity and maternity leave and flexible work schedules are important innovations at the workplace. The way individuals and families use these opportunities, however, will depend on familial and individual values (Lee, 1983).

Most people need to work for pay in order to maintain their families and, increasingly, two wage earners are needed to maintain a reasonable standard of living. Many parents are caught between the desire to be with their children and the need to work overtime or at a second job for added income, especially when children are young. Building and maintaining a career also has costs in terms of family time. Lack of job control and difficulties in changing schedules make it hard to alter the balance of work and family time to meet changing needs.

Parents and children alike identify bad schedules and insufficient contact as what they find worst or most disruptive about jobs (Piotrkowski and Stark, 1984). That families manage to fulfill their basic responsibilities despite such demands on their time is a monument to their resourcefulness. Still, we cannot overlook the costs to children and families of difficult work schedules and extraordinary separations. Understanding these is a critical task facing researchers, practitioners, and policy makers.

References

Abelin, E. L. "The Role of the Father in the Separation-Individuation Process." In J. B. McDevitt and C. F. Settlage (eds.), *Separation-Individuation: Essays in Honor of Margaret S. Mahler.* New York: International Universities Press, 1971.

Ainsworth, M. D. S. "Infant-Mother Attachment." *American Psychologist,* 1979, *34,* 932-937.

Ainsworth, M. D. S., Blehar, M. C., Waters, E., and Wall, S. *Patterns of Attachment: A Psychological Study of the Strange Situation.* Hillsdale, N.J.: Erlbaum, 1978.

Ariès, P. *Centuries of Childhood.* New York: Random House, 1965.

Baron, A. "Protective Legislation and the Cult of Domesticity." *Journal of Family Issues,* 1981, *2,* 25-38.

Beckett, J. O. "Working Wives: A Racial Comparison." *Social Work,* 1976, *21,* 463-471.

Belsky, J., and Steinberg, L. D. "The Effects of Day Care: A Critical Review." *Child Development,* 1978, *49,* 929-949.

Biller, H. B. "Father Absence, Divorce, and Personality Development." In M. E. Lamb (ed.), *The Role of the Father in Child Development.* (2nd ed.) New York: Wiley, 1981.

Blanchard, R. W., and Biller, H. B. "Father Availability and Academic Performance Among Third-Grade Boys." *Developmental Psychology,* 1971, *4,* 301-305.

Booth, A. "Wife's Employment and Husband's Stress: A Replication and Refutation." *Journal of Marriage and the Family,* 1977, *39,* 645-650.

Booth, A., Johnson, D. R., and White, L. "Women, Outside Employment, and Marital Instability." *American Journal of Sociology,* 1984, *90,* 567–582.

Boss, P. G., McCubbin, H. I., and Lester, G. "The Corporate Executive Wife's Coping Patterns in Response to Routine Husband-Father Absence." *Family Process,* 1979, *18,* 79–86.

Bowlby, J. *Maternal Care and Mental Health.* Monograph 2. Geneva: World Health Organization, 1951.

Bowlby, J. *Attachment and Loss.* Vol. 2: *Separation: Anxiety and Anger.* New York: Basic Books, 1973.

Bronfenbrenner, U., Alvarez, W. F., and Henderson, C. R. "Working and Watching: Maternal Employment Status and Parents' Perceptions of Their Three-Year-Old Children." *Child Development,* 1984, *55,* 1362–1378.

Bronfenbrenner, U., and Crouter, A. C. "Work and Family Through Time and Space." In S. B. Kamerman and C. D. Hayes (eds.), *Families That Work: Children in a Changing World.* Washington, D.C.: National Academy Press, 1982.

Chafe, W. H. "Looking Backward in Order to Look Forward: Women, Work, and Social Values in America." In J. M. Kreps (ed.), *Women and the American Economy.* Englewood Cliffs, N.J.: Prentice-Hall, 1976.

Clark, R. A., Nye, F. I., and Gecas, V. "Work Involvement and Marital Role Performance." *Journal of Marriage and the Family,* 1978, *40,* 9–22.

Clarke-Stewart, A. *Daycare.* Cambridge, Mass.: Harvard University Press, 1982.

Cohen, G. "Absentee Husbands in Spiralist Families: The Myth of the Symmetrical Family." *Journal of Marriage and the Family,* 1977, *39,* 595–604.

Cohen, S. E. "Maternal Employment and Mother-Child Interaction." *Merrill-Palmer Quarterly,* 1978, *24*(3), 189–198.

Decker, K. B. "Coping with Sea Duty: Problems Encountered and Resources Utilized During Periods of Family Separation." In E. J. Hunter and D. S. Nice (eds.), *Military Families.* New York: Praeger, 1978.

Degler, C. N. *At Odds—Women and the Family in America from the Revolution to the Present.* New York: Oxford University Press, 1980.

Douvan, E., and Pleck, J. H. "Separation as Support." In R. Rapoport and R. Rapoport (eds.), *Working Couples.* New York: Harper Colophon Books, 1978.

Farber, E. A., and Egeland, B. "Developmental Consequences of Out-of-Home Care for Infants in a Low-Income Population." In E. Zigler and E. Gordon (eds.), *Day Care: Scientific and Social Policy Issues.* Dover, Mass.: Auburn House, 1982.

Farel, A. M. "Effects of Preferred Maternal Roles, Maternal Employment, and Sociodemographic Status on School Adjustment and Competence." *Child Development,* 1980, *51,* 1179-1186.

Farris, A. "Commuting." In R. Rapoport and R. Rapoport (eds.), *Working Couples.* New York: Harper Colophon Books, 1978.

Finn, P. "The Effects of Shiftwork on the Lives of Employees." *Monthly Labor Review,* 1981, *104*(10), 31-35.

Fraiberg, S. *Every Child's Birthright: In Defense of Mothering.* New York: Basic Books, 1972.

Gavron, H. *The Captive Wife.* London: Routledge & Kegan Paul, 1966.

Gerstel, N. R. "The Feasibility of Commuter Marriage." In P. Stein, J. Richman, and N. Hannon (eds.), *The Family: Functions, Conflicts, and Symbols.* Reading, Mass.: Addison-Wesley, 1977.

Gerstel, N. R. "Marital Alternatives and the Regulation of Sex." *Alternative Lifestyles,* 1979, *2,* 145-176.

Gerstel, N. R., and Gross, H. *Commuter Marriage.* New York: Guilford Press, 1984.

Gross, H. E. "Dual-Career Couples Who Live Apart: Two Types." *Journal of Marriage and the Family,* 1980, *42,* 567-576.

Hedges, J. N., and Taylor, D. E. "Recent Trends in Worktime: Hours Edge Downward." *Monthly Labor Review,* 1980, *103* (3), 3-11.

Heyns, B. "The Influence of Parents' Work on Children's School Achievement." In S. B. Kamerman and C. D. Hayes (eds.), *Families That Work: Children in a Changing World.* Washington, D.C.: National Academy Press, 1982.

Hillenbrand, E. "Father Absence in Military Families." *Family Coordinator,* 1976, *25,* 451–458.

Hoch, E. "Working and Nonworking Mothers and Their Infants: A Comparative Study of Maternal Caregiving Characteristics and Infant Social Behavior." *Merrill-Palmer Quarterly,* 1980, *26,* 79–101.

Hoffman, L. W. "Mother's Enjoyment of Work and Effects on the Child." In F. I. Nye and L. W. Hoffman (eds.), *The Employed Mother in America.* Chicago: Rand McNally, 1963.

Hoffman, L. W. "Effects of Maternal Employment on the Child: A Review of the Research." *Developmental Psychology,* 1974, *10,* 204–228.

Hoffman, L. W. "Maternal Employment: 1979." *American Psychologist,* 1979, *34,* 859–865.

Hoffman, L. W. "The Effects of Maternal Employment on the Academic Attitudes and Performance of School-Aged Children." *School Psychology Review,* 1980, *9,* 319–335.

Hoffman, L. W. "Work, Family, and the Socialization of the Child." In R. D. Parke (ed.), *Review of Child Development Research.* Vol. 7. Chicago: University of Chicago Press, 1983.

Hoffman, L. W. "Maternal Employment and the Young Child." In M. Perlmuther (ed.), *Parent-Child Interaction and Parent-Child Relations in Child Development.* Minnesota Symposium on Child Psychology. Vol. 17. pp. 101–127. Hillsdale, N.J.: Erlbaum, 1984.

Hollowell, P. D. *The Lorry Driver.* London: Routledge & Kegan Paul, 1968.

Hood, J., and Golden, S. "Beating Time/Making Time: The Impact of Work Scheduling on Men's Family Roles." *Family Coordinator,* 1979, *28,* 575–582.

Hunter, E. J. *Families Under the Flag.* New York: Praeger, 1982.

Isay, R. "The Submariners' Wives Syndrome." *Psychiatric Quarterly,* 1968, *42,* 647–652.

Kanter, R. M. *Work and Family in the United States.* New York: Russell Sage Foundation, 1977.

Kantor, D., and Lehr, W. *Inside the Family: Toward a Theory of Family Process.* San Francisco: Jossey-Bass, 1975.

Keith, P. M., and Schafer, R. B. "Role Strain and Depression in Two-Job Families." *Family Relations,* 1980, *29,* 483–488.

Kessler, R. C., and McRae, J. A., Jr. "The Effects of Wives' Employment on the Mental Health of Married Men and Women." *American Sociological Review,* 1982, *47,* 216–227.

King, K., McIntyre, J., and Axelson, L. J. "Adolescents' Views of Maternal Employment as a Threat to the Marital Relationship." *Journal of Marriage and the Family,* 1968, *30,* 633–637.

Kirschner, B. F., and Walum, L. R. "Two-Location Families." *Alternative Lifestyles,* 1978, *1,* 513–525.

Lamb, M. E. "Interactions Between Eight-Month-Old Children and Their Fathers and Mothers." In M. E. Lamb (ed.), *The Role of the Father in Child Development.* New York: Wiley, 1976.

Landy, F., Rosenberg, B. G., and Sutton-Smith, B. "The Effects of Limited Father Absence on Cognitive Development." *Child Development,* 1969, *40,* 941–944.

Lee, R. A. "Flexitime and Conjugal Roles." *Journal of Occupational Behavior,* 1983, *4,* 297–315.

Lerner, J. V., and Galambos, N. L. "Maternal Role Satisfaction, Mother-Child Interaction, and Child Temperament: A Process Model." *Developmental Psychology,* 1985, *21,* 1157–1164.

Locksley, A. "On the Effects of Wives' Employment on Marital Adjustment and Companionship." *Journal of Marriage and the Family,* 1980, *42,* 337–346.

Lynn, D. B., and Sawrey, W. L. "The Effects of Father Absence on Norwegian Boys and Girls." *Journal of Abnormal and Social Psychology,* 1959, *59,* 258–262.

Maccoby, E. E. "Effects upon Children of Their Mothers' Outside Employment." In *Work in the Lives of Married Women: Proceedings of the National Manpower Council.* New York: Columbia University Press, 1958.

McCord, J., McCord, W., and Thurber, E. "Effects of Maternal Employment on Lower-Class Boys." *Journal of Abnormal and Social Psychology,* 1963, *67,* 177–182.

Macke, A. S., Bohrnstedt, G. W., and Bernstein, I. N. "Housewives' Self-Esteem and Their Husbands' Success: The Myth of Vicarious Involvement." *Journal of Marriage and the Family,* 1979, *41,* 51–58.

Minturn, L., and Lambert, W. W. *Mothers of Six Cultures: Antecedents of Child Rearing.* New York: Wiley, 1964.

Moen, P., and Moorehouse, M. "Overtime over the Life Cycle: A Test of the Life Cycle Squeeze Hypothesis." In H. Z. Lopata and J. H. Pleck (eds.), *Research in the Interweave of Social Roles.* Vol. 3: *Families and Jobs.* Greenwich, Conn.: JAI Press, 1983.

Moore, K., Spain, D., and Bianchi, S. "Working Wives and Mothers." *Marriage and Family Review,* 1984, *7*(3–4), 77–98.

Moore, T. "Stress in Normal Childhood." *Human Relations,* 1969, *22,* 235–250.

Mott, P. E., Mann, F. C., McLoughlin, Q., and Warwick, D. P. *Shift Work.* Ann Arbor: University of Michigan Press, 1965.

Parke, R. D. *Fathers.* Cambridge, Mass.: Harvard University Press, 1981.

Pedersen, F. A., Cain, R. L., Jr., Zaslow, M. J., and Anderson, B. J. "Variation in Infant Experience Associated with Alternative Family Roles." In L. Laosa and I. Sigel (eds.), *Families as Learning Environments for Children.* New York: Plenum, 1982.

Piotrkowski, C. S. *Work and the Family System.* New York: Macmillan, 1979.

Piotrkowski, C. S., and Katz, M. H. "Women's Work and Personal Relations in the Family." In P. W. Berman and E. R. Ramey (eds.), *Women: A Developmental Perspective.* Bethesda, Md.: National Institutes of Health, 1982.

Piotrkowski, C. S., and Katz, M. H. "Work Experience and Family Relations Among Working-Class and Lower Middle-Class Families." In H. Z. Lopata and J. H. Pleck (eds.), *Research in the Interweave of Social Roles.* Vol. 3: *Families and Jobs.* Greenwich, Conn.: JAI Press, 1983.

Piotrkowski, C. S., and Stark, E. "Job Stress and Children's Mental Health: An Ecological Study." Report prepared for the W. T. Grant Foundation, New York, 1984.

Pleck, E. "Two Worlds in One: Work and Family." *Journal of Social History,* 1976, *10,* 178–195.

Pleck, J. H., Staines, G. L., and Lang, L. "Conflicts Between Work and Family Life." *Monthly Labor Review,* 1980, *103* (3), 29-32.

Presser, H. B., and Cain, V. S. "Shift Work Among Dual-Earner Couples with Children." *Science,* 1983, *219,* 876-879.

Propper, A. M. "The Relationship of Maternal Employment to Adolescent Roles, Activities, and Parental Relationships." *Journal of Marriage and the Family,* 1972, *34,* 417-421.

Radin, N. "The Role of the Father in Cognitive, Academic, and Intellectual Development." In M. E. Lamb (ed.), *The Role of the Father in Child Development.* (2nd ed.) New York: Wiley, 1981.

Renshaw, J. R. "An Exploration of the Dynamics of the Overlapping Worlds of Work and Family Life." *Family Process,* 1976, *15,* 143-165.

Reuter, M. W., and Biller, H. B. "Perceived Paternal Nurturance —Availability and Personality Adjustment Among College Males." *Journal of Consulting and Clinical Psychology,* 1973, *40,* 339-342.

Schachter, F. F. "Toddlers with Employed Mothers." *Child Development,* 1981, *52,* 958-964.

Scott, J. W., and Tilly, L. A. "Women's Work and the Family in Nineteenth Century Europe." In C. E. Rosenberg (ed.), *The Family in History.* Philadelphia: University of Pennsylvania Press, 1975.

Seidenberg, R. *Corporate Wives—Corporate Casualties?* New York: Doubleday, 1975.

Sekscenski, E. S. "Women's Share of Moonlighting Nearly Doubles During 1969-79." *Monthly Labor Review,* 1980, *103* (5), 36-39.

Shinn, M. "Father Absence and Children's Cognitive Development." *Psychological Bulletin,* 1978, *85,* 295-324.

Simpson, I. H., and England, P. "Conjugal Work Roles and Marital Solidarity." *Journal of Family Issues,* 1981, *2,* 180-204.

Smelser, N. J. *Social Change in the Industrial Revolution.* London: Routledge & Kegan Paul, 1959.

Staines, G. L., and Pleck, J. H. *The Impact of Work Schedules on the Family.* Ann Arbor: Survey Research Center, University of Michigan, 1983.

Staines, G. L., Pleck, J. H., Shepard, L. J., and O'Conner, P. O. "Wives' Employment Status and Marital Adjustment." *Psychology of Women Quarterly,* 1978, *3,* 90–120.

Stuckey, M. F., McGhee, P. E., and Bell, N. J. "Parent-Child Interaction: The Influence of Maternal Employment." *Developmental Psychology,* 1982, *18,* 635–644.

Tentler, L. *Wage-Earning Women, Industrial Work, and Family Life in the United States, 1900–1930.* New York: Oxford University Press, 1979.

Thompson, E. P. *The Making of the English Working Class.* New York: Vintage, 1966.

Turner, C. "Dual Work Households and Marital Dissolution." *Human Relations,* 1971, *24,* 535–548.

U.S. Bureau of the Census. *Statistical Abstract of the United States: 1984.* (104th ed.) Washington, D.C.: U.S. Bureau of the Census, 1983.

Wilensky, H. L. "The Uneven Distribution of Leisure: The Impact of Economic Growth on 'Free Time.'" *Social Problems,* Summer 1961, pp. 32–54.

Woods, M. B. "The Unsupervised Child of the Working Mother." *Developmental Psychology,* 1972, *6,* 14–25.

Working Family Project. "Parenting." In R. Rapoport and R. Rapoport (eds.), *Working Couples.* New York: Harper Colophon Books, 1978.

Yarrow, M. R., Scott, P., De Leeuw, L., and Heinig, C. "Child-Rearing in Families of Working and Non-working Mothers." *Sociometry,* 1962, *25,* 122–140.

Zaslow, M., Pedersen, F. A., Suwalsky, J., and Rabinovich, B. "Maternal Employment and Parent-Infant Interaction." Paper presented at the meeting of the Society for Research in Child Development, Detroit, April 1983.

9

Moving to a New Culture: Cultural Identity, Loss, and Mourning

Marsha H. Levy-Warren

Editors' Note: *This chapter illustrates how reactions to a sepa-*
ration event—in this case, the move to a new culture—depend
in large part on the individual's ability to engage in a healthy
mourning process. Levy-Warren, like most of the authors in this
volume, emphasizes the role of inner representations in facilitat-
ing healthy adjustment to loss. She draws an interesting parallel
between the way object constancy allows the child to function
independently and the way clear and stable internal images of
one's culture of origin promote successful adaptation to cultural
relocation.

The author examines the role of culture in the formation
of identity and describes how representations of culture, and
therefore the meaning of culture loss, change through develop-
ment. She looks at how culture has been viewed in psychoana-
lytic theory, focusing on its role in the formation of intrapsychic
structure. Levy-Warren distinguishes culture loss from culture
shock, a more extreme separation reaction in which the loss of
culture is experienced as an internal ego impoverishment. (In
Chapter Twelve, Lerner and Lerner also describe striking differ-
ences in the depressive experiences of patients based on their

300

*internal capacity to mourn.) External factors affecting the sepa-
ration reaction are also delineated: age at relocation, presence
of animate and inanimate objects from the lost culture, circumstances surrounding the relocation (especially degree of choice
and preparation for the move), and differences between the culture of origin and the new culture.*

*Clinical examples provide rich illustrations of the differ-
ence between the natural mourning process of culture loss and
the more pathological melancholic expressions of culture shock.
Levy-Warren also shows how individuals' emotional difficulties
may be shaped by childhood exposure to primary caretakers'
experiences of culture shock, even when presenting patients
themselves have not faced the move to a new culture. In other
patients, there is inadequate recognition of the personal significance of cultural relocation, resulting in an inability to mourn.
Such defensive reactions to separation have been elaborated further in Chapters Three and Six, which discuss variations in
young children's responses to separation.*

Cultural relocation tugs at the very roots of identity. Social science and psychiatric reports alike document the disruption that
occurs when people move from their cultures of origin. What
has yet to be established, however, is just what it is that accounts for the tremendous individual variation in confusion and
disorientation experienced in making such a move (Levy-Warren,
1980).

This chapter examines the disruptions that people experience in separating from their cultures of origin (culture loss, culture shock) and presents a theoretical framework within which
these disruptions can be understood. It describes how culture
comes to be internally represented in the formation of identity
and intrapsychic structure and posits that culture loss is analogous to mourning, while culture shock parallels the more
pathological process of melancholia, as described by Freud in
"Mourning and Melancholia" (1917/1957).

Cultural relocation involves both an internal and an external process of separation. Internal separation occurs within
the context of identity formation; it refers to the growth and

development of mental representations of self and object. External separation is the actual move from one geographical location to another, with an attendant loss of objects and people.

Previous psychoanalytic writings on cultural relocation have discussed a sense of inherent loss and a mourning process (Dellarossa, 1979; Grinberg, 1971), the particular quality of strangeness experienced on arriving in a new culture (Ticho, 1971), and the necessity for a reorganization of identity (Garza-Guerrero, 1974). Just how it is that culture plays a role in the process of identity formation and how cultural relocation, therefore, shakes identity to its core have still to be clearly delineated. This chapter explicates that process, describes factors that influence the disruptiveness of relocation, and concludes with illustrative clinical examples.

Role of Culture in Identity Formation

The registering of culture as part of an individual's identity begins with the mental representations of the relationship between the infant and the need-satisfying object as colored by the social situation in which they form and crystallizes in the development of differentiated mental representations of culture at the close of adolescence. Culture also influences the development of the intrapsychic structures, in that the ego, superego, and ego ideal have important roots in the sociocultural world. These constitute the basis for the significant impact that cultural relocation may have on identity.

The sense of identity has its beginnings in the first mental images of the body (Greenacre, 1958) and proceeds with the development of progressively more differentiated, symbolic, and continuous mental representations of the self and of animate and inanimate objects (Jacobson, 1964; Mahler and Furer, 1968; Schafer, 1968). Internalization of a stable representation of the need-satisfying object ("libidinal object constancy") is the critical aspect of this process (Fraiberg, 1969; Mahler, Pine, and Bergman, 1975), for it permits the child to feel secure even in the absence of the primary caretaker. Establishment of libidinal object constancy takes place within a particular setting, a setting that becomes familiar. That setting alone (that is, one's room or home) will come to evoke comfort through its association with the need-satisfying object.

Representations are, therefore, influenced by the surroundings in which they form. As the child's world expands through the maturation of both emotional and cognitive apparatuses (Hartmann, 1950; Werner, 1957), the cultural coloration of the mental representations becomes more vivid. Winnicott (1981) described the experience of culture as falling into "the potential space between the individual and the environment, that which initially both joins and separates the baby and the mother when the mother's love, displayed or made manifest as human reliability, does in fact give the baby a sense of trust or of confidence in the environmental factor" (p. 121). I further propose that the surroundings themselves have representations, which evoke such comfort as was originally associated with the need-satisfying object. It is these that are the early form of what during adolescence and adulthood become mental representations of culture.

This idea is not without precedent in the psychoanalytic literature. In "Mourning and Melancholia" (1917/1957) Freud writes that mourning can occur in reaction to the loss of an abstraction (which takes the place of a loved person) such as "one's country, liberty, an ideal, and so on" (p. 143). This description suggests the possibility that there are representations for nonobjects such as culture.

Culture is here conceived of as including both concrete and abstract aspects of the environment. That is, its internal representation is through images of people, things, sights, smells, and sounds, as well as values. These are first associated strongly with the most important people in the growing child's life. Then, as representations become more differentiated and the child more individuated, they come to take on their own significance. This process is connected to the development of the capacity for abstraction during adolescence (Piaget and Inhelder, 1969), which makes the world of ideas accessible in a manner never before possible. The first fully elaborated representations of culture itself can, therefore, only take place during adoles-

cence. Culture takes on an increased significance in a person's
life in a variety of ways at this time.

Culture plays a particularly important role both in the
adolescent's representational system and in the reorganization
of intrapsychic structure that occurs during that time. Discussions of the changing superego and ego ideal (A. Freud, 1952;
Blos, 1979) highlight the increased intensity with which the
youth invests the world outside the family of origin. Indeed, the
mature ego ideal, the source of the standards by which self-
esteem is determined at the close of adolescence, derives in large
part from cultural influences.

Culture, however, was always described in psychoanalytic
theory with regard to its role in the formation of intrapsychic
structure. The change from Freud's topographical position in
The Interpretation of Dreams (1900/1953) to his structural position in *The Ego and the Id* (1923/1961) made possible the
first theoretical vision of culture as having an active role in individual development.

The vicissitudes of the influence of culture (external reality) on the development of the ego in its various functions, as
well as the influence of the ego on an individual's adaptation to
culture, have been well documented (Bibring, 1941; Fenichel,
1954; A. Freud, 1967; Hartmann, 1939/1958; Nunberg, 1931;
Waelder, 1936). Freud's final word on the subject, in "An Outline of Psychoanalysis" (1940/1964a), described the ego as determined mostly by an "individual's own experience, that is, by
accidental and contemporary events" (p. 147). It was through
the agency of the superego that the early parental influence was
prolonged. The ego was described as having always to satisfy the
demands of the id, the superego, and reality. It is important to
note that the record of parental influence in the superego included "not only the personalities of the actual parents but also
the family, racial, and national traditions handed on through
them, as well as the demands of the immediate social milieu
which they represent" (p. 146).

The degree of autonomy of the ego from the surrounding
culture has also been a subject of relevant major theoretical
work (Hartmann, 1939/1958; Erikson, 1950; Rapaport, 1958).

The role of the environment in sustaining the defensive and adaptive structures (Rapaport, 1958) and the ways that culture may shape opportunities for ego functioning (Hartmann, Kris, and Loewenstein, 1951) and conditions for adaptation (Muensterberger, 1968) have been given special attention.

In light of the foregoing discussion of the ways culture is integrated in individuals, both intrapsychically and in the formation of identity, it is here suggested that cultural relocation may have an important influence on identity and may create a situation in which fundamental aspects of identity are called into question, depending on the timing and circumstances of the move. When the people, things, sights, smells, sounds, and values around a person change markedly, as happens in cultural relocation, so do the sources of representations, the surroundings in which the intrapsychic structures form, and the situation in which defensive and adaptive mechanisms are sustained. It is in this way that the move reverberates profoundly in the individual in transition.

Impact of Cultural Relocation

A move from one's culture of origin can be seen as similar to the loss of a loved person, which initiates a process of mourning. Bit by bit, the mental representations of people, places, and various kinds of symbols associated with the culture are brought to mind. The representations are first invested with great emotional intensity and then gradually diminish in their emotional significance (Freud, 1917/1957).

In "Analysis Terminable and Interminable" (1937/1964b) Freud wrote about individual differences in the adhesiveness of the libido (p. 241)—the ease or difficulty with which people detach from the important objects in their lives. Variability of secure attachments within the family, just like variability in the adhesiveness of the libido, plays an important role in establishing the intensity of the loss of the culture, as it does in any experience of loss (Freud, 1917/1957). When representations remain intensely connected to the objects themselves rather than having achieved some measure of independence, the loss of the object (or culture) is experienced as a personal impoverishment, rather than an impoverishment in the external world. This is what happens when mourning becomes melancholia (Freud, 1917/1957); this is what is here being proposed as the difference between a feeling of culture loss and a feeling of culture shock.

This is not the same sense of *culture shock* that may be in common use. *Culture shock* has come to refer to a wide range of experiences of loss and disorientation upon entering a new culture (Garza-Guerrero, 1974). It is critical, however, to distinguish between entering a new culture and experiencing an internal ego impoverishment, here denoted as culture "shock," and entering a new culture and experiencing an impoverishment in the external world, here denoted as culture "loss." The distinction is related to the strength, stability, and differentiation of the mental representations that form the core of identity as discussed earlier. A global, nondifferentiated representation remains at a narcissistic, wishful stage of development; the stable representation is at a more realistic, object-related stage.

The timing of a move in a person's life is important in the degree of upset that the experience may engender. A move made with parents within the first five years of life is only a geographical move for the young child. Culture at this time is almost entirely associated with the primary caretakers, so that the "culture" for the child moves with the family. Although the experience of being in a new place may arouse some anxiety, tension specific to the cultural relocation will be present only if it is transmitted through the primary caretakers. The presence of the important loved persons is critical, therefore, in the early years of life. Its importance diminishes over time. Late adolescents and adults who move already have a rather stable and differentiated mental representation of culture. The presence of important loved persons is therefore less critical. It is always a consideration, however, as is the presence or absence of inanimate objects taken from the original culture that might evoke the sense of comfort that originates in the early relationship with the primary caretaker.

The presence or absence of animate and inanimate objects is often influenced by the circumstances of the relocation, another of the important factors to be considered. The degree of choice or necessity and the time of and preparation for relocation influence the kind of loss that is experienced (for example, permanent or temporary, full-scale or partial) and play a major role in the kind of mourning process required. Plans to return to the culture of origin and the expected degree of assimilation to the new culture are also important, particularly insofar as those beliefs are used to ward off the mourning process.

Differences between the culture of origin and the culture of relocation are also significant, for vast differences between the two may allow fewer opportunities for a person to function in ways that sustain self-esteem (Hartmann, Kris, and Loewenstein, 1951; Rapaport, 1958). The consonance of an individual's standards that shape self-esteem ("ego ideal") with societal standards that determine self-worth may vary tremendously. Something that in one culture may be a source of pride may, in the other, be of little or no importance. This might be of particular significance for the adolescent, whose standards are already in a process of transformation: the youth will find a cultural relocation especially difficult if the move is made before stable standards are established.

The experience of culture loss or culture shock is, then, dependent on the stability and differentiation of the individual's mental representations of culture. These representations are, in turn, very much influenced by such factors as the timing of the move in a person's life and the presence of both animate and inanimate objects. The differences between the two cultures may affect the difficulty of the move as well.

The Clinical Situation

Cultural relocation manifests itself in the clinical situation in two major ways. The cultural relocation and mourning process are of primary significance, in the form either of culture shock or of culture loss; or the cultural relocation is of secondary significance, in which case there really has been an inadequate recognition of the personal significance of the move and the consequent need for a mourning process. Illustrations of each of these follow.

When culture shock is present in the clinical situation, either the patient is the person who has moved from another culture and is in shock, or a primary caretaker was in culture shock at a time when the patient was in need of a degree of involvement with the caretaker that was not possible because of that caretaker's melancholic disposition. In the instance of a culture loss, it is usually the patient who has undergone the relocation.

In any case, a clinical picture is always complex and overdetermined. The following case examples are viewed solely from one of many possible perspectives: that of the role of cultural relocation and cultural identity in the overall treatment situation. Cases one, two, and three describe situations in which cultural relocation is of primary significance; case four, a situation in which it is of secondary significance.

Case One: Culture Shock. Mr. M., a twenty-year-old Hispanic, was admitted to a hospital because of hallucinations, delusions, suicidal ideation, and violent behavior toward his wife. He had lost his usual capacity to speak English; in Spanish, he repeated over and over that he had sinned and deserved to die. He carried with him a crucifix and rosary beads.

On meeting with Mr. M.'s wife, the therapist learned that the patient had arrived in this country for the first time three months earlier. Soon after the arrival, he had become increasingly withdrawn, refused to go outdoors, stopped eating, had trouble sleeping, and stopped having sexual relations with his wife.

Once very competent in English, he no longer evidenced any understanding of the language. He began praying every morning, a practice his wife had never seen him carry on in their marriage of two and a half years. She noted, however, that his mother was a very religious woman.

In the ensuing weeks, Mr. M. spoke about his mother a great deal. What evolved was that he had left his country of origin in large part to escape from her criticism and intrusiveness: her disapproval of his marriage to a woman from the United States, his "American" ways, and his complete lack of interest in Catholicism. In his wholesale disconnection from all that was American around him and his return to his "mother tongue" and Catholicism—through what Freud (1917/1957, p. 244) called the "medium of a hallucinatory wishful psychosis" —he expressed his very intense opposition to the loss of his culture of origin, so clearly connected with the primary caretaker of his early years. His suicidal ideation and prominent feelings of guilt were indicative of severe superego condemnation. The cultural relocation brought to the fore the fundamental fragility of not only his sense of culture identity but also his sense of identity as a whole. "Culture" and "mother" remained in an interconnected state; stable, differentiated representations of self, object, and culture were not evident.

Case Two: Culture Shock. Ms. G., a twenty-two-year-old first-year graduate student in modern literature, came for outpatient psychotherapeutic treatment complaining of inability to concentrate on her studies, sleeping problems (including repetitive nightmares), and inexplicable mood swings. She did not know whether she belonged in the field of study she had chosen.

It quickly emerged that Ms. G. had almost never felt she belonged in any group in which she had found herself. The social group in which she had been most comfortable was that of her home-town contemporaries. She was still in touch with many of her school friends, having remained in close contact with them throughout their college years, which had been spent in geographically distant places.

The repetitive nightmares of which she complained were filled with experiences of entrapment: being lost in the woods, caught on a rock in a raging river, unable to find the entrance to a tunnel. Her associations led to her relationship with her mother, a Holocaust survivor, who had been hospitalized for a severe depressive episode during Ms. G.'s pubescence and was remembered as having cried continually during Ms. G.'s early childhood.

At this point, Ms. G. began to recall repeated instances of being told frightening tales of the Holocaust as a young child. She also remembered spending many hours at the homes of school friends, where she was told the fairy tales so much a part of American culture. A picture of a very divided sense of cultural identity gradually emerged: one firmly rooted in the cultural surrounds, the other rooted in the highly charged, painful experiences of her mother in Eastern Europe. No late-adolescent consolidation of identity could be achieved until these various superego and ego identifications and cultural representations had surfaced. Ms. G.'s early relationship with her mother significantly interfered with a clear sense of belonging in a field of study or a social group, for it clouded her capacity to see herself as an individual who was part of a particular culture.

Case Three: Culture Loss. Ms. B., a thirty-four-year-old who had recently arrived from the Middle East, came into outpatient treatment complaining of difficulties in eating and sleeping, an inability to focus on her new job, and a "feeling that the world was not real."

She and her husband, child, and mother had arrived in this country three months before. There had been a long-standing intention to move, for both economic and political reasons, but the actual circumstances of the relocation involved a hasty departure. Both she and her husband had been offered employment if they were able to arrive in three weeks' time.

In treatment, Ms. B. spent most of her time talking about her culture of origin: the food markets she used to wander through on her way home from work; the schools she had attended while growing up; the different smells, sounds, and sights associated with her daily life. She described her vivid dreams about various people and places from "home." She cried, she laughed, she mused, all very much in the service of bringing her culture into the consulting room.

Over the course of several months, Ms. B. began to live more fully in this culture. The food no longer gave her digestive problems; the street noises did not disturb her sleep. The feelings of unreality disappeared. She began to enjoy her job and function well in it. The mourning process for her lost culture was drawing to a close; having spent time recalling and reliving various aspects of her life in her culture of origin, she was ready to live in a new place. The impoverishment was clearly outside Ms. B., making this an instance of culture "loss." Once she was able to affectively recall various aspects of the lost culture, thus allowing herself to mourn, she could engage more fully in the culture in which she now planned to live.

Case Four: Avoidance of Mourning. Ms. C., a twenty-eight-year-old from Central America, came into treatment confused about whether to continue in a long-standing relationship, whether to pursue the career she had chosen, and whether to stay in her current job. She could not resolve her indecisiveness and felt guilty and anxious much of the time.

Ms. C. had left her culture of origin at age seventeen with the intention of attending college in this country and then returning home. After college, she attended a trade school; then she took a position in a training program in her field. While in the program, she met the man with whom she was now in a relationship. They talked periodically about getting married.

At no point in time had Ms. C. truly determined whether she was going to return to her culture of origin or stay here. By maintaining that she might return, she kept active her connection with that culture, which seemed to make it more and more difficult to participate fully in the life she had established for herself here. There had been no mourning process, for she had never allowed herself to leave. "I feel like I have been living for eleven years as a permanent temporary," she noted, "neither here nor there. I have made a life here but never committed myself to really living it."

There were many ways in which Ms. C.'s cultural background and sense of cultural identity played a role in her dilemma. She spoke of having no feeling of being firmly identified with either this culture or that of her origin: it seemed as if she had moved before establishing a clear mental representation of culture. Given that she had moved during her adolescence, it is likely that the maturation of her ego ideal had taken place in different cultures, contributing to the shifts in her self-esteem. Her personal standards for establishing self-esteem would have derived from both the culture of origin and the culture of relocation.

Ms. C.'s emotional investment in avoiding the loss of her culture of origin kept her from sustaining the pleasure she might have experienced from her current cultural life. Bringing these issues to light, which evolved into Ms. C.'s making a decision to stay in this culture, initiated a mourning process that eventually served to help free her to participate more fully in her present life.

Summary of Clinical Cases. In the first case illustration of culture shock, that of Mr. M., stable, differentiated representations of culture had not been adequately formed prior to relocation. Mr. M.'s cultural identity remained rooted in his primary identification with his mother—he could not enter a new culture with a stable sense of himself. In the case of Ms. G., a daughter was unable to achieve a full late-adolescent consolidation of identity, for her cultural representations were split between early identifications with her mother (who had been in culture shock) and somewhat undeveloped representations of her own culture of origin.

Ms. B. evidenced no such lack of differentiation or instability in her cultural identity: hers was a temporary inhibition in reality testing and in her capacity to sustain pleasure, an example of culture loss. Ms. C. was similarly inhibited in her ego functioning: her representations of culture had never become fully developed; a major aspect of her identity had never become fully integrated. She too suffered culture loss.

Conclusion

Just as libidinal object constancy is crucial in a child's capacity to live a life independent of the primary caretaker, so is establishment of clear and stable representations of culture crucial in the capacity of an individual to move from one culture to another. When the representations have remained in their earliest, global, undifferentiated form, the individual is likely to experience what has been defined here as culture shock, a pathological mourning state. The more differentiated representations of culture will permit an experience of culture loss, a normal mourning state.

The age of the person making the move is highly relevant. The younger the individual, the more likely it is that representations will be in a less differentiated form; thus, the more important becomes the presence of significant animate and inanimate objects from the culture of origin. Their presence, in turn, is influenced by the atmosphere in which the move took place—for example, how much choice and planning were exercised.

Several of the relevant factors in understanding the degree of personal disruptiveness of cultural relocation are here introduced; many others will come to light in further work in the area. The theoretical stance set forth provides a framework within which these factors can be discussed and utilized in the clinical situation.

References

Bibring, E. "The Development and Problems of the Instincts." *International Journal of Psycho-Analysis,* 1941, *22,* 102–131.

Blos, P. *The Adolescent Passage.* New York: International Universities Press, 1979.

Dellarossa, G. S. "The Professional of Immigrant Descent." *International Journal of Psycho-Analysis,* 1979, *59,* 37–44.

Erikson, E. H. *Childhood and Society.* New York: Norton, 1950.

Fenichel, O. "Early Stages of Ego Development." In H. Fenichel and D. Rapaport (eds.), *The Collected Papers of Otto Fenichel, Second Series.* New York: Norton, 1954.

Fraiberg, S. "Libidinal Object Constancy and Mental Representation." *Psychoanalytic Study of the Child,* 1969, *24,* 9–47.

Freud, A. "The Mutual Influences in the Development of the Ego and the Id: Introduction to the Discussion." *Psychoanalytic Study of the Child,* 1952, *1,* 42–50.

Freud, A. *The Ego and the Mechanisms of Defense.* (Rev. ed.) New York: International Universities Press, 1967.

Freud, S. "The Interpretation of Dreams." In J. Strachey (ed. and trans.), *The Standard Edition of the Complete Psychological Works of Sigmund Freud.* Vols. 4–5. London: Hogarth Press, 1953. (Originally published 1900.)

Freud, S. "Mourning and Melancholia." In J. Strachey (ed. and trans.), *The Standard Edition of the Complete Psychological*

Works of Sigmund Freud. Vol. 14. London: Hogarth Press, 1957. (Originally published 1917.)

Freud, S. "The Ego and the Id." In J. Strachey (ed. and trans.), *The Standard Edition of the Complete Psychological Works of Sigmund Freud.* Vol. 19. London: Hogarth Press, 1961. (Originally published 1923.)

Freud, S. "An Outline of Psychoanalysis." In J. Strachey (ed. and trans.), *The Standard Edition of the Complete Psychological Works of Sigmund Freud.* Vol. 23. London: Hogarth Press, 1964a. (Originally published 1940.)

Freud, S. "Analysis Terminable and Interminable." In J. Strachey (ed. and trans.), *The Standard Edition of the Complete Psychological Works of Sigmund Freud.* Vol. 23. London: Hogarth Press, 1964b. (Originally published 1937.)

Garza-Guerrero, A. C. "Culture Shock: Its Mourning and the Vicissitudes of Identity." *Journal of the American Psychoanalytic Association,* 1974, 22, 408-429.

Greenacre, P. "Early Physical Determinants in the Development of the Sense of Identity." *Journal of the American Psychoanalytic Association,* 1958, 6, 612-627.

Grinberg, R. "Migracion e Identidad" [Migration and identity]. In *Identidad y Cambio* [Identity and change]. Buenos Aires, Brazil: Kargieman, 1971.

Hartmann, H. "Comments on the Psychoanalytic Theory of the Ego." *Psychoanalytic Study of the Child,* 1950, 5, 74-96.

Hartmann, H. *Ego Psychology and the Problem of Adaptation.* New York: International Universities Press, 1958. (Originally published 1939.)

Hartmann, H., Kris, E., and Loewenstein, R. M. "Some Psychoanalytic Comments on Culture and Personality." In G. B. Wilbur and W. Muensterberger (eds.), *Psychoanalysis and Culture.* New York: International Universities Press, 1951.

Jacobson, E. *The Self and Object World.* New York: International Universities Press, 1964.

Levy-Warren, M. H. "Transcultural Movement Among Puerto Ricans in New York City." Unpublished doctoral dissertation, Department of Psychology, Yale University, 1980.

Mahler, M. S., and Furer, M. *On Human Symbiosis and the*

Vicissitudes of Individuation. New York: International Universities Press, 1968.

Mahler, M. S., Pine, F., and Bergman, A. *The Psychological Birth of the Human Infant: Symbiosis and Individuation.* New York: Basic Books, 1975.

Muensterberger, W. In panel on "Aspects of Culture on Psychoanalytic Theory and Practice," S. W. Jackson, Reporter. *Journal of the American Psychoanalytic Association,* 1968, *16,* 651-670.

Nunberg, H. "The Synthetic Function of the Ego." *International Journal of Psycho-Analysis,* 1931, *12,* 123-140.

Piaget, J., and Inhelder, B. *The Psychology of the Child.* London: Routledge & Kegan Paul, 1969.

Rapaport, D. "The Theory of Ego Autonomy." *Bulletin of the Menninger Clinic,* 1958, *22,* 13-35.

Schafer, R. *Aspects of Internalization.* New York: International Universities Press, 1968.

Ticho, G. "Cultural Aspects of Transference and Countertransference." *Bulletin of the Menninger Clinic,* 1971, *35,* 313-334.

Waelder, R. "The Principle of Multiple Functioning." *Psychoanalytic Quarterly,* 1936, *5,* 45-62.

Werner, H. *Comparative Psychology of Mental Development.* New York: International Universities Press, 1957.

Winnicott, D. W. "The Location of Cultural Experience." In *Playing and Reality.* Harmondsworth, England: Penguin Books, 1981.

10

Impact of Marital Dissolution on Adults and Children: The Significance of Loss and Continuity

Gerald F. Jacobson
Doris S. Jacobson

Editors' Note: *This chapter brings attention to how widespread marital dissolution has become in our society and to the emotional consequences arising from it. The authors point out that the breakup of a marriage and the loss of an intact family must be mourned like any other death. However, unlike an individual's death, which is a sudden and permanent separation, divorce is part of a drawn-out separation process and permits continued contact with the "lost" spouse or parent. While divorcing adults are usually torn between the wish to separate and the wish to maintain their attachment, children of divorce universally seek to restore the family and often pretend the separation is only temporary.*

The Jacobsons view marital dissolution as a series of multiple crises, not a discrete crisis event. Typically, they find two peaks of emotional distress, one at the time of the breakup and another linked to coping with the long-term consequences of the separation. As noted in Chapter Six for a different separation experience, initial distress is a necessary part of the mourn-

ing process of divorce, but prolonged emotional problems are not inevitable. The authors outline three factors that determine how adults will react to divorce: the degree of attachment to the lost spouse, the degree of hostility retained toward the lost spouse, and the degree of ambiguity about the future of the relationship. When divorcing spouses cannot work through the mourning process, emotional difficulties interfere with healthy formation of new relationships. (Psychological impediments to mourning are discussed throughout this volume; see Chapters Nine, Eleven, and Twelve, in particular.)

Like their parents, children of divorce are at increased risk for psychological problems. Several factors shape their coping: their developmental stage, quality of the relationship with each parent, degree of interparental conflict, and parents' emotional well-being. The authors stress that the amount of "time lost" for the child (both with the absent parent and with the custodial parent, who may be less available emotionally) is important to consider: the more time lost (that is, the more separation), the poorer the child's adjustment after divorce.

The chapter offers ideas for clinicians treating divorcing families, emphasizing the importance of working through the multiple losses that may be involved. This may be especially difficult for children, for whom mourning poses special problems (see Chapter Eleven). The effects of marital dissolution may be lifelong, and the conflicts it stirs will be reactivated by other life events involving separation. Recognizing the severe strains facing families coping with divorce and the magnitude of the problem for society, the Jacobsons also offer suggestions for policy and research.

Some transitions are universal; others are not. The former include birth, infancy, childhood, adulthood, decline, and death. Among the most important transitions that are not universal are the beginning and end of a marriage. This chapter will deal with what happens to adults and children when a marriage ends. The terms *marital dissolution, marital separation,* and *divorce* will be used synonymously, although separation and divorce are two distinct events.

There has been an increase in divorce which only recently

has begun to taper off. Divorces in the United States dropped by 3 percent in 1982, to 1,800,000, after a sharp twenty-year rise (National Center for Health Statistics, 1983). Between 1950 and 1970 the number of children involved in divorce almost quadrupled. In 1978 only 63 percent of all children under eighteen lived in a traditional household with both biological parents. The largest proportion of the remainder lived with a single divorced parent or with a remarried parent and a stepparent. Children of divorce are predicted to increase to 30 percent of all children under eighteen in 1990, the largest increase being in those who live with a single divorced parent (Glick, 1979).

Since about 75 percent of divorced women and 80 percent of divorced men remarry (Glick, 1979), many families experience a series of transitions as divorce follows marriage and remarriage follows divorce. To further complicate matters, second marriages end in divorce somewhat more often than first marriages do, and the chain of transitions is then repeated. It is estimated that over one third of the children whose mothers remarry will experience a second marital dissolution before reaching adulthood (National Center for Health Statistics, 1982). Complex and tangled webs of relationships result that were virtually unknown to earlier generations.

This chapter examines the role of separation and loss in marital dissolution and bereavement. In addition to a general consideration of these issues, the chapter will address types of clinical disturbance seen in separation and divorce, as well as factors associated with the mental health of adults and children. The closing sections will discuss issues pertaining to clinical practice and implications for policy and research.

Separation and Loss in Marital Dissolution and Bereavement

Loss of a spouse or parent by divorce invites comparison with loss of a spouse or parent by death. There are similarities as well as differences. Death is a clear and unequivocal event that occurs at a precise moment in time. Divorce, in contrast, is a process rather than an event. Rarely is separation sudden and permanent. Separations and reconciliations may follow one another. There are instances in which couples obtain a legal decree of divorce but continue to live in the same house for years. According to Bohannon (1970, p. 40), some judges refuse to grant decrees of divorce because they cannot condone "litigation by day and copulation by night." G. F. Jacobson (1983) found that three quarters of recently separated or divorced persons who participated in a study had had contact with the former spouse within two weeks of the interview; the same was true for almost half of the longer-term separated and divorced. Similarly, children do not necessarily experience the loss of a major attachment figure. D. S. Jacobson (1978a) studied the impact of divorce on children aged three to thirteen and found that the amount of time spent with noncustodial fathers may decrease, increase, or remain unchanged.

Thus, when divorce occurs, adults and children experience a varying degree of loss of time spent with the spouse or parent. In spite of this variability, divorce does bring a universal loss: that of the sense of being part of a marriage and an intact family. As many divorced persons have said, although no individual dies, the marriage dies. What is lost and therefore needs to be mourned is the belief that a partner or a parent is an enduring and reliable part of one's life. However frequently one sees the partner or parent, the relationship is never again what it once was.

Reactions to loss were initially described by Freud, who emphasized the loss of satisfaction of instinctual needs. He spoke of adhesiveness of the libido and the difficulty of giving up attachments that provided libidinal satisfaction. A major reconsideration of this first psychoanalytic view of loss was Bowlby's model, in which the child's attachment to the mother is thought to be fundamental to all attachments throughout life. Attachment is defined in terms of, among other things, specificity, duration through a large part of the life course, and engagement of emotion. According to Bowlby, anxiety is a uniform response to separation. This response occurs initially in regard to the mother but is repeated whenever there are separations from important people, such as a spouse, later in life.

Weiss (1975, p. 48) applied Bowlby's concept of attachment and separation to the divorce situation. He saw the loss of the marital partner as analogous to loss of the mother for a young child. He described separation distress as accompanying the interruption of attachment and as consisting of "focusing of attention on the lost figure, together with intense discomfort because of the figure's inaccessibility."

It is of interest to compare adults' responses to divorce with the stages of mourning in bereavement, as described by Parkes (1972). The first stage of bereavement, shock and denial, may be seen in divorce, particularly if the separation was unexpected. The next phase is pining and yearning for the lost person. This can occur as well in marital separation. Such yearning is most likely to be expressed by spouses who did not seek the divorce and hence feel abandoned. Some vignettes taken from Hunt and Hunt (1977, p. 4) illustrate this phenomenon. A woman whose husband had just left her said: "I am acting like a frightened child, a little girl who's lost her mummy in the crowd." Another woman illustrated pining and yearning even more directly: "During the night I tossed fitfully . . . only to wake up flailing my arms frantically over the bed, looking for my lost companion . . . I finally piled his side of the bed with boxes of things, pillows, so it would feel heavy as if there were someone there" (p. 46). However, pining and yearning are not universal. Relief and euphoria are often the first reaction to separation (Hunt and Hunt, 1977; Weiss, 1975), although distress may follow.

In addition, the divorced may have an option that the bereaved lack: they can contact the very much alive former spouse and, to a degree, directly assuage the pining. As already mentioned, contacts between separated and divorced spouses are very common, particularly in the early period. Whereas the bereaved can only evoke memories and fantasies of the dead spouse, the divorced can get in touch with them in the flesh. But, as we will see, there are risks involved in taking this course.

The next phase of grief described in bereavement is very important in divorce: anger and protest. Hostility is very common among separating spouses and is usually much more overt than in bereavement. As Fisher (1974, p. 124) said of the separating couple, "Burning with feelings of anger and distrust, they are often told to be friendly and achieve an amicable divorce. I believe there is no such thing as an amicable divorce." Some of the evidence for presence of hostility and its role in divorce will be discussed later in the chapter, in the section on factors associated with mental health.

We now return to the major difference between bereavement and divorce: the presence of a living spouse. As already mentioned, it is possible to interrupt the grief process by resuming contact with the former spouse. This rapprochement, though perhaps allaying some of the anxiety and sadness that resulted from the separation, may end in renewed disappointment. The renewed encounter often triggers intense ambivalent feelings. The conflicts that led to the separation in the first place are now increased, owing to the rage over the loss. Although some couples manage, in spite of these factors, to find a way of relating to each other that is at least tolerable, many find this difficult to achieve. A vicious cycle may then ensue: When the loss of the attachment is too difficult to bear, renewed contacts are made. However, the result of these contacts can be intensely painful, leading to renewed separation. This pain may take a psychological toll, which, in turn, makes the task of working through the separation more difficult.

We now turn our attention to the child's experience of divorce. According to Bowlby (1973), to the extent to which a child experiences the loss of a significant other, he or she may experience acute upset followed by apathy and depression and then loss of interest in that person. Most children, regardless of age, are upset at the time of separation, but the intensity of the reaction is related to the degree of separation, its abruptness, and whether it has happened before. To children who have been exposed to quarrels or physical fighting, it may come as no surprise and may, on occasion, be a relief. Others who have been protected from parental difficulties may be deeply shocked. Divorce inevitably means that the child will spend less time in the noncustodial household, that there will be "time lost." For some, the time lost in the physical presence of the noncustodial parent is minimal and gradual; for others, it is massive and abrupt. Reactions may differ if a separation has happened before. One adolescent asked by one of the authors about her reaction to a recent parental separation said, "This is the fourth time. Ask me about how I felt about the first one—not this one."

Because the amount of "time lost" for the child is so variable, the "pure loss" model must be modified. Unlike adults, children are not torn between the wish to separate and the wish to maintain the relationship. Almost all children want to maintain relationships with both parents (Wallerstein and Kelly, 1980). But children, especially young children, do not have power in this area, and the extent to which parental contact is maintained is determined by the parents themselves. Children may become preoccupied with fantasies about bringing their parents back together, as well as engage in manipulative efforts toward that end. They may pretend the situation is temporary. One little boy whose father had abruptly disappeared told one of the authors that he knew precisely where his father was and that the father would be home as soon as he could. It was a home in which the custodial mother had not been able to allow herself or her child to talk about the situation. Small children may feel guilt, believing that something they did accounted for the separation, thereby instilling in themselves, perhaps, the hope that it can be corrected. This was expressed indirectly by a seven-year-old girl who magnanimously said of her five-year-old brother, "He did it. If he had not bugged Daddy when he talked on the phone, he would not have left. He will not do it again."

In addition to the loss of the noncustodial parent, the child may experience a loss of time and love from the parent in the household (usually the mother), who is preoccupied with her own distress during the acute stage of separation. And children may respond to this double parental withdrawal with behavior problems. They may become concerned, from their vulnerable position, about who will take care of them, who will feed them, with whom they will live—fearful lest they be abandoned by the other parent; that is, if one parent has left, will the other follow suit? Thus, fear of *potential* separation as well as reaction to actual separation must be considered. Research indicates that a high proportion of parents have a difficult time discussing the separation with their children (Jacobson, 1978c; Wallerstein and Kelly, 1980). Reactions of children can be modified by the amount of attention and concern focused on them.

At this time we know little of children's long-range reactions to divorce or the degree to which long-term adjustment is related to the child's initial degree of upset. We do know that how a child reacts is age-related, being based on the emotional and cognitive capabilities he or she brings to the situation. This will be discussed in a later section. Additionally, studies find that family interaction, parental attention, emotional stability, and the degree of change influence the intensity of the acute reaction.

Clinical Disturbance Seen in Separation and Divorce: Nature and Timing

In this section we review empirical evidence on the nature and extent of psychological disturbance seen in adults and children when divorce occurs. In the next section we will look further at factors associated with these disturbances.

In adults, problems commonly seen include depression of various degrees, including depressed mood, loneliness, low work efficiency, trouble sleeping, somatic concerns, and feelings of incompetence (Chester, 1971; Goode, 1956; Hetherington, Cox, and Cox, 1977; Kitson, Graham, and Schmidt, forthcoming; Weiss, 1975). Suicidal and homicidal ideation may be present, and attempts, though infrequent, do occur. Psychotic responses are rare in the absence of predisposition.

One explanation for the disturbance in the separated or divorced comes from the crisis model, which states that any change in an existing equilibrium causes a temporary period of disorganization and upset that usually ends spontaneously in a new equilibrium, which may be on a level of functioning higher than, lower than, or equal to that before the crisis (Caplan,

1961; Jacobson, 1980). However, one of the authors has suggested that in divorce we are not dealing with a single crisis but, rather, with what he has termed, in the title of a book on the subject, "the multiple crises of marital separation and divorce" (G. F. Jacobson, 1983). These multiple crises may occur over a considerable time span; however, the crisis approach suggests that most of the disturbance should occur early in the separation process. This is to some extent true, but there is also evidence that there may be two peaks of distress in adults, one around the time of the breakup and a later one related to long-term adjustment to divorce (Chiriboga and Cutler, 1977; G. F. Jacobson, 1983).

As for children, there is evidence that most experience considerable distress when their parents separate but that this does not inevitably lead to prolonged psychological and behavior problems. As with adults, if crisis is the major cause of distress, one would expect the disturbance to peak early in the dissolution process and then to subside. In fact, most studies have focused on this period—that is, on the "short run," defined as the first year or two after the event. These studies have found evidence of distress in almost all children, most frequently expressed in behavior problems, including increased acting out and antisocial and aggressive behavior, especially in boys, and also in feelings of sadness, anger, and guilt (Fulton, 1978; Hess and Camara, 1979; Hetherington, Cox, and Cox, 1979; Jacobson, 1978a, 1978b, 1978c; McDermott, 1968; Wallerstein and Kelly, 1980; Weiss, 1975). Hetherington reports that there appears to be a reduction in tension at the end of one to two years.

In regard to academic achievement, Hetherington, Camara, and Featherman (1981) found that although most children and parents find divorce a stressful experience, long-term effects may be modified by postdivorce family functioning in a number of areas. When socioeconomic status was taken into account, differences in academic performance between children in one-parent and two-parent households were small. Relatively few children in one-parent homes suffered any serious long-term intellectual deficit. However, children in one-parent homes tended to receive lower grades and lower teacher evaluations.

The authors proposed several interpretations. Circumstances within a one-parent household sometimes result in children's inability to concentrate and use good study habits. In addition, teachers describe children from one-parent homes as more disruptive and less likely to attend school regularly; teachers may rate children more favorably who conform to school routine. Boys were more likely to be adversely affected than girls, a finding that must be considered in light of the fact that most boys were living with mothers and that data on girls living with fathers were not available.

In regard to mental health, evidence on long-term reaction in children is simply not yet in. There are not enough studies to make inferences about personality development or other aspects of later adjustment. There is, however, evidence from a national survey (Zill, 1978) that children of divorce are at about twice the risk of receiving psychiatric attention as children from intact families (13 percent compared with 5.5 percent). The proportion of children receiving such attention is about the same for children of divorce, children of intact families whose parents report "not too happy" marriages, and children of mother-and-stepfather families.

Factors Associated with Mental Health

By no means are all adults and children equally affected by the experience of separation and divorce. It is therefore helpful to understand the factors that mediate between this experience and the adjustment of those involved. In this section we will deal further with these factors in regard to adults and children.

Adults

We will begin with an overview of the many factors that various workers have found to be associated with disturbance and will then go into more detail about the importance of the separation from, and continuing relationship with, the former spouse.

The following is a list, not necessarily complete, culled

from the literature and from our experience of factors reported to be associated with disturbance: (1) separation from and relationship to the former spouse, (2) relationship to children, (3) financial, housing, and employment matters, (4) legal matters, including custody and support, (5) dating and new romantic and sexual relationships, (6) friends and other social supports, (7) sex, age, socioeconomic status, and ethnicity, (8) psychological factors, including personality traits, (9) sex-role attitudes, and (10) level of mental health before the beginning of the marital dissolution process.

Most of the studies have dealt with the early postdivorce period. Although there is no conclusive evidence about the order of the importance of various factors during this period, our reading of the existing evidence is that the extent and nature of the relationship between the separating spouses may be the single most important mediating factor early on. For this reason, issues pertaining to the former spouse will be further discussed. We will deal particularly with attachment, hostility, and ambiguity about the process of separation and divorce.

Attachment. Attachment to the former spouse may take several forms. It may be manifested by reconciliation wishes and by attempts to effect a reconciliation. In other instances, it may be manifested by longing and yearning for the spouse, as previously described. It may be indicated by seeking ways to interact with the spouse, even though these may be hostile. Attachment and anger are far from mutually exclusive. It should be noted that feelings of attachment occur whether or not there is actual contact with the spouse.

Marital attachment was operationalized for research purposes by Kitson (1982), Brown and others (1980), and G. F. Jacobson (1983). Some of the items defining attachment were whether the person missed the spouse, wondering what the spouse was doing, the intensity of the affect, spending a lot of time thinking about the spouse, whether or not a reconciliation was wanted, and amount of time spent in memory and fantasy about the spouse. In all three studies, moderate or higher degrees of attachment were found in 40 to 50 percent of the recently separated or divorced. All three studies showed that greater degrees of attachment were associated with more distress. Thus research findings, as well as clinical experience, confirm that, for the recently separated or divorced, attachment is related to greater disturbance.

Hostility. Feelings of anger between separating spouses are very common. Anger was present in seven out of ten (69 percent) of G. F. Jacobson's (1983) recently separated or divorced respondents, and in nine tenths of this group the anger was related to the separation. Greater anger was associated with more anxiety, depression, and somatic disturbance.

Also of importance is the extent to which anger is manifested in overt hostility to the spouse. This can occur only when there is contact between the spouses. Although there is considerable agreement in the literature that conflict is important in the divorce situation, there is no consensus on how to measure conflict. Emery (1982) suggested that three theoretically relevant aspects of the definition are the process of conflict (that is, hitting, arguing, avoidance), its content (for example, sex, child rearing, money), and its duration. G. F. Jacobson (1983) classified hostility by various types and by whether the person was the source or the recipient of the particular type of hostility. Categories included verbal hostility, such as "putting down" the spouse; divorce-related hostility, such as using financial and custody matters against the spouse; death-related hostility, such as wishing the spouse dead; and physical hostility.

In the recently separated or divorced, hostility was common, ranging from about 90 percent for putting the spouse down or feeling put down by the spouse to 30 percent who experienced death wishes. While some aspects of hostility were greater before the marriage began to break up (as manifested by the couple's starting to discuss the divorce), others increased when the divorce was in process. A number of hostility variables were related to mental health. In most instances, more hostility was associated with more disturbance; this was particularly true of death-related hostility experienced as coming from the spouse. Overall, the findings suggest that some aspects of overt hostility increase disturbance in divorcing adults.

Ambiguity. A third aspect of the relationship to the former spouse associated with mental health is ambiguity. It is manifested by lack of clarity and consistency in one's behavior toward the former spouse; the frequency of changing one's mind about the separation; and the extent to which one assesses the probability of reconciliation realistically, when the judgment of a clinical rater is used as the criterion. Signs of ambiguity were found in 40 to 70 percent of the recently separated or divorced (G. F. Jacobson, 1983). All were associated with significant increases in disturbance. It appears that excessive ambiguity may be both a symptom and a cause of disorder. It may result from the painful perception that one's dilemma appears unresolvable. It may also be symptomatic of confusion, which itself is the result of psychological turmoil that interferes with effective reality testing and problem solving.

Long-Term Adjustment. Factors determining long-term adjustment to separation and divorce are still poorly understood, since most clinical descriptions and formal research studies have dealt with the recently separated and divorced. A continued relationship between the spouses, particularly when stormy, is undoubtedly one factor. However, the research studies mentioned above show that attachment declines with time, and in one study (G. F. Jacobson, 1983) there was no association between attachment and distress in the longer-term separated or divorced. Nevertheless, new crises in the relationship between former spouses may be set off by the remarriage of either partner, as well as by events involving the children, such as graduation or a child's marriage.

As time goes on, it is likely that new relationships, romantic or other, assume greater importance. However, to the extent that the relationship between the former spouses is unresolved, it may interfere with new relationships, including remarriages. Other factors important in long-term adjustment include the financial situation, both absolutely and relative to the predivorce status. This is particularly important for women with children, who may or may not be able to support their families. An important but little investigated area is the relationship of predivorce emotional disturbance to long-term adjustment. Such a disturbance may exert its effect by way of personality traits that impede coping with the life changes associated with divorce.

Children

As already stated, there is evidence that children of divorce are at increased risk of disturbance, the preponderance of studies having been done within two years after parental separation. Although a number of methodological problems beset existing studies (small samples, concentration on white, middle-class families, and different methods of measurement), four major areas have emerged that will be discussed further: parent/child interaction, interparental conflict, emotional well-being of parents, and age-related responses of children. Other factors include those at the psychological level, such as preexisting emotional difficulties of parents and children; the interpersonal level, such as social supports available to parents and children; and the societal level, such as economic changes, stability of households, and life events. We believe that the interrelationships among all these factors in the short and long run following divorce are as important as any single factor in understanding the adjustment of children.

Parent/Child Interaction. There is evidence that adjustment of children after parental separation is associated with their relationships with both parents (Hess and Camara, 1979; Hetherington, Cox, and Cox, 1978; Wallerstein and Kelly, 1980). Continued contact with both parents, when not highly conflictual, can be beneficial. This does not mean that the absence of the noncustodial parent, usually the father, in and of itself accounts for children's problems. It is, rather, the degree of change, the amount of loss, the quantity and quality of parent/child interaction, and other factors, taken together, that affect the well-being of the child. Hess and Camara (1979), for example, studied sixteen white, middle-class, mother-custody families with children aged nine to eleven in which parents had been separated two to three years and a matched group of sixteen intact families. They found that the relationship with each parent was the best predictor of outcome measures. Children who had positive relationships with both parents had lower ratings on measures of stress and aggression and higher ratings on measures of work effectiveness and social peer relationships.

The literature suggests that children of all ages want frequent interaction with the noncustodial parent (Nolan, 1977; Rosen, 1977; Wallerstein and Kelly, 1980) and may retain fantasies of reconciliation for a number of years. The course of the relationship with the noncustodial father is difficult to predict. Some fathers who have a close relationship before separation withdraw afterward, and others who are not close before separation make considerable effort to build and maintain closeness to the child (Wallerstein and Kelly, 1980). The pattern is in part related to the degree of comfort both child and parent feel in the noncustodial relationship.

There are contradictory findings about the relation between frequency of interaction with the noncustodial parent and the child's adjustment. Some studies have found a positive effect, except in situations of high conflict between parents or mental disturbance in the visited parent (Hetherington, Cox, and Cox, 1979; Jacobson, 1978a; Wallerstein and Kelly, 1980; Zill, 1978). D. S. Jacobson found a significant relationship between the number of hours the child lost in the presence of the noncustodial parent during the first year after parental separation and the child's adjustment: the more time lost, the poorer the adjustment. The measure used here, time lost, is relative to the amount of time spent with that parent before the separation. Other studies have found that school-age children, particularly boys, benefit from frequent contact with the father.

However, at least two studies have found that frequency of visits is not related to postseparation adjustment (Kurdek, Blisk, and Siesky, 1981). And D. S. Jacobson (1983), in an ongoing study, has found no relationship between adjustment of children and noncustodial parent contacts in children aged eight to seventeen an average of six and one-half years after parental separation. At least one parent in this study was remarried. Moreover, the study was limited to children who had seen the noncustodial parent at least once in the year before the interview and therefore excluded the extreme situation in which there was no contact at all; on the other end of the spectrum, joint custody cases were also excluded.

The noncustodial parent can have an important role to play in the children's well-being not only directly but also indirectly, through support offered to the custodial parent in child-rearing efforts. A father can relieve a custodial mother from some child-rearing tasks and contribute to more effective parental management through, for example, supporting consistent discipline and control. In both divorced and intact families, it has been found that children are more likely to obey fathers than mothers. Inconsistent discipline can affect child behavior. And two parents provide the child with exposure to more wide-ranging interests and life experiences than one. A parent can serve as a protective buffer between the other parent and the child when things get out of hand. Jacobson (1978c) found that children of divorce receiving greater amounts of parental attention and encouragement to discuss the divorce had significantly fewer behavior problems than those lacking such parental attention and encouragement within the first year after separation.

In sum, the issues in postdivorce parent/child interaction are the quality of the relationships with both parents, how much time the child has lost with the parent no longer in the home, how abruptly the losses have occurred, how much time was lost relative to what existed before, and how the parent not in the home affects the parenting of the custodial parent.

Interparental Conflict. The idea that interparental conflict affects the well-being of children is not new and has been widely reported in the clinical literature. Emery (1982), in a review of current research on parental conflict and children of discord and divorce, reported on what he called the convergence of evidence from studies with methodological flaws. He concluded that a relationship does exist between conflict and children's problems, with a greater effect on boys.

A relationship has been found between marital discord and children's problems in intact marriages (Porter and O'Leary, 1980; Rutter, 1971). Several studies report that children from conflict-ridden intact households are more likely to have problems than those from non-conflict-ridden divorced families

(Hetherington, Cox, and Cox, 1979; McCord, McCord, and Thurber, 1962; Rutter, 1979). Zill (1978) reported that children of divorce are at significantly greater risk of developing mental health problems than children from intact homes where parents report happy marriages. Children from marriages reported to be "not too happy" do not differ significantly from children of divorce (Zill, 1978). Hetherington, in a two-year longitudinal study, examined the impact of interparental conflict on the development of children in divorced and non-divorced families. Divorced and married parents were divided into two groups: high to moderate conflict and low conflict. The results indicated that two years after a parental divorce the high-conflict divorced group exhibited the most adjustment problems.

Clearly, parental conflict does not terminate with the end of marriage. Children may be exposed to escalated conflict after a parental separation as parents go through their own divorce experience over time (see the preceding section on adults). It is reasonable to assume that not only the presence of conflict but its type and duration are important. Openly hostile parents can draw children into the fray. This can intensify conflicting loyalties and interfere with the child's relationship to one or both parents. A high level of conflict can diminish the positive effect of frequent visits to the noncustodial parent. D. S. Jacobson, in her ongoing study of stepfamilies, has found that some parents report reactivation of conflict around the time of the remarriage of a former spouse. This occurred in remarriages that took place an average of six and one-half years after the parental divorce. Areas in which the highest number of parents reported conflict were child support and visiting. These are areas around which continued contacts with former spouses are necessary. They are two of the continuing interfaces in what D. S. Jacobson (1983) has described as the "linked family system" in which the child constitutes the link between two households, affecting and being affected by each.

Interparental conflict can also affect the child indirectly, by influencing the emotional state of the parents. It can, moreover, interfere with the noncustodial parent's acting as a support to the custodial parent with child-rearing tasks during that difficult time when a newly divorced spouse is overwhelmed with new responsibilities for self and children, and it can adversely affect child-rearing practices. These chains of influence emphasize the circular relationship between what goes on with each parent and how it affects the child.

Children can respond to interparental hostility in a number of ways, including staying out of it or manipulating each parent in the interest of the child's own wishes and needs. To the knowledge of these authors, no research to date has addressed the issue of the extent to which parents can separate former spousal roles from parental roles—how well they can separate a conflictual relationship with a former spouse from the relationship with a child. Such knowledge is important in answering such questions as for which families joint custody will work out well.

Emotional Well-Being of Parents. It is well documented that children from families in which a parent has a psychological disturbance are at increased risk of behavior problems (Mednick and McNeil, 1968). There is no reason to believe that this is any less true of children of divorce. As already discussed, separated and divorced persons, on the average, show greater disturbance in many areas than married ones. Mothers who are tense and depressed are more likely to feel negatively about parenting responsibilities and are likely to have less control over a child (Zill, 1978).

One very good parent/child relationship can buffer the negative effects of a disturbed or destructive other parent in an intact family (Hetherington, Cox, and Cox, 1979). However, if in a divorce situation there is interparental conflict, the child's access to the buffering process is limited. Children may have to deal with increased needs of disturbed parents with little outside help, again pointing to the interrelationship of a number of levels in understanding the child's well-being.

Age-Related Responses to Parental Separation. Wallerstein and Kelly (1980) have carried out the only longitudinal study to examine age-related responses of children to parental separation and divorce. This seminal study is based on in-depth clinical observation and generates many hypotheses for research. Wallerstein and Kelly found that children of all ages experience sadness, depression, loneliness, and anger. Ordinarily, those of all ages wish to continue contact with both parents and may fantasize about parental reconciliation.

In the preschool group (Wallerstein and Kelly, 1975), children's reactions included depression, irritability, increased anxiety, especially separation anxiety, increased aggressive behavior, especially in boys, and often some regression. Pervasive neediness commonly ensued and many experienced strong fears of abandonment. Preschool children have limited cognitive abilities with which to understand the reasons for the separation. As a way of dealing with their discomfort, the egocentrism characteristic of their age and restricted cognitive ability lead them to blame themselves for the breakup. Unlike older children, they are unable to seek out, independently, either the noncustodial parent or other social supports.

The initial reaction of latency (school age) children was pervasive sadness, intense strain, and immobilization. For the older latency age group (aged ten to eleven) the most distinguishable feeling was anger. Unlike anger in the younger group, it was more clearly organized and object-directed: these children's capacity to articulate anger was good. It was expressed in the form of temper tantrums and demandingness. One year later some of these difficulties had subsided, but the anger persisted longer than other affective responses (Wallerstein and Kelly, 1976). These school-age children had the cognitive ability to grasp the difficulties of their parents and to be sympathetic as well as angry. Most had loyalty conflicts, and many allied themselves with one parent or the other as a way of dealing with or avoiding conflict. Some were already involved in the developmental tasks of the period when the separation took place; these include academic achievement and relationships with same-sex peers. Their responses varied. For some, parental separation led to disruption of school achievement, development of behavior problems in school, and increased difficulties with peers. Others saw the school as a source of social support and put renewed effort into academic achievement and relied effectively on peers for support.

Most adolescents experienced considerable pain and anger when their parents separated or divorced. Their reactions included sadness and a sense of betrayal. They were more successful than the younger group, after the immediate trauma, in understanding parents' views, assigning responsibility for difficulties, and avoiding loyalty conflicts. They used withdrawal and detachment as a way of dealing with the situation. This involved deidealization of parents and increased awareness of their parents' sexuality. Developmental tasks for the adolescent include resolving conflicts between independence and dependence, developing heterosexual relationships, increasing social skills, and formulating career goals. They had the cognitive ability to address both the emotional and the practical aspects of their situation. They were mobile and able to mobilize a variety of extrafamilial relationships, including those with peers.

Issues in Clinical Practice

Persons in the throes of marital dissolution, particularly in the early stages, may prove a challenge to therapists. Their life situation is highly unstable. Decisions about the spouse and children may need to be made with little time to consider alternatives. The emotional state may involve a high level of distress, including depression, anxiety, rage, and at times suicidal and homicidal ideation (and, more rarely, behavior). They may try to draw the therapist into an adversary relationship toward the spouse or to use the therapist to bring about reconciliation.

The therapist's short-term goal is to reduce acute disturbance and to deal with any risk of destructive or self-destructive behavior. The longer-term goal is to bring about a resolution that maximizes adaptive functioning. The means used to attain short- and long-term goals are similar. The therapist must be attentive to the facts and feelings related to the marital separation. Bringing up what went wrong with the marriage or focusing on long-term characterological issues may be felt as adding yet another burden by someone already overwhelmed by the current situation. It is important to acknowledge that the acute disturbance is an expectable reaction to the stress of marital breakup and to recognize that it will include complex and often contradictory feelings of attachment, anger, and confusion.

The long-term goal is a lasting resolution of the separation issue. Adaptive resolution involves accepting the end of the marital relationship while maintaining appropriate contacts when realistically necessary, mainly in the area of coparenting. Both continued attachment and ongoing hostility can make such a resolution difficult. Some former spouses establish stable relationships, while for others storminess may characterize contacts for months and years. In one instance a couple remarried and redivorced several times, each marriage more conflict-ridden than the one before. Intervention did not completely break this cycle, but it enabled the couple to achieve some understanding of their conflicting need to be and not to be with each other, and as a result of this understanding they were able to reduce the extent to which they involved the children in their interaction.

Most couples fall between the extremes, working out some stability that may, from time to time, be strained by such events as the remarriage of one partner, especially when the other is not remarried, or the birth of children to the former spouse and a new partner. We have seen several instances in which the not-yet-remarried spouse tried to interfere with the new marriage of the other partner, often using the children to that end, not necessarily consciously. A single parent may find that the time when the other parent returns from a honeymoon is precisely the moment when a difficult child absolutely "needs" to be sent to the newly remarried parent, with predictable consequences. The least tense situations tend to occur when both parents have entered into satisfactory remarriages.

One needs to be careful in how much one focuses on the children during the acute separation crisis. Many parents are simply unable to pay very much attention to the children. Excessive focus on them may have the opposite of the desired result: it may create feelings of guilt, which will further impair parenting. The distressed adult must first be helped to feel better if he or she is to be an effective parent. If the parental disturbance lasts very long or if the child's upset is serious, the child should be referred for separate and simultaneous treatment, with the understanding that the parent may not be very helpful early in the child's treatment process.

It is important to keep in mind that the effects of divorce may be lifelong. When one is seeing a person who has ever been divorced, it is worthwhile to inquire into the whereabouts of the former spouse, no matter how many years ago the divorce took place. As mentioned, reactivation of the conflict with the former spouse can be triggered by a variety of events—remarriages and redivorces of spouses, marriages of adult children, and so on. The clinician should therefore be aware that other life events involving separation may evoke feelings about the divorce.

Opinion differs on whether separating spouses should be seen together. Some believe that separation issues can best be worked out when both persons are present. In our experience, seeing separating individuals alone appears to work better. When only those persons are seen together in the office who also live under the same roof, the treatment situation realistically reflects the living situation. By the same reasoning, it is preferable to have a separate therapist see each spouse.

It is also important that clinicians consciously resist the tendency to use their own experience in marriage and, if any, divorce, as a model for their practice. There is a story, perhaps apocryphal, that the factor that most strongly influenced clients' decision to separate or reconcile was the therapist's own status of being married or separated. In any case, directly advising a couple that they should or should not divorce is rarely if ever indicated. It is important to elicit information about all relevant aspects of the situation and to help the client deal with his or her external and psychological realities in the best possible way.

The reasons that marriages fail are beyond the scope of this chapter. There is one rule of thumb: marriages that are threatened by major events not affecting the marital dyad, such as serious illness of children, may have a better prognosis than those in which a long-term alienation exists between the spouses. Clearly, it is not desirable to take any step, particularly that of marital dissolution, impulsively; equally clearly, a rigid stance that marriages must be maintained at all costs is not tenable.

Clinical issues in dealing with children parallel those for adults. Children who are in the midst of parental separation may challenge parents and therapists as they express depression and anger about the losses and disruption in their lives through behavior problems and in other ways. Their wish that their parents reconcile may place additional stress on all. For children, too, it is likely that the turmoil will be self-limiting unless there is a history of preceding difficulty, especially in regard to early parent/child separations—or unless there is continued intense fighting between parents focused on the children's well-being or their loyalties. Short-term goals would be to deal with the acute situation. This would include helping the child with any guilt about the separation and with dealing with loyalty conflicts, including, if necessary, keeping out of the fray. It is important to give attention to children's precise concerns, to elicit aspects of the external and psychological realities as viewed by the child. As previously mentioned, parents may have limited ability to address issues of children meaningfully because of their own immediate turmoil. Children and young people may have an intensified reaction if at the same time there are additional losses, such as the loss of relationships with extended family or, for adolescents, the loss of contact with a strong peer support group. Ideally, a therapeutic contact will lead to the child's acceptance of the situation so he or she can go on to a lasting resolution that involves dealing with each parent realistically.

In our view, it is usually more appropriate to see the child alone or with one parent than with both. Seeing the family together can re-create reconciliation fantasies and cause cognitive confusion about reality. In one situation, for example, the custodial mother of an eleven-year-old girl arranged a birthday party with the noncustodial father in the home in which they had lived before the separation; the child experienced intense anxiety and asked to leave. The remarriage of a parent and the birth of half-siblings may also reactivate feelings about the separation. Of course, any form of therapeutic help needs to be age-related, considered in terms of the child's cognitive capacity and ability to express feelings. While adolescents can seek out treatment resources on their own, young children cannot. Arrangement for treatment for young children can be worked out only with parental support. Group sessions with those who have had similar experiences can provide an atmosphere in which young people can talk out shared problems and participate in a situation in which the quandary of separation is focused on and identified.

Implications for Policy and Research

More than one third of American children will spend part of their childhood living in a household not headed by both biological parents. Adults and children in these families are subject to strains that do not affect intact families. Accordingly, the nature and amount of supports that society should offer these families, and at what points in time, must be determined. These include child-care facilities, health and mental health services, and financial assistance. This matter is especially relevant for ethnic minorities and the poor, for whom the stresses of marital breakup and those of discrimination and poverty may potentiate each other.

A second area of public policy pertaining to divorce involves the legal system. Liberalization of divorce laws, controversial not long ago, is now widely, though not universally, accepted. Today's most controversial issue is the extent to which legislation should foster joint custody. We have already touched on the areas in which research can throw light on this issue.

Research on separation and divorce has sharply increased during the last decade and a half but is still in its early stages. In a recent paper, Kitson and others (1982) have pointed out the limitations of a number of major studies in regard to sample selection. Another issue is the disproportionately large number of studies that have dealt with white, middle-class subjects only. There is need for studies that draw on samples from defined groups, such as geographical areas or school systems. Respondents should represent diverse social-class and ethnic groups. Instruments to measure variables pertaining to the divorce process and outcome variables measuring adjustment, health, mental health in adults and children, and other outcome criteria need to be standardized so that findings can be compared and replicated.

Summary

This chapter contains an overview of the current state of knowledge concerning marital separation and divorce and its relation to the mental health of adults and children. Special attention has been given to the role of attachment and loss.

Loss in divorce is both similar to and different from other types of losses. It is similar in that the adult partners lose the marital bond to the former spouse, and children lose the presence of a parent living in the home. The response to loss is grief, and to some extent the manifestations and working through of grief (for adults) are similar to those occurring when a spouse dies. More often than not, however, spouses maintain some degree of contact with each other and with their children. The nature of this contact, particularly the extent to which it is conflict-ridden, can affect the mental health and well-being of all concerned.

In this chapter we have considered some of the threads in the pattern. We have compared the responses in divorce with those in bereavement, noting similarities and differences. Clinical manifestations often seen in adults and children when divorce occurs have been reported. Factors associated with mental health in adults and children undergoing divorce have been summarized. In adults, special attention has been given to attachment, hostility, and ambiguity concerning the former spouse. In children, parent/child interaction, interparental conflicts, parents' emotional well-being, and age-related responses to marital separation have been discussed. New relationships, social supports, socioeconomic factors, and preexisting disturbance are also associated with mental health. The chapter concludes with implications for clinical practice and for policy and research.

References

Bohannon, P. "The Six Stations of Divorce." In P. Bohannon (ed.), *Divorce and After.* New York: Doubleday, 1970.

Bowlby, J. *Attachment and Loss.* Vol. 2: *Separation: Anxiety and Anger.* New York: Basic Books, 1973.

Brown, P., and others. "Attachment and Distress Following Marital Separation." *Journal of Divorce,* 1980, *3*(4), 303–316.

Caplan, G. *An Approach to Community Mental Health.* Orlando, Fla.: Grune & Stratton, 1961.

Chester, R. "Health and Marriage Breakdown: Experience of a Sample of Divorced Women." *British Journal of Preventive and Social Medicine,* 1971, *25*, 231–235.

Chiriboga, P. A., and Cutler, L. "Stress Responses Among Separating Men and Women." *Journal of Divorce,* 1977, *1*, 95–106.

Emery, R. E. "Interpersonal Conflict and the Children of Discord and Divorce." *Psychological Bulletin,* 1982, *92*(2), 310–330.

Fisher, E. O. *Divorce: The New Freedom.* New York: Harper & Row, 1974.

Fulton, J. A. "Factors Related to Parental Assessment of the Effect of Divorce on Children: A Research Report." Paper presented at the National Institute of Mental Health Conference on Divorce, Washington, D.C., Feb. 1978.

Glick, P. C. "Children of Divorced Parents in Demographic Perspective." *Journal of Social Issues,* 1979, *35*, 4.

Goode, W. J. *After Divorce.* New York: Free Press, 1956.

Hess, R. D., and Camara, K. A. "Post-Divorce Family Relationships as Mediating Factors in the Consequences of Divorce for Children." *Journal of Social Issues,* 1979, *35*(4), 79–96.

Hetherington, E. M., Camara, K. A., and Featherman, D. "Cognitive Performance, School Behavior, and Achievement of Children from One-Parent Households." Report prepared for The Family as Educators Team of the National Institute of Education, 1981.

Hetherington, E. M., Cox, M., and Cox, R. "The Aftermath of

Divorce." Paper presented at the annual meeting of the American Orthopsychiatric Association, New York, Mar. 1977.

Hetherington, E. M., Cox, M., and Cox, R. "The Development of Children in Mother-Headed Families." In H. Hoffman and D. Reiss (eds.), *The American Family: Dying or Developing?* New York: Plenum, 1978.

Hetherington, E. M., Cox, M., and Cox, R. "Family Interaction and the Social, Emotional, and Cognitive Development of Children Following Divorce." In V. Vaughan and T. Brazelton (eds.), *The Family: Setting Priorities.* New York: Science and Medicine Press, 1979.

Hunt, M., and Hunt, B. *The Divorce Experience.* New York: McGraw-Hill, 1977.

Jacobson, D. S. "The Impact of Marital Separation/Divorce on Children: I. Parent-Child Separation and Child Adjustment." *Journal of Divorce,* 1978a, *1*(4), 341–360.

Jacobson, D. S. "The Impact of Marital Separation/Divorce on Children: II. Interparent Hostility and Child Adjustment." *Journal of Divorce,* 1978b, *2*(1), 3–19.

Jacobson, D. S. "The Impact of Marital Separation/Divorce on Children: III. Parent-Child Communication and Child Adjustment." *Journal of Divorce,* 1978c, *2*(2), 175–194.

Jacobson, D. S. "Family Type, Visiting, and Children's Behavior Problems in the Stepfamily: A Linked Family System." Paper presented at the meeting of the American Psychological Association, Anaheim, Calif., Aug. 1983.

Jacobson, G. F. (ed.). *Crisis Intervention in the 1980s.* New Directions for Mental Health Services, no. 6. San Francisco: Jossey-Bass, 1980.

Jacobson, G. F. *The Multiple Crises of Marital Separation and Divorce.* In *Seminars in Psychiatry* series (M. Greenblatt, ed.). Orlando, Fla.: Grune & Stratton, 1983.

Kitson, G. C. "Attachment to the Spouse in Divorce: A Scale and Its Application." *Journal of Marriage and the Family,* 1982, *44,* 379–393.

Kitson, G. C., Graham, A. V., and Schmidt, D. D. "Troubled Marriages and Divorce: A Prospective Suburban Study." *Journal of Family Practice,* forthcoming.

Kitson, G. C., and others. "Sampling Issues in Family Research." *Journal of Marriage and the Family,* 1982, *44,* 965–981.

Kurdek, L. A., Blisk, D., and Siesky, A. E. "Correlates of Children's Long-Term Adjustment to Their Parents' Divorce." *Developmental Psychology,* 1981, *17,* 568–579.

McCord, J., McCord, W., and Thurber, E. "Some Effects of Paternal Absence on Male Children." *Journal of Abnormal Social Psychology,* 1962, *64,* 361–369.

McDermott, J. F. "Parental Divorce in Early Childhood." *American Journal of Psychiatry,* 1968, *124,* 1424–1432.

Mednick, S. A., and McNeil, T. F. "Current Methodology in Research in the Etiology of Schizophrenia: Serious Difficulties Which Suggest the Use of the High Risk Group Method." *Psychological Bulletin,* 1968, *70,* 681–693.

National Center for Health Statistics. "Advance Report of Final Divorce Statistics, 1979." *Monthly Vital Statistics Report,* July 1982, *30*(4), Supplement.

National Center for Health Statistics. *Monthly Vital Statistics Report,* Oct. 5, 1983, *31*(13).

Nolan, J. F. "The Impact of Divorce on Children." *Consultation Courts Review,* 1977, *15,* 25–29.

Parkes, C. M. *Bereavement: Studies of Grief in Adult Life.* New York: International Universities Press, 1972.

Porter, B., and O'Leary, K. D. "Marital Discord and Childhood Behavior Problems." *Journal of Abnormal Child Psychology,* 1980, *8,* 287–295.

Rosen, R. "Children of Divorce: What They Feel About Access and Other Aspects of the Divorce Experience." *Journal of Clinical Child Psychology,* 1977, *6,* 24–26.

Rutter, M. "Parent-Child Separation: Psychological Effects on Children." *Journal of Child Psychology and Psychiatry and Allied Disciplines,* 1971, *12,* 233–250.

Rutter, M. "Maternal Deprivation 1972–1978: New Findings, New Concepts, New Approaches." *Child Development,* 1979, *50,* 283–305.

Wallerstein, J. S., and Kelly, J. B. "The Effects of Parental Divorce: Experiences of the Pre-school Child." *Journal of the American Academy of Child Psychiatry,* 1975, *14,* 600–616.

Wallerstein, J. S., and Kelly, J. B. "The Effects of Parental Divorce: Experiences of the Child in Later Latency." *American Journal of Orthopsychiatry*, 1976, *46*, 256–269.

Wallerstein, J. S., and Kelly, J. B. *Surviving the Breakup: How Children and Parents Cope with Divorce.* New York: Basic Books, 1980.

Weiss, R. S. *Marital Separation: Managing After a Marriage Ends.* New York: Basic Books, 1975.

Zill, N. "Divorce, Marital Happiness, and the Mental Health of Children: Findings from the FCD National Survey of Children." Paper presented at National Institute of Mental Health Workshop on Divorce and Children, Bethesda, Md., Feb. 7–8, 1978.

11

Death of a Parent or Sibling During Childhood

Janice L. Krupnick
Fredric Solomon

Editors' Note: *The authors provide a comprehensive summary of existing knowledge about how children and adolescents fare in response to the death of a family member. Although the chapter takes a research perspective, emphasizing the methodological difficulties that qualify the conclusions reached, it considers clinical and psychoanalytic studies along with more traditional investigations. The authors discuss developmental influences on the capacity to mourn, differences between childhood and adult patterns of grieving, and the fantasies, changes in self-image, and defensive maneuvers that accompany reactions to this most traumatic separation. Clinicians generally agree that healthy mourning requires considerable expression of feelings about the loss. But because children rely on such primitive defenses as denial and regression, even under favorable circumstances the grieving process is likely to take several years. Younger children are more vulnerable to the impact of bereavement, as suggested by Mahler's and Bowlby's developmental studies of separation.*

As with other life transitions that involve loss, the context in which bereavement occurs shapes children's and adolescents' reactions to it. The availability of alternative caregivers is

*important in facilitating adjustment to the loss, as noted else-
where in this volume; see Chapter One on nonhuman primate
responses to loss, Chapter Six on nursery school adjustment,
and Chapter Ten on marital dissolution. Other factors that influence the grieving process include the child's emotional well-
being at the time of the death, the circumstances of the death,
the gender of deceased and bereaved, and the quality of the
child's social support system. The authors summarize the short-,
intermediate-, and long-term consequences of childhood bereavement, suggesting that this trauma renders individuals more
vulnerable to emotional disturbance, especially depression, in
later life. The experience of early bereavement sensitizes the
individual to loss, evoking unresolved grief at subsequent separations. Since life is replete with separation, the impact of early
loss is profound.*

Almost uniformly, when asked to identify the most potent
stressor in ordinary life, researchers and the public have named
the death of a close family member (Holmes and Rahe, 1967;
Rabkin and Streuning, 1976; Elliott and Eisdorfer, 1982; Hamburg, Elliott, and Parron, 1982). In 1982 the Institute of Medicine of the National Academy of Sciences convened a multi-
disciplinary committee to study the health consequences of the
stress of bereavement, at the request of the Office of Prevention
of the National Institute of Mental Health (NIMH). The expert
panel was to evaluate the research literature and to provide its
best judgment about such broad questions as:

- What can be concluded from available research evidence
  about the health consequences of bereavement?
- What further research would be especially important and
  promising to pursue?
- On the basis of both research evidence and informed judgment, are there preventive interventions that should be recommended for more widespread adoption in the health care
  system? Which ones are not yet ready for such adoption but
  should be tested for their value?

The committee's final report was titled *Bereavement: Reactions, Consequences, and Care* (Osterweis, Solomon, and Green, 1984). In the course of the twenty-month study, additional funds were provided by the Marion E. Kenworthy–Sarah H. Swift Foundation that enabled the committee's staff and consultants to thoroughly examine the knowledge base on bereavement during childhood. The present chapter is based on some of the materials prepared for the Institute of Medicine study.

In studies of psychologically disturbed adults, especially those suffering from clinical depression, observers have noted that subjects' backgrounds frequently include a major childhood loss. Clinicians have suggested that bereavement may instigate or exacerbate a wide range of emotional problems during childhood or adolescence and may leave youthful survivors with enduring psychological vulnerabilities. One may hypothesize that it is the developmental immaturity of children, including their underdeveloped capacity for coping, that makes young people a particularly "at risk" population in dealing with the emotional experience and aftermath of significant interpersonal loss.

The exact number of young people who experience the death of an immediate family member is unclear. According to Kliman (1979a), approximately 5 percent of American children (roughly 1.5 million individuals) lose one or both parents by age fifteen. Among lower socioeconomic groups, the proportion may be even higher.

In this chapter, the focus will be on the psychological effects of parent or sibling loss—the types of bereavement believed to have the most serious emotional consequences for children. Because the majority of those who have written about this subject have explored parent rather than sibling loss and because responses to these two types of losses show many similarities, the emphasis will be on children's and adolescents' reactions to the death of a parent. Knowledge about interventions with bereaved children, preventive or therapeutic, is not reviewed here. (See Osterweis, Solomon, and Green, 1984.)

A Comment on the Existing Literature

One cannot make valid assertions about the nature of the bereavement process and its potential impact on children and adolescents without a body of methodologically sound studies on which to draw. Ideally, such studies would include representative samples of bereaved youth who are followed prospectively for several years and who are compared on various psychological dimensions with nonbereaved children. Unfortunately, although there is a sizable literature on the effects of loss during childhood, the number of empirical investigations that meet current research standards is quite small.

One problem is sample selection. Most studies of childhood bereavement have relied on observations of disturbed children in psychotherapeutic or psychoanalytic treatment (Miller, 1971)—groups that may not be representative of all bereaved youth. The studies that have used random samples of grieving children have frequently not included control groups, an omission that makes it difficult to interpret study findings because one does not know what the base rates of problematic behaviors or symptoms might be among nonbereaved subjects. In studies in which control groups were used, it is usually difficult to know whether subjects were matched on important variables, such as gender and age. Furthermore, conclusions about responses to loss in very young children (under age five) have usually been based on observations of institutionalized children who had experienced temporary separations from parents (for example, Bowlby, 1960, 1961, 1963). It is not clear whether the reactions evidenced by children under these circumstances would be comparable to those of children who are bereaved, and one does not know whether the children's behavior in these studies was due to the loss of the parent alone or to the many other simultaneous losses associated with institutional placement. It is also unknown whether the disturbing reactions displayed by subjects in these studies endured over time, since the children who were observed were not followed long enough.

Indeed, the time frame of most studies of childhood bereavement poses a serious problem. Although prospective, longitudinal studies are likely to produce the most reliable data, very few such studies have been carried out. Those that have been done have not followed children all the way to adulthood. A myriad of studies assessing the long-term effects of bereavement in childhood are available, but findings from these studies are suspect because they have almost always been based on retrospective data (see Gregory, 1958). Furthermore, even in the rare prospective studies, methodological shortcomings—such as omission of nonbereaved control groups (Kaffman and Elizur, 1983; Raphael, 1982), failure to observe bereaved children directly (Van Eerdewegh, Bieri, Parilla, and Clayton, 1982), and insufficiently long follow-up (Raphael, 1982; Van Eerdewegh, Bieri, Parilla, and Clayton, 1982)—diminish the ultimate utility of such work.

In spite of a rich clinical literature, limitations on the generalizability of findings from one research study to another have hampered the accumulation of a consistent body of data-based knowledge. For example, it cannot be assumed that findings from studies conducted abroad, in some cases during wartime, are applicable to American children who are not experiencing comparable environmental strain. Important terms, such as *depression, pathological grief,* and *anger,* are commonly used but are generally not clearly defined, so that it is impossible to know whether all researchers are referring to the same behaviors or responses. Standardized instruments that might permit greater generalization across studies are unusual in assessments of children; such instruments have only recently begun to be developed. It seems likely that the different methodological approaches that have been used also account, at least in part, for the different outcomes that have been reported.

Children's Developmental Capacity for Grief

Although it is generally acknowledged that individuals continue to develop and grow throughout the life course, never again are development and growth so rapid and fluctuating as they are during childhood and adolescence. This means that the impact of trauma and the specific reactions it elicits depend largely on the developmental stage of the child when an event occurs. A developmental perspective assumes that the personal meanings and implications of major interpersonal loss will be affected by the child's level of cognitive and emotional maturity.

Considerable confusion and misunderstanding of grieving children have occurred because of adults' expectations that young people will mourn the way that they do. Although children's reactions to loss may be similar to adults' in some respects, particular manifestations and duration are usually quite different.

For instance, soon after the death of a parent or sibling, young children may begin to play games in which they re-create the death or activities related to the funeral; or they might tell visitors or even strangers on the street, "My mother died." Such behaviors, though appearing shallow and uncaring, actually reflect attempts to master the trauma and serve as ways of asking for support. Children may study the reactions of others in order to learn how they should think and feel about their loss. They may repeatedly ask the same questions about the death, less for the factual information than for reassurance that the story has remained the same. The youngster who continues to play after a death as if nothing traumatic had occurred is not showing that the death has had no impact. Rather, this response reflects the intellectual and emotional capacity of the child.

Since losses are so distressing for very young children, they may alternately broach and then withdraw from their emotions in order to avoid becoming overwhelmed. They may not be able to tolerate strong emotions for more than brief periods, and sadness may be evidenced as anger or unruly behavior. Consequently, grief-related reactions may be missed or misunderstood. In addition, because youngsters have strong, immediate needs for caring and relatedness, they will typically shift from observable grief reactions to a rapid search for and acceptance of replacement figures. Whereas adults may grieve intensely for a year or more, children are more likely to express their grief intermittently for a number of years after the death. At successive levels of subsequent development, thoughts and feelings about the loss will typically resurface, needing to be reexamined and resolved. Successful interaction with young people who have experienced parental or sibling loss requires awareness of the unique way in which children grieve. They are unlikely to express their emotions like adults; their manifest behavior should not necessarily be expected to provide insight into their underlying distress. If subsequent psychological development seems inhibited or if psychiatric symptoms emerge following a major loss, professional mental health intervention may be indicated (Kliman, 1980).

Clinicians who have studied grieving children between age four and adolescence disagree about the nature of grieving in children and their ability to resolve major losses adaptively. Some psychoanalysts (Altschul, 1968; Deutsch, 1937; Jacobson, 1965; Wolfenstein, 1966, 1969) feel that the ability to tolerate the intensely painful emotions needed to complete the separation process is not present until adolescence. They assert that children are more likely than adults to use immature defense mechanisms, such as denial, which preclude an adequate working through of a death. These observers see a qualitative difference between children's and adults' responses to the death of a loved person.

Some observers, however, such as Bowlby (1960), emphasize the similarities between the responses of children and adults and suggest that there is an evolutionary basis for the reactions that occur. Bowlby argues that the disagreement over children's capacity for "mourning" rests largely on differing interpretations of terms. It seems that many psychoanalysts use the word *mourning* to describe psychological processes eventuating in a single, specific outcome—namely, detachment—while others regard it more broadly as signifying "a fairly wide array of psychological processes set in train by the loss of a loved person irrespective of outcome" (Bowlby, 1980, p. 17).

Several clinicians have emphasized that if bereavement occurs after the attainment of object constancy (at three to four years of age), it may not result in psychopathology. It is now frequently suggested (Bowlby, 1980; Furman, 1974; Kliman, 1979a) that healthy adjustment can take place if the bereaved child is cared for by a consistent adult who reliably attends to reality needs and encourages the child to express his or her feelings about the loss. Furthermore, the biological changes that are part of development naturally push children toward greater intellectual and emotional mastery and can, under positive circumstances, play a role in children's potential resilience following a loss.

The Grieving Process

The particular ways in which different children express their grief and the duration of the response will vary, depending on an individual child's age, unique personality, and stage of emotional and intellectual development. Children, however, like adults, can be expected to proceed through a sequence of responses to major loss. Bowlby (1960, 1961, 1963, 1980), basing his model on observations of young institutionalized children who were separated from their mothers, identified three discrete phases that follow separation and loss. He found that when a healthy child over the age of six months was separated from his or her mother, the youngster responded with up to a week or more of "protest"—boisterous, rageful, crying behavior indicating an expectation of and insistence on reunion. When such efforts to recover the lost mother failed, there ensued a phase of "despair," characterized by acute pain, unhappiness, and decreasing hope. After this came the final phase, "detachment," during which children acted as if it no longer mattered to them whether their mothers returned. On mother's return, the child might initially avoid and withdraw from her.

In their work with Israeli kibbutz children, Elizur and Kaffman (1982) have also observed a phaselike pattern during the first four years after paternal bereavement. In the first year, after immediately responding to the loss with sadness and grief, the bereaved children began to investigate the meanings and ramifications of the loss they had sustained. They asked realistic questions in an attempt to gain a better understanding of the differences between "dead" and "alive." Children seemed more understanding and accepting of the loss during the second year of bereavement. Anxiety increased significantly, but defensive maneuvers declined. Children were more demanding, restless, and aggressive, and dependency on mothers intensified. During the third and fourth years, there were still signs of excessive dependency in two thirds of the children studied; but anxiety and aggressiveness, which had increased during the second year, declined. By this time, a general trend toward adjustment was evident, although almost 40 percent of a previously normal sample continued to display signs of emotional upset.

Common Ideas, Worries, and Fantasies. Like adults (Krupnick and Horowitz, 1981), bereaved children often experience particular trains of thought after the death of a loved one which are associated with feelings of sadness, rage, fear, shame, and guilt. Three questions, whether directly expressed or not, typically come to mind for most children: Did I make this happen? Will the same thing happen to me? Who is going to take care of me now (or if something happens to my surviving parent)? Adults not only should answer such questions but should take time to hear how the child understands the answer, since miscommunications and misunderstandings may lead to intensified worry or anger.

Feelings of anger are frequently caused by the often-held view that a parent's or sibling's death was a deliberate abandonment. Indeed, 20 percent of the parentally bereaved children studied by Arthur and Kemme (1964) had this idea, one that undermines the child's sense that he or she is adequately cared for.

Observers have noted that bereaved children may worry that their basic physical needs for survival will not be satisfied (Furman, 1974; Kliman, 1968). They may also fear that a fate similar to the one that struck down the deceased parent or sibling may befall them or their surviving caretakers, and they may worry that a dead parent could return to seek revenge (Arthur and Kemme, 1964).

Changes in Self-Image Following Bereavement. Observers of bereaved children (for example, Rochlin, 1959, 1961, 1965; Kliman, 1980) report that they often experience a diminution in self-esteem and self-regard after the death of a parent, possibly because of shifts in self-concept that take place after the loss of an immediate family member.

If children interpret a parent's death as a deliberate desertion caused by the parent's insufficient love for them, they may come to view themselves as unlovable, resulting in persistent low self-esteem (Call and Wolfenstein, 1976). After the death of a caretaker, children may also suddenly view themselves as extremely small and helpless. Recognition that one was unable to control life events that seriously affect the self may contribute to the kind of passivity and apathy that Seligman (1975) described as "learned helplessness," a cause of depression. On the basis of their considerable clinical experience with bereaved children, Erna Furman (1974) and Robert Furman (1973) hypothesize that the tendency toward self-blame and guilt, a fairly universal phenomenon among both bereaved adults and bereaved children, may actually serve as a defense against the more threatening idea that one is vulnerable and helpless in the face of life events. They suggest that if someone feels responsible for a death (even though this notion is totally irrational and psychologically distressing), he or she at least feels some measure of control over the environment.

Bereaved children may also regard themselves as hostile and hurtful. Because children think in egocentric, magical ways, seeing no difference between thought and deed, they may become convinced that it was their own angry feelings or destructive wishes that killed the parent or sibling. A hostile image of the self may be particularly likely to arise if the relationship with the deceased was marked by a good deal of anger or competition, as may be likely when it is a sibling who dies (Blinder, 1972). Relatively universal death wishes toward a parent or sibling can result in postbereavement feelings of responsibility and guilt (Rochlin, 1965; Wahl, 1959), especially if death wishes were particularly intense.

Impact of Identification. Identification with a person who has died, a process that has been described as more common and more dramatic in bereaved children than in adults (Birtchnell, 1969), may simultaneously be both an unconscious defensive maneuver and a conscious effort to emulate the deceased person's admirable traits (Johnson and Rosenblatt, 1981). In moderation, such identification may be enriching for the child (Jacobson, 1957; Kliman, 1980). When such identifications become exaggerated, however, suggesting an adoption of the dead parent's symptoms and death, a child can become quite frightened. Wolfenstein (1969) concludes that this anxiety makes genuinely adaptive identifications in children rare.

According to Johnson and Rosenblatt (1981), socially inappropriate identification with a deceased parent may indicate incomplete or distorted grief. An excessively close identification with an adult may lead to rejection or criticism by peers and a resulting loss of social support. Furthermore, children might feel pressured by adults' encouraging them to assume replacement roles. For example, if a new widow tells her young son that he must now become "the man of the house," the child may feel that he literally has to assume all the roles of his deceased father, such as surrogate marriage partner or emotional confidant to his depressed mother. If the mother later remarries, the son may feel that he was "replaced" because of his inadequate performance.

Children who try to help bereaved parents cope with their loss by "replacing" a dead sibling run the risk of compromising the formation of their own identities. Parents' tendencies to idealize a dead child may encourage overidentification in the surviving youngster as he or she strives to secure the parents' affection by taking on characteristics of the deceased. Such idealization can also make it difficult for surviving siblings to confront their anger at the deceased or at their parents (for example, for failing to prevent the death or for seeming more concerned about the deceased child than about them).

Common Defensive Maneuvers. The defense mechanisms most frequently used by bereaved children in coping with losses include denial, idealization of the dead parent or sibling, inhibition or isolation of grief, identification with the deceased, and displacement.

A good deal has been written (for example, Altschul, 1968; Deutsch, 1937; Jacobson, 1965; Shambaugh, 1961; Elizur and Kaffman, 1982) about the frequent use of denial, which is believed to underlie persistent fantasies of reunion with the deceased. According to Altschul (1968), who notes that denial may continue indefinitely, it may actually be the emotional importance of the deceased person that is denied more than the reality of the death. Wolfenstein (1966) suggests that a defensive, and often maladaptive, splitting of the ego in bereaved children enables them to acknowledge a parent's death while denying its finality.

Another common occurrence is idealization of the dead parent, who is preserved in fantasy as the good parent, while hostility is displaced onto the surviving "bad" parent (Neubauer, 1960). In their study of disturbed bereaved children, Arthur and Kemme (1964) found that this type of idealization was particularly noticeable in girls, who resented efforts to intrude on or devalue fantasized relationships with deceased fathers. Wolfenstein (1966) views idealization of the deceased parent and devaluation of the surviving one as an attempt to undo earlier feelings of hostility toward the parent who died.

Influences on Grieving

Factors that may influence the course and ultimate outcome of grieving in children include the bereaved child's age, developmental stage, and emotional stability; cultural background; circumstances of the death; sex of the deceased and of the bereaved; nature of the child's relationship with the deceased; and nature of the child's support system after the death.

Age, Developmental Stage, and Emotional Stability. It is generally agreed (for example, Alexander and Alderstein, 1958; Bowlby, 1980; Elizur and Kaffman, 1983; McConville, Boag, and Purohit, 1970; Rutter, 1966; Van Eerdewegh, Bieri, Parilla, and Clayton, 1982) that the impact of bereavement may be greater at some ages or developmental stages than at others. Rutter (1966) and Bowlby (1980) have both reported that children younger than five years are more vulnerable to major interpersonal loss than older children. Bowlby has identified children between the ages of six months and four years as a high-risk group, while Rutter speculates that children younger than two are less distressed than three- and four-year-olds because less time has been available to develop emotional ties.

Early adolescence has also been cited as a vulnerable age.

In studies conducted by Rutter (1966), Van Eerdewegh, Bieri, Parilla, and Clayton (1982), and Wolfenstein (1966), it was found that it was mostly adolescent boys who had lost fathers who reacted to parental bereavement with severe depression. In contrast, however, Hilgard, Newman, and Fisk (1960), using retrospective information, found that excellent long-term (into adulthood) adjustments often occurred among individuals who had lost their parent between ages ten and fifteen, if they had experienced an adequate home situation before the death.

A child's prior emotional instability has frequently been cited as a potential factor in postbereavement difficulties. Elizur and Kaffman (1982, 1983; Kaffman and Elizur, 1983), in their studies of Israeli children, found that normal children were also at risk for later psychological problems, although they concede that preexisting emotional difficulties, in combination with other antecedent variables, may intensify negative reactions in the months immediately after a loss. The particular types of emotional disturbances or family problems that tend to place children at greater risk for negative reactions have not been specified.

Cultural Factors. It is generally agreed that social and cultural factors, such as religion, socioeconomic status, and ethnic background, influence an individual's view of and reaction to loss, but there is little empirical evidence to support this claim. Using child interview data, Tallmer, Formanek, and Tallmer (1974) assert that children from lower-class families are more attuned to at least the concept of death, probably because death and violence are more frequent in their social milieu. Studies comparing kibbutz children with urban Israeli children found that differences between the groups in child-rearing techniques, family functioning style, and social setting helped to determine the nature of the problems that emerged after paternal death—although the *overall* rate of adverse emotional sequelae was surprisingly similar in the two groups (Kaffman and Elizur, 1983; Elizur and Kaffman, 1982).

Circumstances of Death. A child's response to parental or sibling death may be seriously affected by the type of death it was—for example, expected or unexpected, in the home or in the hospital. Erna Furman (1974) notes that, for young children, there is no such thing as the "peaceful death" of a parent. Each type of death is linked with its own set of anxieties; the etiology and type of anxiety depend on the particular child and his or her unique situation.

It is generally thought that, for both adults and children, expected deaths are easier to tolerate than sudden losses. When a parent has succumbed to death after a lengthy illness, however, the child may have seen or heard about a series of medical interventions that could have been interpreted as bodily assaults (Furman, 1974). Furthermore, the particular type of injury or illness experienced by the family member may coincide with and give reality to developmentally appropriate but otherwise transient concerns, thereby exacerbating and possibly rigidifying already-existing worries.

Suicide and Homicide. For both adults and children, suicide and homicide are viewed as the most difficult forms of death to accept.

In a study of children's immediate reactions to witnessing suicide attempts and homicides, Pynoos and associates (Pynoos and Eth, 1982; Pynoos, Gilmore, and Shapiro, 1983) found that, regardless of what children have been told, they clearly know, in a fundamental way, what has occurred. They promptly initiate defense mechanisms, such as denial in fantasy, and rework the facts according to developmental phase concerns.

Studies of suicide survivors generally point to a considerable vulnerability to long-term problems. According to Cain and Fast (1966), a clinical sample of forty-five disturbed children who had experienced parental suicide four years earlier displayed such symptoms as obesity, delinquency, fetishism, encopresis, and psychosomatic disorders. They were much more likely than other bereaved children to be psychotic (24 percent, compared with 9 percent) and frequently manifested distortions of communication. Frequently receiving the message that they should not know or tell about the suicide, they were often conflicted about learning and knowing, leading to learning disabilities, speech inhibitions, and disturbances of their sense of reality. In a review of the case material of seventeen adult psychiatric patients who were seen an average of sixteen years after parental suicide (Dorpat, 1972), guilt and depression related to the death, preoccupation with suicide, self-destructive behavior, and absence of grief were evident. As Shepherd and Barraclough (1976) note, however, prebereavement home life for suicide survivors is likely to be abnormal because of the presence of a mentally ill parent. Thus, it is difficult to clarify the degree to which the act of suicide itself exerts an influence on the grieving child.

Gender of Deceased Parent and Bereaved Child. Attempts to locate interactions between the sex of the deceased parent and the bereaved child have yielded contradictory findings. Kliman (1979a, 1979b) has observed that, after age three, grieving for a deceased other-sex parent tends to be more overt, although special anxieties may emerge in children who have lost a parent of the same sex, especially if the child fears that he or she must now become the family's "new mommy or daddy." In samples of disturbed children, Fast and Cain (1966) found that boys who had experienced paternal bereavement felt threatened by, and thus tried to avoid, loving feelings toward their mothers; Arthur and Kemme (1964) found that girls were more likely than boys to idealize dead fathers.

Retrospective studies (for example, Brown, Harris, and Copeland, 1977; Birtchnell, 1970a, 1970b, 1972) suggest that girls, in general, are more vulnerable than boys to the death of a parent and more vulnerable than boys to loss of a father during adolescence (Birtchnell, 1972; Black, 1978; Hill, 1969). Such findings do not hold up in prospective investigations, however, according to Kaffman and Elizur (1983), who noted few differences between boys and girls who experienced paternal death. Rutter (1966), also, though finding significantly higher levels of depression among adolescent boys who lost fathers than among other bereaved youths, concludes that there was no evidence to suggest that psychiatric disorder is more related to the death of a father than mother or vice versa.

Quality of Relationship with the Deceased. As is true of adults, working through a loss may be more complicated if the prior relationship with the person who died was highly ambivalent or dependent (Raphael, 1983). As already described, anger toward the deceased may increase the likelihood of idealization of that person, a defensive maneuver that precludes resolution of grief. In addition, for the very young child who has not yet had the opportunity to develop relationships outside the family, almost all love is invested in parental figures, who assume great responsibility for the child's very survival. Thus, the type of relationship the child is likely to have had cannot be determined in isolation, without considering its interaction with the child's age.

Quality of Support System. Although social support is generally regarded as a buffering variable that can soften the impact of loss, bereaved children must usually rely for support on adults who have been traumatized themselves. Children are likely to look to a surviving parent for help, but in cases of bereavement this individual will have recently been affected by the death of a partner or child.

In place of the atmosphere of stability and consistency that might facilitate a good outcome (Furman, 1974), bereaved children typically experience a situation of chaos, disorganization, and uncertainty. After parental death, disciplinary methods often change, the surviving parent becoming excessively harsh, excessively permissive, or inconsistent. Multiple life-style changes caused by the need to establish living arrangements, possibly including institutional placement, are also not uncommon (Rutter, 1966).

The effects of parental death depend largely on the quality of family relationships before the loss and on the degree to which the home can be maintained and/or reestablished afterward. Protective factors found by Hilgard, Newman, and Fisk (1960) and Elizur and Kaffman (1983) included the presence of a strong, reality-oriented mother who worked and kept the home intact, the ability of a parent to use a network of support outside the home, prebereavement years spent in a home with two compatible parents who had well-defined roles, and parental attitudes that fostered independence and tolerance for separation. "Appropriate" grieving by the surviving parent and avoidance of excessive dependence on a bereaved child may also facilitate satisfactory adaptation following the death of a parent (Hilgard, Newman, and Fisk, 1960).

In cases of parental bereavement, remarriage of the surviving parent may either increase or diminish the support available to the child. In a retrospective study of women who had experienced maternal loss before they were eleven, Birtchnell (1980) found that those who had had poor relationships with mother replacements were vulnerable to depression and anxiety in adulthood. Fast and Cain (1966) note that a bereaved child may resist disciplinary action from, and may experience competitive feelings toward, a stepparent. The child may also unfavorably compare the stepparent with the deceased parent, thereby intensifying feelings of hurt and resentment. However, a sensitive, caring stepparent could provide additional support and could help relieve the burden of emotional dependency that a lonely, unattached parent might place on a child.

After the death of an immediate family member, grandparents, aunts, uncles, and perhaps close family friends could also assist a bereaved child, although the impact of nonparental figures on the course of a child's grieving has not yet been investigated.

Outcomes of Parent or Sibling Loss

It has been suggested that the death of a parent or sibling during childhood or adolescence may lead to a multitude of serious and enduring psychological consequences, including schizophrenia, major depression, and suicide. Responses are usually classified as immediate reactions, which occur during the initial weeks and months after the death; intermediate reactions, which may emerge some years later in childhood or adolescence; and long-range, or "sleeper," effects, which may appear in adulthood either as ongoing reactions or as delayed reactions to the loss.

Immediate Reactions. A range of emotional and behavioral responses may follow the death of a parent or sibling. People who have observed both patient and nonpatient samples of recently bereaved children report that they are frequently sad,

angry, and/or anxious. Behavioral responses may include disturbances in eating and sleeping, difficulties in concentrating and
learning, withdrawal, restlessness, dependency, and regression.
Initial symptom patterns usually depend on the child's age and
developmental phase at the time of the death. For example, it is
common for children under age five to display disturbances in
eating and sleeping and in bowel and bladder habits. School-age
children may become phobic or hypochondriacal, withdrawn,
or overly solicitous of others. Afraid of appearing different
from their peers, adolescents may be uncomfortable expressing
their feelings (LaGrand, 1981).

Intermediate Reactions. Evidence of emotional distress in
children continuing from one to six years after parental or sibling death has been observed in both patient and community
samples.

Studies by Kaffman and Elizur (1979; Elizur and Kaffman, 1982) showed that about 40 percent of normal preadolescent Israeli kibbutz children who lost a father during wartime
continued to display serious psychiatric symptoms, such as soil-
ing, social isolation, and learning problems, more than three years
after their bereavement. By forty-two months postbereavement,
fewer than a third had achieved satisfactory family, school, and
social adjustment. Children with prior emotional problems and
those from families in which marital difficulties had been prominent were more likely to develop pathological reactions than
those with more stable personalities and family backgrounds
(Elizur and Kaffman, 1983).

Both Rutter (1966) and Arthur and Kemme (1964) similarly found an excess of neurotic disturbance in child psychiatric patients who had experienced parental loss. In Arthur and
Kemme's sample, 52 percent of the children displayed conflicts
over independence, 27 percent were excessively dependent on
others, and 39 percent experienced difficulty in defining their
relationship with the other-sex parent four months to two
years after parental death. Sibling death has been associated
with symptoms of depression, such as trembling, sadness, and
crying, in disturbed children as long as five or more years after
the death.

Of note is the finding of frequent depression among adolescent boys who lost a father (Van Eerdewegh, Bieri, Parilla, and Clayton, 1982; Rutter, 1966). Severe depression seems to be most likely in adolescents who are already susceptible to depressive illness (Stone, 1981) and in those whose mothers had depressions preceding their husbands' death.

Parental bereavement has also been correlated with delinquency (Gregory, 1965; Raphael, 1983; Rutter, 1966), school refusal, examination failure, decreased interest in school activities, and dropping out (Black, 1974; Lifshitz, 1976; Raphael, 1983; Van Eerdewegh, Bieri, Parilla, and Clayton, 1982).

Long-Term Reactions. Even though the long-range effects of parental and sibling loss are of most concern, the research evidence in this area is probably the weakest. Links between childhood bereavement and adult neurosis, psychosis, and antisocial behavior have been investigated and generally suggest an increased vulnerability to emotional disturbance later in life. Nevertheless, almost all studies in this area have been retrospective, and specific findings often have been contradictory.

Of most interest have been findings linking childhood bereavement to adult depression. On the basis of his clinical observations, Bowlby (1980) has asserted that profound early loss renders individuals highly vulnerable to later depressive disorders, each subsequent loss triggering an upsurge of unresolved grief initially related to the early bereavement.

The empirical evidence on early loss and depression remains only suggestive, however. In a review of controlled studies investigating the association between bereavement during childhood or adolescence and depression during adulthood, Lloyd (1980) reported that eight of eleven studies (Brown, 1961; Brown, Harris, and Copeland, 1977; Caplan and Douglas, 1969; Dennehy, 1966; Forrest, Fraser, and Priest, 1965; Hill and Price, 1967; Munro and Griffiths, 1969; Roy, 1978) found a significantly higher rate of depressive disorders among the bereaved group; childhood loss of a parent increased the risk of depression by a factor of two or three. In seven of eight controlled studies (Beck, Sethi, and Tuthill, 1963; Birtchnell, 1970a, 1970b; Brown, Harris, and Copeland, 1977; Gay and

Tonge, 1967; Munro, 1966; Sethi, 1964; Wilson, Alltop, and Buffaloe, 1967), early loss was correlated with severity of depression; parental bereavement was associated with psychotic, as opposed to neurotic, depression (Brown, Harris, and Copeland, 1977; Wilson, Alltop, and Buffaloe, 1967). In a recent review of studies on parental death in childhood and later depression, however, Tennant, Bebbington, and Hurry (1980) reported that the data in this area are inconclusive, and Birtchnell (1980) cautions that such factors as the quality of a bereaved child's relationships with subsequent caretakers may be more influential in determining the risk for depression than the experience of bereavement itself.

Some evidence suggests an association between early loss and adult-life impairment in sexual identity, development of autonomy, and capacity for intimacy (Archibald, Bell, Miller, and Tuddenham, 1962; Brown, 1958; Remus-Araico, 1965). Problems in parenting when a bereaved child grows up have been reported, especially for loss of the same-sex parent between ages seven and twelve (Altschul and Beiser, 1984). Increased vulnerability to subsequent criminality has also been documented (Markusen and Fulton, 1971).

Conclusions

Although bereaved children and adults manifest many similar reactions, there are clear differences between them in the time frame and the overt process of grieving. Because children are less mature than adults in their intellectual abilities and their psychic structures, they are more apt to use defense mechanisms, such as denial and regression, that are more primitive than those typically used by adults. Such differences place children at substantially greater psychological risk than adults after the death of a parent or sibling. Denying that a death has occurred, for example, makes it difficult for a child to deal with and work through feelings of loss. Problematic feelings and behaviors associated with the bereavement may emerge months or even years later as a child reworks his or her grief (Kliman, 1979a, 1979b).

One cannot really draw firm conclusions about the long-term consequences of childhood or adolescent loss. For the intermediate term, however, it appears that early bereavement greatly increases the likelihood of depression, school dysfunction, and delinquency. Factors that appear to increase the risk of psychological morbidity following parental or sibling loss during childhood or adolescence include the following: loss before the age of five years or during early adolescence; loss of mother for girls under age eleven and loss of father for adolescent boys; psychological difficulties in the child antedating the death (the more severe the preexisting psychopathology, the greater the risk); problematic relationship with the decreased before the death; emotionally vulnerable surviving parent who becomes overly dependent on the child; inadequate family or community supports or a parent who is unable to make use of an available support system; an unstable, inconsistent environment, including multiple shifts in caretakers and disruption of familiar routines (transfer to an institution could be considered an extreme example); parental remarriage if a negative relationship develops between the child and the stepparent; lack of prior knowledge about death; unexpected death; and experience of parent or sibling suicide or homicide.

References

Alexander, I., and Alderstein, A. "Affective Responses to the Concept of Death in a Population of Children and Early Adolescents." *Journal of Genetic Psychology,* 1958, *93,* 167–177.

Altschul, S. "Denial and Ego Arrest." *Journal of the American Psychoanalytic Association,* 1968, *16,* 301–318.

Altschul, S., and Beiser, H. "The Effect of Parent Loss by Death in Early Childhood on the Function of Parenting." In R. S. Cohen, B. J. Cohler, and S. H. Weissman (eds.), *Parenthood: A Psychodynamic Perspective.* New York: Guilford Press, 1984.

Archibald, H., Bell, D., Miller, C., and Tuddenham, R. "Bereavement in Childhood and Adult Psychiatric Disturbance." *Psychosomatic Medicine,* 1962, *4,* 343–351.

Arthur, B., and Kemme, M. L. "Bereavement in Childhood." *Journal of Child Psychology and Psychiatry,* 1964, *5,* 37–49.

Beck, A. T., Sethi, B., and Tuthill, R. "Childhood Bereavement and Adult Depression." *Archives of General Psychiatry,* 1963, *9,* 295–302.

Birtchnell, J. "The Possible Consequences of Early Parent Death." *British Journal of Medical Psychology,* 1969, *42,* 1–12.

Birtchnell, J. "Early Parent Death and Mental Illness." *British Journal of Psychiatry,* 1970a, *116,* 281–288.

Birtchnell, J. "Depression in Relation to Early and Recent Parent Death." *British Journal of Psychiatry,* 1970b, *116,* 299–306.

Birtchnell, J. "Early Parent Death and Psychiatric Diagnosis." *Social Psychiatry,* 1972, *7,* 202–210.

Birtchnell, J. "Women Whose Mothers Died in Childhood: An Outcome Study." *Psychological Medicine,* 1980, *10,* 699–713.

Black, D. "What Happens to Bereaved Children?" *Proceedings of the Royal Society of Medicine,* 1974, *69,* 842–844.

Black, D. "The Bereaved Child." *Journal of Child Psychology and Psychiatry,* 1978, *19,* 287–292.

Blinder, B. "Sibling Death in Childhood." *Child Psychiatry and Human Development,* 1972, *2,* 169–175.

Bowlby, J. "Grief and Mourning in Infancy and Early Childhood." *Psychoanalytic Study of the Child,* 1960, *15,* 9–52.

Bowlby, J. "Childhood Mourning and Its Implications for Psychiatry." *American Journal of Psychiatry,* 1961, *118,* 481–498.

Bowlby, J. "Pathological Mourning and Childhood Mourning." *Journal of the American Psychoanalytic Association,* 1963, *11,* 500–541.

Bowlby, J. *Attachment and Loss.* Vol. 3: *Loss: Sadness and Depression.* New York: Basic Books, 1980.

Brown, D. "Sex-Role Development in a Changing Culture." *Psychological Bulletin,* 1958, *54,* 232–242.

Brown, F. "Depression and Childhood Bereavement." *Journal of Mental Science,* 1961, *107,* 754–777.

Brown, G., Harris, L., and Copeland, J. "Depression and Loss." *British Journal of Psychiatry,* 1977, *130,* 1–18.

Cain, A., and Fast, I. "Children's Disturbed Reactions to Parent Suicide." *American Journal of Orthopsychiatry,* 1966, *36,* 873–880.

Call, J., and Wolfenstein, M. "Effects on Adults of Object Loss in the First Five Years." *Journal of the American Psychoanalytic Association,* 1976, *24,* 659–668.

Caplan, M., and Douglas, V. "Incidence of Parental Loss in Children with Depressed Mood." *Journal of Child Psychology and Psychiatry,* 1969, *10,* 225–232.

Dennehy, C. "Childhood Bereavement and Psychiatric Illness." *British Journal of Psychiatry,* 1966, *212,* 1049–1069.

Deutsch, H. "Absence of Grief." *Psychoanalytic Quarterly,* 1937, *6,* 12–22.

Dorpat, L. "Psychological Effects of Parental Suicide on Surviving Children." In A. Cain (ed.), *Survivors of Suicide.* Springfield, Ill.: Thomas, 1972.

Elizur, E., and Kaffman, M. "Children's Bereavement Reactions Following Death of the Father: II." *Journal of the American Academy of Child Psychiatry,* 1982, *21,* 474–480.

Elizur, E., and Kaffman, M. "Factors Influencing the Severity of Childhood Bereavement Reactions." *American Journal of Orthopsychiatry,* 1983, *53,* 668–676.

Elliott, G. R., and Eisdorfer, C. (eds.). *Stress and Human Health: A Study by the Institute of Medicine, National Academy of Sciences.* New York: Springer, 1982.

Fast, I., and Cain, A. "The Step-Parent Role: Potential for Disturbances in Family Functioning." *American Journal of Orthopsychiatry,* 1966, *36,* 485–491.

Forrest, A., Fraser, R., and Priest, R. "Environmental Factors in Depressive Illness." *British Journal of Psychiatry,* 1965, *111,* 243–253.

Furman, E. *A Child's Parent Dies: Studies in Childhood Bereavement.* New Haven, Conn.: Yale University Press, 1974.

Furman, E. *Children's Reactions to Object Loss: A Report of the American Psychoanalytic Association.* Washington, D.C.: American Psychoanalytic Association, 1978.

Furman, R. A. "A Child's Capacity for Mourning." In E. J. Anthony and C. Koupernik (eds.), *The Child in His Family: The Impact of Disease and Death.* New York: Wiley, 1973.

Gay, M., and Tonge, W. "The Late Effects of Loss of Parents in Childhood." *British Journal of Psychiatry,* 1967, *113,* 753-759.

Gregory, I. "Studies of Parental Deprivation in Psychiatric Patients." *American Journal of Psychiatry,* 1958, *115,* 432-442.

Gregory, I. "Introspective Data Following Childhood Loss of a Parent." *Archives of General Psychiatry,* 1965, *13,* 99-105.

Hamburg, D., Elliott, G. R., and Parron, D. *Health and Behavior: Frontiers of Research in the Biobehavioral Sciences—A Report of the Institute of Medicine.* Washington, D.C.: National Academy Press, 1982.

Hilgard, J., Newman, M., and Fisk, J. "Strength of Adult Ego Following Childhood Bereavement." *American Journal of Orthopsychiatry,* 1960, *30,* 788-799.

Hill, O. "The Association of Childhood Bereavement with Suicidal Attempt in Depressive Illness." *British Journal of Psychiatry,* 1969, *115,* 301-304.

Hill, O., and Price, J. "Childhood Bereavement and Adult Depression." *British Journal of Psychiatry,* 1967, *113,* 743-751.

Holmes, T. H., and Rahe, R. H. "The Social Readjustment Rating Scale." *Journal of Psychosomatic Research,* 1967, *11,* 213-218.

Jacobson, E. "Denial and Repression." *Journal of the American Psychoanalytic Association,* 1957, *5,* 61-92.

Jacobson, E. "The Return of the Lost Parent." In M. Schur (ed.), *Drives, Affects, Behavior.* New York: International Universities Press, 1965.

Johnson, P., and Rosenblatt, P. "Grief Following Childhood Loss of a Parent." *American Journal of Psychotherapy,* 1981, *35,* 419-425.

Kaffman, M., and Elizur, E. "Children's Bereavement Reactions Following Death of Father: The Early Months of Bereavement." *International Journal of Therapy,* 1979, *1,* 203-229.

Kaffman, M., and Elizur, E. "Bereavement Responses of Kibbutz and Non-Kibbutz Children Following the Death of a Father." *Journal of Child Psychology and Psychiatry*, 1983, *24*, 435-442.

Kliman, G. "Death in the Family." In G. Kliman (ed.), *Psychological Emergencies of Childhood*. Orlando, Fla.: Grune & Stratton, 1968.

Kliman, G. "Facilitation of Mourning During Childhood." In I. Gerber and others (eds.), *Perspectives on Bereavement*. New York: Arno Press, 1979a.

Kliman, G. "Childhood Mourning: A Taboo Within a Taboo." In I. Gerber and others (eds.), *Perspectives on Bereavement*. New York: Arno Press, 1979b.

Kliman, G. "Death: Some Implications in Child Development and Child Analysis." *Advances in Thanatology*, 1980, *4*, 43-50.

Krupnick, J. L., and Horowitz, M. J. "Stress Response Syndromes: Recurrent Themes." *Archives of General Psychiatry*, 1981, *38*, 428-435.

LaGrand, E. E. "Loss Reactions of College Students: A Descriptive Analysis." *Death Education*, 1981, *5*, 235-248.

Lifshitz, M. "Long Range Effects of Father's Loss." *British Journal of Medical Psychology*, 1976, *49*, 189-197.

Lloyd, C. "Life Events and Depressive Disorders Reviewed: Events of Predisposing Factors." *Archives of General Psychiatry*, 1980, *37*, 529-535.

McConville, B., Boag, L., and Purohit, A. "Mourning Processes in Children of Varying Ages." *Canadian Psychiatric Association Journal*, 1970, *15*, 253-255.

Markusen, E., and Fulton, R. "Childhood Bereavement and Behavior Disorders: A Critical Review." *Omega*, 1971, *2*, 107-117.

Miller, J. "Children's Reactions to the Death of a Parent: A Review of the Psychoanalytic Literature." *Journal of the American Psychoanalytic Association*, 1971, *19*, 697-719.

Munro, A. "Parental Deprivation in Depressive Patients." *British Journal of Psychiatry*, 1966, *112*, 443-457.

Munro, A., and Griffiths, A. "Some Psychiatric Nonsequelae of

Childhood Bereavement." *British Journal of Psychiatry,* 1969, *115,* 305–311.

Neubauer, P. "The One-Parent Child and His Oedipal Development." *Psychoanalytic Study of the Child,* 1960, *15,* 286–309.

Osterweis, M., Solomon, F., and Green, M. (eds.). *Bereavement: Reactions, Consequences, and Care—a Report by the Institute of Medicine, National Academy of Sciences.* Washington, D.C.: National Academy Press, 1984.

Pynoos, R., and Eth, A. "Witness to Violence: The Child Interview." Paper presented at the annual meeting of the Academy of Child Psychiatry, Washington, D.C., Oct. 1982.

Pynoos, R., Gilmore, K., and Shapiro, T. "The Response of Children to Parental Suicidal Acts." Paper presented at the annual meeting of the Academy of Child Psychiatry, San Francisco, Oct. 1983.

Rabkin, J. G., and Streuning, E. L. "Life Events, Stress, and Illness." *Science,* 1976, *194,* 1013–1020.

Raphael, B. "The Young Child and the Death of a Parent." In C. M. Parkes and J. Stevenson-Hinde (eds.), *The Place of Attachment in Human Behavior.* New York: Basic Books, 1982.

Raphael, B. *The Anatomy of Bereavement.* New York: Basic Books, 1983.

Remus-Araico, J. "Some Aspects of Early-Orphaned Adults' Analyses." *Psychoanalytic Quarterly,* 1965, *34,* 316–318.

Rochlin, G. "The Loss Complex." *Journal of the American Psychoanalytic Association,* 1959, *7,* 299–316.

Rochlin, G. "The Dread of Abandonment: A Contribution to the Etiology of the Loss Complex and to Depression." *Psychoanalytic Study of the Child,* 1961, *16,* 451–470.

Rochlin, G. *Griefs and Discontents.* Boston: Little, Brown, 1965.

Roy, A. "Vulnerability Factors and Depression in Women." *Psychiatry,* 1978, *133,* 106–110.

Rutter, M. *Children of Sick Parents.* London: Oxford University Press, 1966.

Seligman, M. E. P. *Helplessness: On Depression, Development, and Death.* New York: W. H. Freeman, 1975.

Sethi, B. "Relationship of Separation to Depression." *Archives of General Psychiatry,* 1964, *10,* 486–496.

Shambaugh, B. "A Study of Loss Reactions in a Seven-Year-Old." *Psychoanalytic Study of the Child,* 1961, *16,* 510–522.

Shepherd, D., and Barraclough, B. "The Aftermath of Parental Suicide for Children." *British Journal of Psychiatry,* 1976, *129,* 267–276.

Stone, M. "Depression in Borderline Adolescents." *American Journal of Psychotherapy,* 1981, *35,* 383–399.

Tallmer, M., Formanek, R., and Tallmer, J. "Factors Influencing Children's Concepts of Death." *Journal of Clinical Child Psychology,* Summer 1974, pp. 17–19.

Tennant, C., Bebbington, P., and Hurry, J. "Parental Death in Childhood and Risk of Adult Depressive Disorders: A Review." *Psychological Medicine,* 1980, *10,* 289–299.

Van Eerdewegh, M., Bieri, M., Parilla, R., and Clayton, P. "The Bereaved Child." *British Journal of Psychiatry,* 1982, *140,* 23–29.

Wahl, C. "The Fear of Death." In H. Feifel (ed.), *The Meaning of Death.* New York: McGraw-Hill, 1959.

Wilson, I., Alltop, L., and Buffaloe, W. "Parental Bereavement in Childhood: MMPI Profiles in a Depressed Population." *British Journal of Psychiatry,* 1967, *112,* 761–764.

Wolfenstein, M. "How Is Mourning Possible?" *Psychoanalytic Study of the Child,* 1966, *21,* 93–123.

Wolfenstein, M. "Loss, Rage, and Repetition." *Psychoanalytic Study of the Child,* 1969, *24,* 432–460.

Part Three

Separation, Loss, and Psychopathology: Implications for Treatment

A clinical perspective provides a special view of the centrality of separation and loss in psychological and interpersonal processes. The developmental significance of psychological separateness springs to life in the psychotherapy process, revealing how basic dimensions of inner life are predicated on nuances of the early parent/child relationships—on the nature of closeness and distance, on the quality of attachment and separation. This representational foundation of personality organization describes differential vulnerabilities and capacities to adapt to experiences of separation and loss. An individual's stylistic patterns of coping with interpersonal and psychological loss emerge in the type of psychopathology that may develop and in the nature of the treatment process that unfolds.

Many of the chapters in Part Three explore the theoretical and technical bases for treating individuals who have suffered emotional damage at a very basic level of development, a level of functioning variously discussed in terms of "pre-oedipal issues," "insecure attachment," and "pathology of the self." Variations at this fundamental level of injury are distinguished, and conceptual frameworks are proposed to consider the juxtaposition of more advanced personality problems with these core difficulties in the structure of the self and the organization of the psyche. The final chapter in Part Three considers how different cultural expectations for males and females manifest in different psychological orientations toward interpersonal closeness and hence toward psychological separateness and separation and eventually result in different predispositions to particular clinical syndromes. Although culture clearly shapes the stereotypical nature and relative import of family relationships, we would suggest that certain imperatives of the early parent/child relationship hold across sex and culture: that a reasonable degree of nurturance and a manageable dose of separation together provide an important foundation for the human psyche.

12

Separation, Depression, and Object Loss: Implications for Narcissism and Object Relations

Howard D. Lerner
Paul M. Lerner

Editors' Note: *This chapter offers an in-depth psychological examination of the impact of childhood bereavement on adult personality and psychopathology, viewed both theoretically and through the lens of psychoanalytic treatment. It provides a clinical complement to Chapter Eleven, which reviews research studies on the effects of childhood bereavement. Both chapters emphasize the problematic influence of object loss for the young child. Lerner and Lerner's clinical treatment of the psychology of mourning brings to life the phenomenological meaning of coping with the death of a parent and shows how the structure of the representational world shapes the impact of such profound separations.*

The authors present two clinical cases that illustrate a central point: that object loss will have a very different effect on personality and vulnerability to psychopathology depending on whether the loss affects the cohesion of the self (fosters a deficit in object constancy) or only engenders psychic conflicts within a structurally cohesive self system. In other words, problems stemming from pre-oedipal difficulties versus conflicts originating at the oedipal level are seen not as either/or phenomena but as parts of an interweaving developmental continuum; this view is consistent with the multiplicitous view of psychological structure presented in our introduction. The authors' case discussions illustrate how the retrieval and working through of unresolved grief from early childhood can instigate a progressive developmental unfolding within the treatment relationship. The factors that permit the patient to move beyond the limits imposed by a damaged psychological foundation are discussed in detail in Chapters Thirteen and Fifteen.

Loss of or separation from a significant other is increasingly common and, at the same time, the most poignant of human experiences. Although much of the contemporary literature in psychoanalysis, developmental psychology, and related disciplines emphasizes the crucial role of separation in normal psychological development, the pathogenic significance of early object loss and prolonged separation has long been recognized. Despite considerable research and numerous clinical reports, clinicians and theorists alike remain perplexed about the specific conditions under which loss of or separation from a love object becomes a malignant force. Because reactions to loss are exceedingly complex and are based on a multiplicity of internal and external factors, there is no comprehensive theory that adequately predicts the configuration of one's responses to early loss.

In this chapter we will focus on the impact of early object loss, especially its consequences for one's capacity to be separate and independent and one's vulnerability to depression. We will specify significant internal and external factors that need to be taken into account in understanding the significance and meaning of a loss. In addition, we will argue for and try to demonstrate the clinical and heuristic value of assessing early object loss from a developmental/structural perspective. This is to say that loss of a significant object and relationship at any age has internal and external implications that require assessment. In addition to assessing various developmental lines (A. Freud, 1965), one must distinguish among the individual's current level of functioning, the immediate reaction to the loss, the impact of earlier influences on development, and the effect of the loss on subsequent personality formation (Tyson, 1983).

After a review of the relevant psychoanalytic literature on early object loss, we will present two clinical vignettes that illustrate differing reactions to object loss as well as the complexity of the impact of the loss. Finally, the cases will be discussed from a developmental/structural perspective.

Review of the Literature

As Easer (1974) has noted, psychoanalytic theory has never been a static body of knowledge. From an early concern with identifying the instincts and their vicissitudes during development to a focus on delineating the characteristics, functions, and synthesis of the ego, emphasis is now shifting to a paramount interest in early object relations and their decisive impact on the nature and cohesion of the self system and the quality of later object relations, all within a developmental framework. Paralleling this change in emphasis has been a similar shift in psychoanalytic views of object loss.

Freud's (1917/1957a) original definition of mourning and its distinction from melancholia is still accepted by most clinicians and theorists and may serve as a point of departure for discussing the conceptual and clinical issues related to early object loss. According to Freud (1917/1957a), the distinguishing mental features of mourning are a profoundly painful dejection, loss of interest in the outside world, inability to love, and massive inhibition of all activity. Melancholia involves the identical features as well as "a lowering of the self-regarding feelings to a degree that finds utterances in self-reproaches and self-revilings, and culminate in a delusional expectation of punishment" (p. 244). Freud goes on to note that whereas melancholia, like mourning, may be a reaction to the loss of a loved object, it differs in that "one cannot see clearly what it is that has been lost. . . . [The person] knows *whom* he has lost but not *what* he has lost in him" (p. 245). These observations led Freud to conclude that "in mourning it is the world which has become poor and empty; in melancholia it is the ego itself" (p. 246).

The process of mourning involves a gradual relinquishment and severing of emotional ties to the lost object and a corresponding displacement of the libidinal cathexis onto (or attachment to) other objects. According to Freud, "Each single one of the memories and situations of expectancy which demonstrate the libido's attachment to the lost object is met by the verdict of reality that the object no longer exists; and the ego, confronted as it were with the question whether it shall share this fate, is persuaded by the sum of the narcissistic satisfactions it derives from being alive to sever its attachment to the object that has been abolished" (1917/1957a, p. 237). Melancholia too involves a withdrawal of libido from the lost object. However, rather than being displaced onto other objects, the libido, by means of regressive identification, is withdrawn back into the ego. In this way the object loss is transformed into an ego loss, and the conflict between the ego and the lost object is experienced as a "cleavage" within the ego.

Anna Freud (1960), in her characteristic, deceptively simple way, describes mourning as "the individual's effort to accept a fact in the external world and to effect corresponding changes in the inner world" (p. 54). In keeping with shifts in emphasis in psychoanalytic theory noted earlier, her focus is on structural considerations, as contrasted with her father's earlier interest in the economic model.

Speaking from outside the mainstream of psychoanalytic tradition, Bowlby (1960) has also had much to say about mourning. He observed and outlined a specific sequence of responses that follow on a child's removal from the mother and placement with strangers—protest, despair, and detachment. He suggested that the phase of protest is associated with separation anxiety, despair with grief and mourning, and detachment with defense. Postulating that attachment behavior is an instinctive response, part of an inherited behavioral repertoire initiated when the mother figure is available, Bowlby hypothesizes that separation anxiety and protest ensue when the mother figure is temporarily unavailable. He asserts that grief and mourning reactions occur in infants and children wherever the responses mediating attachment are activated and the mother figure continues to be unavailable. It follows from Bowlby's observations and formulations that infants subject to object loss and deprivation of mother love are capable of mourning in the adult sense from the age of six months on. According to Bowlby, his "principal aim" was to "demonstrate that the responses to be observed in young children on the loss of the mother figure differ in no material respect from those observed in adults on the loss of a loved object" (1960, p. 10).

In contrast with Bowlby's position, debate abounds in psychoanalysis over when, if at all, children are capable of mourning in a comparable way to adults (A. Freud, 1960). Authors point to the complex ego functions involved in mourning, such as a concept of reality, an ability to take cognitive distance, a capacity to bear pain, and a capacity to summon an inner image of the object in its absence. They question whether children have these requisite capacities.

Similar questions are raised with respect to at what age children reach sufficient levels of ego development to comprehend the concept of death as well as the idea of its finality (Wolf, 1958; Schur, 1960; Spitz, 1960; Shambaugh, 1961; Wolfenstein, 1966; Furman, 1974). Developmental achievements including self/other differentiation, grasping the distinction between animate and inanimate objects, understanding time (especially a future perspective), and reality testing appear essential in order for the child to conceive of death as involving the cessation of certain functions. Furman (1974), on the basis of clinical and observational studies, found that children, with help, can understand the finality of death and hence are capable of mourning once object constancy has been achieved, at approximately age three and a half to four. Others question Furman's timetable; Walsh (1979) regards age nine as a critical developmental point for the child's ability to conceive of death, while Wolfenstein (1966) extends the developmental attainment of a mourning capacity until late adolescence. Behavior observed in children before this stage, Wolfenstein regards as an "inhibited emotional response" characterized as "mourning at a distance."

Despite disagreement on when the child is capable of comprehending death and experiencing mourning, there is consensus that early parent loss has a traumatic impact and that the younger the child, the more devastating the effects. Nagera (1970) uses the concept "developmental interference" to explain why. He suggests that, unlike the adult, the child is not a finished product but, rather, is in the midst of a multiplicity of developmental processes, processes that require for their normal unfolding the presence of the absent object. Consequently, internal developmental processes interfere with the possibility of mourning, which can only take place simultaneously with or in subordination to age-appropriate developmental needs. Nagera (1970) states: "It is not sufficiently taken into account that if the relevant objects are absent, especially during certain stages, it is in the nature of many of these developmental phases to re-create the objects anew: to make them come to life in fantasies or to ascribe such roles as the developmental stage requires to any suitable figures available in the environment. It is partly this developmental need that opposes the normal process of mourning. . . . Thus, relevant objects are brought to life again and again in order to satisfy the requirements of psychological development" (p. 367). In essence, Nagera distinguishes between the child's overt reactions to loss, secondary to the developmental disturbance occasioned by the loss, and real mourning reactions to the object loss. Implicit in Nagera's formulation is the notion that children defend against loss and the accompanying pain for the adaptive purpose of negotiating developmental tasks that lie ahead.

Other investigators have reported observations similar to Nagera's and have also tried to identify and describe the defensive processes used. Both Meiss (1953) and Wolfenstein (1966) indicate that object loss in children and adolescents leads to a heightened adaptive and defensive identification with the lost parent that differs in important ways from the normal process of identification and the generally accepted definition of mourning. Specifically, the identification does not involve a gradual decathexis, or "letting go," of the lost object but an intensification of the loss. In tandem with idealization of the object and denial of the loss (and in keeping with the observation of Nagera, 1970), a study by Wolfenstein (1966) found that children and adolescents harbor a fantasy that the dead parent will return. The denial and fantasy serve an important developmental and adaptive purpose—that is, the maintenance and integrity of the ego.

The massive defensive response to loss in children is presented in a moving way by Shambaugh (1961) in his account of a normal seven-year-old boy who began analysis because of the impending death of his mother. Most of the experience the child underwent in mourning was not visible to the adult world around him. After the death he did not appear to have suffered a loss but, rather, became energetic, hyperactive and restless, distractible, and almost euphoric; there was a global suppression of actual events and associated feelings. Mention of the loss evoked anger and denial, play was drenched with aggression, and there was an increase in oral and dependent needs. There was also a marked increase in magical thinking and enhanced narcissism manifested in fantasies of omnipotence, independence, and invulnerability.

Although children use a variety of defenses when confronted with loss, most observers point to the crucial role of denial (Wolfenstein, 1966). The use of denial in children perhaps contributes to adults' belief that the child is not unduly upset by the loss—a belief that leads adults to collude with the child in denying the loss.

In addition to the notion of loss as a "developmental interference" and the attempts to explicate the child's defensive reaction to the loss, other investigators have drawn attention to the psychosexual stage the child is in when the loss occurs and the impact of the loss on drive development. Meiss (1953) offered the sensitive account of a five-year-old boy who had just entered the stage of oedipal conflict when his father died. At the time of the death, the boy was beginning to experience normal, stage-appropriate hostile and aggressive feelings toward him. The untimely death erased any opportunity the child might have had to experience the love and affection the father would have displayed toward him in spite of the boy's own feelings. As a response to the loss, the child's developmental need to regard his father as omnipotent and omniscient continued to pervade his thinking, unaltered by the experience of reality. His powerful desires for his father to disappear had been traumatically realized, and hence he lacked the opportunity to learn that wishes are not the same as deeds. Under these circumstances, the child's oedipal passions were intensified as he entertained highly charged but ambivalent fantasies of his father's return to life.

In keeping with contemporary trends within psychoanalysis, attention is increasingly being paid to the consequences of object loss for the child's narcissism and emerging sense of self. Many authors note a flight into narcissism occasioned by object loss, taking the form of enhanced omnipotence and grandeur, but the implications of these observations for theory and treatment have not been fully elaborated. Wolfenstein (1966) refers to the narcissistic dimension of the parent/child relationship that underlies the deep implications of loss; that is, "the child still conceives of the parent as part of himself," and loss of the object can leave the child in a "developmental vacuum" (p. 106) unless a substitute is found. An overemphasis on the body or the self-image as a consequence of object loss can result in what Atwood (1974) terms a "narcissistic imbalance" manifested in ideas of grandiosity and invincibility. Atwood (1974) describes a child who had had a nonambivalent relationship with a lost parent and then developed salvation fantasies in which he assumed the role that the lost parent had played for him. Feelings of despair and helplessness were projected onto others. Atwood (1974) states: "The traumatically intensified need for comfort and security is satisfied indirectly and vicariously through constant attention to the real or imagined needs of others" (p. 256). Treatment involved the therapist's assuming what seemed to the patient significant functions of the lost parent. Being allowed to develop a transference enabled the child to complete the mourning process successfully.

Tyson (1983), in particular, has examined the impact of object loss on narcissistic equilibrium from a developmental perspective. He identified three central dimensions of narcissism—omnipotence, self-constancy, and self-esteem—and then outlined the impact of loss along each dimension. Tyson cogently points out that the impact of the loss will vary with the degree of self/other differentiation and the developmental level of mental representations. That is, he reminds us that psychic structure formation is dependent on objects for growth and maintenance and that the impact of loss on these structures will covary with the degree to which the structures are internalized and thus autonomous from the sustaining object.

In summary, a review of the psychoanalytic literature on early object loss indicates that although most authors accept Freud's original definition of mourning, there is considerable disagreement on whether children are capable of mourning in a comparable way to adults. Despite this controversy, there is unanimous agreement that the impact of loss on personality structure formation is dramatic, intense, and complex and is dependent on a multitude of internal and external factors, including level of ego and drive development, mitigating aspects of defense, availability of substitute objects, and the degree to which inner psychic structures have become autonomous from the supporting object.

Clinical Cases

Case 1. When the patient initially sought treatment, she was a twenty-seven-year-old, married, childless writer who was suffering from intense depressive feelings associated with the death of her father. Since the father's death from cancer of the bowel, about one year earlier, she had lost considerable weight, was experiencing sleep disturbances including frequent nightmares of either being chased or her father's having to choose between herself and another woman and his inevitably choosing the other woman, recurring self-reproaches about her being a disappointment to both her parents, nagging feelings of guilt, painful feelings of being orphaned, and intrusive obsessive thoughts of harm befalling her younger brother. When the patient was fourteen, her mother had died of breast cancer, having progressively suffered and deteriorated over a nine-month period. The father's death had also reawakened feelings of sadness, emptiness, and bleakness that she associated with the earlier death of her mother.

The older of two, the patient was born into a close, tight-knit Italian family who lived in a small, rural western Canadian community. The patient's brother was three years younger. The patient described her childhood, initially, in idyllic terms. However, in time, both she and her analyst came to understand the excessive compliance and accommodation expected of her by her parents. Being the only Italian family in the small community prompted heightened closeness, forbade overt rebelliousness, and permitted few opportunities for separation. Though quite popular and an outstanding student, the patient dated little in high school and did not feel part of any particular peer group.

In her analysis the patient filled the early hours with feelings associated with her father's death as well as excessive concerns and worries about her brother. Although she could recognize and voice disappointment and resentment at the financial mess her father had left—he had accumulated numerous debts because of business failures—the more painful aspects of his death were being displaced onto her brother and expressed through obsessive concerns about him. Despite the appropriateness of this content, something very different was occurring in the transference. Quickly coming to the fore was her self-diminishing, self-devaluing, self-reproachful style of presentation as well as her vigilance and heightened sensitivity to the analyst's feelings, thoughts, and comments. For example, she would often preface her remarks with "I know you would think such-and-such, but this is the way I feel about it." Thus, she would anticipate, often correctly, the analyst's reaction, cast it into a harsh, critical, attacking statement, and then deny its validity. In this regard the patient appeared to be using her heightened sensitivity to ward off anticipated assaults on her self-esteem. Initially, the analyst felt disarmed by this maneuver; however, as he empathized with the pain and vulnerability underlying the sensitivity, the defense gradually began to give way. As the hypersensitivity itself became the focus of therapeutic scrutiny, the content of the analytic hours began shifting from experiences involving the patient's father to those involving her mother.

As her mother came to the center of the analytic stage and the patient could begin to recognize, tolerate, and express the full range of her intense ambivalent feelings, she was able to mourn the loss of her mother in a total and unabashed way. In this respect, then, the hypersensitivity and continuous vigilance had served to ward off, in the person of the analyst, the loving, devoted, and competent but intrusive and impinging mother of childhood who had inordinate difficulty permitting the patient genuine independence and autonomy.

With the working through of the mourning and the relationship with the patient's mother, gradual changes began to appear in the transference. Progressively, the patient began to comment on and complain about the analyst's overly cautious, unnecessarily delicate handling of her. She wondered why her occasional latenesses were taken so lightly, why he was not encouraging and pushing her to be more productive, and why he was not actively forcing her to confess her more intimate, intense, and erotic feelings, especially those toward him. In essence, her complaints had to do with her analyst's "not grabbing hold of her." She could understand this, in part, as resulting from his kindness and his having to maintain a role of neutrality. More basically, however, she took his sensed nonreactivity as confirmation of her long-standing feelings of being dull, boring, unintelligent, and, even more specifically, unattractive and undesirable to men. What she failed to recognize was that her hypervigilance and heightened sensitivity had inhibited and dampened her analyst's capacity to respond to her in a more intense and emotional way. As these reactions were explored, what quickly emerged were highly charged, intense feelings of rage toward her father—toward his passivity, nondemonstrativeness, and nonresponsiveness. She felt that he not only had never "grabbed hold of her" but also had never taken pride and delight in her as a woman, never given her a sense of "specialness," never permitted her to feel that she could have a significant impact on him. With the emergence, then, of rage and disappointment toward the unavailable oedipal father who aroused feelings of mortification by choosing other women over herself, as well as failing to confirm her sense of adequacy as a woman, the patient could then mourn his loss in a more genuine and unashamed manner.

Case 2. The patient, a thirty-six-year-old, twice-divorced interior designer, sought treatment soon after the painful termination of a nine-month relationship with a married man five years her junior. With the realization that her intimate, romantic involvements with married or in some other way unavailable men were becoming a distinct pattern, she became obsessed with the thought that she was destined to spend the rest of her life unmarried and essentially alone. This coincided with being told by a palm reader that she had been "fated" by her father's death—that is, she would forever have difficulty in relationships with men, and there was nothing she could do about it.

The youngest of three girls, she experienced the first of several losses at age six when her father died of a brain tumor. When she was nine, her mother had a severe stroke, resulting in paralysis to one side of her body and loss of speech. After her mother's stroke, a distant, uninvited uncle intruded on and split up the family. The two older sisters were sent to boarding school; the patient and her mother were taken to the uncle's farm in a small, rural community. During the next several years, a maternal grandmother died, the patient's oldest and favorite sister married and moved to a distant city, and she and her mother were frequently and thoughtlessly shifted from relative to relative. When the patient was sixteen, her mother suffered another stroke and died. Thus, by midadolescence, she had lost both parents and a grandmother through death, had lost a sister through marriage, and had, essentially, reared herself.

The patient began analysis by providing, in a highly controlled and typically affectless manner, with the assistance of a carefully prepared log, a comprehensive, exhaustively detailed chronicle of her life, beginning with her father's death and extending through other deaths and losses, her two marriages and subsequent divorces, the birth of her daughter, her cervical cancer confirmed and operated on soon after her daughter's birth, and her many and varied affairs. As she spent each analytic hour meticulously recalling and detailing each of these events in its entirety, the analyst gradually became aware of her inordinate need for control, defensive use of compliance, excessive investment in self-sufficiency, yearning for but intense fear of belonging (alienation), long-standing search for the ideal man, and overriding desire to feel genuine. Throughout this period, her analyst, paradoxically, felt himself an ignored (dead) bystander watching her, in her characteristic self-reliant manner, conduct her own analysis, as well as a captive (controlled masochism) audience that was being constantly monitored to ensure that he, or his attention, not wander off. As well, he experienced himself as a *protective container* into which she was pouring the hardships and suffering that life had visited on her. Respectful of the dangerous, unwanted, intrusive uncle of childhood, he confined his infrequent remarks to attempts to empathize and to recognize with her the immense pain and sadness that had accompanied her much of her life. She responded to these comments with genuine but controlled and muted gratitude—as if they were unexpected, unsolicited, mildly intrusive, but nonetheless precious gifts.

In the eleventh month of treatment, the first extended break occurred. During the three-week separation from analysis, the patient's efforts to be in control and entirely self-sufficient failed to quiet and contain intense feelings of emptiness, loneliness, and isolation as well as the unbearable but persistent thought that her analyst would never return to her. As these more spontaneous thoughts and feelings, together with the accompanying defenses, were jointly scrutinized, the patient, for the first time, could openly and undefensively grieve the death of her father, which had occurred more than thirty years before. With the activation and release of the grief she began to recapture a flood of early memories—painful ones, such as the time, during the onset of his illness, when he got lost while the two of them were out driving and she had to direct them home; but also fond and pleasurable memories, including how, before his illness, he was able to infect her with his joyful, fun-loving, devil-may-care attitude toward life. As she filled her treatment hours with these forgotten experiences, so time away from treatment was spent in a desperate and unwavering attempt to totally recapture and reclaim her lost father. For the first time since his funeral, she visited his grave site, not once but weekly. In her search for more information about him, neglected relatives were contacted, hospital records secured, and stashed-away photo albums hungrily explored.

Amidst this frantic search she reported the following dream: "I went to the hospital to visit my father. Two people were in the room and my father was furthest away. It was the first time in a very long time I had seen him. I walked in the room and he recognized me. He had only one eye. Where his right eye once was, skin had grown over it. I felt that he felt self-conscious. I hugged and held him for a long time with my hand behind his head and kissed the right side of his face, the side with the missing eye. I sensed that he knew I was not repulsed by him. Later, I moved to the other side of the bed, and from that perspective he looked the same as always. I then began having a conversation with the man in the other bed. I had vague sexual feelings toward him which I can't explain."

Two associations to this dream, one involving her view of her father from the left side, were especially significant. Seeing him in the dream with the right side of his face covered over by a layer of skin evoked a highly painful, previously repressed memory. She recalled that during his illness he was sent to a world-renowned hospital in another city for brain surgery. In meeting him on his return at the local railroad station, she recalled her being stunned, mortified, repulsed, and horrified by his appearance. He looked like a broken, damaged, deformed shadow of the father she had once known. Clad in pajamas and a bathrobe, with a bandage covering one side of his head, he had lost considerable weight, his color was ashen, and he was helplessly confined in a wheelchair. His fly lay open, exposing his genitals. This she found profoundly humiliating, both for him and for herself. Her other association, to the left-side view, involved dramatically different feelings. She felt elated, almost ecstatic, and rather disbelieving that, for the first time since his death, her mind could conjure up a full, total, undisguised inner image of him.

Discussion

With the emergence of a broadened developmental perspective in psychoanalysis (Mahler, Pine, and Bergman, 1975), new models of personality formation are beginning to appear. Whereas earlier models were derived from theories of drive and impulse/defense configurations, these newer models issue from theories of structure and structure formation in psychic development. These latter views start from the notion that development involves the growth and differentiation of psychological functions that crystallize into more stable psychic structures. Psychic conflict may occur among these various structures and may lead to psychopathology, as in earlier views, but in addition, the structures themselves may be pathological as a result of incomplete or arrested development.

This distinction between psychopathology as a result of conflict among structures and as a result of structural arrest has been further elaborated by Tolpin and Kohut (1980) in their differentiation between neurotic pathology and self-pathology. According to these authors, neurotic pathology (structural conflict) is thought to originate in later childhood at a time when self/other differentiation exists and when the various agencies of the mind (id, ego, superego) have been firmly established, so that the child is able to experience oedipal passions. Symptoms occur when libidinal and aggressive drives create a danger situation, anxiety is mobilized, defenses are erected and are only partly successful, and a compromise solution is fashioned in the form of a neurotic symptom. By contrast, self-pathology begins in earlier childhood, at a time when the psychic structures themselves are still in formation. Symptoms in this instance occur when an insecurely established self is threatened by dangers of psychological disintegration, fragmentation, and devitalization.

From a developmental perspective, the distinction drawn by Tolpin and Kohut between structural conflict and structural arrest or deficit, despite its clinical utility, seems an oversimplification. We are in agreement with Tyson (1983) that, rather than a dichotomy, one is dealing here with a continuum involving the extent to which psychic structures have been internalized and thus have gained some degree of autonomy from the sustaining and refueling object.

Viewed from this perspective, the patient in Case 1 could be seen as having achieved higher developmental levels of psychic structure formation than the patient in Case 2. In Case 1 there was much evidence that the patient had attained self/other differentiation, her core instinctual conflicts were basically at an oedipal level, the losses she had experienced exerted minimal impact on her sense of self and of objects, and her low self-esteem was rooted in feelings of mortification associated with oedipal loss rather than in major disturbances in her self system. While the patient's developmental level of mental representations was relatively high, those aspects of each of her parents that, owing to pain and discomfort, she had come to disown were quickly retrievable and relived in the transference and readily related to the major dynamic conflict. Before entering treatment, she had already begun the mourning process. Through treatment the patient was able to recapture repressed and disowned aspects of her lost objects and thus mourn their loss in a more complete way.

The patient in Case 2, by contrast, manifested a precarious sense of self/other differentiation. As indicated in the case material, throughout the early phases of treatment, the major resistance was posed by the patient's excessive self-sufficiency. As Modell (1975) has pointed out, severe environmental trauma can induce the formation of a false self organization, including the illusion of omnipotent self-reliance. Because the sharing and communication of affects is object-seeking, the illusion that nothing is needed from others and that one can provide one's own emotional sustenance removes the individual from the fear of closeness to objects by denying any instinctual demand to be made on the object. With this patient, associated with closeness and defended against by the illusion of self-sufficiency were profound fears of loss and abandonment as well as fears of losing her autonomous sense of self. In addition to the fragile self/ other differentiation, the patient's conflicts were at an oral-narcissistic level. As evidenced by the false self, there was little sense of self-continuity or identity, and her mental representations were at a lower developmental level. The patient's failure to establish a satisfactory, long-term sexual relationship and her tendency to choose unavailable men were not true manifestations of an unresolved oedipal struggle. Rather, they signified an oedipal conflict compounded and influenced by an earlier-based defect in psychic structure—namely, a failure in the internalization and representation of her father. Only by rediscovering and reclaiming her lost father through treatment was she able, paradoxically, to lose him, mourn the loss, and then work through her oedipal conflicts.

Because of the differing levels of mental representation and differing degrees of self/other differentiation, the depressive feelings experienced and the processes involved varied between the two cases. To use formulations detailed by Blatt (1974): The patient in the first case manifested depressive affect involving both anaclitic and introjective features. In addition to disturbances in sleep and appetite, she experienced painful feelings of loss, a sense of inferiority, unexplainable feelings of guilt, and a tendency toward self-reproach. Although separations rekindled the feelings of loss, she could nonetheless tolerate the experience without fearing abandonment by the object. By contrast, the depressive affect experienced by the second patient was more fully of an anaclitic nature. Her experience involved profound feelings of loss, emptiness, depletion, and at times deadness. Once invested in the object, she found separation especially painful. As noted in the clinical material, separations evoked feelings of loss and abandonment, together with the fear that the object would completely vanish and never return.

In distinguishing mourning from melancholia, Freud (1917/1957a) noted that whereas both were reactions to object loss, in the latter the lost object had been experienced with ambivalent feelings and that, rather than a displacement of libido onto other objects, through regression the libido was withdrawn into the ego. Although Freud had written "On Narcissism" (1914/1957b) three years before and thought of "Mourning and Melancholia" as an extension of that paper, several ideas contained in "On Narcissism" were not developed as fully as they might have been in the later paper. Specifically, in "On Narcissism" he drew an important distinction between a true object relation and a narcissistic object relation, noting that the latter involves an object choice on the basis of the need for the object and the function it serves. Implied in his concept of narcissistic object relation is that the object is not regarded as a separate entity but, rather, as part of the self and is used to serve a function that is normally internalized and carried out intrapsychically. If one applies the idea of narcissistic object relation to melancholia, then aspects of melancholia described by Freud, such as the unclearness of what is lost and the sense of the self (ego), not the world, as empty and poorer, make clear and compelling theoretical sense.

Freud's early writings, particularly "On Narcissism" and "Mourning and Melancholia," cast in the light of recent advances in psychoanalytic theory and related disciplines, have crucially important significance for assessing and treating individuals who have suffered object loss.

Developmental/Structural Assessment. A careful developmental/structural assessment of the patient's object relations and narcissistic status, both at the time of object loss and later, permits the clinician to explore the dynamics and constituent elements of subjective pain, particularly narcissistic injury (Tyson, 1983), on a developmental/structural continuum in relation to self/object differentiation, the progressive formation of mental representations, and the gradual attainment of self- and object constancy. Loss of the primary caretaking object prior to some degree of self/object differentiation is a qualitatively different experience from loss of a meaningful relationship in later years. A developmental/structural assessment further distinguishes among the immediate effect of object loss, the influence of earlier factors on development, and the impact of object loss on later development. Such an assessment contributes directly to the formation of accurate, appropriate, and tactful treatment interventions, which can be formulated on a developmental/structural continuum.

Treatment Implications. Conceptions of psychopathology as the result of psychic conflict and unconscious yearnings and fears invite models of treatment that emphasize interpretations and insights revolving around the clash of drives and defenses; treatment is seen as a special kind of education, and the therapeutic relationship as a unique laboratory for exploring and unearthing the critical dynamics as they emerge in the transference. Conceptions of psychopathology predicated on developmental arrest and the consequent impairment of psychological structure formation, by contrast, invite models of treatment that emphasize the psychological substrate and nutriments necessary for growth and development. Treatment is seen as a "second chance" for development, with a special kind of parenting, the interpretive process as a model of growth-promoting interactions, and the therapeutic relationship as a substitute for the nuclear family as the matrix for individuation and growth.

Summary

Loss of or separation from a significant other is one of the most poignant and painful human experiences. A review of the evolving psychoanalytic literature indicates that the impact of early object loss on personality development is dramatic, intense, exceedingly complex, and dependent on a multitude of internal and external factors, including level of ego and drive development, developmental level of defenses and mental representations, availability of substitute objects, and the degree to which inner psychological structures have become autonomous from the supporting object. We have advanced and clinically illustrated a developmental/structural perspective through two cases in which the impact of object loss on object relations and narcissism is viewed on a developmental continuum in relation to self/object differentiation, level of mental representation, and degree of self- and object constancy. Formulations derived from an integration of Freud's early notions of narcissism and his distinction between mourning and melancholia adumbrate more recent advances within psychoanalytic developmental, object relations, and self theories. Models of structural conflict and developmental arrest have important implications for assessment and treatment.

References

Atwood, G. "The Loss of a Loved Parent and the Origin of Salvation Fantasies." *Psychotherapy: Theory, Research, and Practice,* 1974, *11*(3), 256.

Blatt, S. J. "Levels of Object Representation in Anaclitic and Introjective Depression." *Psychoanalytic Study of the Child,* 1974, *29,* 107-158.

Bowlby, J. "Grief and Mourning in Infancy and Early Childhood." *Psychoanalytic Study of the Child,* 1960, *15,* 9-52.

Easer, R. "Empathic Inhibition and Psychoanalytic Technique." *Psychoanalytic Quarterly,* 1974, *43,* 557-580.

Freud, A. "Discussion of Dr. John Bowlby's Paper." *Psychoanalytic Study of the Child,* 1960, *15,* 53-62.

Freud, A. *Normality and Pathology in Childhood: Assessment of Development.* New York: International Universities Press, 1965.

Freud, S. "Mourning and Melancholia." In J. Strachey (ed. and trans.), *The Standard Edition of the Complete Psychological Works of Sigmund Freud.* Vol. 14. London: Hogarth Press, 1957a. (Originally published 1917.)

Freud, S. "On Narcissism: An Introduction." In J. Strachey (ed. and trans.), *The Standard Edition of the Complete Psychological Works of Sigmund Freud.* Vol. 14. London: Hogarth Press, 1957b. (Originally published 1914.)

Furman, E. *A Child's Parent Dies: Studies in Childhood Bereavement.* New Haven, Conn.: Yale University Press, 1974.

Mahler, M. S., Pine, F., and Bergman, A. *The Psychological Birth of the Human Infant: Symbiosis and Individuation.* New York: Basic Books, 1975.

Meiss, M. "The Oedipal Problem of a Fatherless Child." *Psychoanalytic Study of the Child,* 1953, *7,* 216-219.

Modell, A. "A Narcissistic Defense Against Affects and the Illusion of Self-Sufficiency." *International Journal of Psycho-Analysis,* 1975, *56,* 275-282.

Nagera, H. "Children's Reaction to the Death of Important Objects: A Developmental Approach." *Psychoanalytic Study of the Child,* 1970, *25,* 360-400.

Schur, M. "Discussion of Dr. John Bowlby's Paper." *Psychoanalytic Study of the Child,* 1960, *15,* 63-84.

Shambaugh, B. "A Study of Loss Reactions in a Seven-Year-Old." *Psychoanalytic Study of the Child,* 1961, *16,* 510-522.

Spitz, R. A. "Discussion of Dr. John Bowlby's Paper." *Psychoanalytic Study of the Child,* 1960, *15,* 85-94.

Tolpin, M., and Kohut, H. "The Disorders of the Self: The Psychopathology of the First Years of Life." In S. I. Greenspan and G. H. Pollock (eds.), *Psychoanalysis and the Life Cycle.* Washington, D.C.: National Institute of Mental Health, 1980.

Tyson, R. L. "Some Narcissistic Consequences of Object Loss: A Developmental View." *Psychoanalytic Quarterly,* 1983, *52,* 205-224.

Walsh, F. "Concurrent Grandparent Death." *Family Process,* 1979, *17,* 457-483.

Wolf, A. W. M. *Helping Your Child Understand Death.* New York: Child Study Association, 1958.

Wolfenstein, M. "How Is Mourning Possible?" *Psychoanalytic Study of the Child,* 1966, *21,* 93-123.

13

Increments of Separation in the Consolidation of the Self

Frank M. Lachmann
Beatrice A. Beebe
Robert D. Stolorow

Editors' Note: *The authors present a theoretical explanation and clinical case illustration of a concept they have developed for treating patients who suffer from the structural vulnerability of inadequate self/object differentiation. This concept, called "increments of separation," refers to (1) the steps that mark the separation-individuation pathway in psychotherapy for the patient who has suffered a developmental arrest in the structuralization of the self and (2) the symbolic meanings evoked by experiences of separation and separateness that reflect and affect the experience of the self. The notion of increments of separation not only provides a way to understand the structural vulnerabilities of the self and the symbolic meanings of separation but also serves as a technical framework actually used with patients to organize the bizarre and frightening fantasies, intense affective reactions, and fragmented states they may experience. In addition, therapist and patient use of the "increments" framework to articulate advances and retreats in the separation process permits anticipation and better management of the expectable therapeutic side effects of disorganization, heightened excitation, and depression.*

*The authors describe a ten-year, intensive, psychoanalyti-
cally oriented treatment of a psychotic patient who entered
psychotherapy experiencing delusions, hallucinations, and severe difficulties with self/object differentiation. The case material explains the therapeutic use of the concept of increments of
separation with this patient to assist the developmental journey
that began in a psychological world in which self and other were
predominantly merged and in which separation was tantamount
to the wish to destroy or be destroyed. Although the authors
depart from Mahler's theory of separation and individuation in
their theoretical approach (for example, in their views of aggression and psychological structure), they recommend a technical
stance consonant with Mahler's view of what facilitates the
separation process in childhood: that the nurturing object
understand and accept the urge for and fear of separateness. We
would like to note that, contrary to the current psychiatric emphasis on medication management and the often-expressed pessimism about true psychological recovery for seriously disturbed
patients, the case presented here offers a profound illustration
of the resilience of human potential, given the requisite therapeutic effort, however herculean.*

> "Forward development is in all respects frighten-
> ing to the individual concerned, if there is not left
> open the way back to total dependence" [Winni-
> cott, 1972, p. 8].

Considerable attention has been paid to the distinction between
psychopathology that reflects arrests in the structuralization of
self-experience and psychopathology that reflects a self in conflict (Stolorow and Lachmann, 1980). Although these types of
psychopathology are not mutually exclusive, it is of particular
clinical importance, especially for patients with severe disturbances, to specify those instances in which one is more salient
than the other. A previous work by two of us (Lachmann and
Beebe, 1983) described the treatment of a patient in whom the
therapist facilitated the structuralization and consolidation of a
fragmented self through clarifying and acknowledging steps
taken by the patient in disentangling himself from states of mer-

ger. These steps were termed "increments of separation." In the present chapter we illustrate and elaborate on the clinical and theoretical utility of this concept.

In patients who are best understood as arrested at a level of insufficient self/object differentiation, separation issues occupy a central position in the treatment. We use the term *differentiation* to refer to the psychological process through which self and object are distinguished from each other and *separation* to refer both to the capacity to maintain this distinction and to the diminution of the imperative need for the object's actual continued presence. In the treatment of these patients, difficulties in both differentiation and separation are routinely evident. They suffer both from the structural vulnerability of insufficient self/object differentiation and from the imperative need for the object's physical presence to maintain self-cohesion. These difficulties cut across a variety of traditional diagnostic categories.

The use of the concept of increments of separation has been illustrated in a previous publication (Lachmann and Beebe, 1983). The therapist introduced this concept in the treatment to underscore that any particular step taken by the patient in the direction of greater autonomy was not equivalent to his fantasy that separation meant total isolation and death. Reciprocally, this concept was used to indicate that a retreat from any particular step of separation did not immediately signal a remerger with the feared and enticing mother imago of his childhood. The notion of increments of separation thereby afforded the patient a safety zone and a sense of greater control, since any particular step did not have to be equivalent to his "all or none" fantasy. The therapist's introduction of this concept thus aided the patient in organizing his continual back-and-forth oscillations into manageable proportions, which, in turn, gradually enabled him to modify his fantasy that to separate meant to die. Encapsulated here is the slow process whereby psychic structure is gradually established by minute transformations.

The concept of increments of separation provides a framework for organizing the fluctuations of steps toward separation and their defensive undoing or reversal through remergers. The concept channels into the process of separation and self/object differentiation specific aspects of psychopathology, such as alterations in the sense of time and difficulties in the modulation of affect. It thus can help to structure the entire process of self-consolidation. Furthermore, both patient and therapist can use this framework to anticipate the expectable fluctuations in the separation process and thereby temper the secondary reactions of undue excitement, disorganization, or despair that often disrupt advances and retreats.

Clinical experience has demonstrated the extent to which separation from a primary object can acquire a variety of meanings. These meanings, in turn, profoundly affect the capacity to separate, to tolerate the separation, to maintain self-cohesion in the face of separation, and to reengage in more developmentally advanced ways with the object from whom one has separated. Implicit are two views of separation difficulties, one emphasizing their symbolic meaning and the other their basis in structural vulnerability. Clearly these must be intimately interrelated. Both views are necessary in the approach to clinical material, although one aspect is at times more salient than the other. Addressing increments of separation enables us to relate material that is replete with symbolic meanings about separation to the structural vulnerabilities in which such meanings take form.

Thinking of certain therapeutic occurrences as increments of separation is a crucial addition to the therapeutic stance. By articulating the advances and retreats in the separation process, we can focus attention on the structural implications of various events that otherwise might be investigated only in terms of their symbolic meanings. For example, in the clinical material discussed below, the patient's dream in which his girlfriend is depicted as castrating and dead is interpreted in terms of the structural advances that make this imagery possible, rather than as a symbolic manifestation of the patient's pathology. By viewing material in terms of advances and retreats in separation, events that would not on the surface be immediately linked to differentiation and separation can thus be drawn into the separation process.

The concept of increments of separation is useful in enabling the patient to alter the nature of his or her attachment to objects. When minute fluctuations of the separation process are carefully addressed, each step provides an opportunity for slightly altering the patient's perception of the object and the associated concept of self. With each incremental advance, the object can be characterized in more specific, subtle, and/or complex ways. This increasing articulation of the perception of the object enhances the sense of its psychic presence and concomitantly decreases the imperative need for its physical availability. Thus, movement along the continuum from merger to self/object differentiation involves the patient's awareness of the various minute increments of the separation process. This awareness facilitates increasingly articulated and differentiated images of the object, of the self, and of the relationship of self to object.

The framework of increments of separation addresses four major areas of pathology: time, affect, self/object differentiation, and gradations of experience. For example, as in the case of Burton, described below, the experience of time may be accelerated, stopped entirely, or interfered with, as was inferred from the patient's fears of having a terminal disease and his suicidal preoccupations. Affective states may be grossly unmodulated, with one affect entirely dominating the person's experience—as, for example, when Burton experienced himself as totally evil and murderous. The affective disturbance here lies not in the fact that the patient experienced himself as evil but, rather, in his perception of himself as *nothing but* evil. Lack of self/object differentiation can be inferred from fluctuations between homicidal and suicidal states. The patient experienced both self and object as evil, and he was interchangeably both killer and victim. In each of these areas of pathology, gradations of experience tend to be lost, so that an "all or none" quality predominates.

In the previous publication of Burton's treatment, clinical material was understood and interpreted in terms of the predominance of either developmental deficit or psychological conflict. The patient's subjective states shifted back and forth from difficulties in maintaining self-cohesion to more consolidated structuralizations that permitted him to defensively ward off conflictual wishes. Periodically, the patient's psychological survival depended on remergers with maternal images. In the ninth year of his treatment, interpretations could be offered that addressed such mergers as a defensive undoing of newly consolidated strengths. These interpretations were aimed at enabling the patient to acknowledge and integrate his strivings to differentiate himself from an archaic mother image and his corresponding wish to separate from his wife, who had come to embody this archaic image. It thereby became possible for him to maintain self-cohesion in the face of these strivings and wishes, rather than to succumb to a self-fragmenting process in which he perceived himself as a murderer, as an evil betrayer, or as dead.

In the previous publication, we distinguished between merger and identification. By *merger* we mean a fantasy of oneness and/or experience of union with another person whose qualities are felt as one's own. In addition, the distinction between self and object cannot be maintained, as an archaic oneness theme dominates experience and obscures its complexity. The loss of the capacity to maintain a distinction between self and object and the domination of experience by one overriding theme also occur in fragmentation states. However, whether a merger experience becomes a fragmentation state depends on the person's capacity to tolerate the affects aroused and on the degree to which higher-level functions are only transiently suspended and thus readily recoverable or become lost and unavailable. The term *identification* is reserved for those processes in which wished-for or feared qualities of others are incorporated and integrated into an already well-structured sense of self.

We define *self-consolidation* as a state in which one experiences oneself as a functional unity or whole, whereby affects can be tolerated and used as signals, and divergent themes in the sense of self can be tolerated and integrated (Stolorow and Lachmann, 1980). We define *self-fragmentation* as a state in which one theme completely dominates the sense of self, accompanied by powerful, archaic, and disorganizing affects. By *structuralization* we mean an increasingly articulated and complex subjective world into which diverse experiences are assimilated and in which self and objects achieve the status of being whole, differentiated, and consolidated, and this status is relatively irreversible.

The consolidation of the sense of self can be understood along three dimensions: temporal continuity, structural cohesion, and the capacity to maintain its positive affective coloration (Stolorow and Lachmann, 1980). A degree of consolidation of the sense of self along these three dimensions is a prerequisite for the emergence of psychological conflict. For example, in the treatment of patients whose clinical material reflects self-fragmentation and insufficient self-consolidation, interpretations are aimed at enabling them to attain or maintain self-cohesion. To a large extent, the treatment described below was guided by an understanding of deficit pathology and the need to address developmental arrests. When there was evidence of sufficient structuralization, interpretations addressed conflicts and wishes that the patient needed to ward off.

The Case of Burton

Burton began his fifth attempt at psychotherapeutic treatment at age twenty, as a college sophomore. He felt that life was not worth living, he complained of his self-destructiveness, and he described his extensive involvement with drugs (LSD, Ritalin), periodic alcoholism, stealing (for which he had already spent a month in jail), and persistent suicidal and homicidal ideation. In addition to these more chronic states and activities, the immediate stress motivating him to seek treatment was his panic states centering on fears of "imminent disintegration."

Burton suffered from a long-standing psychotic disorder that included delusions and auditory hallucinations. He heard a persecutory voice, located "at the back of my mind," criticizing him, mocking him, and telling him to kill himself. Because of this voice, he felt split into two persons—one who acted and one who mocked him. In addition, he believed that he would "harness the world's forces and become the personification of total wisdom and power." He experienced visual illusions, such as his girlfriend's face so vividly changing into that of a gorilla that he fled from her in panic. His auditory hallucinations of a buzzing sound about to explode were derived from repetitive childhood nightmares involving a series of boxes containing "a buzzing noise which eventually exploded into an atomic bomb." He felt he was losing his sense of being alive and believed he had a terminal disease. He also experienced difficulties in concentration—racing thoughts, states of stimulus barrage, lapses of memory, and states in which he felt he was outside his body. Time was experienced as either speeding up or in danger of stopping.

In the context of the chronicity and extent of Burton's psychic disorganization, his strengths were impressive. He used his rich imagination and considerable intellectual ability to articulate his experience with sensitive self-reflection. He was able to be intensely concerned about his friends in a warm, caring way. Despite his suicidal tendencies and pervasive despair, the vitality of his struggle suggested a passionate commitment to life, which had allowed him to keep alive his wish for human contact.

By the ninth year of psychoanalytic therapy, most of which occurred on a schedule of three sessions a week, the delusional and hallucinatory states were no longer in evidence. His use of psychedelic drugs stopped after the first year of treatment when it was interpretively linked to his suicidal fantasies. The homicidal tendencies reached their height after the second year of treatment when he hospitalized himself for two weeks after coming very close to throwing a man into the path of an oncoming car during a drunken brawl. Thereafter, although he was extensively involved with a fantasy of himself as Jack the Ripper, he did not appear to be in danger of enacting this fantasy. In the third year of the treatment, he married Liz, a psychotic, heroin-addicted woman whose stance toward him replicated his most frightening and alluring fantasies about his mother. She was the inconstant, tantalizing, self-destructive witch-mother whom he would save and who would then enable him to survive. Part of their routine sexual play involved Liz threatening Burton with a knife during intercourse. During the four years of this marriage, Burton reacted to his perception of Liz as evil by perceiving himself as evil as well. Whenever Liz would reject him, take drugs, or disappear all night, Burton's hard-won, tentative integrations of good and bad self- and object images would again disintegrate. Isolated fragments of the merged self- and object images would then predominate. Burton would simultaneously want to murder the malevolent object and kill the monstrous self. He would then become dangerously suicidal.

When Liz abruptly left him, in the seventh year of treatment, Burton became psychotically depressed and was hospitalized for six weeks at the insistence of the therapist. The severe depression continued for a full year after the hospitalization, despite a sophisticated antidepressant drug program. During the year following hospitalization, despite his consistently severely depressed mood, the treatment succeeded in using Burton's ideal of himself as a scholar to stem the tide toward remerger with Liz. Increasingly he was able to combat his urgent wishes to contact her. Therapeutic interventions conveyed an understanding of his distress, which enabled him to tolerate it better. In spite of the severe depression, he maintained a high academic standing.

During the ninth year of treatment, Burton began to address and explore his eventual termination of treatment and the impending separation from the therapist. By this time, he was a teaching fellow at a graduate school and was arranging to live in the same house as his new girlfriend, Sybille. His relationship with his parents was strained, but he enjoyed the support of good friends and the respect of his professors and students. All these achievements had been slowly acquired over the preceding years of his therapy and signaled a stability in his life that he had not previously known. During the tenth and final year of treatment, Burton married Sybille, a caring, stable woman, and at a follow-up two and a half years after termination, he reported that he enjoyed fatherhood and academic success.

Burton's core problem was his arrest at a level of insufficient self/object differentiation. The "object" was an archaic image of his mother as evil. Self and object were predominantly experienced as merged, and to separate meant to murder and/or be murdered. Oscillations between partial separations and re-mergers marked the treatment. He remerged at times because he lacked sufficient structuralization to maintain a sense of self as aggressive and separate and at other times because he needed to defend himself against the murder.

Therapeutic Action of Increments of Separation

The interpretive use of the concept of increments of sepa-ration can be schematized as follows:

1. Viewing an aspect of the patient's material (productions, associations, behavior, or dreams) as reflecting an incre-ment of separation. The therapeutic focus is on the struc-ture or formal organization of the material, rather than on its symbolic or manifest content. Criteria for designating an aspect of the material as an increment of separation are as follows:
    a. Any progress in the ordering of experience along the time dimension toward the establishment of a se-quence of past, present, and future.
    b. Any progress in the capacity to tolerate strong af-fect and to integrate divergent affects.
    c. Progressive consolidation of increasingly differen-tiated and complex perceptions of self and object.
2. Clarifying and acknowledging an aspect of the patient's ma-terial as reflecting an increment of separation. Whereas in calling the patient's material an increment of separation, therapeutic attention is paid to the structure of the mate-rial and its relevance for the separation process, once an in-crement of separation has been identified, the therapist's acknowledgment of this shift as an indication of separation may have therapeutic consequences.

The patient may respond in a number of ways. If the in-tervention is entirely consonant with the patient's experience and psychological organization, he may offer his own transla-tion or application of this increment. We understand this translation as an indication of increased structuralization. No further work with that particular separation issue is indicated at that moment.

Alternatively, the patient may respond with a sense of loss, which we understand as "work in progress." The therapist needs to convey an understanding of this reaction as an expectable part of the working-through process.

The most frequently encountered reaction of the patient is an attempt to undo or reverse the increment of separation. It is important to distinguish between defensive undoing of structural attainments and reversals stemming from structural fragmentations. In defensive undoing, we infer that there has been some consolidation of the increment of separation but that conflicts were thereby evoked. Typically, then, wishes are warded off through the defense of undoing. In contrast, structural fragmentation implies a psychological organization as yet unable to tolerate the increment of separation.

The requisite therapeutic response to instances of undoing is interpretation of the defense, of the wishes that are thereby warded off, and of the danger that makes this warding off necessary. With instances of fragmentation, the therapist should convey an understanding and acceptance of the patient's inability to maintain the structural advance and of his or her need to reverse the self state associated with it. In so doing, the therapist introduces a model for gradations of experience, in which "all or none" experiences can be modulated. That is, reversals of increments of separation need not be equated, as the patient frequently equates them, with total loss of progress or with total remerger with an archaic object. Instead, the therapist introduces a developmental model of expectable advances and retreats in the separation process. The therapeutic relationship and interventions thereby function as a facilitating medium (Winnicott, 1965) to avert further disintegration and to permit the arrested developmental process to resume once again.

Clinical Illustrations

At the beginning of the ninth year, Burton struggled with the idea of accepting the finality of his divorce and tried to stop pursuing his ex-wife, Liz. However, he was as yet unable to sustain this sense of separateness from his former wife, and he reacted with renewed efforts to revive his merger with her. Telephoning her quickly reinstated a sense of having remerged with her. Furthermore, he tried to reverse his intolerable sense of separation by asserting that it was Liz, not he, who was setting the boundaries: "She is shutting me out, killing me; I'll kill her." The rapid, continual oscillations between feelings of being killed by Liz and killing her, between considering himself "evil" and her "evil," signaled a return to a state of insufficient self/object differentiation.

For the next several weeks, Burton's imperative need for Liz's actual, physical presence waxed and waned. He "needed" to be with Liz, to repair the rift. This "need" was interpreted by the therapist as a reversal of an increment of separation. The therapist conveyed her understanding of the dreaded meanings of his moves toward autonomy and also conveyed that his revival of merged states did not have to be equated with total loss of his progress—that is, with a dreaded total loss of self. Therapeutic interventions focused primarily on the vulnerability in the structure of his experience and secondarily on the meaning of separation.

Burton's decision no longer to pursue Liz indicated a rudimentary sense of self as aware, "deciding," and thereby actively participating in the process of separation. Thus, first, this increment was predicated on the acquisition of a capacity for some (temporary) restraint and self-awareness in that Burton restrained, for the moment, his previously imperative need to act in pursuing Liz. Second, this increment momentarily furthered the elaboration of psychological structure capable of organizing experience, as opposed to his simply acting and reacting impulsively. In deciding to pursue Liz "no longer," Burton indicated that he had at least a fleeting but distinct memory of a time when he could not restrain himself, thus organizing his experience along a time dimension, comparing present with past. In deciding not to act and thus to (temporarily) tolerate his painful affect state, Burton enhanced his use of time as a dimension along which to order and structure his experience.

Clarifying and acknowledging these increments of separation—that is, the momentary consolidation of the sense of self as aware and deciding and the use of a time perspective—and interpreting the ensuing retreats and reversals of these increments of separation did not, however, forestall urgent wishes toward remerger. Time perspective and self/object differentiation had been precariously established and were quickly lost.

The ensuing disorganization culminated in a self-fragmentation in the form of a suicidal state containing a revival of a merger with his mother as dying. Burton described his state as "a subjective car accident. I have fallen asleep. I am living in the middle of the unconscious. . . . It's like my mother dying, I can't handle the pain, I'm passing out . . . I want to blow my brains out, I want to lose myself now." Images of himself and his mother as dying were interchangeable. The therapist offered interpretations of his inability to tolerate the intense affects and his loss of the germinal self/object distinction, which resulted in his "losing" himself and becoming suicidal. These reversals of the prior fleeting increments of separation were accepted by the therapist. However, she reintroduced the vanishing time dimension by pointing out that Burton imagined he would be trapped in this feared state forever. These interpretations enabled him to progress from his suicidal and merged position to an acceptance of a more differentiated dependent state. He felt unable to take care of himself and overtly acknowledged his need for the therapist. He dreamed of a woman who let him suck her breasts and whom he identified as the therapist. The sense of merger with his mother as dying and of "losing" himself was replaced by his recognition of his dependent wishes. He could now use these images to comfort himself in the face of the dread of murderous separation.

The therapist articulated Burton's movement from a position of merger to one of dependence as an increment of separation. This achievement was inferred from his advance to a state in which he experienced himself as dependent and the therapist as a "supplier" somewhat differentiated from him. Thus he reintegrated perceptions of himself as not only aggressive but also needy. His newly acquired capacity to sustain a differentiated image of the therapist as a source of comfort enabled him to tolerate powerful, painful affects and stemmed the tide of fragmentation. In the face of fears of losing control, wishes to give up his hold on life, and a dread of succumbing to a full-scale regression, Burton was able to glean comfort from expressing wishes to be cared for by the therapist. His fear of regression—that is, his fear that he would become suicidal again—could now be interpreted as a *defensive* reaction to the increments of separation he had achieved. Thus, his fear that he might give up was interpreted as his attempt to undo his progress. He had reached a point where he felt both dependent longings and erotic feelings toward the more differentiated therapist. This achievement stirred up memories of his frightening erotic, dependent attachment to his mother. He attempted to combat these dangerous erotic and dependent wishes by undoing his newly consolidated, more advanced state.

To summarize, we have provided illustrations of increments of separation and their use in the therapeutic process. In the first example, a self-fragmentation necessitated the therapist's acceptance of the reversal of Burton's fleeting structural attainments. Her understanding and acceptance of the propensity to fragment served to convey a more encompassing sense of time, in contrast to the patient's dread of being trapped immediately and forever in his panicked state. The therapist's acceptance of the reversal of the increment of separation also enabled Burton to reconsolidate. In the second example, a defensive reaction prompted the therapist to interpret those conflicted wishes that threatened to impel the patient to undo his structural attainments.

The dream of "sucking on the therapist's breasts" offered a variety of possible therapeutic stances. Although the meanings of dependency along the lines of its implications as a resistance, as a regressive defense, and as an erotic transference could all have been explored, none of these stances would have directly addressed the crucial structural advance implied in the shift from merger to more differentiated dependence. Viewing this shift as an increment of separation illustrates the contribution that an understanding of this concept can make to the patient's struggle to separate.

With his sexual and dependent wishes less embattled and in the foreground, Burton was able to feel panicked and rageful about his sexual dependence on Liz. The therapist helped Burton spell out his fear that his separation from Liz would entail the loss of his sexuality. In the following sessions, Burton reiterated this theme: "I feel more resigned to the end of my relationship with Liz: I can live, but my sexual life ends." He continued conflictually, both more resigned to losing Liz and filled with rage. He struggled with these feelings: "I'm losing a part of myself; I'm resisting it. I feel like an abandoned child, I feel wronged. I can't give her up—I feel chained to a dead person." The therapist was able to connect these thoughts to Burton's tie to his mother and his early dreams in which alternately he or his mother was locked in a coffin with the other outside. Further, she reminded him of his lifelong dread that to move away from his mother would result in the death of both. In response, Burton appreciated the degree to which Liz reevoked his experience with his mother. He said, "I can't take all my experiences seriously."

Disentangling his sexuality from Liz, "resigning" himself to her loss, and recognizing the archaically rooted depth of his loss experience were all acknowledged as major moves in the differentiation process and as increments of separation. Burton nevertheless became severely depressed, feeling suicidal and evil, as if his "whole existence" were "falling apart." He was able to maintain the "holding environment" he had established with the therapist, stating that he felt considerably closer to her. He took comfort in expressing his wish to be taken care of, yet he still experienced this closeness as a further step away from Liz and a betrayal of her. The suicidal depression was interpreted as a retaliatory torture of himself for the moves away from Liz. The intensity of his feelings was seen in terms of his conflicted reaction to the considerable progress he had made, prompting his wish to undo it.

Now Burton could maintain a capacity for self-comforting, without the disintegration and loss of object images seen in previous episodes. The success of the interpretation of undoing based on a conflict model may have been possible because of a preceding period of *some* consolidation of self/object differentiation, as noted above in the "dependent transference." Furthermore, the therapist's view of Burton as engaged in conflict offered him a more organized view of himself than he himself held but one with which he was now able to identify.

Burton was able to comfort himself with the therapist's interpretations of his suicidal depression as "retaliatory torture," and he began to make interpretations similar to those the therapist had made. In a chagrined manner, he summarized these by saying: "It is my resistance to getting better." In the following sessions, Burton continued to maintain his recognition that his depressive reactions were part of what he called his "resistance."

By this point Burton had developed the capacity to understand his dreads and fantasies in relation to his past experience. In his statements "I can't take all my experiences seriously" and "It's my resistance to getting better," Burton demonstrated both his capacity to further parcel and refine his experience (in contrast to the more global, "all or none" mode of experiencing) and his capacity to be aware of this articulation. Burton's statements are examples of the patient's own translation of an increment of separation and can be understood as reflecting developmental achievements in which the consolidation of a process of separation played a pivotal role. Although the therapist never explicitly made these interpretations to Burton, his statements convey the extent to which his ability to view his experience in a perspective of time, with graded intensities, and with further self/object differentiation had become an increasingly available resource.

The therapist's time frame had been introduced and was gradually assimilated by the patient. Whereas the patient's experience heretofore had been of rapidly oscillating, global, and overwhelming shifts, the therapist's articulation of individual points of advance and retreat in the separation process had transformed the patient's experience into more manageable segments. Each clarification of points of advance and retreat created an opportunity for the patient's experience to be further articulated, self-awareness enhanced, and images of self and object reorganized. Rapidly oscillating subjective states were thereby transformed into structures of increasing differentiation and complexity.

Three dreams illustrated further increments in Burton's developing capacity to separate from Liz. In the first dream Burton sat with Liz but tried not to tell her how angry he felt, because he was so glad to be next to her. Yet he could also not help telling her something angry, maybe that she was unfaithful. He then felt anxious, in the dream, that she would leave him. In the second dream he made love to her but discovered that "her pussy looked like a wound." Meanwhile, Liz told him of her other sexual relationships. In a third dream, Burton described "something frozen in the freezer, left there too long: cold, gray, dead. My relationship with Liz died. In the dream someone finally went too far. It's so sad, gone forever. Things that are rotted can't be brought back to life."

Acknowledging aspects of Liz as damaging, castrating, rotten, or dead marked a further increment of separation. In accepting the loss of Liz, Burton accepted a degree of differentiation that, like "death," was irreversible. Thereafter a shift occurred in his pathological enmeshment with Liz, toward a consolidation of disparate self fragments. From this point on, the affective intensity mobilized in working through the separation and loss experience shifted from Liz to the therapist.

From these dreams we infer that further increments of separation have taken place, and these were formulated as such for Burton. First, with respect to self/object differentiation, he and Liz are depicted as separately consolidated entities, each with personal affects and motivations that can be at variance. Second, aspects of experience are ordered along the dimension of time, such that the past is relegated to the past—the relationship is irretrievable. The developmental advances noted in these dreams remained active in his subsequent waking life. Although this material contains symbolic reference to loss and separation, the therapist emphasized the increments of separation implicit in these dreams. She thereby drew this material into the separation process, thus highlighting Burton's structural attainments. Nevertheless, he experienced himself as murderous as a consequence of this increment of separation ("I'm killing something off"), which led him again to remerge with a malevolent object, simultaneously wanting to kill himself and Liz. He stated, "I'm thinking of going to kill her, it's not just a fantasy, I began planning every move, I felt afraid of what would happen."

Although Burton's remerger with a malevolent object was characteristic of him when he felt monstrous for separating, this time his response was more moderate and short-lived than in the past. By the next session he had been able to help himself by a strategy of "not doing anything to allay anxiety"—that is, tolerating the anxiety. He spontaneously acknowledged the defensive aspect of his regressive "going crazy" and the "responsibility in choosing not to go crazy." It is striking that Burton was able to reconsolidate on his own between sessions, by experiencing himself as "responsible" and tolerating his anxiety.

Growing out of his experience of "choice" regarding his ability to withstand a regressive move and face his enormous loss, there emerged signs of increased self-consolidation: "There is growth in separation. It's becoming who you are," he summarized.

Implications for Child Development

In this chapter we have shown how the concept of increments of separation can be used to reinstate a thwarted process of self/object differentiation within a therapeutic relationship. This clinical finding, we believe, holds important implications for the understanding of early psychological development.

It seems evident that the accretion of psychological structure and the attainment of self/object differentiation are closely interrelated facets of a unitary developmental process. On the one hand, we have shown that increments of separation contribute vitally to the structuralization of the sense of self, specifically with respect to its distinctness, its continuity in time, and the modulation and gradation of its affective tone. On the other hand, such structural attainments, in turn, make possible further advances in self/object differentiation.

A developmental framework emphasizing increments of

separation stands in sharp contrast to the traditional view stressing the presumed role of "aggressive drive deployment" in fueling early thrusts toward separation. It is our view that some consolidation of self/object differentiation is a prerequisite for tolerance of hostile feelings toward objects and that phase-inappropriate arousal of aggressive affect can seriously impede the separation process by rendering the increments of separation too conflictual and by irreparably disrupting the requisite facilitating object relationship (see Stolorow and Lachmann, 1980, chap. 8).

It is our belief that the process of self-demarcation and self/object differentiation requires a facilitating tie to the surround throughout the course of development (see Atwood and Stolorow, 1984, chap. 3; Kohut, 1977). The stance that we have found successful in revitalizing an arrested separation process in the therapeutic situation bears on what may be optimal for early psychological development. The parent, like the therapist, must be able to understand and accept both the child's minute steps toward greater separation and their temporary reversals. Such a parent would neither need to cling to archaic states of oneness with the child nor require the child's unwavering progress toward autonomy because of a fear of such oneness. It is from pathogenic situations such as these that early efforts to separate acquire their conflictual meanings. For example, we infer that Burton's mother felt inseparable from her son from her profound reaction to his phase-appropriate independent strides. Her response was to withdraw, take to her bed for days, and to accuse him, "Your words are like bombs." She presumably needed to cling to archaic states of oneness with Burton, and he perceived that his efforts to separate were experienced by her as psychologically damaging. Exemplified here are strivings for distinct selfhood that become linked with fantasies of omnipotent destructiveness. Furthermore, when the child's need to retreat to less differentiated states is rejected, such longings for remerger can become the source of intense, sometimes chronic feelings of shame and self-loathing.

The therapeutic stance described parallels the parent's ability to enjoy the child's growth toward greater self-definition and accept the child's need, on occasion, to return to less differentiated modes of experience. The gradual developmental process that we call increments of separation may then be optimally facilitated. As was true of Burton, adult patients with arrests in the separation process revive their need for just such a facilitating context in the analytic transference relationship that becomes established.

References

Atwood, G., and Stolorow, R. D. *Structures of Subjectivity: Explorations in Psychoanalytic Phenomenology.* Hillsdale, N.J.: Analytic Press, 1984.

Kohut, H. *The Restoration of the Self.* New York: International Universities Press, 1977.

Lachmann, F. M., and Beebe, B. "Consolidation of the Self: A Case Study." *Dynamic Psychotherapy,* 1983, *1,* 55–75.

Stolorow, R. D., and Lachmann, F. M. *Psychoanalysis of Developmental Arrests: Theory and Treatment.* New York: International Universities Press, 1980.

Winnicott, D. W. *The Maturational Processes and the Facilitating Environment.* New York: International Universities Press, 1965.

Winnicott, D. W. "Basis for Self in Body." *International Journal of Child Psychotherapy,* 1972, *1*(1), 7–10.

14

Transitional Phenomena
and Psychological Separateness
in Schizophrenic, Borderline,
and Bulimic Patients

Alan Sugarman
Lee S. Jaffe

Editors' Note: *This chapter examines the developmental deficits characteristic of patients with four types of serious disturbance: symbiotic schizophrenia, paranoid schizophrenia, bulimia, and borderline personality pathology. By considering the developmental origins of psychopathology, the authors bring together the sometimes divergent perspectives of ego psychology and object relations, using case examples.*

Sugarman and Jaffe underline the centrality of the childhood psychological task of achieving separateness from parents, accomplished through the formation of progressively more differentiated and integrated representations of self and other. As representational capacities develop, the child internalizes the ability to regulate internal states and experiences a new sense of agency. Four stages in the development of a healthy self-representation are delineated; these are linked both to Mahler's separation-individuation sequence and to Piagetian descriptions of cognitive developmental advances. When environmental or con-

stitutional factors interfere with these normal progressions in the representational world, individuals remain psychologically unseparated and unable to maintain crucial self-regulatory functions and, hence, manifest severe psychopathology.

Sugarman and Jaffe propose a developmental line of "transitional" phenomena that promote the separation process. Depending on the status of their representational world, individuals may accord transitional properties to their own bodies, to inanimate and animate objects, to fantasies, and to abstractions. Thus, for the paranoid schizophrenic, fantasies serve a transitional function; a megalomaniac self-view offers pseudo self-sufficiency, and a fantasy world of evil helps to regulate aggression and defend against the wish for merger. The bulimic shores up a tenuous self/other boundary by gorging and purging, taking in and forcing out. The body serves as a vehicle for venting dependent and aggressive urges, and food becomes a symbol for relationships. Expansion of the concept of the transitional object into a progressive developmental sequence of "transitional phenomena" is a novel idea with useful clinical implications.

This chapter follows the common psychoanalytic practice of pinpointing the specific developmental origins of each type of pathology (for example, locating "the paranoid's fixation point . . . in the transition between the differentiation and practicing subphases" of Mahler's separation-individuation sequence). As discussed in the introduction, we take issue with this way of viewing psychological disturbance, suggesting instead that intrapsychic structures form within a complex context of multiple, usually ongoing, problems in the developmental environment. Thus, in our view, personality takes on particular shadings as a result of an interpersonal and constitutional nexus that defies such parsimonious specification. Nonetheless, the degree of severity of pathology does relate, however broadly, to a timetable of development: in general, the earlier and more profound the disruption in adequacy of caregiving, the more severe the disturbance.

Our purpose in this chapter is twofold: first, to elaborate the intrapsychic imprint that marks the self-representations of individuals who experience inadequate parental care during their early years and, second, to explore the forms of transitional phenomena that help such individuals compensate for the intrapsychic deficits that constantly threaten to disrupt their psychological adaptation to the environment. Developmentally, the roots of these deficits lie in an early mismatch between organismic needs and environmental responsiveness. With each developmental task that encounters neglect or interference, the child fails to internalize key self-regulatory capacities, and severe psychopathology eventually results. In spite of the deficits caused by various developmental interferences, the child can develop independent means of fostering emotional adaptation and promoting internalization of regulatory functions in the form of different types of transitional phenomena. In this way separation-individuation is fostered. When development follows a normal course, earlier forms of transitional phenomena are but way stations that are reintegrated into more advanced forms as the child grows older. But when psychological growth is severely encumbered, the earlier forms of transitional phenomena can be retained by the adult as an attempt to maintain the self-regulatory functions that are basic to psychological survival. One such self-regulatory function is the developmentally based capacity to maintain psychological separateness from others and to establish a sense of personal identity. Thus, transitional phenomena are those mechanisms that the individual uses to bridge the sense of aloneness and psychological separateness that increases with development. Winnicott (1971) used the term *transitional object* in reference to the young child's reliance on blankets, toys, or favorite stuffed animals as parental substitutes. Our model expands the concept of transitional object to include a range of levels of transitional phenomena existing throughout development (Sugarman and Jaffe, 1983; Sugarman and Kurash, 1982a, 1982b).

    In what follows, we will outline some basic aspects of the separation-individuation process, present a summary of our model of the development of the self-representation, and cover some general considerations about pathological deviations in the ontogeny of the self-representation. With these general propositions as a foundation for viewing particular clinical syndromes, we will detail the object relational deficits in four types of severe psychopathology—symbiotic schizophrenia, paranoid schizophrenia, bulimia, and borderline personality pathology— and then explore the various forms of transitional phenomena that can be employed to regulate a fragile sense of psychological separateness.

Intrapsychic Aspects of Separation

Although many authors agree that separation conflicts are germinal to later psychopathology, there is not yet any integrated model that details how these early problems with separation and individuation predispose the infant and later the child to develop psychopathological symptoms. The more precise we can be in articulating these connections, the better we will be equipped to clarify to patients the meaning of their symptoms, and the better we will be able to teach parents the nuances of "good enough" parenting so as to prevent severe psychopathology in later life.

We believe that an emphasis on the development and expansion of the self-representation via a progressive internalization of self-regulatory functions offers the greatest potential for clarifying the relation between early separation experiences and severe psychopathology. Every human infant possesses an innate potential for self-regulation, which requires a facilitating environment to promote development (Sugarman and Jaffe, 1983). Consequently, the capacity to regulate inner states, provided initially by the environment, becomes "internalized" and increasingly integrated into the self-representation. Thus, intrapsychic structure may be viewed as including a variety of regulating, integrating, and adaptive functions previously performed by the caretaker. In part, this process of "transmuting internalization" involves a "depersonalizing" of the object representation with which the regulatory functions were associated (Tolpin, 1971). That is, the developing child's inner focus shifts from the global totality of the object representation into a differentiated emphasis on its specific functions. Consequently, the child's own self-representation is enriched, and the growth of intrapsychic structure allows him or her to perform the functions previously exercised by the other but in a fashion divested of the other's personal attributes (Sander, 1983). Only in this way can a genuine psychological emancipation from the primary caretakers develop.

The continued encounter with "just sufficient frustration" promotes such internalization, resulting in a continual expansion of the self-representation and an increasing sense of self-as-agent (Schafer, 1968). This expansion facilitates the formation of a differentiated internal world that is separated from the external one by increasingly complex, developmentally induced intrapsychic boundaries. Little in the way of distinction between self and object or inner and outer will emerge without a sense of being willful, or intentionally affecting the environment. Unless willing precedes satisfaction, need gratification will remain experienced as magically present when desired or as occurring at arbitrary and meaningless times. The life course, especially nodal developmental stages, can be characterized by the gradual predominance of the reality principle over the illusion that internal need states will automatically summon satisfaction and hence regulation (Freud, 1911/1958; Winnicott, 1971; Krystal, 1978). If gratification of need states is not linked to intention, the child and later the adult will experience frustration and satisfaction as arising from without rather than under the egis of an active, intentional self. Consequently, the progress of individuation and psychological separation will be arrested.

Thus, intrapsychic development can be recast as promoting an ever greater sense of psychological separateness from the caretaker through this expanded self-representation and sense of agency. Similarly, severe psychopathology may be viewed as the consequence of this failure to separate psychologically, because the self-representation remains empty and tenuously defined. Elsewhere (Sugarman and Jaffe, 1983) we have delineated a series of developmental stages that are key passages in the formation of this increasingly differentiated and integrated self-representation. Furthermore, we have suggested that a developmental line of transitional phenomena exists that facilitate the transitions between these key stages. Transitions from one stage of development to another precipitate strains within the individual and between the individual and the external environment. Transitional phenomena are turned to during such times in order to reduce this strain and allow the regaining of inner/outer equilibrium.

The specific form of transitional phenomena will differ at each stage because of maturational and developmental shifts in cognitive functioning, defensive functioning, libidinal focus, affect organization, and the demands of the environment. Despite such manifest differences, all transitional phenomena promote an ever-increasing independence by facilitating a developmentally sequential internalization of key regulatory functions. By promoting separation, they help the individual to cope with painful emotions and to forestall regression. Often, the absence of transitional phenomena in the context of undue trauma results in a regression to a more primitive level of adaptation; either the inner or outer world becomes overemphasized to the detriment of the other. Poor differentiation between the representations of self and other or between inner and outer occurs because of a failure to internalize key regulatory functions.

Four stages in the development of the self-representation and significant shifts in level of psychological separation and individuation have been delineated (Sugarman and Jaffe, 1983). The earliest stage is characterized by sensory-motor, need-satisfying capacities (Edgcumbe and Burgner, 1972), when an inability to distinguish pleasurable sensation from the pleasing object keeps the infant's fledgling sense of self ephemeral and tenuous. Autoerotic stimulation fosters the emergence of an inner sense of intentionality and mastery (Sander, 1983). Thus, the body serves as a transitional phenomenon (Sugarman and Jaffe, 1983; Johansen, 1983).

The second stage coincides with the practicing and rapprochement subphases of separation-individuation, when the toddler's sense of self is increasingly differentiated as he or she learns to anticipate and search for desired objects (Mahler, Pine, and Bergman, 1975; Jacobson, 1964). Symbolization occurs and is reflected in the attainments of both object permanence (Greenspan, 1979) and self permanence (Lewis and Brooks-Gunn, 1979). Such representations of self and others remain locked into the spatial and temporal contexts in which they were encountered, however, and this dependence on the external world for maintenance of the sense of self-as-agent limits the toddler's ability to separate psychologically. A sense of being an independent agent is a sense of psychological causality that is acquired only with the attainment of evocative constancy (Wolff, 1969). Inanimate objects act as the transitional phenomenon that promote this accomplishment (Sugarman and Jaffe, 1983).

Oedipal issues usher in the third stage of development in self-representation. As the increasingly differentiated, complex, and integrated self- and object representations become more symbolic, the oedipal- and latency-aged child gains greater interpersonal independence. By the end of latency, complex and hierarchically organized systems of self- and object representations will emerge. Such an in-depth representational world promotes greater independence from parents and a better sense of self. Fantasy is used at this stage as the transitional phenomenon that facilitates this more complex representational network (Sugarman and Jaffe, 1983).

The advent of formal operational thinking in adolescence ushers in the last stage of development. New-found cognitive abilities integrate a wider array of internal states and modes of representation. "Wishes, feelings, fears, internalized prohibitions, different self- and object representations, realistic perceptions, anticipations of the future, and memories of the past can best be considered within a closed system leading to relatively stable identity" (Greenspan, 1979, p. 216). Only abstract transitional phenomena such as new philosophies, political interests, or art forms offer the complexity necessary to further internalization and expansion of the adolescent's identity (Sugarman and Jaffe, 1983). At this level, transitional phenomena no longer serve the more primitive function of helping the individual cope with the psychological experience of loss, separateness, or lack of closeness. Rather, this advanced level functions to promote a more autonomous sense of self that is not linked to interpersonal dependence.

Psychopathology: Struggles with Psychological Separation

It has been necessary to review our model of psychological development in order to provide the framework for understanding severe psychopathology from a developmental perspective. Our model has emphasized the psychological separation from parents through the formation of an ever more individualized and integrated sense of self as the major adaptive task of development. Psychoanalytic theoreticians have debated the relative importance of self- and object representations compared with ego functions for quite some time. An "either/or" attitude about the relative value of an object relations or an ego-psychological model has appeared, preventing the necessary synthesis of both perspectives, a synthesis that can explain personality functioning in all its complexity. That is, the roles of cognition, perception, motivation, and impulse regulation must be understood within the context of the interpersonal environment from which these capacities arise.

Such a synthesis must take cognizance of the hierarchical nature of personality functioning and not err as do many ego psychologists (for example, Bellak, Hurvich, and Gediman, 1973) in assuming that all personality functions play an equal role in determining behavior (Horner, 1975). We suggest that ego functions such as cognition or sense of reality be viewed as subordinated, secondary functions that arise out of the interpersonal mother/child matrix (Sugarman, 1986b). "If id, ego, and superego have their origins in interactions with the environment that are internalized interactions transposed to a new arena, thus becoming intrapsychic interactions, then psychic structure formation and individuation are dependent on object relations" (Loewald, 1978, p. 498). As self- and object representations differentiate and integrate, psychological boundaries are developed and affects are neutralized, promoting the development of reality testing, defensive functioning, and so on. No longer is there the need for primitive affects to signal distress and summon caretakers. These ego functions then promote further development within the self- and object representations in a spiraling fashion (Sugarman, 1986b).

Thus, severe psychopathology may be understood as a failure to develop or to maintain self- and object representations. Clinical experience with such patients easily demonstrates that such individuals have poorly differentiated and unintegrated representations of themselves (Bursten, 1978). The emotional drain posed by therapeutic work with such patients results partly from the necessity that the therapist lend so much of himself or herself in order to compensate for their deficiencies. The failure of individuals with severe psychopathology to internalize key regulatory functions at the appropriate developmental stages leaves such patients continually dependent on others to provide such regulation. That is, they remain psychologically unseparated from caretakers.

Most of their symptoms, then, may be understood as misguided attempts to use developmentally primitive transitional phenomena to internalize regulatory functions that should have been internalized long ago. Under optimal circumstances, the developmental line of transitional phenomena forms a vertical decalage in which all previous forms are present but are subordinated to the most advanced one; hence, the most advanced form is manifest while earlier forms remain latent. The decalage disappears under the regression of severe psychopathology, and the hierarchical organization of transitional phenomena is absent. In general, the less severe the psychopathology, the greater the range of transitional phenomena available, and the more the reliance on advanced ones.

We will now describe four major types of severe psychopathology and the ways in which patients suffering from them use more primitive transitional phenomena. We have focused on these four syndromes—schizophrenia, paranoia, bulimia, and borderline personality organization—because they constitute a considerable portion of the severe types of modern-day psychopathology.

Schizophrenia: A Failure to Internalize
Homeostatic Mechanisms

Numerous clinicians have indicated that nonparanoid types of schizophrenia can be traced to the most basic problems in separating from the symbiotic relationship with the mother (Frosch, 1979; Mahler, 1968; Rinsley, 1980; Meissner, 1978; Searles, 1965). Rinsley (1980) has gone even further and has differentiated an autistic type of schizophrenic, arising out of insufficient symbiotic relations with the mother, from a symbiotic schizophrenic, characterized by a failure to "hatch" out of the symbiotic orbit. In cases of symbiotic schizophrenia, a hypersymbiotic mother/infant bond has continued the omnipotent symbiotic dual unit of mother and child. Serious psychic disorganization is the eventual result of being faced with the reality of a separation for which the child has never been psychologically prepared. Such individuals are left excessively vulnerable to real object losses and separations because of their continued dependence on the caretaker for emotional supplies and other key ego functions (Rinsley, 1980).

The shift in understanding schizophrenia as outlined above, from a primary focus on id demands overwhelming a fragile ego, has resulted in a more optimistic treatment outlook. Rather than viewing schizophrenics as without object relations and untreatable, we can view them as having very primitive object relations characteristic of the symbiotic stage of development. The early origin of this disorder suggests that these patients are so consumed with struggles to retain or reobtain basic homeostatic regulation that just the maintenance of basic rhythmic patterns such as sleep/wake or hunger/elimination cycles and the attempt to integrate sensory modalities requires inordinate effort. Their self-representation is so fragmented and so undifferentiated from their object representations that the question of self-regulation seems almost academic. What point is there to self-regulation if a sense of self is all but absent? As a result, the treatment approach to symbiotic schizophrenia includes an awareness that the patient lacks object constancy and will require frequent sessions; an awareness that progress must be measured by years, not months, of therapy; and finally, a preparedness for the powerful countertransference reactions provoked by the schizophrenic's tendency to merge with the therapist and the strain that this places on the therapist's boundaries.

Clinical Manifestations of Fusion and Lack of Homeostatic Regulation

Not surprisingly, the schizophrenic's interpersonal relationships and internal representations of self and other are distorted and primitive (Pao, 1979). It is important to realize that these patients are prone to lose their self/other boundary if one is to avoid attributing to them a greater sense of intentionality and control than they actually have. The clinician, whose self/other boundary is more firmly delineated, may find it difficult to appreciate the experience of individuals who do not have such boundaries. A therapeutic perspective can be maintained only if one consciously reminds oneself of this model. For example, the tendency of symbiotic patients to disregard matters of hygiene to the point that health can be endangered could be experienced as repulsive by the clinician. The smearing of feces, projectile vomiting, and a more general lack of cleanliness are common characteristics of such people. Therefore, it is crucial to remember that they lack a sufficient sense of self-as-agent and subjective sense of themselves to regulate this behavior, and they frequently lack a sufficient awareness of the therapist to consider their impact on him or her. This assault on the therapist's ego boundaries is exhausting and is one of the most difficult aspects of such patients.

In fact, exhaustion and anger are the two most common countertransference reactions to what often feels like the schizophrenic's relentless pursuit of merger at all costs. Both these countertransference reactions may be understood as defensive boundary-delineating mechanisms against such incorporativeness. Such patients fail to maintain object constancy and remain fixated at a developmental level characterized by sensory-motor thinking and magical hallucinations (Ferenczi and Rank, 1916; Mahler, 1968; Rinsley, 1980). Because separation has never been managed, the appearance of a potential caretaker precipitates hopes for fusion and fears of engulfment, while the absence of such a person feels like a catastrophic loss. Hence, the schizophrenic has been viewed as suffering from a need/fear dilemma (Burnham, Gladstone, and Gibson, 1969).

These patients' self- and object representations also lack stability; attachments are withdrawn easily and in some ways mirror the infant's distractibility. Patients show a persistence of predepressive anxiety and its associated failures in normal internalization and structuralization (Klein, 1935, 1946/1975, 1948; Rinsley, 1980). Primitive superego precursors remain primitive and unintegrated and hence are not incorporated into the early ego (Kernberg, 1966; Rinsley, 1968). The self-representation is fragmented at the level of the body ego. Body parts and products are confused with persecutory introjects and viewed as powerful and dangerous. Thus, they are disowned, projected, and isolated in an attempt to protect both self and others (Rinsley, 1980). The awkward motor coordination mentioned by Spitz (1971) may well derive from such mechanisms.

Thus, one of the most fundamental levels on which schizophrenic symptomatology is manifested has to do with an alienation from the body. Such individuals seem to have an excessive insensitivity to their basic bodily functions; they seem not to be aware of the urge to defecate, vomit, and so forth until such urges can no longer be ignored. Internal regulation of such functions is lost, so that they must be externally regulated by others, who are experienced as essentially undifferentiated from the self. Consequently, one often treats schizophrenics like newly trained toddlers by checking whether they need to go to the bathroom, for example, or whether they are full and should not eat any more.

Because such patients are so alienated from their bodies, sexual impulses are poorly regulated and usually infused with aggressive or more primitive libidinal aims. For example, one chronic schizophrenic patient, as a matter of course, exposed his genitals to any new female staff member attending his ward group meeting. Another, when discussing his sexual fantasies in therapy, would refer to the female genitals as a "womb" (he included a portion of the body from above the knees to below the breasts). Both examples reflect the schizophrenic's lack of self/ other boundaries and lack of awareness of the other's feelings. Often, it appears that the erogenous zones of sexual pleasure are not integrated into the person's sense of self and are inappropriately experienced in terms of body image, emotional context, and interpersonal relationships (Rinsley, 1980; Fliess, 1961; Freud, 1905/1953, 1914/1957).

Such a lack of self/other differentiation leads to a striking breakdown in ego functioning by disrupting thinking and distorting reality testing. By many clinical standards, thinking disturbances are the defining feature of schizophrenic pathology, while impaired reality testing is the index of a psychotic condition. Condensation, displacement, autistic logic, and other primary process mechanisms as well as drive-laden content give these patients' thinking either a crude, drive-dominated quality or a bizarre, ethereal, otherworldly quality. One chronic schizophrenic, for example, spent most of his therapy sessions discussing his wish to "grok," a science fiction term for empathic, intuitive telepathic communication. Through such ideas he was expressing his wishes to fuse, or merge, with the therapist. Every time he realized such hopes were unattainable, he retreated in depressed fury, regressing quickly under the impact of his anger. Causal thinking and the ability to distinguish thought from fantasy become impossible without attempts at self-as-agent and awareness that others are separate from oneself.

But despite their fragmentation, schizophrenics do maintain enough of a sense of self to experience a lack of self-esteem. Their low self-esteem is painful to watch because it is so thinly veiled. The patient mentioned above, in his attempts to "grok," would expand his fantasies of titular ascent because of distant familial ties to royalty.

Transitional Phenomena Used by Schizophrenics

Body as Transitional Phenomenon. The schizophrenic's unintegrated and severely regressed sense of self is reflected in an impoverished use of transitional phenomena. These patients have less access to transitional phenomena than patients suffering from other severe psychopathological disorders. Because such individuals have regressed to the point that they are still struggling to achieve a homeostatic equilibrium between themselves and the environment, they are struggling to develop and maintain the basic rhythmic patterns of the newborn, such as sleep/waking, hunger/satiation, and arousal/quiescence (Greenspan, 1981). Such a primitive struggle at self-regulation necessitates a primary reliance on the body as a transitional phenomenon. And indeed, autoerotic behavior seems a primary preoccupation of many schizophrenics. It is common on long-term inpatient wards to find these individuals spending most of their waking hours lying in bed masturbating, unless they are prevented from doing so by staff. Such behavior may be viewed as an adaptive effort to regulate interpersonal sexual and/or aggressive impulses. These behaviors can also be viewed as an attempt to maintain a primitive sense of well-being akin to the infant's fusion with the mother.

Likewise, illicit drugs are used by some schizophrenics in an attempt to maintain a sense of well-being. A review of the literature on opiate addiction, for example, indicates a consistent subgroup of schizophrenic addicts who seem to have turned to the drug to regain homeostatic equilibrium (Blatt, Wilber, Sugarman, and McDonald, 1984).

Inanimate Objects as Transitional Phenomena. It is commonly recognized that inanimate objects can serve transitional functions, thus helping to regulate inner states. What is unusual, in the case of the schizophrenic, is the use of people *as if* they were inanimate. One patient belonged to a psychodrama group and included the group as an integral part of his weekly schedule. On closer investigation it was discovered that he in no way involved himself in the group's activities, nor did he have a relationship with the therapist, at least in any conventional sense. When it was suggested to the patient that he discontinue the group, however, or when his going was even brought up for discussion, he became anxious and decompensated, and if not reassured, he developed delusions. Because of the limited capacity these patients have for communicating, it was difficult to learn the exact functions that this patient's group facilitated. It seems unlikely that the group was merely a routine, as he could tolerate other changes in schedule, such as those involving his therapy hour. Rather, it seems that the group and group leader were experienced as though he had regained a childhood state of symbiotic belonging. Even though the patient had no appreciation for his group leader as a person, he seemed to derive a sense of safety and security from contact with the group.

Fantasy as Transitional Phenomenon. Occasionally fantasy is used as a transitional phenomenon. Although the severe ego impairment usually prevents access to this more advanced phenomenon, some schizophrenics do seem able to use fantasy to obtain some degree of narcissistic regulation (Freud, 1914/ 1957). One such person, for example, developed an idyllic world of kings, princes, and princesses, all designed to counteract his pervasive sense of being defective, inadequate, and unappealing to women. The themes had the simplicity, the emphasis on good triumphing over evil, and the adulation of beautiful women so characteristic of oedipal- and latency-aged children. Nonetheless, the essential motive for these fantasies was his fear of being abandoned rather than an interest in competitive victory.

Paranoia: An Effort to Ameliorate Narcissistic Injury

The paranoid psychoses have been least directly tied to early problems in separation and individuation. Meissner (1978), however, in his opus on paranoia, does indicate that the practicing subphase has key importance in the etiology of such pathologies. He links the sense of autonomy developed during the practicing subphase to the central role of conflicts around autonomy and control so characteristic of paranoid symptomatology. We also believe that the clinical syndrome of paranoia is best understood as deriving from the anxieties attendant on this early period of development.

According to Klein (1935), the paranoid position is characterized by projection of aggressive drive derivatives onto the maternal object. Persecutory anxiety then ensues, which necessitates pathological defenses centered on splitting. Further development is precluded, for the intensity of the aggression makes progression into the depressive position and its attendant guilt too anxiety-provoking. Thus, Klein focuses on the inner environment and drive regulation. If one adds an insensitive, frustrating, or even abusive caretaking environment as another source of the intense aggression of this period, paranoia can be traced to interpersonal problems in separation-individuation as well.

In many ways paranoid personalities and paranoid schizophrenics appear far more integrated than the undifferentiated schizophrenics just described. A review of the research studies on these syndromes (Blatt and Wild, 1976) demonstrates a preponderance of evidence that paranoid schizophrenics outperform nonparanoid schizophrenics on almost all the cognitive or perceptual tasks developed by experimental psychologists. Thus, one must conclude that the self-representations of these individuals are more integrated and more capable of self-regulation than those of undifferentiated schizophrenics.

Despite this conclusion, clinical experience with paranoid personalities (Bursten, 1973) or paranoid schizophrenics (Meissner, 1978) reveals that such self-definition is fragile. In fact, the paranoid individual seems to be in an almost perpetual struggle to maintain his sense of being different and unique. Controlling, argumentative, and distancing modes of relating are all maneuvers to avoid a sense of passivity, helplessness, and weakness. These patients maintain a pseudo autonomy and a denial of interpersonal neediness as a veneer covering their fragile sense of self-as-agent. In this regard, it is important to view their struggles and aggression as encounters with forces they experience as alien and frightening. Actually, they still experience agency as external, although they will go to great lengths to obscure the shame and humiliation felt over what they perceive to be an underlying inadequacy and incompetence. Viewed from this perspective, introjective depression (Blatt, 1974; Lerner, Blatt, and Johnson, 1983) and feelings of worthlessness and guilt lie at the root of many paranoid conditions. It is precisely those hostile introjects that are subject to projective defenses.

Developmentally, the paranoid's fixation point lies in the

transition between the differentiation and practicing subphases (Sugarman, 1984). It is the practicing subphase, with its developmental emphasis on motoric development and a rapid expansion of abilities, that deserves to be thought of as paralleling the psychosocial struggles with autonomy versus shame and doubt (Sugarman, Quinlan, and Devennis, 1982). Erikson's (1950) equation of these conflicts with the anal phase links such a struggle to the end of the practicing phase, with the last major attainment of control over one's body, instead of realizing that the struggle over autonomy begins with early motility. Such a broadening of the time frame covered by this expansion of an active sense of self helps to explain the interplay of anal-sadistic and oral-aggressive derivatives in the psychodynamics of paranoia.

Clinical Manifestations of Severe Narcissistic Injury

At root, then, the core failure in self-regulation in these patients revolves around self-esteem regulation, which is compounded by problems in drive regulation, ego functioning, and object relations. The grandiosity and egocentrism underlying the delusional and/or overly inferential thinking of these individuals seem to reflect interpersonal attempts to maintain a self-image of being capable, active, and potent. Bursten (1973) attributes the grandiose self-representation of the paranoid personality to a pathological and self-defeating attempt to avoid the shame at having inadequacies revealed to others and to oneself. Certainly the egocentrism at the core of the paranoid schizophrenic's delusional system implies a desperate need to assume that the world revolves around, and is interested in, the patient. Intensive psychotherapy with such individuals invariably reveals significant deficits in self-esteem, which are defended against by such delusions. One such patient was convinced that his family had hospitalized him in order to get at an inheritance from his father. Similarly, he assumed that his therapist was motivated only by the desire to "bleed him dry" of his resources. Haughtily and disdainfully he would disclaim his need for treatment or for intimate relationships with his family. As therapy progressed, a picture of a shy, unassuming, and self-conscious boy growing up under the dictatorial domination of a highly narcissistic father emerged. He had never felt able to measure up to his father's standards and had misinterpreted his father's self-absorption as a reflection of his own basic undesirability and weakness. His father's brazen promiscuity and gambling became idealized standards to which he aspired but which he could not reach. Only as his anger surfaced and his realization of his father's inability to love emerged could his feelings of inadequacy and the need for his paranoid defenses subside.

Paranoid individuals so desperately seek to feel capable and active that they must fend off any suggestion of dependent longings. Consequently, drive regulation becomes impaired. For over seventy years psychoanalysts have been aware of the role of latent homosexuality in paranoia (Freud, 1911/1958). In fact, both homosexual and heterosexual impulses are kept out of conscious awareness. Reaction formation, projection, and reversals serve to distance the homosexual impulses, while isolation of affect, intellectualization, and projection transform the heterosexual ones. Only recently, however, have psychoanalysts recognized the interpersonal distancing implicit in such drive attenuation. Such patients cannot tolerate even the momentary fusions of sexual experiences. Homosexuality avoids the danger of the engulfing mother but still leaves the patient with the narcissistic humiliation of a socially unacceptable wish. The above-described patient, for example, would plead to perform fellatio on his therapist in order to incorporate the therapist's strength and power, just as he had overidentified with his father to escape the symbiotic pull to his narcissistically frustrating, depressed mother.

More recently (Meissner, 1978; Sugarman, 1984) psychoanalysts have realized that aggressive drive regulation is a significant problem in its own right with these individuals. Anger is no longer viewed solely as a transformation of homosexual love via reaction formation. Rather, these individuals feel inordinately angry over a variety of perceived deprivations, in part to maintain emotional distance and to preclude the danger of fusion associated with dependent wishes. But such primitive rage prevents the integration of what remain as emotionally polarized self- and object representations (Kernberg, 1975). Such extreme splitting and primitive anger leave the paranoid schizophrenic at risk for violent outbursts.

Not surprisingly, internalization of benign object relations, as well as maintenance of interpersonal relationships, is a problem for these individuals. The fear of symbiotic regression, with its inevitable helplessness and vulnerability, creates intense anxiety or even panic. Consequently, they use a variety of defenses against wishes for merger by creating interpersonal and emotional distance between themselves and others. At the extreme, deanimation and devitalization are used to create sterile, cold representations of self and other in an effort to disavow all needs for human contact. Blatt and Wild (1976) suggest that these maneuvers are somewhat successful. That is, the walling off of any sense of human neediness does help the ego to function more effectively. Once one accepts the distorted initial premise of a delusion, the rest of it is highly logical and coherent.

Such devitalized representations help to maintain a sense of strength and autonomy at the most basic level of body representation. Hypochondriacal concerns are often forerunners of a paranoid episode because of the paranoid's anxiety about erosion of strength and autonomy in his body. Often the Rorschach percepts reveal a deanimating of body parts in another attempt to regain a sense of being strong, capable, and independent. One such patient perceived the upper detail of Card X on the Rorschach as "the human backbone greatly larger than it should be. ... The spine has great strength in the picture, its size. And to me it almost looked metallic, you know. It almost looked like, I almost call it a metallic rod that giant turbines run by, it looked so strong" (Sugarman, 1984, pp. 419–420).

Transitional Phenomena Used by Paranoids

Fantasy as Transitional Phenomenon. Paranoid patients present an interesting use of transitional phenomena from different stages. In general, they rely on fantasy in order to create and extend their elaborate delusional systems. In fact, they seem incapable of distinguishing between fantasy and reality to the point that the loss of such a distinction has been described as the hallmark of delusional thinking. Via fantasy they can regulate their self-esteem through megalomaniac self-appraisals. Furthermore, the fantastic delusions of the paranoid help him cope with difficulties around object relationships. He creates a world populated by evil, menacing figures against whom he must be on guard so that he need not fear giving in to repressed, passive-dependent longings. His fantasy world gives him a pseudo self-sufficiency, ensuring that he will not feel the need to risk real interpersonal relationships, along with the impulses and fears they stimulate in him. Fantastic enemies are far safer than a real person with whom interpersonal intimacy is possible.

Inanimate Objects as Transitional Phenomena. As the paranoid process (Meissner, 1978) escalates, however, fantasy no longer seems to offer the haven it once did. As a result, the content of the fantasies changes, and delusions of being persecuted by malevolent others give way to delusions of being influenced by machines (Tausk, 1919/1948) or other inanimate objects. Thus, the form or structure of the transitional phenomenon is fantasy, but the content now becomes an inanimate object. At this point we can view the paranoid as having regressed to a stage wherein deanimated transitional phenomena are used because even fantastic, animated transitional phenomena feel too real.

The paranoid patient uses his deanimated representations to maintain a desperate, rigid pseudo autonomy because fantasied others are no longer safe. The extreme stability, consistency, and safety of fantasied attachments to inadequate objects maintain the paranoid's tenuous hold on the self/other boundary and yet allow him to feel that the object is always available if needed.

For example, one paranoid adolescent secretly hoarded Ninja weapons, which he would not use on others. When deprived of them during hospitalization, he began to fashion other weapons from furniture and room accessories. As long as he had a weapon, he could relate to other patients on the unit. Agitation and regression would follow discovery and confiscation of each weapon, however.

Just as the practicing toddler finds the blanket more predictable and simultaneously less engulfing than the mother, the paranoid patient feels safer with deanimated objects. Furthermore, such deanimation helps to prevent a regression in which a sense of self-as-agent would be lost. Affect regulation is also facilitated by deanimated transitional phenomena. Such objects are even less likely to invite emotion than fantasied humans. Thus, when vital fantasies can no longer bind strong emotional impulses, the paranoid further estranges himself from his feelings by relating to inanimate objects. In addition, should these transitional objects become the targets of displaced rage, they are as unlikely to retaliate as are the toys the toddler periodically abuses (Sugarman, 1984). Eventually, interpersonal distortion increases, however, as such extreme estrangement from emotional involvement with others or oneself results in a pervasive unclarity about what is and is not real.

Bulimia: A Maintenance of the Self/Other Boundary

In recent years an awareness has developed that bulimia, a syndrome characterized by gorging and vomiting, must be distinguished from anorexia nervosa, a disorder characterized by refusal to eat. Until this realization, bulimia had been considered just a variant of anorexia nervosa (for example, Bruch, 1973; Sugarman, Quinlan, and Devennis, 1981). The finding of a significant group of normal-weight women who maintain their normal weight by purging themselves through vomiting or laxative abuse after binging on large quantities of high-calorie food has emphasized that bulimia does not necessarily involve an attempt at weight reduction. Given this difference in the function and phenomenology of weight loss, it seems reasonable to assume that the unconscious motivations for bulimic symptoms will differ from those for anorexia.

Even when one recognizes the separate existence of the bulimic syndrome, however, the diagnostic picture remains unclear. There are bulimics who use their binge/purge cycles to lower their weight in a fashion similar to anorectics. Furthermore, some bulimics have a history of anorexia nervosa prior to the onset of bulimic symptomatology. It is our belief that these two instances of bulimia associated with or originating in anorecticlike restriction of weight represent a far more pathological ego structure and developmentally more primitive motivational system than either normal-weight bulimia or pure anorexia. This clinically derived impression is buttressed by research that finds that these bulimics show a greater degree of body-image distortion than anorectics (Button, Frangella, and Slade, 1977), a more vulnerable self/other boundary (Sugarman, Quinlan, and Devennis, 1981), and a consistent tendency to perceive their parents as more disturbed (Kramer, 1983).

Although bulimia as a symptom picture can be present in a variety of ego organizations, the bulimics who show either significant weight loss or a history of anorexia frequently show a developmental trauma in the transition from the differentiation to the practicing subphase (Sugarman, Quinlan, and Devennis, 1981). A variety of family problems, including violation of transactional boundaries and parental under- or overinvolvement, result in inhibition of the normal strivings for autonomy and activity associated with the practicing subphase. Parental, usually maternal, overinvolvement and overcontrol or underinvolvement leads the destined bulimic to suppress her natural tendencies for growth and independence.

The caretaker's inability to tolerate or promote her child's separateness prevents the child from developing a firm boundary between self- and object representations. Such a developmental arrest leaves the child fixated at a level of sensory-motor self- and object representations (Blatt, 1974). As a consequence, the bulimic fails to develop the ability to evoke a representation of the mother in her absence (evocative object constancy). For her, an absent mother is tantamount to a lost mother; and she has not internalized the maternal capacity to soothe and regulate her own internal tension, emotion, or mood. As a result, fantasies of fusion with the soothing and fulfilling mother are generated. Thus, the bulimic engages in a perpetual struggle to gratify her intense needs to be dependent and yet to maintain a sense of autonomy and a consolidated self/other boundary.

A brief vignette will demonstrate the clinical utility of an object relations view of the bulimic's struggles. One bulimic patient, a month before her analyst's vacation, dreamed that she was breast-feeding a baboon. After refusing to associate to the dream, she talked about her jealousy over her stepfather's love of a sister and how she wanted him for herself. Although the obvious oedipal theme, from a classical perspective, might lead to an interpretation about the analyst's leaving the patient for another woman, in this case the oedipal theme served a defensive function. The associative link following the dream revealed the primacy of the patient's pre-oedipal wishes for closeness, her anaclitic mode of relatedness, and her difficulty with feelings of loss. An oedipal interpretation would have been experienced by the patient, and rightly so, as an empathic failure. Thus, in working with such bulimic patients, an understanding of their problems in the early development of object relations is indispensable.

Clinical Manifestations of a Tenuous Self/Other Boundary

Despite the developmentally primitive nature of her object relations, the bulimic seems able to circumscribe conflicts well enough so that many ego functions are maintained. However, more pervasive problems exist in regard to less visible ego functions. For instance, the bulimic's sense of reality is often distorted. Such patients commonly report a quasi-dissociated state while engaged in the binge/purge cycle. At such times they feel detached from others and enjoy a temporary sense of isolation and superiority. The sense of control allows them to avoid dependent longings and the risk of losing differentiation between self and others. Time perspective seems altered in these instances as the bulimic's frenzied, frenetic behavior makes the present so intensely prominent that a sense of past and future recedes into the background. Their own experience is paramount, and a sense of others recedes.

Judgment is another ego function that suffers in these patients. The intensity of their dependency needs and ambivalence about having them met can result in excessive acting out in psychotherapy. One such patient, for example, became promiscuous without using birth control and abused drugs and alcohol to excess, only to drive home from wherever she had ingested these substances while highly intoxicated. She seemed to show no ability to plan or to anticipate the consequences of her actions at these times, despite her high intelligence. This behavior was interpreted as a reaction to feeling deprived in the maternal transference as well as an expression of the way she used rage to ward off any genuine closeness and intimacy.

Perhaps the most severe ego disruption shown by bulimic patients involves body ego. Their histories often reveal excessively early toilet training or excessively rigid restrictions on physical activity during the separation-individuation process. Deprived of the opportunity to pursue physical autonomy and free choice, the toddler turns her urge to discriminate and manipulate against herself (Erikson, 1950). Because the body is so important for developing this sense of autonomy, it is the body against which the bulimic turns her impulses (Sugarman and Kurash, 1982a). This body-ego distortion is so important a factor that research has found that the degree of body-image distortion is the best predictor of treatment outcome (Garfinkel, Moldofsky, and Garnor, 1977). One such bulimic patient developed phobiclike fears of sitting in public because her body might become stuck in the chair, despite its true condition resembling emaciation. The fear allowed her to further isolate herself and avoid the risk of interpersonal contact, with its potential revival of dependent wishes. Consistent with the above research, she dropped out of treatment in the first few weeks.

Bulimics have demonstrated difficulty in regulating both sexual and angry feelings. Often they show a condensation of feelings derived from different developmental levels, so that sexual activity is often used to gratify dependency needs. That is, the frantic promiscuity evident in many of these individuals is designed to allow them to be held and to feel loved rather than to gain genital pleasure. Thus, intensive psychotherapy with these patients is likely to be marked by sexual acting out of their desire to have the therapist gratify their dependent wishes.

Female therapists report the presence of homosexual fantasies involving dependency needs displaced from the therapist. For example, a fascination with other women's breasts often expresses the wish to be a suckling child at an unconscious, symbolic level.

Frustration of these dependent needs in the therapy renders the patient vulnerable to developmentally primitive rage. One such patient frequently reported being furious for the entire day because her analyst was not providing sufficient care in the form of verbal activity and reassurance. Another patient would find herself brooding about past hurts and slights and then developing elaborate vengeful fantasies. It is not just this oral aggression that troubles the bulimic. Another source of the temper so often seen in these women is their anger over feeling forced to comply or submit. Anything that feels like an imposition is likely to result in sudden, obstinate withholding or passive-aggressive behavior. These struggles for control both highlight the bulimic's fear of losing her sense of independence and can be used defensively to create distance from the desired object. Interpersonal transactions are conflictual for these women because their sense of self feels so tenuous. The failure to develop a representation of the caretaker that can be maintained in the caretaker's absence renders the bulimic vulnerable to feeling empty, helpless, and hopeless. Any prolonged separation from the current love object leaves her feeling isolated and cut off from the loved one in a fashion similar to her mother's unavailability during childhood. Consequently, the bulimic harbors intense wishes to obtain an idealized state of perfect reunion in which all her needs would be known and met without her having to express them. Of course, such unrealistic hopes are impossible to meet and only guarantee further disappointment and disillusionment. The bulimic would be doomed to disappointment even if these wishes were gratified, however; for as soon as another person becomes too close and important to her, she experiences that person as demanding or expecting something. Consequently, bulimics manage to spoil or ruin relationships in an unconscious attempt to maintain a fragile sense of autonomy.

Not surprisingly, self-esteem is a source of difficulty in bulimic women. Because of the early maternal unavailability and subsequent failure to internalize a soothing, accepting caretaker, the bulimic has an ego ideal imbued with the high demands and expectations for perfection associated with the maternal introject. A major source of resistance in treatment is the frequent conviction that the therapist must be as condemning and judgmental as she is. This externalization of her ego ideal allows her to cling to the illusion of omnipotent perfection and consequent acceptance by her mother. It also allows the bulimic to maintain an internal relationship with mother and not destroy her with oral and narcissistic rage.

Transitional Phenomena Used by the Bulimic

The Body as Transitional Phenomenon. The body, of course, is the preferred transitional phenomenon of the bulimic (Sugarman and Kurash, 1982a). Through the use of her body, the bulimic attempts to maintain a sense of psychological separateness and individuation. Because the self- and object representations of the bulimic are sensory-motor, the object can be represented only at the moment of need gratification. Only through action or motor sequences can a sense of self as active agent and a sense of the mother as separate and stable be obtained. Gorging and vomiting become actions that promote self/other differentiation. They also help the bulimic with affect regulation. The devouring and regurgitation of food acts as a concrete metaphor for these patients' interpersonal relationships. To the therapist they often seem to want more and more and yet ultimately spoil and devalue what they are given. Thus, bulimics use their bodies to somatically discharge dependent and aggressive impulses in an effort to maintain some control. Taking in food is equivalent to giving in to their craving for symbiotic reunion; purging attenuates the anxiety of being controlled by the now-internalized mother. In a symbiotic way, separation from and aggressive rejection of the mother can be achieved while avoiding the danger of actually enacting this with the mother. One patient would immediately feel that her entire body had become enlarged after eating and, in panic and revulsion, would vomit. Ego functioning is facilitated through the demarcation of the body ego. Inside and outside are so rigidly defined that ego functions that presuppose such boundaries are strengthened. Narcissistic regulation is also attained through the use of the body. Purging helps to temporarily attenuate the self-loathing precipitated by the binge. Furthermore, it fosters an illusory sense of self-control. Ultimately, however, the bulimic is humiliated by being confronted by her tenuous control over her essential neediness.

Objects as Transitional Phenomena. Other individuals are often used as transitional phenomena by the bulimic, and she abuses them just as she does her own body. The bulimic's lack of appreciation of the independent status of others as individuals with their own needs leads to considering them merely as need-gratifying objects. One sees an expectation that the other exists only in regard to the bulimic's needs, which is a perspective more characteristic of the toddler's attitude toward his blanket than the relationships of a mature adult. Others are turned to in attempts to fill the empty, desolate void within the bulimic. In this way bulimics attempt to compensate for their lack of evocative object constancy. Frequently, drugs are a less cumbersome transitional object used by the bulimic both to compensate for her inner emptiness and to regulate intense drives. They are more predictable and less demanding than people. Even narcissistic regulation is temporarily fostered as alcohol is often used to muffle the recriminations of a sadistic externalized superego and to attenuate the anxiety about fusion associated with penetration and orgasm. One such patient seemed able to enjoy intercourse only when alcohol had obliterated her self-awareness.

Fantasy as Transitional Phenomenon. The fact that the bulimic does have access to fantasy in order to foster self-regulation is often unappreciated. These individuals' concreteness and emphasis on immediacy of need gratification often make them appear lacking in higher-level cognitive attainments. But treatment in intensive psychotherapy often reveals a host of unconscious fantasies. In fact, if used appropriately, the making conscious of such fantasies can often allow the bulimic to give up her more primitive modes of self-regulation. Oftentimes, the fantasies can become a means of regulating self-esteem as the bulimic becomes more and more aware of her wishes to be looked at and admired, much as a toddler looks to her mother for unconditional appreciation and love. At the same time, affect regulation is enhanced by the expansion of the self-representation involved in fantasy. The more the bulimic fantasizes about sexual or aggressive impulses, the greater sense of self-awareness and autonomy from them occurs. Her judgment can also benefit from fantasy; in fantasy consequences can be anticipated and active planning can take place, expanding the use of self-as-agent and promoting a sense of adult mastery. Finally, the emergence of fantasy in therapy often marks the beginnings of evocative object constancy and the coalescence of a treatment alliance, because a rudimentary internalization of the therapist's stable and consistent caring and acceptance has occurred.

Borderline Personality Organization: An Effort at Self-Integration

A spate of articles over the last twenty years (Kernberg, 1967; Horner, 1975; Mahler, 1971; Masterson, 1972, 1976; Sugarman, 1979; Sugarman and Lerner, 1980; Sugarman, Bloom-Feshbach, and Bloom-Feshbach, 1980) have linked borderline personality organization to an early arrest in the separation-individuation process, usually the rapprochement subphase. Masterson and Rinsley (1975) suggest that the mother's withdrawal of emotional support during the rapprochement subphase provides a leitmotif to the borderline child's subsequent development. Thereafter, the child feels "caught in a dilemma, wherein regressive clinging is supported, and efforts toward separation and growth are met by a withdrawal of the maternal supplies needed to promote ego development and further separation-individuation" (Sugarman and Lerner, 1980, p. 32). Such parental inability to tolerate the child's developmentally appropriate ambivalence, aggression, and autonomy interferes with the key developmental task of this stage—the integration of affectively polarized self- and object representations into unified, more comprehensive, and realistic ones. Kernberg (1967) suggests that an innate surplus of aggression in the toddler may also interfere with such integration. Whatever the blend of nature and nurture, such a developmental arrest precludes several key personality characteristics: (1) the mastery of separation anxiety, (2) an affirmation of basic trust, (3) the deflation of symbiotic omnipotence and idealization, (4) a firming up of a core sense of self (Spear, 1980; Spear and Sugarman, 1984), (5) the establishment of ego control and impulse regulation, and (6) the replacement of primitive defenses by more mature ones like repression and intellectualization (Lerner and Lerner, 1980; Lerner, Sugarman, and Gaughran, 1981; Sugarman and Lerner, 1980).

Despite the widespread use of the borderline diagnostic concept over the last two decades, tremendous unclarity about its meaning and applicability still exists. Although Kernberg (1967), in his major reformulation of this syndrome, emphasized that it refers to a stable disturbance in personality functioning, one continues to see terms such as *borderline schizophrenic* or *borderline psychotic* in the literature. It is crucial to realize that this form of psychopathology is not a variant of schizophrenia or any other psychotic disorder (Sugarman, 1980). Equally misunderstood, however, is Kernberg's emphasis that it is a structural diagnosis that intersects character style. That is, any type of personality style can be organized at a borderline level, just as at a neurotic or a psychotic level. It is incorrect to think that a diagnosis of borderline personality disorder is sufficient in itself. One must clarify both the style and the level of organization, such as "an obsessive personality organized at a borderline level." *DSM-III* makes this error when it includes "borderline personality disorder" as an Axis II disorder rather than appreciating the need to specify both style and structural level. Yet, the variety of psychodynamics and defenses used by the various personality styles organized at this level makes it difficult to state generalities about their regulatory problems (Sugarman and Lerner, 1980). Consequently, we will restrict our discussion to the infantile personality (Kernberg, 1967; Sugarman, 1979), a hysterical personality organized at the borderline level. It is this type of borderline patient to which the *DSM-III* criteria apply and to which clinicians refer when they speak globally about "the" borderline patient.

Clinical Manifestations of Poor Self-Integration

Because the developmental fixation point of most character structures organized at a borderline level lies at the transition from the practicing to the rapprochement subphase, the regulatory capacities of these patients tend to be less disrupted than those of the prior three groups. Kernberg (1967) reports a common observation that an interaction among defensive structure, affect organization, and nature of internalized object representations allows some of these individuals to demonstrate surprisingly good instrumental skills and vocational and/or intellectual achievement. The capacity of narcissistic personalities who are also organized at a borderline level to perform well in these spheres, despite profound pathology in object relations, has received particular comment (Sugarman, 1979; Masterson, 1981). Nonetheless, borderline patients do demonstrate impairments in self-integration because their representations of both self and others remain dichotomously organized around gratifying and frustrating affect states.

Consequently, the infantile personality has severe problems in interpersonal relationships. In general, patients with a borderline personality organization have self-representations that are tenuously maintained (Bursten, 1978). Despite their erratic and unstable behavior, such individuals maintain a surprisingly stable way of organizing and relating to the world. It is as though their whole *modus operandi* for living were designed around their consistent strategies for integrating and shoring up their inherently precarious sense of self (Bursten, 1978). Because these patients have failed to traverse the rapprochement subphase successfully, their self- and object representations remain unintegrated (Kernberg, 1967). Their early representations of self and other, which were encoded along globally affective lines (good, gratifying, pleasurable; or bad, depriving, unpleasurable), have not been integrated, owing to an excess of negative representations, which exists for either constitutional or experiential reasons (Kernberg, 1966). Consequently they vacillate between unrealistic perceptions of themselves or others as either all good or all bad. Numerous problems in interpersonal relationships are reported to be among their most troublesome symptoms (Sugarman, 1979; Gunderson, 1977). Furthermore, they have failed to develop evocative object constancy and are thus left vulnerable to separation anxiety (Rinsley, 1980), anaclitic depression (Sugarman, 1979), a sense of aloneness (Adler and Buie, 1979), and concreteness (Sugarman, Bloom-Feshbach, and Bloom-Feshbach, 1980; Sugarman and Kurash, 1982b).

A number of interpersonal strategies for managing this failure to integrate self- and object representations are used unconsciously. Some types of borderline personalities use a defense of withdrawal and distancing to avoid stimulation of the wishes for closeness associated with their failure to separate and individuate. Other types mold themselves to the way those around them are or to what others expect in an effort to feel more whole and individuated. Individuals with infantile personalities seem to seek out others mainly in an effort to discover in reality the positive representations of an idealized caretaker. In this way, they try to avoid feeling deprived by preventing the emergence of the powerful, "bad" self- and object representation.

Such an unpredictable and vacillating sense of self and other accompanies a difficult integration and modulation of drives and their related emotions. Kernberg (1967) has suggested that borderline individuals are born with an overabundance of aggressive drives, which prevents them from experiencing and representing a sufficiently positive experience of themselves and others to neutralize their anger. The relative balance between nature and nurture is always difficult to ascertain and will always vary with the individual. But our clinical experience coincides with that of a number of other clinicians (Masterson and Rinsley, 1975; Shapiro, Zinner, Shapiro, and Berkowitz, 1975) who suggest that the familial environment of such individuals often stimulates or provokes intense rage. Mothers are often so depriving or so enveloping that anger about being either ungratified or unable to separate is inevitable. Regardless of specific etiology, however, the major descriptive studies of these patients report that they are prone to erratic and awesome displays of rage, a fact that speaks to their basic problem in affect regulation (Grinker, Werble, and Drye, 1968; Gunderson, 1977).

Sexual impulses are also problematic for borderline patients. Because they are so desperate for contact, their sexual behavior has an indiscriminate and frenzied quality. Commonly, sexual urges are fused with dependent ones so that intercourse is used in an attempt to meet primitive needs to feel loved unconditionally. One infantile patient, for example, performed fellatio on every male patient on her ward in an effort to be loved and appreciated. The self-devaluation implicit in such behavior highlights another aspect of these patients' confused emotions. Often sexual feelings are so heavily colored by hostile ones that sexual behavior takes on a masochistic or sadistic quality. Another borderline couple's most exciting sexual moments came as he masochistically sucked her toes to her sadistic commands.

Self-esteem is, of course, a problem for individuals who have such a labile and unpredictable sense of self and others. At moments when the positive self- and object representations are in ascendance, these patients have grandiose images of themselves and an idealized picture of others. Psychotherapists working with borderline patients report the common experience of being worshiped as the best therapist in the world while gratifying the patient and being viewed as the worst, most incompetent one as soon as they fail to meet some need. Because of their arrest in separation-individuation, the ego ideal of borderline patients remains organized around the powerful, highly idealized early caretaker. Because of the failure to realize the limitations of the parent figure(s), the ego ideal is not modified through development. Consequently, the goals toward which the borderline individual strives and the persons whom he or she wishes to emulate remain unrealistically high and unreachable. This leaves the borderline plagued by doubts of self-worth or lovableness. Fast (1975) has commented on the inability of

such individuals to achieve their vocational potential because of
the underlying fear that they cannot meet such grandiose self-
aspirations.

Compared with the other syndromes discussed in this
chapter, the developmentally later trouble spot of borderline
pathology allows greater ego development. Kernberg (1967)
states that the borderline suffers from nonspecific ego weakness. That is, the regulatory functions subserved under the ego
are relatively intact; reality testing and thought processes are
generally adequate. But the fragility of ego functions is nevertheless evident in such patients' potential to suffer rapid and
transient regressions in thinking and reality testing when they
feel unloved, unsupported, or abandoned. Strong emotions such
as anger, depression, or desire are stimulated by this interpersonal void and prompt rapid regression (Knight, 1954; Zilboorg,
1941).

Transitional Phenomena Used by the Borderline Personality Organization

Fantasy as Transitional Phenomenon. Fantasy is the most
common transitional phenomena used by borderline patients in
their efforts to better integrate self- and object experiences and
to manage regressive longings. As a consequence, they often
show a blatant disregard for consensual validity in their interpretations of interactions with others. Causality and natural
laws are avoided or distorted to conform to their preconceived
understanding of interpersonal relationships (Sugarman and Kurash, 1982b). Borderline patients are noteworthy for their tendencies to interpret the world along fantastic lines (Chethik and
Fast, 1970; Fast, 1975; Leichtman and Shapiro, 1980; Lerner,
Sugarman, and Barbour, 1985; Sugarman, 1986a). Distorted interpretations of the world help to maintain the illusion that external reality corresponds to subjective reality and help to prop
up fragile self-esteem and self-coherence. Furthermore, the emphasis on fantasy creates a sense of inner vitality that defends
against a more basic sense of passivity, helplessness, emptiness,
and isolation from others. Such a vitalization of self-representa-

tion also promotes a clearer differentiation between self and other and a better adaptation to the social environment. Being able to fantasize also helps the borderline to avoid enacting many primitive feelings directly. For example, one borderline couple encouraged each other to imitate the other one's current idealized sexual partner, and in this way they avoided seeking out overt affairs. At the same time they avoided the regressive fears of merger with each other.

Objects as Transitional Phenomena. Objects seem to be the other noteworthy form of transitional phenomenon used by such individuals. Some borderline patients literally retain their original transitional objects. For example, one adolescent patient carried her blanket everywhere in the hospital. But drugs (Lidz, Lidz, and Rubenstein, 1976; Sugarman and Kurash, 1982b) are among the most common transitional objects used by the borderline (Modell, 1963; Rosenthal, 1981). Thus, drugs may become the borderline individual's only claim to membership in his or her peer group. This is a misguided attempt to revamp infantile parental representations and replace them with more mature ones. Separation anxiety and/or anaclitic depression are consequently attenuated. Furthermore, marijuana, a drug favored by many borderline adolescents, allows a more abstract and deeper subjective experience of inner states (Sugarman and Kurash, 1982b). Borderline patients report an ability to "get into things" better while high; thus, there is an increase in cognitive and affective intuitiveness. For a moment they replace the toddler's "love affair with the world" with a love affair with symbols. Thoughts and feelings are reflected on, played with, and explored in a manner reminiscent of the toddler's use of his transitional object. But, in a capacity more akin to the toddler's blanket, the gamut of paraphernalia associated with drugs is also clung to and included in the drugs' transitional functions.

Although human beings do not meet the usual criteria for an inanimate object, the ruthless tyranny exercised over them by the borderline individual indicates that they are equated with the blanket. That is, the infantile personality lacks an awareness that the other is a whole and autonomous individual with separate needs and wishes. Rather, the other is a "part object," a term used to indicate that others are treated as though their only function were to help borderline individuals regulate their own inner states.

Abstraction as Transitional Phenomenon. Abstraction is even less available as a transitional phenomenon for such patients. Although borderline individuals may be quite intellectual or creative, they are noted for never being able to live up to what seemed their early promise. In therapy, such failures are usually found to result from the vulnerability of their abstract capacities to intrusion by self-aggrandizing or self-disparaging fantasies. Such individuals are so reliant on fantasy in order to maintain an integrated sense of self and a differentiated sense of the other that their potential for this more advanced transitional phenomenon is disrupted easily. Only with successful treatment and an integration of the self-representation can the borderline patient's ideational capacities be realized.

Summary

In conclusion, we suggest that the four types of severe psychopathology considered herein (schizophrenia, paranoia, bulimia, and borderline personality organization) originate out of early developmental difficulties in separation and individuation. That is, early developmental interferences occur and forestall an ability to continue the process of psychological separation from parental figures. The normal separation-individuation process culminates in traversal of the adolescent developmental stage (Blos, 1967; Schafer, 1973). For such an experience of being psychologically separate, there must be a parallel increase in the sense of the self as individuated and self-regulated. This sense is based on the formation and subsequent development of internal representations of both self and important others. These representations emerge out of the infant's earliest interactions with caretakers and follow a developmental sequence parallel to that of cognitive development. Representations become progressively more abstract and integrated the higher the developmental stage. Gradually, a variety of regulatory functions are internalized and integrated into the self-representation. Transitional phenomena play a particularly important role as vehicles for the internalization of such capacities. They help the developing child to navigate the transitions between stages, during which the regulatory functions occupy an intermediate position between the environment and the self-representation.

Individuals who suffer from the psychopathologies we have described have failed to internalize the regulatory functions that promote individuation and separation. Their developmental disturbances have left them arrested at or regressed to primitive stages of interpersonal relatedness. Despite such interpersonal failures, they, like all human beings, strive to maintain some emotional connectedness with others. Consequently, many of their symptoms can be viewed as pathological attempts to use primitive transitional phenomena to internalize regulatory functions and remain interpersonally engaged. Thus, these pathological transitional phenomena indicate a continuing struggle to gain or maintain a more mature sense of separateness and autonomy. It is our hope that attending to these transitional phenomena may ultimately help clinicians to formulate more precise treatment strategies that will facilitate the patient's developmental and interpersonal strivings.

References

Adler, G., and Buie, D. "Aloneness and Borderline Psychopathology: The Possible Relevance of Child Development Issues." *International Journal of Psycho-Analysis,* 1979, *60,* 83-96.

Bellak, L., Hurvich, M., and Gediman, H. K. *Ego Functions in Schizophrenics, Neurotics, and Normals.* New York: Wiley, 1973.

Blatt, S. J. "Levels of Object Representation in Anaclitic and Introjective Depression." *Psychoanalytic Study of the Child,* 1974, *29,* 107-157.

Blatt, S. J., Wilber, C., Sugarman, A., and McDonald, C. "Psychodynamic Theories of Opiate Addiction: New Directions for Research." *Clinical Psychology Review,* 1984, *4,* 159–189.

Blatt, S. J., and Wild, C. *Schizophrenia: A Developmental Analysis.* Orlando, Fla.: Academic Press, 1976.

Blos, P. "The Second Individuation Process of Adolescence." *Psychoanalytic Study of the Child,* 1967, *22,* 162–186.

Bruch, H. *Eating Disorders: Obesity, Anorexia Nervosa, and the Person Within.* New York: Basic Books, 1973.

Burnham, D., Gladstone, A., and Gibson, R. *Schizophrenia and the Need-Fear Dilemma.* New York: International Universities Press, 1969.

Bursten, B. "Some Narcissistic Personality Types." *International Journal of Psycho-Analysis,* 1973, *54,* 287–299.

Bursten, B. "A Diagnostic Framework." *International Review of Psycho-Analysis,* 1978, *5,* 15–31.

Button, E., Frangella, F., and Slade, P. "A Reappraisal of Body Perception Disturbance in Anorexia Nervosa." *Psychological Medicine,* 1977, *7,* 235–243.

Chethik, M., and Fast, I. "A Function of Fantasy in the Borderline Child." *American Journal of Orthopsychiatry,* 1970, *40,* 756–765.

Edgcumbe, R., and Burgner, M. "Some Problems in the Conceptualization of Early Object Relationships: Part I. The Concepts of Need Satisfaction and Need Satisfying Relationships." *Psychoanalytic Study of the Child,* 1972, *27,* 283–314.

Erikson, E. H. *Childhood and Society.* New York: Norton, 1950.

Fast, I. "Aspects of Work Style and Work Difficulty in Borderline Personalities." *International Journal of Psycho-Analysis,* 1975, *56,* 397–403.

Ferenczi, S., and Rank, O. "Stages in the Development of the Sense of Reality." In S. Ferenczi and O. Rank, *Sex in Psychoanalysis.* Boston: Badger, 1916.

Fliess, R. *Ego and Body Ego.* New York: International Universities Press, 1961.

Freud, S. "Three Essays on the Theory of Sexuality." In J.

Strachey (ed. and trans.), *The Standard Edition of the Complete Psychological Works of Sigmund Freud.* Vol. 7. London: Hogarth Press, 1953. (Originally published 1905.)

Freud, S. "On Narcissism: An Introduction." In J. Strachey (ed. and trans.), *The Standard Edition of the Complete Psychological Works of Sigmund Freud.* Vol. 14. London: Hogarth Press, 1957. (Originally published 1914.)

Freud, S. "Psycho-Analytic Notes on an Autobiographical Account of a Case of Paranoia (Dementia Paranoides)." In J. Strachey (ed. and trans.), *The Standard Edition of the Complete Psychological Works of Sigmund Freud.* Vol. 12. London: Hogarth Press, 1958. (Originally published 1911.)

Frosch, J. *The Psychotic Process.* New York: International Universities Press, 1979.

Garfinkel, P., Moldofsky, H., and Garnor, D. "Prognosis in Anorexia Nervosa as Influenced by Clinical Features, Treatment, and Self Perception." *Canadian Medical Association Journal,* 1977, *117*, 1041-1045.

Greenspan, S. I. *Intelligence and Adaptation.* New York: International Universities Press, 1979.

Greenspan, S. I. *Psychopathology and Adaptation in Infancy and Early Childhood.* New York: International Universities Press, 1981.

Grinker, R., Werble, B., and Drye, R. *The Borderline Syndrome.* New York: Basic Books, 1968.

Gunderson, J. "Characteristics of Borderlines." In P. Hartocollis (ed.), *Borderline Personality Disorders: The Concept, the Patient, the Syndrome.* New York: International Universities Press, 1977.

Horner, A. "Stages and the Processes in the Development of Early Object Relations and Their Associated Pathologies." *International Review of Psycho-Analysis,* 1975, *2*, 95-105.

Jacobson, E. *The Self and the Object World.* New York: International Universities Press, 1964.

Johansen, K. "Transitional Experience of a Borderline Patient." *Journal of Nervous and Mental Disease,* 1983, *171*, 126-128.

Kernberg, O. "Structural Derivatives of Object Relationships." *International Journal of Psycho-Analysis,* 1966, *45*, 236-253.

Kernberg, O. "Borderline Personality Organization." *Journal of the American Psychoanalytic Association,* 1967, *15,* 641–685.

Kernberg, O. *Borderline Conditions and Pathological Narcissism.* New York: Jason Aronson, 1975.

Klein, M. "A Contribution to the Psychogenesis of Manic Depressive States." *International Journal of Psycho-Analysis,* 1935, *196,* 145–174.

Klein, M. "Mourning and Its Relation to Manic Depressive States." In M. Klein, *Contributions to Psychoanalysis.* London: Hogarth Press, 1948.

Klein, M. "Notes on Some Schizoid Mechanisms." In M. Klein, *Envy and Gratitude and Other Works.* New York: Delacorte Press/Seymour Lawrence, 1975. (Originally published 1946.)

Knight, R. "Management and Psychotherapy of the Borderline Schizophrenic Patient." In R. Knight and C. Friedman (eds.), *Psychoanalytic Psychiatry and Psychology.* New York: International Universities Press, 1954.

Kramer, S. "Bulimia and Related Eating Disorders: A Family Systems Perspective." Unpublished doctoral dissertation, California School of Professional Psychology–San Diego, 1983.

Krystal, H. "Self Representation and the Capacity for Self Care." *Annual of Psychoanalysis,* 1978, *6,* 209–246.

Leichtman, M., and Shapiro, S. "An Introduction to the Psychological Assessment of Borderline Conditions in Children: Borderline Children and the Test Process." In J. Kwawer, H. Lerner, P. Lerner, and A. Sugarman (eds.), *Borderline Phenomena and the Rorschach Test.* New York: International Universities Press, 1980.

Lerner, H., Blatt, S. J., and Johnson, C. "Three Forms of Paranoia." Unpublished manuscript, University of Michigan, 1983.

Lerner, H., Sugarman, A., and Barbour, C. "Patterns of Ego Boundary Disturbance in Neurotic, Borderline, and Schizophrenic Patients." *Psychoanalytic Psychology,* 1985, *2,* 47–66.

Lerner, H., Sugarman, A., and Gaughran, J. "Borderline and

Schizophrenic Patients: A Comparative Study of Defensive Structure." *Journal of Nervous and Mental Disease,* 1981, *169,* 705-711.

Lerner, P., and Lerner, H. "Rorschach Assessment of Primitive Defenses in Borderline Structure." In J. Kwawer, H. Lerner, P. Lerner, and A. Sugarman (eds.), *Borderline Phenomena and the Rorschach Test.* New York: International Universities Press, 1980.

Lewis, M., and Brooks-Gunn, J. *Social Cognition and the Acquisition of the Self.* New York: Plenum, 1979.

Lidz, T., Lidz, R., and Rubenstein, R. "An Anaclitic Syndrome in Adolescent Amphetamine Addicts." *Psychoanalytic Study of the Child,* 1976, *31,* 317-348.

Loewald, H. "Instinct Theory, Object Relations, and Psychic Structure Formation." *Journal of the American Psychoanalytic Association,* 1978, *26,* 493-506.

Mahler, M. S. *On Human Symbiosis and the Vicissitudes of Individuation.* Vol. 1: *Infantile Psychosis.* New York: International Universities Press, 1968.

Mahler, M. S. "A Study of the Separation-Individuation Process and Its Possible Application to Borderline Phenomena in the Psychoanalytic Situation." *Psychoanalytic Study of the Child,* 1971, *26,* 403-424.

Mahler, M. S., Pine, F., and Bergman, A. *The Psychological Birth of the Human Infant: Symbiosis and Individuation.* New York: Basic Books, 1975.

Masterson, J. *Treatment of the Borderline Adolescent: A Developmental Approach.* New York: Wiley, 1972.

Masterson, J. *Psychotherapy of the Borderline Adult: A Developmental Approach.* New York: Brunner/Mazel, 1976.

Masterson, J. *The Narcissistic and Borderline Disorders.* New York: Brunner/Mazel, 1981.

Masterson, J., and Rinsley, D. "The Borderline Syndrome: The Role of the Mother in the Genesis and Psychic Structure of the Borderline Personality." *International Journal of Psycho-Analysis,* 1975, *56,* 163-177.

Meissner, W. W. *The Paranoid Process.* New York: Jason Aronson, 1978.

Modell, A. "Primitive Object Relationships and the Predisposition to Schizophrenia." *International Journal of Psycho-Analysis,* 1963, *44,* 282-290.

Pao, P. N. *Schizophrenic Disorders: Theory and Treatment from a Psychodynamic Point of View.* New York: International Universities Press, 1979.

Rinsley, D. "Economic Aspects of Object Relations." *International Journal of Psycho-Analysis,* 1968, *49,* 38-48.

Rinsley, D. *Treatment of the Severely Disturbed Adolescent.* New York: Jason Aronson, 1980.

Rosenthal, P. A. "Changes in Transitional Objects: Girls in Mid-adolescence." *Adolescent Psychiatry,* 1981, *9,* 214-222.

Sander, L. "Polarity, Paradox, and the Organizing Process in Development." In J. Call, E. Galenson, and K. Tyson (eds.), *Frontiers of Infant Psychiatry.* New York: Basic Books, 1983.

Schafer, R. *Aspects of Internalization.* New York: International Universities Press, 1968.

Schafer, R. "Concepts of Self and Identity and the Experience of Separation-Individuation in Adolescence." *Psychoanalytic Quarterly,* 1973, *42,* 42-59.

Searles, H. *Collected Papers on Schizophrenia and Related Subjects.* New York: International Universities Press, 1965.

Shapiro, E., Zinner, J., Shapiro, R., and Berkowitz, D. "The Influence of Family Experience on Borderline Personality Development." *International Review of Psycho-Analysis,* 1975, *2,* 399-412.

Spear, W. "The Psychological Assessment of Structural and Thematic Object Representations in Borderline and Schizophrenic Patients." In J. Kwawer, H. Lerner, P. Lerner, and A. Sugarman (eds.), *Borderline Phenomena and the Rorschach Test.* New York: International Universities Press, 1980.

Spear, W., and Sugarman, A. "Dimensions of Internalized Object Relations in Borderline and Schizophrenic Patients." *Psycho-Analytic Psychology,* 1984, *1,* 113-129.

Spitz, R. A. *The First Year of Life: A Psychoanalytic Study of Normal and Deviant Development of Object Relations.* New York: International Universities Press, 1971.

Sugarman, A. "The Infantile Personality: Orality in the Hysteric Revisited." *International Journal of Psycho-Analysis,* 1979, *60,* 501-513.

Sugarman, A. "The Borderline Personality Organization as Manifested on Psychological Tests." In J. Kwawer, H. Lerner, P. Lerner, and A. Sugarman (eds.), *Borderline Phenomena and the Rorschach Test.* New York: International Universities Press, 1980.

Sugarman, A. "The Use of Deanimated Transitional Phenomena in Paranoid Conditions." *Bulletin of the Menninger Clinic,* 1984, *48,* 418-426.

Sugarman, A. "An Object Relations Understanding of Borderline Phenomena on the Rorschach." In M. Kissen (ed.), *Assessing Object Relations Phenomena.* New York: International Universities Press, 1986a.

Sugarman, A. "Self Experience and Reality Testing: Synthesis of an Object Relations and an Ego Psychological Model on the Rorschach." In M. Kissen (ed.), *Assessing Object Relations Phenomena.* New York: International Universities Press, 1986b.

Sugarman, A., Bloom-Feshbach, S., and Bloom-Feshbach, J. "The Psychological Dimensions of Borderline Adolescents." In J. Kwawer, H. Lerner, P. Lerner, and A. Sugarman (eds.), *Borderline Phenomena and the Rorschach Test.* New York: International Universities Press, 1980.

Sugarman, A., and Jaffe, L. S. "A Developmental Line of Transitional Phenomena." Paper presented at the annual meeting of the American Psychological Association, Anaheim, Calif. Aug. 1983.

Sugarman, A., and Kurash, C. "The Body as a Transitional Object in Bulimia." *International Journal of Eating Disorders,* 1982a, *1,* 57-67.

Sugarman, A., and Kurash, C. "Marijuana Abuse, Transitional Experience, and the Borderline Adolescent." *Psychoanalytic Inquiry,* 1982b, *2,* 519-538.

Sugarman, A., and Lerner, H. "Reflections on the Current State of the Borderline Concept." In J. Kwawer, H. Lerner, P. Lerner, and A. Sugarman (eds.), *Borderline Phenomena and the Rorschach Test.* New York: International Universities Press, 1980.

Sugarman, A., Quinlan, D., and Devennis, L. "Anorexia Nervosa as a Defense Against Anaclitic Depression." *International Journal of Eating Disorders,* 1981, *1,* 44-61.

Sugarman, A., Quinlan, D., and Devennis, L. "Ego Boundary Disturbance in Anorexia Nervosa: Preliminary Findings." *Journal of Personality Assessment,* 1982, *45,* 455-561.

Tausk, V. "On the Origin of the Influencing Machine." In R. Fliess (ed.), *The Psychoanalytic Reader.* New York: International Universities Press, 1948. (Originally published 1919.)

Tolpin, M. "On the Beginnings of a Cohesive Self: An Application of the Concept of Transmitting Internalization to the Study of the Transitional Object and Signal Anxiety." *Psychoanalytic Study of the Child,* 1971, *26,* 316-352.

Winnicott, D. W. *Playing and Reality.* New York: Basic Books, 1971.

Wolff, P. "The Developmental Psychologies of Jean Piaget and Psychoanalysis." *Psychological Issues,* 1969, Monograph 5.

Zilboorg, G. "Ambulatory Schizophrenias." *Psychiatry,* 1941, *4,* 149-155.

15

The Process of Psychotherapy: Separation and the Complex Interplay Among Empathy, Insight, and Internalization

Jesse D. Geller

Editors' Note: *This chapter tackles the complex task of deline- ating the various influences of separation on modification of representational structures during the psychotherapy process. Geller begins by observing that separation events, experiences of either actual or symbolic loss, are common precipitating factors motivating the desire for treatment. He examines the develop- mental role of separation and loss experiences in forming repre- sentations of self and other and notes how these internalized transactions are replayed in the transferential and realistic inter- personal interaction within the treatment relationship. The chapter emphasizes therapy recommendations most relevant for patients who have insufficient structuralization of the self (that is, those who lack object constancy or who have suffered early insecure attachment). Such patients are unfinished in their de- velopment along the separation-individuation continuum and hence are more prone to react strongly to events involving a realistic or symbolic separation. Geller notes the separations in- herent in the treatment process—ends of sessions, therapist vaca-*

tions, professional affective distance, inevitable empathic failures, and termination of the treatment. The therapist's attention to the separation reactions evoked by these experiences provides a way to rework the unresolved affect, pathological defenses, primitive inner structures, and problematic interpersonal patterns that have evolved from the earliest object relationships.

Traditional therapeutic approaches, especially psychoanalysis, have emphasized the role of insight in the psychological change process. Geller suggests a special complementary role for other affective and interpersonal processes, for both patient and therapist. Therapeutic change is deemed to operate through reconstruction of inner representational structures based on the new internalizations fostered by the empathically charged treatment relationship.

Geller introduces many theoretical and technical issues, including the phenomenology of inner representations, the cognitive structure and modality of representation, a life-span developmental view of individuation, and the stereotypical patterning of representational and interpersonal constellations in different characterological categories of patient. Although the scope and complexity of the topics surveyed may be difficult to follow at times, the reader's clarity of focus will be facilitated by maintaining an overview of the author's creative attempt to portray how the inner representational world can be brought to awareness and rendered amenable to constructive modification. The chapter is also somewhat ambiguous about the implications of the psychoanalytic theoretical distinction between levels of internalization. Questions remain about which kinds of patients might benefit from the therapeutic suggestions Geller proposes, especially those technical strategies related to the sensory dimension of fantasy and affect.

> It is the image in the mind that binds us to our lost
> treasures, but it is the loss that shapes the image.
>
> —*Colette*

Psychotherapy has become one of the major resources in our culture for helping individuals come to terms with the accumulating experiences of separation and loss endured during a lifetime. Every day psychotherapists provide consolation and understanding to individuals who have suffered separation by exclusion, rejection, abandonment, betrayal, and disillusionment. As the meanings and rituals associated with death have become more secularized, psychotherapists have increasingly assumed the solemn responsibility of enabling the bereaved to complete what Freud (1917/1957) called the "work" of mourning. Therapists are regularly called on to help individuals manage the raw and often violent emotions that accompany the dissolution of a marriage or love affair. Many of their patients are people who are having difficulty dealing with externally imposed endings or transitions: receiving a promotion, graduation from a training program, the aftermath of compulsory retirement, inability to honor publication deadlines, curtailment of activities due to accidents and disease, the "empty nest," and so forth. Some come to therapy because they feel afraid whenever separated from the familiarity and security of their homes. Still others seek psychotherapy because they have lost faith in their capacity to achieve an autonomous feeling of identity (a "self") clearly marked off from the key persons in their lives.

The theories of psychopathology that guide the work of psychotherapists grant varying degrees of importance to the universal themes of separation and loss. Rank (1924/1952) was an early advocate of the view that all neurotic symptoms could be interpreted as an expression of the thesis and antithesis of separation and union. Freud (1926/1959) came to regard separation anxiety as the primal, prototypical anxiety. Existential

The author wishes to acknowledge the support and wisdom of the friends, colleagues, and family members who helped during the writing of this chapter.

psychotherapists (for example, Boss, 1963; May, 1961) have always given particular importance to the idea of separateness and its relation to loneliness, awareness of nonbeing, a sense of responsibility, and the struggle to achieve personal freedom. More recently, the processes of separation and individuation have been assigned new prominence among psychotherapists influenced by the object relations theorists within psychoanalysis (for example, Fairbairn, 1952; Loewald, 1962; Winnicott, 1965; Guntrip, 1969; Mahler, 1979; Kernberg, 1976; Searles, 1977; Stolorow and Ross, 1978; Meissner, 1981; Mahler, Pine, and Bergman, 1975), the self psychology of Kohut (1971, 1977), and the attachment theory of Bowlby (1969, 1973).

My own efforts to grapple with the multiform ways in which separations present themselves in psychotherapy are based on a selective integration of psychoanalytic and existential teachings, along with the contributions of developmental cognitive psychologists (Piaget, 1954; Bruner, 1964; Werner, 1961). Though differing in important respects, therapists working in these traditions share the belief that a phenomenologically based, developmentally informed, empathic appreciation of the ways individuals internally represent interactions with others and act in behalf of, or in response to, these representations is essential to understanding the diversity and complexity of the processes set in motion by separations and losses, whether actual or symbolic. The emerging view in the psychoanalytic literature is that the predominant emotional tone, painfulness, and duration of the feelings induced by the loss or threatened loss of a relationship, as well as the meanings ascribed to those feelings, are prefigured by the mental models of relationships that populate an individual's "representational world" (Sandler and Rosenblatt, 1962). There is growing consensus that, to the extent that individuals have failed to acquire realistic and cohesive representations of themselves as separate and different from others and feel incapable of functioning independently, they are vulnerable to severe and prolonged reactions to the stress of separations (for example, Blatt, 1974; Horowitz, Wilner, Marmar, and Krupnick, 1980). There is also an increasing acknowledgment that patients who suffer from impairments in the formation and consolidation of the representational capacities that underlie development of the distinction between self and non-self, the special type of symbolization involved in "person constancy," and the abilities required to experience and express ambivalence or conflict have great difficulty in participating efficaciously in a psychotherapy in which the primary responsibility for bringing about lasting and beneficial changes is assigned to insight and the processes of working through.

Patients whose problems with separation and loss are correlated with impairments in these capacities have challenged psychoanalytically informed therapists to reexamine their models of the therapeutic action of psychotherapy. This reexamination is resulting in a more systematic study of a paradigm of psychotherapy in which insight plays a role *secondary* to the complex interplay between empathy and the internalization of patient/therapist relations. At the center of many of these investigations is a concern with discovering the conditions that would best promote the creation of "new" therapeutic cognitive/affective representations of the functional aspects and qualities of the therapy relationship. Psychotherapists guided by this concern make the fundamental assumption that when mental models of relationships develop in the direction of becoming increasingly embodied, differentiated, and hierarchically organized, they advance the journey toward a constructive acceptance of the separateness, uniqueness, autonomy, historicity, and finitude of the self and others.

The primary aim of this chapter is to extend the implications of these trends and assumptions for the individual psychotherapy of adult patients. I will argue for a model of psychotherapy that assigns complementary roles to insight and to that form of internalization known as introjection in explaining how events happening in the two-person psychotherapy relationship move patients toward successive levels of maturity in dealing with the crises of separation that prompted their entrance into therapy. To illustrate the value of this perspective, I will focus on the therapeutic potential of sustained, empathically infused inquiries into the problematic nature and quality of patients' reactions to the spatial, temporal, and interpersonal boundaries that separate them from their therapists. Every issue to be discussed within this perspective is linked to the view that exploring patients' unique modes of negotiating the separations, losses, transitions, and endings woven into psychotherapy itself concurrently (1) facilitates the conscious recovery and reconstruction of damaging mental models of relationships (acquired as a function of early attachment- and separation-related events) so that they can be expressed in the form of differentiated feelings and memories, independent of overt behavior, and (2) activates, at the introjective level of symbolization, the processes that preserve and replicate, within self-experience, the beneficial interactions originally experienced during therapy sessions.

For reasons that will become gradually apparent, the following questions can profitably serve to organize these inquiries: What characteristics does a patient ascribe to his or her therapist? What roles or functions does the therapist serve for the patient? What are the emotional consequences for the patient of the therapist's failure or unwillingness to meet his or her needs, expectations, or wishes? Can the patient maintain a durable, positive attachment to the therapist regardless of fluctuations in need states or externally imposed frustrations?

One cannot conceive of separation apart from attachment or from the interdependence of self and others. Similarly, attachment and separation, like frustration and gratification, are polar principles. Separations and attachments are also sources of frustration and gratification. When patients have been chronically separated from the affectionate and caring concern of valued others, they tend to respond in a particularly problematic way both to the frustrating aspects of separations and to the gratifications made possible by intimate attachments to others. Throughout this chapter particular attention will be given to the therapeutic challenges posed by patients suffering from this twofold difficulty. To conclude, I will briefly discuss the ways therapists define, order, and negotiate the tasks arising during the termination phase.

The Work Structure of Psychotherapy

Establishing and Regulating Boundaries. Psychotherapy can be differentiated from other forms of human relatedness in a variety of ways. From an open-systems perspective, the psychotherapeutic enterprise can be differentiated from other aspects of the interpersonal environment on the basis of discontinuities of time, space, and task definition (Astrachan, Flynn, Geller, and Harvey, 1971). Temporal, spatial, and interpersonal boundaries of various kinds are also woven into the work structure of psychotherapy.

To begin with, all psychotherapies, whether explicitly time-limited or not, terminate. The very success of a psychotherapy signals the readiness of the relationship to end. Second, psychotherapy takes place only in an environment created, maintained, and sanctioned by the therapist. John Updike (1966) has commented that the settings where therapists work occupy an ambiguous terrain, midway between an office and a home. Therapists pledge confidentiality and protect the relationship from external interruptions and distractions. For example, within the intimate confines of individual psychotherapy, a patient's significant others are excluded from sessions. The role requirements of psychotherapy are such that therapists also have primary responsibility for defining the temporal parameters of the relationship, including length of sessions, interval between sessions, their availability during intersession intervals, timing and duration of their vacations, and in some instances the total duration of the psychotherapy. Sessions are typically scheduled at regular, and therefore predictable intervals. Encounters with therapists are rhythmically spaced. Therapeutic sessions also have a more or less fixed duration, and therapists avoid or limit contact with their patients in extratherapeutic situations. Most therapists in private practice continue to follow Freud's (1913/1958) recommendation of "leasing a definite hour" to each patient. Whether to charge, as Freud further recommended, full fee for missed or canceled appointments as a deterrent to motivated absences remains a source of perennial controversy.

Much needs to be learned about the management of the temporal parameters of psychotherapy. Current guidelines for the optimal duration and frequency of sessions are not empirically grounded, and recommendations tend to be idiosyncratic. Langs (1976) advocates a frequency of two sessions a week, with increases for patients who are psychotic or imminently so or who are "acting out." By contrast, Saul (1972) recommends a basic frequency of three sessions a week. In Weiner's (1975) view, a week is the maximum interval across which a patient is likely to work consistently on his or her problems. Writing of psychoanalysis, Glover (1955) suggests that after forty-eight hours there is a "dwindling" of responses to the "average current stimulus" of the analyst.

Therapists are empowered to establish, regulate, and limit transactions across the temporal and spatial boundaries that differentiate psychotherapy as a social system from the rest of the interpersonal environment. This empowerment highlights the status inequalities that separate the positions of patient and therapist. Psychotherapists not only function as symbols of authority but also occupy a *position* of authority. Most broadly stated, psychotherapists, in their roles as institutionally sanctioned experts, have the primary responsibility for defining the tasks and division of labor required to accomplish the work of psychotherapy (Geller, Astrachan, and Flynn, 1976). As conceptualized here, it is the imposition of these tasks that transforms a relationship between two individuals into a therapeutic situation and which sets in motion a benignly influential and healing process.

The Search for Synthetic Solutions: The Importance of Empathy. The tasks that therapists impose on themselves require the synthetic resolution of a wide variety of polarities. Rhythmic oscillations between commitment and detachment, gratification and frustration, immediacy and deferral, passion and decorum, levity and gravity, emotional understanding and intellectual comprehension, talking and listening, and so on are required to practice psychotherapy creatively. In their search for a vocabulary to describe the coordinations or integrations required to optimize a patient's adaptation to the therapeutic process, therapists have invented such terms as *participant observation, benign impartiality, detached concern, selective authenticity,* and *disciplined subjectivity.* In the terminology of Piaget (1954), therapeutic competence entails assimilating patients into one's existing conception of the rules, rituals, and roles of psychotherapy while, in a complementary fashion, accommodating the work structure to effect a better fit with the unique needs and circumstances of each patient.

Empathy provides a means for synthesizing Piaget's dual imperatives and makes an indispensable contribution to honoring the uniqueness of each individual. In his most recent statement, Rogers (1975) describes empathy as a "complex, demanding, strong, subtle, and gentle *process* . . . of entering the private perceptual world of the other and becoming thoroughly at home in it. It includes being sensitive, moment to moment, to the changing felt meanings which flow in this other person . . . delicately without making judgments, seeing meanings of which he/she is scarcely aware, but not trying to uncover meanings of which the person is totally unaware, since this would be too threatening. It includes communicating your sense of his/her world as you look with fresh eyes at elements of which the individual is fearful. . . . To be with another in this way means that for the time being you lay aside the views and values you hold for yourself in order to enter another's world without prejudice" (p. 4).

Psychotherapists of diverse persuasions regard this way of discovering and conveying the subjective meanings of an individual's experience as the most important element in their concept of the ideal therapist (Raskin, 1974). Moreover, empirical research indicates that trying to comprehend and share empathically in the psychological states of patients facilitates self-exploration and correlates positively with various independent criteria of successful therapeutic outcomes (for example, Bergin and Strupp, 1972; Kurtz and Grummon, 1972; Kazdin, 1980). What will be emphasized here is the ways in which empathically conveyed understandings move patients, via successive approximations, toward the establishment of more meaningful, coherent connections between disparate, and perhaps disavowed, aspects of experience. Empathic interventions so conceived serve to combine, unite, and synthesize that which has been kept apart.

Survival of the Enterprise. The decision to enter therapy is not made easily or once and for all. It is commonly preceded by lengthy, agonized conflict and a series of unsuccessful prior attempts to master a particular "problem in living" either self-reliantly or with the help of friends and relatives (Farber and Geller, 1977). Moreover, many patients begin therapy compromised in their ability to collaborate with therapists in a mutually satisfying pursuit of solutions to the troublesome aspects of their lives. These difficulties often make their first appearance in the form of dysfunctional responses to the tasks therapists impose on their patients. These tasks, in varying proportions, require self-reflectiveness, free recall of past events, intimate self-disclosure, the development of an emotional attachment to the therapist, cognitive processing of "new" information, attentiveness to nonverbal behavior, and accommodations to the ambiguities and work structure of therapy as defined by the therapist. Establishment of a genuinely collaborative and emotionally honest relationship often requires repeated clarification of the relevance of these tasks to the goals of therapy (Bordin, 1976). In order to erode obstacles to the development of what has been called a "working alliance" (Greenson, 1967) or a "therapeutic alliance" (Friedman, 1969), a therapist must consider patients' initial expectations of how the therapy relationship should or will proceed, as shaped by their characterologically based styles of helpseeking (Rickers-Ovsiankina, Berzins, Geller, and Rogers, 1971). Failure to attend empathically to this task can intensify a patient's suffering, can jeopardize the continued existence of the enterprise, and may prompt patients to leave psychotherapy before they can experience its benefits.

In actual practice therapists often fall short of being empathic, and many therapies terminate before desired or planned-for outcomes are achieved. There is, in fact, a high attrition rate during the initial phase of psychotherapy, the first ten sessions (Baekeland and Lundwall, 1975). Garfield's (1978) comprehensive review of the literature finds that clinics typically report that 50 percent or more of their patients withdraw from therapy before the eighth session and over 65 percent before the tenth. In some comprehensive mental health centers, over 50 percent of patients from minority group backgrounds drop out of therapy after only *one* interview (Sue, 1977; Geller, 1986).

Although "premature terminations" are commonplace

and are a source of deep concern to clinicians, very few studies have sought out their determinants. One notable exception is a retrospective study of early terminators by Kline, Adrian, and Spevak (1974). These investigators found that ex-patients weighed the "perception" that their therapist was not interested in them most heavily in their decision to drop out of therapy. Moreover, about half the patients who were recontacted reported that they had sought help elsewhere after dropping out of therapy, leading the authors to conclude that many patients who terminate prematurely are not lacking in motivation to obtain help, as professionals often assume, but, rather, are reacting to the failure to find it.

That a psychotherapy may be in danger of ending prematurely can be inferred from the ways a patient responds to the external boundaries that encircle the therapeutic enterprise and the interpersonal boundaries that differentiate the positions of patient and therapist. Here I would include such warning signals as rigid accentuations of the status inequalities that separate therapist and patient, dependently demanding requests for extratherapeutic gratifications, tendencies to agree or disagree indiscriminately with the therapist, uncertainties about the privacy of bodily and mental experiences (and consequent withholding of "secrets"), confusion over the distinction between the therapist's professional role and his or her personality, and functional restrictions in the ability to retain the distinction between self and other while experiencing empathic closeness.

Insight and an Atemporal Perspective on Relationships. Empathic exploration of the nature, origins, and significance of these interactional phenomena plays a predominant role in some therapies, a lesser one in others, but is of some importance in all therapies. The pursuit of such understandings recommends itself for a variety of reasons. A focus on the patient's behavior *in* therapy is consistent with the widely held belief that for interpretations to be effective, they must be directed to the patient's concrete experience (Hammer, 1968). As Strachey (1934) said, "For an interpretation to be 'transmutative,' it must be 'emotionally immediate.' The patient must experience it as 'something *actual*' " (p. 136). Extending the implications of this technical principle, I would argue, following Gill (1982), that if patients are to benefit from insight into their methods of coping with the stress of separations in the essential relationships in their lives, they must experience and reflect on these methods within the "here and now" context of the transference. Reliance on transference interpretations derives from the assumption that, during the course of therapy, patients relive and reenact, rather than merely talk about, their prototypical reactions to the loss or threatened loss of relationships. Goleman (1984) expressed this conviction as follows: "Of course, each kind of leave-taking is distinct in many ways from all others, with its own intrinsic problems, pain, and promise. Nevertheless those who study the momentous departures in life often find common strands that bind them, and it is possible to see in any good-bye the texture and the lessons of all those that preceded it and that will follow" (p. 26).

As I understand the concept, transference is a particular instance and potential liability of the universal tendency to perceive and cognitively structure new experiences on the basis of the enduring, and often unconscious, schemata, or mental models, that people construct of persons and of transactions with them (Singer, 1985). All relationships to varying extents are influenced by spontaneously recurring attempts, made unknowingly, to perceive and feel toward others as if they represented important figures from the past. A psychoanalytically designed therapeutic situation distinguishes itself by providing patients with repeated and varied opportunities to learn how their efforts to collaborate with the therapist as a "real person" are distorted by the biasing influence of defensive displacements and the projection of mental models of relationships that are reacted to without awareness of their existence or significance.

Such inquiries help patients to discriminate more clearly between the past and the present and to develop a more integrated perspective on the evolution of persons and relationships over time. A stylistic analysis of a patient's use of language can reveal whether the patient is alienated from his or her personal past, lives in ceaseless transition, or appreciates that events and interactions have significance from the vantage point of the time at which they occurred. Patients whose sense of personal continuity is impaired have great difficulty in telling "stories" about themselves that have a clearly intelligible beginning, middle, and end. Statements are made about the self or others as if they were applicable at any point in time, whether past, present, or future.

By linking sessions together thematically, therapists can help patients to recognize their continuity in time, as well as challenge directly and immediately an atemporal perspective on relationships. Interconnected narratives increase an awareness of the relations that exist between what was, what is, and what will be. This function can also be served by working within the context of a precise, time-limited therapy contract. Mann (1973) maintains that such a structural framework mobilizes the personal meanings that separations and endings have for patients with greater clarity than psychotherapies that leave open the question of duration. Whether or not a termination date is set early on, clinical experience supports the hypothesis that dealing with separation anxieties from the very beginning of therapy prevents overwhelming crises at the time of termination. Ends of hours, canceled sessions, and vacations, as well as intrahour ruptures of attachment, including pauses or breaks—actual or impending—in the flow of the therapeutic dialogue are "apprenticeships" (Edelson, 1963) during which patients and therapists can struggle to acquire the understanding and skills to handle the end of therapy constructively.

I believe that when transference-based interpretations of patients' responses to these mini-separations are empathically and developmentally informed, they facilitate the growth and differentiation of the representational capacities that enable a patient to derive maximum benefit from the processes and results of insight and internalization. The rest of this chapter is devoted to the hypothesis that insight and internalization reactivate the processes of "representational differentiation and consolidation" (Schafer, 1973b) and, in so doing, conjointly bring about enduring changes in a patient's sense of self, capacity to organize conflicts, and ability to maintain secure and real-

istic "internal working models" (Bowlby, 1969, 1973) of attachment to individual beloved persons during their physical absence. According to the hybrid perspective that guides my
work, the representational capacities underlying these sectors of
the personality unfold according to developmental principles
and timetables, are influenced by the phase-specific tasks, crises,
and conflicts of early childhood, and shape the unique route
that the individual travels in dealing with the recurrent crises of
separation encountered during the life course. To clarify the implications of these assumptions, I will next compare the varying
types of difficulty that neurotic, schizoid, and borderline patients have with the evocative challenges posed by the gratifying
and frustrating aspects of psychotherapy. In responding to these
diagnostic categories, the reader is encouraged to bear in mind
that "every man is in certain respects (a) like all other men, (b)
like some other men, and (c) like no other man" (Kluckhohn
and Murray, 1949, p. 53).

Separation and the Representation of Conflict

Separations, as distinct from endings or permanent losses,
initiate a process that is completed by the reunion of the participants in a relationship. Separation, in this sense, implies both
moving away from and coming back together. That the therapist decides when, where, and for how long he or she will be
available complicates this cycle and charges it emotionally. On
the one hand, the rhythmic regularity with which therapists
space therapeutic sessions can reintroduce a sense of congruent
order into lives more accustomed to anarchy. It is not uncommon for patients in once-weekly psychotherapy to define the
beginning and ending of each week as occurring on the day of
their therapy session. The regular recurrence of sessions presents
concrete evidence of the therapist's reliability and trustworthi-
ness. On the other hand, the time limitations and spatial restrictions that therapists impose on their patients are sources of conflict. They activate patients' problematic relations with "authority figures." Like the "abstinent" (Freud, 1917/1957) therapist's neutrality, restricted rate of verbalization, impersonal

diction, and refusals to provide advice or affirmations about actions taken, the spatial and temporal boundaries that separate patient and therapist are also *real* deprivations.

The very human imperfections of the "good enough" psychotherapist confront patients with still another potent source of conflict. All therapists make mistakes, perhaps the most important of which are the failures of empathy that inevitably occur during a lengthy and ambitious psychotherapy. In the ordinary conduct of psychotherapy, empathic failures take various forms, such as premature interpretations, accurate but narrowly apprehended interpretations, inadvertently intrusive assertions of certainty ("You *must* have felt . . ."), generalities that compromise a patient's uniqueness, and defensively prompted retreats from empathic immersion in a patient's psychic reality. Empathic failures such as these are, for patients, mini-experiences of separation and loss. They engender a feeling of not being recognized or understood and, hence, of being alone.

Individuals beginning therapy vary enormously in their readiness and ability to recognize, tolerate, and deal openly with the felt internality of the conflicts, depressive states, and memories of unempathic parenting precipitated by the varying sources of separation and frustration inherent in psychotherapy. Individuals who fall within the normal-neurotic range of functioning can usually be expected to experience the contradictory tugs of conflict exerted by feelings that can be localized, distinguished, and described. They tend to organize conflicts in terms of feelings that are differentiated with respect to their ideational and affective components and, when testing the limits of their therapist's authority or availability, do so within the work structure of therapy, as defined by the therapist. Once they have established an emotional attachment to their therapists, enforced separations occasionally arouse within them complex blends of love and hate, relief and regret, deprivation and longing. Intermittently, the status inequalities and power differentials that separate the positions of patient and therapist provoke similar conflicts as well as interpersonal struggles for mutuality and autonomy. And, in response to their therapists' failures of empathy, patients suffering from neurotic character disorders are apt, at varying levels of intensity, to feel sad, fearful, lonely, needy, helpless, self-hating, hostile toward others, apathetic, withdrawn, or hypochondriacal. In general, these feelings and struggles do not overwhelm the therapeutic alliance but, rather, serve to catalyze more or less frank discussions of the personal, especially unconscious, meanings for the patient of the inherently frustrating limits on the relationship to the therapist. These discussions bring conflicts that originated in childhood and the defenses associated with them into consciousness and, in an inseparable fashion, initiate qualitative changes in a patient's capacity to benefit from the opportunities for interpersonal learning made available in therapy. Gradually, these discussions uncover and attenuate a patient's being influenced and gratified by the "nonspecific" healing ingredients of psychotherapy (Frank, 1973; Strupp, 1976).

A therapist's empathy and interpretations, as offered, occur within a context in which information is concurrently being transmitted by voice quality, gaze, facial expressions, limb movements, posture, odor, touch, and the animate and inanimate objects that inhabit the therapist's office. These nonlexical contributions to the therapeutic situation convey, *indirectly,* the therapist's empathy, as well as calmness, nonintrusiveness, interest, hopefulness, gentleness, respect, and competence. Moreover, interpretations always contain implicit statements about the therapist himself and his emotional attitudes toward the patient. As Rycroft (1956) has noted, a "correct" interpretation says, in effect, "I am still here. I have been listening to you. I understand what you are talking about. I remember what you said yesterday, last week, last month, last year. I have been sufficiently interested to listen, and remember, and understand. Also you are not the only person to have felt this way. You are not incomprehensible. I am not shocked. I am not admonishing you or trying to get you to conform to any ideas of my own as to how you should feel or behave" (p. 472). As a totality, these implicit, nonlexically conveyed messages embody the therapist's so-called nonspecific contributions to the therapeutic dialogue.

Opinions differ on just what conditions must exist if the

insights resulting from accurate interpretations are to initiate enduring changes in the ways patients cope with the stress of separations. The majority opinion among analytic therapists is that successful participation in an insight-oriented therapy demands the capacity to bring to awareness the simultaneity of the opposing feelings, impulses, beliefs, and goals that structure the inner experience of conflict (for example, Krystal, 1979). Schafer (1973a) would additionally argue that it is not expanding awareness itself that promotes growth and change but, rather, the free and open communication of expanded awareness within the context of a relationship that is consistently experienced as benignly influential. My own view is that, for insights to achieve their desired ends, the patient must also be capable of storing, reproducing faithfully, and yielding to the "corrective emotional experiences" (Alexander and French, 1946) carried by the therapist's specific and nonspecific contributions to the therapeutic dialogue.

The Schizoid Dilemma. These various conditions are not prevailing during the opening phases of the treatment of patients who have defensively withdrawn into enduring maladaptive states of separateness. Patients whom Guntrip (1969) would call schizoid "stand apart" from their bodies, from conflicts, and from intimate relationships. A schizoid patient's characteristic orientation to the external world is never to become attached to anybody or anything that might become indispensable. Although such patients complain of feeling trapped inside a "plastic bubble" or a "cocoon" or behind a "sheet of glass," allowing nothing of emotional importance to leave or enter, they nevertheless rigidly attempt to maintain "an illusion of self-sufficiency" (Modell, 1976) early in therapy. Schizoid patients have pronounced needs for privacy and dignity. They experience the invitation to speak truthfully about themselves as inherently subversive and are extremely reluctant to acknowledge that they have "wishes" or that, for the gratification or relief of "needs," benign, predictable, and giving others must exist in the external world. In their efforts to avoid conflicts and disappointments, they may try to forsake all desires for unity, belonging, and love. Because "wishes are to the mind as

needs are to the body" (Rieff, 1961, p. 79), pronounced schizoid tendencies alienate individuals from their bodies as well as
from interpersonal relationships. Furthermore, schizoid patients
experience an absolute contradiction between the state of being
authentically involved *in* an experience and simultaneously
bringing self-reflectiveness to bear on that experience. Consequently, they are alienated as well from the concrete and palpable aspects of their own experience.

The conscious efforts of schizoid patients to attend to
the "perceptual reality" of the therapeutic dialogue are also
more or less disembodied. Schizoid patients are cut off from access to the physicality of the therapeutic situation. Like grief's
self-absorption, schizoid detachment precludes receptivity to
interpersonal influence or to the external cues that convey com-
passion. Though exquisitely sensitive to variations in their therapists' depth of involvement, schizoid patients cannot feel the
animating presence of their therapists or the bodily closeness
implicit in all forms of verbal intimacy. They are unable to tolerate subjective awareness of the therapist's caring concern and
genuine interest. They cannot look directly at their therapists
and risk seeing whether there is the possibility of gratifying
chronically disavowed wishes for consolation or forgiveness.
They cannot risk feeling with an empathic therapist who appreciates their loneliness, their stoic self-reliance, and their hyper-
developed sense of irony. In brief, because of pronounced tendencies toward disembodiment and emotional inaccessibility,
schizoid patients lack intimate knowledge of whether or not
their therapists are conveying the nonspecific healing ingredients of psychotherapy. Given that the same processes make
possible sensitivity to and awareness of one's own and another's
bodily states, the insights produced by schizoid patients are
therefore in danger of remaining colorless, sterile, and disappointingly nontransformative.

Equally formidable therapeutic challenges are posed by
patients suffering from borderline personality disorders (Kernberg, 1976). Whereas schizoid patients begin each hour as if
they were greeting a stranger, borderline patients, early in therapy, develop an intense addictionlike attachment to their ther-

apist. They cling to their therapist's concrete presence as if the therapist were an irreplaceable object of use. Yet, like schizoid patients, they have great difficulty assimilating the sensuous fullness of the therapeutic dialogue. Consequently, they are significantly less capable of constructing, inwardly sustaining, and internalizing the realistic and comforting representations of their therapists than normal-neurotic patients. They seem to use their therapists like a drug whose positive effects wear off rapidly between sessions. Further complicating therapeutic work with borderline patients is their greater difficulty than neurotic patients in coherently formulating and talking openly about the negative feelings, images, cravings, and ideas activated by the disappointments and separations intrinsic in psychotherapy.

The Borderline Condition and a Reduced Sense of Conflict. In order to preserve our illusions, certainty, and innocence, we all occasionally "keep apart," or actively dissociate, mutually contradictory perspectives on ourselves or others. Investigations of the cognitive functioning of borderline patients indicate that they, by contrast, rigidly adopt an undialectical, either/or stance toward distinctions of all kinds—for example, yes/no, inside/outside, male/female, weak/strong, dependent/independent, self/nonself (Kernberg, 1976). Patients who chronically segregate positively and negatively charged attributes into such dichotomous categories do not, strictly speaking, experience intrapsyshic conflict or ambivalence. Rather, they are vulnerable to emotional turmoil, emotional upheaval, and precipitous transitions between all-encompassing "good" and "bad" moods (Geller, 1984).

Borderline patients are particularly notorious for the radically discontinuous ways in which they alternate between extreme polarized and dissociated states of mind and roles vis-à-vis their therapists. Often within a single hour they will both pick a fight and demand proof of emotional support, only to refuse warmth when given. They may report suicidal feelings and immediately thereafter ask to reduce the frequency of their sessions. They may relate to the therapist first as a powerful, omniscient figure worthy of being supplicated, only to treat him or her, soon after, as an individual to be demeaned and depreciated. Concomitantly, they may rapidly fluctuate between a view of their situation as futile and of themselves as totally worthless, hopeless, and helpless and the megalomaniacal illusion that complete recovery or cure is imminent.

Though obvious to their therapists, these sudden shifts and contradictions are not apparent to patients, for whom there exist separate divisions of "good" and "bad" selves, as well as actively kept-apart "good" and "bad" others. As Horowitz and Zilberg (1983) have observed, "The patient is the 'I,' the therapist is the 'you,' without the recognition of there being, simultaneously and potentially, another 'I' and another 'you' " (p. 289).

Excessive reliance on defenses such as splitting, denial, and projective identification (Kernberg, 1976) can impair the ability to tolerate the felt experience of simultaneously activated, incompatible dispositions to action. Like the early stages of grief, an "authoritarian" (Adorno, Frenkel-Brunswik, Levinson, and Sanford, 1950) style of information processing limits the distinctiveness, variety, and communicability of the feelings available to an individual. Accordingly, when patients habitually dissociate mutually contradictory self- and object representations, "regression" can be discerned in the nature, as well as the handling and expression, of the affects that are provoked by the stress of separations.

I regard affects as regressed to the extent that they are represented in awareness without significant psychic elaboration, symbolization, or ideation. Affects that are located in close proximity to the primitive trunk of emotion are almost totally somatic. They are "unstructured," are lacking in specific meanings, and are difficult to translate into emotion words. Like pervasive moods, affects in their regressed forms blur the distinction between the experienced self and the experienced world. During adulthood, affect regression does not generally manifest itself as a total or unchangeable phenomenon but as ever changing in clinical picture and severity (Arlow and Brenner, 1964). However, regression may proceed to the point where an individual characteristically feels out of control, vulnerable to impulsive action, and "dis-eased" when dealing with ruptures of attachment from valued others.

These various tendencies can be discerned in the commonly reported observation that borderline patients respond to enforced separations from their therapists with suicidal gestures, morbid disturbances of self-esteem, and various psychophysiological disturbances, including psychomotor retardation or agitation. This constellation of symptoms has been found to differentiate "pathological grief" from the normal depressions that accompany acute bereavement (Jacobs and Kosten, 1983). When suffering in this way, borderline patients feel "entitled" to engage their therapists in transactions across the spatial and temporal boundaries that separate the therapist from the patient. During these hoped-for extratherapeutic interactions (for example, telephone calls, unscheduled visits), they are given to expressing feelings of helpless distress, confusion, impotence, impending disintegration, or even death, in a dependently demanding and/or paranoid fashion.

At times, even the most well-timed or accurate interpretation cannot contain borderline patients within the contractually agreed-on temporal framework of the therapy relationship. When working with them on an outpatient basis, psychotherapists must therefore delicately integrate the explicit exercise of their "managerial" functions (Newton, 1973) and their empathic responsibilities. A therapist can remain empathically attuned to the borderline patient's efforts to cope with intersession intervals by bearing in mind that the length and breadth of time, as experienced, are relative. When the patient is experiencing imperious longings and uncertainties, even a momentary separation can feel like a prolonged or even permanent loss. A disregulated conception of time, not simply entitlement, hostile impulses, or the wish to control the therapist, is visible in the borderline patient's efforts to cope with separations. Consequently, the work requires the ability to maintain a firm, programatic, and objective stance toward transactions across the external boundaries between patient and therapist; otherwise, the therapy relationship could duplicate the chaos of the borderline patient's other relationships. Clinical experience substantiates that clear definition of the roles of patient and therapist, including an authoritative and predictable stance toward transactions "outside" therapy, is inherently reassuring to patients who are rendered confused and disorganized by separations, notwithstanding the storminess of their transactions at the ends of hours.

A therapist can infer from the "exit lines" (Gabbard, 1982) that he or she uses to indicate that a session is over how guilty or how comfortable he or she feels about imposing time limits and spatial restrictions on a particular patient. "We will continue next time" promotes a process-oriented view of therapy without the implicit coercion to be found in the concluding statement "We will talk more about that next week." By comparison, some exit lines obscure the therapist's authority (for example, "We *have* to end now") or apologize for this authority (for example, "I'm sorry, our time is up for today").

To effectively exercise one's authority while remaining empathically attuned to the psychic reality of patients suffering from the more profound forms of character pathology taxes the emotional maturity and technical skills of the most seasoned therapist. Borderline patients inevitably arouse intense and disquieting feelings of grandiosity, anger, and confusion in their therapists. However, when patients are relentlessly avoidant of intimacy and authenticity, the therapist faces struggles with boredom, sleepiness, and loneliness. Such countertransference reactions are implicated in precipitously ended as well as unnecessarily prolonged therapy relationships. However, like the mini-separations that punctuate the therapeutic process, therapists can turn to advantage countertransference-based ruptures of attachment by empathizing with their emotional consequences for a patient. In this regard, Kaiser (1965) placed the management and understanding of a therapist's inclination to withdraw emotionally from his or her patient(s) at the core of his theory of psychotherapy. My efforts in this direction are guided by the assumption that giving patients the opportunity to experience and express (at progressively higher levels of organization) their "disappointments" in the person of the therapist and the process of therapy opens up the possibility of nurturing the development of the representational capacities needed to reconcile the flaws, contradictions, and paradoxes inherent in *all* persons and relationships and to facilitate formation of more recognizable, desomaticized, and communicable memories of childhood attachments and separations. The conceptual starting point for this clinical strategy is the hypothesis that the processes that promote maturation of differentiated affects and those that give rise to creation of evocative memories are correlated and mediated by the process of introjection.

The Processes and Products of Introjection

Introjection is an evolving concept within psychoanalytic theory (Meissner, 1981) and bears many similarities to the proliferating array of schemalike concepts being advanced by social and cognitive psychologists (Singer, 1985). According to the theoretical model that guides this chapter, introjection is that form of internalization which gives rise to the creation of cognitive/affective representations of the reciprocally contingent nature and dyadic structure of the self-in-relation-to-others. This view is consistent with Loewald's (1962) hypothesis that what is internalized is relations with external objects, not the objects themselves. (In psychoanalytic parlance, an object may be a person, a psychological or physical part of a person, a tool, an inanimate aspect of the environment, or a symbol. When human objects are referred to here, I shall use the term *other*.) The hypothesis that it is *relationships* to others rather than others themselves that are internalized suggests that whenever a person brings to awareness "evocative memories" (Fraiberg, 1969) of a significant other, discernible cues or signs that they are occurring, inextricably, against a background of evocative memories of the self should be present. The crux of Sullivan's (1953) theorizing pointed in this direction.

There are accumulating research data to support the conclusion that schematic representations of the self and others are not merely the imaginative by-products of fantasy but have the capacity to organize and directly influence attention, memory, and the felt appraisal of experience (Singer, 1985). In a similar vein, psychoanalytic theorists presume that introjects have the capacity to replace relations to an external object, to stabilize them, or to supplement them with relations to mental representations of an internalized object (Cameron, 1961; Dorpat, 1979; Giovacchini, 1975; Volkan, 1976). Though integral components of behavioral systems, the roles or functions that the objects of an introjected relationship serve for an individual are not necessarily consciously perceived. The available evidence suggests that the mental models of relationships acquired specifically as a function of early attachment- and separation-related events tend to operate outside conscious awareness and to resist dramatic change (Main, Kaplan, and Cassidy, 1985).

When brought to awareness, the objects of introjected relationships are experienced as separate, to lesser or greater degrees, from the subjectively grasped sense of self. Temporary suspension of the reflective self-representation that one is daydreaming enables individuals to experience the objects of introjected relationships that are brought to consciousness as "imaginary felt presences" existing within the confines of the mind or body or both (Schafer, 1968). Individuals conceive of their relations with these presences as analogous to their relations to an external object, including those that have been lost in actuality. This tendency is implicated in the experience of conflict, including the contradictory nature of grief. Bereaved individuals often treat painful memories and constantly recurring images of loved ones who have been lost as "cherished burdens" (Moffat, 1982). Moffat describes as follows her own paradoxical reaction to the passing of grief: "Feeling better, more frequently surprised by joy, as was Wordsworth, I also felt a sense of betrayal of my husband, even though I rationally knew that sustained grief would be morbid. Because grief may become a substitute for the dead one, giving up our grief can be the greatest challenge of mourning" (p. xxvii).

Psychotherapy can be critical in assisting the process of mourning (see Chapter Twelve), in facilitating the surrendering of the internalized relationship (the introject), and in working through the natural ambivalence of loss (anger, or repressed anger and guilt). A primary focus of a psychotherapy guided by these basic goals would consist in the "externalization" of mental models of relationships to the extent that differentiated conflicts and memories, with specific meanings, could materialize in the privacy of consciousness.

The Language of Conflict. The metaphors an individual uses to group and explain the opposing tendencies that constitute the experience of conflict provide a valuable avenue for exploring the emotional and conceptual maturity with which that person conducts relationships with mental representations of internalized others. At the introjective level of symbolization, action fantasies, varying in the extent to which they rely on the metaphor of internalized persons, arise during efforts to resolve or master emotional conflicts. Individual differences along this continuum tend to be correlated with the security of a person's attachments. Patients who are able to sustain contact and communication with absent others also tend to organize conflicts involving their separateness in terms of real and imagined transgressions against vividly constituted representations of autonomous, approving and/or disapproving whole human figures. In their fantasies, their differentiated strivings and wishes for autonomy are confronted with the antithetical values and prohibitions of persons, groups, and/or a vast array of nonhumans personified with human qualities, such as pets, institutions, and deities.

During development, abstractions and moral principles increasingly come to serve as symbolic substitutes for imagistic representations of persons in positions of authority. Some patients speak as if they were in bondage to moral absolutes such as duty or truth; others, as if they were being assailed, persecuted, or gratified by, and in passive relation to, imagistic representations of their parents' moral commands. Prior to the achievement of "secondary autonomy" (Hartmann, 1939/ 1958), either stylistic choice implies a diminished feeling of conscious self-determination.

Individuals who have great difficulty maintaining lively internal relationships with realistically conceived human beings tend to speak as if they were dominated and driven by the part properties of persons (for example, the voice of conscience, a wagging finger) or quasi-human figures and creatures (for example, monsters). When individuals who are functioning at the lower levels of "person constancy" imaginatively gaze within, they discover the presence of vague and unassimilated "pressures," "forces," and ameboid "things" or "shadows" which have the property of "otherness" and which render them unable to perform various actions. At still more regressed levels, the other's felt presence can be unconsciously represented in the chronic persistence of rigidly held and stereotyped facial expressions, gestures, postures. Here, bodily pain may not be distinguishable from the painful feelings that conflicts inspire within and between people.

Self/Other Differentiation and the Narcissistic Condition. In some pathological states, the objects of an introjected relationship may be phenomenologically confused with or mistaken for the subjectively grasped sense of self. The link between incompletely differentiated self- and object representations and regressive reactions to ruptures of attachment is recognized in Kohut's (1971) concept of the "selfobject." Selfobjects are described by Kohut and Wolf (1978) as those "objects which we experience as part of our self; the expected control over them is therefore closer to the concept of the control which a grown-up expects to have over his own body and mind than the concept of control which he expects to have over others" (p. 414). Kohut regards a person as suffering from a narcissistic personality disorder to the extent that he or she is dominated by the need to use the therapist as a selfobject in order to maintain self-esteem, vitality, a sense of purposiveness, personal coherence, and temporal stability.

According to Kohut, a tenuous or fragmented sense of self and the felt inability to perform these functions for oneself are diagnostic of the traumatic effects of childhood disillusionment with idealized parents. He believes that patients so impaired seek, in a regressive manner, to re-create within the context of selfobject transferences the subject-centered gradiosity of early childhood and the small child's belief in the possibility of merging with the calmness, infallibility, and omnipotence of perfect parental figures. Clinical manifestations of narcissism, so conceived, include the failure to acknowledge that the therapist exists outside the role of "my therapist" and the expectation that the therapist will serve as a symbiotic partner who totally shares and participates in the patient's experience. When functioning narcissistically, patients do not perceive their therapists as having a separate existence of their own; the therapist is perceived exclusively from the perspective of the satisfaction and frustration of the patient's wishes. For Kohut, empathic attunement requires of the therapist the capacity to allow for and respond flexibly to a patient's needs for such an idealizing relationship as well as the patient's fears of and defenses against merging with an idealized symbiotic partner. At the extremes, narcissistic patients manifest an inability to distinguish clearly between imaginative fantasies about the therapist and memories that are based on real events or the more objective characteristics of the therapist. In essence, narcissistic patients are embedded in their own point of view without clearly being aware that they have a point of view.

That a selfobject transference is emerging can be inferred from the emotions a patient experiences when the therapist fails or is unwilling to serve a function that the patient believes he or she should perform. When disappointed by their therapists, individuals who are moving toward individuation experience a variety of intelligible depressive states that are accompanied by a contemplative appreciation of imperfections or a willingness to forgive, with a wistful acknowledgment of the universal longing for preambivalent relationships. Levinson and others (1978) coined the term *de-illusionment* to describe this constellation of focused, neutralized, and thoughtlike feelings and reactions. By contrast, when patients are in the throes of an idealizing selfobject transference, disappointments give rise to physiologically diffuse and conceptually vague feelings of devitalization, worthlessness, panic, despair, and inconsolability. Disappointments, experienced at such regressed levels of affectivity, call into question the overall acceptance or rejection of the relationship and are expressed either in hatefulness and excessive demands or in emotional withdrawal.

Central to Kohut's position is the belief that patients suffering from narcissistic personality disorders require the opportunity gradually and fully to experience an idealizing transference within the context of a relationship in which the therapist functions empathically as a selfobject and in which the patient experiences the therapist as unempathic at times, at conscious and preconscious levels. Kohut recommends neither the acceptance of idealizations nor their manipulation but, rather, an empathic exploration of real, imagined, and provoked disruptions of idealization and the discovery of the precipitating events that lead to the disruptions of the idealizing transference. He maintains that the pursuit of such empathic understandings promotes both the gradual appropriation to consciousness of the traumatic effects of unempathic parenting and the "transmuting internalizations" that bring about "structural leaps" in the development of a cohesive sense of self.

In adopting this position, Kohut echoes and expands on Freud's seminal hypothesis that activation of the processes of introjection requires the loss or threatened loss of an object as a precondition. Freud's (1917/1957, 1923/1961) investigations of moral development and mourning led him to this hypothesis. He invoked the concept of introjection to explain how the guiding, restraining, punishing functions originally imposed on children by their parents were re-created on the intrapersonal terrain of self-experience (that is, in the superego). Freud believed that the shift from regulation by the environment to self-regulation, as mediated by introjection, required as a precondition the relinquishment of ambivalently held aggressive and sexual impulses toward the parents.

The pivotal role of relinquished relationships in activating the processes of internalization reappears in Freud's overarching conclusion that "the character of the ego is a precipitate of abandoned object cathexes and contains the history of those object choices" (1923/1961, p. 23). Schwaber (1971, p. 147) summarizes the essence of Freud's views as follows: "When we lose persons important to us or have to give up an earlier mode of relating to them, we try nonetheless to keep them with us by setting up a remembrance within the ego. If then we rage unconsciously at being deserted, or give vent to old ambivalences toward them, we suffer because we are angry at what has become an aspect of ourselves. . . . The superego is a special grouping of identifications within the ego distilled from our earliest and most important loves and losses, our parents."

In the context of therapy, these remembrances and identifications assume individual forms within the evolving transferential phenomena. In accord with classical psychoanalytic technique, idealizations are routinely interpreted as transference resistances against acknowledgment of components of the oedipus complex such as hostile-rivalrous attitudes (Gedo, 1975). Kernberg (1976) alternatively regards idealizations as a defense against pre-oedipal primitive envy and aggression. According to Kohut's point of view, idealization transferences may defensively serve these functions, and they may also serve to prevent reactivation of unbearable states of rage, sorrow, helplessness, and other primitive residues of the traumatic effects of unempathic parenting.

It is extremely difficult to differentiate trauma from pathogenic influence in general. Inferences from clinical data have led me to the view that when patients seem driven to experience the therapeutic situation as necessarily and relentlessly disappointing, they may be demonstrating, as precisely as they can, lexically inexpressible memories of separations and losses that operated like traumas in their effects during childhood. In a similar vein, Lipin (1963) has reasoned that when patients rigidly hold the conviction that the therapist will be cold, unresponsive, unreliable, unpredictable, arbitrary, and deliberately humiliating, or when they repetitively interact with their therapists in ways that invite rejection, they may be doing so not only for defensive purposes but in order to produce replicas of memories that have never been fully conscious or capable of relatively organized expression. Cohen (1980) likewise believes that his research supports the view that memories of childhood traumas are not withdrawn from consciousness merely because of their offensive contents but, rather, overwhelm the capacity to form memory traces. He maintains that they "are not only unrecallable in the ordinary sense that repressed memories are. Rather, they are unavailable for recall because they do not employ adequate mental representations even in the unconscious" (p. 423).

The various psychotherapy literatures have emphasized clinical strategies for helping patients *recover* repressed representational memories and percepts that, at one time, were consciously known. Far less attention has been devoted to helping patients *construct* memories, revived and repeated in the transference, which are unconscious because they have never been coherently formulated.

Forms of Representing the Forgotten Past. My own efforts to discover and describe the structure of unconscious memories and fantasies draw heavily on the view that character-based cleavages and restrictions in gaining access to one's personal past often result from imbalances in the *forms* of representation that encode the affective and cognitive components of internalized interpersonal experiences. I am using the term *form* here to refer to the end products of the enactive or sensory-motor, imagistic, and symbolic modes or systems of processing new experiences, constructing inner models of experiences, and representing past experiences to awareness (Piaget, 1954; Bruner, 1964). Selective reconstructions of persons or events, in their physical absence, can take place in one or more of these modes of representation. For example, memories of the "weight," or "heaviness," of loss may be enacted behaviorally, through the assumption of various postures, gestures, and facial expressions. Memories of losses encountered during the earliest stages of development are organized exclusively at a sensory-motor level of representation (Schimek, 1975). This aspect of the forgotten past is continuously presented to others in the form of an individual's personal style of bodily movement (Geller, 1978). When representations of an event find expression in the imagistic mode, individuals reexperience sensory/perceptual processes similar to those that were activated when the event actually occurred. There is growing evidence that it is in the imagistic mode that unresolved traumatic episodes, disavowed self-appraisals, and conflicted interpersonal fantasies may enter awareness after a prolonged period of repression (Singer, 1974). Such imaginings may include vivid nightmares, obsessively reviewed pictorializations of scenes involving an estranged other, and memories of the way the other smelled or tasted. Symbolic representations predominantly include intrusive repetitions of or reflections on the elements of a memory that are namable by words and their grammatical organization. The process of recalling to mind a flow of verbal meanings that stand for a memory to which they are related can obviously arouse intense feelings. Nevertheless, enactive and imagistic representations stand in closer proximity to actual, immediate physical experience than do more abstract and symbolic forms of representation.

Bruner's (1964) studies of cognitive growth show that, during the course of development, the processes of differentiation result in the articulation of functional boundaries between the enactive, imagistic, and lexical modes of representation. Thus, not only do these modes acquire their own unique properties, but their relations may come to be either mutually facilitating and congruent or, to varying extents, disjunctive. Insofar as a memory is encoded in more than one of these modes of representation (Crowder, 1970), crucial aspects of that memory may be "lost" because of the inability to translate information from one mode to another. It is impossible for a unitary memory trace to materialize when the modes of representation that bring information to consciousness are dissociated from one another. When "enactive memories" (Dorpat, 1983) that are cut off from access to imagistic and symbolic representations of the "same" event are reactivated, unsuspectingly and without warning, in response to some stimulus, remembering is functionally equivalent to repeating the experience. Because each mode organizes the "reality" of an event differently, changes in the relations among modes can prompt far-reaching changes in the vividness, duration, intensity, amount of detail, and emotional meanings of a particular memory.

Like Horowitz and Zilberg (1983), I believe that "neurotic styles" (Shapiro, 1965) of information processing impose significant functional restrictions on one's capacity to explore, coordinate, and integrate the enactive, imagistic, and lexical modes of representation. Consequently, my working clinical model prominently includes strategies that initiate qualitative changes in the relations among the sensuous modes of representation that are called into play during the therapeutic dialogue.

In order to extend one's awareness of these forms of sentience, one must temporarily liberate the mind from practical purposes, including the search for hidden meanings. It requires a leap of faith for some patients and some therapists to attend to the esthetic surface of experience as it emerges into consciousness. In order to gain intimate knowledge of the processes of formulation which culminate in mental contents and which precede speech, it is necessary, moreover, to allocate attention in a sensuously receptive manner (Deikman, 1974). I actively encourage patients to "recognize" or "sense" how they organize, selectively, the content of experience while using and translating among the enactive, imagistic, and symbolic modes of representation. With varying degrees of skill and anxiety, they begin to recognize how the process of recalling a memory can be aborted at various preparatory levels of formulation before the memory appears clearly in consciousness. They also discover how inhibitions to awareness, as revealed by discontinuities in experience, occur at the boundaries between these representational systems (Horowitz, 1972). In turn, progressive elaboration and integration of the relations between modes of representation help patients bring to awareness, more readily and vividly, dissociated and lexically inexpressible memories, some of which may never have been fully conscious or capable of being given relatively organized expression. Viewed from this perspective, the therapeutic process is not so much a matter of "lifting" repressions as a means of providing patients with structuralizing and humanizing experiences.

I have found metaphors particularly useful in stimulating multimodal memories—that is, in connecting or reconnecting modes and levels of expressive functioning. Recasting abstract statements (Patient: "I felt criticized when you said the hour was over . . .") into body-centered metaphors (Therapist: "You looked like I slapped you across the face when I . . .") strengthens the concreteness and palpability of subjective awareness. Promoting these changes enriches a patient's conscious efforts to attend to external reality and the state of the body itself. Appropriately chosen metaphors thus provide patients with emotionally significant information and increase the likelihood that

they will "take in" and constructively remember recent interactions with the therapist. These two sources of gain make a required and inseparable contribution to the unfolding of the representational capacities that enable an individual to attain an
integrated and constant sense of "Self."

Empathy, Introjection, and the
Journey Toward Individuation

Many rival versions of what constitutes the "Self" coexist
without final reconciliation (Horowitz and Zilberg, 1983).
Some theorists (for example, Schafer, 1973b) regard the Self as
a superordinate self-representation, a summary formulation considering at once all of the following: the bodily me, the realization that one is not the other but a being in one's own right,
narcissistic aspirations driven by and experienced as ambitions,
the emotions of pride and humiliation, extensions of the self,
including identifications with possessions (both animate and inanimate), as well as loyalties to groups, nations, abstract moral
values, and religious ideals, self-images of present abilities, sta-
tuses, roles, and the pursuit of long-range goals regarded as central to personal existence and the sense of futurity (Allport,
1955). Still others (for example, Kohut, 1971) find it useful to
postulate the existence of a synthesizer, or "self of selves,"
which transcends and is responsible for the inward unity among
all the principal functions and properties that have been attributed to the Self. Whether or not a distinguishable, substantive
single Self exists, the component elements of the selves of the
patients seeking psychotherapy exist in varying degrees of contradiction, disjointedness, or integration.

A person can be said to be approaching individuation
(Jung, 1965) when the representations that constitute his or
her sense of self are coordinated, complexly organized, and coherently interrelated so that they add up effortlessly to form an
invisible whole. Persons who are moving toward individuation
possess a valued, coherent, and stable identity that springs from
and comprises all the "persons" within them. They live comfortably in and with the knowledge that a basically solid sense

of self is not monolithic in nature (Searles, 1977). Their subjective experience is characterized, to borrow a phrase from Loewald (1976), by a sense of "unity within multiplicity." Moreover, when a person's identities are differentiated and hierarchically arranged, the distinction between the self and the external world feels substantial and natural.

Various benefits accrue to individuals who possess these attributes. Individuals who feel secure in their own identities are able to erect a firm line of demarcation between themselves and the pressures and influences of the external world. They know which experiences, feelings, and opinions are peculiarly their own. The consolidation of an *initial* adult identity also brings with it an increased capacity to reexperience symbioticlike modes of relatedness for a variety of adaptive purposes.

Giving as well as receiving empathy presumes the ability to participate in intimate exchanges in which there is an interpenetration of self and other. Parents or therapists who can extend themselves, selectively and nonintrusively, into the experience of their children or patients are able to discover ways of providing care that are empathically attuned to the children's or patients' particular needs. When in need of help themselves, individuals who feel secure in their own identities can enter into and use relationships in which there is a blending or sharing of the functions and experiences of valued others. They can, for example, augment and alter their capacity for human relatedness through the medium of "identificatory love" (Loewald, 1976). According to Loewald, identificatory love is a form of mentation that "does not structure or divide reality into the poles of inner and outer, subject and object, self and others" (p. 39). This fluid and "symbiotic" mode of relatedness enables individuals who possess an overriding sense of identity to relinquish, in controlled and reversible ways, the burdens of defining the self in terms of separateness from others. In situations of deep intimacy, identificatory love enables individuals who have developed a stable sense of self to "take in," or introject, functional aspects of a caring relationship and, in so doing, expand or refine attributes that may not be adequately represented in their own personalities.

Internalization and the Psychotherapy Relationship. The development of new, more caring images of self and other is thus facilitated when patients constructively accept the relaxation of the boundaries between themselves and their therapists brought about by participating in reciprocal exchanges having the quality of rhythmic synchronization (Geller, 1985). Introjection takes advantage of the fact that rhythmic synchronization of the therapeutic dialogue inspires mutuality and co-oscillation and makes it easier (or at least possible) to cross the boundaries separating patient and therapist. When these conditions prevail, patients, without their knowledge or consent, begin to imitate, to mirror, the nonspecific healing ingredients of psychotherapy as embodied in their therapists' habits, mannerisms, facial expressions, and vocal qualities. Mirroring an empathic therapist's calm bodily state (or imagined calm bodily state) and warm facial expressions initiates changes in a patient's experience of diffuse and poorly localized sensations having to do with muscle tension, posture, temperature, equilibrium, vibration, rate and depth of breathing, and resonance. By yielding to the bodily changes brought about by such reciprocal coanesthetic (Spitz, 1965) stimulation, patients increasingly learn how to empathize with themselves. This form of softening ego boundaries, on a bodily level, provides, I believe, one of the bases that make possible nondefensively motivated forms of introjecting the "atmosphere" of being in the presence of an empathic therapist.

It will be recalled that psychoanalytic use of the concept of introjection is intertwined with the view that it is the structure of a disrupted or relinquished relationship that is preserved in the form of an introject. What is being suggested here is that introjection can also operate silently and spontaneously, like the incidental learning that occurs in conditioning paradigms, when patients do not need to cling rigidly to their sense of self. In a similar vein, Eagle and Wolitzky (1982, p. 353) quote Rangell as concluding that in the analysis of neurotic patients there is "a constant series of microidentifications." What is further being suggested here is that the wish to reexperience symbiotic modes of relatedness is not in itself pathological or immature, nor does the need to suspend the boundaries that separate self and other necessarily entail a defensive retreat from intrapsychic autonomy. In fact, working with patients who expect that feeling and thinking with an empathic therapist will overwhelm, perhaps irreversibly, an already tenuous and fragmented sense of self necessitates clinical strategies that promote the maturation, rather than the relinquishing, of the wishes and capacities to participate in symbiotic modes of relatedness.

Individuals who are uncertain about their existence as separate beings are seriously threatened by their positive yearnings and unsatisfied longings for empathy. To be known, empathically, jeopardizes the precarious sense of individuality, cohesion, and stability of patients who feel that the distinction between self and others is illusory and artificial. Consequently, warmth, concern, consensus, and tenderness, expressed either by the therapist or by the patients themselves, are experienced as more threatening than gratifying. This need/fear dilemma achieves terrifying proportions in the lives of schizophrenic patients (Laing, 1965). Many "first breaks" with reality are precipitated by the dissolving sense of self brought about by a re-experiencing of "merging" or "fusing" with caring others.

When patients have never established a clearly delineated sense of self as separate from the external world, promoting access to symbiotic modes of relatedness requires as a precondition the progressive differentiation of the "bodily me." Developmental cognitive psychologists and clinical psychoanalysts agree that the process of emerging from "embeddedness" (Schachtel, 1959) originates in the acquisition of the ability to distinguish oneself as a physical body that is separate from the bodies of others. According to the epigenetic principle of development (Erikson, 1959), the emergence of the ability to recognize and localize coanesthetic representations of the "bodily me" serves as a lifelong anchor for self-awareness and forms a necessary foundation of a body image, which, in turn, resides at the core of the adult's efforts to become a whole self. Directing attention to the organic continuity of the stream of sensations that arise within the body can provide patients who are in doubt with the surest evidence of their separate existence.

A psychotherapy that is specifically designed to promote individuation in patients for whom reexperiencing symbiotic modes of relatedness with caring others is extremely difficult should prominently include repeated and varied opportunities to experiment with being close while maintaining comfortable access to the distinction between self and nonself. Such opportunities arise from the invitation to oscillate between experiencing and reflecting on fears of and defenses against taking in the therapist's empathy and interpretations. By drawing a patient's attention to the concrete, immediate, palpable presence of the therapist, transference-based interpretations temporarily attenuate or eliminate impediments to the flow of accurate information from therapist to patient. Concurrently, therapists can increase the fullness of the information flowing toward them by making greater use of clarifications and confrontations. These interventions can be used to bring into sharper focus patients' needs for and fears of empathic closeness. In making decisions about how to space apart sound and silence, I am guided by the view that dysrhythmic human interactions engender separation anxiety and that patients experience as unempathic, at conscious and preconscious levels, their therapist's inability or unwillingness to accommodate to their "obligatory rhythms" (Kestenberg, 1966). Consequently, I try to delicately adjust my rate of vocalization, as well as my verbal utterances, to meet the idiosyncratic rhythmic requirements of each patient. For example, the sounds of a therapist's voice reassures patients who feel alone when expected to speak at length about themselves under minimal guidance. Likewise, dependently demanding patients misconstrue their therapist's interest as disappointingly inadequate unless the therapist is frequently and expressively brought to speech. By contrast, in order not to feel intruded on or entrapped, emotionally inaccessible patients require a therapist who limits his or her verbal output, as well as motility. Allowing and responding to these idiosyncratic patterns of the individual will make it possible to move the therapeutic dialogue in the direction of greater mutuality and reciprocity. Patients who have adopted the tactics of alienation are gradually encouraged to risk being close to their therapists and, indeed, even to go so far as to invite their therapists to become benignly influential introjected presences in their representational worlds.

Functional Significance of Introjection. The "new" cognitive/affective representations that patients create from their relations with their therapists vary in ease of evocation, affective tone, aliveness, felt proximity to actual experience, vividness, and a host of other formal properties (Geller, Smith-Behrends, and Hartley, 1982). Their conscious manifestations are more or less vulnerable to "contamination" (Volkan, 1976) by preexisting mental models of relationships. Newly created representations can also be characterized in terms of their functional significance for a particular individual. As early as 1934, Strachey spoke of a patient's introjection of the analyst as an auxiliary superego that helps to modify the patient's harsh superego. More recently, object relations theorists have sensitized clinicians to the possibility that "therapist introjects" (Giovacchini, 1975; Dorpat, 1979) can serve a much wider variety of functions, from wish fulfilling to problem solving (Atwood and Stolorow, 1980).

Let us briefly review some of the ways in which the ability to evoke in specific, perceptlike detail, under conditions of relaxation, the felt presence of an empathic therapist can both provide temporary respite from the burdens of self/other differentiation and promote such differentiation. Introjected representations of the therapeutic situation can function similarly to the "transitional objects" of infancy (Winnicott, 1953). They can symbolically reunite a patient with soothing images of the therapist during separations. At the onset of therapy, the furniture, plants, paintings, and books in the therapist's office, as well as the clothing worn by the therapist, may have no personal meaning, except for the concrete, momentary pleasures they provide. By contrast, patients who are moving in the direction of personalizing and internalizing the therapeutic process may symbolically re-create the familiar surroundings in which the therapist is embedded in order to relieve the pain associated with the frustrations and real limits of the therapy relationship and to assuage more generalized feelings of loneliness. While using therapist introjects in order to be soothed or consoled, patients may, unwittingly, enter more comfortably what Winnicott (1953) calls the "transitional mode of experience." In this mode the demarcation between the self and extrapersonal space is temporarily suspended, rather than negated. Winnicott observes that "it is an area not challenged, because no claim is made on its behalf except that it shall exist as a resting place for the individual engaged in the perpetual human task of keeping inner and outer reality separate yet interrelated" (p. 91). According to Winnicott, while functioning in this "intermediate area of experiencing," an individual can endow objects, concepts, or reevoked memories with lifelike qualities and roles while retaining an appreciation of their objective properties. Access to this mode of experiencing may be a psychic precondition for the "taking in" of empathy and makes possible the experience and appreciation of the therapist as simultaneously real and current, as well as transferential and historical. Therefore, even as patients are using images of the therapist as an aid in avoiding, limiting, or curbing anxiety-laden fantasies, they may be strengthening their ability to form fantasies in which reliable representations of the self-in-relation-to-others are preserved.

The dyadic structure of introjected relations with the therapist provides patients with a way to contain clashing tendencies and entertain differing perspectives on the same event. Introjected images of the therapist may assert, deny, or question a state of affairs. They may be called forth like the imaginary companions of childhood in order to gratify wishes that might otherwise be repressed or squelched. While acknowledging such desires in the other, through the medium of creative play, patients have the opportunity to stand at a distance and discover new ways of sublimating their drives. As previously noted, en route to acquiring their own autonomous values and the capacity for self-regulation, children rely on the ethical standards—both approving and forbidding—of first real and then internalized parental figures. In a similar fashion, therapist introjects can serve as inner directives that shape decisions about goodness, safety, pleasure, and survival.

Though adaptive and reparative, these functions do not

directly increase a patient's insight into the motivational and developmental origins of his or her problems in dealing with separation and loss. Rather, introjection strengthens the ego functions required for gaining emotionally intensified and intimate knowledge of oneself. In other words, the functions of observing, listening, thinking, remembering, judging, and recognizing are enhanced by the creation of introjected representations of the new modes of relatedness and information processing made available in psychotherapy.

A patient's capacity and motivation for gaining such emotionally charged self-knowledge can serve as an important guide in determining whether the termination of therapy for that individual is going to be a "prologue" (Ekstein, 1965) to further growth and development.

The Process of Terminating Therapy

For a variety of reasons, the *process* of terminating therapy, in itself, may be the most crucial aspect of a patient's treatment experience. During the extended leave-taking of the termination phase of therapy, highly influential role relationship schemes are revived, often for the first time, with clarity. The imminent ending of the relationship has the power to provoke the emergence of transference paradigms that may have been inaccessible during the initial and working-through stages of therapy. For example, the working out of the conflicts and coalitions between the "I's" and "you's" that structure the experience of separation guilt usually peak during the termination phase. (*Separation guilt* refers to the conviction that to become oneself, to be fully separate, will deprive, betray, damage, or even kill the "other." The other potentially includes former states of self that are left behind during the progressive development of a sense of self.) Moreover, it is during this phase of the relationship that patients and therapists confront most poignantly the limit on what therapy can accomplish.

Assessing Readiness for Termination. A systematic approach to the question of how to arrive at the decision to terminate a psychotherapy is still lacking. Kauff (1980) has observed that termination has been most often treated in the various psychotherapy literatures as an "isolated event" or as "the end point of the working-through phase of therapy." Kauff has recommended the use of Mahler's description of disturbances originating during a period extending from infancy to roughly four years of age, designated as the "separation/individuation" period, as a paradigm for understanding the meaning of termination as a continuing process within the total therapeutic experience. This perspective may be too restrictive. Recent investigations of adult development have revealed that the quest for individuation is far more lengthy and complex than has usually been imagined. Jung (1965) believed that individuation may not be achievable till the fifth decade of life. The work of Erikson (1959), Gould (1972), Vaillant (1977), and Levinson and associates (1978), however, also carries the implication that we are not condemned to repeat, perpetually and stereotypically, the nature and outcome of our earliest attachments to and separations from our parents. What evidence is available suggests that although the adult's reactions to attachments and separations reveal the enduring influence of childhood prototypes, the process of individuation is potentially carried forward by the ever-changing constellation of developmental tasks that confronts us as we age. Existing theories of psychotherapy have not as yet integrated an adult development perspective into their investigations of how the unique separations and losses of each developmental era can serve to reorganize the quality and substance of mental models of relationships.

The literature has focused mainly on developing criteria to assess readiness to terminate psychotherapy. Many criteria have been suggested. Frequently they reflect idealized conceptions of psychological health or the authors' values and personal philosophy of life (for example, Rogers, 1961; Horney, 1966). Relief from symptoms is probably the most frequently cited criterion (Luborsky and others, 1980). But because symptomatic improvement is unreliable as a sole measure of successful treatment, therapists are apt to rely on supplementary criteria to assess whether a decision to consider termination is appropriate (Dewald, 1961).

Other criteria frequently mentioned in the psychoanalytic literature include the capacity for love, the capacity for work, the capacity for mourning, genital primacy, the changing nature of recurring dreams, and the removal of defenses and resistances by interpretation (see Firestein, 1978, for a review of this literature). An undercurrent of dissatisfaction is betrayed in every effort to find adequate criteria to document the efficacy of psychotherapy in ways that are acceptable to academicians and to institutions that financially support the professional practice of psychotherapy. I rely on multiple and patient-specific criteria to negotiate the fact that all endings are, more or less, arbitrary, and I accept the equally humbling realization that all therapies are "incomplete."*

The Therapist's Stance During the Termination Phase. Of increasing importance to some therapists are criteria that focus attention on the therapist's relationship to the patient as it changes during the process of termination or affects that process (Balint, 1950; Edelson, 1963). Expressive of this view is the hypothesis that the work of therapy is being successfully accomplished if, among other things, patients can assume roles and functions for themselves that their therapists had previously fulfilled for them. To this end, attention is devoted during the terminal phase of psychotherapy to working through the dependency elements in the relationship (Firestein, 1978). Among psychoanalytic therapists there is considerable disagreement on whether this task is or should be facilitated by shifting the

---

*Therapies that terminate prematurely for reasons external to the therapy relationship are commonplace. For example, the realities of clinical work are such that therapists-in-training often impose administratively dictated endings on their patients. Most psychotherapy training programs are organized in such a way that student therapists change settings once a year and therefore terminate annually with the majority of their patients. This educational policy deprives many therapists of the opportunity to learn how to bring a therapy relationship to a mutually agreed-on "natural conclusion." In parallel, Keith (1966) has expressed concern over the iatrogenic consequences for patients of being left by one's therapist and/or transferred to a new therapist. Despite their ubiquity and importance, externally imposed premature terminations have received relatively scant attention in the literature (Lenzer, 1955; Pumpian-Midlin, 1958; Dewald, 1965; Whitaker, 1966; Sher, 1970; Glenn, 1971; Mikkelson and Gutheil, 1979).

structure of the relationship in a more egalitarian direction. In order to foster a patient's perception of the therapist as a real person, Buxbaum (1950) advocates becoming more spontaneous and self-disclosing. Hurn (1971) maintains that the analyst has no need to present himself as a "human being," since the entire analytic process leads inevitably to the patient's perception of "the analyst-as-he-is." Weigert (1952) takes yet another approach to this issue. Weigert believes that when therapists find themselves no longer needing to maintain a cautiously objective and neutral stance, a timely termination is approaching because the resolution of the countertransference goes hand in hand with the resolution of transference. In other words, she does not advocate role-playing this shift for technical reasons but, rather, believes that a therapist's felt readiness to engage in a more egalitarian relationship parallels the disappearance of the resistances of transference and consequently provides an important barometer of the approaching successful end of treatment. Possibly the most extreme version of this attitude is found in Searles's belief that "a successful psychoanalysis involves the analyst's deeply felt relinquishment of the patient, both as being a cherished infant and as being a fellow adult who is responded to at the level of genital love" (1965, p. 297).

An alternative hypothesis is that such changes signal a patient's growing capacity to form or symbolically create, during and outside treatment hours, enduring introjected representations of real and imagined patient/therapist interactions. A patient's greater readiness to receive help tacitly encourages some therapists to become more expressive, open, active, and spontaneous—that is, increasingly egalitarian—at the outset of the termination phase. This shift entails a change in the rhythmic structure of the therapeutic dialogue. Therapists who limit themselves to correctly timed, sparingly employed interpretations implicitly set themselves above and apart from their patients; a give-and-take conversational style is more likely to induce feelings of equality in a patient. As previously posited, rhythmic coordination of patient/therapist relations may be one of the interactional bases that permit nondefensively activated forms of introjection.

Ideally, a therapist's orientation to termination should evolve out of an understanding of his or her relationship with the particular patient and what it has meant to that patient. Realization of this goal depends, in large part, on a therapist's ability to adapt his or her depth of involvement, activity level, and expressiveness to fit the unique needs and circumstances of each patient. Studies by Geller and Nash (1975) and Greene and Geller (1980) suggest that therapists, especially beginners, experience a change in their depth of involvement during the termination phase and that this shift may be expressive of an internally consistent and possibly generalized orientation to ending relationships. It appears that beginning therapists tend to move in the direction of seeking either greater intimacy with or increasing distance from their patients as termination approaches. Unrestrained expression of either disposition during the final weeks of therapy may seriously undermine a patient's efforts to achieve autonomy. For example, therapists who, in the extreme, "act out" their need to withdraw from the relationship and from the pain of termination might well be experienced as rejecting or as prematurely stopping the work of therapy, and those therapists who need to get closer to their patients prior to the imminent ending might unwittingly inhibit the expression of anger and resentment, arouse regressive urges within their patients, or make it more difficult for them to experience, without separation guilt, the desire to leave therapy.

Introjection and the Continuation of Therapy After Termination. Dorpat (1979) has written: "Identifications are made with the subject's representations of objects, not with the actual object. It is not correct to say that one identifies with a person. Rather, one identifies with one's conscious or unconscious representation of that person" (p. 36). Following Dorpat, I assume that introjection must logically precede identification if the functions and qualities originally ascribed to the therapist are to be transformed into representations of the self as regulatory agent. Nevertheless, in the absence of normative data, it is impossible to determine whether the use of fantasies of the therapeutic relationship is a transitional mode en route to autonomous self-regulation or whether their continued use is *necessary* for autonomous self-regulation.

In order to examine empirically this and other hypotheses presented in this chapter, phenomenologically based models of both the representational forms that organize and present to awareness representations of the self-in-relation-to-others and the corresponding affects that accompany such representational forms must be created. As a first step in this direction, we have developed a methodology for investigating the content, formal properties, and functions of patients' representations of the therapeutic relationship (Geller, Smith-Behrends, and Hartley, 1982). Data from a sample of 206 psychotherapists (who themselves had been patients in psychoanalysis, psychotherapy, or both) show that the creation of multimodal representations of the therapeutic relationship and those that are used for the purpose of continuing the therapeutic dialogue is correlated with self-perceived change and growth. Moreover, our data indicate that, in situations of stress and also during sleep, the need for visual, tactile, or auditory contact with "personifications" of the therapist may continue to appear long after termination. In addition, preliminary analyses of the dreams of our subjects in which the therapist appears in the manifest content suggest that the therapeutic relationship is experienced differently according to the patient's sex. Consistent with Gilligan's (1982) understanding of women's development, the dreams of the female patients in our sample were infused with a greater preoccupation with separation and loss, and a greater acceptance of needs for relatedness, than the dreams of the male patients.

Finally, our findings suggest that an assessment of a patient's motivational priorities to discover what functions therapist introjects can serve may prove to be a sensitive index of that patient's readiness to enter the terminal phase of psychotherapy. Edelson (1963, p. 23) describes the relationship between internalization and the outcome of psychotherapy as follows: "The problem of termination is not how to get therapy stopped, or when to stop it, but how to terminate so that what has been happening keeps on 'going' inside the patient. The problem of termination is not simply one of helping the patient to achieve independence in the sense of willingness to function in the physical absence of the therapist. Most basically it is a problem of facilitating achievement by the patient of the ability to 'hang on' to the therapist (or the experience of the relationship with the therapist) in his physical absence in the form of a realistic intrapsychic representation (memories, identification associated with altered functioning) which is conserved rather than destructively or vengefully abandoned following separation, thus making mastery of this experience possible."

With this perspective in mind, I have become particularly attentive to the articulation and recurring use of fantasies of the therapeutic relationship to practice the "new" modes of looking at, listening to, talking to, and being with others that are made available during psychotherapy sessions. Symbolic re-creation of the therapeutic dialogue in the form of evocative memories provides patients with a model for continuing, in the privacy of consciousness, the work of expressive and exploratory psychotherapy. The dyadic structure of introjected relations with the therapist provides patients with a sympathetic audience before whom they can grasp and reveal that which, as yet, cannot be discussed with others. When cognitive/expressive fantasies are used in this way, they not only contribute to the temporary relief of inner turmoil but also promote acquisition of a generalizable skill for repairing affectional bonds and dealing with stressful situations, dysfunctional fears, and inhibitions in everyday life. If the psychotherapeutic process is to independently endure the physical absence of the therapist, it must have an afterlife in the form of such enduring, beneficial cognitive/affective representations. Thus, introjection of the therapeutic dialogue not only helps to preserve the gains derived from therapy but ensures the survival of the process after termination.

References

Adorno, T. W., Frenkel-Brunswik, E., Levinson, D. J., and Sanford, N. *The Authoritarian Personality*. New York: Harper & Row, 1950.

Alexander, F., and French, T. M. *Psychoanalytic Therapy*. New York: Roland Press, 1946.

Allport, G. W. *Becoming*. New Haven, Conn.: Yale University Press, 1955.

Arlow, J., and Brenner, C. *Psychoanalytic Concepts and the Structural Theory.* New York: International Universities Press, 1964.

Astrachan, B. M., Flynn, H. R., Geller, J. D., and Harvey, H. H. "A Systems Approach to Day Hospitalization." In J. H. Wasserman (ed.), *Current Psychiatric Therapies.* Orlando, Fla.: Grune & Stratton, 1971.

Atwood, G., and Stolorow, R. "Psychoanalytic Concepts and the Representational World." *Psychoanalysis and Contemporary Thought,* 1980, *3,* 267–290.

Baekeland, F., and Lundwall, L. "Dropping Out of Treatment: A Critical Review." *Psychological Bulletin,* 1975, *82,* 737–783.

Balint, M. "On the Termination of Analysis." *International Journal of Psycho-Analysis,* 1950, *31,* 196–201.

Bergin, A. E., and Strupp, H. H. *Changing Frontiers in the Science of Psychotherapy.* Chicago: Aldine-Atherton, 1972.

Blatt, S. J. "Levels of Object Representation in Anaclitic and Introjective Depression." *Psychoanalytic Study of the Child,* 1974, *29,* 107–157.

Bordin, E. S. "The Working Alliance: Basis for a General Theory of Psychotherapy." Paper presented at the annual meeting of the American Psychological Association, Washington, D.C., Sept. 1976.

Boss, M. *Daseinsanalyse and Psychoanalysis.* New York: Basic Books, 1963.

Bowlby, J. *Attachment and Loss.* Vol. 1: *Attachment.* New York: Basic Books, 1969.

Bowlby, J. *Attachment and Loss.* Vol. 2: *Separation.* New York: Basic Books, 1973.

Bruner, J. S. "The Course of Cognitive Growth." *American Psychologist,* 1964, *19,* 1–15.

Buxbaum, E. "Criteria for the Termination of an Analysis." *International Journal of Psychoanalysis,* 1950, *31,* 184–193.

Cameron, N. "Introjection, Reprojection, and Hallucination in the Interaction Between Schizophrenic Patient and Therapist." *International Journal of Psycho-Analysis,* 1961, *42,* 86–96.

Cohen, J. "Structural Consequences of Psychic Trauma: A New Look at Beyond the Pleasure Principle." *International Journal of Psycho-Analysis,* 1980, *61,* 421–432.

Crowder, R. G. "The Role of One's Own Voice in Immediate Memory." *Cognitive Psychology,* 1970, *1,* 157–178.

Deikman, A. J. "Bimodal Consciousness." In R. E. Ornstein (ed.), *The Nature of Human Consciousness.* New York: Viking Press, 1974.

Dewald, P. A. "Reactions to Forced Termination of Therapy." *Psychiatric Quarterly,* 1961, *39,* 102–125.

Dorpat, T. L. "Introjection and the Idealizing Transference." *International Journal of Psychoanalytic Psychotherapy,* 1979, *7,* 26–51.

Dorpat, T. L. "Denial, Defect, Symptom Formation and Construction." *Psychoanalytic Inquiry,* 1983, *3,* 223–253.

Eagle, M., and Wolitzky, D. L. "Therapeutic Influence in Dynamic Psychotherapy: A Review and Synthesis." In S. Slipp (ed.), *Curative Factors in Dynamic Psychotherapy.* New York: McGraw-Hill, 1982.

Edelson, M. *The Termination of Intensive Psychotherapy.* Springfield, Ill.: Thomas, 1963.

Ekstein, R. "Working Through and the Termination of Analysis." *Journal of the American Psychoanalytic Association,* 1965, *13,* 57–58.

Erikson, E. H. "Identity and the Life Cycle." *Psychological Issues,* 1959, Monograph 1.

Fairbairn, W. D. *An Object-Relations Theory of the Personality.* New York: Basic Books, 1952.

Farber, B., and Geller, J. D. "College Student Attitudes Toward Psychotherapy." *Journal of the American College Health Association,* 1977, *25,* 301–307.

Firestein, S. K. *Termination in Psychoanalysis.* New York: International Universities Press, 1978.

Fraiberg, S. "Libidinal Object Constancy and Mental Representation." *Psychoanalytic Study of the Child,* 1969, *24,* 3–47.

Frank, J. D. *Persuasion and Healing.* (Rev. ed.) Baltimore: Johns Hopkins University Press, 1973.

Freud, S. "Mourning and Melancholia." In J. Strachey (ed. and trans.), *The Standard Edition of the Complete Psychological Works of Sigmund Freud.* Vol. 14. London: Hogarth Press, 1957. (Originally published 1917.)

Freud, S. "On Beginning the Treatment: Further Recommendations on the Technique of Psychoanalysis." In J. Strachey (ed. and trans.), *The Standard Edition of the Complete Psychological Works of Sigmund Freud.* Vol. 12. London: Hogarth Press, 1958. (Originally published 1913.)

Freud, S. "Inhibitions, Symptoms and Anxiety." In J. Strachey (ed. and trans.), *The Standard Edition of the Complete Psychological Works of Sigmund Freud.* Vol. 20. London: Hogarth Press, 1959. (Originally published 1926.)

Freud, S. "The Ego and the Id." In J. Strachey (ed. and trans.), *The Standard Edition of the Complete Psychological Works of Sigmund Freud.* Vol. 19. London: Hogarth Press, 1961. (Originally published 1923.)

Friedman, L. "The Therapeutic Alliance." *International Journal of Psycho-Analysis,* 1969, *50,* 139–153.

Gabbard, O. "The Exit Line: A Manifestation of Heightened Transference-Countertransference at the End of the Hour." *Journal of the American Psychoanalytic Association,* 1982, *30,* 579–599.

Garfield, S. L. "Research on Client Variables in Psychotherapy." In A. E. Bergin and S. L. Garfield (eds.), *Handbook of Psychotherapy and Behavior Change: An Empirical Analysis.* (2nd ed.) New York: Wiley, 1978.

Gedo, J. "Forms of Idealization in the Analytic Transference." *Journal of the American Psychoanalytic Association,* 1975, *23,* 485–505.

Geller, J. D. "The Body, Expressive Movement, and Physical Contact in Psychotherapy." In J. L. Singer and K. S. Pope (eds.), *The Power of Human Imagination.* New York: Plenum, 1978.

Geller, J. D. "Moods, Feelings, and the Process of Affect Formation." In L. Temoshok, L. S. Zegans, and C. Van Dyke (eds.), *Emotions in Health and Illness: Foundations of Clinical Practice.* Orlando, Fla.: Grune & Stratton, 1984.

Geller, J. D. "The Role of Rhythm in Psychotherapy." Paper

presented at the conference of the National Coalition of Arts Therapy Associations, New York, Nov. 1985.

Geller, J. D. "Racial Bias in the Evaluation of Patients for Psychotherapy." In L. Comas-Diaz and E. H. Griffith (eds.), *Clinical Practice in Cross-Cultural Mental Health.* New York: Wiley, 1986.

Geller, J. D., Astrachan, B. M., and Flynn, H. "The Development and Validation of a Measure of the Psychiatrist's Authoritative Domain." *Journal of Nervous and Mental Disease,* 1976, *162,* 410–422.

Geller, J. D., and Nash, V. "Termination from Psychotherapy as Viewed by Psychiatric Residents." Unpublished manuscript, 1975.

Geller, J. D., Smith-Behrends, R., and Hartley, D. "Images of the Psychotherapist: A Theoretical and Methodological Perspective." *Imagination, Cognition, and Personality,* 1982, *1,* 123–146.

Gill, M. *Analysis of Transference.* Vol. 1. New York: International Universities Press, 1982.

Gilligan, C. *In a Different Voice: Psychological Theory and Women's Development.* Cambridge, Mass.: Harvard University Press, 1982.

Giovacchini, P. L. "Self Projections in the Narcissistic Transference." *International Journal of Psychoanalytic Psychotherapy,* 1975, *4,* 142–166.

Glenn, M. L. "Separation Anxiety: When the Therapist Leaves the Patient." *American Journal of Psychotherapy,* 1971, *25,* 437–442.

Glover, E. *The Technique of Psychoanalysis.* New York: International Universities Press, 1955.

Goleman, D. "Saying Goodbye Speaks Volumes." *New York Times,* Apr. 3, 1984, p. 26.

Gould, R. L. "The Phases of Adult Life: A Study in Developmental Psychology." *American Journal of Psychiatry,* 1972, *129,* 521–531.

Greene, L. R., and Geller, J. D. "Effects of Therapists' Clinical Experience and Personal Boundaries on Termination of Psychotherapy." *Journal of Psychiatric Education,* 1980, *7,* 31–35.

Greenson, R. *The Technique and Practice of Psychoanalysis.* New York: International Universities Press, 1967.

Guntrip, H. *Schizoid Phenomena, Object Relations, and the Self.* New York: International Universities Press, 1969.

Hammer, E. F. (ed.). *Uses of Interpretation in Treatment: Technique and Art.* Orlando, Fla.: Grune & Stratton, 1968.

Hartmann, H. *Ego Psychology and the Problem of Adaptation.* New York: International Universities Press, 1958. (Originally published 1939.)

Horney, K. *New Ways in Psychoanalysis.* New York: Norton, 1966.

Horowitz, M. J. "Modes of Representation in Thought." *Journal of the American Psychoanalytic Association,* 1972, *20,* 793-819.

Horowitz, M. J., Wilner, N., Marmar, C., and Krupnick, J. L. "Pathological Grief and the Activation of Latent Self-Images." *American Journal of Psychiatry,* 1980, *137,* 1157-1162.

Horowitz, M. J., and Zilberg, N. "Regressive Alterations of the Self Concept." *American Journal of Psychiatry,* 1983, *40,* 284-289.

Hurn, H. T. "Toward a Paradigm of the Terminal Phase." *Journal of the American Psychoanalytic Association,* 1971, *19,* 332-348.

Jacobs, S., and Kosten, T. R. "Depressive Syndromes During Acute Bereavement: Indications for Professional Intervention." *Yale Psychiatric Quarterly,* 1983, *6,* 4-13.

Jung, C. G. *Memories, Dreams, Reflections.* New York: Vintage Books, 1965.

Kaiser, H. *Effective Psychotherapy: The Contributions of Helmuth Kaiser.* New York: Free Press, 1965.

Kauff, P. F. "The Termination Process: Its Relationship to the Separation-Individuation Phase of Development." *International Journal of Group Psychotherapy,* 1980, *29,* 51-66.

Kazdin, M. *Research Design in Clinical Psychology.* New York: Harper & Row, 1980.

Keith, C. "Multiple Transfers of Psychotherapy Patients." *Archives of General Psychiatry,* 1966, *14,* 185-190.

Kernberg, O. *Object Relations Theory and Clinical Psychoanalysis.* New York: Jason Aronson, 1976.

Kestenberg, J. S. "Rhythm and Organization in Obsessive-Compulsive Development." *International Journal of Psychoanalysis*, 1966, *47*, 151–159.

Kline, F., Adrian, A., and Spevak, M. "Patients Evaluate Therapists." *Archives of General Psychiatry*, 1974, *31*, 113–116.

Kluckhohn, C., and Murray, H. A. *Personality in Nature, Society, and Culture.* New York: Knopf, 1949.

Kohut, H. *The Analysis of the Self.* New York: International Universities Press, 1971.

Kohut, H. *The Restoration of the Self.* New York: International Universities Press, 1977.

Kohut, H., and Wolf, E. S. "The Disorders of the Self and Their Treatment: An Outline." *International Journal of Psycho-Analysis*, 1978, *59*, 413–425.

Krystal, H. "Alexithymia and Psychotherapy." *American Journal of Psychotherapy*, 1979, *33*, 17–31.

Kurtz, R. R., and Grummon, D. L. "Different Approaches to the Measurement of Therapist Empathy and Their Relationship to Therapy Outcomes." *Journal of Consulting and Clinical Psychology*, 1972, *39*, 106–115.

Laing, R. D. *The Divided Self.* Baltimore: Pelican Books, 1965.

Langs, R. *The Bipersonal Field.* New York: Jason Aronson, 1976.

Lenzer, A. S. "Countertransference and the Resident on Leaving His Patient." *Journal of the Hillside Hospital*, 1955, *4*, 148–157.

Levinson, D. J., and others. *The Seasons of a Man's Life.* New York: Knopf, 1978.

Lipin, T. "The Repetition Compulsion and 'Maturational' Drive-Representatives." *International Journal of Psycho-Analysis*, 1963, *44*, 389–406.

Loewald, H. W. "Internalization, Separation, Mourning, and the Superego." *Psychoanalytic Quarterly*, 1962, *31*, 483–504.

Loewald, H. W. *Psychoanalysis and the History of the Individual.* New Haven, Conn.: Yale University Press, 1976.

Luborsky, L., and others. "Predicting the Outcomes of Psychotherapy: Findings of the Penn Psychotherapy Research Project." *Archives of General Psychiatry*, 1980, *37*, 471–481.

Mahler, M. S. *The Selected Papers of Margaret S. Mahler.* Vol. 2: *Separation-Individuation.* New York: Jason Aronson, 1979.

Mahler, M. S., Pine, F., and Bergman, A. *The Psychological Birth of the Human Infant: Symbiosis and Individuation.* New York: Basic Books, 1975.

Main, M., Kaplan, N., and Cassidy, J. "Security in Infancy, Childhood, and Adulthood: A Move to the Level of Representation." In I. Bretherton and E. Waters (eds.), "Growing Points of Attachment Theory and Research." *Monographs of the Society for Research in Child Development,* 1985, *50* (1-2, Serial No. 209).

Mann, J. *Time-Limited Psychotherapy.* Cambridge, Mass.: Harvard University Press, 1973.

May, R. (ed.). *Existential Psychology.* New York: Random House, 1961.

Meissner, W. W. *Internalization in Psychoanalysis.* New York: International Universities Press, 1981.

Mikkelson, E. J., and Gutheil, J. "Stages of Forced Termination: Uses of the Death Metaphor." *Psychiatric Quarterly,* 1979, *51,* 15-27.

Modell, A. " 'The Holding Environment' and the Therapeutic Action of Psychoanalysis." *Journal of the American Psychoanalytic Association,* 1976, *24,* 285-309.

Moffat, M. J. *In the Midst of Winter: Selections from the Literature of Mourning.* New York: Random House, 1982.

Newton, P. M. "Social Structure and Process in Psychotherapy: A Sociopsychological Analysis of Transference, Resistance, Change." *International Journal of Psychiatry,* 1973, *11,* 480-509.

Piaget, J. *The Construction of Reality in the Child.* New York: Basic Books, 1954.

Pumpian-Midlin, E. "Comments on Techniques of Termination and Transfer in a Clinic." *American Journal of Psychotherapy,* 1958, *12,* 455-459.

Rank, O. *The Trauma of Birth.* New York: Brunner/Mazel, 1952. (Originally published 1924.)

Raskin, N. "Studies on Psychotherapeutic Orientation: Ideology in Practice." *AAP Psychotherapy Research Monographs.* Orlando, Fla.: American Academy of Psychotherapists, 1974.

Rickers-Ovsiankina, M., Berzins, J. I., Geller, J. D., and Rogers,
    G. W. "Patients' Role Expectations in Psychotherapy: A The-
    oretical and Measurement Approach." *Psychotherapy*, 1971,
    8, 124-127.
Rieff, P. *Freud: The Mind of the Moralist*. New York: Double-
    day, 1961.
Rogers, C. R. *On Becoming a Person*. Boston: Houghton Mifflin
    1961.
Rogers, C. R. "Empathic: An Unappreciated Way of Being."
    Counseling Psychologist, 1975, *5*, 1-10.
Rycroft, C. "The Nature and Function of the Analyst's Com-
    munication to the Patient." *International Journal of Psycho-
    Analysis*, 1956, *37*, 469-471.
Sandler, J., and Rosenblatt, B. "The Concept of the Represen-
    tational World." *Psychoanalytic Study of the Child*, 1962,
    17, 128-145.
Saul, L. *Psychodynamically Based Psychotherapy*. New York:
    Science House, 1972.
Schachtel, E. G. *Metamorphosis: On the Development of Af-
    fect, Perception, Attention, and Memory*. New York: Basic
    Books, 1959.
Schafer, R. *Aspects of Internalization*. New York: International
    Universities Press, 1968.
Schafer, R. "The Termination of Brief Psychoanalytic Psycho-
    therapy." *International Journal of Psychoanalytic Psycho-
    therapy*, 1973a, *2*, 135-148.
Schafer, R. "Concepts of Self and Identity and the Experience
    of Separation-Individuation in Adolescence." *Psychoanalytic
    Quarterly*, 1973b, *42*, 42-59.
Schimek, J. G. "A Critical Re-examination of Freud's Concept
    of Unconscious Mental Representation." *International Re-
    view of Psychoanalysis*, 1975, *2*, 186-197.
Schwaber, P. "Freud and the Twenties." *Massachusetts Review*,
    1971, *10*, 133-147.
Searles, H. F. "Oedipal Love in the Countertransference." In
    H. F. Searles, *Collected Papers on Schizophrenia and Related
    Subjects*. New York: International Universities Press, 1965.
Searles, H. F. "Dual and Multiple-Identity Processes in Border-

line Ego Functioning." In P. Hartocollis (ed.), *Borderline Personality Disorders: The Concept, the Patient, the Syndrome.* New York: International Universities Press, 1977.

Shapiro, D. *Neurotic Styles.* New York: Basic Books, 1965.

Sher, M. "The Process of Changing Therapists." *American Journal of Psychotherapy,* 1970, *25,* 278–282.

Singer, J. L. *Imagery and Daydream Methods in Psychotherapy and Behavior Modification.* Orlando, Fla.: Academic Press, 1974.

Singer, J. L. "Transference and the Human Condition: A Cognitive-Affective Perspective." *Psychoanalytic Psychology,* 1985, *2,* 189–219.

Spitz, R. A. *The First Year of Life: A Psychoanalytic Study of Normal and Deviant Development of Object Relations.* New York: International Universities Press, 1965.

Stolorow, R., and Ross, J. "The Representational World in Psychoanalytic Therapy." *International Review of Psychoanalysis,* 1978, *5,* 247–256.

Strachey, J. "The Nature of the Therapeutic Action of Psychoanalysis." *International Journal of Psycho-Analysis,* 1934, *15,* 127–159.

Strupp, H. H. "The Nature of the Therapeutic Influence and Its Basic Ingredients." In A. Burton (ed.), *What Makes Behavior Change Possible?* New York: Brunner/Mazel, 1976.

Sue, S. "Community Mental Health Services to Minority Groups: Some Optimism, Some Pessimism." *American Psychologist,* 1977, *32,* 616–624.

Sullivan, H. S. *The Interpersonal Theory of Psychiatry.* New York: Norton, 1953.

Updike, J. *The Music School.* New York: Fawcett, 1966.

Vaillant, G. E. *Adaptation to Life.* Boston: Little, Brown, 1977.

Volkan, V. D. *Primitive Internalized Object Relations.* New York: International Universities Press, 1976.

Weigert, E. "Contribution to the Problem of Terminating Psychoanalyses." *Psychoanalytic Quarterly,* 1952, *21,* 465–472.

Weiner, E. *Principles of Psychotherapy.* New York: Wiley, 1975.

Werner, H. *Comparative Psychology of Mental Development.* New York: Science Editions, 1961.

Whitaker, C. "The Administrative Ending in Psychotherapy." *Voices*, 1966, *2*, 69–73.

Winnicott, D. W. "Transitional Objects and Transitional Phenomena: A Study of the First Not-Me Possession." *International Journal of Psycho-Analysis*, 1953, *34*, 89–97.

Winnicott, D. W. *The Maturational Processes and the Facilitating Environment.* New York: International Universities Press, 1965.

16

Contradictory Values in the Study of Separation and Attachment: Implications for Depression and Schizophrenia

Helen Block Lewis

Editors' Note: *This chapter traverses a complicated and exten-*
sive conceptual landscape, starting with an examination of the
biases and values underlying scientific and theoretical views of
attachment and separation and ending with a biological/cultural/
psychological explanation of sex differences in psychopathol-
ogy. Lewis questions the neutrality of viewing individuation and
autonomy as the goals of mental health and suggests that sepa-
rateness and separation have negative as well as positive con-
comitants. She argues that the emotional connectedness and
interpersonal orientation that differentially characterize women
have been devalued in society and in scientific circles by such
androcentric (male-biased) thinkers as Freud, Piaget, Kohlberg,
and Levi-Strauss. Lewis finds that the work of these and other
scholars diminishes the importance of parenting, love, and affec-
tionate ties and elevates the significance of more "masculine"
domains, including autonomy in social relations, affective con-
trol, competition, and morality based on guilt. Using a blend of
theory, research, and clinical observation, Lewis explores the

515

*divergent emotional pathways underlying sex differences in psy-
chology and behavior, particularly highlighting the "moral"
emotions of shame and guilt.*

*Lewis's focus on shame and guilt is connected to her in-
terest in individual differences in cognitive style. Herself a pioneering developer of the work on field dependence, Lewis ana-
lyzes the cognitive/perceptual tasks used to assess degree of
field dependence for their connections with psychoanalytic
coping styles. Such patterns define the individual's level of differentiation of the self, a deep dimension of psychological structure that shapes defenses, object relations, capacity for empathy, sensitivity to separation, and many other factors.*

*One question raised by this chapter is how to reconcile
the beneficial aspect of separateness with the positive value of
interpersonal relatedness. It might be noted that some developmental theories, such as Loevinger's, view a truly integrated
level of individuation as entailing both a heightened sensitivity
to and interest in object relations and a differentiated capacity
for autonomous and self-reliant functioning.*

The concept of separation as it is used in much of present-day
psychology implies a number of positive values. For example,
the differentiation of the self out of an infantile symbiosis
(Mahler, Pine, and Bergman, 1975) has been viewed as the
achievement of separation. Mahler and her associates write of
the self as "an awareness of separateness" and as a "cognitive
affective achievement" that is a "precondition of true object
relationships" (p. 6).* Differentiation of the self out of an undifferentiated infant/mother matrix of experience is the forerunner of such valued characteristics as autonomy, competence,
and independence. In this line of thinking both children's and

*It is worth noting, in passing, that Mahler, Pine, and Bergman treat *self*
and *self-awareness* as synonymous. The failure to distinguish between self
and self-awareness is a fundamental epistemological error that has led
many to assume that because the infant appears to be without self-awareness, it does not have a self—that is, a registration or organizing center. We
now know that infants are "organized" beings, implying a "self" at birth.
(For a fuller treatment of the concept of self, see Lewis, 1958.)

adults' difficulties in tolerating separation imply such negative characteristics as dependence and incompetence. Yet the "object relationships," or attachments, that are so basic to human development themselves have a positive value. They involve affectionate behavior and feelings, and they issue in the positive emotions of happiness and joy. Separation, in contrast, can evoke hurt feelings of rejection and of humiliated fury. When bereavement is the stimulus, separation can also evoke the negative feelings of sadness, loss, and depression.

As I shall show in this chapter, this contradiction of values around separation and attachment is endemic in our culture. It has been reflected in many broad areas of psychology, such as the development of cognitive styles from childhood to adulthood and sex differences in cognitive styles and in mental illness. This chapter will examine the contradiction in values as it emerges in these areas.

Our thinking about separation has been embedded in a familiar concept of infancy that has long governed psychology—the concept of human infancy as a big, buzzing, blooming confusion (James, 1890) or as governed by the chaotic Id (Freud, 1923/1961a). Another line of thinking about separation that is much less developed in psychology is based on our newer knowledge of infants' amazingly complex social capacities, which predispose them to attachment. Neonates, far from being undifferentiated or symbiotic, are highly organized individuals, capable of differentiated responses. For example, infants only thirty-six hours old can discriminate and imitate adult facial expressions of happiness, sadness, and surprise (Field, Woodson, Greenberg, and Cohen, 1982). Neonates' movements are synchronized with adult speech (Condon and Sander, 1974). Newborns can discriminate and prefer the sound of their mothers' voices (DeCasper and Fifer, 1980). Neonates discriminate the sound of other newborns crying, and they respond by crying themselves (Simner, 1971). This high level of social "competence" in infants (Stone, Smith, and Murphy, 1973) suggests that they can be thought of as having an organized self.

This evidence also suggests that infant and mother are separate selves from the beginning, at the same time that it emphasizes the fundamentally social nature of the human organism. The new evidence about infancy thus reveals a dialectic between an initial (separate) organization of the infant self and human attachment, in which attachment is what fosters the continued and developing separation of the self. From this dialectic it follows that difficulties at separation have a positive value, reflecting the existence of lifelong attachment bonds. Absence of difficulty in separation at any particular stage of life may reflect a dehumanized or pathological self.

Human beings are unique creatures on earth in that they all live in a cultural order that recognizes and ritualizes lifelong personal attachments. Cross-cultural studies show that people in all societies grieve and mourn on bereavement (Rosenblatt, Walsh, and Jackson, 1976). From the standpoint of a lifelong attachment system, separation is normally a temporary condition, evoking behavior designed to maintain the attachment system. Some form of substitute attachment normally replaces separation, whether the substitute is another person or a symbolic love affair with some interesting things in the world or both. Separation, moreover, especially when it results from hostility or anger, normally evokes the moral emotions of shame and guilt, which press toward renewed and restored attachment.

It is a fascinating historical fact that our present-day awareness of the centrality of the emotional attachment system throughout life has been derived mainly from the phenomena of separation. Freud's theoretical system, put forward in "The Interpretation of Dreams" (1900/1953), began with a model of the lone infant's behavior in the absence of its caretaker. Freud deduced from this model that all thought and behavior are roundabout ways of seeking the original missing gratification. His focus on the lone infant led him to a drive-reduction model of human development, a model that derived attachment from the taming or reduction of the sexual partial instincts. In this view, attachment was always a shaky substitute for the original, primal infantile "narcissism" or "autism" (Freud, 1917/1957; Mahler, Pine, and Bergman, 1975).

During the 1950s Bowlby (1969), following a line of research that began with studies of wartime separation, evolved his concept of a biologically given, goal-corrected attachment system, in part from the work of the ethologists. In this formulation, he broke with Freud's drive-reduction theoretical system. The work of Harlow and Harlow on nonhuman primates opened up another major line of investigation, in which separation of infants from their mothers could be systematically varied in a way not ethically possible with human beings. Severe distress, closely paralleling human infant distress, could be observed in rhesus monkey infants separated from their mothers (Seay, Hansen, and Harlow, 1962). These results were "in general accord with expectations based upon the human separation syndrome described by Bowlby" (p. 132). Work with primates (Harlow and Mears, 1979) convinced the Harlows that "the so-called primary drives of hunger, fear, rage, and pain are actually socially disruptive, and not the proper prerogative on which to form the foundation of behavior of social animals such as men and monkeys. The most fundamental social motives are various forms of love or affection . . . even though men's motives may be more subtle and more persistent" (p. 8). In their handbook on infancy, Stone, Smith, and Murphy (1973) are in agreement with the Harlows and with Bowlby that attachment must be accounted for in its own right. Attempts to derive it (in Freudian theory or in "dependency" theories) from so-called primary drives have been unsuccessful.

It is instructive to realize that the relative neglect of attachment behavior can be traced, in part, to an androcentric bias in evolutionary biology during much of the nineteenth and twentieth centuries. As Elaine Morgan showed in her witty *Descent of Woman* (1972), the image of Tarzan, the aggressive Mighty Hunter coming down out of the trees, has dominated speculation about the course of evolution from primate forms. Central to this picture is the response of the individual to conditions of predation; natural selection favors the aggressivity of males. This was the prevailing context for Freud's lone infant learning to master deprivation. Morgan suggests, in contrast, that human evolution was determined also by the survival needs of a hypothetical female primate ancestor, carrying her clinging infant. Although Morgan is not an academic scholar, the usefulness of some of her ideas has been confirmed in a recent re-thinking of the evidence about the origin of our species (Love-joy, 1981). Lovejoy suggests that both the fossil record and demographic analysis implicate "an already established hominid character system, which included *intensified parenting and so-cial relationships*" (italics added) as the condition *preceding* ad-vanced material culture and the development of the human brain.

Ethologists have also called attention to the social condi-tions governing even the narrowest physiological responses (Chance, 1980). Studying animal behavior in the wild, rather than in the laboratory alone, has led ethologists to discover that adult animals' social relationships are as important as their rela-tionship to the physical environment, if not more so (Chance, 1980, p. 87). Two distinct patterns of social organization have been discerned in nonhuman primates: a "hedonic" and an "agonic" mode of social cohesion. In the agonic mode, which is originally based on responses to the threat of physical danger, the threat has been encapsulated within the group by the exis-tence of a dominant male who serves as the focus of social at-tention but who is also a "negative social referent." In the he-donic mode, which also fosters group cohesion, other animals are "positive social referents," in the context of which eating, sleeping, resting, and grooming take place. Chance points out that the existence of the hedonic mode of social interaction has been the "single most important discovery" resulting from ethologists' focus on patterns of social attention in primate groups. "The integrity of the . . . hedonic system has been hid-den as its components—involving body contact (as in grooming [or] sitting or sleeping next to), relaxation, and exploration—appear at different times. . . . Only when the elimination of dan-ger occurs, as within the core of a territory, or when the young are in the presence of the mother and in contact with her, has the hedonic system been seen as a single piece" (p. 89).

Chance suggests that the reason for the relatively late dis-covery of a hedonic mode was that ethology developed initially from the study of birds and fishes, whose social relations are phasic and are constructed on agonic forms. Another reason that seems equally plausible is the prevailing androcentrism in science, which regards affectional ties as secondary derivatives of individualistic drives. Attachment has thus been neglected not only in evolutionary theory but also as a central "biological" source of humanity's lifelong difficulties with separation.

The contradiction in values connected with the concept of separation is particularly well illustrated in the research on the cognitive style called field dependence. As we shall see in a moment, Witkin's formulations and reformulations of his differentiation construct (Witkin, Goodenough, and Oltman, 1979) reflect the difficulty created by the dialectic between separation and attachment. The research on field dependence, in turn, has had wide ramifications in many areas of psychology. Sex differences in this cognitive style dimension have been shown to be paralleled by congruent differences in adult personality and "superego" style, as well as sex differences in vulnerability to the two major functional adult mental illnesses: depression and schizophrenia. The hypothesis that there are sex differences in the attachment pattern, beginning early in development, is a compelling one, but one that encounters severe difficulties if the contradiction in values around the concept of separation is not addressed. In the remainder of this chapter, I shall first discuss the contradiction in values in the research on field dependence and the resulting theoretical difficulties. I shall then turn to the contradiction in values in understanding sex differences in field dependence and personality. Finally, I shall discuss the sex differences in proneness to depressive and schizophrenic illness, in which the contradiction in values around separation may even play a role in symptom formation (Witkin and others, 1954/1972, 1962).

Field Dependence and the Conflict of Values Around Separation

The research on field dependence grew unexpectedly out of Wertheimer's (1912) interest in the problem of the nature of human nature. Wertheimer puzzled over the question whether the self should be understood as an "egotistical" product or a product of interaction between the self and the "field." Gestalt theory, with its emphasis on the organization of the field, rather than on random stimulus-response connections, would predict that even the perception of the upright in space was not an "egotistical" product but a function of the self in relation to the organization of the field.

Wertheimer observed that two sets of experimental factors ordinarily come together to enable us to determine with great accuracy how far our bodies are "off" from the true vertical and how far objects are off from their usual orientation. Under ordinary circumstances kinesthetic feedback from the pull of gravity on the body combines with visual perception of the vertical and horizontal in space to give us a large fund of information on which we base our automatic and very accurate judgments of the position of the body and of objects in space. Wertheimer designed a method of separating the visual from the postural cues in the perception of the upright, predicting that a test of their relative potency would favor the visual cues over the self-centered, or "egotistical," body cues as the more potent determinant. Wertheimer's original experiment had confirmed his hypothesis; later experiments by Gibson and Mowrer (1938) had contradicted Wertheimer's findings. Asch and Witkin (1948; Witkin and Asch, 1948) were attempting to reconcile this discrepancy when Witkin made his observations about individual differences (the most probable reason for the discrepancy). It should be noted that, in the main, Wertheimer's hypothesis has been confirmed: people do tend, on the average, to be influenced by the prevailing visual cues in their perception of the upright in space; they are not "self-centered."

The idea that there are individual differences in self-perception of the body's position in space was quite unpredicted by Gestalt theory, which emphasized the compelling nature of a visual form of organization for everyone. But it did fit a psychodynamic way of thinking in which the self's relation to others and to the world is the inheritor of tensions between the ego and superego (Freud, 1923/1961a).

New Look investigators during the 1950s were busy trying to evolve experimental situations in which Freudian defenses and developmental phases could be put to test. In this atmosphere, Witkin's "accidental" discovery of what turned out to be stable and significant differences in people's perception of the upright in space could be used to test Freudian thinking. A person whose mode of orienting in space was "self-centered" could be expected to have a personality that fit this cognitive style. The resulting characterology involves "internal" autonomy rather than "external" dependency. This characterology is reminiscent of Freud's libidinal types (1931/1961c). A field-independent person's superego would be dominated by internal "fear of conscience" (guilt), while a field-dependent person's superego would be more vulnerable to "loss of love" or "other-connected" shame.

In Witkin's theory, people who are influenced by "external" cues and who therefore show difficulty in orienting themselves in space and in disembedding geometrical forms from context are thought of as less "differentiated." Less differentiated (more field-dependent) persons are hypothesized to be less separated from others. Thus, Witkin, Goodenough, and Oltman (1979) write: "A system that is more differentiated shows greater self/nonself segregation, signifying definite boundaries between an inner core . . . and the outer world, particularly other people. In a less differentiated system, in contrast, there is greater connectedness between the self and others" (p. 1127).

A contradiction in values surrounding the concept of separation creates theoretical difficulties in understanding field dependence/independence. On the one hand, ontogenetic development of cognitive functioning proceeds from field dependence to field independence. In perception of the upright in space, for example, both cross-sectional and longitudinal data show progressive decreases in the effect of the visual field until the teenage years (Witkin, Goodenough, and Karp, 1967). The evidence for restructuring factors (as reflected in the ability to disembed visual-spatial figures) shows similar developmental trends (Witkin and others, 1962). It is obvious, moreover, that children function less autonomously in interpersonal situations than adults. So far, we have looked at separation and field independence as having positive values.

On the other hand, there is evidence to suggest that field-dependent people may be emotionally closer to other people. Field-dependent people get along better with others. For example, groups of subjects with field-dependent participants may be more effective in working out disagreements and conflicts than groups consisting entirely of field-independent participants (Oltman and others, 1975). Field-dependent people are more popular with others (Oltman and others, 1975) and are more successful at occupations that feature personal relationships (for example, MacKinnon, 1962; Quinlan and Blatt, 1972).

Field-dependent people are more likely to rely on others' judgments in ambiguous social situations (Witkin, Goodenough, and Oltman, 1979). They may be either more "suggestible" or more "trusting." They more often talk about themselves and prefer to be closer to others (Greene, 1976; Sousa-Poza and Rohrberg, 1976). They more often prefer to be with people (Coates, Lord, and Jacobovits, 1975). In short, field-independent people represent some negative values regarding separation, especially emotional distance from other people.

Another line of investigation into field dependence also yields an important contribution in values concerning separation. This is the line of evidence that comes from cross-cultural studies. There is now a large body of evidence on subsistence-level cultural groups (Witkin and Berry, 1975; Berry, 1976) indicating that members of hunting/gathering economies tend to be relatively field independent, while agricultural/sedentary groups tend to be relatively field dependent. We know from archeological evidence that primitive people were nomadic hunters and gatherers of food, who learned to cultivate crops and domesticate animals about 8,000 years ago. As an agricultural economy developed, people began to settle in a more sedentary village life. It is therefore plausible to assume that there has been an evolutionary trend from field independence to greater field dependence, as economies moved historically from hunting/gathering to agricultural. This assumption gains additional credence when the adaptive consequences of hunting and farming economies are examined in relation to the kinds of situations in which people with a field-dependent or a field-independent cognitive style function most effectively.

The activities involved in hunting and gathering require the ability to extract key information from the surrounding field for the location of game and other food. Moreover, the hunter must be continuously aware of his location in space if he is to return home safely. We may imagine, therefore, that cognitive restructuring skills are particularly adaptive in the life of the hunter/gatherer. In contrast, only minimal social skills may be required. The hunter leads a relatively isolated life. The size of the social group is limited by the food-producing capacity of the local environment. The hunter, therefore, usually travels in family-size bands with relatively loose social structures characterized by minimal differences among social roles and little permanent political authority. These conditions place a premium on individual autonomy (see, for example, Witkin and Berry, 1975).

The typical agricultural group is very different in these respects. Its more sedentary existence places less demand on cognitive restructuring skills, but interpersonal relationships become much more important. The development of agriculture made possible a marked increase in group size and led to diversity of social roles and social stratification along with elaborate rules of conduct governing behavior among group members. The regularities required by planting and harvest and the need to accumulate food supplies for consumption between harvest periods would contribute to the development of social institutions that control individual autonomy. It is easy to suppose that the interpersonal orientation and social skills of field-dependent people would be particularly adaptive in subsistence-level farming cultures (Witkin and Berry, 1975).

Theories of development commonly propose that evolutionary change and ontogenetic change proceed in the same direction. Against this background we see that the evidence leads to a contradiction. Evolutionary change proceeds toward an increasing elaboration of social structure and of field dependence, unlike ontogenetic development. The idea that evolution proceeds from field independence to field dependence suggests that the values of Tarzan, the Mighty Hunter, are positive only for one set of adaptive requirements. The values of social cohesion and emotional closeness also serve adaptive requirements.

This contradiction in values also calls our attention to a very important distinction that needs to be made when we think about separation. Two main lines of differentiation can be discerned in the segregation of the self from the nonself. One involves the self's response to people; the other, the self's response to "things," including such animate objects as plants or animals (other than pets).

The usefulness of this distinction is exemplified by the fascinating research on the relation between infants' concepts of person permanence and object (thing) permanence. Bell (1970) explored a suggestion by Piaget that infants develop a concept of persons' independent existence (when not present in perception) even more quickly than they develop a homologous concept of inanimate objects. Piaget's notion was based on his realization of the emotional salience of the mother. Bell devised scales to test person permanence and inanimate-object permanence in infancy. Infants who were more advanced in the concept of person permanence than in inanimate-object permanence were identified as having a "positive decalage." Infants who were more advanced in their concept of inanimate-object permanence than person permanence were identified as having a "negative decalage." Of thirty-three infants tested, twenty-three fell into the "positive" group. All of these twenty-three infants turned out to be securely attached to their mothers. Seven of the thirty-three infants were identified as having a "negative decalage." These were all anxiously attached to their mothers. (The remaining three infants were distributed among all three strange-situation response classifications.) Bell's findings have since been replicated (Ainsworth, Blehar, Waters, and Wall, 1978).

These findings suggest that the development of person constancy may be basic to the development of object constancy. At the least they suggest that under ordinary circumstances one can expect that person permanence and inanimate-object permanence will develop in tandem. They also suggest that, at the extremes of emotional disturbance, the two tracks of response to "person" and "thing" may develop at each other's expense. At one extreme, early difficulty in maintaining a satisfactory adjustment to others may express itself in withdrawal from them into a substitute attachment or interest in the physical world. This is a pattern that has been described, for example, for autistic boys. Such a preoccupation with inanimate objects in space could foster development of a field-independent cognitive style through emotional deficit. In another pattern that has been described for symbiotic girls, difficulty in separating the self from significant others may be expressed in an inability to bear separation from the mother and in an almost total lack of interest in the physical world. Such a pattern would foster field dependence by another kind of emotional default. Still another pattern of stable emotional attachment would presumably predict a self both interpersonally adept and field independent. The evidence about field dependence in children does indeed give us a glimpse of this pattern, but only among girls (Coates, Lord, and Jacobovits, 1975).

Beginning at about age eight and continuing into adolescence and adulthood, males are slightly but significantly more field independent than females (Witkin, 1965; Berry, 1976). The picture in early childhood, however, is different. Little girls, especially at age five, are likely to be more field independent than little boys (Coates, Lord, and Jacobovits, 1975). Among little boys, the evidence suggests that field independence goes with an orientation toward things (Kogan, 1976). We turn now to the contradiction in values about separation as it is reflected in the research on sex differences in field dependence.

Sex Differences in Field Dependence

Tests of field independence have been developed for use with preschool children as young as three years of age (Coates, 1974). Coates cites nine studies on preschool children, eight of which yielded evidence that little girls are more field independent than little boys. Among five-year-olds in particular, the difference favoring little girls was especially pronounced. It should be noted that this result holds for other cognitive styles as well as field dependence. Kogan (1976) tells us that "sex differences in cognitive styles and strategies are pervasive during the preschool years and almost uniformly favor females" (p. 121).

In an earlier study, Coates had found that preschool children of both sexes whose teachers rated them as autonomous, achievement striving, independent, and goal-directed were significantly more field independent on the Preschool Embedded Figures Test (PEFT). Coates (1974) links these findings with the general finding (Maccoby and Jacklin, 1974) that little girls are more positive in their social behavior than boys, while boys show a higher level of aggression. She cites the considerable evidence that a high level of aggression operates to impair boys' analytic ability and so may account for girls' early advantage in field independence. The evidence on field dependence in little girls thus suggests that the development of a sound attachment bond parallels the development of an articulated mode of perceiving things in the world. So far, in the benign atmosphere of childhood, especially in the nursery school, good things go together.

The evidence on sex differences in field dependence among adults suggests, in contrast, that by the time of adulthood, social skills and a differentiated approach to things in the world have taken divergent tracks. The emotional closeness and interpersonal skills linked to field dependence are also more prevalent in women, while men are superior in cognitive restructuring as well as more impersonal and aggressive in their social behavior (Maccoby and Jacklin, 1974). How shall we understand this change from childhood to adulthood?

In their recent theoretical reformulation, Witkin, Goodenough, and Oltman (1979) imply that the two tracks of development generally occur at each other's expense. Cognitive restructuring skills do not foster interpersonal closeness, and vice versa. But this formulation tends to ignore the fact that in childhood the tracks are parallel, at least in five-year-old girls. Beginning at adolescence our male-dominated competitive culture pushes men to develop cognitive restructuring skills and impersonal behavior and to devalue emotional closeness and attachment, which have relatively little value in the marketplace. It simultaneously fosters and devalues women's emotional closeness and attachments, while making fewer demands on their cognitive restructuring skills. Recognizing the culture's contradictory values thus suggests that interpersonal skills and cognitive restructuring skills need not be divergent tracks of development. This possibility, in turn, suggests that depression and schizophrenia, the two great categories of functional mental illness, may represent an extreme divergence in which cognitive restructuring skills and interpersonal skills do develop at each other's expense.

Field Dependence and "Superego Style": Shame and Guilt

Robust evidence has been accumulating ever since our first report (Witkin and others, 1954/1972) linking field dependence and depression (for example, Levenson and Neuringer, 1974; Newman and Hirt, 1983). Similarly, there is evidence linking paranoia and field independence (Witkin, 1965; Johnson, 1980).

That women in our society are more prone to depression than men, while men are more prone to paranoid schizophrenia than women, has been well known since accurate statistics began to be assembled, well before World War II. In a paper published almost three decades ago (Lewis, 1958), I speculated that this sex difference in the two great functional mental disorders might be somehow related to the almost ubiquitous sex difference in field dependence. But it was not until the 1960s' revival of the women's liberation movement that I began to glimpse the way in which women's depression and men's paranoia are both caricatures of women's and men's stereotypical roles in a male-dominated, exploitive society. The image of an affectively overwhelmed, selfless woman, helpless to stop her own suffering (usually at the hands of a man), is in sharp contrast to the image of an emotionally shut-down man, ideationally overwhelmed by a compelling mission to rectify guilt, even if this means killing people. In these two caricatures, depressed women are excessively ashamed, while paranoid men are obsessed with the ideation of guilt.

From this reasoning it followed that field-dependent people should be more prone to shame, while field-independent people should be more prone to guilt. During the 1960s, two colleagues and I (Witkin, Lewis, and Weil, 1968) planned and executed a study in which we predicted that field-dependent patients would be more prone to shame than guilt in their first therapeutic encounters, while field-independent patients would be more prone to guilt than shame. When we undertook our study, shame was indeed a neglected phenomenon. Its neglect may be understood in part as a reflection of the positive values for separation and autonomy as contrasted to attachment. The "autonomous" superego mode is clearly guilt, which is self-initiated and self-propelled. Shame, in contrast, is an experience that directly involves the "other's" disapproval or scorn and so more clearly reflects its origins in attachment.

In our experimental study, the transcripts of the first two psychotherapy sessions of "pairs" of field-dependent and field-independent patients in treatment with the same therapist were assessed for their implied affective content, using Gottschalk and Gleser's (1969) reliable and valid method. As predicted, field-dependent patients showed significantly more shame anxiety than guilt anxiety, while field-independent patients showed significantly more guilt than shame. As predicted, also, field-dependent patients showed more self-directed hostility. The success of these predictions encouraged me to undertake a thorough phenomenological analysis of the experiences of shame and guilt with particular reference to the position and role of the self in both states. The transcripts of 180 psychotherapy sessions of nine patient/therapist pairs were among the sources for my analysis, in which symptom formation *in statu nascendi* could be traced from evoked, undischarged states of shame and guilt (Lewis, 1971).

A brief word on the subject of definition. I use *shame* to refer to a family of affective/cognitive states in which embarrassment, mortification, humiliation, feeling ridiculous, chagrin, disgrace, and shyness are among the variants. These states differ widely in their cognitive content, but they are similar in their focus on the *self*-in-the-eyes-of-the-other as the center of acute, painful awareness. "Guilt" is a family of affective/cognitive states with themes of responsibility, fault, obligation, and blame for particular events—that is, for *things* done or not done.

As I have shown at great length in *Shame and Guilt in Neurosis* (Lewis, 1971), the transcripts of the psychotherapy sessions contained many examples of the way unresolved states of shame and guilt evolved into symptoms. Without Freud's prior descriptions of the "primary process" transformations of thought and feeling that take place under the press of strangulated affect, my interpretations could not have been made. The transcripts illuminated how shame and guilt function to maintain threatened affectional ties with significant others. Unresolved shame could be seen to maintain affectional ties at the expense of self-esteem, leaving the self in a state of depression. Unresolved guilt could be seen to maintain affectional ties at the expense of the self's rational judgment about the attribution of guilt or blame, including obsessive ideas of persecution.

Contradictory values about separation and attachment became apparent in my attempts to conceptualize shame. For example, Freud's theory of the superego, which required the internalization of the castration threat, made superego and guilt synonymous. In many quarters, therefore, shame was not regarded as a genuine superego state. The absence of the castration threat in women's development led Freud to assume their less developed form of sense of guilt and, by default, their greater proneness to a less highly developed form of conscience, shame. In this line of thinking, shame was made synonymous with only one of its meanings, being caught or found out. The other-connected imagery in shame also resulted in its being considered only a precursor of a fully formed conscience. Because of its "objective" quality (Heider, 1958), guilt was considered a higher-order response than shame, the more "subjective" experience.

I have recently found much support for my struggle to formulate shame and guilt as equally developed superego experiences in the work of Norma Haan (1978) and Carol Gilligan (1983), two students of Kohlberg who have taken him to task for his androcentric bias. Not only Kohlberg and Piaget but Freud and Levi-Strauss must also be included in this criticism. Haan's work was stimulated in part by the finding that American women are frequently found to be morally less mature than men on Kohlberg's scale. Haan argues that the "moral reasoning of males who live in technological, rationalized societies . . . and who defensively intellectualize and deny interpersonal and situational details is especially favored in the Kohlberg scoring system" (p. 287).

Gilligan (1983), for example, has persuasively argued that the social sciences lack an adequate theory of moral development because of their androcentric bias. She contrasts the "ethic of care," which women more often voice in solving moral dilemmas, with the "ethic of responsibility," more often voiced by men. This description of a sex difference in moral thought is actually not too different from Freud's descriptive statement that women's superego "is never so inexorable, so impersonal, so independent of its emotional origins" as men's (Freud, 1925/ 1961b, pp. 257–258). What is at issue here is the theoretical place for the "ethic of care." Gilligan suggests that including it in theory "restores the concept of love to the moral domain, uniting cognition and affect by tying reflection to the experience of relationship" (p. 120). It is particularly in the behavior of infants and their caretakers that we can now see how closely cognition and affect are united and how "reflection" is connected to the experience of relationship.

Contradictory Values About Separation in Depression and Schizophrenia

We come, finally, to the way in which the two major functional mental illnesses reflect our culture's contradictory values about separation and attachment. A few words, first, about the contrast between depression and schizophrenia. Although the contrast is between two very gross categories, there is cross-cultural evidence that primitive people distinguish between depression and schizophrenia in much the same terms as we do (Murphy, 1976). Two widely separated non-Western groups, the Eskimo of northwest Alaska and the Yoruba of tropical Nigeria, both label as "crazy" such phenomena as "talking to oneself, screaming at someone who does not exist, making strange grimaces, becoming strange and violent" (p. 1022). Although they have no single label that covers both anxiety and depression any more than we do, they have many phrases in their vocabulary for excessive emotional responses in such neurotic symptoms as "shaking and trembling all over," "unrest that prevents sleep," "extreme bashfulness which is like a sense of shame," "crying with sadness," and "head down" (p. 1024).

The biochemists, looking for their biochemical markers of mental illness, also recognize the important distinction between schizophrenia, which involves the "stress of social interaction," and depression, which is a "stress reaction to social loss" (Barchas, Akil, and Elliot, 1978, p. 967). And although we do not as yet have any worldwide evidence that women are more prone to depression than men or less prone to paranoid schizophrenia, there is good evidence in our own society.

One other brief word about the difficulties of establishing the evidence about sex difference in proneness to depression and schizophrenia. Some researchers—for example, Gove and Tudor (1973) and Chesler (1972), who relied on Gove and Tudor's evidence—have concluded that women in our society are more prone to mental illness in general than men, as a reflection of their oppression by men. Although I do not at all disagree with the idea that women are oppressed, and by men, a careful review of the evidence suggests that the important question is not which sex is more often mentally ill but how the sexes differ in kind of illness. There is unanimous agreement that women are more often depressed than men. The evidence that men are more prone to fall ill of schizophrenia is more ambiguous, mainly because of changing use of diagnostic criteria in schizophrenia. When, however, rates for schizophrenia and manic-depressive psychosis are assessed by first admissions to state hospitals (and by readmissions), men—especially between the ages of fifteen and thirty-five—are more frequently admitted for schizophrenia, and women for manic-depressive psychosis (Malzberg, 1959). The rates for schizophrenia, moreover, far exceed the rates for bipolar depression, and they closely parallel the statistics for poverty and social disorganization (Faris and Dunham, 1939; Levy and Rowitz, 1973; Dohrenwend and Dohrenwend, 1976). Highest admissions for schizophrenia come from areas where the population is poor and where there are substandard housing, high residential mobility, high unemployment, and high male delinquency. The rates for manic-depressive illness, in contrast, do *not* parallel social conditions. This difference in the extent to which the two major psychoses are influenced by socioeconomic factors makes sense of men's proneness to schizophrenia as a reflection of their place in the front line of economic battle. Women's greater proneness to depressive psychosis as well as depressive neurosis reflects the casualties of women's primary involvement with the family as their front line of struggle.

It has been suggested in some quarters, notably by Hammen and her associates (Hammen and Pedesky, 1977), that women's greater proneness to depression is an artifact of their greater freedom to report illnesses and to express their feelings, rather than to a genuine susceptibility to depressive illness. In an elegant study of the question of susceptibility, Radloff and Rae (1979) showed that even when various precipitating factors that might produce depression are controlled, the sex difference in depression remains, leading to the conclusion that there is a genuine susceptibility factor in women's proneness to depression.

This difference in susceptibility reflects the difference in acculturation process for the two sexes. First, women's reproductive function casts them in the role of primary caretaker of others, and second, the acculturation process is especially different for the two sexes when the social order is characterized by male domination and exploitiveness.

A brief description of what I mean by the acculturation process is necessary at this point. A fundamental assumption is that the organization of culture is our species' unique adaptation to life. The principal evolutionary change from primate to human life is the emergence of human culture as our species' biological adaptation, with a concomitant increase in the extent and impact of nurturant social forces on human, as contrasted to primate, behavior. We are thus social animals by biological inheritance. Human beings are the most thoroughly domesticated, the most long-lastingly affectionate, and the most moral animals on earth. All human cultures, whatever their level of technological development, are organized around a system of morality that governs human behavior from birth to death (a circumstance that may shortly destroy us all in a nuclear war).

Human acculturation (and resulting morality) begins in the earliest affectional interaction between the infant and his or her caretakers in the nuclear family. We now know, thanks to the work of the Harlows, Bowlby, Spitz, Mahler, Ainsworth, and a host of researchers whose work grew out of Freud's observations, that infant development thrives in this affectional interaction and is injured in its absence. We now know that there are specific, long-lasting, universal attachment emotions that arise in and accompany the affectional infant/caretaker interaction. Delight, joy, interest, pride, and laughter occur when attachment is maintained; protest, humiliated fury, righteous indignation, anxiety, shame, and guilt occur when attachment is threatened. The two superego emotions, shame and guilt, function so as to restore threatened affectional bonds.

The human nuclear family is the transmission belt for the culture's morality, which is imbibed along with parental nurturance, beginning with mother's milk. It is thus always a transmission belt for affectionate values. The nuclear family is sometimes also, as in our own society, a transmission belt for exploitive values and for the maintenance of male supremacy. The contradiction or ambivalence between these positive and negative values can drive people crazy, as Freud was the first to describe. It is likely to drive women and men crazy in different ways, as the statistics on depression and schizophrenia suggest, both because of the sex difference in reproductive function and because of the subordinate power of women that is widespread in exploitive, male-dominated societies.

Let us look first at the way the sex difference in reproductive function operates in the acculturation process. We are here immediately confronted with an emotionally charged question, since differences in reproductive function have been used by (mainly male) thinkers, of whom Freud was only one, to "explain" women's subordinate power. But let us try to put aside this separate issue of women's subordination. It is a fact that the XX and XY chromosome pairs, which each release a different pattern of hormones, make women and not men genetically equipped to bear and suckle children. The existence of a mother/infant affectional system guiding the behavior of both parties is now an established empirical fact of mammalian behavior, including our own.

But the importance of this genetically based maternal function in the differing acculturation patterns of the two sexes is very hard to consider outside of the androcentric values implicit in our culture. For example, in their monumental work on sex differences, Maccoby and Jacklin (1974) accept a genetic basis for aggression in males. But they do not accept the parallel hypothesis that nurturant behavior in women has a genetic base, in spite of the fact that a genetic factor clearly determines childbearing, while no known genetic factor has been unearthed for male aggression or warfare. Maccoby and Jacklin note that women in all cultures are thought to be more nurturant than men. They also insist that the evidence for women's greater sociability is a myth—a conclusion that is, in my opinion, not at all congruent with the evidence cited in their book. It is clear, however, that Maccoby and Jacklin are afraid—quite rightly so— that women's greater sociability makes them "easier to exploit." Women who are protesting their own subjugation may well fear that hypotheses about their greater sociability may be used to help keep them in their place. But this is a danger only if there is a tacit agreement (among women as well as men) that the "superior" values in the world are aggression and egotism.

Let us look, then, at what evidence there is for the thesis of women's greater sociability. Several lines of evidence converge to support this hypothesis (Lewis, 1976). The first comes from studies of sex differences in neonate behavior. Even at two to three days of age, girls are more responsive than boys to the sound of another newborn's cry. Two- to three-day-old girls show more reflex smiling and sucking than boys. Newborn girls are more sensitive than boys to touch, taste, and pain. They are also more sensitive (as measured by shorter EEG latency) to light and sound. Females, moreover, retain this greater sensory sensitivity into adulthood. It is a characteristic especially useful for caretakers.

A second line of evidence comes from older infants. Girls are more responsive to the human face than boys, who, in turn, are more responsive to geometric designs. Girls babble more than boys and are generally superior in language development—another useful attribute of caretakers.

A third line of evidence comes from studies of sex differences in mother/infant interaction. The fascinating information that has emerged from studies of monkeys is that mother monkeys treat the two sexes differently. Mothers punish their male infants more than their females; they pay them less attention and carry them around less. (This finding among primates has a forerunner among mice: female pups are retrieved by their mothers more often than male pups.) No one yet understands the basis for this difference in mother/infant interaction among monkeys. But it can contribute to a greater sociability among female monkeys than among males.

This conjecture is paralleled by evidence that female monkeys are less injured by maternal deprivation than males (Sackett, 1974). Similarly, females raised in isolation are less injured in their curiosity, in their social behavior, and in their learning capacity. As Sackett puts it, summarizing the findings of experiments on maternal deprivation, females are the "buffered sex." Perhaps they can take being reared in isolation better than males because they have some kind of edge in sociability to begin with.

The findings among monkeys are neatly paralleled by findings about sex differences in mother/infant interaction among ourselves. No one, of course, has done experiments rearing children in social isolation. But careful techniques of direct observation reveal that mothers treat their boy babies quite differently than their girls. Close observation of middle-class mothers and their first infants by Howard Moss (1974) showed significant differences in handling at three weeks and again at three months of age. Mothers held their three-week-old boys farther from their own bodies. They more often held a boy baby in a sitting or standing position—what the observers called "stressing the baby's musculature." Mothers stimulated and aroused their boy infants more than their girls, and they attended to them more than their girls. In sharp contrast, the only thing mothers did more of with their girl babies was imitate them. One does not need to be a psychoanalyst to interpret these findings as meaning that mothers were less easy with infants of the male sex and were expressing their sense of sameness with girls by imitating them.

By the time the infants were three months old, an important sex difference had emerged in the mother/infant interaction. Male infants, even at three weeks, had cried more, fussed more, and been more irritable than girls. Girl infants slept more and cried less than boys. For males, who were more irritable to begin with, the correlation between the total time they cried and the amount of attention they got from their mothers was negative. The more boys cried, the less their mothers attended them. For girl infants, in contrast, the amount of time they cried and the amount of attention they got were positively correlated. As Moss points out, the evidence here joins the evidence of a number of other studies that boys are more subject to inconsolable emotional reactions while girls are more readily soothed by maternal intervention.

Infantile autism has been reported more often in boys than girls in the ratio of four to one (Taylor and Ounsted, 1972). Although the evidence connecting infantile autism and adult schizophrenia is contradictory, autistic children are like some adult schizophrenics in a failure of emotional communication and an "obsessive" interest in things (Goldfarb, 1974).

The reasons for the favorable treatment of girl infants by their mothers and for the smoother interaction between mothers and their girls are still very mysterious. But being a same-sex caretaker may be an important factor facilitating maternal care of girls, while being of the opposite sex may complicate maternal care of boys. It was Freud who developed the earliest hypothesis about this factor. But Freud, with his customary androcentrism, could see only greater difficulties ahead for women in their object choice. It was Margaret Mead (1949), largely under Horney's influence, who first suggested that having a different-sex caretaker made the development of gender identity harder for boys. David Lynn (1962) also pursued this line of reasoning, suggesting that girls have only to learn a lesson in "mother-person emulation," while boys have to "solve a problem" in mother-person differentiation and then form an identification with a relatively distant father. Freud's predictions about women's greater troubles with either object choice or gender identity have not been confirmed. On the contrary, although men are less likely than women to apply for psychiatric help in general, many more men apply for help with homosexuality than women. Men are by far more often subject to distortions of their sexuality in the form of transvestism, fetishism, exhibitionism, voyeurism, child molesting, incest, and rape. These distortions of their sexuality form an avenue along which men march into the statistics on schizophrenia (Lewis, 1976, 1978).

Let us now briefly recapitulate the story so far. Women's genetically based reproductive function may make them more sociable than men, beginning in infancy. Their genetics would thus operate in the same direction as cultural prescriptions that train girls to be mothers in their turn. It requires an intuitive leap of understanding to connect women's greater sociability to their greater vulnerability to depression, which is, above all, the experience of sadness over social loss. The same intuitive leap of understanding connects men's lesser sociability with their proneness to schizophrenia, the illness of emotional shutdown.

The differences between the sexes that I have so far been describing are responses to the quality and type of nurturing environment in which both sexes thrive. When it comes, however, to the effects of an exploitive society that spreads its gospel of domination even into the family, sociability or attachment loses its charm. It is, in fact, a capacity that is devalued or else sanctified in a warring, exploitive society. In identifying with their mothers, women are at the same time identifying with the devalued, sometimes sanctified sex. Women have to struggle not to devalue their "other orientation" in a world that often ridicules and shames attachment. As Bowlby (1973) points out, failure to understand loss as a given of the attachment system has made it seem "childish, even babyish to yearn for the presence of a loved figure or to be distressed during her (or his) absence" (p. 80). Men, who are encouraged to be aggressive and competitive, are thereby encouraged to renounce their affectionateness, as well as to scorn it. They are thus more vulnerable to guilt. Specifically, my hypothesis is that depression is connected to a greater proneness to shame, while paranoia is connected to greater proneness to guilt.

Direct evidence for the role of shame in depression has not been easy to obtain, mainly because there are too few easily usable, reliable, and valid shame measures. But there is nevertheless some information (Lewis, 1986). Hoblitzelle (1982) has developed a reliable and valid measure of shame and has found evidence of a significant correlation between shame and depression. A recent study that attempted to refine the exact target of people's self-blame (Peterson, Schwartz, and Seligman, 1981) carefully distinguished between blaming the self for *behaviors* and blaming the self for its *character*. This is, in fact, very close to the distinction I have drawn between the "thing" focus, or objective character, of guilt and the self, or personal, focus in shame. The depressive symptoms of eighty-seven women undergraduates correlated with blame directed at their own *characters*, while blame directed at *behaviors* was correlated with a lack of depressive symptoms. I do not know whether the same result would obtain for men.

On the side of paranoia and guilt, the evidence is mainly from the symptomatology itself, which is, quintessentially, the projection of guilt. Colby (1977), in his studies of computer-simulated paranoia, suggests that a shame/humiliation model is preferable to a homosexual, hostility, or homeostatic model. Although this is in apparent contradiction to my view that guilt is the more proximal state out of which paranoia forms, the discrepancy between Colby's view and my own may be more apparent than real. Colby actually suggests that the paranoid forestalls the threat of humiliation by a strategy of "blaming others" for "wrongdoing"—that is, projecting guilt. It seems to me quite in keeping with the fact that women do not give up their affectionateness, however, only devalue it, that the clinical picture in depression involves no bizarre distortions of gender identity. On the contrary, the symptoms of depression are as familiar to all of us and as mundane as depressed mood. Men, in contrast, are required by our exploitive society to function in the world as if aggression and not affectionateness were the stuff of which they are made. No wonder that Schreber's (Freud, 1911/1958) paranoid mythology, by means of which he functioned at least for a few years, became that he had a special mission on earth to rectify evil by teaching human beings that God's will is the cultivation of feminine voluptuousness. Schreber's attachment needs were still showing in his distorted thinking.

Summary

To summarize some of the main points that emerge when we explore the contradiction of values surrounding separation and attachment: Our present-day awareness of the centrality of the emotional attachment system throughout life has been derived mainly from studying the phenomena of separation. There is now evidence to support the existence of a dialectic between an initial, separate organization of the infant's self and its attachment to the caretaker, in which attachment fosters the continued and developing separation of the self. The relative neglect of attachment can be traced, in part, to an androcentric bias in evolutionary theory, which emphasized the skills of the independent male hunter rather than the nurturant behavior of mothers as determinants of evolutionary change.

Research on the cognitive style of field dependence especially highlights the contradiction of values surrounding separation and attachment. There is evidence that, in childhood, a sound attachment bond goes with both prosocial behavior and field independence. Evidence also suggests that, at least from adolescence onward, there is an inverse relationship between the cognitive restructuring skills that are apparent in field-independent people and the interpersonal, social skills that are more apparent in field-dependent people. Beginning at adolescence, our male-dominated culture pushes men to develop cognitive restructuring skills and impersonal behavior. The culture also devalues women's attachments and women's work, while making fewer demands on their cognitive restructuring skills. Women become more field dependent, more shame-prone, and more

prone to depression than men. Men become more field independent, more guilt-prone, and more prone to schizophrenia, especially paranoia. Sex differences between the major functional
psychoses thus reflect the contradiction of values within our
culture.

References

Ainsworth, M. D. S., Blehar, M. C., Waters, E., and Wall, S. *Patterns of Attachment: A Psychological Study of the Strange Situation.* Hillsdale, N.J.: Erlbaum, 1978.

Asch, S. E., and Witkin, H. A. "Studies in Space Orientation I and II." *Journal of Experimental Psychology,* 1948, *38,* 325–337, 455–477.

Barchas, J., Akil, H., and Elliot, G. "Behavioral Neurochemistry: Neuroregulation and Behavioral States." *Science,* 1978, *200,* 964–973.

Bell, S. "The Development of the Concept of the Object as Related to Infant-Mother Attachment." *Child Development,* 1970, *41,* 291–311.

Berry, J. *Human Ecology and Cognitive Style.* New York: Wiley, 1976.

Bowlby, J. *Attachment and Loss.* Vol. 1: *Attachment.* New York: Basic Books, 1969.

Bowlby, J. *Attachment and Loss.* Vol. 2: *Separation: Anxiety and Anger.* New York: Basic Books, 1973.

Chance, M. "An Ethological Assessment of Emotion." In R. Plutchik and H. Kellerman (eds.), *Emotion: Theory, Research, and Experience.* Vol. 1. Orlando, Fla.: Academic Press, 1980.

Chesler, P. *Women and Madness.* New York: Doubleday, 1972.

Coates, S. "Sex Differences in Field Dependence Among Preschool Children." In R. Friedman, R. Richart, and R. Vande Wiele (eds.), *Sex Differences in Behavior.* New York: Wiley, 1974.

Coates, S., Lord, M., and Jacobovits, E. "Field Dependence-Independence, Social and Non-social Play, and Sex Differences in Preschool Children." *Perceptual and Motor Skills,* 1975, *40,* 195–202.

Colby, K. "Appraisal of Four Psychological Theories of Paranoid Phenomena." *Journal of Abnormal Psychology,* 1977,
86, 54–59.

Condon, W., and Sander, L. "Neonate Movement Is Synchronized with Adult Speech." *Science,* 1974, *183,* 99–101.

DeCasper, A. J., and Fifer, W. "Of Human Bonding: Newborns
Prefer Their Mothers' Voices." *Science,* 1980, *208,* 1174–
1176.

Dohrenwend, B. S., and Dohrenwend, B. P. "Sex Differences
and Psychiatric Disorders." *American Journal of Sociology,*
1976, *81,* 1447–1454.

Faris, P., and Dunham, H. *Mental Disorders in Urban Areas.*
Chicago: University of Chicago Press, 1939.

Field, T., Woodson, R., Greenberg, R., and Cohen, D. "Discrimination and Imitation of Facial Expression by Neonates." *Science,* 1982, *218,* 179–181.

Freud, S. "The Interpretation of Dreams." In J. Strachey (ed.
and trans.), *The Standard Edition of the Complete Psychological Works of Sigmund Freud.* Vols. 4–5. London: Hogarth Press, 1953. (Originally published 1900.)

Freud, S. "Mourning and Melancholia." In J. Strachey (ed. and
trans.), *The Standard Edition of the Complete Psychological
Works of Sigmund Freud.* Vol. 14. London: Hogarth Press,
1957. (Originally published 1917.)

Freud, S. "Psycho-Analytic Notes on an Autobiographical Account of a Case of Paranoia (Dementia Paranoides)." In J.
Strachey (ed. and trans.), *The Standard Edition of the Complete Psychological Works of Sigmund Freud.* Vol. 12. London: Hogarth Press, 1958. (Originally published 1911.)

Freud, S. "The Ego and the Id." In J. Strachey (ed. and trans.),
*The Standard Edition of the Complete Psychological Works
of Sigmund Freud.* Vol. 19. London: Hogarth Press, 1961a.
(Originally published 1923.)

Freud, S. "Some Psychical Consequences of the Distinction Between the Sexes." In J. Strachey (ed. and trans.), *The Standard Edition of the Complete Psychological Works of Sigmund Freud.* Vol. 19. London: Hogarth Press, 1961b. (Originally published 1925.)

Freud, S. "On Libidinal Types." In J. Strachey (ed. and trans.),

The Standard Edition of the Complete Psychological Works of Sigmund Freud. Vol. 21. London: Hogarth Press, 1961c. (Originally published 1931.)

Gibson, I., and Mowrer, O. "Determinants of the Perceived Vertical and Horizontal." *Psychological Review,* 1938, *45,* 300-323.

Gilligan, C. "Do the Social Sciences Have an Adequate Theory of Moral Development?" In N. Haan, P. Bellak, M. Robins, and P. Sullivan (eds.), *Social Sciences: Moral Inquiry.* Berkeley: University of California Press, 1983.

Goldfarb, W. "Distinguishing and Classifying the Individual Schizophrenic Style." In S. Arieti (ed.), *Handbook of Psychiatry.* 2nd ed. New York: Basic Books, 1974.

Gottschalk, L., and Gleser, G. *The Measurement of Psychological States Through the Content Analysis of Verbal Behavior.* Berkeley: University of California Press, 1969.

Gove, W., and Tudor, J. "Adult Sex Roles and Mental Illness." *American Journal of Sociology,* 1973, *78,* 812-835.

Greene, L. "Effects of Field Dependence on Affective Reactions and Compliance in Dyadic Interactions." *Journal of Personality and Social Psychology,* 1976, *34,* 569-577.

Haan, N. "Two Moralities in Action Contexts: Relationships to Thought, Ego Regulation, and Development." *Journal of Personality and Social Psychology,* 1978, *36,* 286-306.

Hammen, C., and Pedesky, C. "Sex Differences in the Expression of Depression." Paper presented at the annual meeting of the American Psychological Association, Toronto, August 1977.

Harlow, H. F., and Mears, C. *The Human Model: Primate Perspectives.* New York: Wiley, 1979.

Heider, F. *The Psychology of Interpersonal Relations.* New York: Wiley, 1958.

Hoblitzelle, W. "Developing a Measure of Shame and Guilt and the Role of Shame in Depression." Unpublished doctoral predissertation, Department of Psychology, Yale University, 1982.

James, W. *Principles of Psychology.* Vol. 1. New York: Holt, 1890.

Johnson, D. "Cognitive Organization in Paranoid and Non-paranoid Schizophrenics." Unpublished doctoral dissertation, Department of Psychology, Yale University, 1980.

Kogan, N. *Cognitive Styles in Infancy and Early Childhood.* Hillsdale, N.J.: Erlbaum, 1976.

Levenson, M., and Neuringer, C. "Suicide and Field Dependency." *Omega,* 1974, *5,* 181–185.

Levy, R., and Rowitz, R. *The Ecology of Mental Disorders.* New York: Behavioral Publications, 1973.

Lewis, H. B. "Over-differentiation and Under-individuation of the Self." *Psychoanalysis and the Psychoanalytic Review,* 1958, *45,* 3–24.

Lewis, H. B. *Shame and Guilt in Neurosis.* New York: International Universities Press, 1971.

Lewis, H. B. *Psychic War in Men and Women.* New York: New York University Press, 1976.

Lewis, H. B. "Sex Differences in Superego Mode as Related to Sex Differences in Psychiatric Illness." *Social Science and Medicine,* 1978, *12,* 199–205.

Lewis, H. B. "The Role of Shame in Depression." In M. Rutter, C. Izard, and P. Read (eds.), *Depression in Young People: Developmental and Clinical Perspectives.* New York: Guilford Press, 1986.

Lovejoy, C. "The Origin of Man." *Science,* 1981, *216,* 341–349.

Lynn, D. "Sex Role and Parental Identification." *Child Development,* 1962, *33,* 555–564.

Maccoby, E. E., and Jacklin, C. N. *The Psychology of Sex Differences.* Stanford, Calif.: Stanford University Press, 1974.

MacKinnon, D. "The Personality Correlates of Creativity: A Study of American Architects." In G. Nielson (ed.), *The XIVth International Congress of Applied Psychology.* Vol. 2. Copenhagen: Munksgaard, 1962.

Mahler, M. S., Pine, F., and Bergman, A. *The Psychological Birth of the Human Infant: Symbiosis and Individuation.* New York: Basic Books, 1975.

Malzberg, B. "Important Statistical Data and Mental Illness." In S. Arieti (ed.), *American Handbook of Psychiatry.* New York: Basic Books, 1959.

Mead, M. *Male and Female*. New York: Morrow, 1949.

Meltzoff, A., and Moore, M. "Imitation and Facial and Non-facial Gestures." *Science,* 1977, *198,* 75–78.

Morgan, E. *The Descent of Woman*. New York: Bantam Books, 1972.

Moss, H. "Early Sex Differences and the Mother-Infant Interaction." In R. Friedman, R. Richart, and R. Vande Wiele (eds.), *Sex Differences in Behavior*. New York: Wiley, 1974.

Murphy, J. "Psychiatric Labeling in Cross-Cultural Perspective." *Science,* 1976, *191,* 1019–1028.

Newman, R., and Hirt, M. "The Psychoanalytic Theory of Depression: Symptoms as a Function of Aggressive Wishes and Field Articulation." *Journal of Abnormal Psychology,* 1983, *92,* 42–49.

Oltman, P., and others. "Psychological Differentiation as a Factor in Conflict Resolution." *Journal of Personality and Social Psychology,* 1975, *32,* 730–736.

Peterson, C., Schwartz, S., and Seligman, M. E. "Self-Blame and Depressive Symptoms." *Journal of Personality and Social Psychology,* 1981, *41,* 253–260.

Quinlan, D., and Blatt, S. "Field Articulation and Performance Under Stress: Differential Predictions in Surgical and Psychiatric Nursing Training." *Journal of Consulting and Clinical Psychology,* 1972, *39,* 517.

Radloff, L., and Rae, D. "Susceptibility and Precipitating Factors in Depression: Sex Differences and Similarities." *Journal of Abnormal Psychology,* 1979, *88,* 174–181.

Rosenblatt, P., Walsh, P., and Jackson, D. *Grief and Mourning in Cross-Cultural Perspective*. New Haven, Conn.: Human Relations Area Files Press, 1976.

Sackett, G. "Sex Differences in Rhesus Monkeys Following Varied Rearing Experiences." In R. Friedman, R. Richart, and R. Vande Wiele (eds.), *Sex Differences in Behavior*. New York: Wiley, 1974.

Seay, B., Hansen, E., and Harlow, H. F. "Mother Infant Separation in Monkeys." *Journal of Child Psychology and Psychiatry,* 1962, *3,* 123–132.

Simner, A. "Newborn Response to the Cry of Another Infant." *Developmental Psychology,* 1971, *5,* 136–150.

Sousa-Poza, J., and Rohrberg, R. "Communicational and Interactional Aspects of Self-Disclosure in Psychotherapy: Differences Related to Cognitive Style." *Psychiatry*, 1976, *39*, 81–91.

Stone, L. J., Smith, H. T., and Murphy, L. B. (eds.). *The Competent Infant*. New York: Basic Books, 1973.

Taylor, D., and Ounsted, C. "The Nature of Gender Differences Explored Through Ontogenetic Analysis of Sex Differences in Disease." In C. Ounsted and D. Taylor (eds.), *Gender Differences: Their Ontogeny and Significance*. Baltimore: Williams & Wilkins, 1972.

Wertheimer, M. "Experimentelle Studien über das Sehen von Bewegung" [Experimental studies on the perception of movement]. *Zeltschrift für Psychologie*, 1912, *61*, 161–265.

Witkin, H. A. "Psychological Differentiation and Forms of Pathology." *Journal of Abnormal Psychology*, 1965, *70*, 317–336.

Witkin, H. A., and Asch, S. E. "Studies in Space Orientation III and IV." *Journal of Experimental Psychology*, 1948, *38*, 603–614; 762–782.

Witkin, H. A., and Berry, J. "Psychological Differentiation in Cross-Cultural Perspective." *Journal of Cross-Cultural Psychology*, 1975, *6*, 4–87.

Witkin, H. A., Goodenough, D. R., and Karp, S. "Stability of Cognitive Style from Childhood to Young Adulthood." *Journal of Personality and Social Psychology*, 1967, *7*, 291–300.

Witkin, H. A., Goodenough, D. R., and Oltman, P. "Psychological Differentiation: Current Status." *Journal of Personality and Social Psychology*, 1979, *37*, 1127–1145.

Witkin, H. A., Lewis, H. B., and Weil, E. "Affective Reactions and Patient-Therapist Interaction Among More and Less Differentiated Patients Early in Therapy." *Journal of Nervous and Mental Disease*, 1968, *146*, 193–208.

Witkin, H. A., and others. *Personality Through Perception*. New York: Harper & Row, 1954; Westport, Conn.: Greenwood Press, 1972.

Witkin, H. A., and others. *Psychological Differentiation*. New York: Wiley, 1962.

Afterword: Converging Themes in the Psychology of Separation and Loss

Jonathan Bloom-Feshbach
Sally Bloom-Feshbach

The different contributions to this volume point to several common themes in the psychology of separation. Identifying the often hidden separation component in a situation reveals structural parallels among many phenomena, including, for example, the inner struggles of adolescents leaving home, of immigrants adjusting to new cultures, of children facing parental death, and of psychotherapy patients coping with the limits of treatment relationships. The purpose of this afterword is to highlight some of the trends that emerge from the volume, as well as to indicate some areas of incomplete knowledge that warrant further inquiry.

Although the universal importance of separation for young children is well accepted, there remains theoretical controversy about the psychoanalytic theory of separation-individuation that conceptualizes separation in terms of a process of psychological differentiation. This debate not only divides the research-oriented developmentalist from the clinician but emerges within the psychoanalytic approach itself. Although many clinicians retain the language of traditional psychoanalysis

549

(such as *ego, superego,* and *introjection*), there appears to be a trend, both in this volume and in the field, away from the classical structural theory toward a representational model emphasizing the level of differentiation and articulation in the imagos of self and other (see Chapters Twelve through Fifteen). The view that mental representations of transactions with early parenting figures form the building blocks of psychological structure is part of a growing consensus in behavioral science. As such, it holds promise for bridging the disciplinary gap between the ethological/developmental attachment researchers and the proponents of a psychoanalytic/clinical approach to the study of separation.

Central to a representational model must be a structural dimension that describes the degree of differentiation in the level of representation. This dimension is a significant omission in the attachment concept of the internal working model. It constitutes a major thrust in the psychoanalytic understanding of the role of separation both in the development of psychological schemata and in the response of the psyche to separation experiences. Although the term *object constancy* carries theoretical baggage such as libido and symbiosis, the essence of the concept appears to remain valid and pivotal: that there is an internal representational capacity that regulates interpersonal autonomy and affect modulation. Both object relational and self psychology perspectives emphasize the degree of differentiation and integration of the self- and object representations in reframing this same idea. Such language is more in line with the research evidence that a germinal and interpersonally oriented self exists from the start. Some chapters in this volume integrate the language and theory of several psychoanalytic approaches, finding roots for the psychology of the structure of the self, and for the psychology of the conflicts of the self, even in Freud's early writings.

Structural differences in individuals' representational schemata produce qualitatively different psychological universes, where the meanings of closeness, sexuality, discord, and separation vary in predictable ways. The clinical evidence suggests that these universes are finite in structure and tend to converge into recognizable psychological configurations. For children, three types of attachment relationship have been delineated by the Ainsworth methodology; for adults, defensive styles (Horowitz, 1976) as well as levels of ego development (Loevinger, 1976) have been defined.

Whatever the preferred conceptualization—*object constancy, self structure,* or *security of attachment*—deficient early caregiving brings into being a developmentally impaired psychological world. What is the role of separation and loss in this process? Separation is the boundary, the end point, of interpersonal closeness or attachment. Throughout this volume, separation has been accorded a symbolic meaning as well as a literal one. Hence, a person can feel alone and separated from a loved one even in the presence of that person. Psychological distance can be worse than overt conflict in creating a feeling of abandonment, because at least parties in conflict interact. Anger and discord in the love bond, short of murderous rage, are less problematic than unexpressed anger and conflict that cannot be communicated, because unexpressed feelings create a wall, a separation. The child's feeling of being unloved or ambivalently loved is produced both through a lack of loving interaction and through an empathic distance that renders the child isolated and prematurely separate. An additional problematic pattern of loving occurs when the parent's overinvolved, intrusive ties to the child interfere with natural developmental urges toward independence and separateness. For a healthy, separate sense of self to develop, a child must be able to enjoy closeness as well as autonomy, feeling that the path toward independence is supported and that the doorway of dependence remains open.

The infant needs closeness—tactile, affective, and interpersonal. Leaving aside the debates about symbiosis and about adult/infant similarity, the child harbors a wish for and fear of merger that parallels the struggles of the disturbed adolescent or adult. As the clinical section of this volume shows, advances toward and retreats from self-cohesion and psychological autonomy can be defined in terms of incremental degrees of separation.

The literature on children's responses to bereavement brings into focus the potentially powerful impact of object loss on development. A heightened degree of separation and loss in the micro-interactions of the parent/child relationship, though not identifiable as a clear-cut trauma, can have similar effects. Hence, the child who has not developed a secure interpersonal foundation will not have the capacity to structurally represent and affectively cope with more advanced psychological dilemmas, such as competition and intimacy. In this way, a complex mosaic of troubled parenting transactions as well as traumatic experiences of loss may disrupt and limit the developmental course.

In the face of increasing maternal employment, professionals, policymakers, and the general public have turned their attention to the kind of care that prospering infants—and healthy children—need. As Piotrkowski and Gornick note (see Chapter Eight), there is no definitive scientific resolution of this issue. Research generally indicates that within certain limits (for example, when the degree of separation required is not too extensive, when the nature of work is satisfying, and when familial support is available) maternal employment does not appear harmful and may even benefit the developing child. However, recent evidence and re-evaluation of the literature raise troubling questions about potential negative effects on personality development created by alternative child care arrangements during the first year of life (Belsky, 1986). The possibility of impediments to attachment deriving from too much work-related separation is a sensitive but critical issue for further investigation.

It is evident that events of loss occur in a context that influences their meaning and affects the quality of eventual adjustment. For monkeys and humans, for children and adults, the ultimate implications of particular separation events will be shaped by the individual's emotional well-being and developmental status, the nature and quality of preexisting relationships, and the availability of alternative objects. Dimensions of the loss itself are also important, including its magnitude and expectability. Chapter One, describing nonhuman primate reactions to separation, reported the provocative finding that competing adaptational demands (such as having to work to obtain food) may diminish the pain of "mourning," preventing disguised or delayed depression. We see an analogue of this finding in the healthy function served by human defenses. In our clinical experience, some combination of expression of distress and adaptive distraction from painful events promotes the work of mourning. As Chapter Six illustrates, distress is expectable and necessary in the face of loss, but prolonged or overly intense reactions may signal a separation problem.

The role of separation in adult development is clearly an arena for further thought and investigation. The study of adult development is itself a new and controversial topic, even apart from considering the role of separation. The work of Levinson and associates (1978) and the chapter by Cohler and Stott in this volume suggest that the intrapsychic focus on separation and individuation is particularly relevant to child and adolescent development. Levinson's concept of the "life structure" and Cohler and Stott's view of "interdependence" both imply that discussion of development in adulthood should emphasize the network of relationships outside the self; put differently, for the adult, the very definition of self is interwoven with interpersonal, work, and community ties.

The broadening of roles and the expansion of the self during adulthood are reflected in the continual modification of the representational world. Later representational development necessarily rests on the foundation established during early childhood. Each new layering of representational structure is affected by the existing structures, and each new composite structure continues to shape further internalizations. Thus, mastery of separation experience predicated on a solid emotional core facilitates the adult's capacity to undergo the developmental "mourning" instigated by inevitable changes in self-image, relationships, and work and family roles. For example, obsessional decision-making dilemmas in adults who cannot let go of alternatives (such as whether to get married or which career path to select) may at root reflect separation difficulties evoked by the need to relinquish something. Such "letting go" of choices constitutes accepting and working through a loss (Viorst, 1986). Similarly, separateness and independence must be achieved before true interdependence is possible. Thus, psychological autonomy is a precondition for many facets of adult development, especially the capacity to establish and maintain relationships characterized by true intimacy and mutuality (as opposed to the dependent yearnings for closeness rooted in a lack of separateness). The adult representation of self and other may combine the many domains of inner schemata, ranging from the core foundation through the psychosocial experience of latency and adolescence to the increasingly interpersonal networks of the adult years.

This web of representational structures suggests the metaphor of an Oriental rug, in which the warp and weft define the basic foundation of the carpet (its structure), while the knots define the content. The design elements of the knotted portion give the rug its perceptible quality and meaning, but the foundation layer makes this level possible. However, even the knotted portion has structural as well as content features. Similarly, in representation, there are a number of significant psychological templates which provide the content of thought and feeling but which also have structural elements. Representation of culture is such a template. Though not as deep a structure as the core level of internalized early transactions, the representation of culture has a profound influence on the meanings of life experience. As Levy-Warren's chapter suggests, the representation of culture is intimately linked to identity. Culture functions like temperamental differences in shaping tendencies toward separateness or motivations for closeness. But both culture and temperament are secondary to the overriding human need for relationships and the attendant grief of loss. Similarly, sex differences may function like cultural templates, influencing interpersonal transactions, psychological responses, and the affective valences of closeness and separateness. But in spite of the feminine inclination toward and special capacity for empathy and interpersonal relatedness, sex differences are ultimately outweighed by the common human object-seeking (attachment) motivations. This universality of basic separation processes is not surprising in light of the biological need for human beings to remain attached in the face of an extended (in evolutionary terms) period of infantile dependence. Separation reactions, as regulators of

the interpersonal boundary, serve to promote the intense interpersonal ties through which human mutuality and culture are
transmitted.

The relationship between internalization and separation is
another important issue, one that has generated considerable
clinical attention but little empirical scrutiny. We know that
some experience of distance or separateness from a love object
fosters the taking in, or imitation, of properties of that object.
The conditions governing this phenomenon are not well understood. For example, we need to clarify the different mechanisms underlying different levels of internalization (in psychoanalytic terminology, the differences among incorporation,
introjection, and identification). A central question is whether
the conditions influencing the internalization of more basic affective properties of caregiving interactions (such as whether an
interpersonal sequence is nurturant, distance-promoting, aggressive, and so on) differ from the conditions determining the
internalization of more differentiated features of love objects.

Because separation and loss are ubiquitous in human development and in the course of life, psychological difficulties reflective of them frequently emerge. As a result, the etiology and
treatment of psychopathology are replete with separation-related
phenomena. Among the various constellations of psychological
dynamics linked to separation is a defensive pattern most widely identified in studies of childhood bereavement. Children have
a tendency to interpret parental death as a deliberate desertion
for which they are responsible. Krupnick and Solomon (Chapter
Eleven) cite the work of Erna and Robert Furman, who suggest
that the nearly universal tendency toward self-blame and guilt
in bereaved children and adults is not simply internalized rage
but is a defense against the more upsetting reality that one is
helpless and lacks control over such threatening life events. The
powerful gratification of feeling in control is reflected in a "passive into active" defensive maneuver that renders the self an active initiator, rather than a passive victim, of abandonment.
Although the motivation to achieve self-control and mastery
over problematic affects and experiences is a normal adaptational process, under extreme circumstances and for some indi-

viduals such efforts at control become self-destructive. Nevertheless, the suffering evoked by guilt and self-blame may feel preferable to the more painful experience of being a helpless victim.

This neurotic defensive process is often evident in the way individuals cope with nonbereavement separations and losses as well. Further, this process manifests not only at an intrapsychic level but also at a behavioral level, where individuals unconsciously reenact circumstances and relationships that recapitulate traumatic loss: people who have suffered frequent geographical moves may keep finding themselves compelled to migrate to new areas; individuals traumatized by divorce in childhood may unconsciously seek marriages destined to fail; those who have experienced inadequate parental nurturance may remain mistrustful and distant and hence alienate potential friends and lovers; and individuals from abusive families may unconsciously gravitate to abusive therapists. These and many other examples of traumatic interpersonal loss that magnetize the individual toward repetition reveal the deep human yearning for self-control and illustrate the serious consequences of unexpressed affect that spills into action. One main goal of working through unresolved feelings of loss is to restructure the inner schemata that impel reenactment of the loss. This can be accomplished in the normal course of living or within the more systematic structure of a psychoanalysis or psychotherapy.

Another separation theme that bears mention is the attachment relationship to inanimate objects. This phenomenon is readily observable in children's love of their schools, in adults' ties to alma mater or workplace, and in long-term patients' "institutional transference" to hospital or clinic. Houses, neighborhoods, and athletic teams are commonly invested with enduring affect. The intensity of these attachments parallels what one observes in object relationships. Sugarman and Jaffe's chapter on transitional phenomena expands the attachment sphere to include fantasies, eating habits, and other symbolic domains that facilitate coping with deficits in interpersonal connectedness and self-differentiation. Ties to inanimate objects may be especially important for those who lack libidinal object constancy and self-cohesion, as these individuals may have a tendency to gravitate away from human ties, toward inanimate attachment bonds. Lewis's chapter reviews the concept of negative decalage, noting that the appearance of infant representation of *nonhuman* objects prior to representation of people is associated with insecure attachment patterns. This further explains why changes in the therapist's office and appearance, appointment schedule, and other routines are so disruptive to more disturbed patients.

Treating the patient with profound deficits in self- and object representations has been greatly facilitated by the contemporary shift toward a pre-oedipal developmental emphasis on separation and psychological separateness. The application of psychoanalytic techniques to the treatment of narcissistic, borderline, and psychotic patients in recent years has been clinically exciting and has spawned considerable theoretical attention to the kinds of issues raised in this volume. Several chapters in each of the three parts note theoretical and technical considerations relevant for therapeutic work with such patients. Treatment recommendations, such as Lachmann, Beebe, and Stolorow's concept of increments of separation or Geller's emphasis on the modality of representation, have distinct curative influences. However, we think that such techniques share the general feature of promoting *self-observation* within the *interpersonal* context of the therapist/patient relationship. Individuals who lack object constancy, who are impaired in psychological differentiation, have a serious deficit in the capacity to stand outside their emotional fluctuations. Such individuals have not progressed beyond the pre-oedipal level, and as Kernberg notes, the oedipal phase is not simply a stage when particular conflicts with competition and sexuality come to the fore. Rather, the oedipal stage ushers in an entire reorganization of the mind, in which the child's competitive strivings are represented in perspectives extending outside the self (fantasizing how one parent envisions the other parent's relationship with the child). This developmental shift in cognitive and affective functioning, occurring with the emergence of a new Piagetian stage, produces a greater capacity for tolerating self-criticism and lays the groundwork for continued psychological differentiation. Individuals who successfully traverse this developmental course evolve cohesive, affectively integrated psychological structures that permit self-observation—a key ingredient for psychotherapeutic change. But the developmentally impaired individual whose early parenting relationships have wrought havoc in the core self- and object representations possesses only conflict-ridden, fragmented, and emotionally polarized domains of self-experience with which to work on healing the self. For the clinician, one of the psychological puzzles of each psychotherapy is finding a way to ally with a healthy part of the patient's inner world. This positive object tie promotes the patient's identification with the therapist's caring and inquiring professional stance. Through this process the patient begins to build a capacity for constructive self-observation. Finding the eye in the emotional storm of the disturbed patient is facilitated by the repeated invitation to join with the therapist in using a perspective that encourages self-reflection.

Throughout this volume the dual roles of separation have been highlighted: separations produce painful but potentially growth-promoting experiences. Human development and the course of life transitions confront the individual with many experiences of separation and loss, on both the practical and the symbolic level. These experiences spur growth in the relinquishing of the familiar and habitual and in the reaching forward to new possibilities. Developmentally appropriate and emotionally manageable separation experiences are healthy and growth-promoting, while unexpected, severe, and developmentally asynchronous separations are psychologically problematic. In spite of the theoretical debates, alternative disciplinary allegiances, and differential emphases on research or on clinical knowledge, converging perspectives about the psychology of separation have emerged in the contributions compiled here. We believe that the breadth and significance of separation issues provide a unique vantage point from which to study human development, both normal and pathological. We hope that this volume will promote increased understanding of and interest in the psychology of separation and will constitute one additional step toward a more differentiated, integrated perspective of separation.

References

Belsky, J. "Infant Day Care: A Cause for Concern?" *Zero to Three,* 1986, *6*(5), 1–7.

Horowitz, M. *Stress Response Syndromes.* New York: Jason Aronson, 1976.

Levinson, D. J., and others. *The Seasons of a Man's Life.* New York: Knopf, 1978.

Loevinger, J. *Ego Development: Conceptions and Theories.* San Francisco: Jossey-Bass, 1976.

Viorst, J. *Necessary Losses.* New York: Simon & Schuster, 1986.

Name Index

Subject Index

poral context of, 68-69; themes on, 552

Melancholia, concept of, 377-378

Memory, psychoanalytic theory of, 91-92

Men: and field dependence, 527-529; and schizophrenia, 533-534. *See also* Fathers; Parents

Menstruation, in adolescence, 156

Merger: identification distinct from, 401; in infancy, 21-22; and schizophrenia, 494

Metaphors, for multimodal memories, 490-491

Mitigation stage, in bereavement, 238

Mother/child relationship: history of views on, 4-5; and nursery school entry, 219-220, 223-224; and psychoanalytic theory, 8; rhythmicity in, 78; sex differences in, 537-539; and strange situations, 119-125. *See also* Parent/child interaction

Mothers: avoidance of, 69-76; good and bad images of, 139-140; loss of, 63-86; and object relationship, 90; responses to separation from, 115-118; responsive, 277-278; as secure base or as secure haven, 121, 123; and work-related separations, 273-279; in work force, 270. *See also* Parents; Women

Mourning: in adulthood and in childhood, 117; avoidance of, 311-312; capacity for, 152; concept of, 99, 351, 377-378; and culture, 303; process of, 378; and psychotherapy, 482-483

N

Narcissism: clinical manifestations of injury in, 432-434; and object loss, 382-383, 392; and object relations, 375-395; and paranoia, 430-436; and self/other differentiation, 484-488

National Academy of Sciences, Institute of Medicine of, 346-347

National Center for Health Statistics, 318, 343

National Institute of Mental Health, 346

National Institute on Aging, 166n

Neurotic pathology, self-pathology distinct from, 389

Nigeria, mental health concepts in, 532-533

Normal autism, and separation-individuation, 9, 14, 16, 172

Norway, work absence studies in, 282

Nursery school entry: analysis of, 207-231; background on, 207-209; and departure protest, 210, 215, 221-222; and eventual adjustment, 217-218; findings on, 218-221; index of problems at, 214-216; literature on, 209-212; research needed on, 226; sample for, 212-213; and separation and emotional adjustment, 221-226; and separation problems, 223; and separation-related data, 213-214; and shift work, 281; study of, 212-218

O

Object constancy: and adolescent/parent separation, 252; concept of, 91, 92, 139; libidinal, 9, 302-303, 312; and nursery school entry, 222; and person constancy, 526-527; psychoanalytic theory on, 91-92; and separation, 37; and separation-individuation, 172, 173, 174n; themes in, 550

Object loss: depression and separation related to, 375-395; impact of, 551-552; and narcissism, 382-383, 392

Object relations: in adolescence, 155-156; and adolescent/parent separation, 235; central role of, 89-91; developmental/structural